AF594011

# A Community Connection

SECOND EDITION

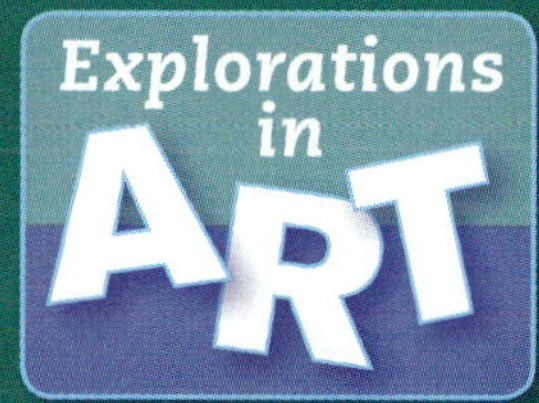


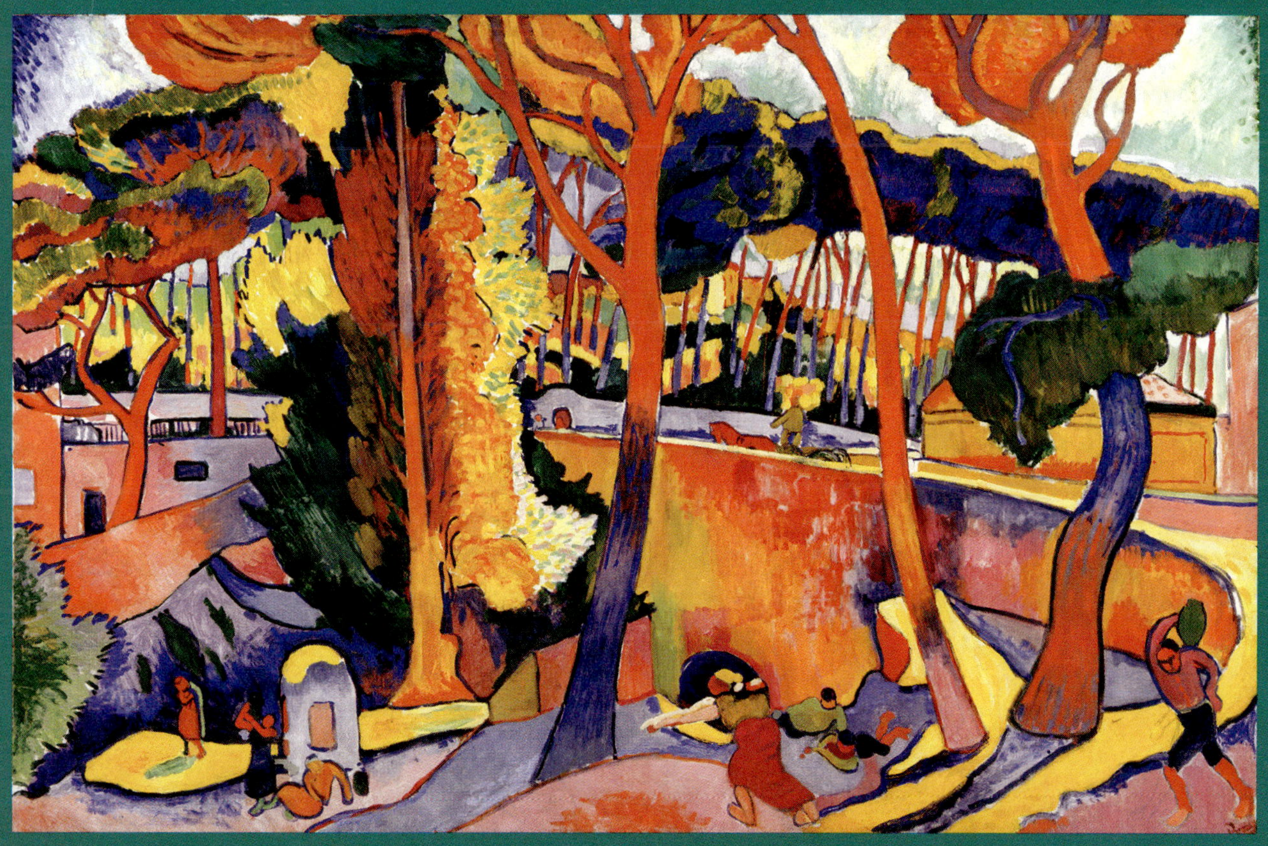

Davis Publications, Inc. 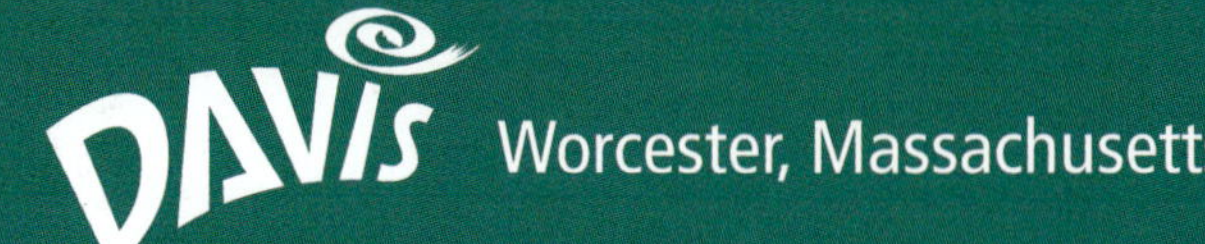 Worcester, Massachusetts

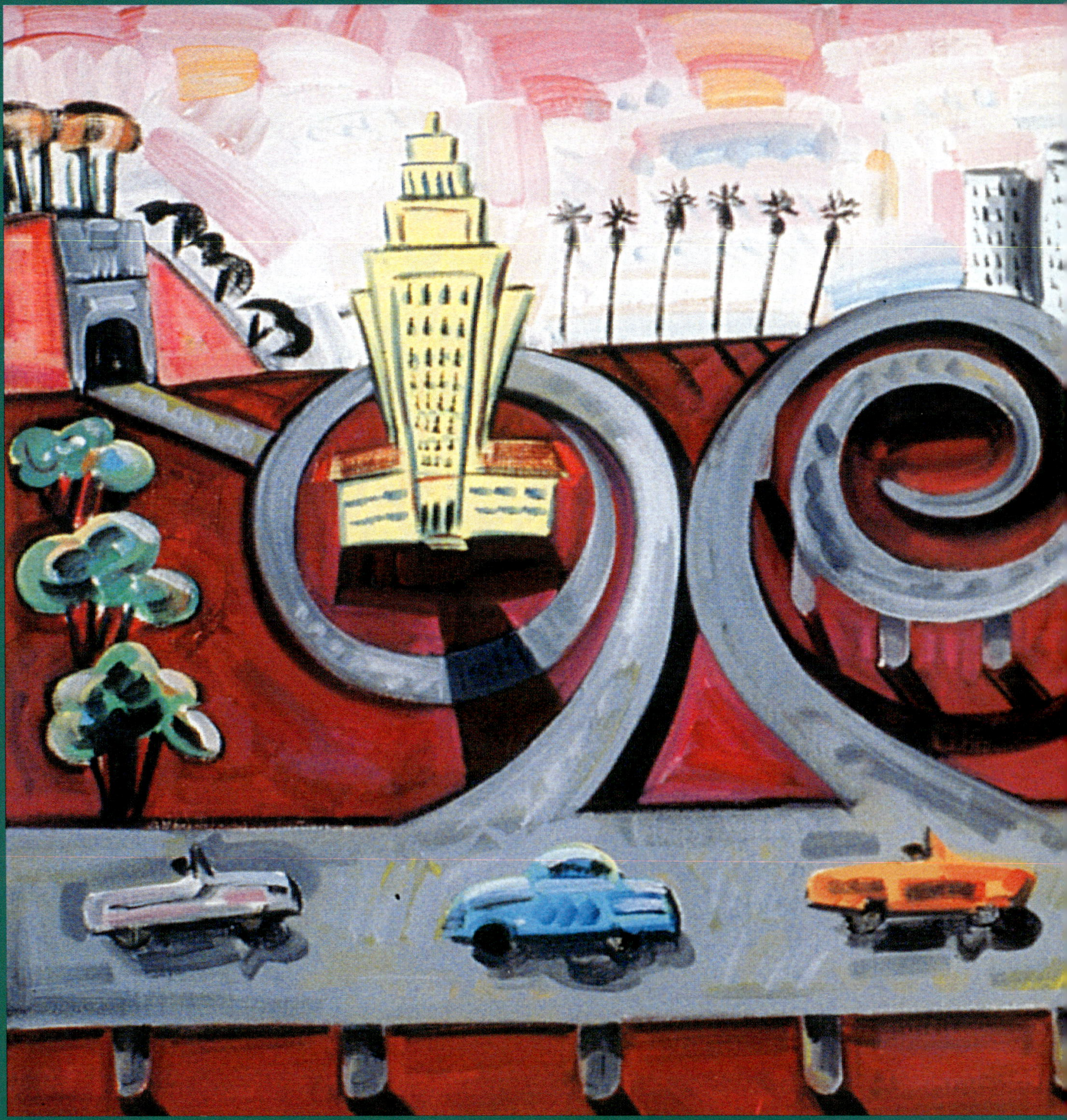

# A Community Connection

SECOND EDITION

Marilyn G. Stewart and Eldon Katter

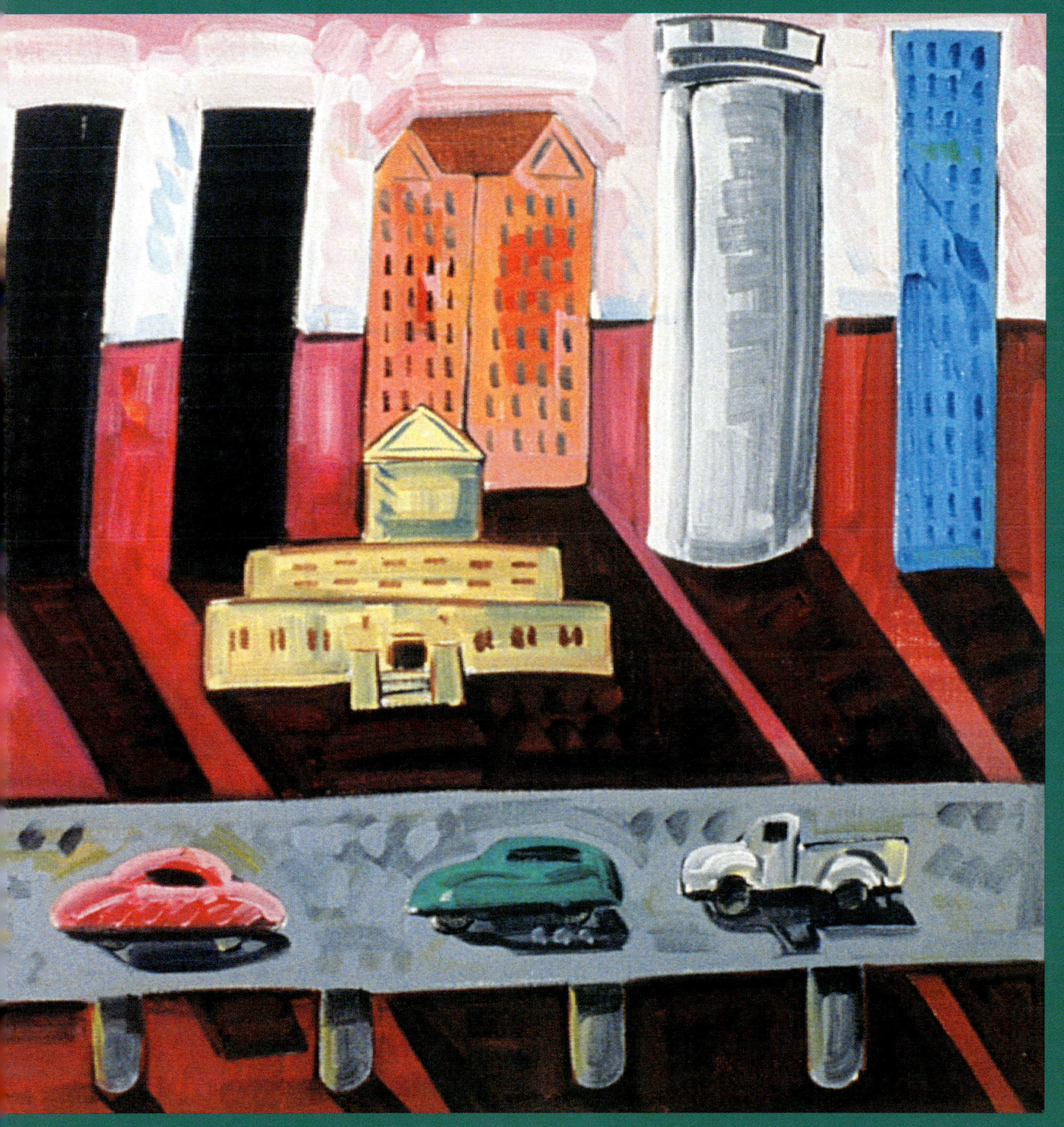

**Reviewers**

Donna Andrich
Houston, Texas

Jaci Hanson
Art Education Consultant
Winter Haven, Florida

BettyAnn Plishker
Fairfax County Public Schools
Annandale, Virginia

Sharon Warwick
National Consultant
Denton, Texas

Cindy Walker
Art Consultant
Chesterfield, Missouri

**Educational Consultants**

Laurel Archambault
Henry James Memorial School
Simsbury, Connecticut

Marissa Ashton
Thomas Prince School
Princeton, Massachusetts

Jennifer Bowden
Huffines Middle School
Flower Mound, Texas

Louisa Brown
Atlanta International School
Atlanta, Georgia

Monica Brown
Laurel Nokomis School
Nokomis, Florida

Anita Cook
Thomas Prince School
Princeton, Massachusetts

Robin W. Cutler
Grafton Middle School
Grafton, Massachusetts

Dale Dinapoli
Archie R. Cole Junior High School
East Greenwich, Rhode Island

Cappie Dobyns
Sweetwater Middle School
Sweetwater, Texas

Judith Durgin
Merrimack Valley Middle School
Penacook, New Hampshire

Suzanne Dyer
Bryant Middle School
Dearborn, Michigan

Elaine Gale
Sarasota Middle School
Sarasota, Florida

Cathy Gersich
Fairhaven Middle School
Bellingham, Washington

Rachel Grabek
Chocksett Middle School
Sterling, Massachusetts

Emma Golding
Thomas Prince School
Princeton, Massachusetts

Sandra Gordon Hersch
Norrback Elementary
Worcester, Massachusetts

Jenny Hersh
Thomas Prince School
Princeton, Massachusetts

Janey Hood
Mount Vernon Middle School
Mount Vernon, Missouri

Maryann Horton
Camels Hump Middle School
Richmond, Vermont

Robin Jackson
Advent Episcopal School
Birmingham, Alabama

Anne Jacques
Smith Middle School
Fort Hood, Texas

Alice S. W. Kepley
Penn View Christian School
Souderton, Pennsylvania

Bunki Kramer
Los Cerros Middle School
Danville, California

Karen Larson
Plum Grove Junior High School
Rolling Meadows, Illinois

Marguerite Lawler-Rohner
Fred C. Wescott Junior High School
Westbrook, Maine

Karen Lintner
Mount Nittany Middle School
State College, Pennsylvania

Betsy Logan
Samford Middle School
Auburn, Alabama

Sara Macaulay
Winsor School
Boston, Massachusetts

Patricia Mann
T.R. Smedberg Middle School
Sacramento, California

Shannon McBride
Riverdale Grade School
Portland, Oregon

Deborah A. Meyers
Colony Middle School
Palmer, Alaska

Phyllis Mowery-Racz
Desert Sands Middle School
Phoenix, Arizona

Kaye Passmore
Notre Dame Academy
Worcester, Massachusetts

Sandy Ray
Johnakin Middle School
Marion, South Carolina

Susan Rushin
Ponoco Mountain Intermediate School South
Swiftwater, Pennsylvania

Roger Shule
Antioch Upper Grade School
Antioch, Illinois

Betsy Menson Sio
Jordan-Elbridge Middle School
Jordan, New York

Elizabeth Sio
37 East Street
Skaneateles, New York

Sharon Siswick
Islesboro Central School
Islesboro, Maine

Karen Skophammer
Manson Northwest Webster Community School
Barnum, Iowa

Evelyn Sonnichsen
Plymouth Middle School
Plymouth, Minnesota

Ann Titus
Central Middle School
Galveston, Texas

Sindee Viano
Avery Coonley School
Downers Grove, Illinois

Karen Watson-Newlin
Verona Area Middle School
Verona, Wisconsin

Shirley W. Whitesides
Asheville Middle School
Asheville, North Carolina

Jason Ohler
Nome Elementary School
Nome, Alaska

**Program Authors**

Marilyn G. Stewart
Eldon Katter

**Writers**

Judy Douglass
Tracy Ellen
Kaye Passmore
Cory Perewiznyk
Kathleen Walck
Nancy Walkup
Tara Young

**Project Staff**

*President and Publisher*
Wyatt Wade

*Content Editor*
Claire Mowbray Golding

*Editor*
Reba Libby

*Product Manager*
Barbara Place

*Design*
WGBH Design:
Tong-Mei Chan
Tyler Kemp-Benedict
Greta Merrick
Jonathan Rissmeyer
Douglass Scott
Michelle Vaira

With extremely helpful image guidance from Karl Cole, Curator of Images

*Production*
Chrysalis Publishing Group

*Editorial Assistants*
*Photo Acquisitions*
Jane McKeag
Abigail Reip
Donna Young

*Illustrator*
Susan Christy-Pallo

*Photography*
Tom Fiorelli

*Manufacturing*
Georgiana Rock



Library of Congress Control Number 2008931902

Printed in the United States of America

ISBN: 978-0-87192-882-5

1 2 3 4 5 6 7 8 9 RRD 15 14 13 12 11 10 09 08

Cover: André Derain, *Turning Road, L'Estaque*, (detail) 1906. Oil on canvas, 51" x 76 ¾" (129.5 x 195 cm). Museum of Fine Arts, Houston. Gift of Audrey Jones Beck. ©2000 Artists Rights Society (ARS), New York/ADAGP, Paris.

Title Page: Frank Romero, *Downtown*, 1990. Oil on linen, 24" x 48" (61 x 121.9 cm). Courtesy of the artist.

# A Letter from the Authors

Dear Student,

We are delighted that you'll be using *A Community Connection* as your art textbook this year.

Our goal in writing this book was to offer you experiences in art that will matter to you today and remain part of your thinking well into the future.

We hope this textbook will inspire you to notice the art all around you. We also hope it will help you express your own ideas and feelings through art in its many forms—drawing, painting, sculpture, photography, printmaking, fiber arts, ceramics, graphic design, and their countless combinations.

You may wonder why we chose the book's unit titles. Each unit focuses on a "big idea" such as Nature, Messages, or Daily Life. These ideas have been important to people around the world throughout history. As you learn about them, we hope you'll begin to see that ideas like these connect you to people who may live far away, people you will never meet. These are the ideas that make us all human. These are the ideas that form the basis for the art people make, no matter when or where they live.

Enjoy finding the connections!

**Marilyn G. Stewart** is Professor of Art Education, Kutztown University of Pennsylvania. She is co-author, with Eldon Katter, of *Explorations in Art 1–5*, author of *Thinking Through Aesthetics*, co-author, with Sydney Walker, of *Rethinking Curriculum in Art*, and series editor of the Art Education in Practice series, all published by Davis Publications. Her honors and awards include 1998 Eastern Region Higher Education Art Educator of the Year, 2006 Pennsylvania Art Educator of the Year, and 1997–98 Getty Education Institute for the Arts Visiting Scholar. A frequent speaker and consultant, she has conducted more than 160 staff development institutes, seminars, or workshops in over 25 states.

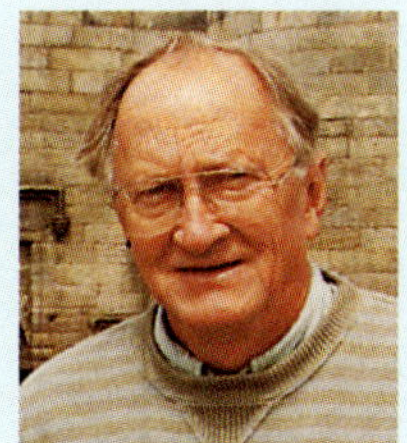

**Eldon Katter** is Emeritus Professor of Art Education at Kutztown University. He is co-author, with Marilyn Stewart, of *Explorations in Art 1–5*, former editor of *SchoolArts*, and former president of the National Art Education Association. He has taught art in elementary schools in Illinois and Massachusetts. As a Peace Corps volunteer in the 1960s, he taught art at a teacher training school in Harar, Ethiopia. He also worked for the Teacher Education in East Africa project in Kampala, Uganda.

# An Introduction to Art

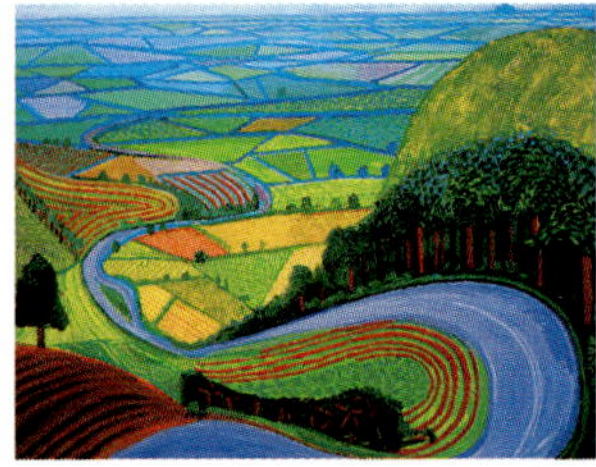
p. xx

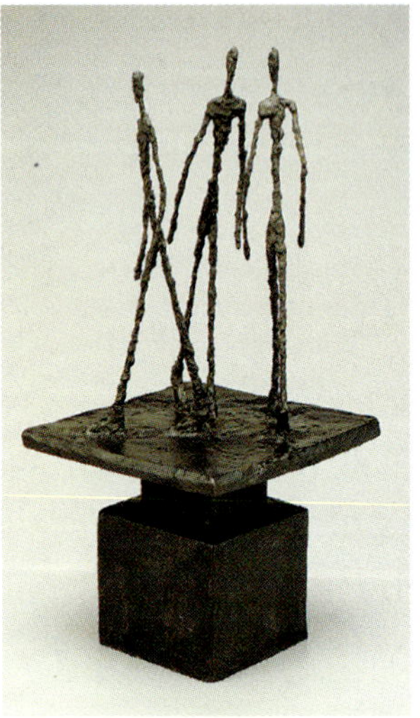
p. xxx

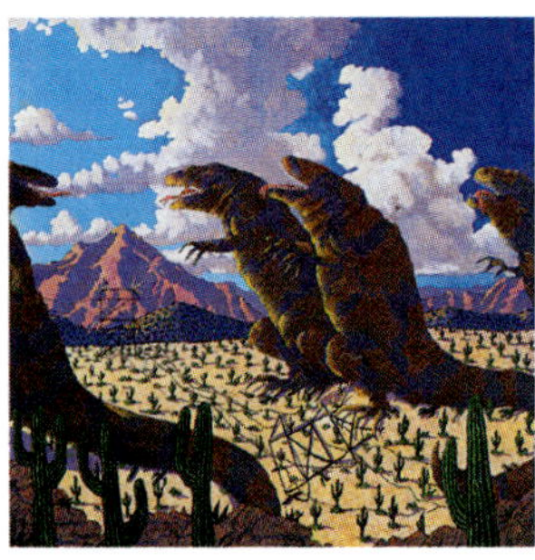
p. xxxi

# Unit 1 Art and Messages

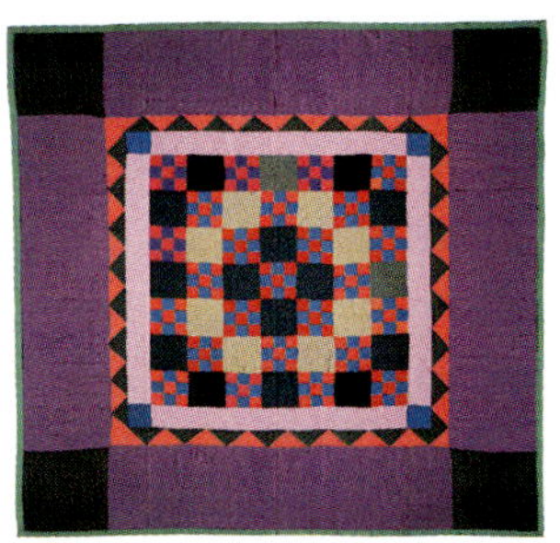
p. 4

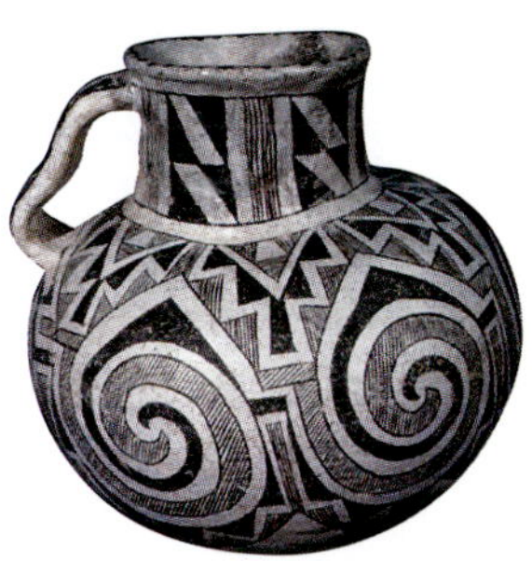
p. 17

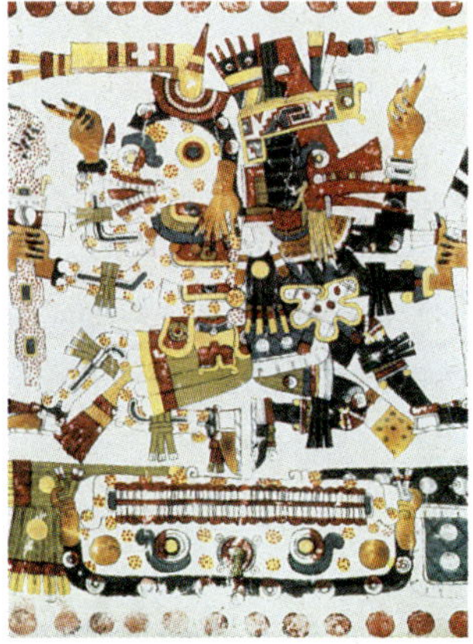
p. 22



**Unit 1 Artists**

# Unit 2 Art and Daily Life

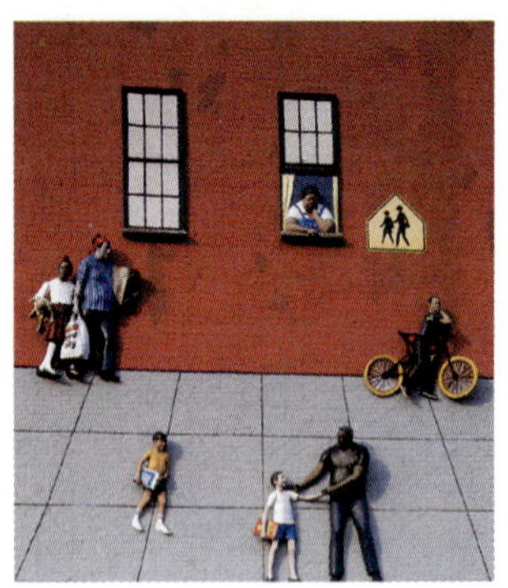
p. 32

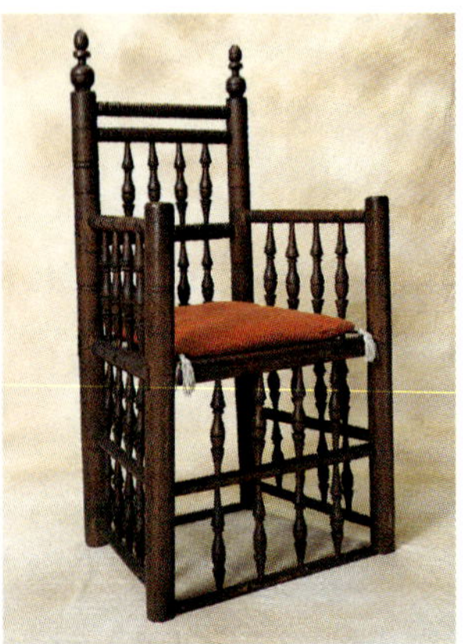
p. 48

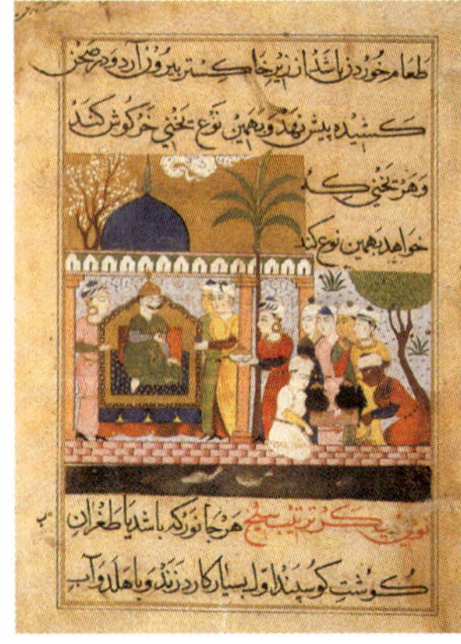
p. 51



**Unit 2 Artists**

# Unit 3 Art and Belonging

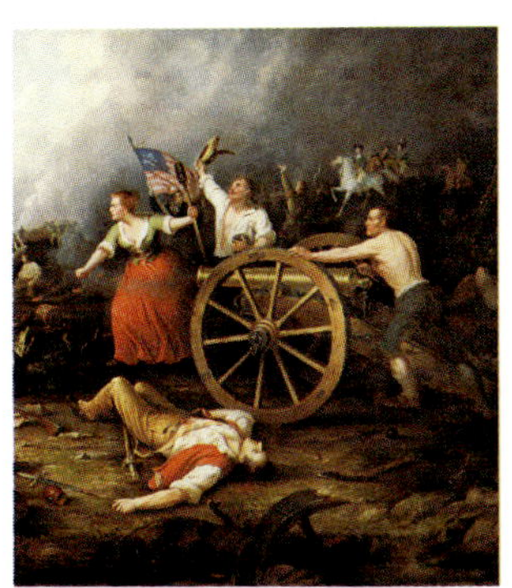
p. 66

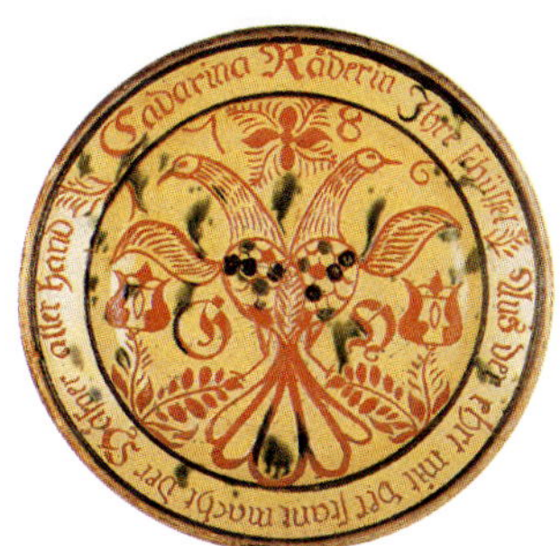

p. 79

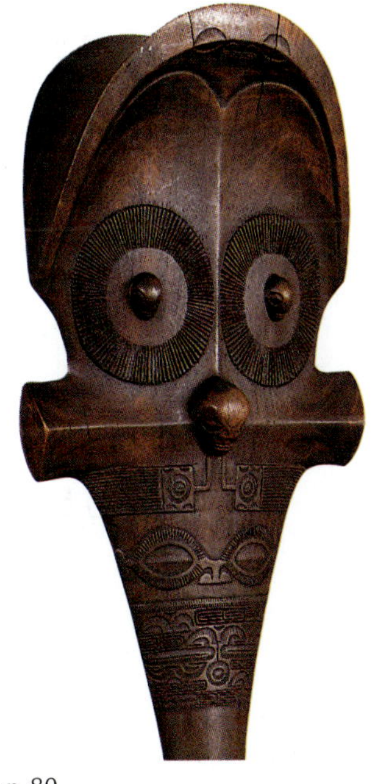
p. 80



**Unit 3 Artists**

# Unit 4 Art and Places

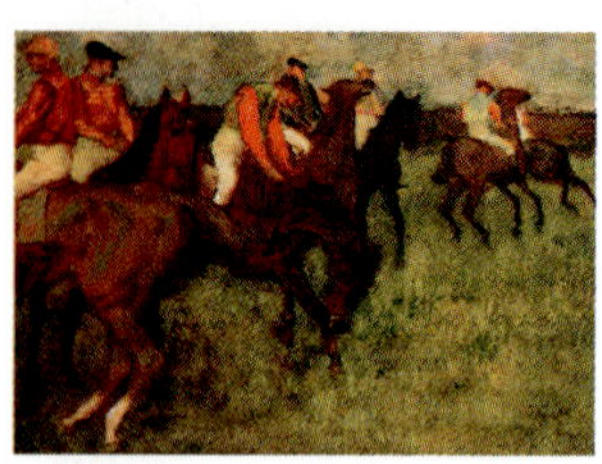
p. 98

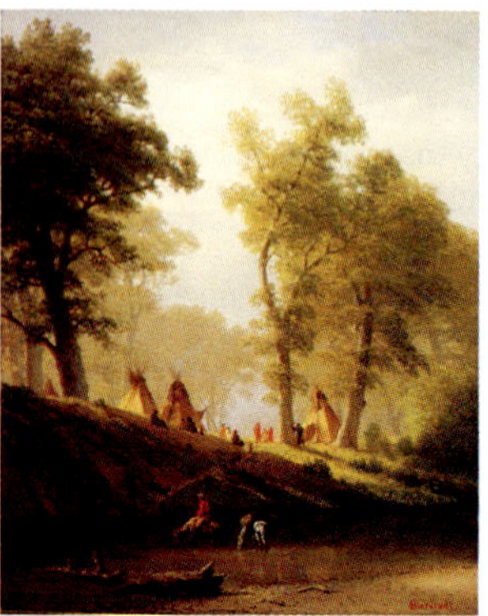
p. 107

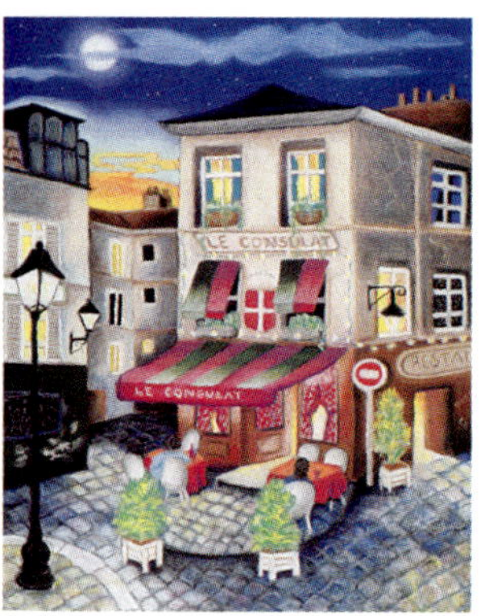
p. 120



**Unit 4 Artists**

# Unit 5 Art and Nature

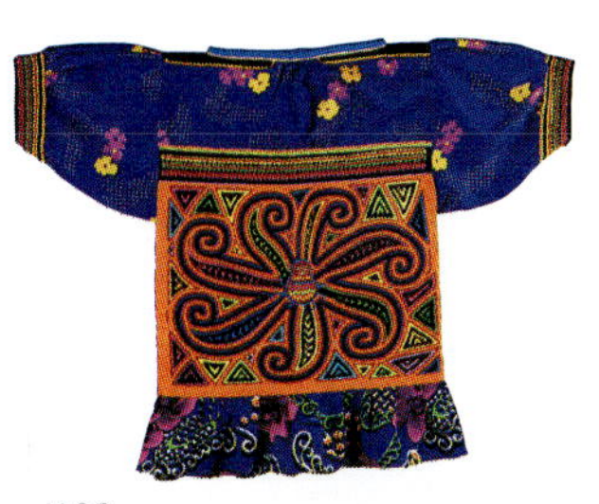
p. 129

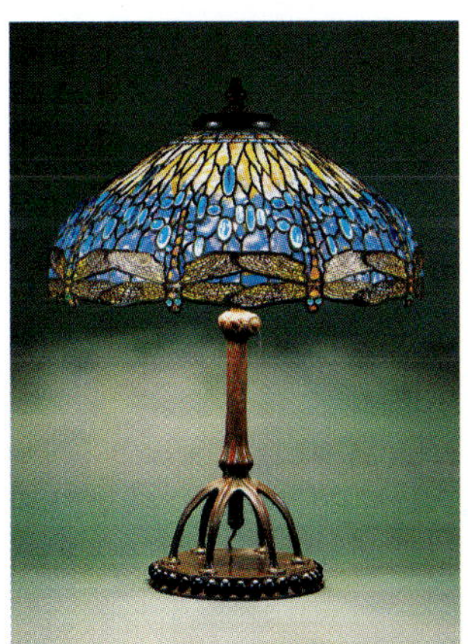
p. 138

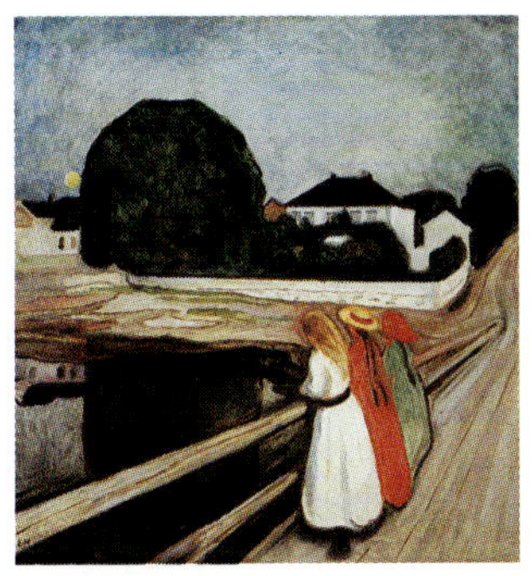
p. 141



**Unit 5 Artists**

# Unit 6 Art and Change

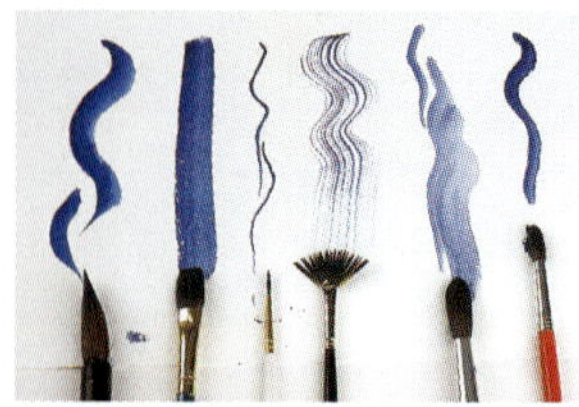
p. 160

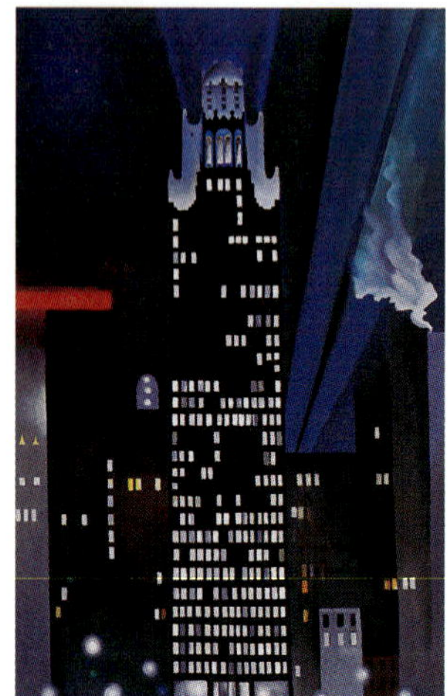
p. 166

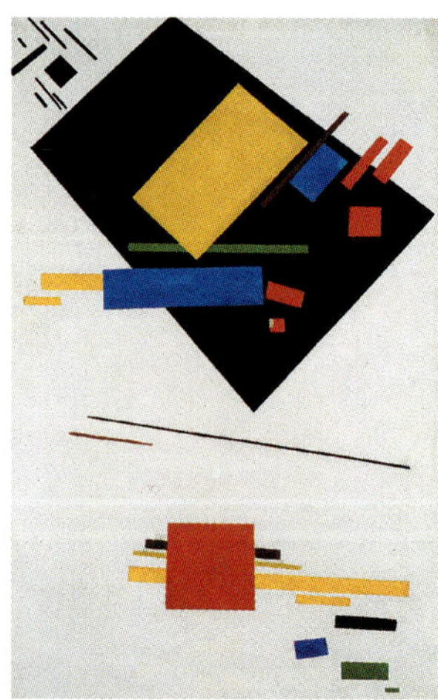
p. 171



**Unit 6 Artists**

# Unit 7 Art and Celebration

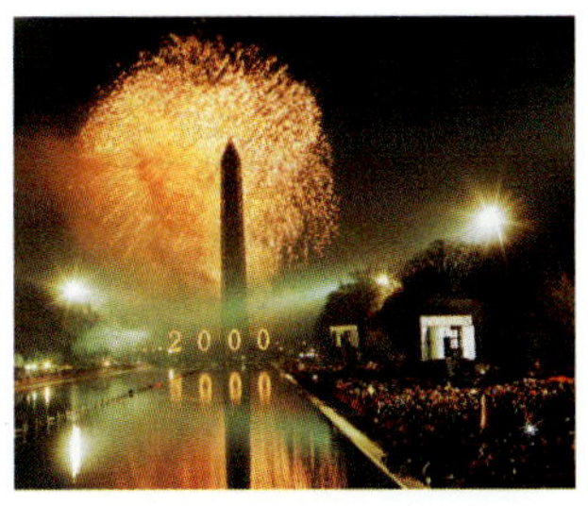
p. 188

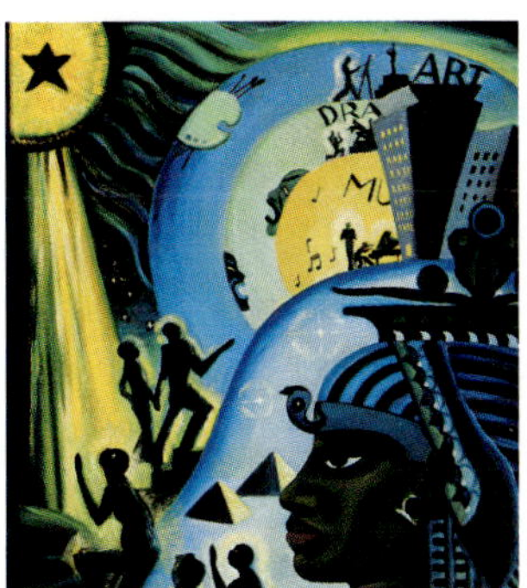

p. 198

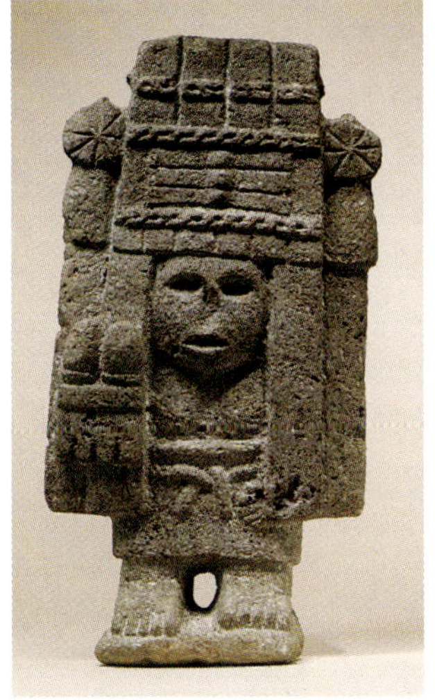
p. 208

# Unit 8 Art and Making a Difference

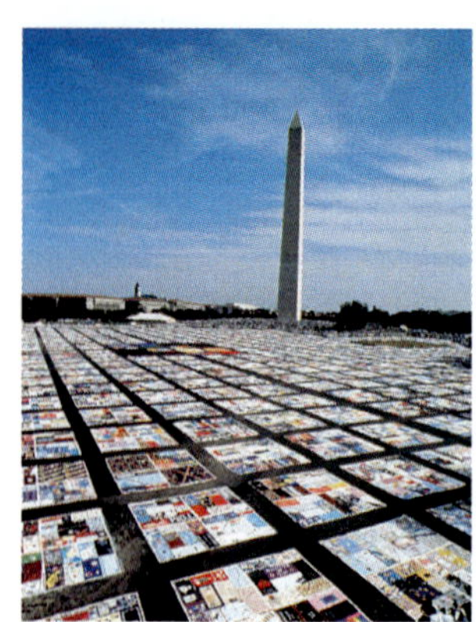
p. 216

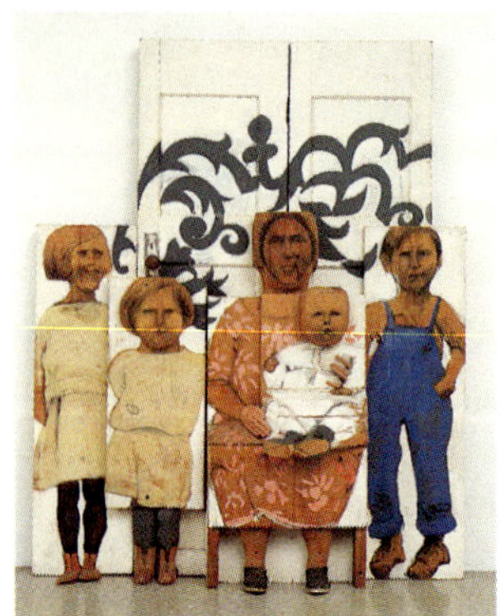
p. 227

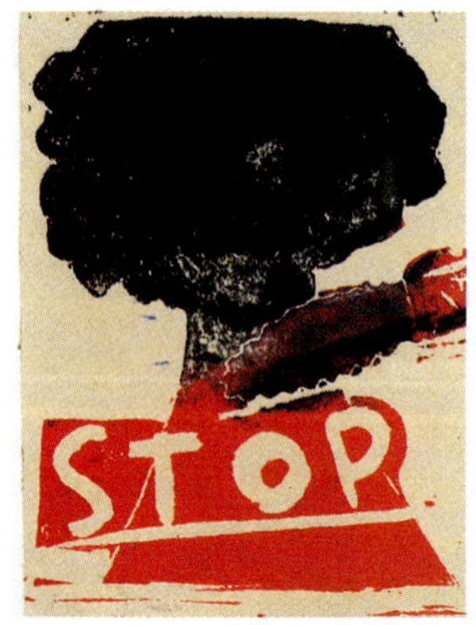

p. 237



**Unit 8 Artists**

# Unit 9 Art and New Directions

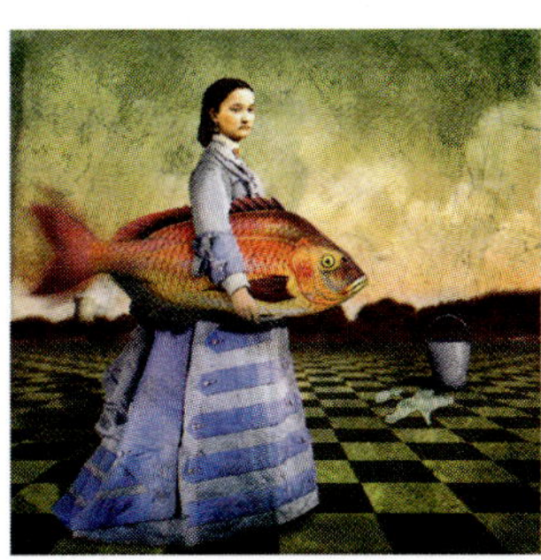
p. 249

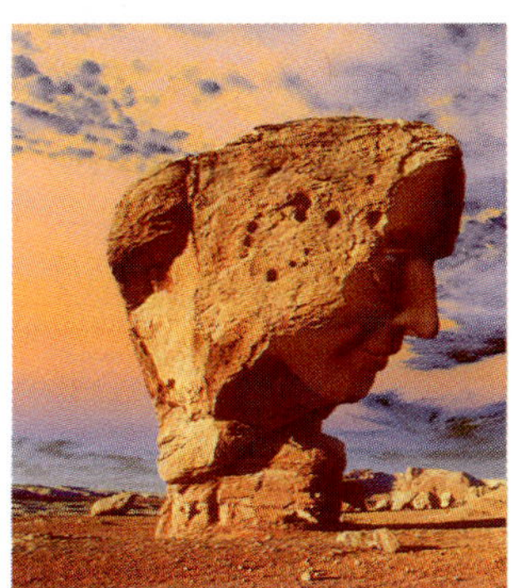
p. 253

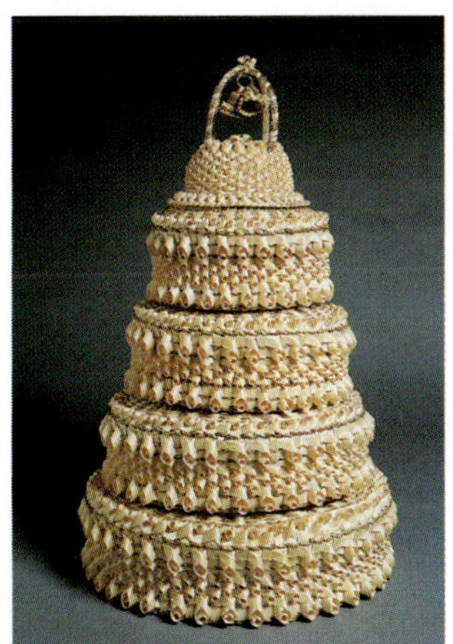
p. 263



**Unit 9 Artists**

## Student Handbook

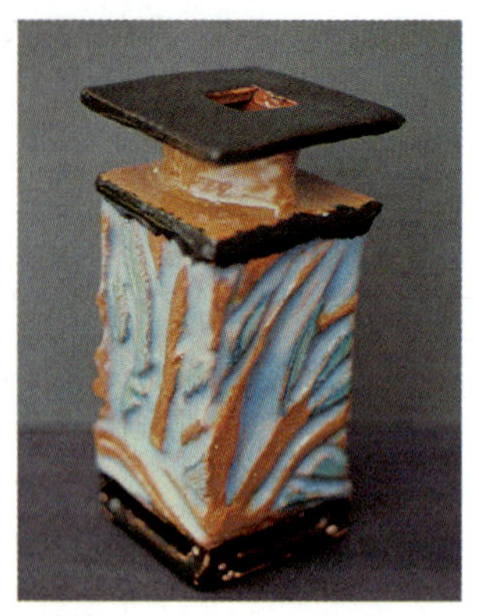
p. 277

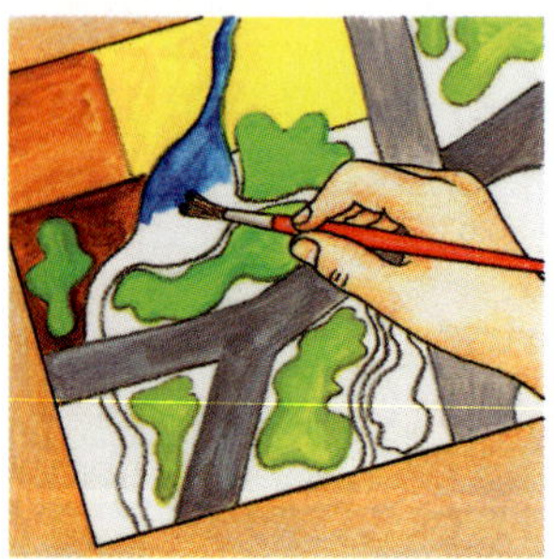
p. 301



## Resources

# Art Is a Community Connection

**What is a community? You might think community means simply your city or town.** But do you belong to a sports team? Do you go to a church or temple, or participate in a club at school? Those groups are communities, too.

People everywhere like to tell others what is special about where they live or what they do. All over the world, art helps people tell these things.

In this book, you'll learn about the many different ways that communities have used art to communicate. As you look at the artworks on these pages, think about the communities you belong to. How is art a part of those communities? How can art help connect your community to other communities? And why are community connections so important to human beings?

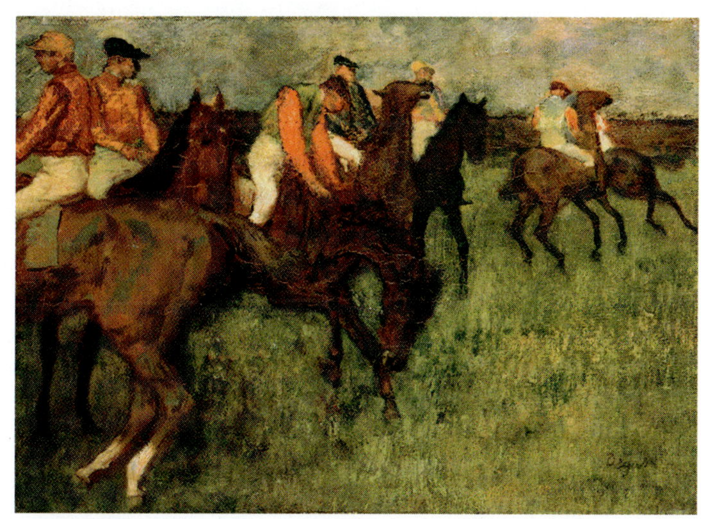

Edgar Degas, *Jockeys,* 1886–90. See page 98.

Romare Bearden, *Pittsburgh Memories,* 1984. See page 13.

Unit 1

# Art and Messages

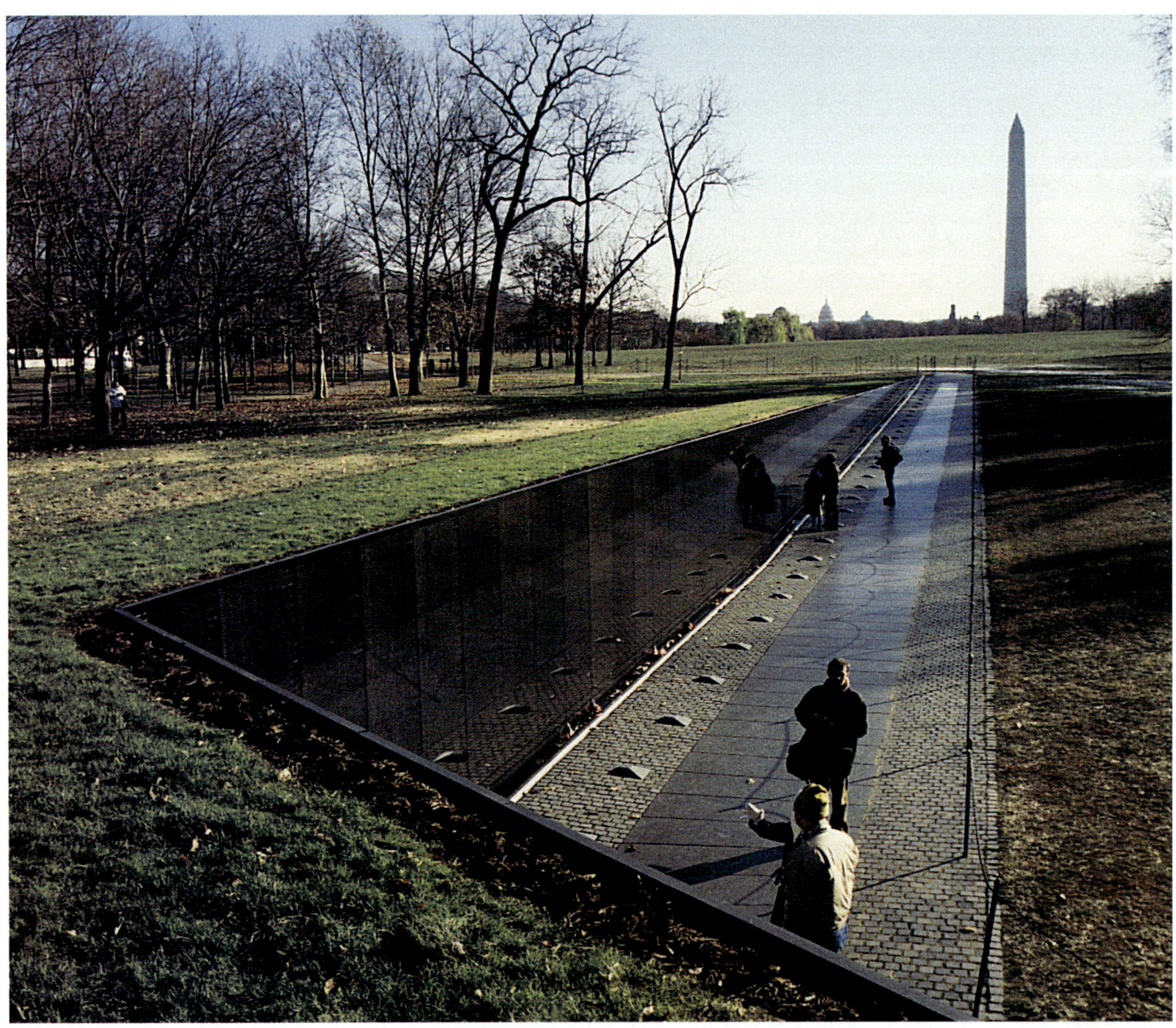

Fig. 1–1 **When visitors come to the wall, they read and touch the engraved names and see their own reflections in its surface. What message might the wall give them?**

Maya Lin, *Vietnam Veterans Memorial*, 1982. Black granite, 493' long (150 m). Constitution Gardens, Washington, DC. Photo by Robert Hersh.

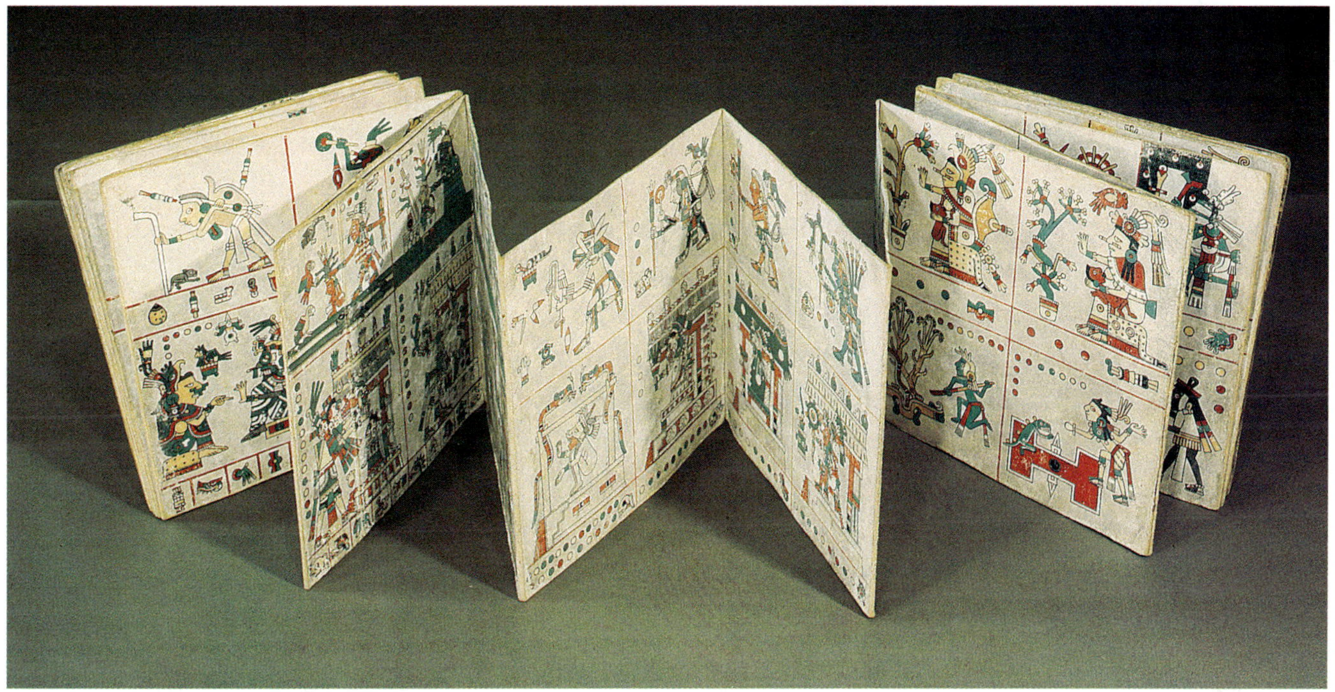

**From the air, it looks like a large V-shaped gash in the ground. As you approach it on foot, you see a gently sloping walkway beside a smooth dark wall.** Up close, you can read the names of all the Americans who died or were reported missing in the Vietnam War. *The Vietnam Veterans Memorial* (Fig. 1–1) has become a symbol for the loss of human life due to war. Its message has been sent throughout this nation and around the world.

Fig. 1–2 **We can learn a great deal about the Aztec culture from its books, called codices. In what way is Aztec picture writing like the pictures you see in comics?**

Mexico, Mixtec style, *Codex Fejervary-Mayer* (shown partially unfolded), ca. 1400 CE. Beaten deerskin and limewash. Liverpool Museum, Liverpool, Great Britain. Werner Forman/Art Resource, New York.

Messages from artworks are also sent within smaller areas. Artworks can tell about the important interests and concerns that community members share.

**In this unit, you will learn:**

- How artists express the ideas and feelings of communities through their artwork.
- How to use shapes and symbols to send your own messages.
- How to identify symbols and messages in artworks.

# Visual Messages

Communication is the exchange of information, thoughts, feelings, ideas, opinions, and much more. It can be spoken, written, or take a visual form. To communicate, you need a sender (someone who creates a message) and a receiver (someone who understands the message). As you have grown up, you have learned how to speak and write the language of your community. You've learned to understand visual messages. Many of those visual messages are sent to you through art.

## Communicating Beliefs and Values

Artworks often tell about a community's beliefs and values. The quilt in **Fig. 1–3** was made by members of the Amish community, a religious group in North America. The Amish believe in living simple, quiet lives. This is reflected in their quiltmaking traditions. Amish quilts communicate the ideas of simplicity and quality through the use of solid colors and geometric shapes.

Communities also communicate values through their heroes and legends. In *Southwest Pietà* **(Fig. 1–4)** Luis Jiménez uses larger-than-life-sized figures to tell a moving story that blends Aztec and European history.

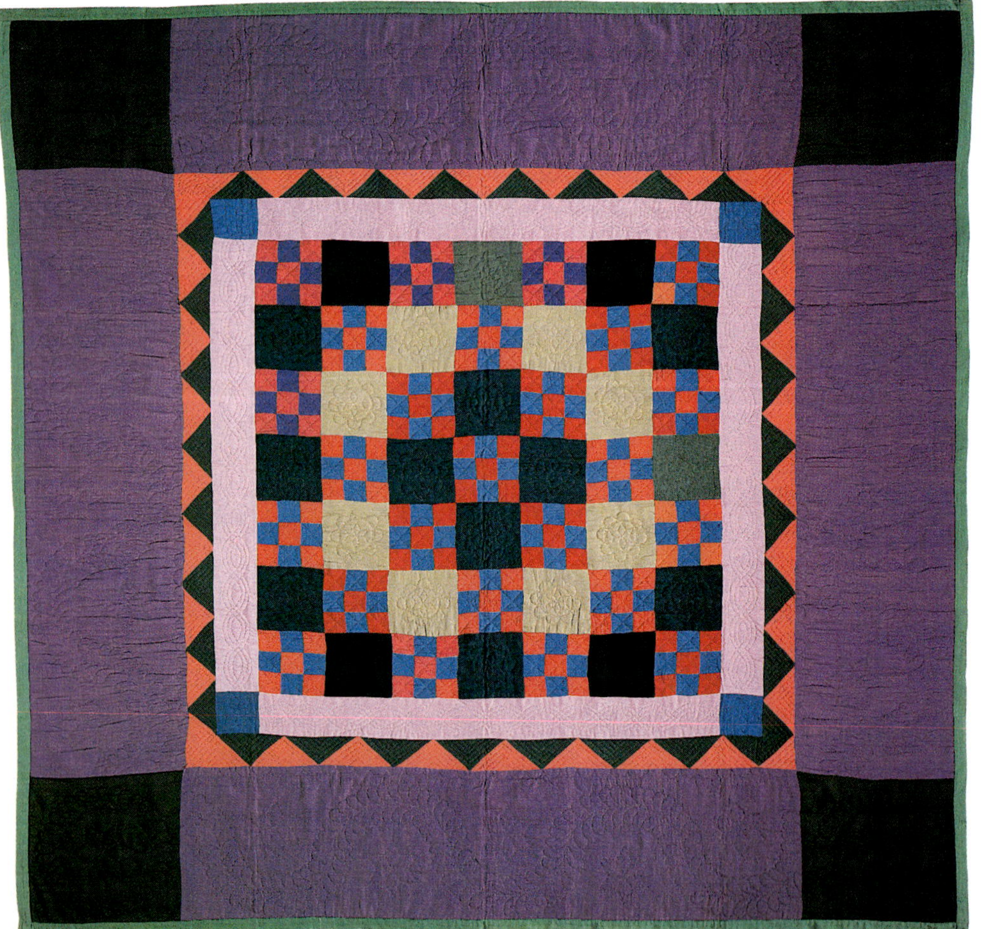

Fig. 1–3 **This quilt has a pattern of geometric shapes and stitched objects. Which of the quilt's designs represent the Amish idea of simplicity? Of quality?**

Anonymous Amish quiltmaker, member of the Zook family, American, *Ninepatch*, Lancaster County, Pennsylvania, ca. 1930. Pieced wools, 80" x 80" (203.2 x 203.2 cm). Private Collection, Photo courtesy of The Quilt Complex.

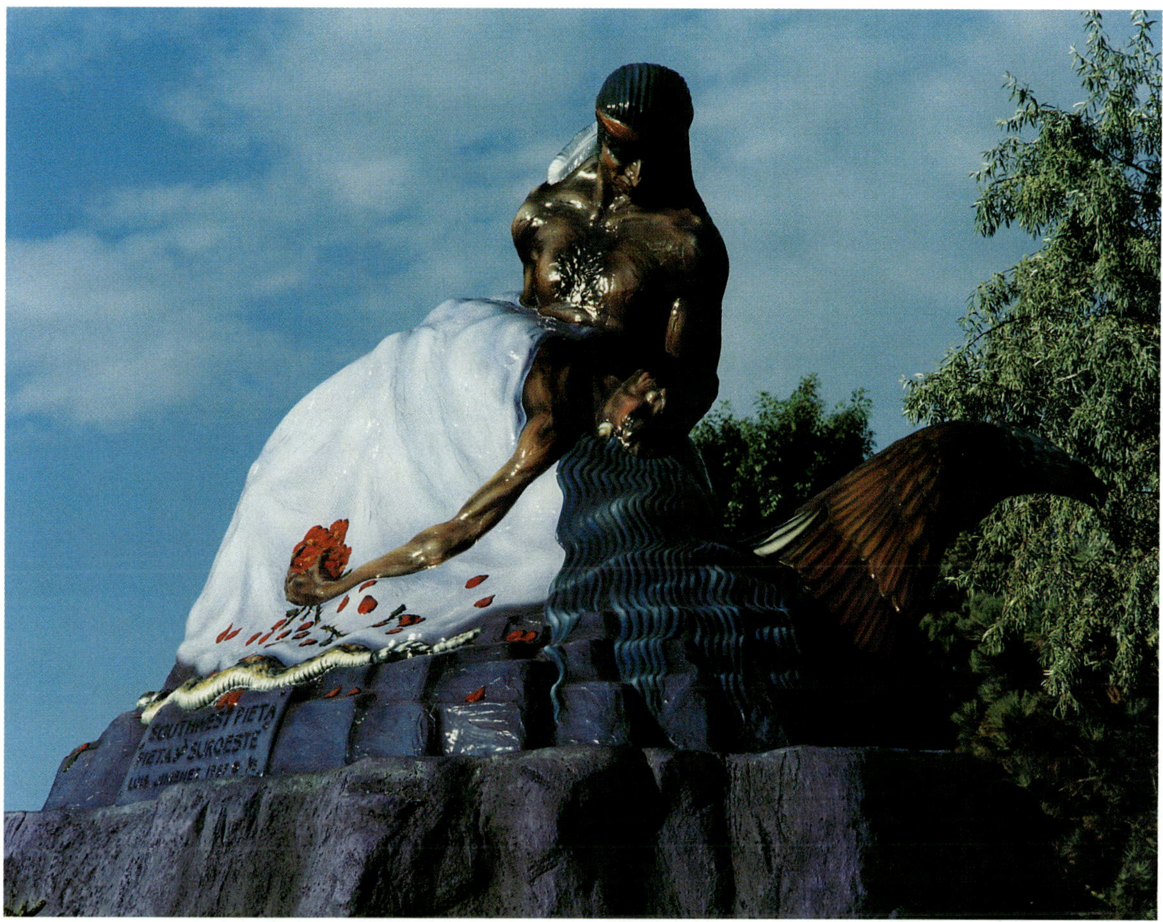


Fig. 1–4 **Some artworks show figures from community legends. This sculpture is titled *Southwest Pietà*. "Pietà" can mean mercy or pity. What kind of message does the sculpture send?**

Luis Jiménez, *Southwest Pietà*, Albuquerque, New Mexico, 1983. Fiberglass. Photograph by Bruce Berman. ©2000 Luis Jiménez/Artist Rights Society (ARS), New York.

## Meet Luis Jiménez

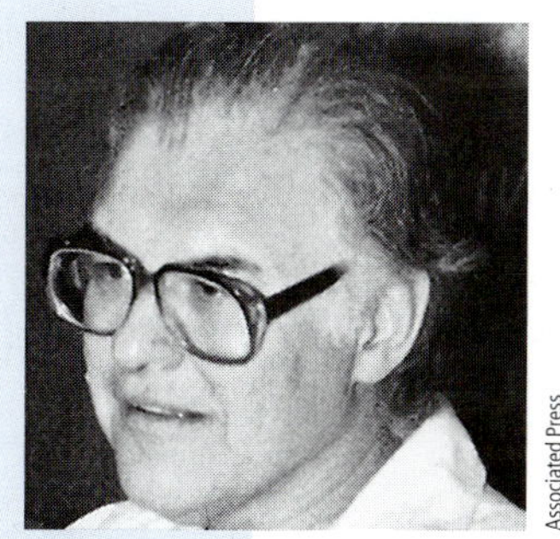

Associated Press

Luis Jiménez, the son of a Mexican immigrant, was born in El Paso, Texas. He worked in his father's neon sign shop and learned how to work with large pieces of metal. At 20, he went to the University of Texas at Austin. Although he had planned to major in architecture, he switched to fine art.

Jiménez is known for making large sculptures out of a common industrial material—fiberglass. Inspired by Mexican artists like Diego Rivera, he proudly depicted Mexican culture. His work focuses on common people without trying to make them beautiful. It is displayed across the United States.

**"People have often said to me that my work raises issues… that's part of what artists do… Art has the obligation to take us to a different place."**

— Luis Jiménez (1940–2006)

**Teaching and Telling** Communities rely on artworks to show how their members work and play. They use art to tell stories about historical events and special places. People depend on artists to observe life and, through their artworks, show others what they see.

It is sometimes easy to see the connection between an artwork and the life of a community. However, in artworks such as the *Thompson Indian River Shield* (Fig. 1–5), the meaning of the materials and images is not as clear. We might guess what the symbols mean, but we need to know more about the community to understand the artwork's message.

**Finding Clues to Meaning** Many of the artworks we see were made hundreds and even thousands of years ago. Some were made in faraway places. Because of this, we may never know their full meaning. However, we might understand an artwork better by looking at its details and learning about the community in which it was made. For example, an object or symbol that is repeated in the artwork might mean something special to the community. We can sometimes find clues to its meaning.

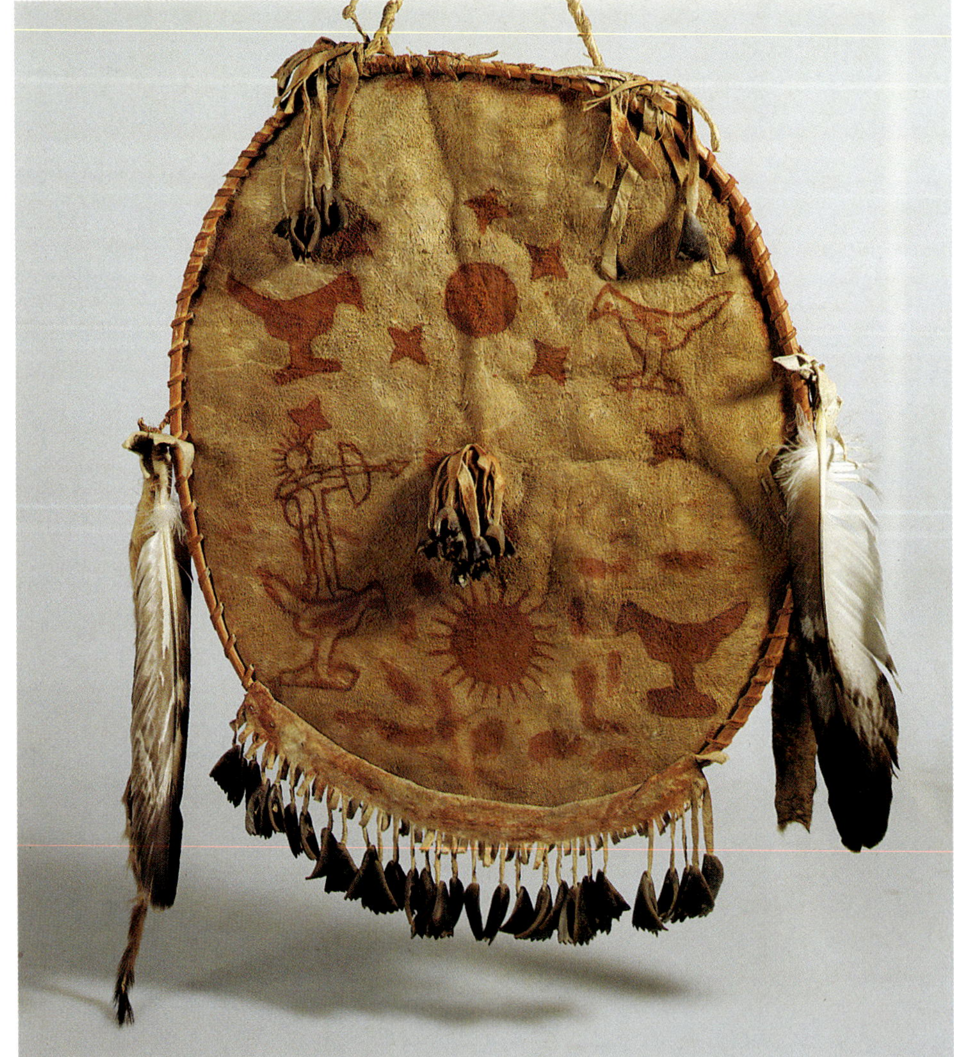

Fig. 1–5 **Artists from Native American cultures often use natural materials and symbols from nature. What natural materials and symbols can you identify in this shield?**

Canada, *Thompson Indian River Shield*, no date. Deerskin stretched on a wooden hoop. Peabody Museum, Harvard University. Photograph by Hillel Burger.

## Studio Time

### A Special Place

Working individually or in a group, create a symbol to show how your community is unique or special.

- Finish the following prompt: "I am from a place (that or where…)." For example, you might say, "I am from a place where a river flows through the center of town," or "I am from a place that values reading."
- Compile a list of the completed prompts from the class.
- Using the list as your guide, create a set of symbols to represent your community.
- Choose appropriate colors. Consider using your design for a poster or banner.

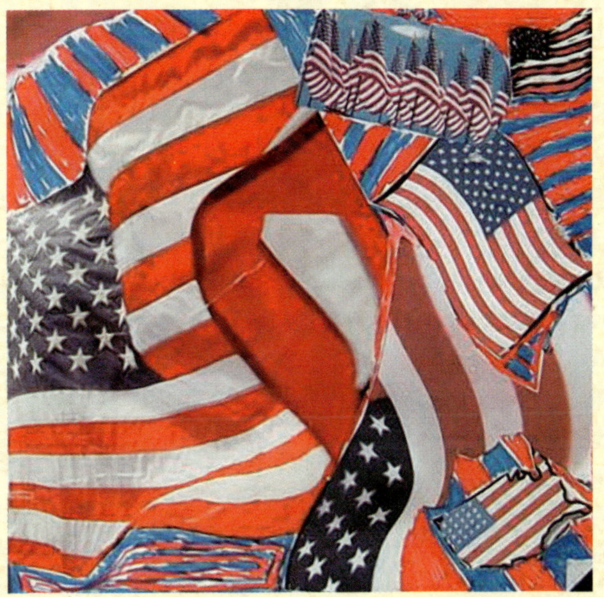

Fig. 1–7 Student artwork

Reflect on the message your symbol conveys about your community.

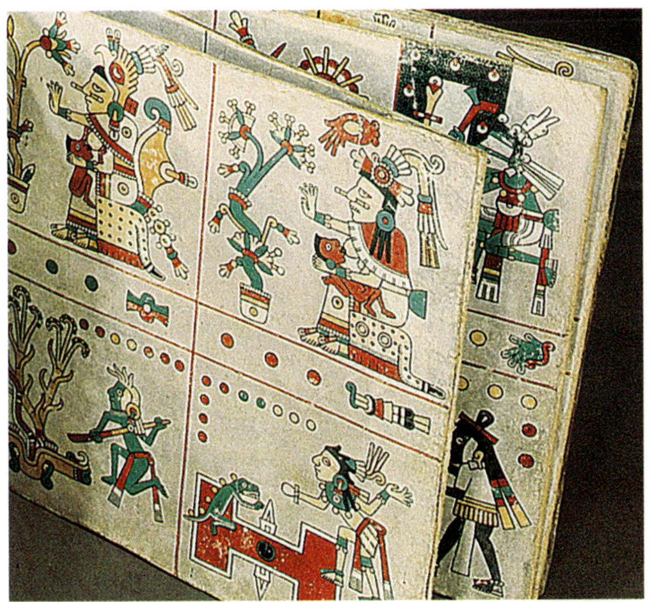

Fig. 1–6 **Look at the details in this close-up view of the codex that appears in full in Fig. 1–2. What patterns or repeated images do you see?**

Mexico, Mixtec style, *Codex Fejervary-Mayer* (shown partially unfolded), ca. 1400 CE. Beaten deerskin and limewash. Liverpool Museum, Liverpool, Great Britain. Werner Forman/Art Resource, NY.

### Check Your Understanding

**1.** In your own words, explain the roles of the sender and receiver in understanding messages communicated through art.

**2.** Compare and contrast the messages that are communicated in **Figs. 1–3** and **1–4**.

**3.** How do people in a community use artworks?

# Graphic Design

If you have looked around you at all today, you've probably seen an example of graphic design. Graphic design is the art of combining words and images to create a message. Graphic designers create packages, labels, and logos for products and businesses. They create the look of magazines, maps, posters, signage for roads and buildings, and exhibits for museums. They design billboards, and create advertisements in newspapers and magazines. They're responsible for the look of greeting cards and books.

The messages expressed in graphic designs help people decide whether to buy a product or service. Graphic designs can inform and persuade people, causing them to support other people, groups, and ideas. Graphic designs also help people identify places and services in the community.

**Effective Graphic Design** A successful graphic design may use mostly words, type, and color to send its message, such as the one shown in Fig. 1–8. Here, the text sends a strong message all by itself. Or a graphic design might rely on a combination of text and images, as in Fig. 1–9. There are many possible solutions to any design problem. Graphic designers are always trying to find the most effective ones.

**Observe** Look again at Fig. 1–9. What words are largest? Smallest? Which are most brightly colored? Which are easiest to read? What has the artist done to produce these effects?

**Tools:** Pencil, paper, and markers.

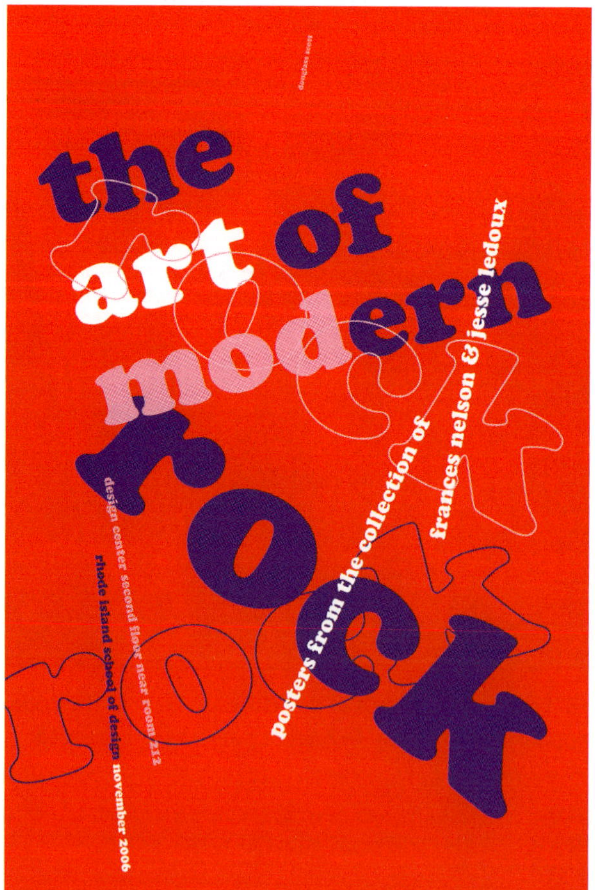


Fig. 1–8 **How are color and lettering used to draw your attention to this graphic design?**

Douglass Scott, *The Art of Modern Rock,* 2006. Digital print, 11" x 17" (27.9 cm x 43.2 cm). Courtesy of the designer.

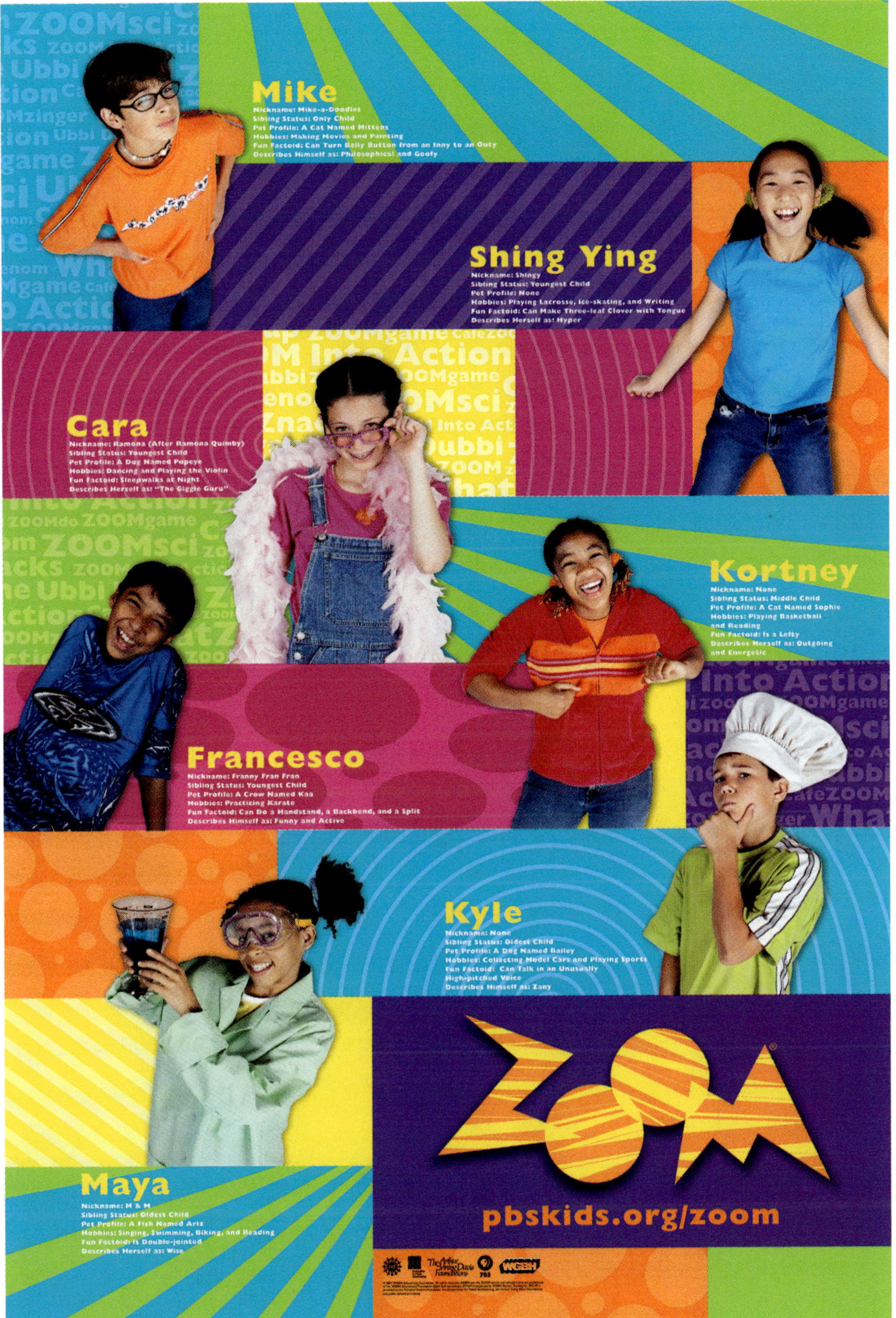


Fig. 1–9 **How did the artist use color and images to promote the show *ZOOM*? What is the most important element in the graphic?**

Peter Lyons, *Zoom*, 2004. Offset lithography, 22" x 33" (55.9 cm x 83.8 cm). Courtesy of WGBH Design.

## Practice: Lettering

- Draw two parallel lines 3" apart across a sheet of paper.
- Choose a simple font, such as Times Roman or Arial. Print out an entire alphabet of the font.
- Choose a word or phrase to copy in the style of your chosen font.
- Draw the word or phrase, paying careful attention to sizes and spacing of letters.

**The Design Process** Most graphic designs start with a need to communicate a message. For example, when a company needs to advertise a new product, it might ask a graphic designer to design a magazine ad. This is a design problem to be solved. To solve the problem, the designer must do the following:

- Find out who the audience is, how big the ad will be, and where the ad will be placed.
- Play with ideas by drawing, painting, photographing, or using computers.
- Develop several clear, possible solutions.
- Present the solutions to the company.
- Revise one solution according to the company's desires.
- Produce the final ad.

A graphic design that is simple, clear, and unified can be spotted at a distance. To make the design simple, choose only the most important ideas to illustrate. To attract attention to a design, include a clear center of interest. Use colors to suggest moods or feelings.

**Observe** Look carefully at the images, colors, and lettering used in Figs. 1–10 and 1–11. Where is the type in each? Where are the images? What colors have been used? What elements stand out most clearly? Why?

**Tools:** Paper, pencils, and markers.

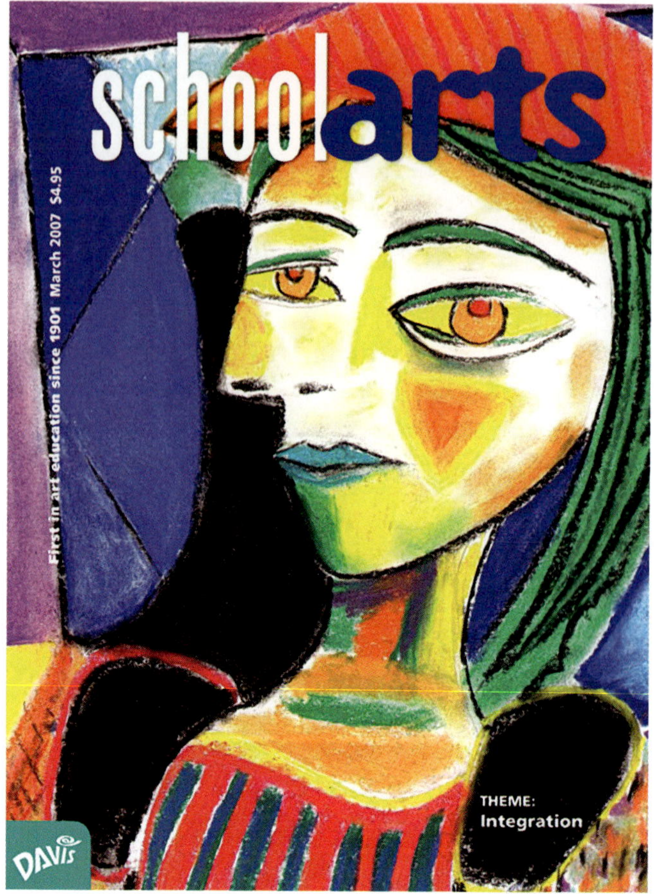


Fig. 1–10 **How has the designer of this magazine cover attracted attention? Where is the center of interest?**

*Self Portraits in the Classroom.* Cover, *SchoolArts* Magazine, March 2007. Courtesy of Davis Publications, Worcester, MA.

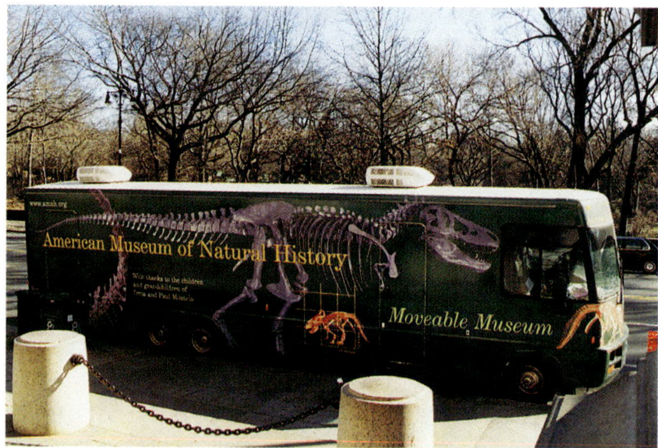


Fig. 1–11 **Why can the side of this bus be considered an example of graphic design?**

American Museum of Natural History, *Mobile Museum*, 2000. Courtesy of the American Museum of Natural History.

### Practice: The Design Process

- Choose a simple image to go with the word you made in the previous practice session. The word and image should work together to form a message.
- Think about placement and size. Will the word be larger than the image? Should the image be larger than the word? Why?
- Think about colors to use. What colors help communicate your message and attract your attention?

### Check Your Understanding

1. What can graphic designs provide to people in communities?
2. Compare and contrast the images, colors, and lettering used in Figs. 1–10 and 1–11.
3. Describe an example of graphic design. How do the colors, letters, and images express a message?

## Studio Time

### An Illustrated Word

Create a graphic design out of one word. For example, the word *ice* might have letters that look like chunks of carved ice. The word *flower* could have letters that resemble flowers.

- Choose a word that represents something you might find in your community.
- Plan your design, using cut paper to make the basic letter shapes. What colors can you use?
- Make several sketches.
- Choose your best sketch and create your finished graphic design.

Reflect on how the features of the letters relate to the word.

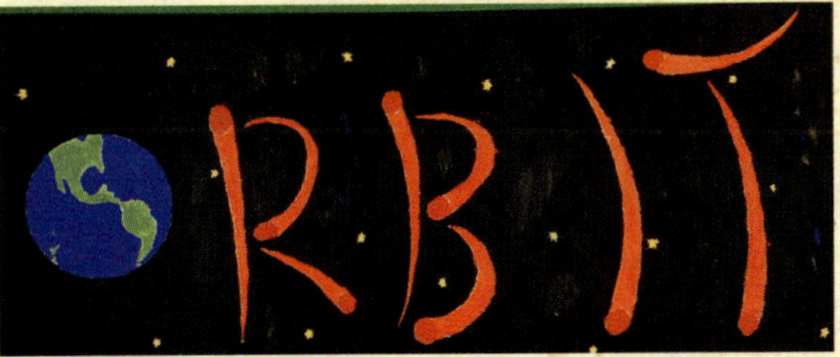


Fig. 1–12 Student artwork

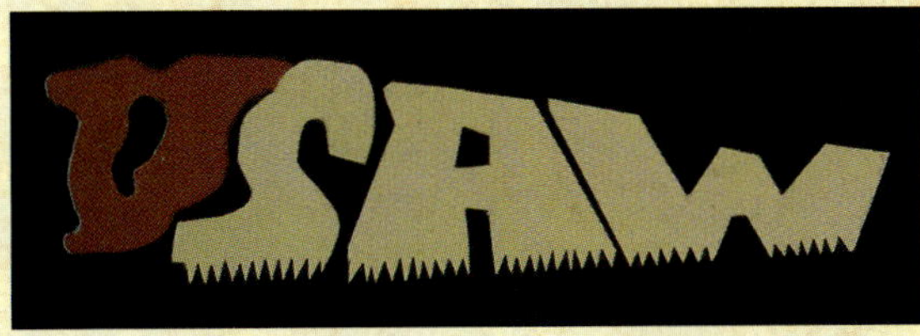


Fig. 1–13 Student artwork

# A Telling Collage

## Studio Background

You are part of many different communities. Your family is a community, for instance. Your school is another kind of community. Clubs are communities, too.

**In this studio exploration, you will use collage techniques to tell about the communities you know best.** To create a collage, an artist pastes flat materials, such as pieces of fabric and paper, on a background. Some artists combine collage with drawing and painting. Artists use collage to express their thoughts, feelings, and ideas about a subject.

### You Will Need

- magazines
- drawing paper
- pencils
- glue
- markers
- paint (optional)

## Step 1 Plan and Practice

- Think about the communities to which you belong. They might be geographical communities, or clubs and groups.
- Ask yourself: Which of these communities influence the decisions I make? Which ones affect my behavior, my clothing, or the way I spend my time?
- Rank the communities in terms of their importance.

**Things to Remember:**

✓ Choose images that best describe you and the communities in which you participate.

✓ Show how you rank the importance of your communities by how they are arranged.

✓ Arrange your images in a way that communicates a clear message about your community.

## Inspiration from Our World

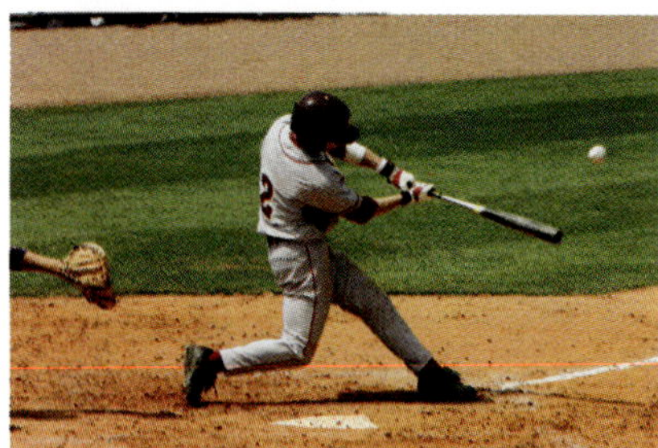

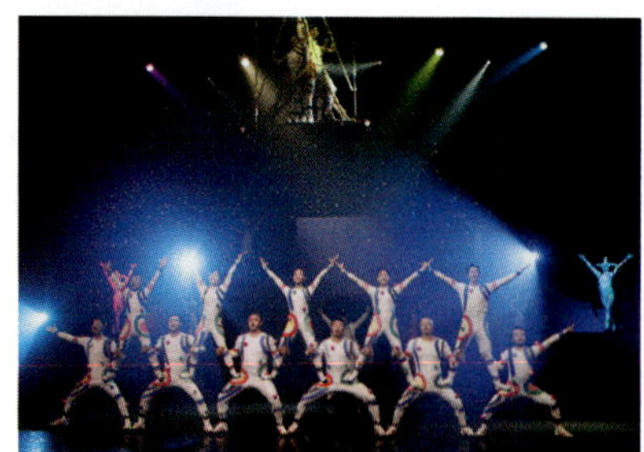

PR Newswire.

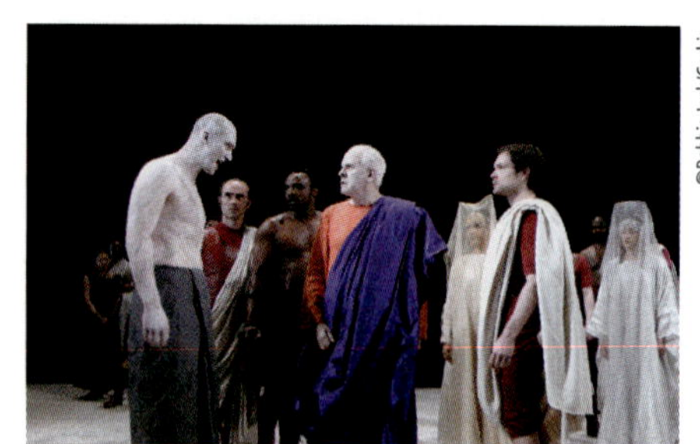

©Robbie Jack/Corbis.

## Inspiration from Art

Collage is a French word for pasted paper. In a collage, flat materials such as paper, fabric, news clippings, or photographs are pasted on a background. Collage artists may also use pieces of natural materials (twigs, seashells) and other odds and ends. They might add details, shapes, and colors with markers, crayons, or charcoal.

Romare Bearden created many collages about life in big cities. In *Pittsburgh Memories* **(Fig. 1–14)**, he remembers his grandmother's boardinghouse in Pittsburgh, Pennsylvania. With shapes, colors, and details, he shows a picture of the community there. For *Cloak of Heritage* **(Fig. 1–15)**, artist Kevin Warren Smith chose photographs of Native Americans to help express ideas about his heritage.

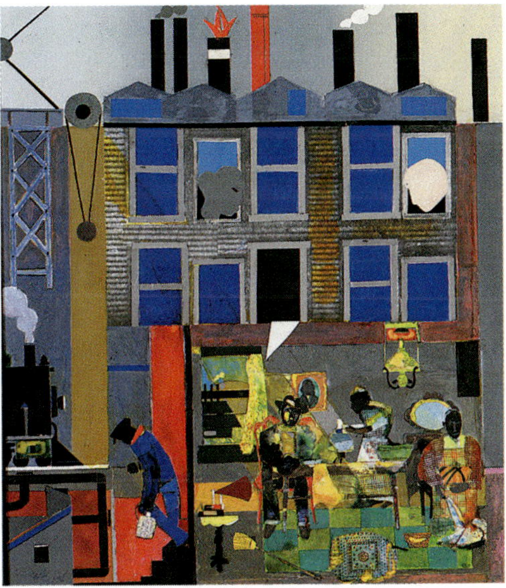

Fig. 1–14 **What thoughts and feelings might the artist be expressing in this collage? Why do you think so?**

Romare Bearden, *Pittsburgh Memories*, 1984. Collage on board, 28 5/8" x 23 1/4" (72.7 x 59.7 cm). The Carnegie Museum of Art, Pittsburgh (Gift of Mr. and Mrs. Ronald R. Davenport and Mr. and Mrs. Milton A. Washington). ©Romare Bearden Foundation/Licensed by VAGA, New York, NY.

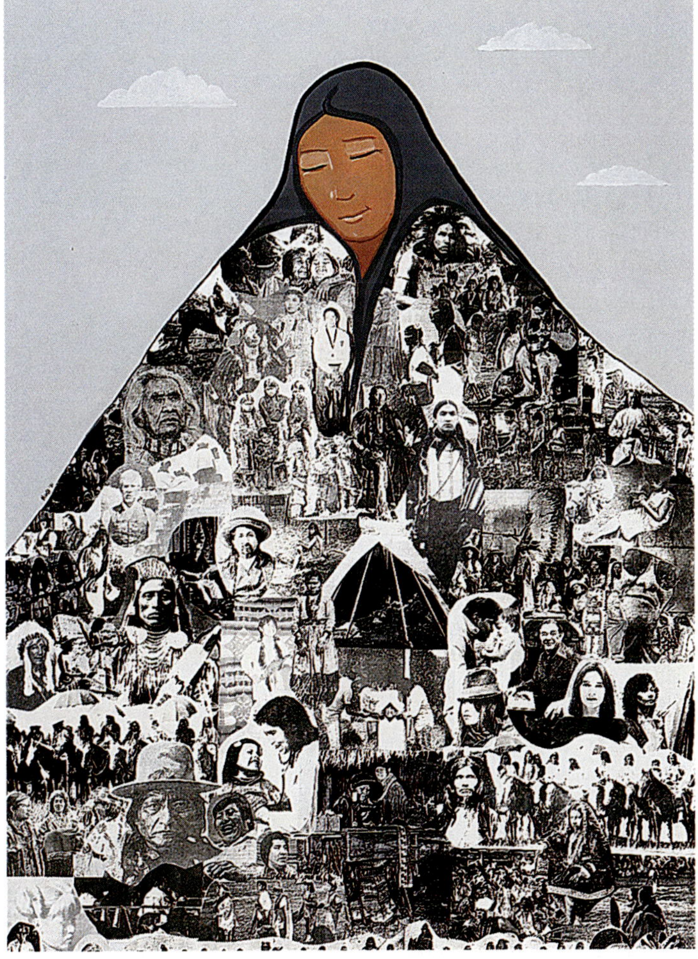

Fig. 1–15 **The subject matter of Kevin Warren Smith's work often focuses on Native American themes. How has the artist made the woman who wears the cloak seem important?**

Kevin Warren Smith, *Cloak of Heritage*, 1991. Acrylic and collage on canvas, 24" x 36" (61 x 91.4 cm). ©Kevin Warren Smith.

## Step 2 Begin to Create

- **Look for and cut out magazine images that symbolize your membership in multiple communities.**

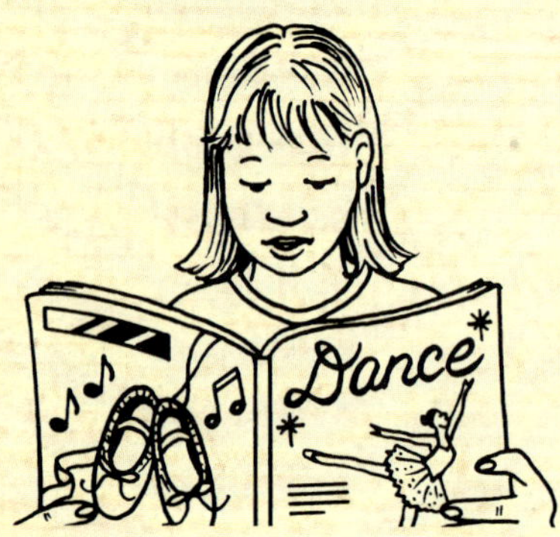


- You may wish to include your own drawings or cut-paper designs.
- Do not use letters or words.
- Arrange the images on a background using the principles of design: balance, rhythm, proportion, emphasis, pattern, unity, and variety.
- **Try different arrangements before pasting the images.**

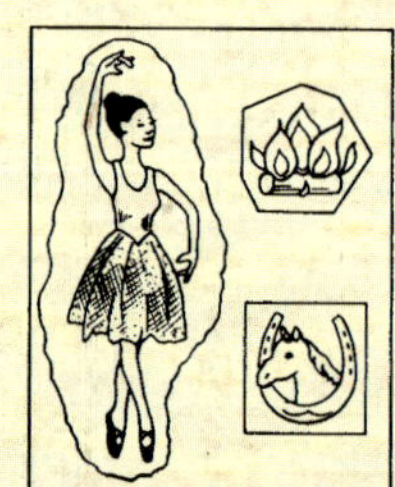
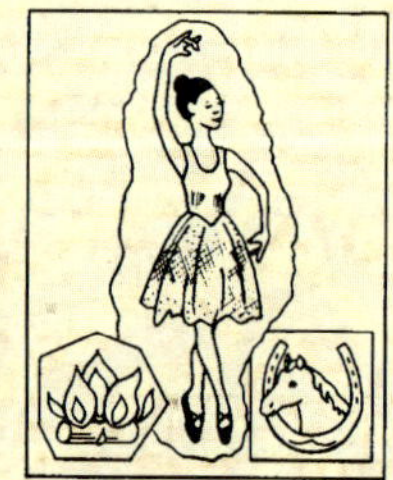
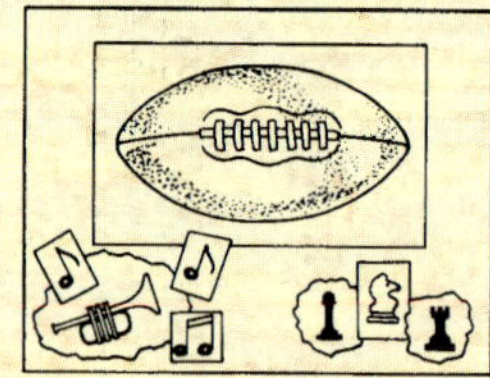
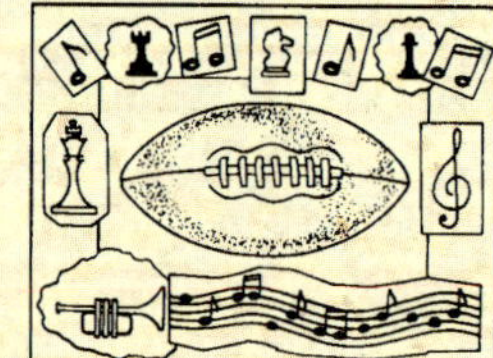

- Choose an arrangement that expresses a message about your community memberships and their rank.
- **Glue the images to the background.**

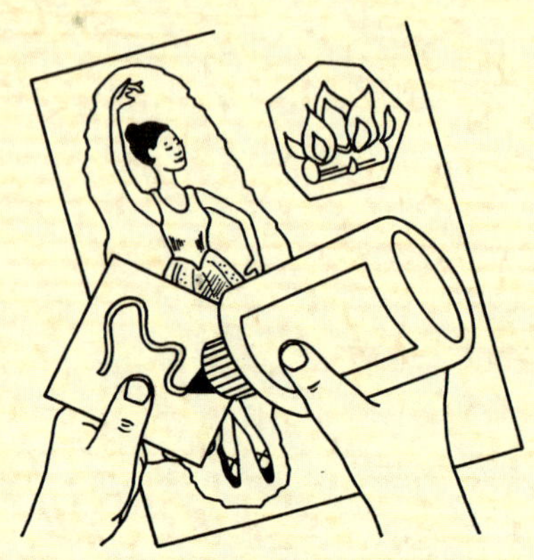

## Step 3 Revise

**Did you remember to:**

✓ Choose images that best describe you and the communities in which you participate?

✓ Show how you rank the importance of your communities by how they are arranged?

✓ Arrange your images in a way that communicates a clear message about your community?

Adjust your work if necessary. In your sketchbook, make a note of your revisions and why you made them.

### Step 4 **Add Finishing Touches**

- Use markers, colored paper, or paint to add meaning to your collage.

### Step 5 **Share and Reflect**

- Display your completed collage with those of your classmates.
- Take turns describing what you see in each other's artworks. Can you name the communities to which each student belongs?
- Discuss how each artist has arranged pictures to express a message.

## Art Criticism

**Describe** What does the artist show in this collage?

**Analyze** How did the artist arrange the images in this collage?

**Interpret** What do you think this collage says about the interests of the artist?

**Evaluate** What makes this a successful collage?

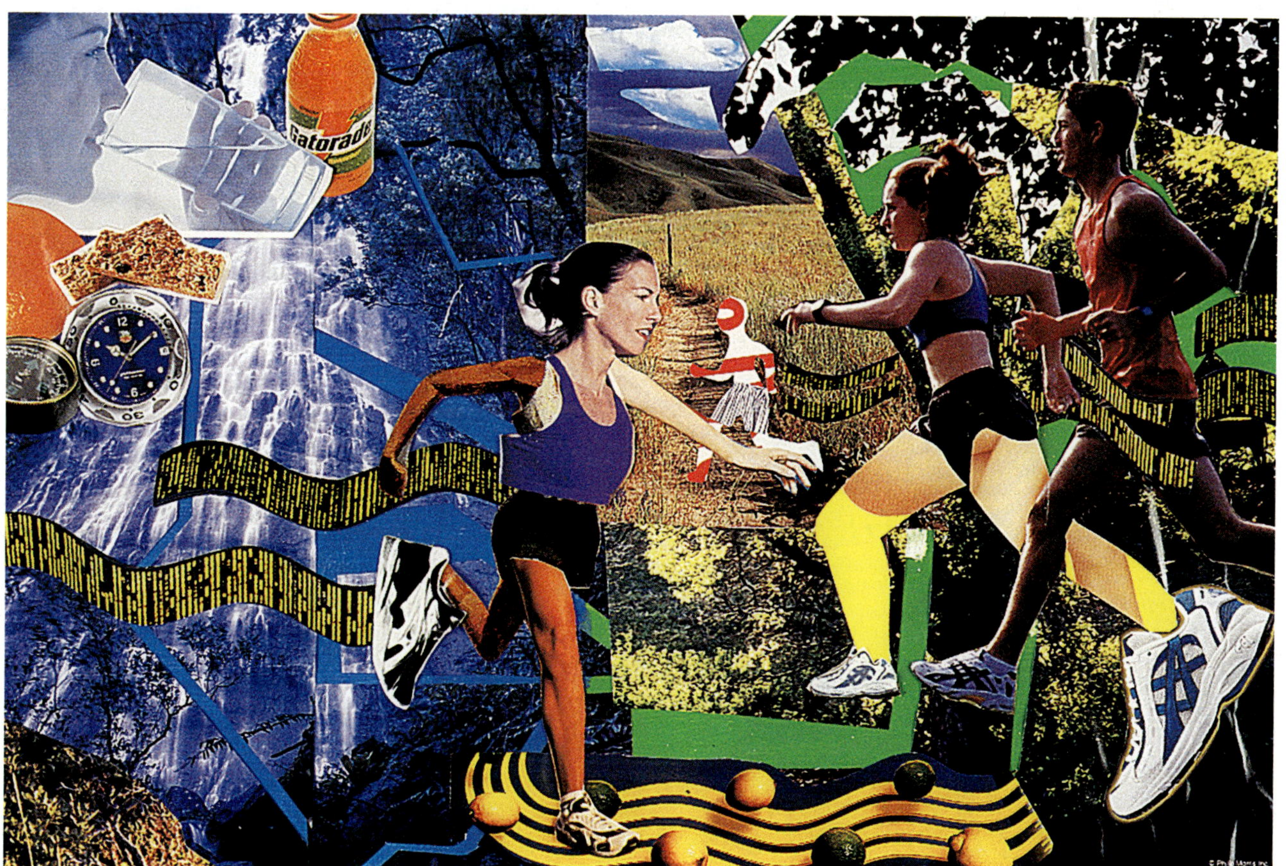


Fig. 1–16 Student artwork

# Art in Early North America

The first peoples to populate the North and South American continents probably came from Asia across the frozen Bering Strait more than ten thousand years ago. They migrated slowly eastward into what are now Canada and the northern United States. Eventually, some moved farther south. The ancient southwestern part of the United States became the home of three Native American cultures—the Hohokam, the Mogollon, and the Ancestral Puebloans. Each had its own special way of life.

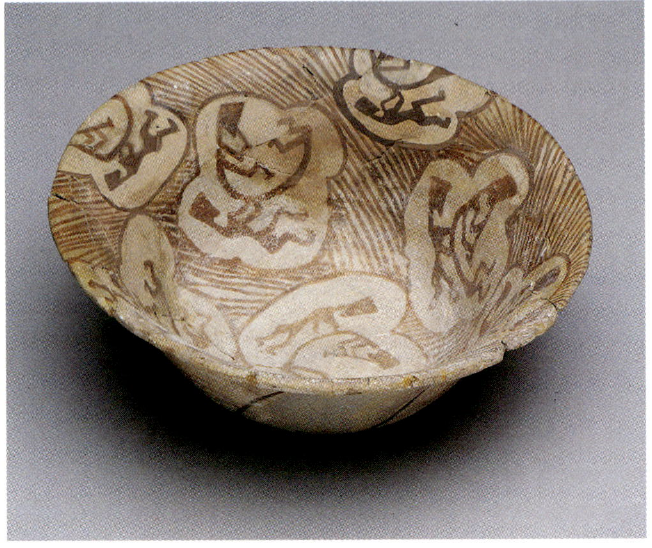

Fig. 1–17 **The figures on this bowl are Kokopeli, a sacred flute player who had a hump-back. What might this tell us about values in Hohokam culture?**

Hohokam, *Red-on-Buff Bowl*, 9 panels with Kokopeli ("hump backed flute player") design, classic period 1100–1400 AD. Ceramic, diam. 6 ¾" (17.2 cm) x d. 2 ¾" (17.2 x 7 cm). Gift of Paul Clute. Museum of Indian Arts and Culture/Laboratory of Anthropology, Museum of New Mexico. Photograph by Blair Clark.

**Community Messages** Archaeologists and art historians can often tell where an ancient pottery jar or bowl or woven basket came from by studying its form and decoration. Each ancient Native American community used colors, lines, shapes, and patterns in unique ways. The designs and patterns meant something special to the people who lived at the time.

The Hohokam lived in what is now Arizona. They created red-on-buff painted designs that showed symbols of animals, masked dancers, and gods **(Fig. 1–17)**.

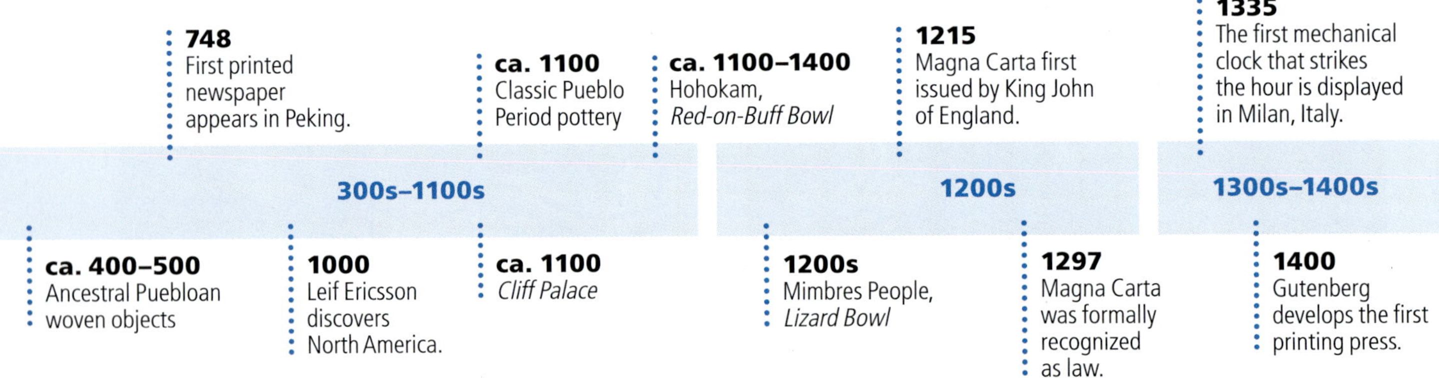

The Mimbres were a Mogollon people who lived in what is now New Mexico. They created elegant black-on-white designs on pottery bowls. These designs were both geometric and organic. Geometric designs include shapes such as squares and triangles. Organic designs include irregular shapes from nature (Fig. 1–18).

Ancestral Puebloan potters lived in the Four Corners region of Utah, Colorado, Arizona, and New Mexico. The Ancestral Puebloans also used black-on-white patterns (Fig. 1–19), but they were very different from the patterns of the Mimbres.

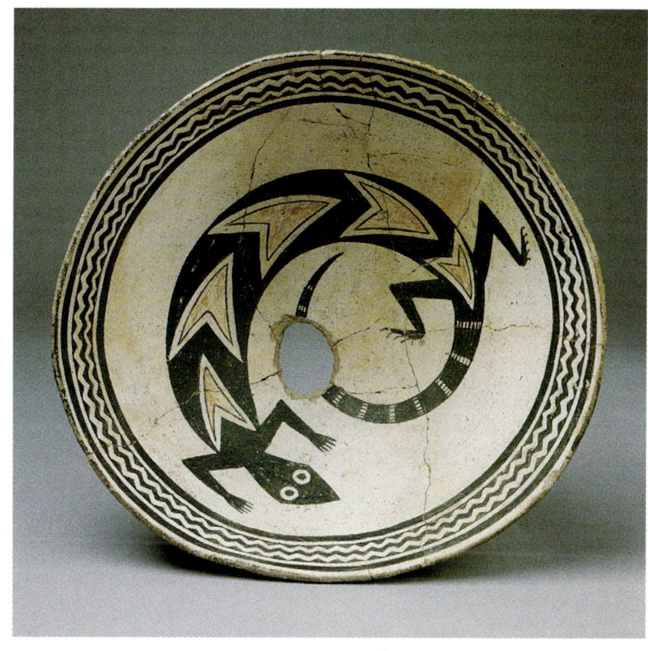

Fig. 1–18 **This painted bowl shows a lizard. How is the design on this vessel different from the others shown in this lesson?**

Mimbres People, *Lizard Bowl*, 13th century. Polychrome, Peabody Museum, Harvard University. Photograph by Hillel Burger.

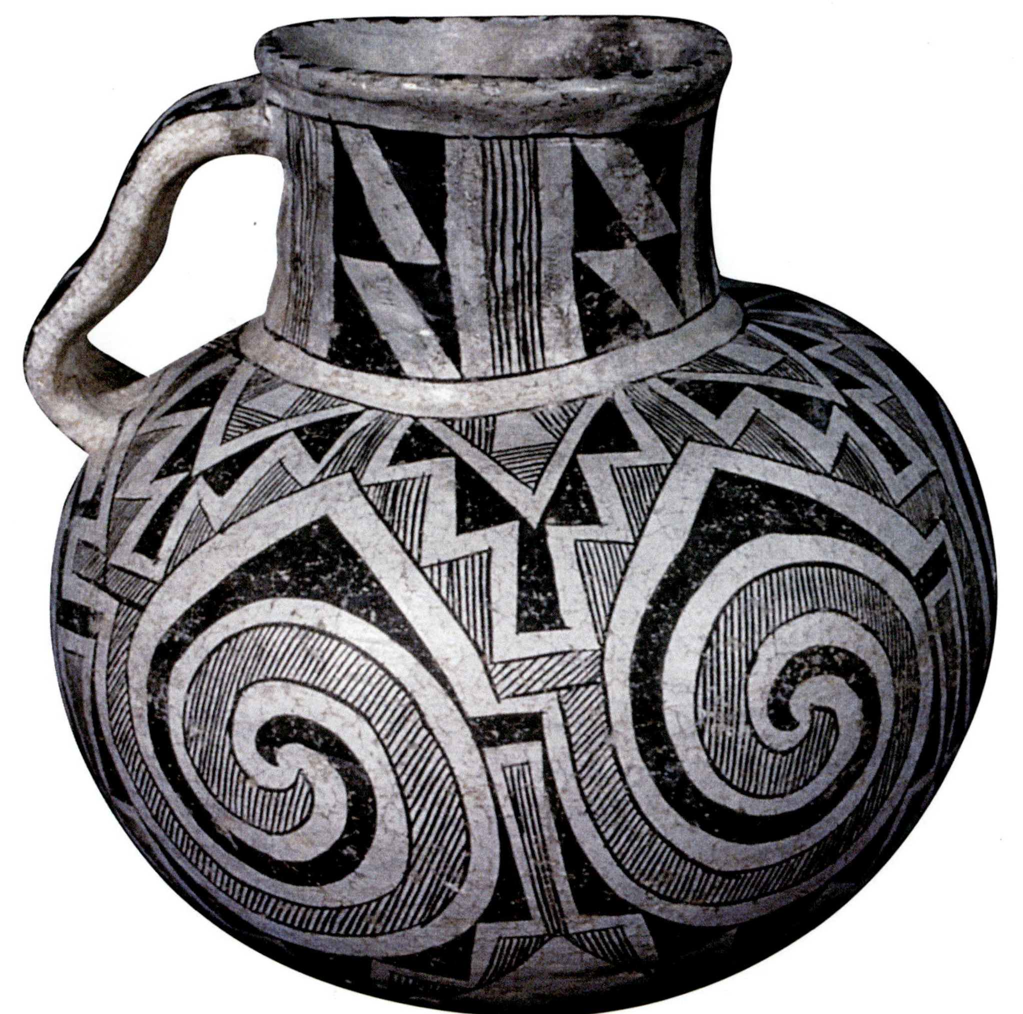

Fig. 1–19 **The Ancestral Puebloans painted their pottery with a dye made by boiling a plant called woodland aster. What repeated elements can you see in this pattern?**

Native American, Tularosa, *Black-on-White Pitcher*, ca. 1000–1200 AD. Ceramic, h. 7 ⅛" (18 cm) x d. 6 ⅞" (17.5 cm) x circum. 23" (58.4 cm). Courtesy of the Maxwell Museum of Anthropology, University of New Mexico, Albuquerque, New Mexico.

**An Early Community** The Ancestral Puebloans, sometimes called the Anasazi, were some of the first people in the southwestern United States to live in caves and rocky cliffs. After living in pit houses, they established communities along the canyon walls of a huge plateau in southwestern Colorado. The structures, called pueblos, are much like modern apartment buildings with sections two, three, and four stories high.

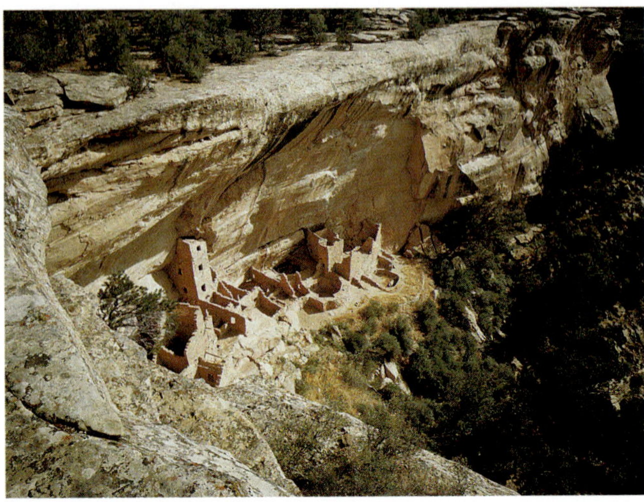

Fig. 1–20 **The pueblo had rounded ceremonial rooms, called kivas. How did the design of the structure make it easy for people to communicate with one another?**

Colorado, Mesa Verde National Park, *Cliff Palace*, ca. 1100 AD. David Muench Photography.

The Ancestral Puebloans were skillful weavers and sophisticated potters **(Figs. 1–19 and 1–21)**. They also made beautiful turquoise jewelry. Their art forms were adorned with symbols and patterns similar to those used on baskets. Some are similar to pictographs that people painted on cliff walls long ago. To the Ancestral Puebloans, these symbols told about identity, status, or group membership. Early artworks were used to tell stories, to teach young children about adult roles, and to communicate with the spirit world.

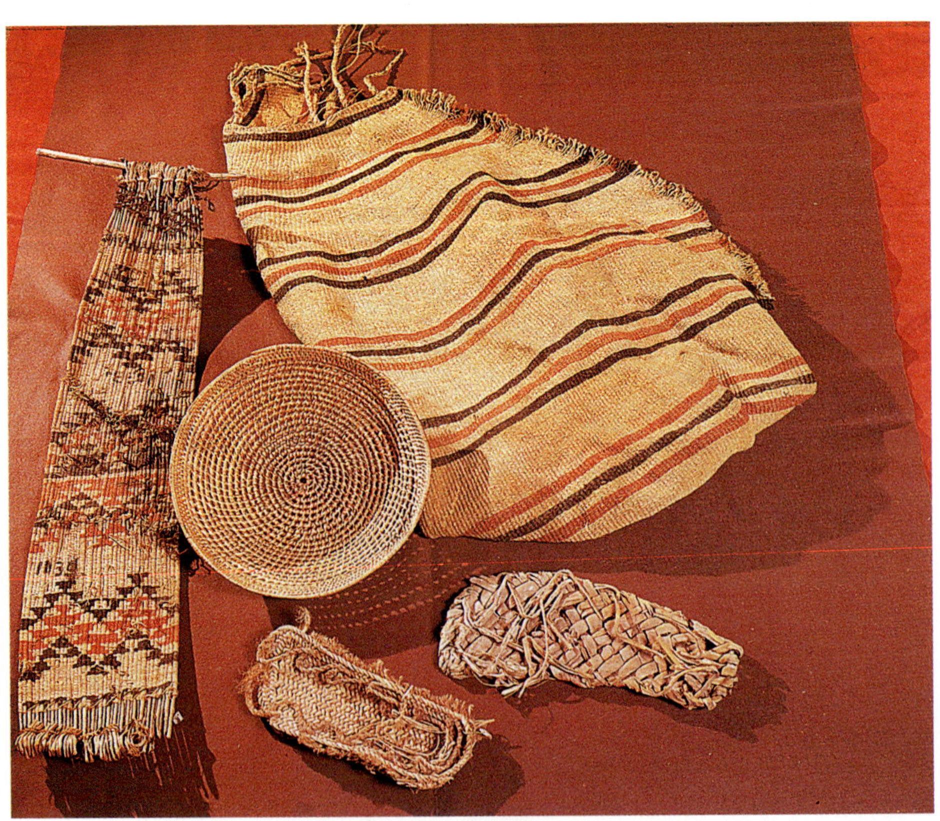

Fig. 1–21 **Early archaeologists called the early period of Pueblo culture the "Basket Maker" phase. How are these woven designs similar to the painted decorations on the pottery vessels?**

American, New Mexico, Anasazi, *Bruden band, silver basket, sack, cliff dwellers sandal, and sandal made of unsplit yucca blades*, ca. 400–500 AD. Courtesy of the Department of Library Services, American Museum of Natural History.

## Meet Pueblo Potters

Native Americans in the southwestern United States have been making pottery for over 2,000 years. Women pass techniques down through the generations. Girls learn by watching their grandmothers, mothers, and aunts. They continue their ancestors' traditions, respectfully using the earth to form vessels for daily and ritual use, or for sale. Traditionally, pottery was made for practical uses, although it was also artistic.

In the 1880s, the railroad was built across the United States. Pueblo communities became tourist attractions, and Pueblo potters started making their work to sell to tourists as souvenirs. In the early 1900s, Pueblo pottery began to be recognized as a fine art and displayed in museums. Many Pueblo potters proudly use traditional techniques, avoiding commercial clay and pigments, potter's wheels, and kilns. Their pottery is made by hand out of local, natural materials. It connects them to their ancestors, even as they create their own unique designs.

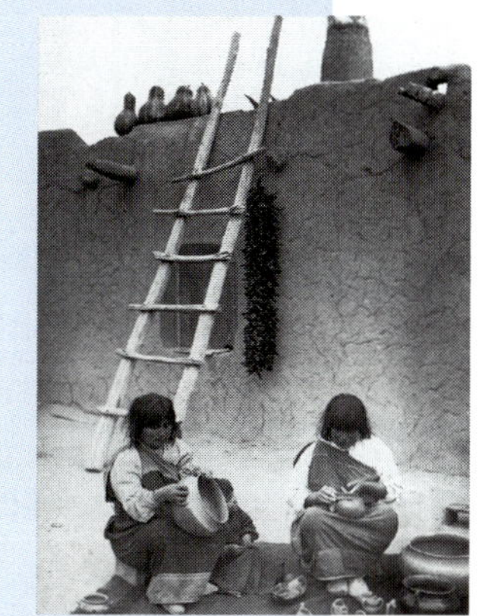
©CORBIS

**"When you hold a Pueblo pot in your hands, you feel a tactile connection through the clay to the potter and to centuries of tradition."**

— Website, Museum of Indian Arts and Culture

## Studio Time

### Identity Banner

Design a cut-paper banner or flag that displays a personal symbol.

- Think of simple shapes that express something about yourself. The shapes can be geometric or organic.
- Plan your design. Sketch the main shapes first.
- Use contrasting colors of paper to make your shapes stand out from the background.
- After you make your cut-paper design, try creating one using felt and stitchery.

Reflect on how you can re-create your design using felt and stitchery.

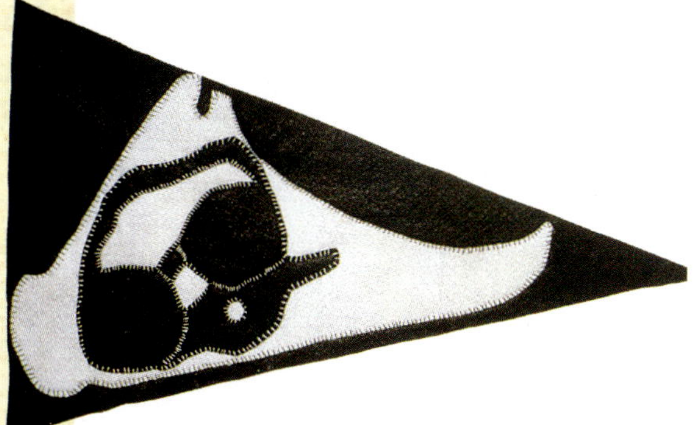

Fig. 1–22 Student artwork

## Check Your Understanding

1. Who were among the early settlers in the southwestern United States? Which state did each group live in?
2. Compare and contrast the artworks of the Hohokam, the Mogollon, and the Ancestral Puebloan cultures.
3. What do the artworks on this page tell you about the materials that were available to the Ancestral Puebloans?

# The Art of Mesoamerica and South America

**Planned Communities** Beginning around 1500 BCE, the people in the Mesoamerican region built civilizations based on agriculture. Throughout history, several different cultures or groups formed within this area. The Mesoamericans were skilled in city planning and architecture, and developed skills in sculpture, painting, pottery, and jewelry-making.

Each of these groups built planned communities that met their specific needs. People of the Olmec culture created ceremonial centers with large sculptures of warriors, priests, and athletes. The Mayans built cities, such as Chichen Itza, with pyramids, palaces, courts, and many dwellings. The Aztecs borrowed many ideas from Mayan art. One of their largest cities, Tenochtitlán, was destroyed in 1521. Present-day Mexico City was later built on this site.

In South America, the Andean cultures of Peru also developed large public architecture and sculpture. Their planned communities filled the needs of their military rule, and provided space for their religious and agricultural ceremonies.

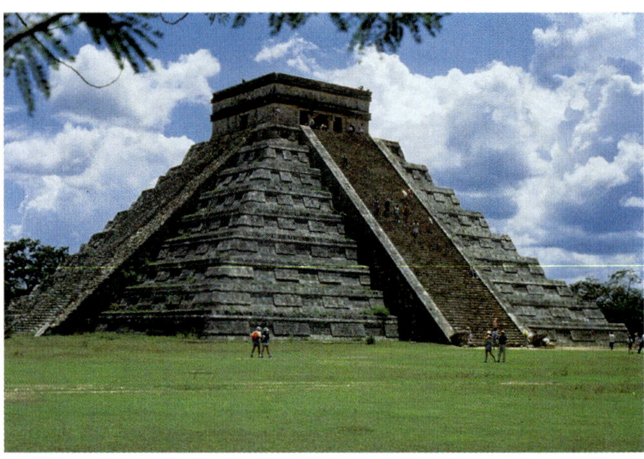

Fig. 1–23 **The surfaces of this Mayan platform pyramid are carved with decorations representing Quetzalcoatl, the sun god. What do the decorations suggest about the purpose of the pyramid?**

Pre-Columbian Mexico, *Chichen Itza Castle*, from Northeast, ca. 12th–13th century. Courtesy of Davis Art Slides.

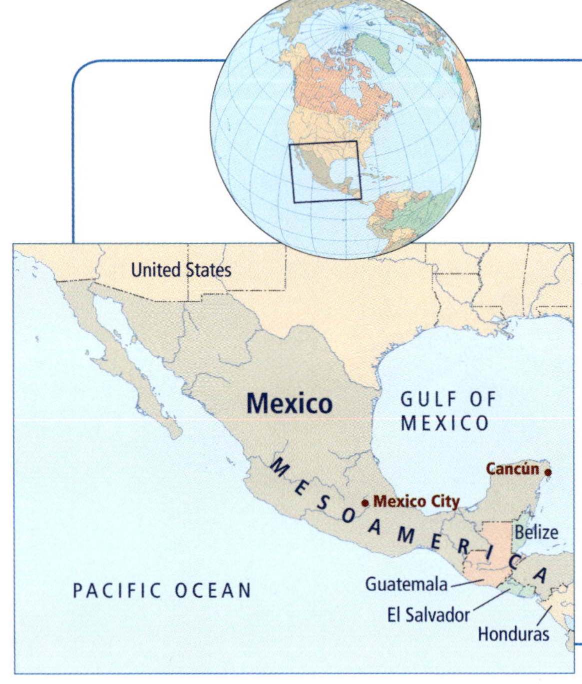


## Social Studies Connection

**Mesoamerica** extends from present-day Mexico south to Honduras. Farther south lies the vast continent of South America. Over 3000 years ago, the people in these areas developed communities. Some of the world's great civilizations developed here. Between 1492 and 1521, much of Mesoamerica and South America was conquered by Spain. Art historians use the term pre-Columbian to describe the period before the Spanish conquered this region. Pre-Columbian means the time before Columbus arrived.

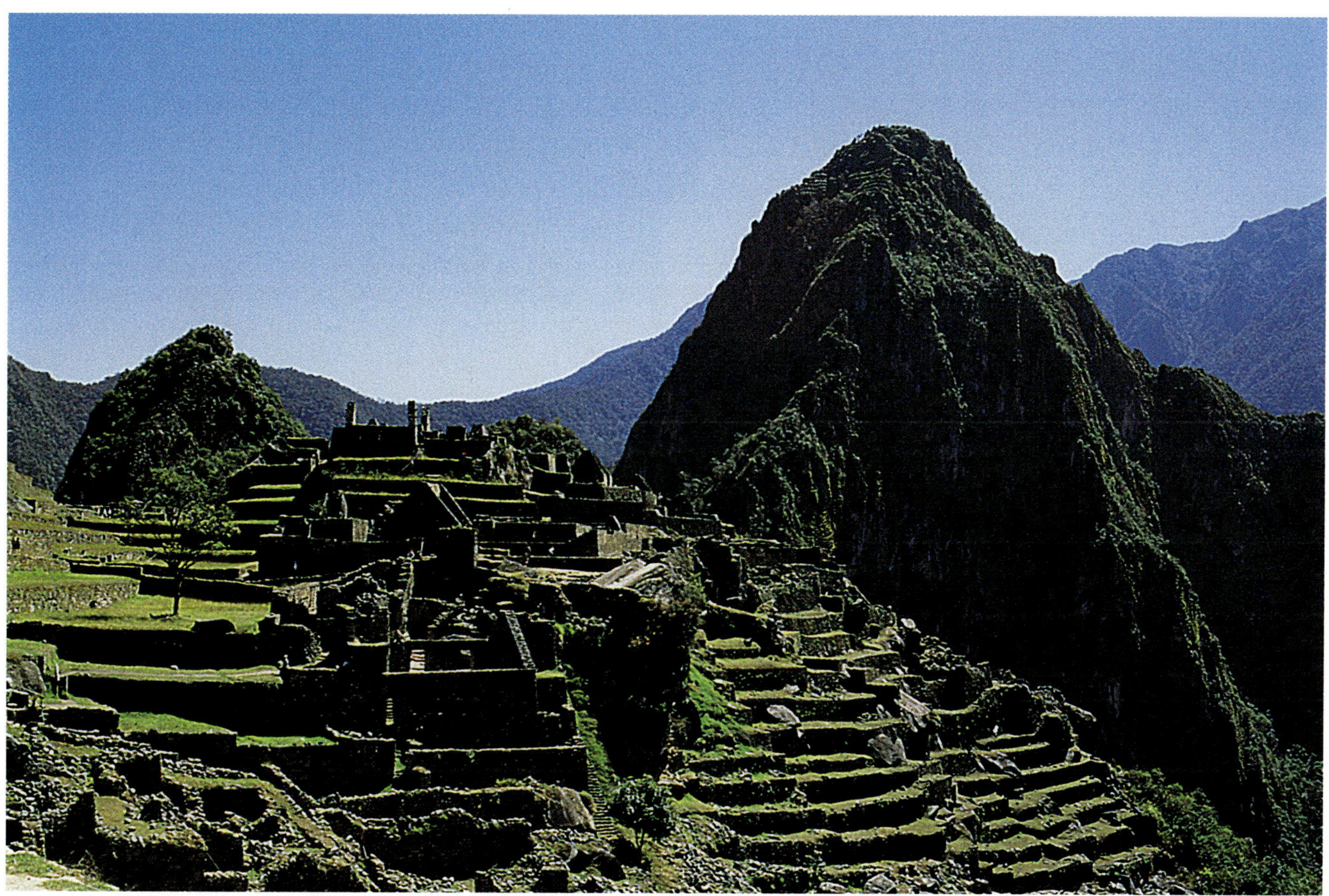

Fig. 1–24 **The Inca city of Machu Picchu was built as a royal estate and religious center. The carefully cut stones fit together so well that mortar was not necessary.**

Pre-Columbian Peru, *Machu Picchu* (General View), 15th century. Photograph by David DeVore.

## Visual Culture

In this lesson, you have learned about the design of Mesoamerican communities around plazas and markets. Consider the plans and layouts of your city, town, or neighboring communities. Look at maps of towns in your region. Identify towns that have a basic grid plan, or cities that have streets radiating from a monument circle. Notice that some towns have a "town square" while others may have a long "main street." Also compare and contrast the layout of shopping malls, shopping plazas, and strip malls.

## Communicating with Symbols

Imagine a time when there was no such thing as paper. How would you communicate your ideas and thoughts? How would you keep track of those things you now record on calendars? For the Aztec farming communities of Mesoamerica, calendars were important. The Aztecs used calendars to plan planting and harvesting cycles. They developed complex stone calendars with unique forms of picture writing **(Fig. 1–26)**.

The Aztec people eventually learned to make paper from the bark of trees. Scribes wrote on strips of this paper to form a codex. A codex is a book with pages folded like an accordion, held together with hinges instead of a spine. Trained scribes used signs and pictures in these books to keep religious, historical, and government records.

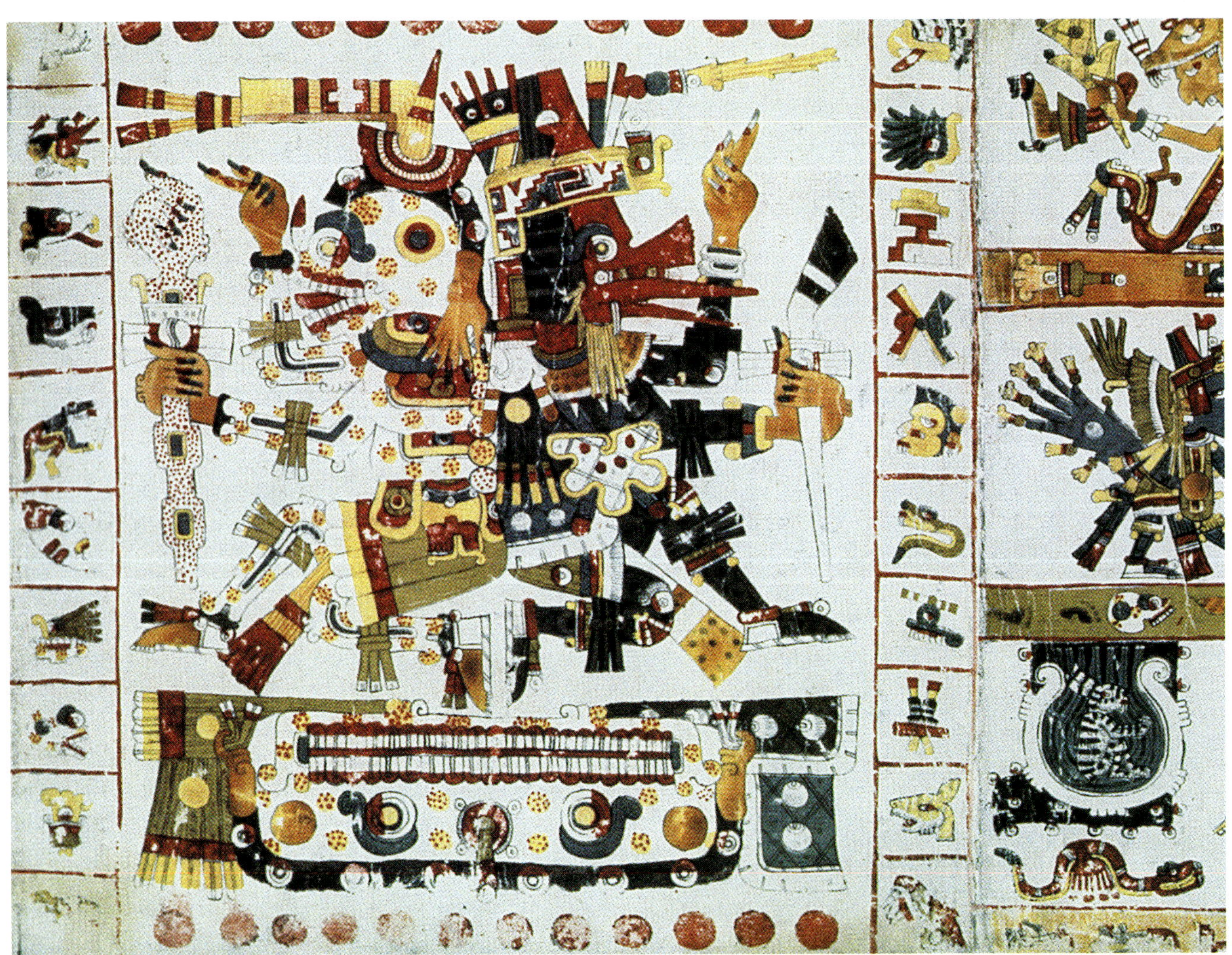

Fig. 1–25 **This Aztec codex shows the death god and the lord of life surrounded by the Aztec calendar. Compare it to the calendar shown in Fig. 1–26.**

Mexico, Aztec, *Codex Borgia*, ca. 1400 CE. Pigments on deerskin, 10 5/8" x 3 15/16" (27 x 10 cm). Courtesy of Davis Art Slides.

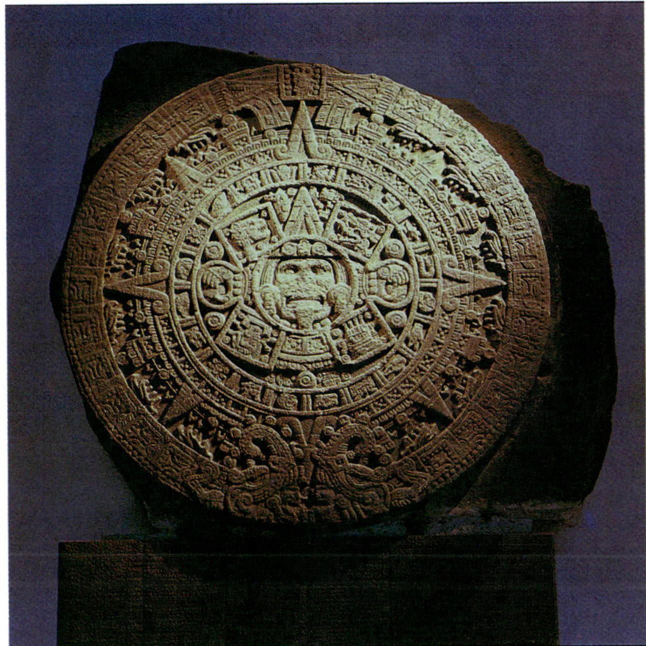

Fig. 1–26 **This calendar is thirteen feet in diameter and weighs twenty-four tons. If you found an object like this, what clues would help you guess that it's a calendar?**

Mexico, Aztec, *Calendar Stone*, 1325–1521 AD. Weighs 24 tons and is 13' (3.9 m) in diameter. National Museum of Archaeology, Mexico City. Photo Researchers, Inc. ©George Holton.

## Meet the Aztecs

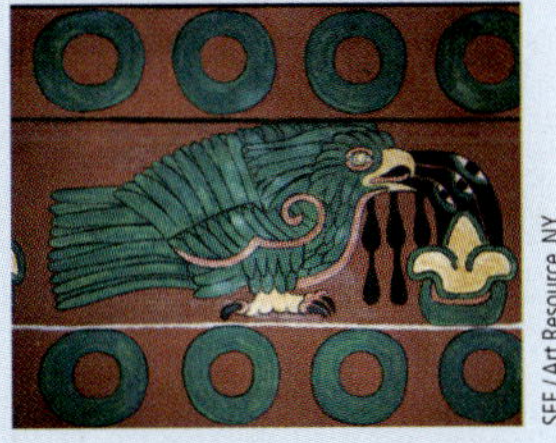
SEF / Art Resource, NY.

The Aztecs migrated from the North into the Valley of Mexico as early as the 1200s. The civilization ruled over much of Mesoamerica until it was conquered by Spain in the 1500s. The Aztec civilization was a complex one, with a written language and a large number of people who were able to read. Diaries, written histories, and other documents have revealed a great deal about how the Aztecs lived.

When the Aztec civilization was at its peak, it had a total population of about 15 million people—nearly the same size as the state of Florida today.

## Studio Time

### A Message in a Book

Make an accordion-fold book full of symbols to convey a message.

- Plan and sketch your message. Plan a sequence of simple images to make it clear.
- Fold paper strips to make a series of square pages. Join the strips together with smaller strips.
- Draw your message in your book. Make decorative front and back covers.

Reflect on how your symbols help send a message.

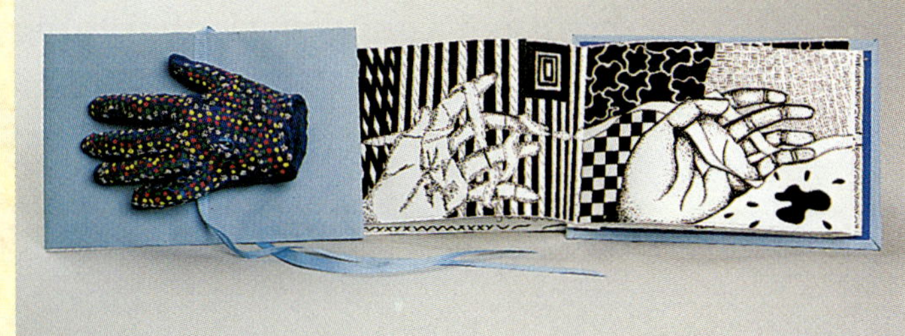

Fig. 1–27 Student artwork

## Check Your Understanding

1. What kind of community centers did the Olmec create?
2. Compare how Aztec communities recorded important information in the past to how you record important information now.
3. Imagine your own world without paper. What would you use as a surface to write on?

# 3-D Messages

## Studio Background

Whether it's worth a thousand words or not, sometimes one picture just isn't enough to get a message across. A montage is a collage that is created from multiple photographs. Artists who create photomontages use parts of magazine and newspaper images, as well as photographs, to help them tell a story. Montages can also include drawing or painting.

**In this studio exploration, you will create a three-dimensional (3-D) montage that sends a message.** Your montage should have the attention-getting quality of a good work of graphic design.

### You Will Need

- magazines
- newspapers
- stiff cardboard
- ruler
- scissors
- X-Acto™ knife
- tape
- glue

### Safety Note

Use knives and other sharp tools with extreme care to avoid cuts and other accidents.

## Step 1 Plan and Practice

- Think carefully about the message you will create. Will it be a comfortable message? An angry one? A message about your school, your hometown, your friends, or family?
- Collect photographs from magazines, newspapers, or your home. Look for photographs that will best send your chosen message. Will you use photographs of people, objects, or places?
- How will you create an interesting 3-D shape? How can you use colors and shapes that give your work graphic punch?

### Things to Remember:

- ✓ Use images that send your message clearly.
- ✓ Use colors and shapes that help reinforce your message.
- ✓ Make your 3-D form interesting from all sides.

## Inspiration from Our World

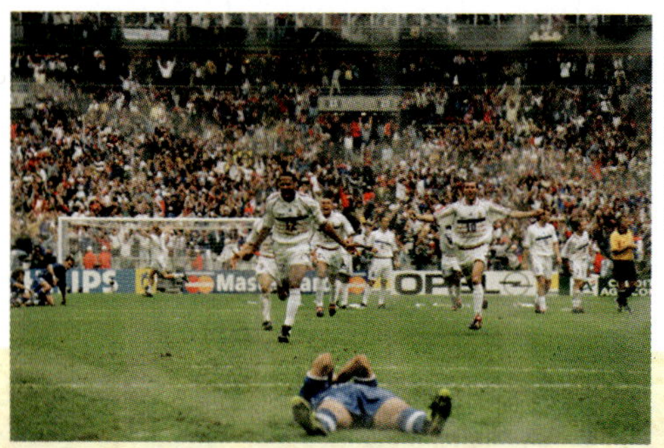

©Dimitri Lundt/TempSport/Corbis

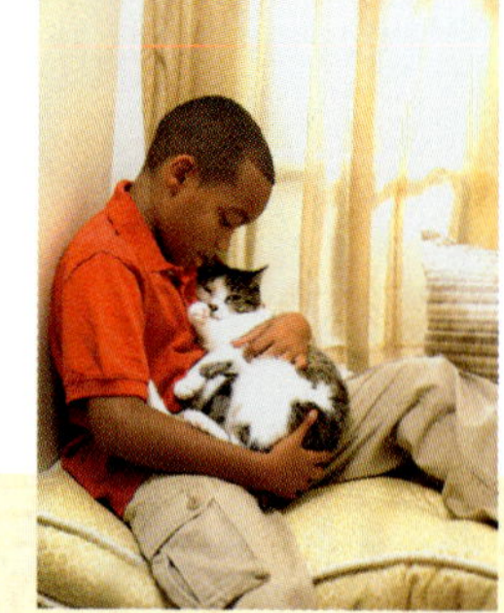

©David Shopper/Corbis

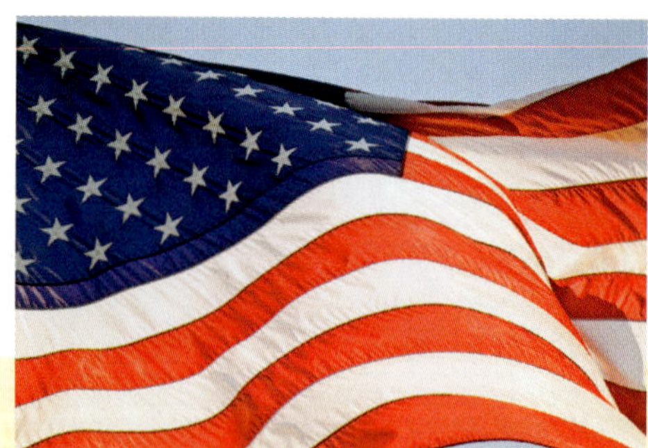

## Inspiration from Art

Artists have been combining photographic images for almost as long as photography has been around. In the early 1900s, a group of European artists created artworks by combining parts of photographs. They named this process *montage*. These artists were from an art movement called Dada. Dada artists were known for arranging images and words in nonsensical ways. They rejected traditional art styles and materials. The Surrealists were a group of artists who created artworks based on dreams and fantasy. The Surrealists and other artists found that the art of montage could be used to suggest new meanings, or say surprising things.

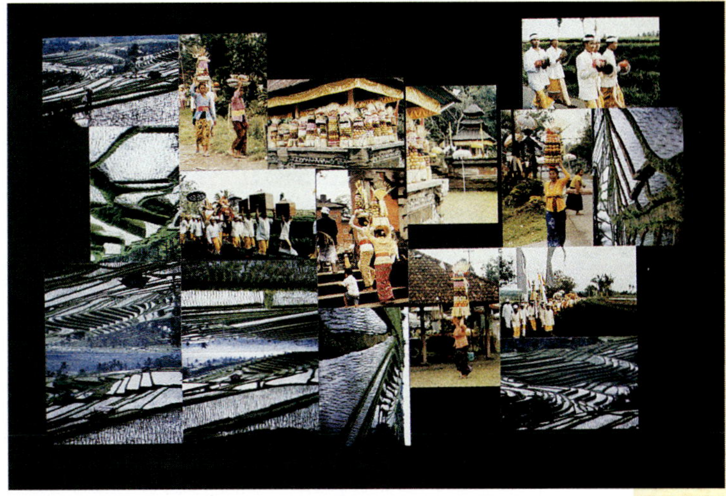

Fig. 1–29 **Nagano invented the word photofusion to describe his process of assembling photos into panoramic views. How is Nagano's "story" different from Revelle's (Fig. 1–28)?**

Paul Nagano, *Balinese Offerings,* 2000. Photofusion, 22" x 32" (55.9 x 81.3 cm). Courtesy of the artist.

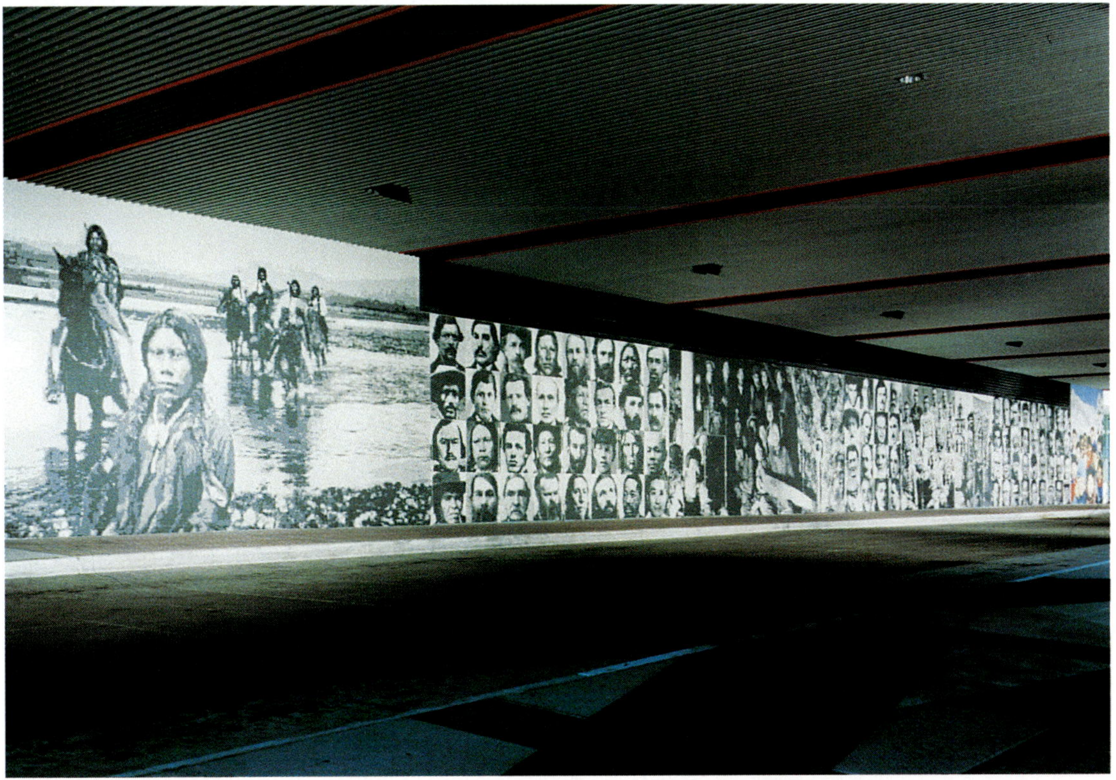

Fig. 1–28 **This ceramic tile mural uses photographs of people who helped shape the character and spirit of Colorado. What other artworks in this book could be considered photomontage?**

Barbara Jo Revelle, *Colorado Panorama: A People's History of Colorado.* Courtesy of the artist.

## Step 2 **Begin to Create**

- **Create a cardboard form. Cut, score, and fold flat pieces of cardboard, or use slotting techniques and tape to join cardboard pieces.** Try to create a form that will help express your message.

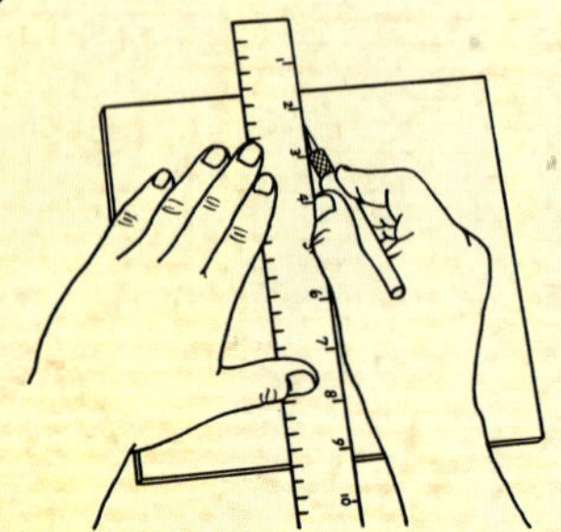

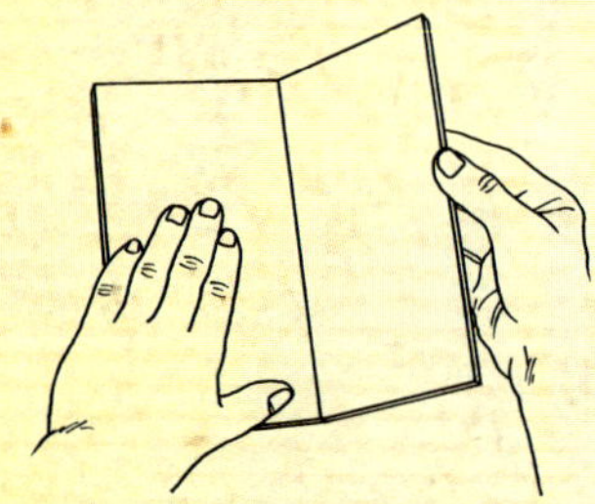

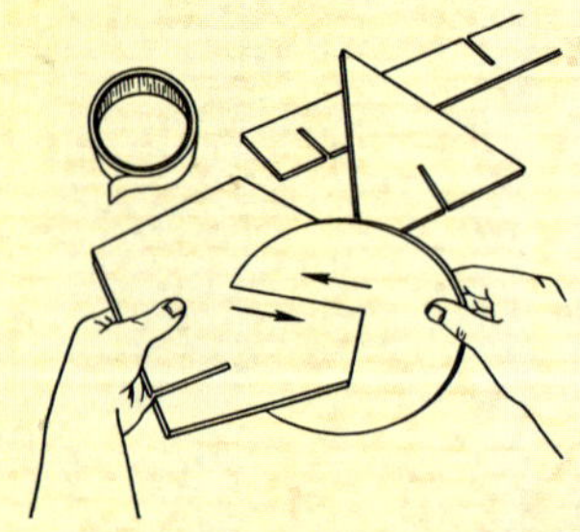

- Try arranging your images in different ways on your cardboard base. Which images work well together? What surprising combinations can you come up with? As you work, you may need to find additional photographs.
- Choose colored papers and drawing media to make your message more powerful.
- **When you are satisfied with your arrangements, glue the photographs in place.**

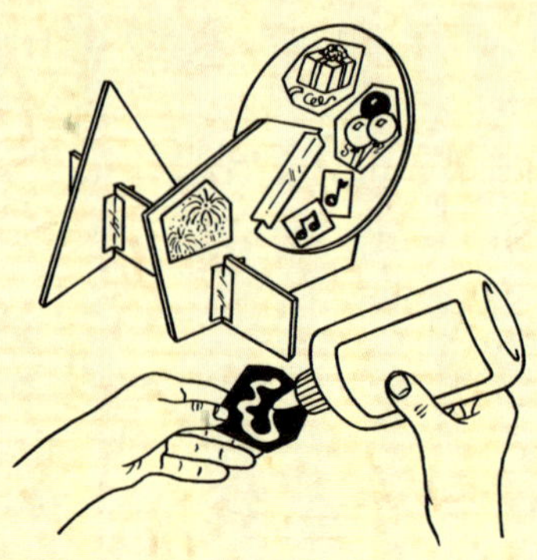

## Step 3 **Revise**

**Did you remember to:**

✓ Use images that send your message clearly?

✓ Use colors and shapes that help reinforce your message?

✓ Make your 3-D form interesting from all sides?

Adjust your work if necessary. In your sketchbook, make a note of your revisions and why you made them.

## Step 4 **Add Finishing Touches**

- Add details if necessary to help reinforce your message.
- Make sure all edges are securely glued down.

### Step 5 **Share and Reflect**

- Share your artwork with a classmate. Talk about the decisions you made and how you think the photographic images work together to send a message.
- Write a short paragraph about your artwork that will help others better understand its meaning.
- Display the statement and your artwork with those of your classmates.
- Take time to look at their work and read the accompanying statements.

## Art Criticism

**Describe** How would you describe this artwork to someone over the phone?

**Analyze** How did the artist unify the many parts of this sculptural form?

**Interpret** What do you think the artist attempted to communicate through this artwork?

**Evaluate** What do you like about this artwork?

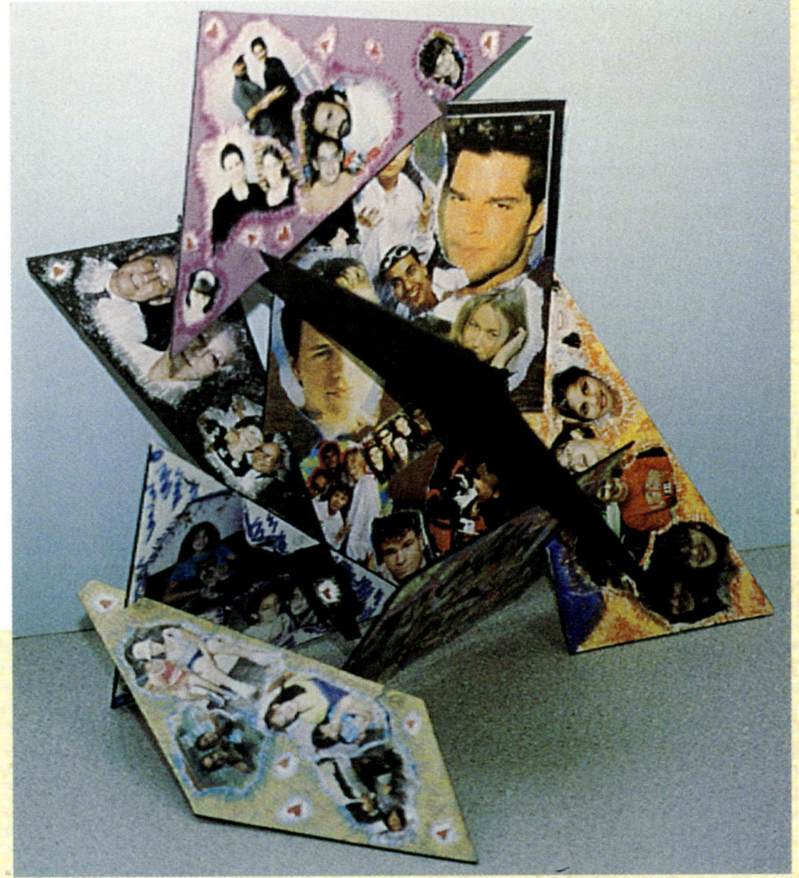

Fig. 1–30 Student artwork

## Math

**How can a quilt made of simple geometric shapes tell a story?** Amish quilts contain only the most basic geometric shapes: squares, triangles, and rectangles. Despite their simplicity, the designs of these quilts are powerful. The distinctive patterns, the width of borders, and the size of the blocks "tell" about their Amish origins. What kind of geometric designs could you make by using only squares, rectangles, and triangles?

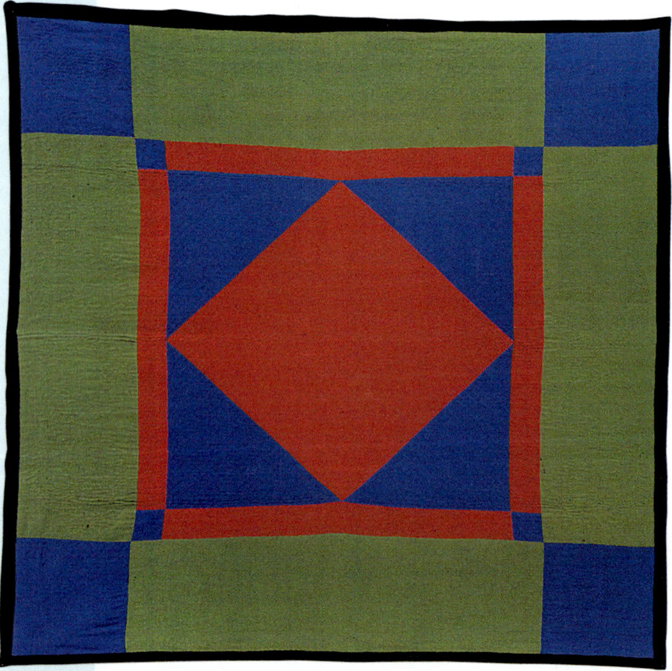

Fig. 1–31 **This Amish quiltmaker chose these colors and geometric shapes to create a powerful work of art. What type of balance do you see in this quilt?**

Rebecca Fisher Stoltzfus, *Diamond in the Square Quilt*, 1903. Wool with rayon binding added later, 77" x 77" (195.6 x 195.6 cm). Collection of the Museum of American Folk Art, New York. Gift of Mr. and Mrs. William B. Wigton. 1984.25.1

## Theater

**Visual art communicates important messages about communities.** Theater and the theatrical tradition of storytelling also does this. Many cultures use stories to educate children and adults. The Cherokee people of the Southeast use stories to tell about the Cherokee culture. They also remind adults of those values. Stories are told at family gatherings, community events, and during everyday conversation.

Fig. 1–32 **Another culture using music and dance as a way to tell stories is found in Bali. The Balinese dance called Barong tells the story of good versus evil.**

Bali, Indonesia, Barong Play: *Rangda, the Witch, Appears.* Courtesy of Davis Art Slides.

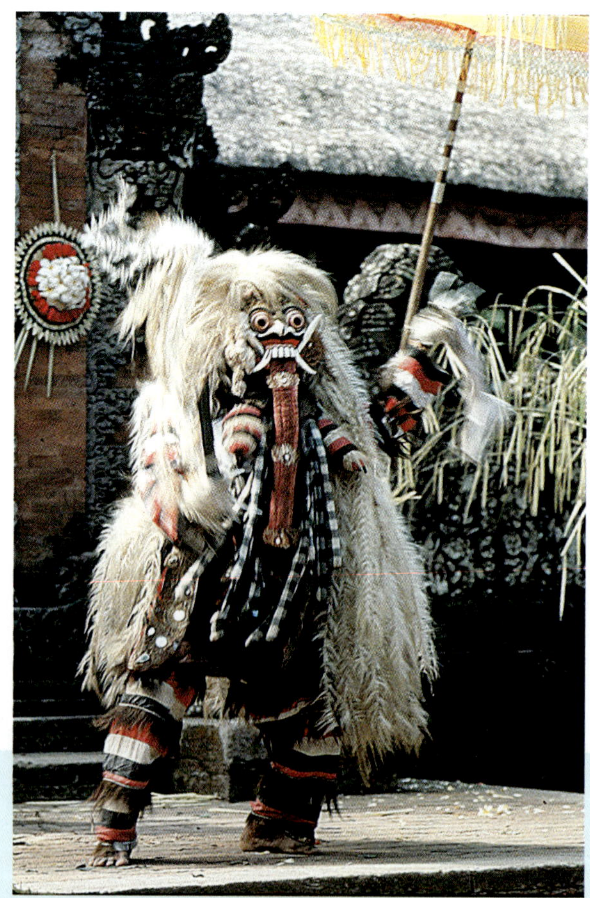

## Careers **Scenic Designer**

**Imagine making a scene from the past or future "come alive."** A scenic designer is responsible for the appearance of the stage. Scenic designers must do a lot of planning to create detailed and realistic stage sets. They need to think about lighting and the use of space. They make sketches and models to present to the director. Once a design is final, they work with the set-construction crews. Why might a scenic designer need to understand the ways actors will move throughout the stage area?

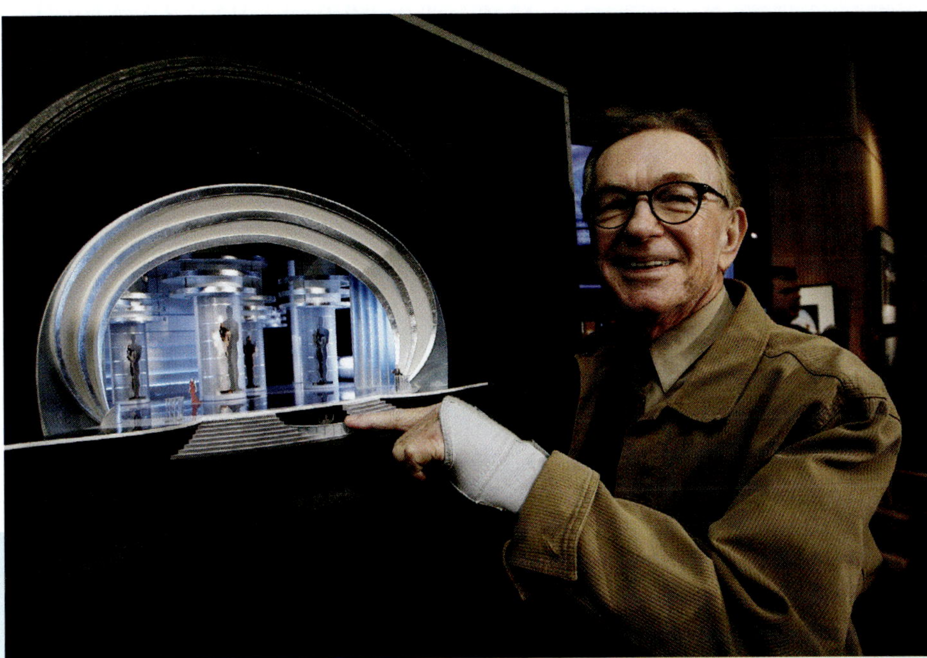

Fig. 1–33 **Set designer Roy Christopher points to a set for the Academy Awards.**

©Mario Anzuoni/Reuters/Corbis. ©Academy of Motion Picture Arts and Sciences®.

## Daily Life

**What are your favorite television shows?** Do you prefer shows that are made-up or shows based on real life? Television programs and commercials present views of life today that may or may not be true. A lot of what we see on TV is written for a teenage or young-adult audience. Discuss some of these shows with your classmates. How realistically do these shows reflect your life and the life of your peers?

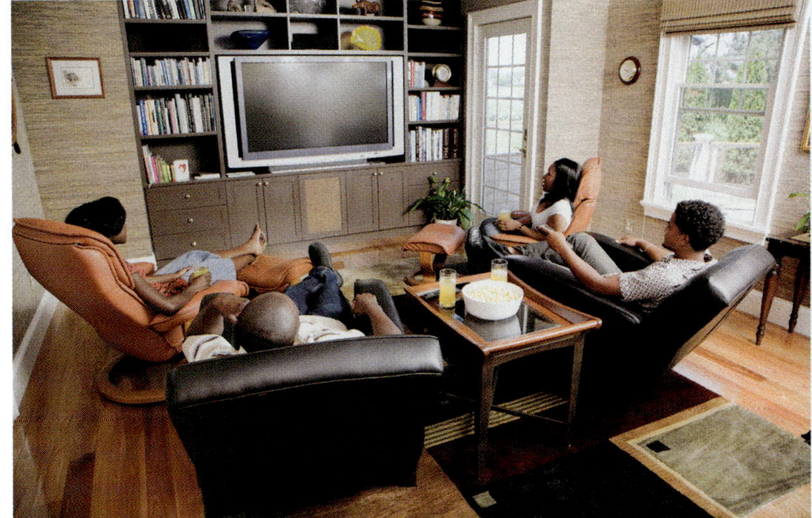

Fig. 1–34 Jack Hollingsworth/Getty Images

## Vocabulary Review

Match each art term below with its definition.

**collage**
**pueblos**
**codex**
**graphic design**
**communication**

1. Native American structures built in the southwest
2. artwork created when flat materials, usually paper, are pasted together on a background
3. a type of book, used by the Aztecs, whose pages are hinged together on both sides like an accordion
4. the exchange of information, thoughts, feelings, ideas, opinions, etc.
5. packages, labels, and logos created by designers for products and businesses

## Aesthetic Thinking

Discuss what many people say is the difference between craft and fine-art traditions. Do you agree or disagree? Use images or real objects to support your claim.

## Write About Art

Museum curators often write short texts—called labels—that are placed next to works of art to provide information to museum visitors. When you look at this photograph, what's the first question that comes to mind about the artwork? Write a label of about fifty words that answers that question. (You may need to do a little research.)

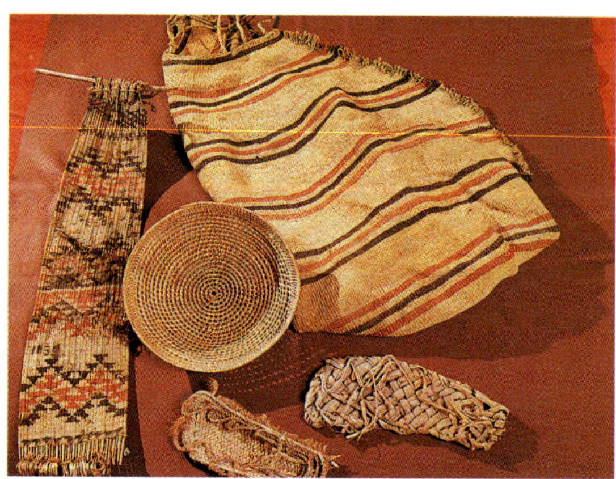

Fig. 1–35 **In addition to baskets, the Ancestral Puebloans wove sacks, sandals, and other useful objects.**

American, New Mexico, Anasazi, *Bruden band, silver basket, sack, cliff dwellers sandal, and sandal made of unsplit yucca blades*, ca. 400–500 AD. Courtesy of the Department of Library Services, American Museum of Natural History.

## Art Criticism

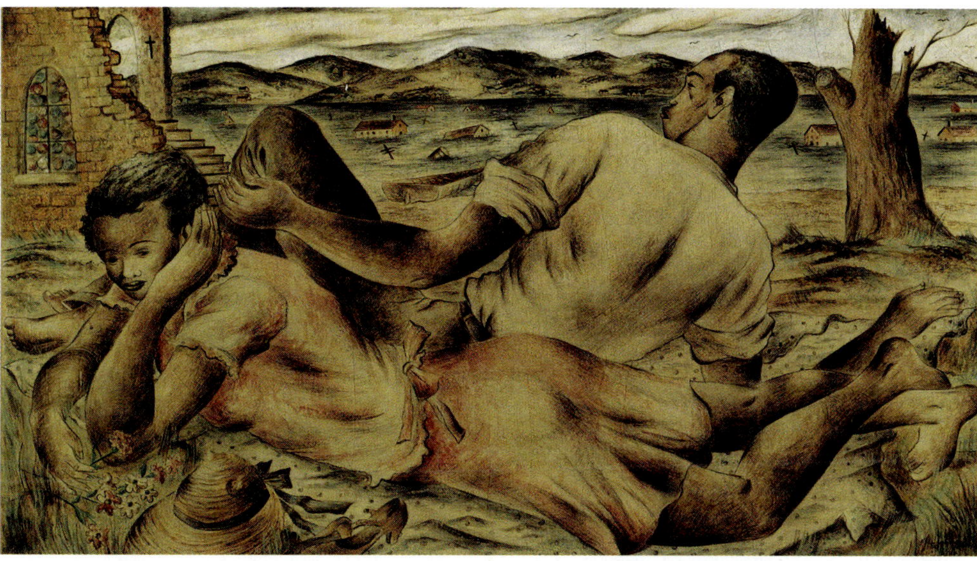

Fig. 1–36 Eldzier, Cortor, *Southern Landscape (Southern Flood)* c. 1939–40. Tempera and gesso on board 20" x 34" (51 x 86.4 cm). Brooklyn Museum 2006.2. Gift of Mr. and Mrs. Abraham Adler and bequest of Laura L. Barnes, by exchange.

**Describe** What do you see in this painting?

**Analyze** What types of shapes does the artist repeat in this painting?

**Interpret** How would you describe the mood of the painting?

**Evaluate** The artist has said that the two figures "represent youth with hope," in contrast to the devastation of the flood. How do you think he created a sense of hope in these two figures?

Library of Congress, Prints & Photographs Division, Carl van Vechten Collection, [reproduction number, e.g., LC-USZ62-54231]

## Meet the Artist

**Eldzier Cortor** (born 1916) was born in Virginia. He moved with his family to Chicago as a child, and later attended the Art Institute there. Cortor traveled throughout the Caribbean in the late 1940s, and taught for a time in Haiti. Most of his prints and paintings focus on images of an African-American woman who, he said, "conveys a feeling of eternity."

## For Your Portfolio

Create an artist's statement form for an artwork you made in this unit. Include a place for your name and date, the media and techniques used, how your artwork sends a message, and how satisfied you are with this completed artwork and why.

## For Your Sketchbook

Fill some sketchbook pages with different visual ways you can tell about the communities of which you are a member. You might, for example, develop a symbol for each geographical and shared interest community.

Unit 2

# Art and Daily Life

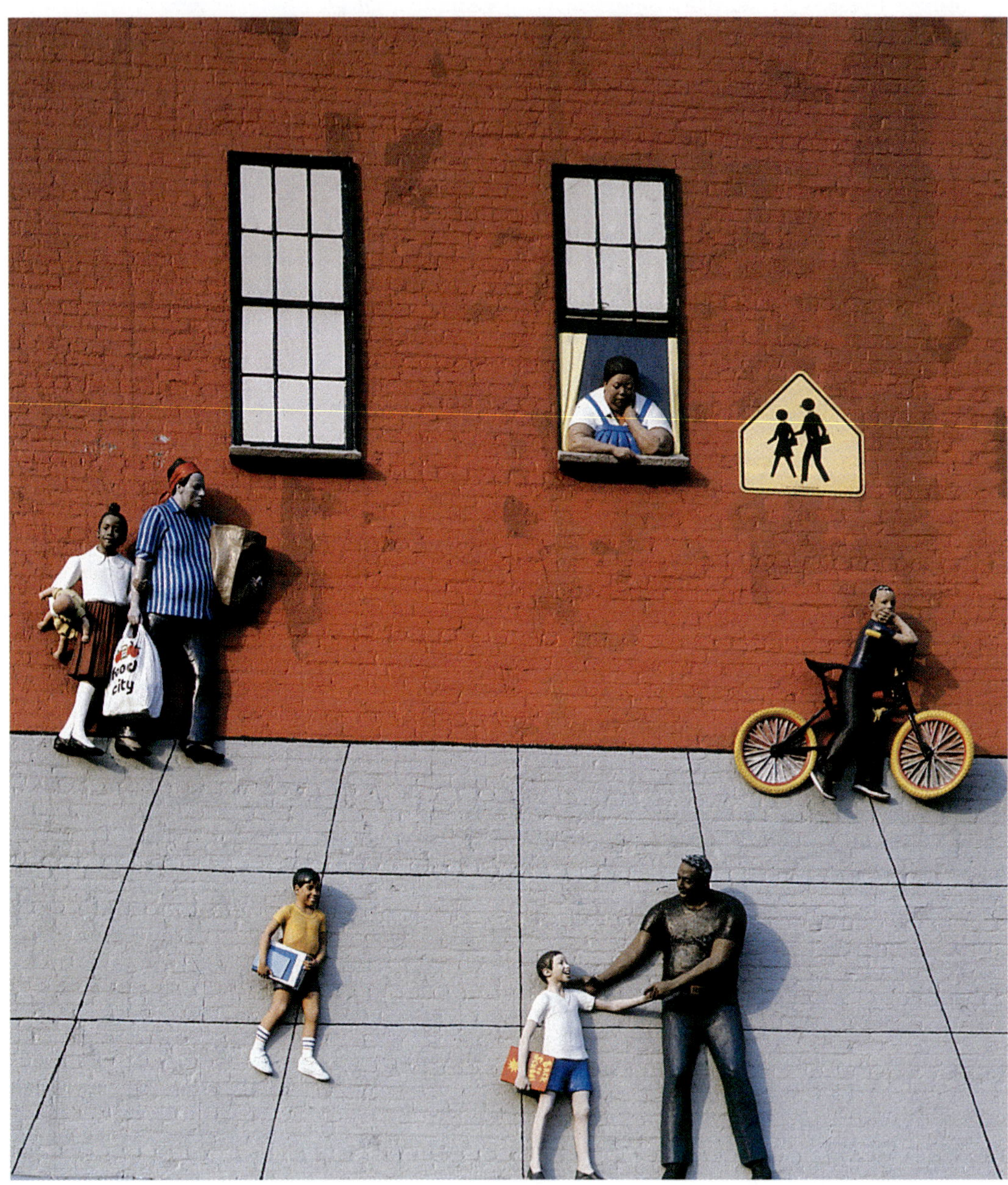


Fig. 2–1 **This scene is displayed on a building in the South Bronx. What does the artwork tell you about daily life in this community?**

John Ahearn, *Back to School*, 1985. Permanent outdoor mural at Walton Avenue and 172nd Street, Bronx, NY. Courtesy of Alexander and Bonin, New York.

## Recording Daily Colonial Life

Meeting basic needs in their new land challenged North American colonists. They had to make the things they could not bring from Europe. Those who knew a craft tradition helped by making things that were needed. Artworks by European printmakers, engravers, and painters are visual records of the colonists' early settlements. The artworks shown in **Figs. 2–17** and **2–18** are scenes of daily life in early communities in New York and Virginia.

**A Common Art Background** Colonial art owes much to the memories and experiences of the early settlers. The people who built the colonies were familiar with art created during the European Renaissance. Some were also familiar with art from ancient Greece and Rome. This shared knowledge is one reason why we can see similarities in the crafts, painting, sculpture, and architecture created by different North American communities.

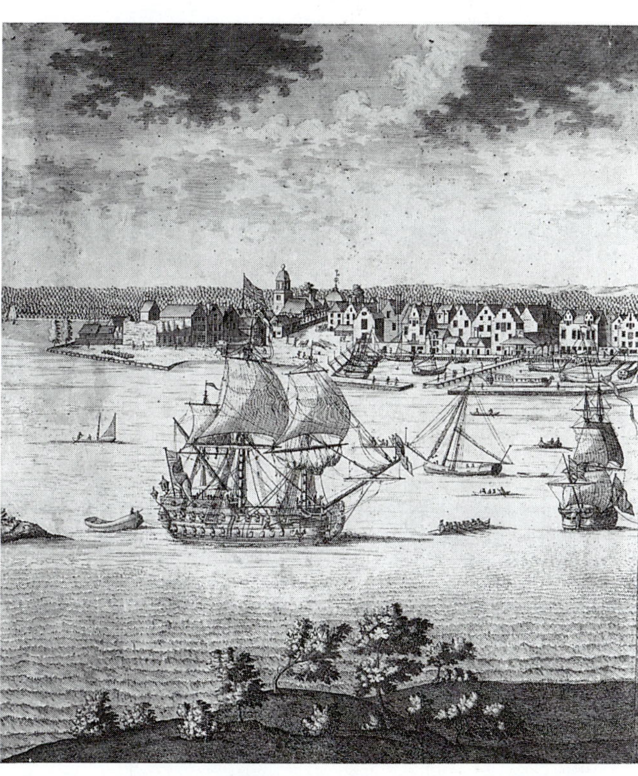

Fig. 2–17 **What does this image tell you about daily life in New York in the early 1700s? How might it be different today?**

William Burgis, *View of New York from Brooklyn Heights* (detail: section one), 1716–18. Engraving after drawing, 20 $\frac{7}{8}$" x 17 $\frac{15}{16}$" (53 x 44.7 cm). Collection of the New York Historical Society.

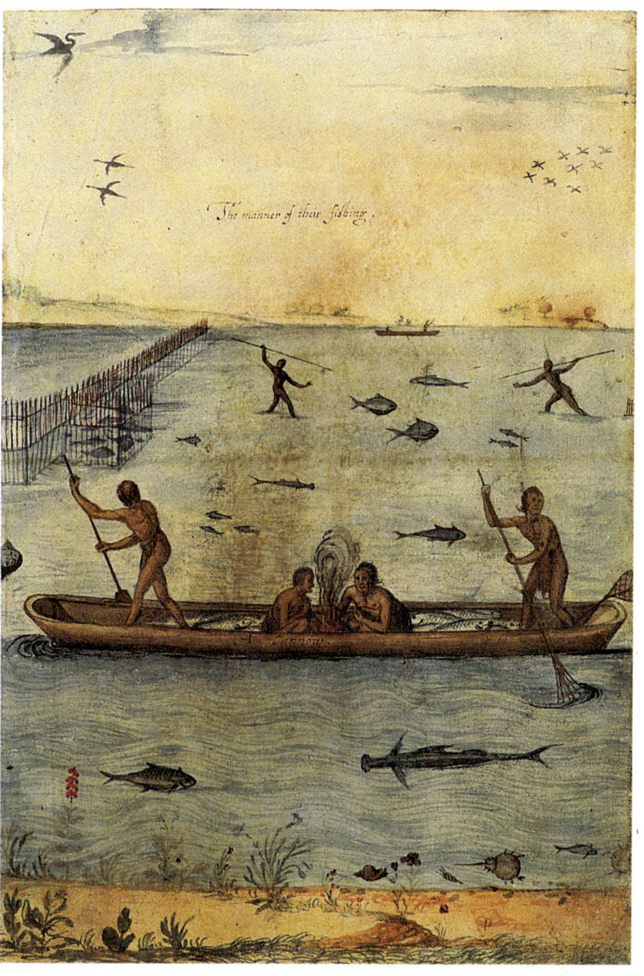


Fig. 2–18 **This watercolor painting shows one glimpse of what colonial life was like in Virginia. What details from daily life do you see?**

After original watercolor by John White, *Indians Fishing*, Virginia, 1585. Watercolor touched with gold. Courtesy of the Trustees of the British Museum. ©Copyright The British Museum.

## 2.4 Continued

**Art in the Home** Colonists along the East Coast created decorative items for daily use in wood, silver, and other metals. Women created fine quilts, needlework, and homespun weaving. The major influences on art in the thirteen colonies came from England.

In the New England colonies, portraits for the home were popular. Many portraits show settlers in fine clothes, posed as if they were privileged Europeans.

Most painters were self-taught. They traveled from one town to another to paint signs and houses. These artists were known as *limners*. In their spare time, limners painted portraits of the colonists. Eventually, some artists moved beyond portrait painting and created historical paintings as well.

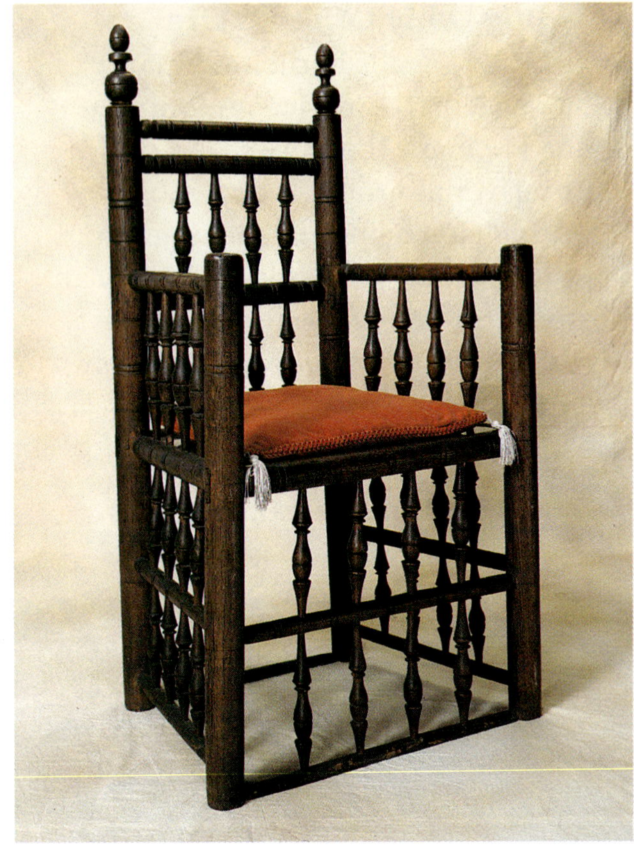

Fig. 2–19 **Chairs were luxury items in many early New England homes. Why do you think this chair was considered to be luxurious?**

Plymouth Colony, *Bradford Chair*, 1630. Black ash, seat wood, 46" x 24" x 19" (116.8 x 61 x 48.3 cm). Pilgrim Society, Pilgrim Hall Museum, Plymouth, MA.

### Check Your Understanding

**1.** Why do colonial artworks from different communities share some similarities?

**2.** How is the colonial bowl shown in Fig. 2–21 similar to a bowl you use today? How are they different?

**3.** Why do you think some settlers posed for portraits as if they were privileged people from Europe?

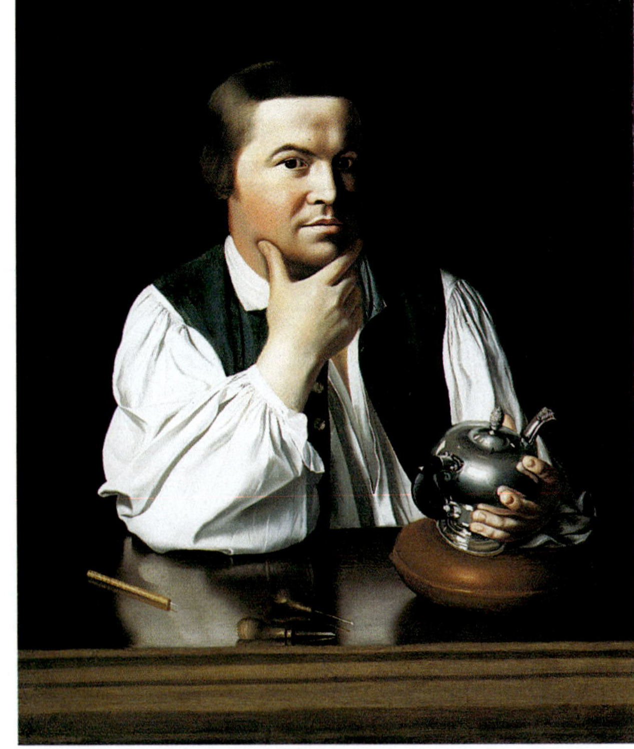

Fig. 2–20 John Singleton Copley, *Paul Revere*, 1768. Oil on canvas, 35 ⅛" x 28 ½" (89.2 x 72.4 cm). Gift of Joseph W. Revere, William B. Revere and Edward H. R. Revere. Courtesy of Museum of Fine Arts, Boston. Reproduced with permission. ©1999 Museum of Fine Arts, Boston. All Rights Reserved.

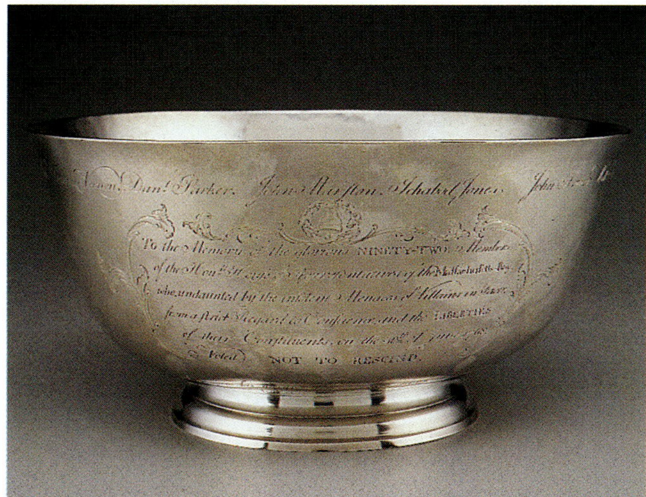

Fig. 2–21 **This bowl is a well-known piece of American silver. For whom might the artist have made this bowl? For what might the bowl have been used?**

Paul Revere, *Sons of Liberty Bowl*, Boston, 1768. Silver, 5 ½" x 11" (14 x 27.9 cm). Gift by Subscription and Francis Bartlett Fund. Courtesy of Museum of Fine Arts, Boston. Reproduced with permission. 

## Studio Time

### Interpret an Object

Draw an imaginative interpretation of an object that is an important part of your everyday life.

- Study your object carefully. Use markers or watercolors to create your interpretation of it.
- Plan your composition by using the principles of design. What will you emphasize? What rhythms can you show? How will you use normal, ideal, or exaggerated proportions? How can you use other principles of design to create a definite mood or feeling?

Reflect on the decisions you made in interpreting your subject.

## Meet Paul Revere

Paul Revere (1734–1818) is well known for warning American colonists that the British were coming during the Revolutionary War. Fewer people know that Revere was a master silversmith, a political cartoonist, an engraver, and designer of the first paper money used by the colonial government.



Revere learned to work silver as an apprentice at his father's shop in Boston. When Revere was 20, his father died. After the Revolution, he successfully ran the shop and started several other businesses. Revere used his talent and skills as a silversmith to create various pieces. He was well known as a designer and craftsman of elegant silverware and tea sets, such as the bowl shown in **Fig. 2–21**.

**"His work, highly praised during his lifetime, is regarded as one of the outstanding achievements in American decorative arts."**

—The Paul Revere House, website

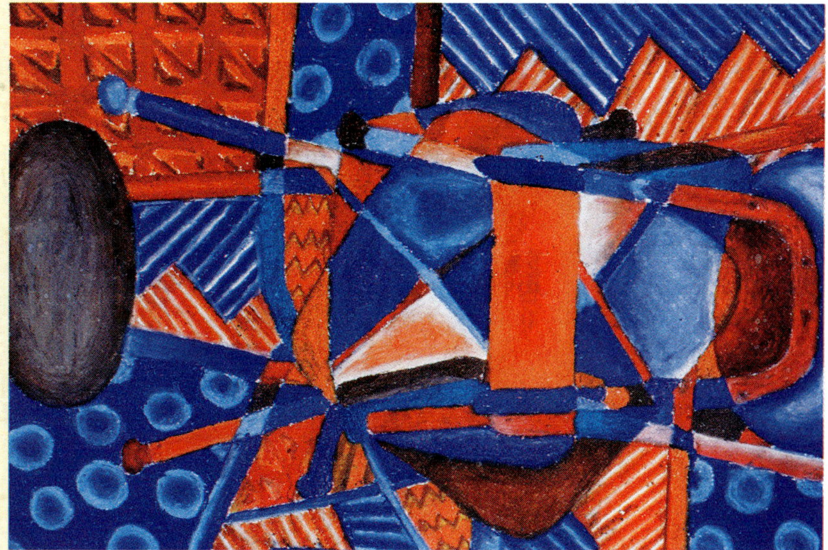

Fig. 2–22 Student artwork

# An Indian Empire

Indian artworks differ from one part of the country to another and from one time period to another. In part, this is because of India's class structure and its many different religions. The Hindu, Muslim, and Buddhist religions each have a strong influence on the way people are shown in Indian art.

One major theme in India's art is the pursuit of a purposeful life. Some artworks show how people should seek an ideal life. Others reveal the daily-life activities of the different social classes, from nobility to peasants.

Fig. 2–23 **What does this illustration tell you about farming in India?**

Miftah al Fuzula, *Oxen Ploughing*, 15th century. Gouache on paper. British Library, Oriental and India Office Library.

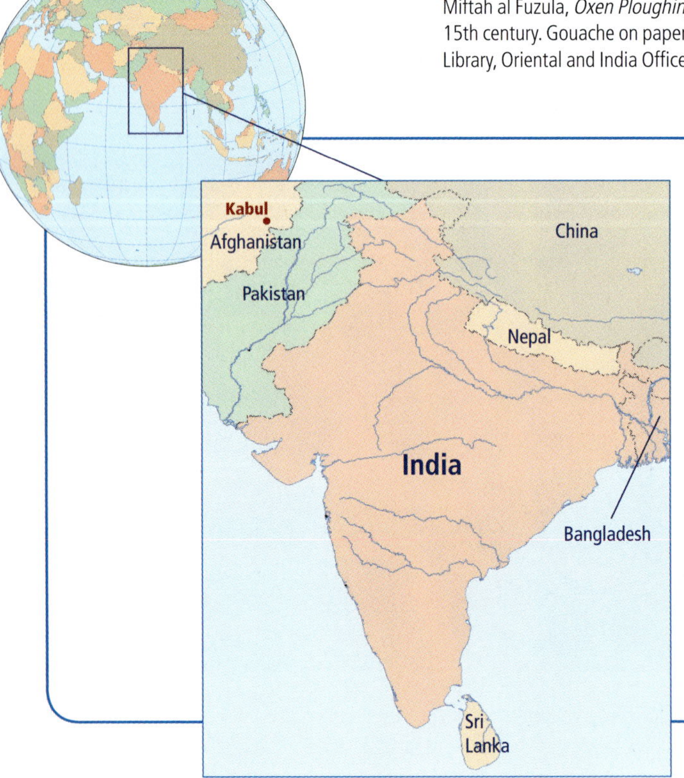


## Social Studies Connection

About 5000 years ago, the first known civilization developed in the Indus Valley, the area now known as **India**. Many different people settled in this land. Aryans, Persians, Greeks, and Muslims each blended elements of their civilizations with the Indian culture. For thousands of years, Hinduism and Buddhism were the native religions in India. Then, in the 1500s and 1600s, the Mughal Empire came to rule most of India. The Muslim Mughal rulers developed a culture that blended Middle Eastern and Indian elements.

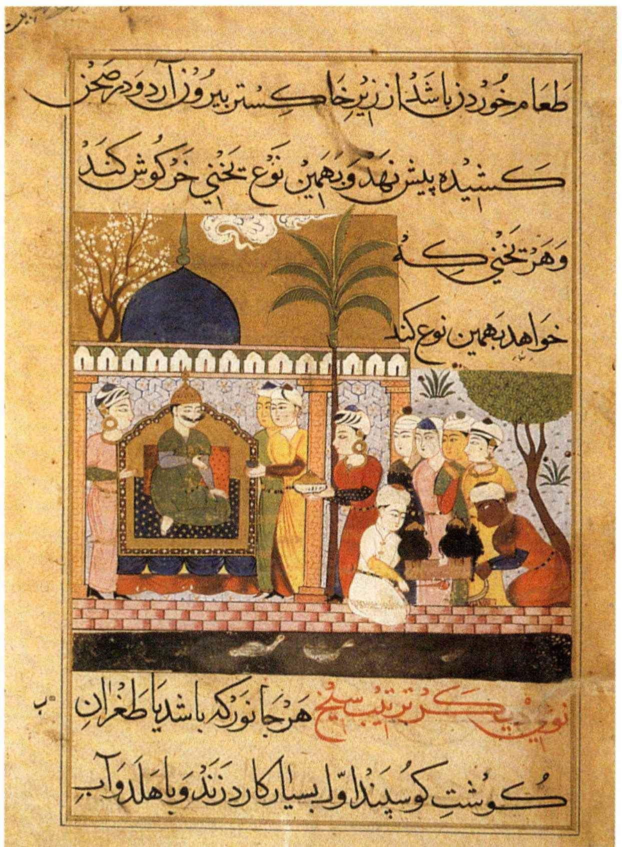

Fig. 2–24 **This is a cookbook page from the 1500s. Why might the sultan have wanted this book illustrated for his son?**

Ni'mat-nama, *The Preparation of Hare Soup*, 1500–10. Gouache on paper. British Library, Oriental and India Office Library.

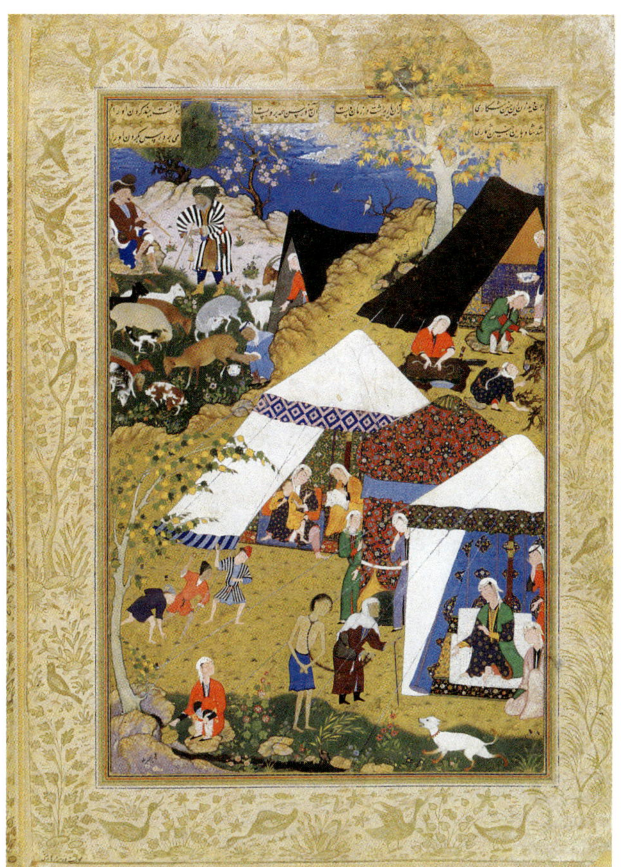

Fig. 2–25 **There are many things going on in this camp scene. What do you see that tells you about daily life in India during the 1500s?**

M. Ali, *Camp Scene, Khsa of Nizami*, 1539–43. Gouache on paper. British Library, Oriental and India Office Library.

**Miniature Paintings** Miniature paintings were primarily used for book illustration and became especially popular in the 1400s. A miniature is a very small, detailed painting. Subjects for the paintings came from Hindu legends and everyday life. Artists used bright colors to create the paintings.

Before the Mughal Empire was established in 1526, paintings were created in small commercial studios. Soon after the empire was established, the production of paintings shifted to royal court workshops.

### Visual Culture

Decoration and ornament are important in the art and architecture of India. Consider the ways people in your town, community, or neighborhood use ornament and decoration. Pay attention to the way people decorate lawns, streets, windows, houses, and even school hallways and classrooms. Notice how some ornaments and decorations are seasonal or for special occasions. Think about why people decorate and when decorations might, or might not, be appropriate. When does enhancing become distracting?

## Meet Farrukh Beg

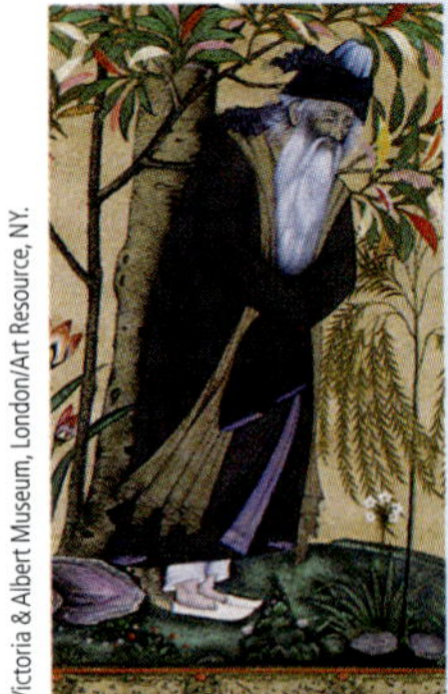



Farrukh Beg (1547–ca. 1615) was most likely born in Persia (present-day Iran). He trained as a painter, and eventually entered the service of Mirza Hakim, Emperor Akbar's half-brother, in Kabul. When Hakim died in 1585, Beg traveled to Fathpur Sikri and became one of Akbar's court painters.

In 1605 Akbar died. Beg spent eight years painting in south central India before rejoining the court of Akbar's son Jehangir. Beg became one of Jehangir's most favored court painters. On one of his paintings, Jehangir named Beg "wonder of the age."

**"If any other person has put in the eye and eyebrow of a face, I can perceive whose work the original face is, and who has painted the eye and eyebrows."**

— Emperor Jehangir of the Mughal Empire from 1605 to 1627.

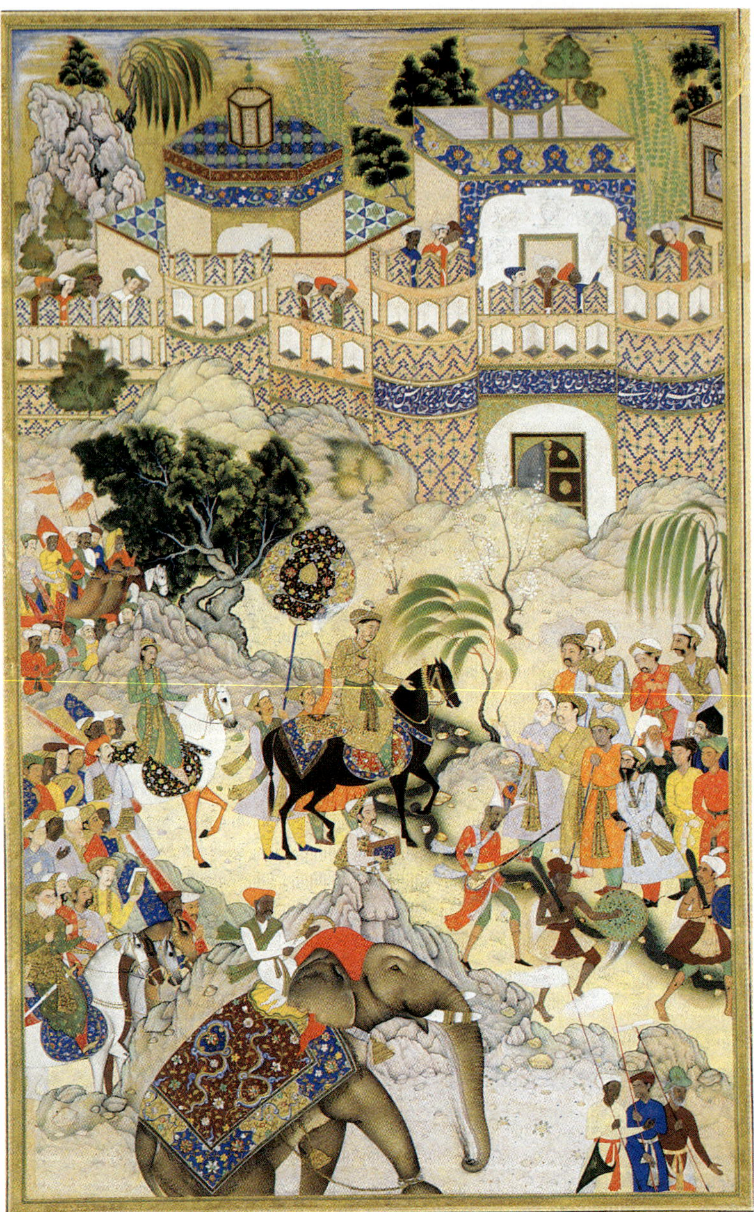

Fig. 2–26 **Notice the rich detail in this painting. How might the artists have exaggerated the reality of this event?**

Farrukh Beg, *Akbar's Entry Into Surat,* Akbar-nama, ca. 1590. Gouache on paper, 14 7/8" x 9 9/16" (37.9 x 24.3 cm). Trustees of the Victoria & Albert Museum.

**The Court Workshop** Emperor Akbar ruled the Mughal Empire in India from 1556–1605. At the start of his reign, he set up a workshop for court artists. The workshop community grew to more than 100 artists. It produced images of daily court life and garden scenes that told the story of Akbar's reign.

Muslim and Hindu artists often worked together on paintings. They shared in the creation of general outlines, portrait heads, landscapes, and coloring. The workshop artists blended color with calligraphy and detailed realism. The artists created a unique style by combining Hindu ideas, European realism, Persian composition, and Muslim discipline.

The court workshop tradition continued during the reigns of the next two emperors. But the well-known workshop was abolished at the end of Shah Jahan's rule in 1658. After that, the artists made their livings selling their art on the streets and in city marketplaces.

### Check Your Understanding

1. How did the religions of India's communities influence art?
2. Study the image in Fig. 2–25. How was daily life in India at the time of this painting different from your daily life now? How is it similar?
3. Why do you think Emperor Akbar decided to set up a workshop for court artists?

## Studio Time

### A New Look at What's Familiar

Create an imaginative collage about a daily-life event.

- Think about what you will show. What does the interior or exterior space look like? What do people do there? What objects do they use?
- Look at works by Mughal artists for inspiration: How do they organize space?
- Include drawing in your collage.

Reflect on how you have organized the space in your collage.

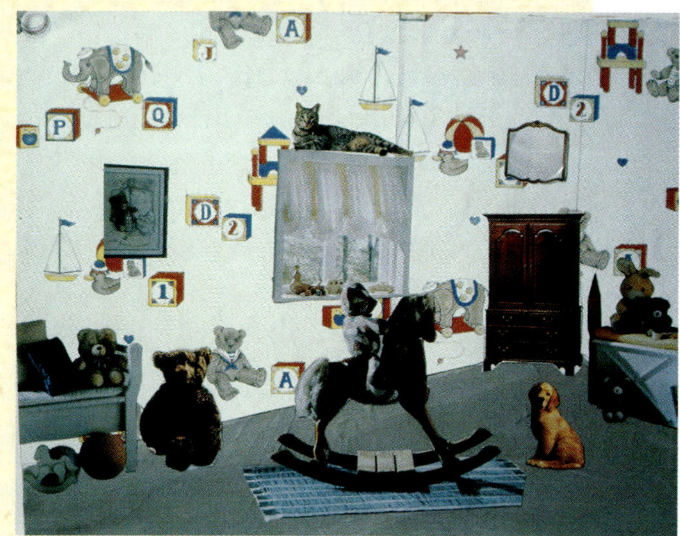

Fig. 2–27 Student artwork

# Function with Flair

## Studio Background

Think of how often you use boxes, bags, and plastic storage bins at home and at school. What do you think people living in earlier times used for containers? Many made clay pots in hundreds of different shapes and sizes. They added many features to make the pots both functional and beautiful. The forms and features of the pots varied depending on where the people lived, what they needed, and how they passed along their culture's traditions.

**In this studio exploration, you will create a clay container that can be used in daily life. Decorate your container imaginatively.** Like generations of pottery makers, you will explore the coil method to make a decorated and functional object. You will use slip to join the coils. Slip is a thick liquid made of clay mixed with water.

### You Will Need

- clay
- rolling pin
- two flat sticks
- water
- slip
- paintbrush
- clay tools, such as a fork, spoon, wooden dowel
- sheet of plastic or large plastic bag

## Step 1 Plan and Practice

- Determine what uses your container will have.
- Decide what your container will look like. Think about how to make the container's form and decorations unusual and personal.

**Things to Remember:**

✓ Use neat, even coils to build your container.

✓ Make the shape of your container symmetrical.

✓ Embellish the container in a way that makes it distinctive.

## Inspiration from Our World

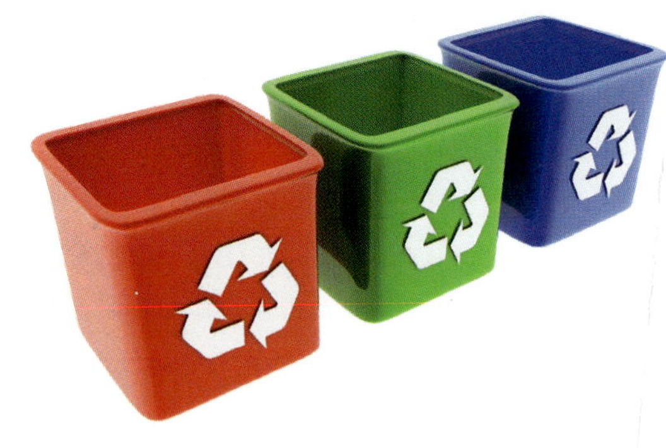

## Step 4 Add Finishing Touches

- **Decorate your container before firing.** You can add small balls or coils of clay for a relief design. You might also carve a design directly into the clay's surface.

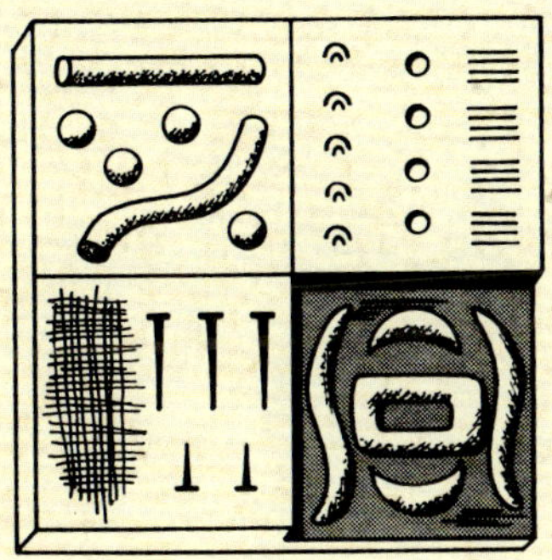

## Step 5 Share and Reflect

- Display your completed work. In a small group, discuss the form, function, and decoration of your container. What purpose can your container serve in daily life? How did you design your container so that it would perform this function? How do your decorative features add to the container?
- What do your container's form and decorations say about your community?
- How do you feel about working with clay? Why?

## Art Criticism

**Describe** What do you see?

**Analyze** How do you think the artist formed and decorated this container?

**Interpret** What do you think is the purpose or function of this container?

**Evaluate** What did the artist do especially well in designing this container?

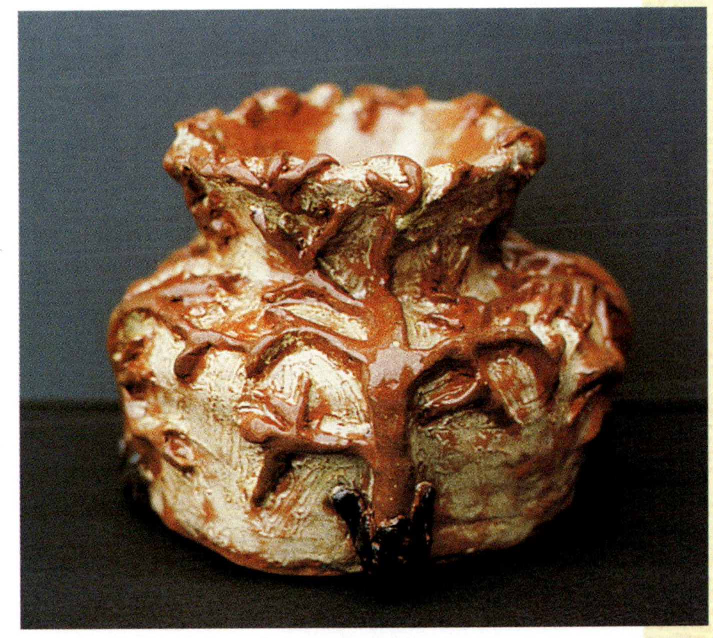

Fig. 2–29 Student artwork

## Science

**Each Native American pueblo in New Mexico traditionally uses a particular color of clay for its pottery.** For example, the pueblo San Ildefonso is well known for its heavy-walled black pottery. Acoma is known for its creamy-white clay. Why do you think there are differences among pueblos? Each pueblo gathers the natural materials (gypsum, sand, and clay) only from its own reservation. This process makes the pottery unique to each pueblo.

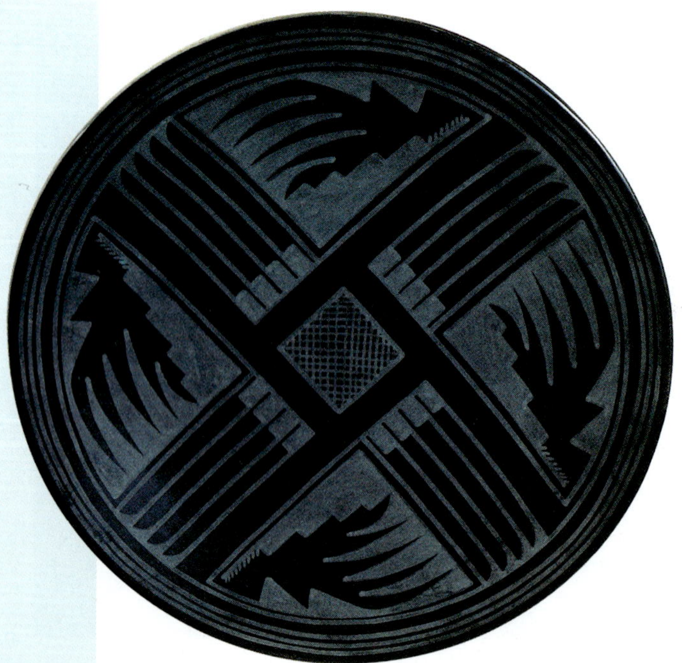

Fig. 2–30 **Maria Martinez made well known the technique of black-on-black pottery you see pictured here. She made the pots and her husband, Julian, put designs on them.**

Maria and Julian Martinez, *Bowl*, n.d. Clay, height: 7" (17.8 cm). National Museum of American Art, Smithsonian Institution, Washington, DC/Art Resource, NY.

## Dance

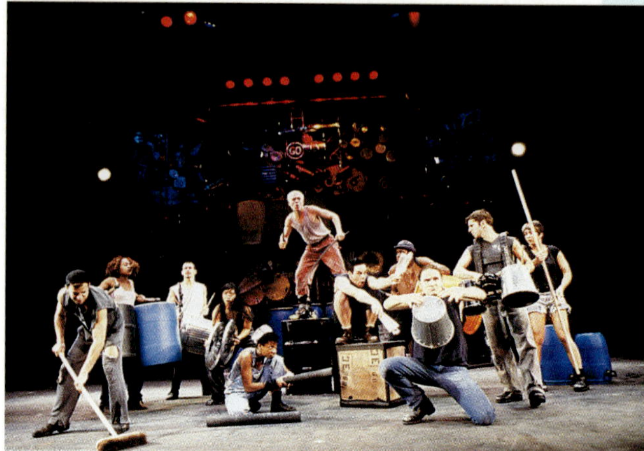

Fig. 2–31 ***STOMP* cast members create music using objects like brooms and plastic containers. What object do you use daily that could be used to make music?**

*Cast members of the musical* STOMP. Photo ©Junichi Takahashi. Courtesy of Takahashi Studios, New York.

**Visual art may show scenes of daily life or may be used in daily activities or rituals.** Dance can also be a part of daily life. What movements do you use during different daily activities? In what ways are those movements like dance? Think of some chores or other responsibilities you have. If you were to create a dance to help you with your daily work, what would it look like?

## Careers **Interior Designer**

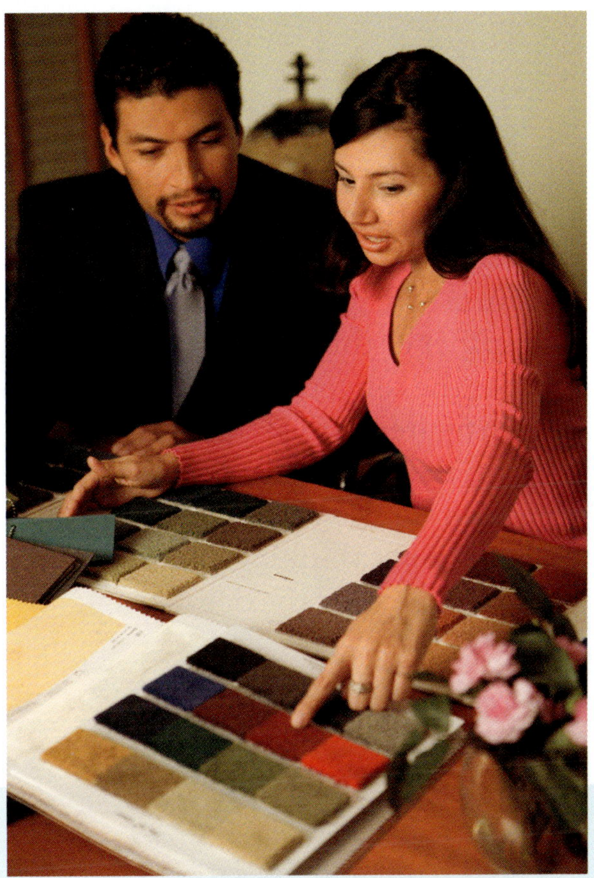

**Do you often rearrange furniture or want to repaint rooms in more appealing colors? Interior designers are responsible for planning the look and function of inside spaces.** These may include the spaces where we live, work, and play. Interior designers may work with clients to select furniture, wall and floor coverings, and art elements. Interior designers have to be skilled at working with color, fabric, and furniture. They must have good communication and budgeting skills.

Fig. 2–32 ©Somos Images/Corbis

## Daily Life

**What are some outdoor activities that take place in your neighborhood after school or on the weekends?** Maybe people chat on their front steps, walk their pets, or play games on the sidewalk. Why do you think ordinary subjects like these are found in art? In art, a representation of a scene from everyday life is called a genre scene. How could the daily life of your neighborhood be shown through art? What subject would you choose for a genre painting?

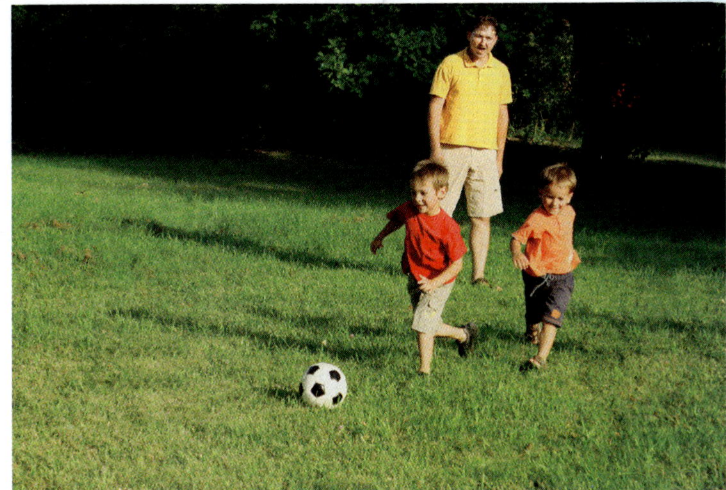

Fig. 2–33

## Vocabulary Review

Match each art term below with its definition.

**mixed media**

**miniature**

**portrait**

**bisqueware**

**proportion**

**contour drawing**

1. an artwork that shows a specific person or group of people
2. the relation of one thing to another in size, amount, number, or degree
3. a drawing that shows only the edges of objects
4. any artwork that is made with more than one medium
5. ceramic that has been fired once but not glazed
6. a very small, detailed painting

## Aesthetic Thinking

Drawing was not appreciated as an art form until the 1600s. Why do you think that was the case? How is drawing a unique art form?

## Write About Art

Write a short script to accompany this painting. Assign each character a name and a role. In your script, capture what each person is saying to another or thinking to himself. How does the conversation between the two figures in the foreground differ from that of the two figures in the background? What is the single figure in the front thinking? What secret thoughts could the dog have?

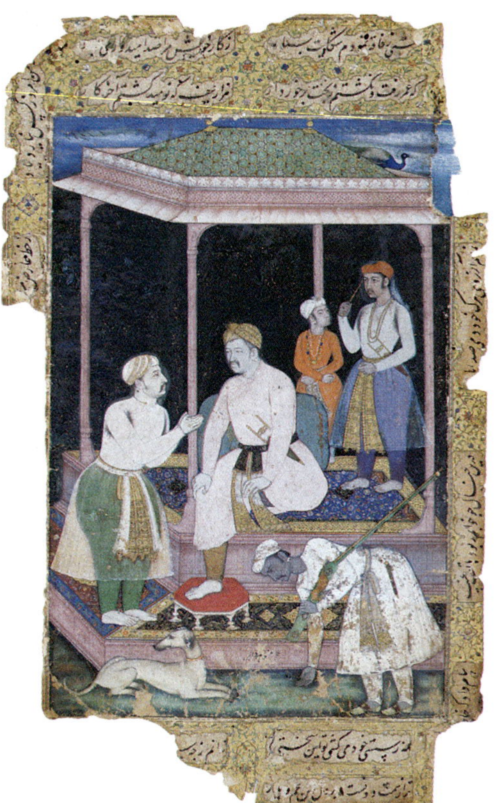

Fig. 2–34 **In this scene, Akbar is shown greeting an old friend in a garden pavilion. Do you think daily life in Akbar's court was formal or informal? What makes you think so?**

Manohar Das, India, *Akbar Receives Mirza 'Aziz Koka*, 1602. Opaque watercolor and gold on paper, 7 ¼" x 4 ¾" (18.4 x 12.1 cm). Cincinnati Art Museum, Gift of John J. Emery 1950.289a.

## Art Criticism

**Describe** What do you see in this painting?

**Analyze** How does the artist use texture in this work?

**Interpret** Why do you think Degas shows only part of the horse on the left, as if he is trotting off the page?

**Evaluate** Why do you think Degas chose to show these horses and jockeys before the race instead of during or immediately after it?

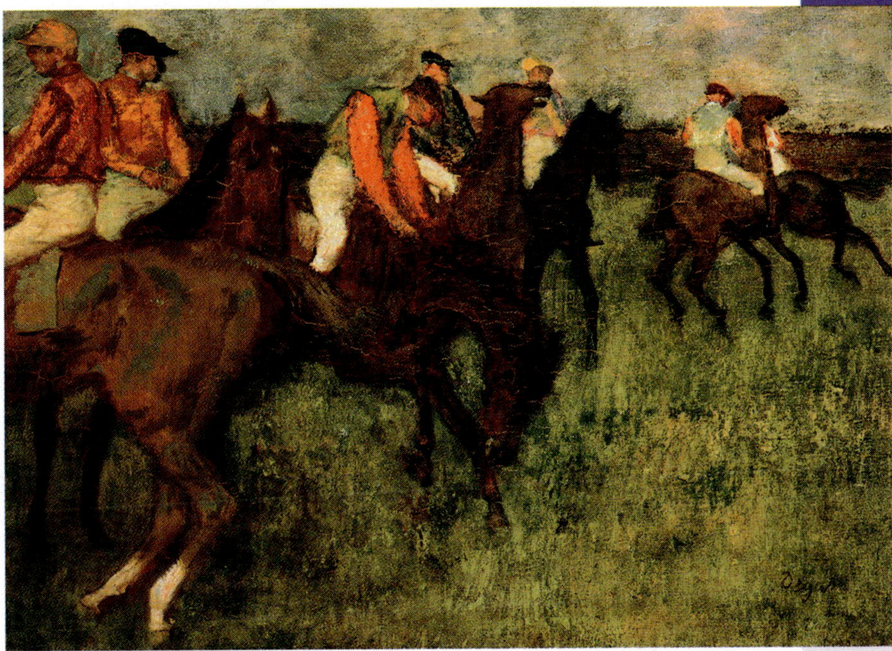

Fig. 2–35 Edgar Degas, *Jockeys*, 1886–90. Oil on paper, 10 ¼" x 14 3/16" (26 x 36 cm). Private Collection. Photo: Visual Arts Library/Art Resource, NY.

## Meet the Artist

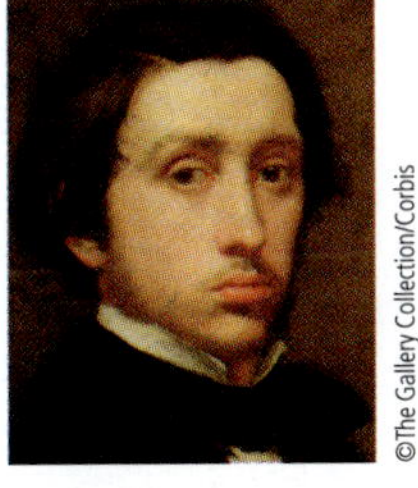

©The Gallery Collection/Corbis

**Edgar Degas** was born in Paris. He worked in a variety of media, including painting, drawing, printmaking, sculpture, and photography. Degas focused on a few key subjects in his work, exploring each of them in great depth. These included ballet dancers, women bathing, portraits, and horses and jockeys.

**"It is essential to do the same subject over again, ten times, a hundred times. Nothing in art must seem to be chance, not even movement."**

—Edgar Degas (1834–1917)

## For Your Portfolio

Select an artwork in this textbook that sends a clear message about daily life in a community. Describe the work in detail. Think about how the arrangement of the parts helps convey the intended message. Date your response and add it to your portfolio.

## For Your Sketchbook

Design a page in your sketchbook for writing visually descriptive impressions of daily life scenes in your community. Refer to these poetic descriptions when developing ideas for future artworks.

Unit 3

# Art and Belonging

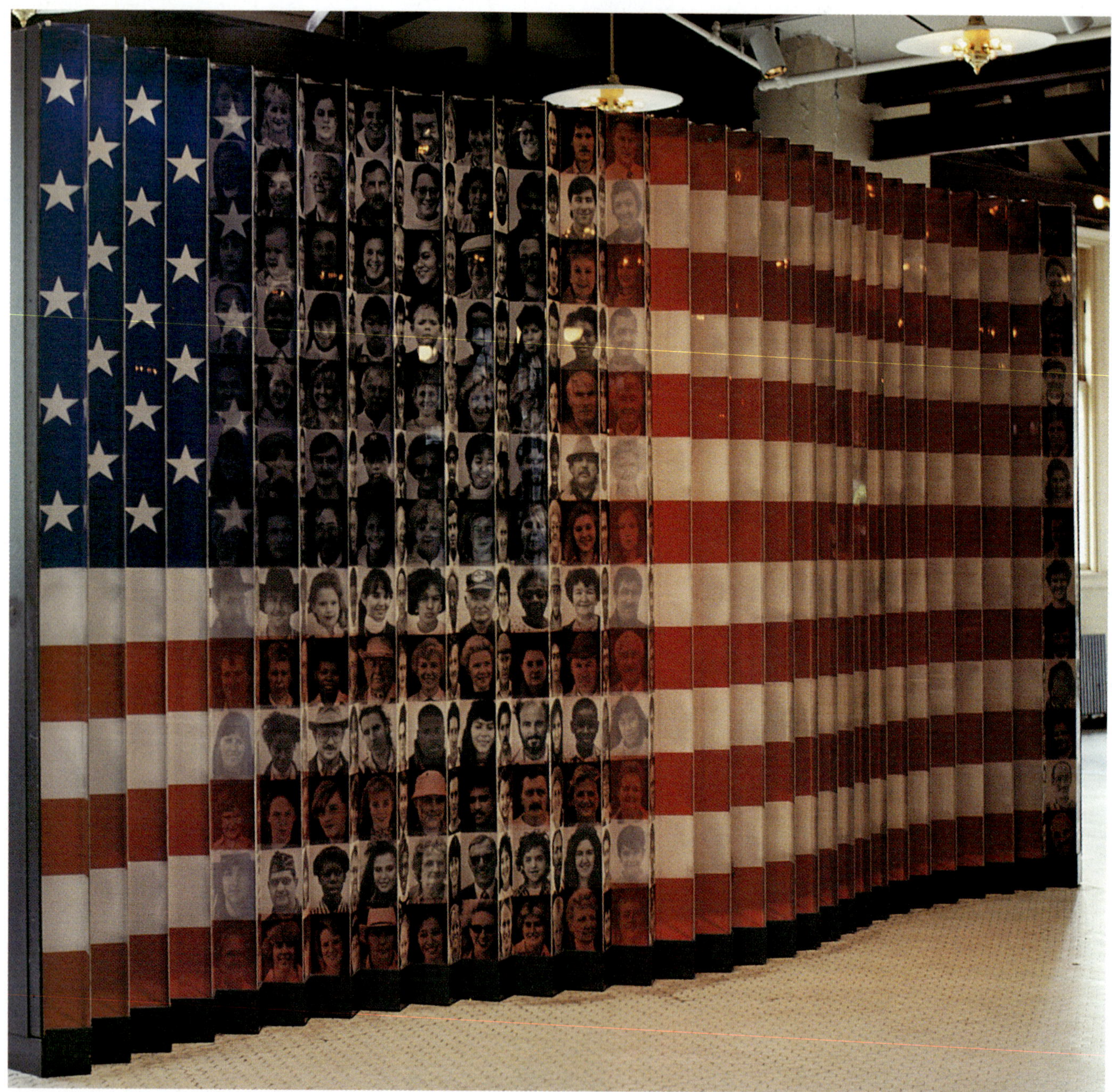

Fig. 3–1 **What does this flag, with its many different faces, say to you?**

Pablo Delano (photographer of faces), Installation designed by MetaForm/Rathe/D&P (The Liberty/Ellis Island Collaborative), *Flag of Faces*, Ellis Island, 1990. 8' 8" x 16' 6 ¾" x 2" (264.2 x 504.8 x 5.1 cm). Exhibit installation at the Ellis Island Immigration Museum, National Park Service/Statue of Liberty National Monument.

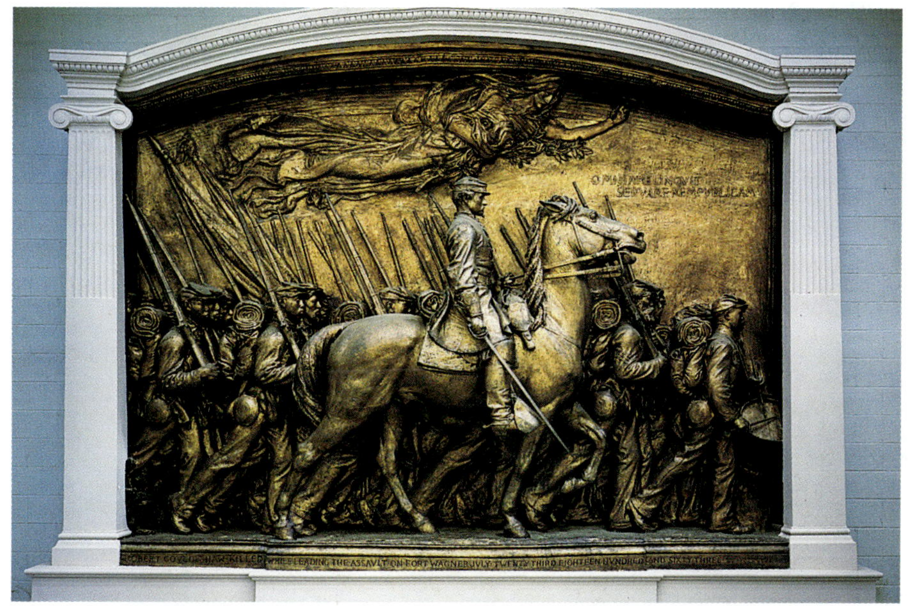

Fig. 3–2 **What does this artwork seem to say about belonging to a community of soldiers?**

Augustus Saint-Gaudens, *Shaw Memorial* (Final Version), 1900. U.S. Department of the Interior, National Park Service, Saint-Gaudens National Historic Site, Cornish, New Hampshire.

**Do you know where your ancestors are from? How did your family arrive in America?** In the late 1800s and early 1900s, millions of people from around the world came to live in the United States, looking for a better life.

Artworks can express what it means to belong to a community, whether that community is as large as a country or as small as a neighborhood. *Flag of Faces* **(Fig. 3–1)** shows people whose ancestors journeyed here seeking a new home. Although it sends a message about a whole nation, other artworks tell about belonging to local communities throughout the world.

**In this unit, you will learn:**

- How artists reveal and honor values and beliefs through their work.
- How to use modeling, carving, and assemblage techniques expressively.
- How to identify symbols of belonging in artworks from around the world.

# Art Reveals Beliefs

**Public Monuments** Look around your town or city. Do you see artworks in public places that mean something special to the local people? Many artists create monuments for public places—places where people gather or pass by every day.

A monument is a public sculpture that reminds people of an important event or person in the area's history. Monuments represent ideas that are important to the people who live in the area.

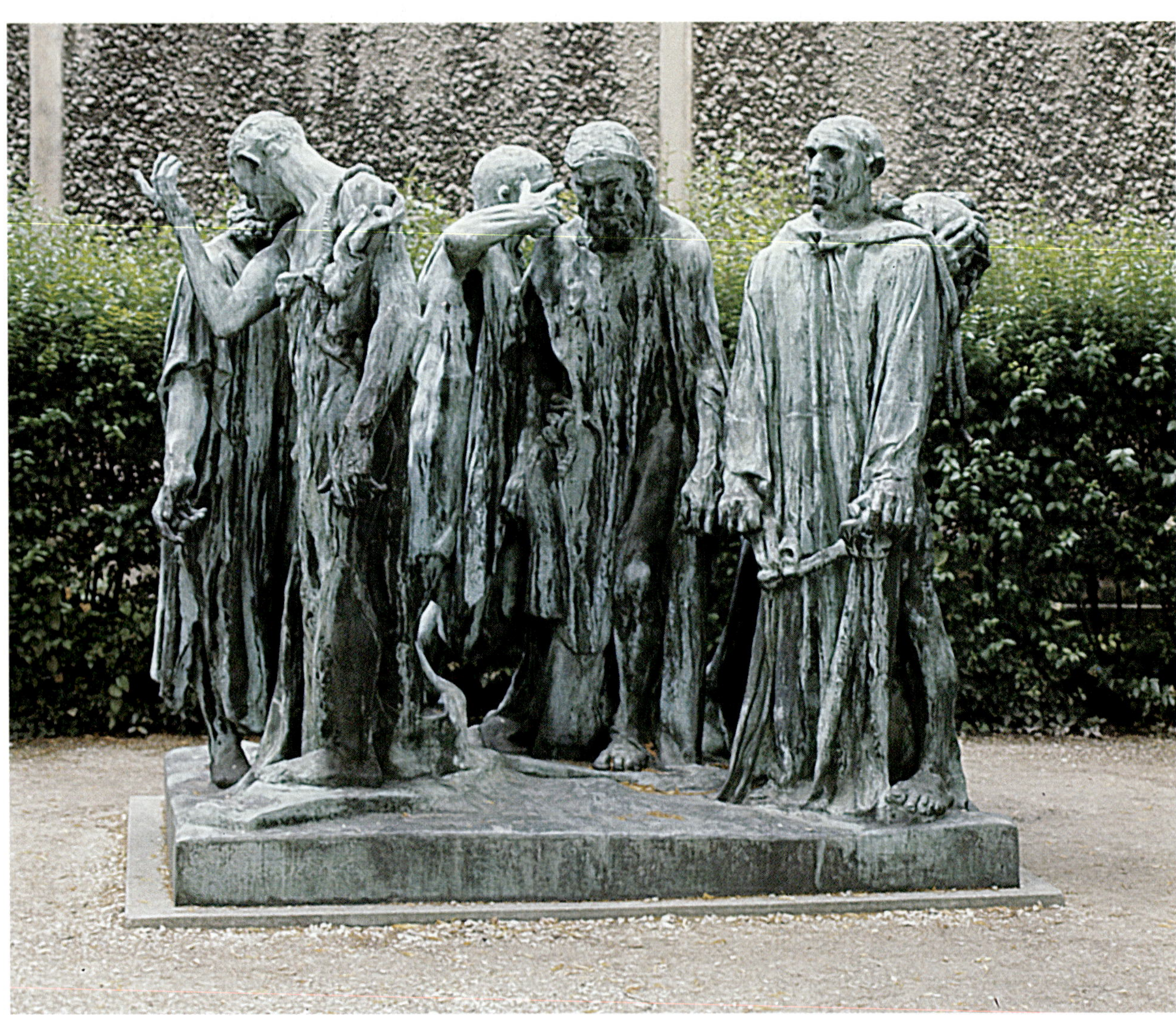

Fig. 3–3 **How does this sculpture represent the heroism of the burghers?**

Auguste Rodin, *The Burghers of Calais*, 1884–85. Bronze, 81 7/8" x 55 1/8" x 74 3/4" (208 x 140 x 190 cm). Musée Rodin, Paris, France. Courtesy of Art Resource, New York.

**Public Tributes** Public monuments can remind us of events, time periods, or people that are important to the community. They commemorate, or honor, the events and people that have shaped the histories of towns, cities, and even countries. The sculpture of *The Burghers of Calais* (Fig. 3–3) was created for the town of Calais, France. The burghers, or leaders, of the town offered their lives in exchange for the town's safety during the Hundred Years' War. The sculpture shows the six men facing death. It tells us that the people of this town value bravery and feel bound together by their beliefs.

## Meet Auguste Rodin

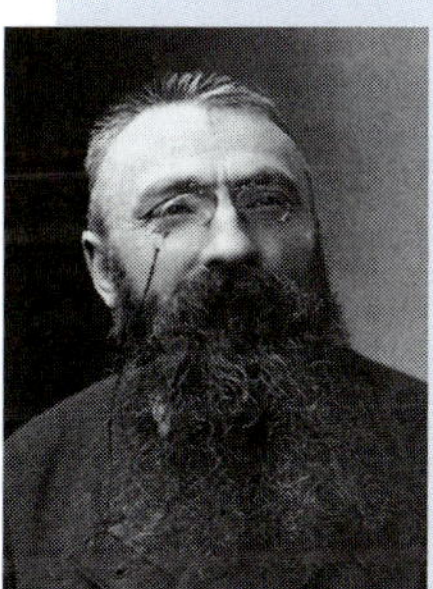

©Bettmann/CORBIS

Auguste Rodin was born in France. He studied drawing and sculpture at the Ècole Impériale de Dessin, a school for craft and design.

To earn money, he made sculptures for public places. One of his first masterpieces, *The Vanquished*, was criticized because it was so realistic that people believed he had cast it from a real person. To convince them of his skill, he made his next realistic sculpture larger than life-size.

Eventually, Rodin earned international success and employed up to 50 assistants to help turn his clay maquettes into powerful bronze sculptures.

**"Art is contemplation. It is the pleasure of the mind which searches into nature..."**

— Auguste Rodin (1840–1917)

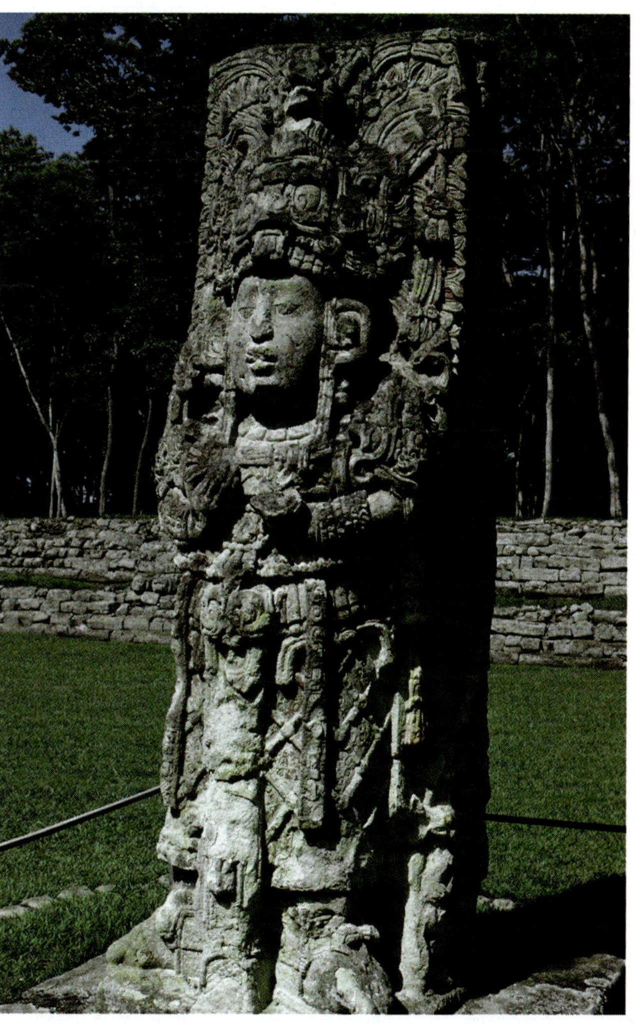

Fig. 3–4 **What details on this sculpture tell you that it represents an important person?**

Maya Culture, *Stele H from Copan: Ruler Eighteen Rabbit*. Stone with paint traces, 141" (358.14 cm) high.

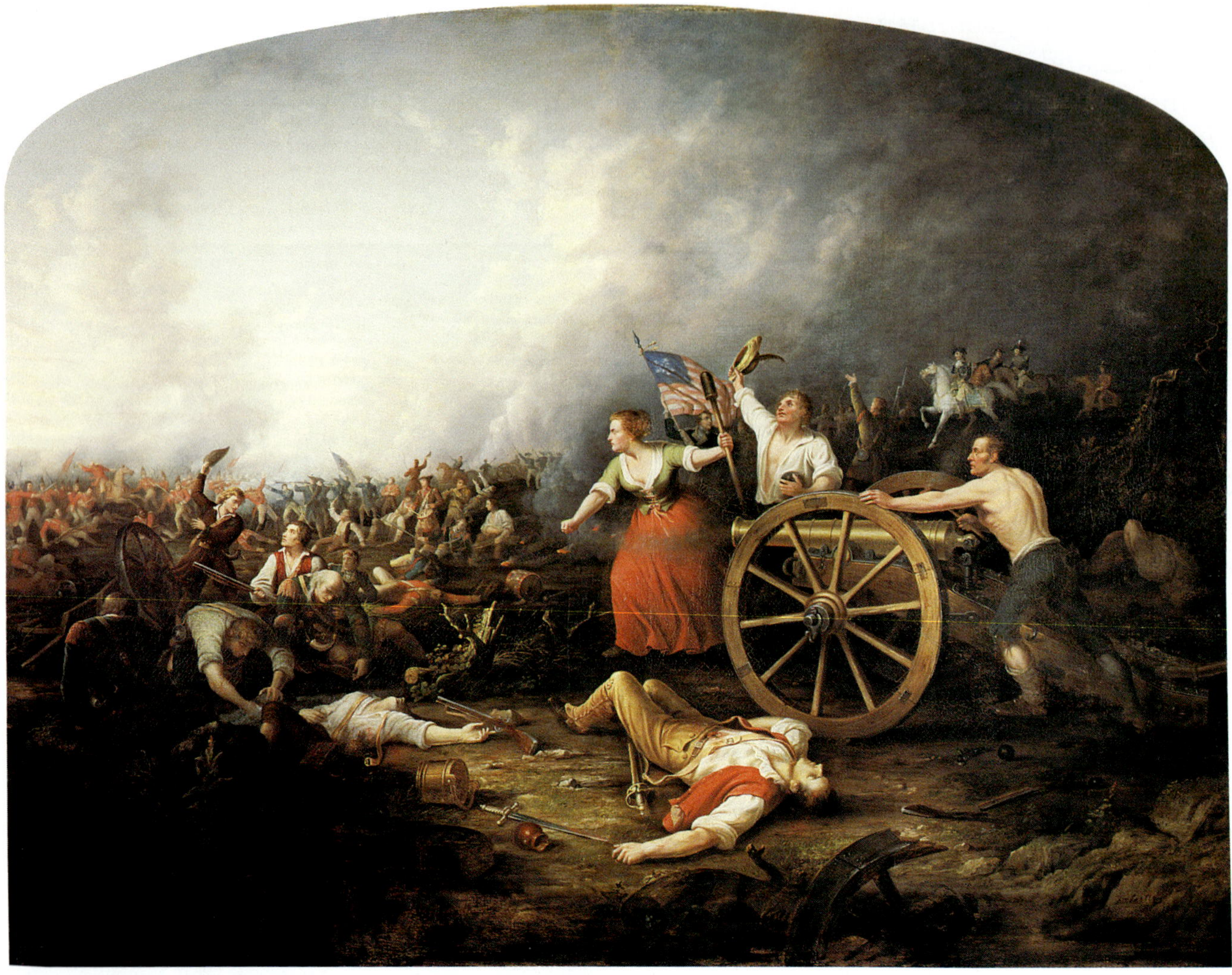

Fig. 3–5 **How does this painting commemorate Molly Pitcher's bravery? How might other important women be shown in commemorative artworks?**

Dennis Malone Carter, *Molly Pitcher at the Battle of Monmouth*, 1854. Oil on canvas, 42" x 56" (106.7 x 142.2 cm). Gift of Herbert P. Whitlock, 1913. Courtesy of Fraunces Tavern Museum, New York City.

**Art Honors Heroes and Leaders** Who are your heroes? Professional basketball players? Actresses? Someone in your neighborhood? Heroes and leaders are people who do things that represent the values and beliefs of a community. Local heroes are an important source of pride for the people who live in the area. They help create a sense of belonging because everyone honors or respects them for the same reasons.

Artworks help record the stories of heroic actions and deeds that are often told and retold within a community. The painting of Molly Pitcher tells the story of an American Revolutionary War heroine **(Fig. 3–5)**.

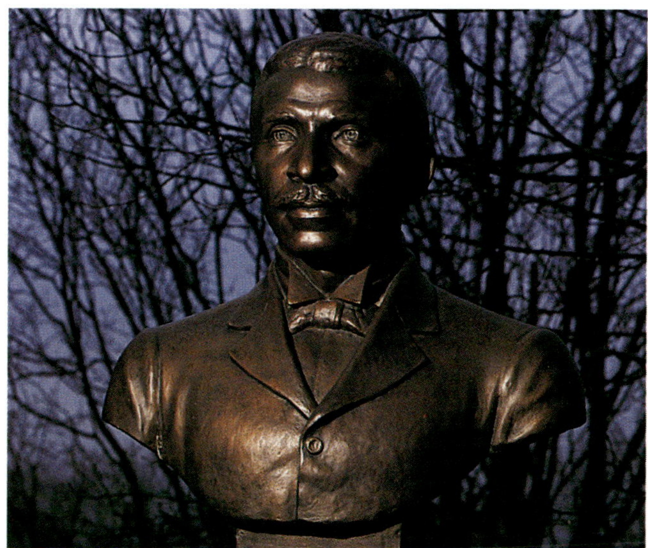

Fig. 3–6 **This sculpture commemorates George Washington Carver, who developed agricultural products that could be grown in the South. What commemorative sculptures have you seen?**

Richmond Barthé, *George Washington Carver*, 1977. Hall of Fame, Bronx Community College, New York City. Bronze. Photo ©1999 Frank Fournier.

Molly Pitcher's birth name was Mary Ludwig McCauley. She earned the nickname Molly Pitcher because she carried pitchers of water to soldiers during the Battle of Monmouth. Another example, the sculpture of George Washington Carver (Fig. 3–6), commemorates his contributions and importance as a great scientist.

### Check Your Understanding

1. What is the purpose of a public monument?
2. Select two artworks from this lesson and compare how each honors or gives tribute to an individual, event, or time period.
3. Name one of your heroes and tell how you might show this person in a sculpture.

## Studio Time

### Recording a Community Story

Choose an important event from a community story to draw.

- Sketch your ideas. Think about how you will organize your work. What people will you include? Will you create a particular setting? From what point of view will you draw the scene?
- Select your best sketch and use it to create your final colored pencil drawing. Sketch the large areas first, and then add smaller features and details.

Reflect on how well your drawing documents a community event.

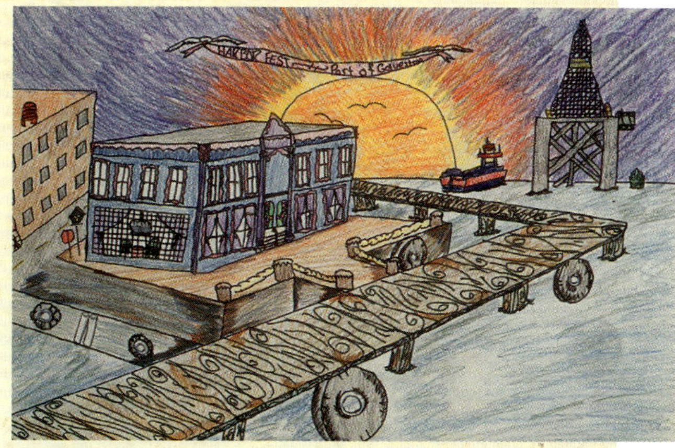

Fig. 3–7 Student artwork

## 3.2 Skills and Techniques

# Sculpture

Have you ever picked up a rock or a piece of wood because you liked its shape or texture? Nature creates beautiful forms. Since the earliest times, people have used their own methods and tools to shape materials into beautiful forms. Forms are objects that have three dimensions: height, width, and depth. Artworks that have three dimensions are called sculpture.

Communities throughout history have created sculptures for different reasons. Ancient people created sculptures of their gods and ancestors. These were used in community rituals, worship, or celebrations. More recent sculptures often show leaders or individuals and groups that people admire. Some sculptures are requested by a city or town to show something special or unique about the community.

**Form and Balance in Sculpture** Forms are solid and fill space. The space that a sculpture fills is the *positive space*. The space surrounding the inside and outside edges of a sculpture is the *negative space*.

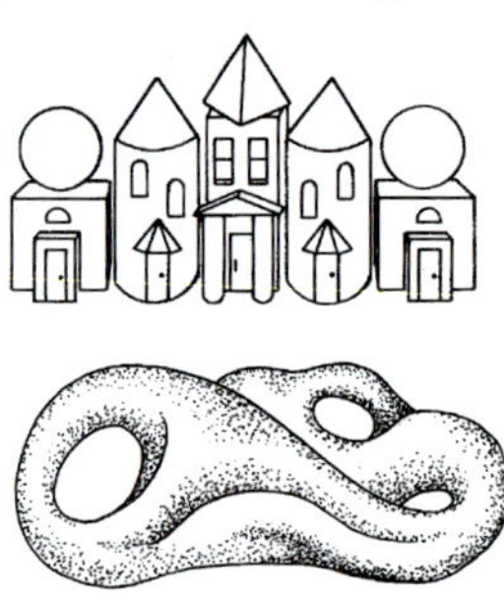

Balance occurs in an artwork when all its parts have equal visual weight. If you drew an imaginary line through a drawing and both halves were mirror images, the artwork would have *symmetrical balance*. If the two halves were not mirror images, but the artwork still looked visually balanced, then the artwork would have *asymmetrical balance*. The third kind of balance is *radial balance*, in which the parts of the design seem to radiate, or spread out, from the center of the artwork.

Fig. 3–8 **What ideals do you think are represented by this tribute to community workers? How does the form of this sculpture convey these ideals?**

Miere Laderman Ukeles, *Ceremonial Arch Honoring Service Workers in the New Service Economy*, 1988. Steel arch with materials donated from New York City agencies, 11' x 12' 4" x 9' 1" ( 335.3 x 148 x 109 cm), Courtesy Ronald Feldman Fine Arts, New York.

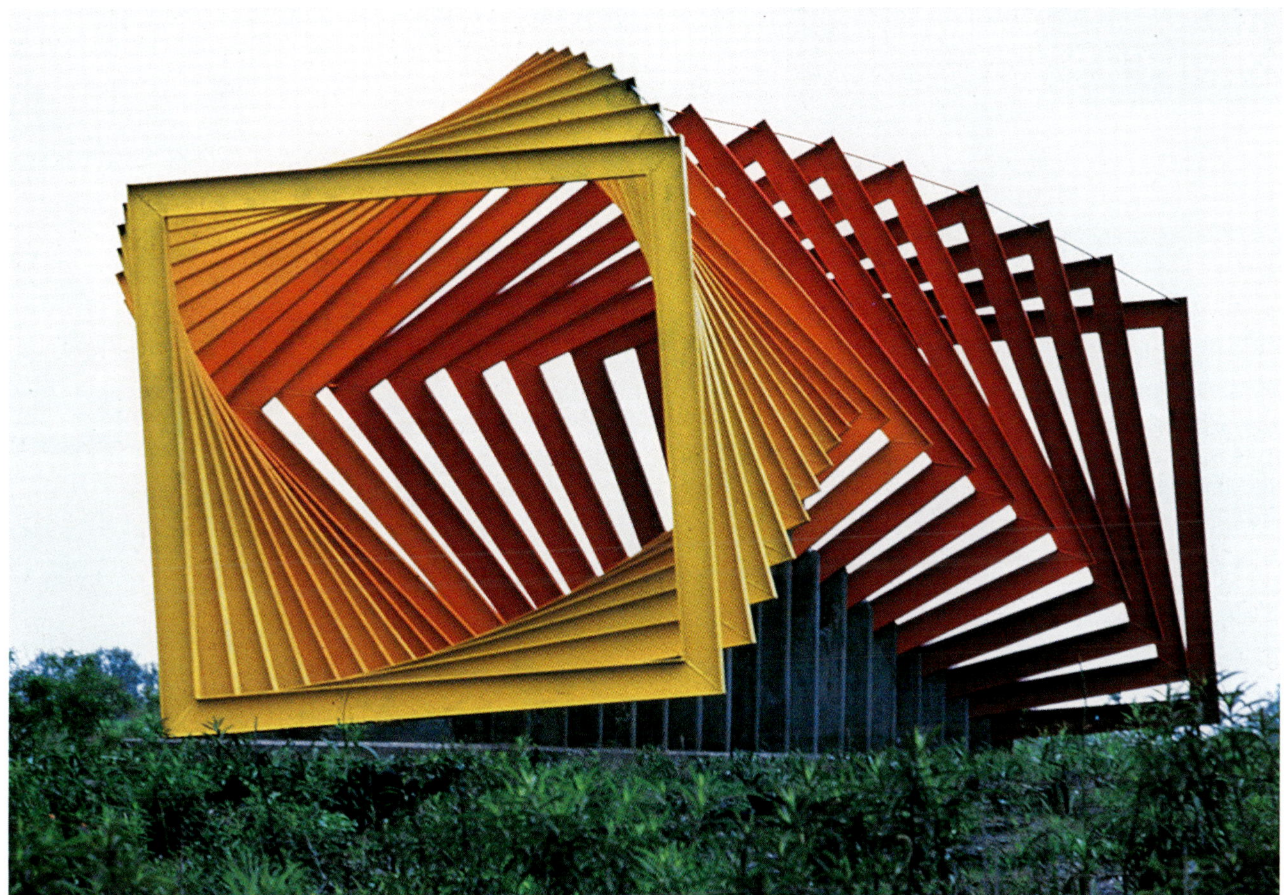

Fig. 3–9 **Why do you think this artist used so much negative space in her sculpture?**

Helen Escobedo, *Coatl (snake)*, 1982. Steel I-beams, 19' 6" x 48' 9" (6 x 15 m). National University of Mexico.

**Observe** Look at Fig. 3–8. Study its form. How would you describe the positive and negative space? What kind of balance does the sculpture have?

**Tools:** Examples of sculptures and colored pencils.

### Practice: Identifying Form and Balance

- Choose an example of a sculpture to study and sketch or trace its form.
- Use colored pencils to color in the positive space of the sculpture. Leave the negative space white.
- Using a pencil, draw a faint line through the center of your sketch. Use the line to help you identify the kind of balance used.

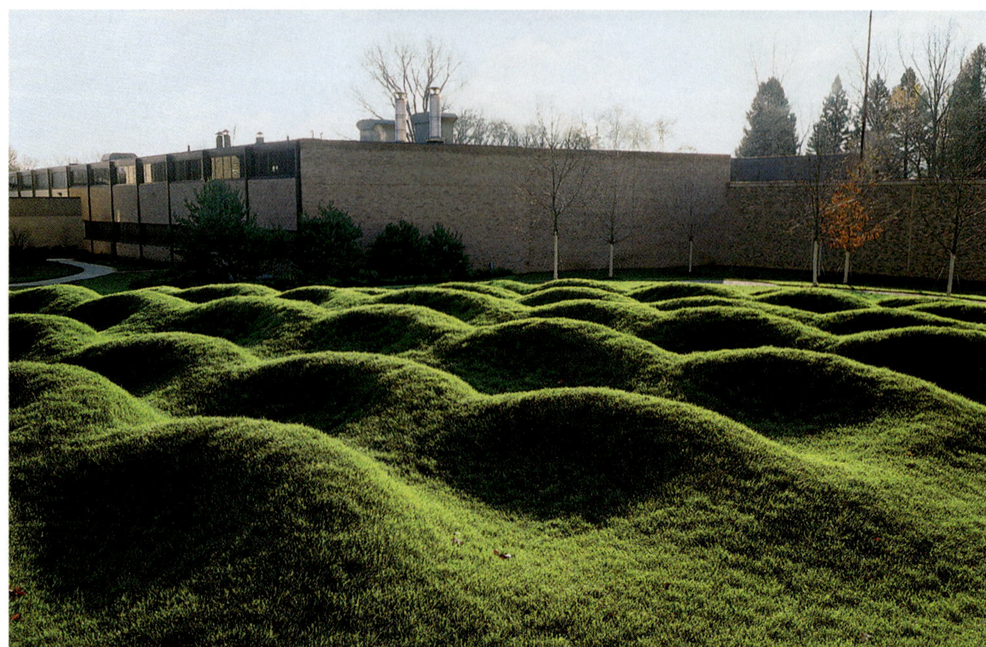

Fig. 3–10 **What kind of sculpture is pictured? How do you think it was created?**

Maya Lin, *Wave Field*, 1993–95. Sculpted earth; 100' x 100' (30.5 x 30.5 m). University of Michigan, Ann Arbor, MI. An art:21 artist.

**Materials and Methods** Traditional materials for sculptures include stone, wood, clay, ivory, and cast metal, such as bronze. Traditional ways to create sculpture involve carving, modeling, and casting. Today, many sculptors combine discarded materials to create sculptures. Discarded materials used in sculpture are called found objects. Some artists use construction equipment to create sculptural forms from the environment. These forms are called earthworks. Sculptures can be made to last for centuries or for only a short time.

**Observe** Look at Fig. 3–10. Imagine that the sculpture is the size of your desktop. How might you have created those forms in clay? Would you use your fingers? A tool? An object?

**Tools:** Modeling clay or ceramic clay.

### Practice: Modeling

- Modeling is the process of using your hands and a few simple tools to shape soft materials.
- Start with a lump of clay about the size of an egg. Soften the clay by working it with your hands.
- Experiment with the clay. Can you make holes in it? Can you twist it? How thin can you make it without piercing it?
- Make three very different shapes with the clay, one at a time.

### Check Your Understanding

1. What materials and methods are commonly used to create sculpture?
2. How is sculpture different from painting and drawing? How is it similar?
3. How can a sculpture be used to relay a message to a community?

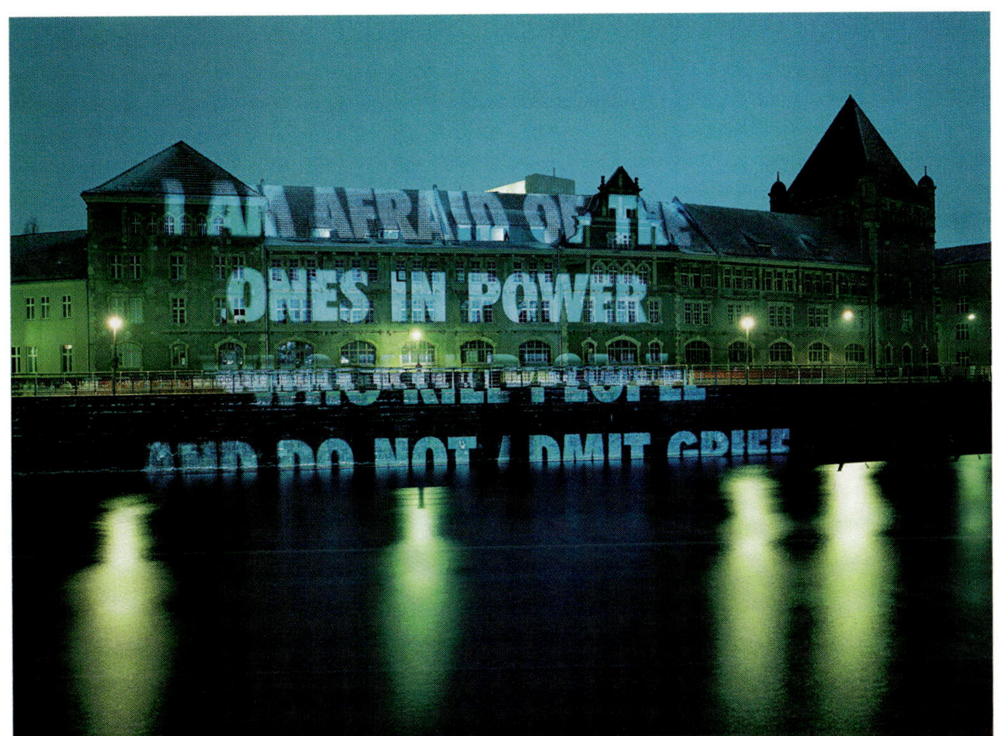


Fig. 3–11 **The text from this work, "I am afraid of the ones in power who kill people and do not admit grief," was projected on the Museumshöfe in Berlin.**

Jenny Holzer, *Xenon for Berlin*, 2001. Light projection. Museumshöfe, Berlin. Text (pictured) *Mother and Child*, 1990. Photo: Attilio Maranzano ©Jenny Holzer Studio/Art Resource, NY.

## Studio Time

### A Community Hero

Think about a person you admire. Your hero might be someone who lives in your community or someone who lives elsewhere in the nation or world. You may choose to depict a hero from the past or present.

- Create a clay sculpture of one of your heroes by pinching and pulling the clay into the shapes you desire.
- To join two pieces of moist clay, scratch both surfaces and apply slip, or watery clay, and press the parts together. Smooth the joints.
- To finish your clay sculpture, use a stamp or scratch the surface to add texture, or glazes to add color.

Reflect on the choices you made in characterizing your hero.

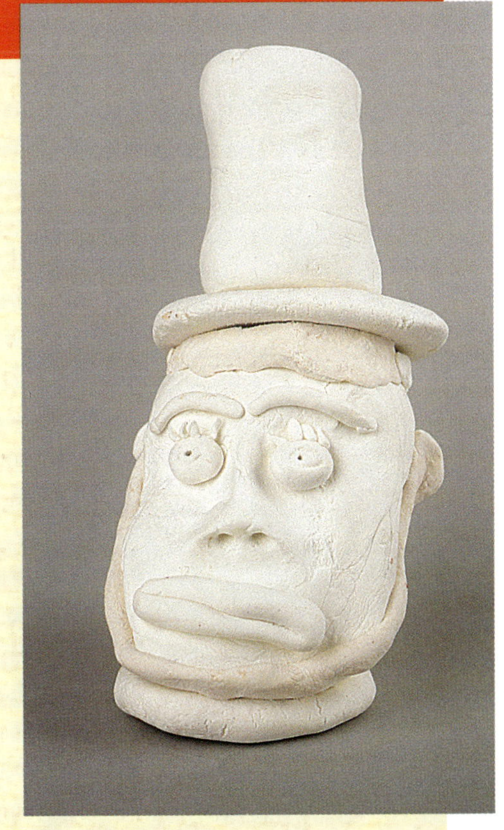

Fig. 3–12 Student artwork

# A Commemorative Maquette

## Studio Background

Traditionally, large sculptures are carved from stone or wood. Artists must plan their sculptures carefully before they actually create them. They sketch their ideas first and often make maquettes of the larger sculpture. A maquette is a small-scale model.

**In this studio exploration, you will carve a plaster maquette for a large sculpture that honors an event, person, or group in your community.** Where might such a sculpture stand? How big might it be? What materials could you use to create it? Visit a large sculpture or monument that already exists in your town or city for inspiration. Spend some time walking around it. Look at every side of the sculpture and notice how each side flows into the next. When you think about your own sculpture, imagine it from every side.

### You Will Need

- sketch paper
- pencil
- waxed carton
- plastic bucket
- plaster powder
- rubber gloves and dust mask
- water
- carving tools
- paint and paintbrush

## Step 1 Plan and Practice

- Sketch your ideas on paper. The idea for your sculpture must be suitable for carving.
- Think about a basic shape that you can use for your maquette.
- Imagine all sides of your sculpture and sketch each one. Keep your idea simple.

## Inspiration from Our World

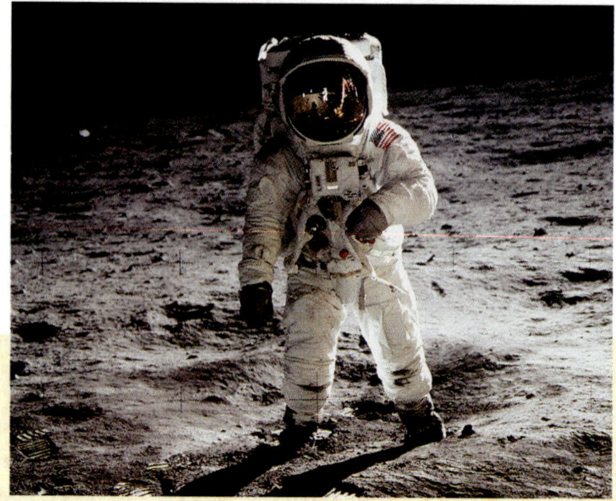

NASA

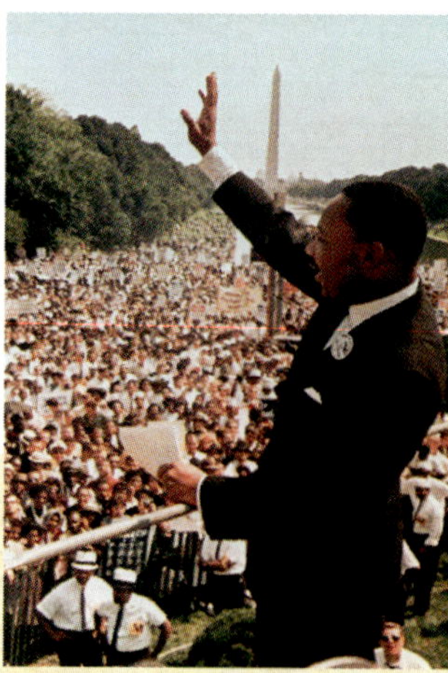

AP Photo

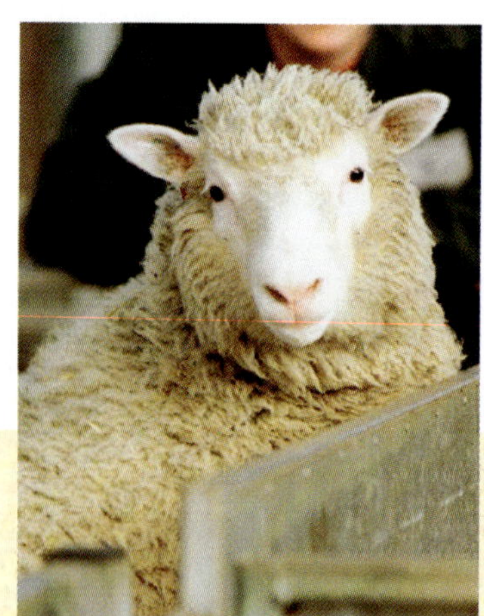

AP Photo/Paul Clements

**Things to Remember:**

- ✓ Carve rough forms first.
- ✓ Include details that help express your ideas about your subject.
- ✓ Consider all sides and angles of your sculpture while creating your maquette.

## Inspiration from Art

Carving and cutting are called *subtractive processes* in sculpture, because you take away material with cutting tools. Large monuments and sculptures are often carved from blocks of stone or wood. Sometimes they are cut from cast metal, or shaped with tools before they are assembled.

Large sculptures must be carefully planned, because mistakes in carving or cutting are difficult or impossible to correct. Maquettes allow artists to try out and develop their ideas first. Artists carve maquettes from inexpensive material, such as Styrofoam™ or plaster. Then they refer to their maquettes when they create the actual sculpture.

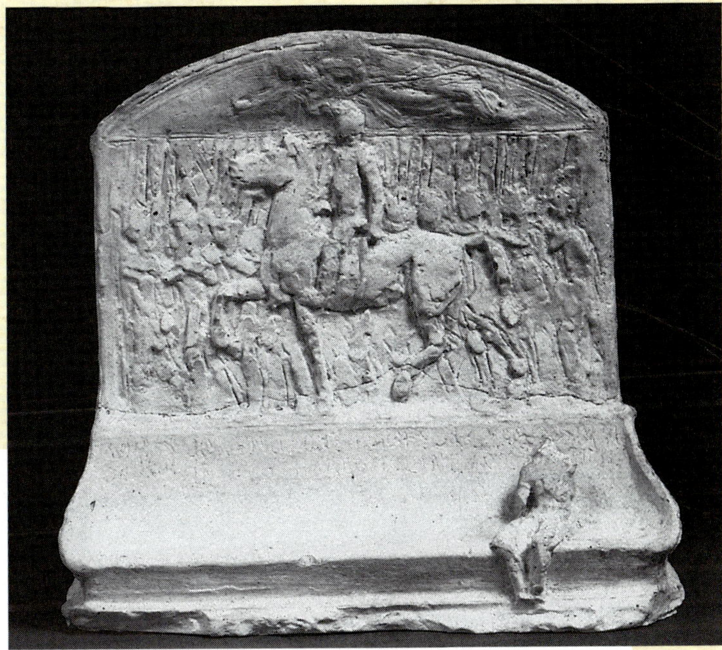

Fig. 3–13 **This maquette is called a sketch. How does this remind you of sketches you have made when planning a two-dimensional artwork?**

Augustus Saint-Gaudens, *Maquette for the Robert Gould Shaw Memorial*, 1883. Plaster, 15" x 16" (38.1 x 40.6 cm). U.S. Department of the Interior, National Park Service, Saint-Gaudens National Historic Site, Cornish, NH.

Artist Augustus Saint-Gaudens created many monuments in his lifetime. The *Robert Gould Shaw Memorial* **(Fig. 3–2, page 63)** in Boston, Massachusetts, is considered to be his finest work. This monument of the Civil War honors African-American soldiers. How might the maquette for this monument **(Fig. 3–13)** have helped the artist shape his ideas?

# 3.3 Studio Exploration Continued

## Step 2 **Begin to Create**

- **Cut a waxed carton to the basic dimensions you want for your maquette.** Will it be tall and thin or short and stout? What other dimensions can you think of?

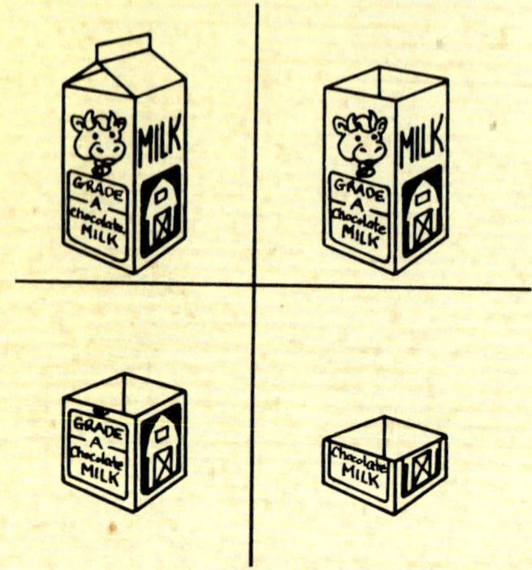


- Fill a plastic bucket about halfway with warm water, and put on rubber gloves and a dust mask. **Sift the plaster powder through your fingers into the water until an island forms in the middle of the bucket.** After a few minutes, stir the mixture slowly with your hand. Break up any lumps. If your mixture is too thick, add a little more water.

**Safety Note** Always wear rubber gloves and a dust mask or respirator when mixing plaster.

- Pour the plaster into the carton. Gently tap the carton to pop any air bubbles that may have formed. Let the plaster harden, then remove the carton.
- **Use a chisel to carve the rough forms first.** Then use a rasp or file to smooth and define the edges of your forms. Carve small details with a paint scraper or sandpaper. Work slowly and carefully. Look at all sides of your work often as you carve.

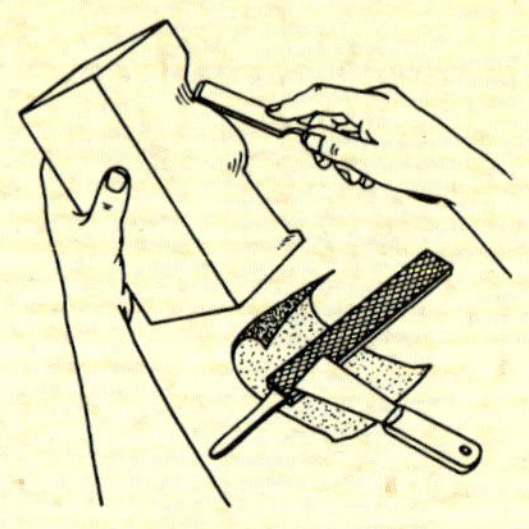

**Safety Note** Hold or clamp your form to keep it from slipping as you work. Always carve away from your body. Keep fingers and hands clear of the carving tool. Wear goggles to protect your eyes. Keep a safe distance from other students to avoid flying chips.

## Step 3 **Revise**

**Did you remember to:**

- ✓ Carve rough forms first?
- ✓ Include details that help express your ideas about your subject?
- ✓ Consider all sides and angles of your sculpture while creating your maquette?

Adjust your work if necessary. In your sketchbook, make a note of your revisions and why you made them.

## Step 4 **Add Finishing Touches**

- You might choose to paint your maquette. Imagine how a large sculpture made from your maquette would look. Choose colors that will best represent your subject.

## Step 5 **Share and Reflect**

- Display and discuss your work with your classmates. Are all sides of your work interesting? What does your sculpture tell about the event, person, or group that you wish to honor? What messages about your community's values and beliefs do the sculptures convey?

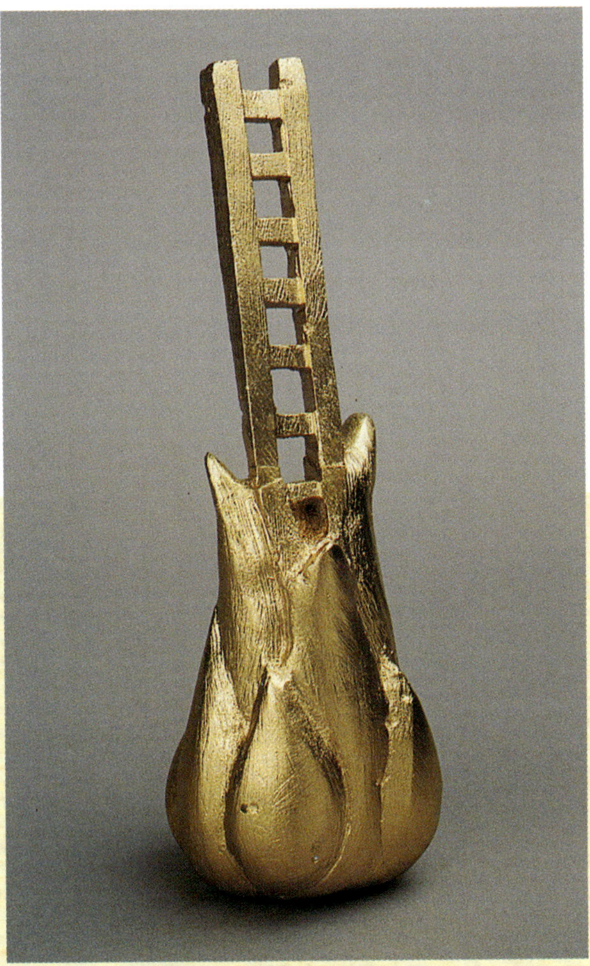

Fig. 3–14 Student artwork

## Art Criticism

**Describe** What forms do you recognize in this sculpture?

**Analyze** How are the parts arranged?

**Interpret** What heroic group do you think this sculpture honors?

**Evaluate** What makes this artwork successful?

# Art and Independence

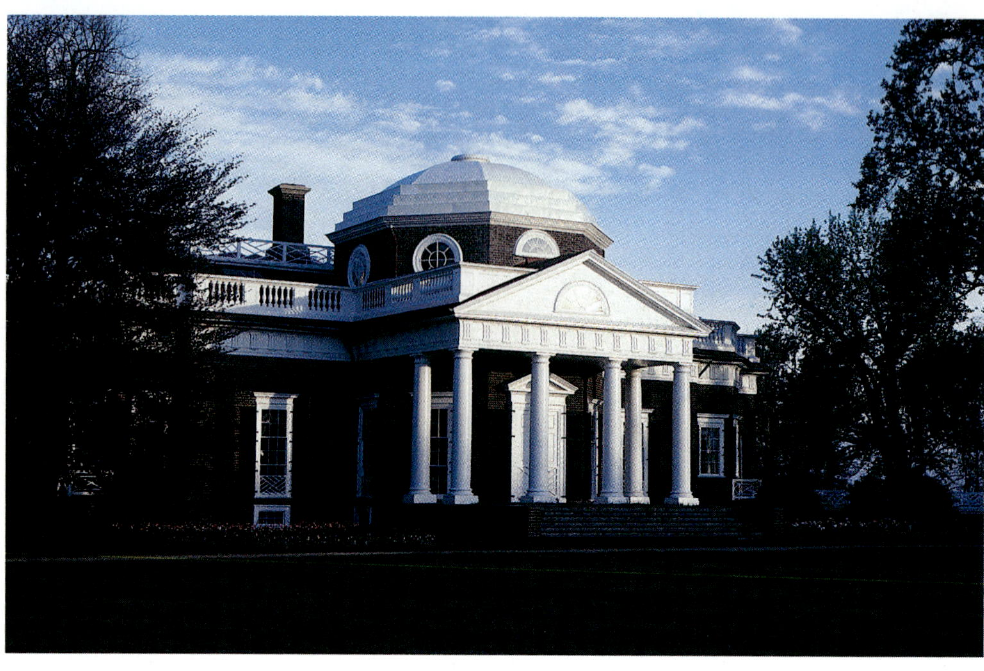

Fig. 3–15 **Most Neoclassical-style buildings are symmetrical and have the same number of windows on each side of a center door. What other elements of classical architecture can you identify?**

Thomas Jefferson, *Monticello*, Charlottesville, Virginia, 1769–84. 44.7' x 87.9' x 110' (13.6 x 26.8 x 33.5 m). Photograph by Robert Llewellyn.

When people form new groups, they often try to create a style that identifies the group. For example, when the new nation of the United States formed, artists tried to capture the spirit of its national identity. Portraits of leaders and paintings about historical events became popular subjects.

In their artworks, artists recorded the nation's fight for independence. Many looked to the classical art and architecture of ancient Greece and Rome for inspiration. This renewed interest in classical approaches to art became known as the Neoclassical style. The sculpture of George Washington **(Fig. 3–17)** reflects the nation's adoption of Greek and Roman ideals.

**1700s**

**1769** Jefferson, *Monticello*

**1783** The Treaty of Paris is signed, recognizing the United States' independence.

**1786** Huebner, *Earthenware Plate*

**1788** *Marriage Chest of Margaret Kernan*

**1800s**

**1806** Noah Webster assembles the first American dictionary.

**1814** Francis Scott Key composes *The Star Spangled Banner* during the War of 1812.

**1815** Krimmel, *Election Day in Philadelphia*

**1840** Greenough, *George Washington*

**1848** The first women's rights convention is held in Seneca Falls, NY.

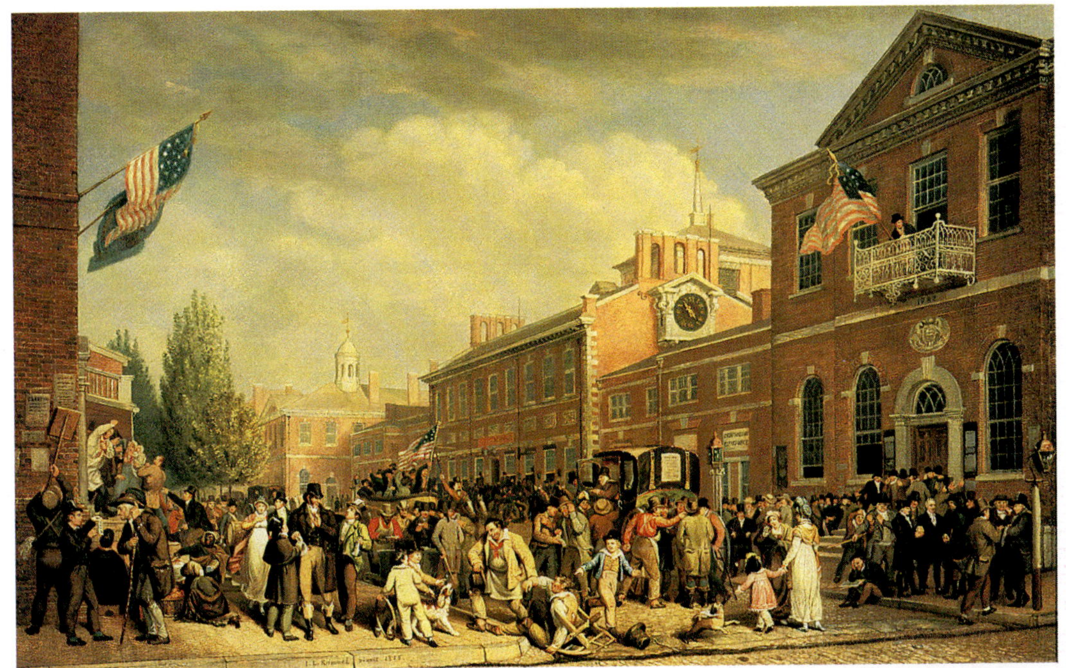

Fig. 3–16 **This painting is a celebration of community, with figures representing several social classes. In this picture of an election, what important ideal of government is being celebrated?**

John Lewis Krimmel, *Election Day in Philadelphia*, 1815. Oil on canvas, 16 3⁄8" x 25 5⁄8" (41.6 x 65.2 cm). Courtesy of The Henry Francis du Pont Winterthur Museum.

**Neoclassical Style** The Neoclassical style included painting, sculpture, and architecture. Some sculptures of human figures express ideals such as truth and justice. Other artworks show important historic events. Artworks such as *Election Day in Philadelphia* (Fig. 3–16) document the workings of democracy in the United States. As large cities developed, sculptures appeared in community parks and public buildings for all to see.

Buildings in the Neoclassical style include features of Greek and Roman architecture. Some have the large Doric, Ionic, or Corinthian columns seen in Greek structures. These buildings are sometimes called *Greek Revival style*, which is a fancier version of the Neoclassical style of architecture. Large Greek Revival homes became popular in the southern United States. Thomas Jefferson promoted the Neoclassical style through the design of his own home in Virginia (Fig. 3–15).

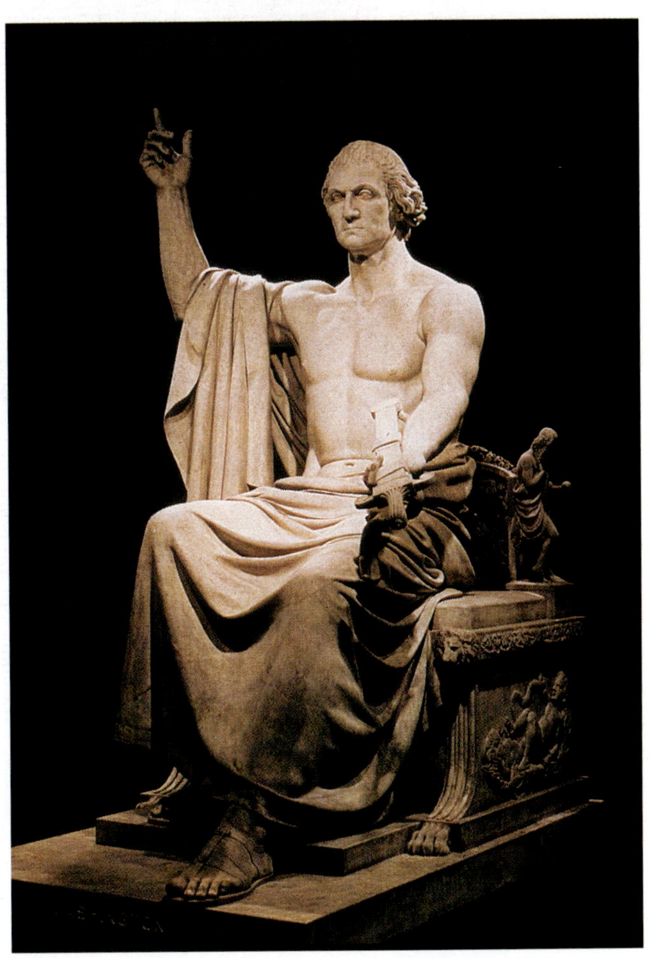

Fig. 3–17 **Why might this sculptor have portrayed a national leader in a Roman toga?**

Horatio Greenough, *George Washington*, 1840. Marble, 133 7⁄8" (340 cm) from back to front of base. National Museum of American Art, Smithsonian Institution, Washington, DC/Art Resource, NY.

**Signs of Belonging** A nation is made up of many different smaller communities, each with its own unique style and identity. Designs seen in local art are often connected to the region's weather or to the background of the people who live there. For instance, winter scenes are common in the art of New England. What designs do you think identify other regions of the United States? Why?

In the years following American independence, rural Pennsylvania was home to a rich folk art tradition. The German and Swiss settlers in Pennsylvania were called Pennsylvania Germans or, sometimes, Pennsylvania Dutch. They made furniture, pottery, and glassware based on the traditions of their homelands. In their craft, they used a decorative style that goes back to the Middle Ages. Their style continues to identify this region of the United States today.

### Check Your Understanding

1. What are the characteristics of the Neoclassical style of architecture?
2. How is the portrait of George Washington in Fig. 3–17 similar to the portrait of Paul Revere in Fig. 2–20? How are they different?
3. How did Pennsylvania German folk art reflect a belief in tradition?

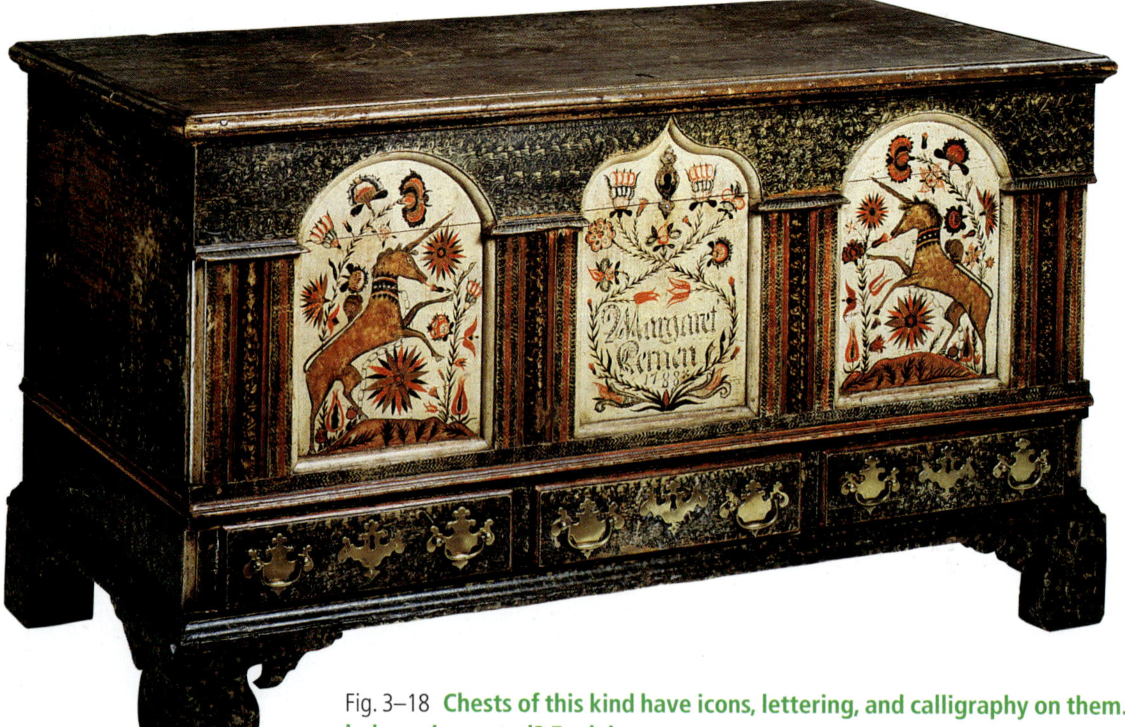


Fig. 3–18 **Chests of this kind have icons, lettering, and calligraphy on them. What kind of balance is created? Explain.**

Pennsylvania German, *Marriage Chest of Margaret Kernan*, 1788. Painted tulipwood, 28 ⅜" x 50" x 24" (72.1 x 127 x 61 cm). Courtesy of The Henry Francis du Pont Winterthur Museum.

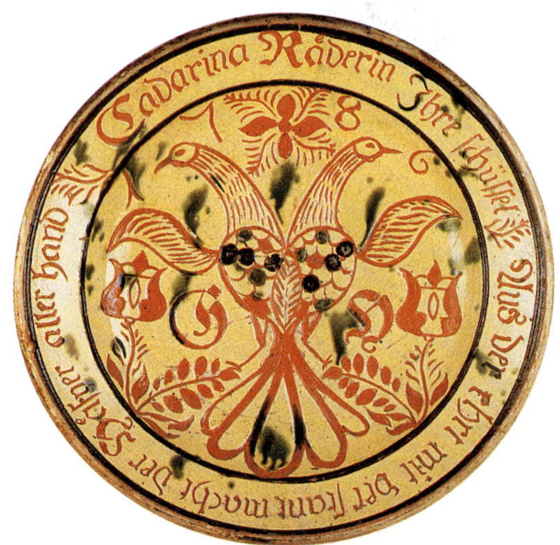

Fig. 3–19 **The inscription on this plate reads, "Catharine Raeder, her plate. Out of the earth with understanding the potter makes everything." What shape is formed by the bodies of the two doves?**

George Huebner, *Plate, inscribed to Catharine Raeder*, 1786. Earthenware, 2" x diam. 12 ⅝" (5 x 32 cm). Philadelphia Museum of Art. Gift of John T. Morris.

## Meet the Pennsylvania Germans

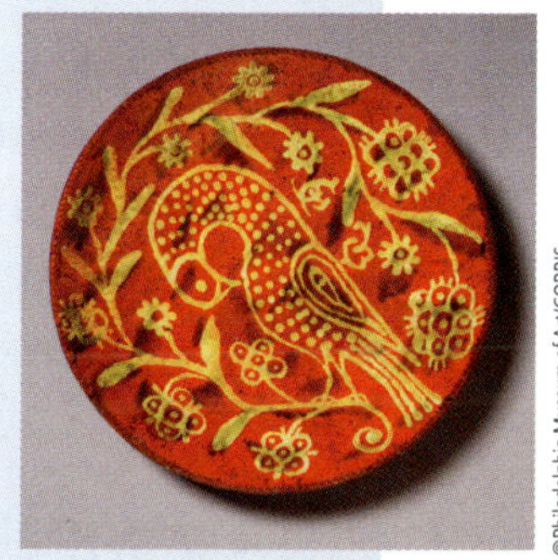



The Pennsylvania Germans are the people who left the German Rhineland in the 1600s and 1700s to escape persecution. They were called "church people" and came to Pennsylvania seeking religious freedom.

For the Pennsylvania Germans, the home was valued as a special place. Sharing and working together as a family were important ideals. This was reflected in framed "blessings" or sayings for the home. These sayings were often painted or embroidered by young women to show off their handwriting and needlework skills.

Pennsylvania German artists painted wooden chests in vivid colors with simplified tulips, birds, and prancing unicorns **(Fig. 3–18)**. They rubbed wet paint with a corncob to produce marbleized effects. The same rich floral patterning is also seen in their pottery and glass. Potters used a technique called sgrafitto. In sgrafitto, designs are scratched onto a clay object through a thin layer of colored slip. Then the pottery is glazed and fired.

**"The Pennsylvania Dutch...were virtually the only people in America in Colonial days who had a strong, imaginative feeling for color and design..."**

— J. George Frederick,
*Pennsylvania Dutch Cookery*

## Studio Time

### Decorative Plates

Design and make a decorative plate.

- Plan your plate. What shapes, colors, and symbols might you include?
- Design a decorative border.
- What design elements and principles will help you express your idea? Will you use symmetrical or radial balance?
- Create your plate using clay or another material.

Reflect on what you did to create balance.

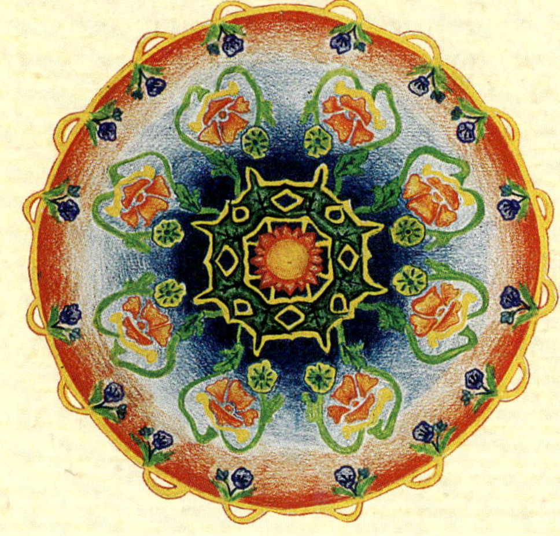

Fig. 3–20 Student artwork

# Art of Polynesia

**Art and Community Life** People around the world have different ways of showing that they belong to a community. Many have also found ways to show their status, or importance, in that community. In the South Pacific region, people show their importance through the objects they use and things they give to others.

Much of the art in Polynesia is created for ceremonial use. Decorations can symbolize a person's status or identity. In some island cultures, people wear jewelry and body tattoos to show identity and status. **Fig. 3–21** shows the head of a war club from the Marquesas Islands. Notice its tattoo pattern. This pattern identifies the owner of the club.

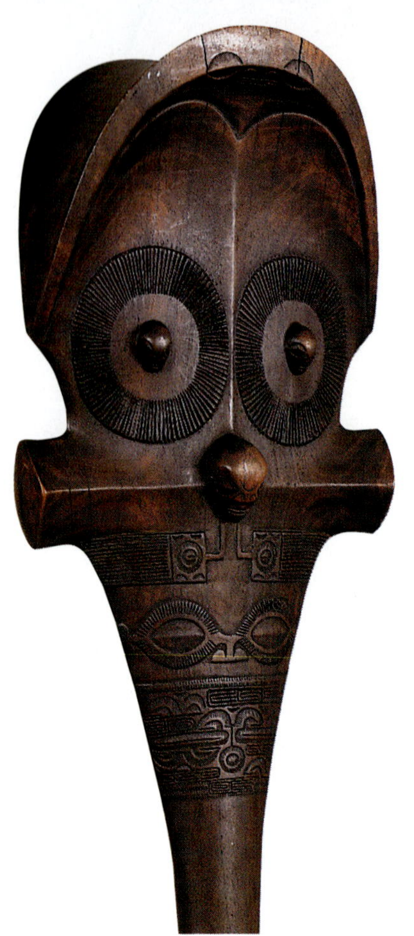

Fig. 3–21 **The patterns in the lower half of each Polynesian club identify the owner. How would you describe the lines and shapes carved there?**

Marquesas Islands, *Head detail of war club*, late 18th century. Hardwood, length: 63" (160 cm). Peabody Essex Museum, Salem, Massachusetts.

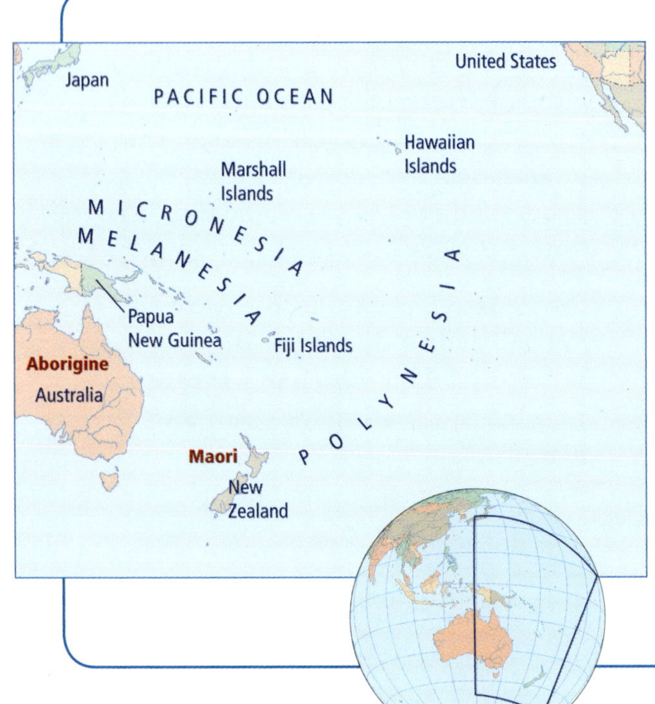


## Social Studies Connection

The term **Polynesia** comes from the Greek *polus* (many) and *nesos* (island). The waters of the South Pacific Ocean surround thousands of diverse and isolated islands. The South Pacific Rim, as it is sometimes called, includes six major cultures. One of these cultures is Polynesia.

Polynesia is a vast triangle about 5000 miles along each side with corners at New Zealand, Hawaii, and Easter Island. Tahiti, in the Society Islands, marks the geographic center of Polynesia. Polynesian art reflects the people of the South Pacific. Many of these people were explorers who set out on unknown seas to find and settle new lands.

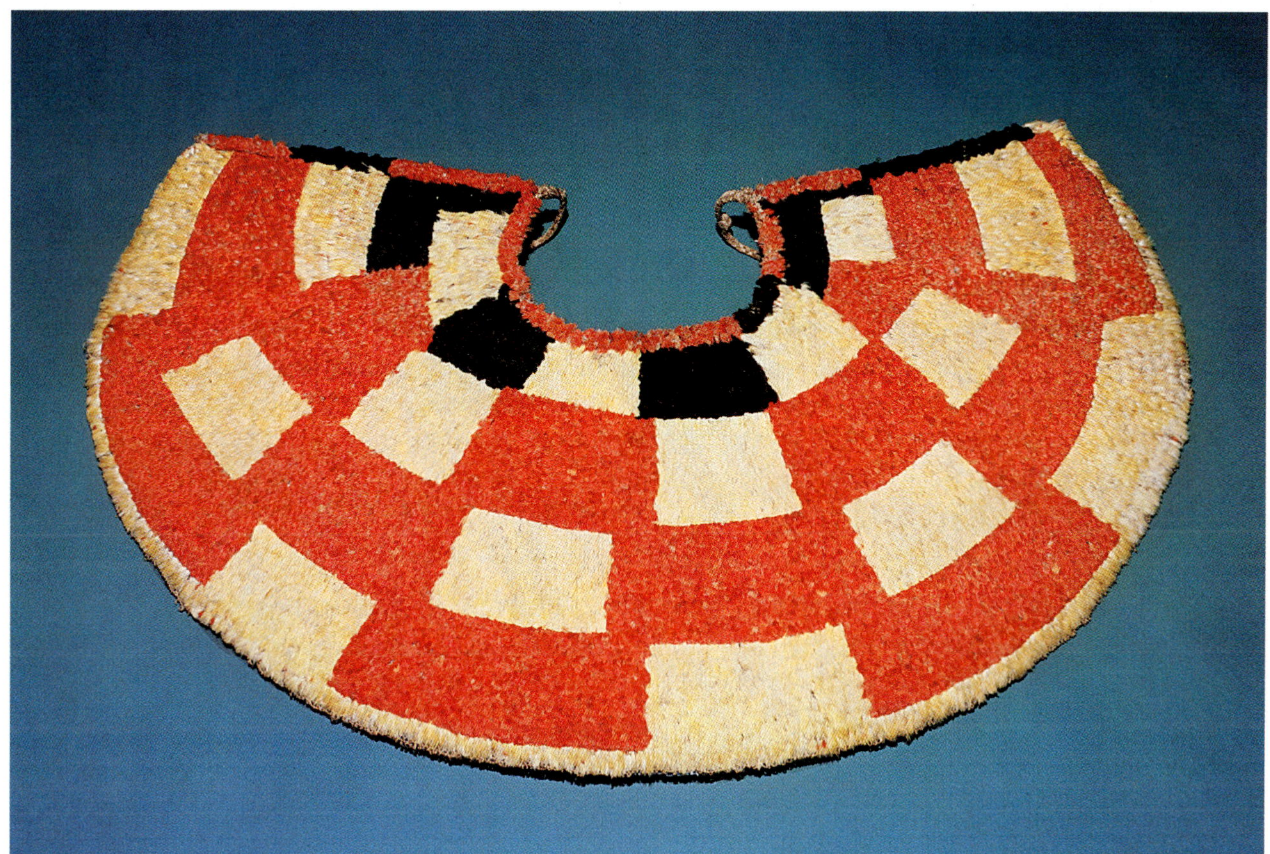

Fig. 3–22 **The Hawaiians crafted beautiful objects, including featherworks. The privileged noble class wore feather capes such as this one. Why might feathers have symbolized importance in this community?**

Hawaii, *Starbuck Cape*, ca. 1824. Red, yellow, and black feathers, length 16.5" x front 14.5" x neck 21.5"x base 85" (42 x 36.8 x 54.6 x 216 cm). Courtesy of Bishop Museum, Seth Joel.

Traditionally, the quality and craftsmanship of a Polynesian man's weapons, clothing, and tattoos reflected his place in the community. So did the size and height of his house. Women didn't have as much need for status symbols. However, if they owned certain fans and ornaments, they were important in the community.

Polynesian artworks were originally made from natural materials without the use of metal tools. Local materials such as raffia, bark cloth, tusks, shells, and feathers are often combined in dramatic ways. Look at the Hawaiian feather cape in **Fig. 3–22**. Feathers are highly valued in Hawaiian culture. Feather capes were one way people showed that they belonged to this community.

### Visual Culture

In this lesson you learned that in many Polynesian island cultures, people wear jewelry and body tattoos for status and to show group membership. Consider how people in your school and neighboring communities use visual clues, colors, and symbols to communicate group membership and status.

**Maori Master Carvers** Some areas of Polynesia are well known for particular art forms. The Maori of New Zealand are excellent carvers. A great master carver is called *tohunga*, meaning craftsman-priest. Tohungas have high social rank and special status in the community.

Some of the most spectacular works by tohungas are prow and stern (the front and rear ends of a boat) ornaments. Notice the skillfully carved open spiral motif in Fig. 3–25. A motif is a repeating pattern.

Among the Maori, the size, height, and adornment of the house are related to the owner's importance in the community. All houses are highly respected as symbols of living ancestors. The ridge beam of the house represents the ancestor's backbone, and the rafters stand for his ribs. The face boards on the front of the house represent his outstretched arms. A mask at the peak of the face boards symbolizes his face.

### Check Your Understanding

1. What is a tohunga?
2. How is the Maori house in Fig. 3–23 similar to houses in your community? How is it different?
3. How does Polynesian art show ways that people belong to their communities?

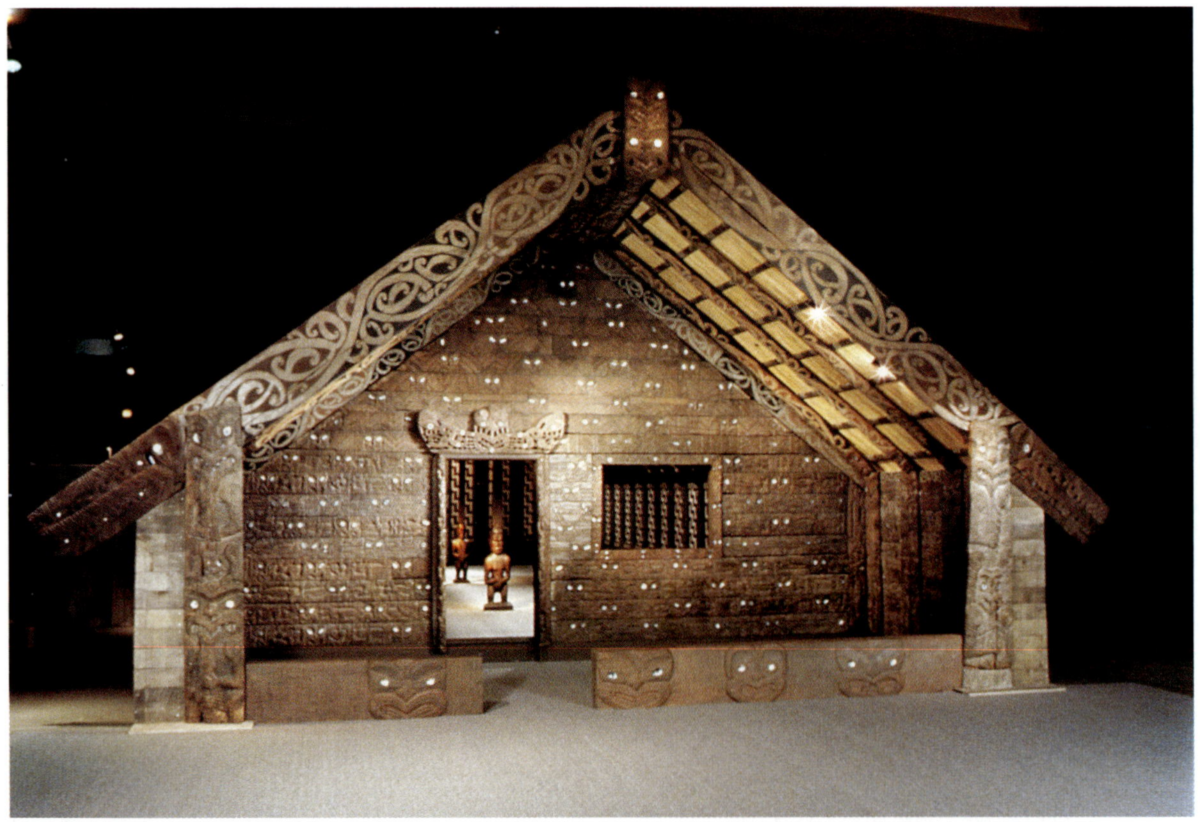

Fig. 3–23 **Notice the many pairs of eyes on the Maori house shown here. What might they symbolize?**

*Maori House*. The Field Museum of Natural Histroy, Chicago, Illinois.

## Studio Time

### Individual Assemblage

Use found objects or wood scraps to create an assemblage that expresses your individuality.

- Plan your assemblage. Include an expressive pattern or motif that you can repeat throughout the sculpture.
- Will wood scraps or found objects fit your idea best? Or a combination?
- Glue largest pieces together first. Experiment before you glue. Then add details.
- Paint or finish your assemblage, or leave it as is.

Reflect on how your assemblage expresses your individuality. Is your sculpture interesting from all sides?

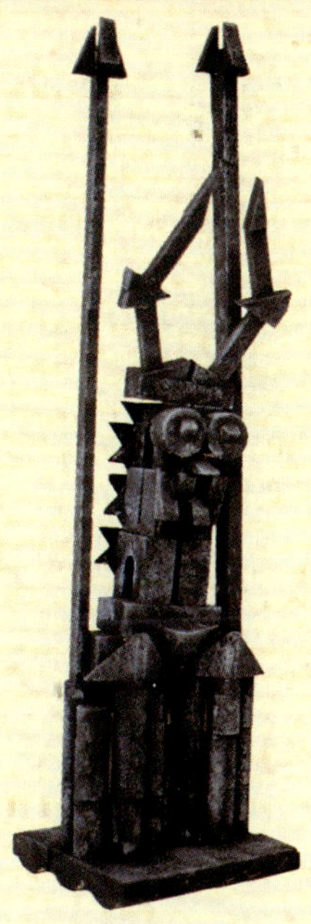

Fig. 3–24 Student artwork

### Meet the Maori

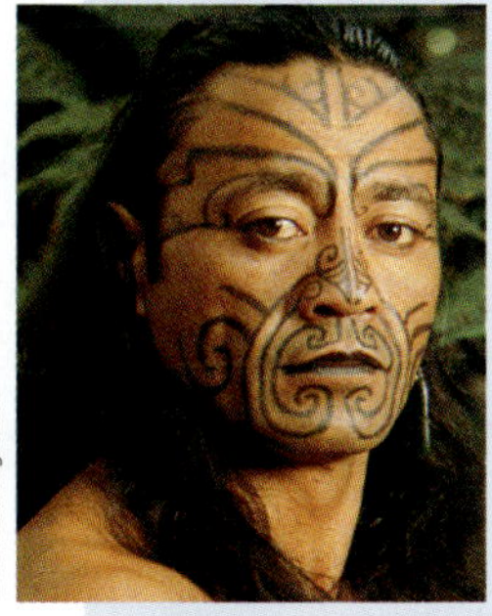



The Maori are ethnic Polynesians who arrived on New Zealand around 800 CE. Their culture was based on agriculture, fishing, and the hunting of birds. Wood, bone, and jade carving was both an art and a necessity: the Maori used tools made from these materials for catching and preparing food and for protection.

Maori religious and political beliefs are reflected in their carving and literature. They value land and their ancestors. The Maori believe that the real meaning of beauty can be found in detailed surface decorations. They use these decorations in three forms of art: the canoe, the meeting house, and body art.

**"It was the concept of it all, the idea that we were playing such an important role to save Maori art. Everyone has a reason in life. This was my reason."**

— Clive Fugill, Master Carver

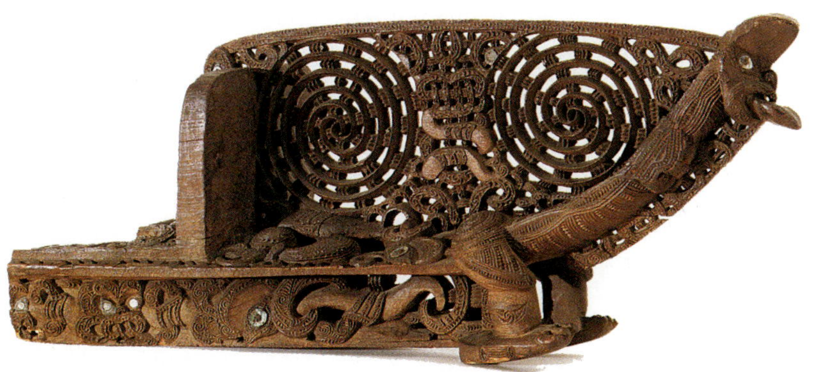

Fig. 3–25 **This prow ornament was designed to help a canoe move swiftly through the water. What other functions might this prow ornament have served?**

New Zealand, Maori, East Coast, North Island, *Canoe Prow*, ca. 1800–1900. Wood and paua shell, 19 11/16" x 16 1/8" x 46 5/8" (50 x 41 x 118.5 cm). Photography by Museum of New Zealand Te Papa Tongarewa.

# Collaborative Sculpture

## Studio Background

Sometimes artists collaborate with communities to create artworks. To collaborate means to work together. Collaborative artworks are made for many reasons, such as addressing the concerns of a community or honoring people or events. When artists and communities work together on an artwork, they choose the subject matter, plan the artwork, and create it as a group.

**In this studio exploration, you will work with classmates to create a sculpture that pays tribute to your community by showing group identity or commemorating a community event or hero.** Your group will choose your subject together. Then, you will sketch a plan for the sculpture and choose the materials that will best express your ideas.

### You Will Need

- sketch paper
- pencil
- variety of sculptural materials
- related sculpture tools

## Step 1 Plan and Practice

- Work with your group to create a plan for your sculpture. What group or event will you show? How can your sculpture be designed to show group identity or commemorate a community event or hero? Will assemblage or another form of sculpture send your message more clearly? Sketch your ideas.
- Determine the steps necessary to complete the project. Decide who will be responsible for each section or phase of the project. For example, one person might collect the materials, another might arrange them, and another might assemble them into the sculpture.

### Things to Remember:

✓ Work together as a team, sharing responsibilities for designing and creating the sculpture.

✓ Consider all sides of your sculpture during the creation process.

✓ Show group identity or commemoration through your sculpture.

## Inspiration from Our World

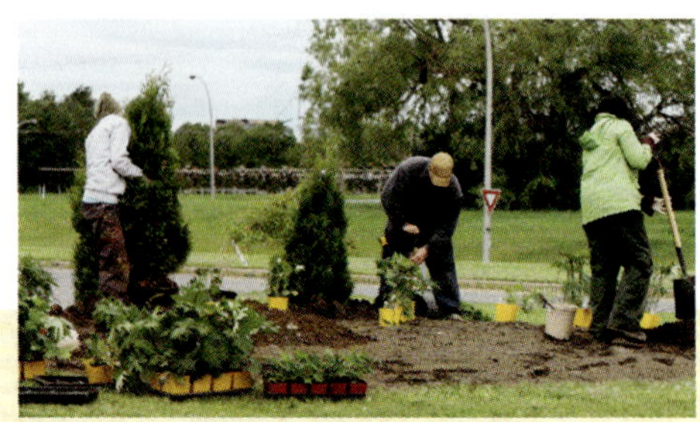

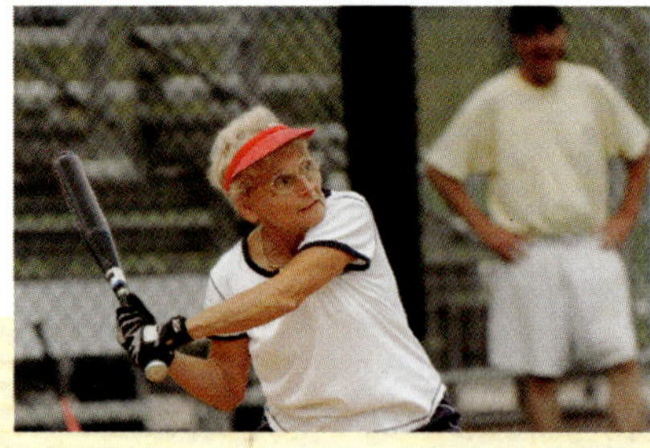

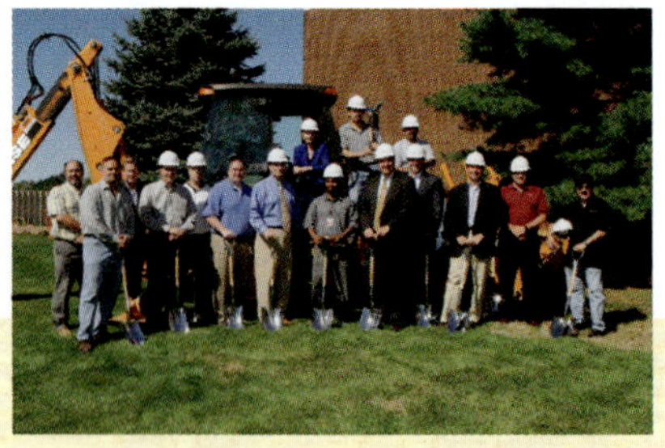

PR Newswire

## Careers **Sculptors**

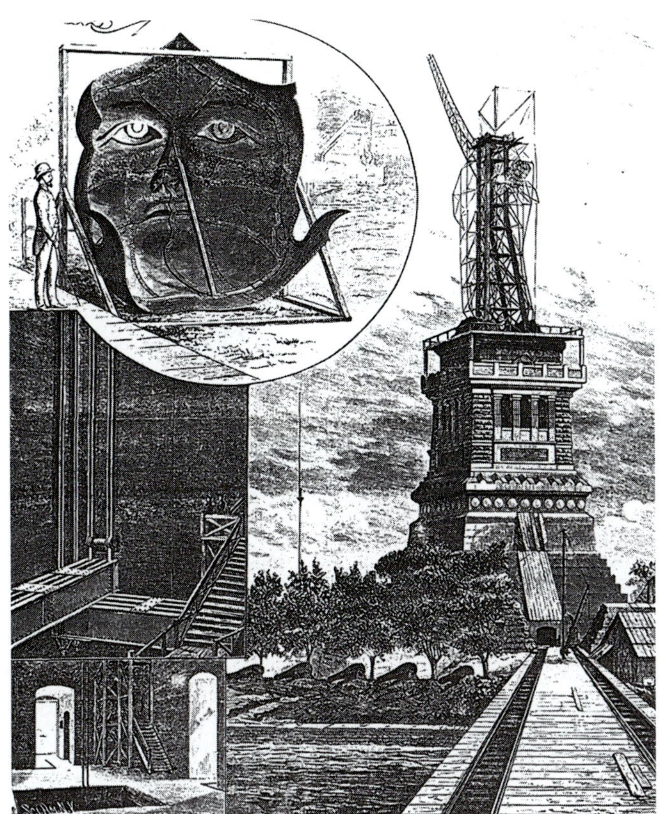

**How do you think huge sculptures like the Statue of Liberty are created?** In the late 1800s, French sculptor Frédéric-Auguste Bartholdi designed the Statue of Liberty. He used a process that is still used by sculptors today. Like Bartholdi, most sculptors design a public work to fit a specific place for a particular purpose. Sculptors create initial sketches and small-scale models for their design. They work with many other people to complete monumental works.

Fig. 3–31 **Sculptors often have many details to work out when creating "site-specific" sculptures.**

*Statue of Liberty Under Construction*, 1886. Illustration from "The Scientific American," August 14, 1886. Courtesy of the Statue of Liberty National Monument, New York.

## Daily Life

**Which groups do you belong to?** Do you relate more to older people or people your own age? Today, young people have a big impact on popular culture. In earlier times, adults paid little attention to the stage between childhood and adulthood. As a result, teenagers were usually treated like adults and made their own decisions. How does this compare to being a teenager today? What makes teenagers feel like they belong in their family, in school, or in the community?

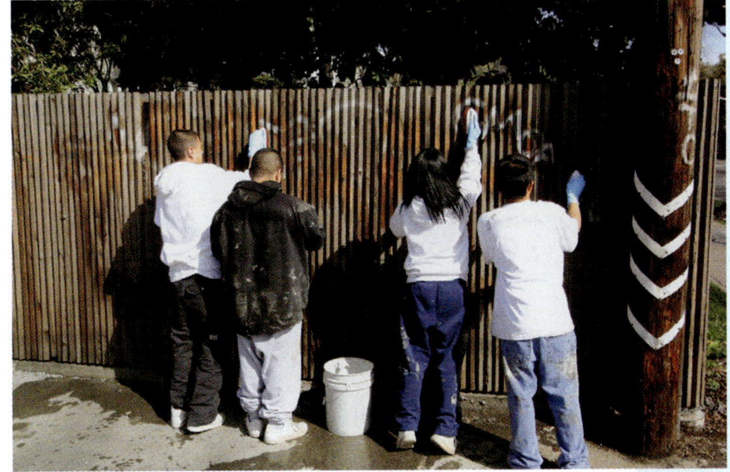

Fig. 3–32

# Unit 3 Vocabulary and Content Review

## Vocabulary Review

Match each art term below with its definition.

**monument**

**commemorate**

**maquette**

**sgrafitto**

**found objects**

**earthworks**

1. discarded materials
2. an artwork created for a public place that preserves the memory of a person, event, or action
3. a small-scale model of a larger sculpture
4. artworks created from the environment
5. to honor the memory of someone or something
6. a technique where designs are scratched onto a clay object through a thin layer of colored slip

## Aesthetic Thinking

Monumental artworks sometimes require many artists to complete. How do you think the experience of working with others would differ from working alone? When would you choose one way of working over another?

## For Your Portfolio

Look through this unit and select one artwork from the past. Describe the work with careful attention to detail. How does this artwork suggest group membership and ideals?

## Write About Art

Imagine that you are a city planner proposing this bridge design to the local government for approval. Write a short explanation of why you chose this design and how you think it represents the community.

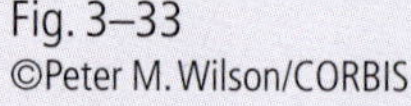

Fig. 3–33
©Peter M. Wilson/CORBIS

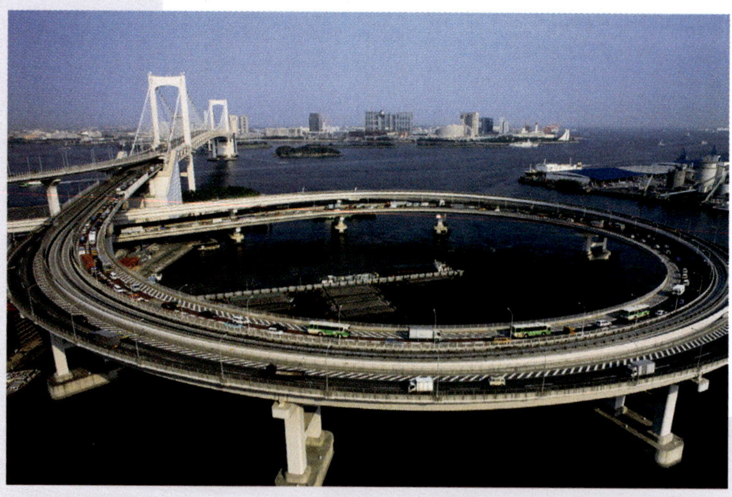

## Art Criticism

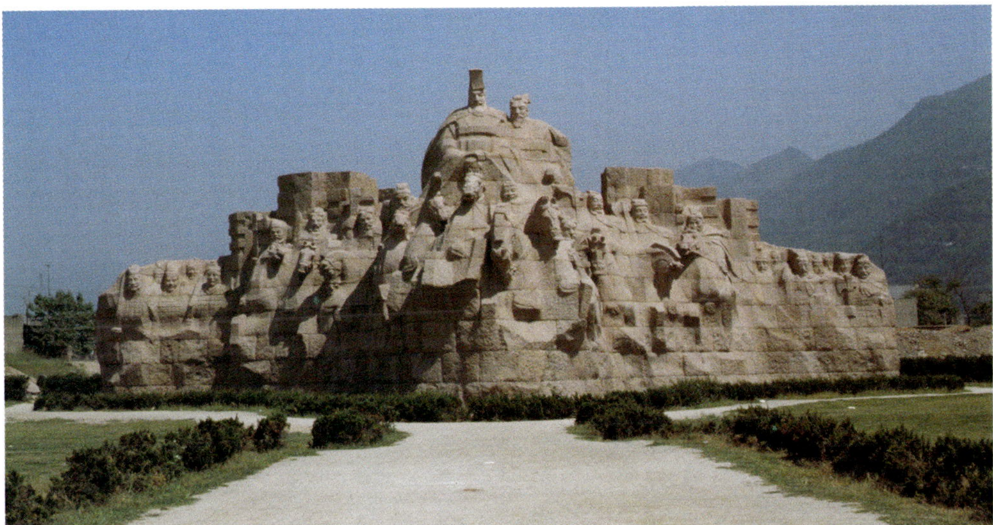

Fig 3–34 Wang Tian Ren, Ge De Mao, Meng Xi Ling, *Emperor Qin Unifying China*, Xi'an, 1993. Granite. Reprinted by permission of the University of Washington Press. Photo by John T. Young.

**Describe** What do you see in this sculpture?

**Analyze** Which figure do the artists emphasize in this sculpture? How?

**Interpret** How would you feel standing next to this sculpture? What message do you think the enormous scale conveys?

**Evaluate** When you first saw this picture, how old did you think the sculpture was? Why might these contemporary artists have chosen to make the sculpture look like it could be an ancient monument?

## Meet the Artists

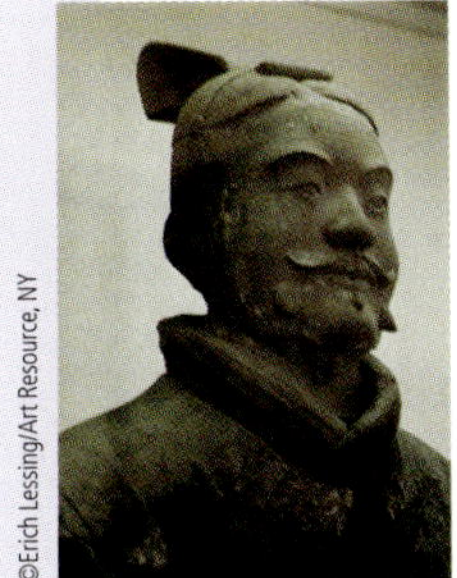



**Qin Stonemasons and Sculptors**

The Qin Dynasty in China lasted only fifteen years, from 221 BCE until 206 BCE. Emperor Qin directed several major engineering and construction projects, including the Great Wall of China. He also ordered the construction of a giant tomb guarded by more than 8,000 figures of soldiers and horses called the "Terra Cotta Army," in which each of the larger-than-life-size figures is unique.

**Fig. 3–34** commemorates Emperor Qin's unification of China.

## For Your Sketchbook

Design a page in your sketchbook for generating a list of words that are associated with belonging. For example, list words that describe friendship, responsibility, loyalty, or ownership. Create visual symbols, or icons, for each of these words.

Unit 4

# Art and Places

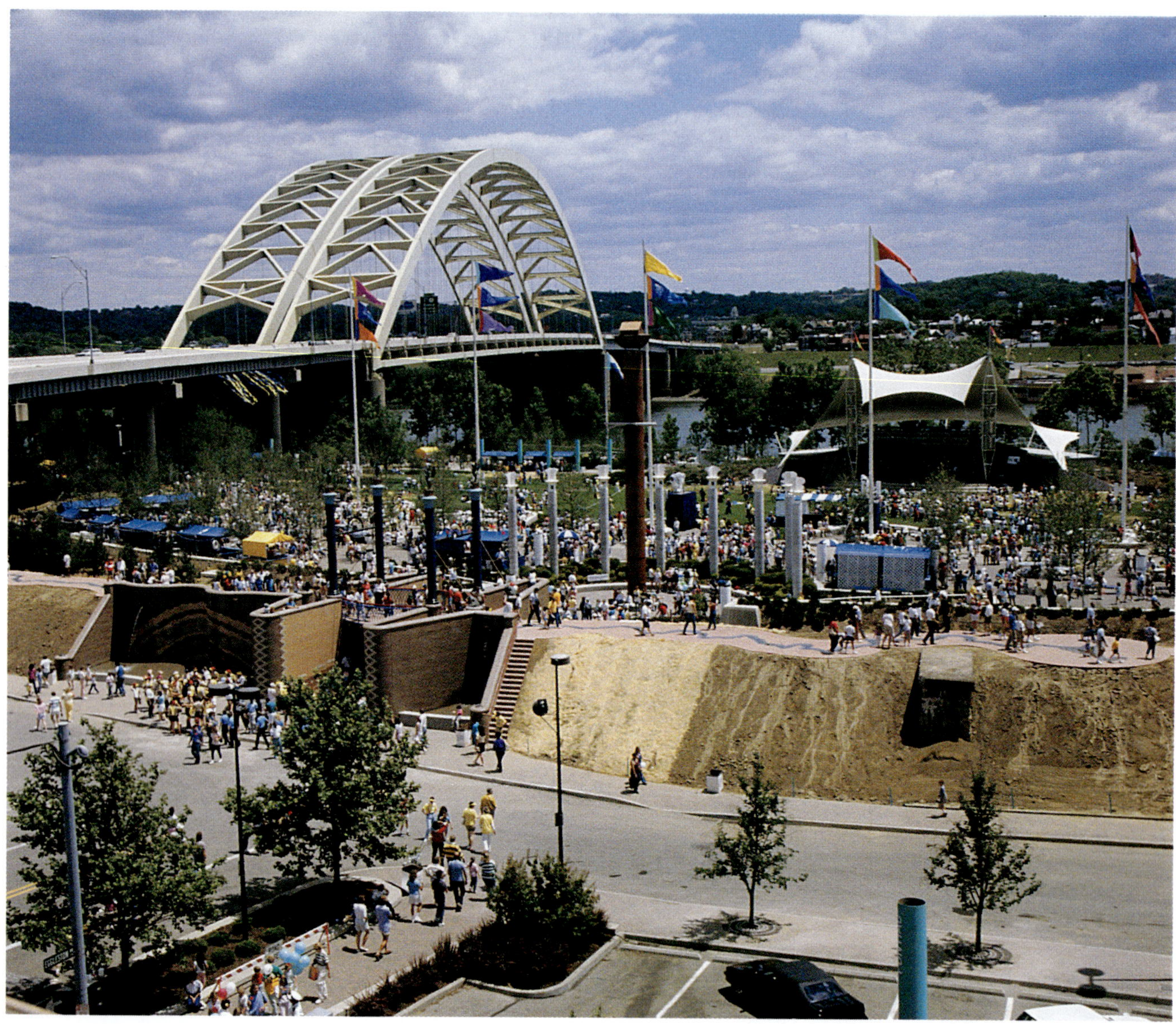

Fig. 4–1 **Imagine designing a gateway to your own town or city. What features would you include to remind people of its history?**

Andrew Leicester, *Cincinnati Gateway*, 1988. Bronze, steel cast iron, polychrome masonry, stone, water and plant materials 480' x 145' x 65' (146.3 x 44.2 x 20 m). Sawyer Point Park, Cincinnati, Ohio. Photo copyright Andrew Leicester.

**Every place has a history. Think about one of your favorite places—maybe a park, a library, or a farm.** Who were the people who created that place? What did they do there? How did they feel about the place? There are many ways for you to find out. Artworks can often provide some of the clues. They can inspire people to think in new ways about the history of a place. Artworks tell visitors that places, like people, have stories about their past.

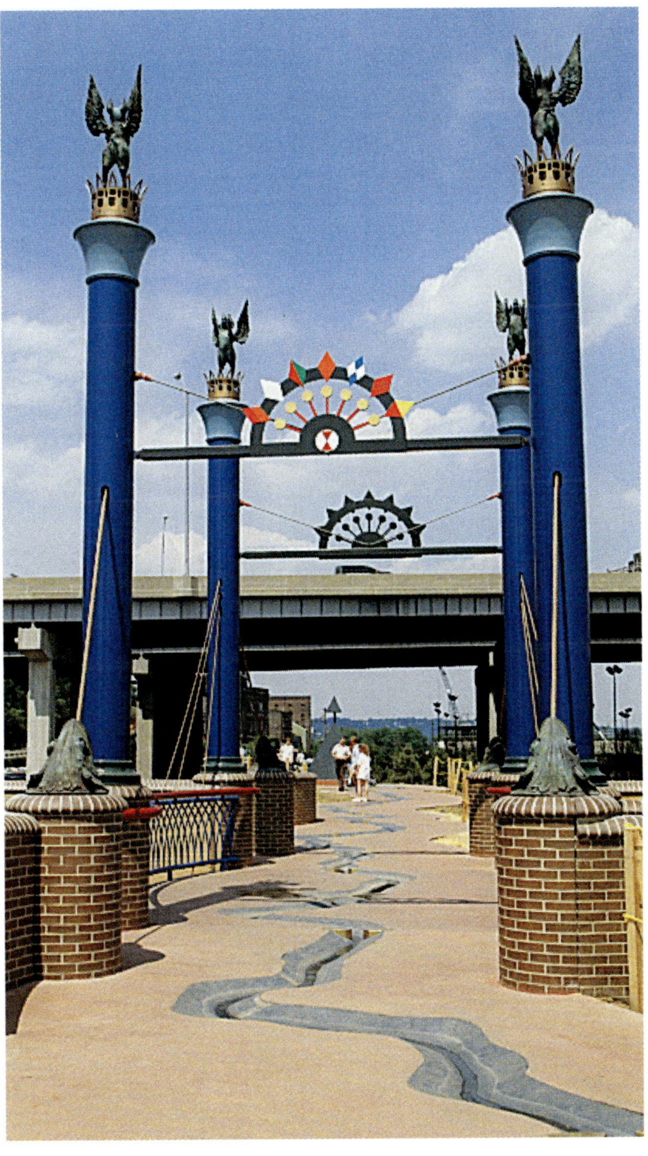

**In this unit, you will learn:**

- How artists help connect communities to places through their artworks.
- How to create depth in drawings and paintings by using two-point perspective.
- How to view artworks as ways of telling the stories of places.

Fig. 4–2 **This is a detailed picture of the entrance to the park pictured on the previous page.**

Andrew Leicester, *Cincinnati Gateway*, (detail) 1988. Bronze, steel cast iron, polychrome masonry, stone, water and plant materials 480' x 145' x 65' (146.3 x 44.2 x 20 m). Sawyer Point Park, Cincinnati, Ohio. Photo copyright Andrew Leicester.

# Common Places

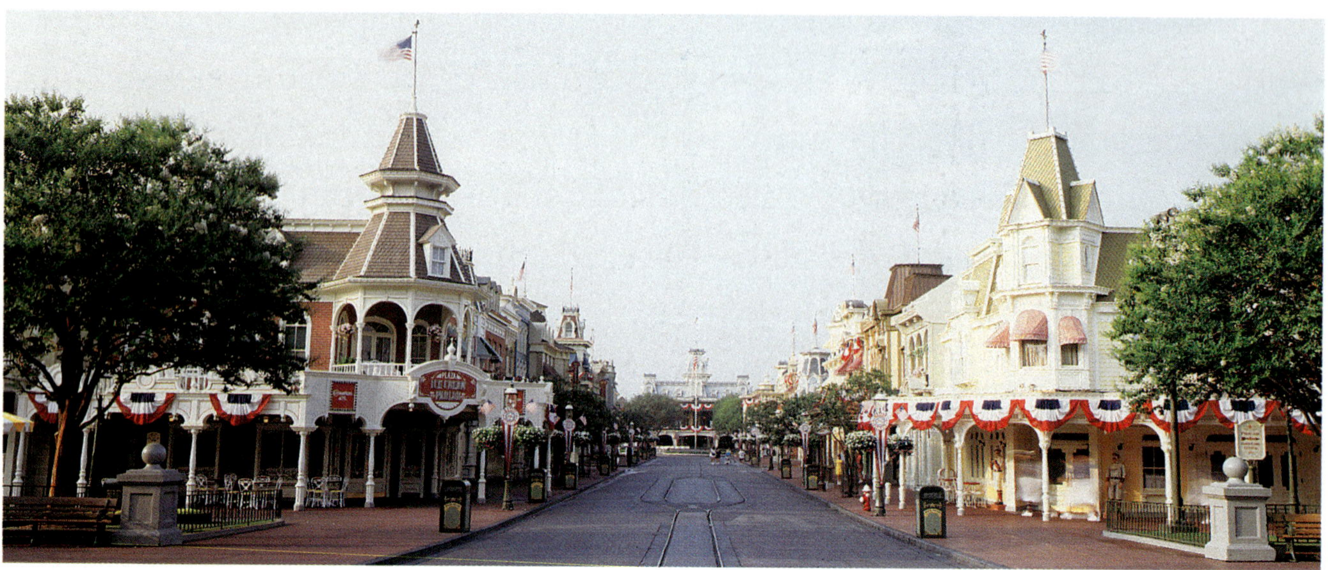

Fig. 4–3 **How does this main street, designed by Walt Disney, look like the main street in your town or city?**

*Panoramic view of Main Street, U.S.A.*, in the Magic Kingdom Park at the Walt Disney World Resort. ©Disney Enterprises, Inc.

People need places to meet, shop, and celebrate events. Artists and architects design and create plazas, town squares, shopping malls, gardens, parks, and cultural centers. Sometimes, the places they design become famous and symbolize the community.

**A Place Called Main Street** When we think of a town or city, we think of its center. Most towns grew up around a place where people gathered to exchange goods and ideas. In many towns, that place is "Main Street." When drawing or painting an image of a city or town, artists often show its center because that's where things happen.

But artists show us more than the way places look in real life. They show us ideas about places. Berenice Abbott spent several years photographing the city of New York. Sometimes she photographed the city from the air or during different times of day. Other times she focused on details of buildings and bridges. How did she call attention to the awesome strength and size of a city bridge in **Fig. 4–4**?

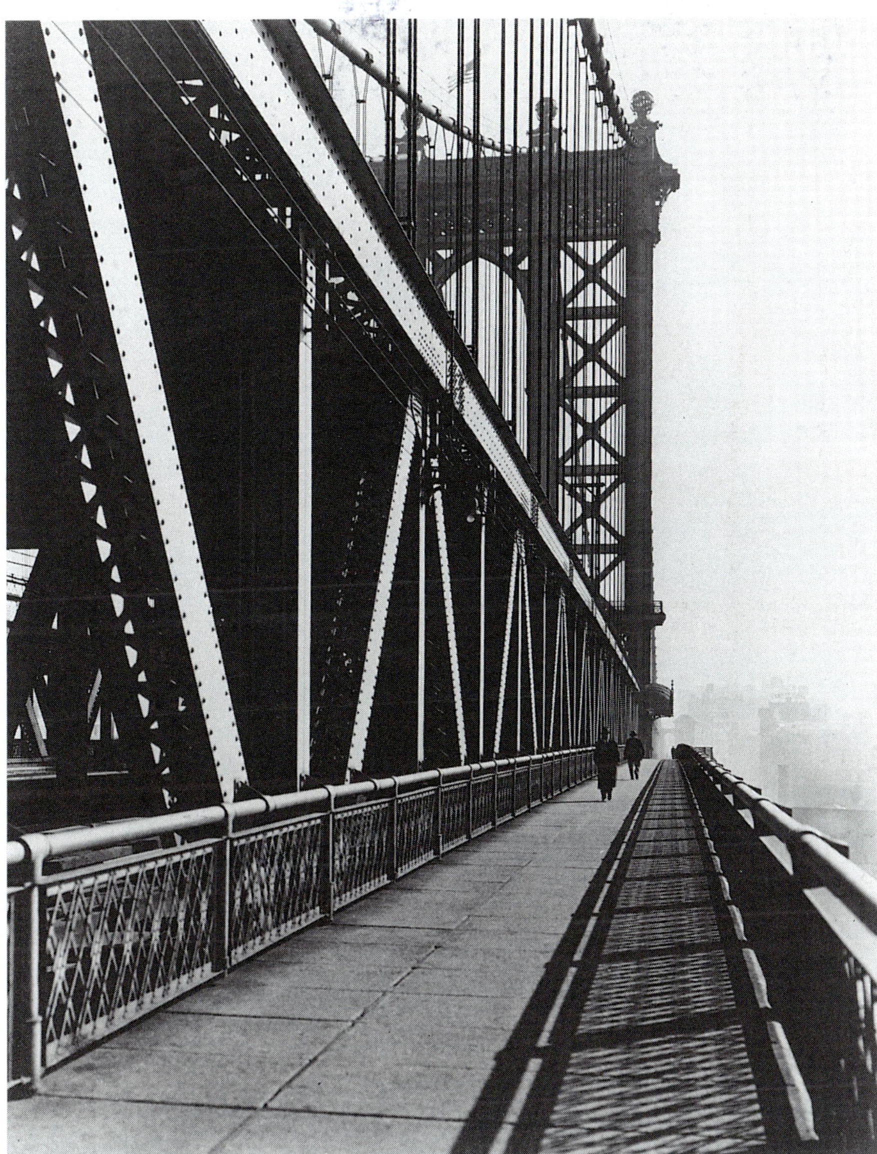

Fig. 4–4 **In cities, people often look to the sky to feel a sense of space. How does this artist capture the feeling of space in Manhattan?**

Berenice Abbott, *Walkway, Manhattan Bridge, New York*, 1936. Silver gelatin print. Museum of the City of New York.

## Meet Berenice Abbott

Berenice Abbott was born in Springfield, Ohio. She was in her mid-twenties and living in Paris when she met the well-known American photographer Man Ray. He wanted to train a new darkroom assistant who didn't already know photography, so he hired Abbott. She had a natural talent for photography and was soon taking portrait photographs of artists, writers, and the very wealthy. She had her first Paris exhibition in 1926, when she was just 28.

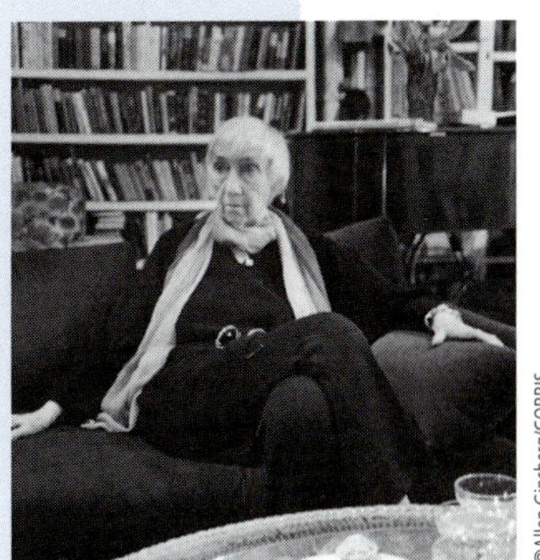



When Abbott returned to America, she fell in love with New York. She began photographing the old and new of the changing city and growing skyscrapers. The project took ten years.

**"The challenge for me has first been to see things as they are, whether a portrait, a city street, or a bouncing ball. In a word, I have tried to be objective."**

—Berenice Abbott (1898–1991)

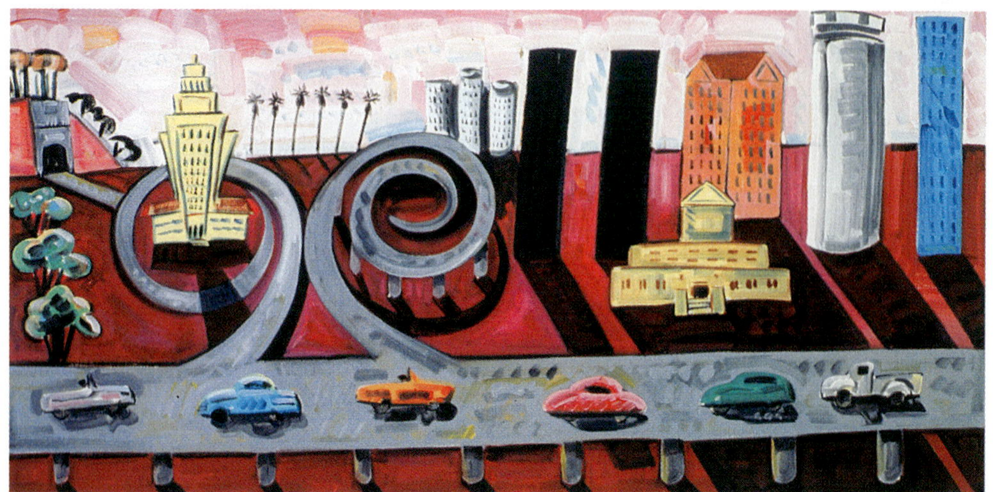

Fig. 4–5 **California is known for its many cars and freeways. In what ways does the artist capture the spirit of Los Angeles?**

Frank Romero, *Downtown*, 1990. Oil on linen, 24" x 48" (61 x 121.9 cm). Courtesy of the artist.

**The Spirit of Places** People tend to mark places that mean something to them. Sometimes they mark them with memorials. Memorials are artworks or other objects that help people remember where important events took place or where famous individuals lived. By creating artworks that celebrate special places, artists help people remember the history and significance of these places. Artists look at our communities carefully, then show us new ways to see them. They think about what makes a place unique and interesting, and use their ideas to create artworks.

By making paintings, drawings, and prints of places, artists can show us what is most unique or special—not common—about a place. Wayne Thiebaud's *Downgrade* (Fig. 4–6) shows a landscape feature that is common in the San Francisco Bay area. California artist Frank Romero (Fig. 4–5) highlights the importance of cars and freeways in Los Angeles.

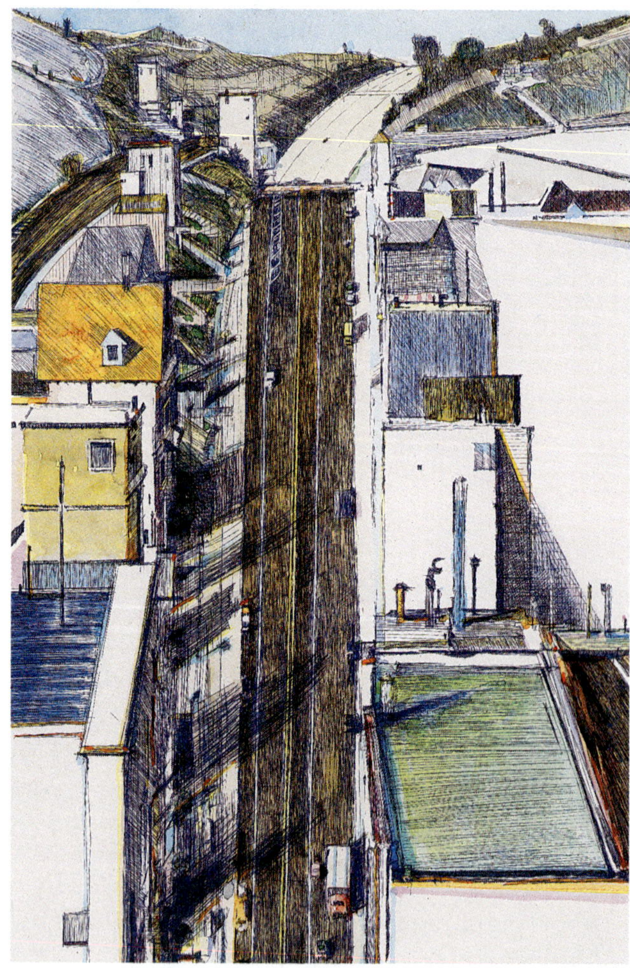

Fig. 4–6 **This artist often uses San Francisco as his subject matter. How has he used line to convey the idea of a place with long, steep hills?**

Wayne Thiebaud, *Downgrade*, 1979. Aquatint and watercolor over hard-ground etching, 20" x 30" (50.8 x 76.2 cm). Image courtesy of the Campbell-Thiebaud Gallery, San Francisco, CA. ©Wayne Thiebaud/Licensed by VAGA, New York, NY.

**Wilderness Places** Artists of the Hudson River School strongly believed in the ideals of their country. They wanted to show everyone the beauty of the United States. This nationalistic spirit led them to explore and document wilderness places throughout North America. Inspired by nature, their paintings provided national images of majestic landscapes and community centers that many people still recognize.

Many other artists also traveled west and painted the unknown American landscape. Their artworks document the settlement of western territories.

## Meet Sally Cover

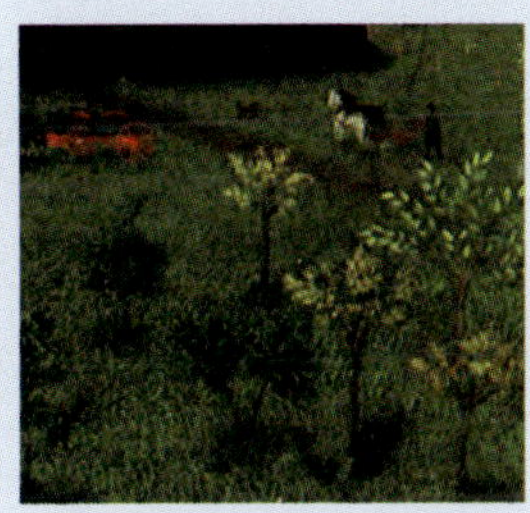
Detail of Homestead of Ellsworth L. Ball.

As one of ten children growing up on a farm in the western United States, Sally Cover (1853–1936) taught herself art by sketching local scenery. Throughout her life, she moved around to various western states, painting the land and people that she encountered. She often worked in oil and watercolor.

Cover's painting of the homestead of Ellsworth Ball shows the open, flat landscape and humble farms of the high plains of Nebraska in the late 1800s.

## Check Your Understanding

1. What art styles influenced the way American artists represented place in the early 1800s?
2. How does the Romantic style differ from the Realistic style, and why did American artists in the early 1800s blend these styles?
3. How did art affect the geographical expansion of North American communities?

## Studio Time

### Memories of Place

Using oil pastels, create a drawing of a place in nature that you remember.

- Capture what you think is beautiful about the place. Note details that others might miss at first glance.
- Sketch your composition. Then fill in the largest background areas using light and dull colors.
- As you work toward the foreground, brighten your colors and add more details.

Reflect on how your choice and placement of colors help to create a sense of place.

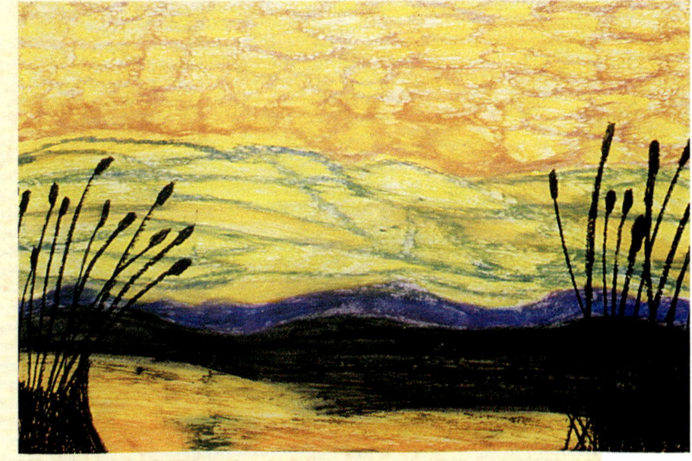
Fig. 4–18 Student artwork

# Japanese Places in Art

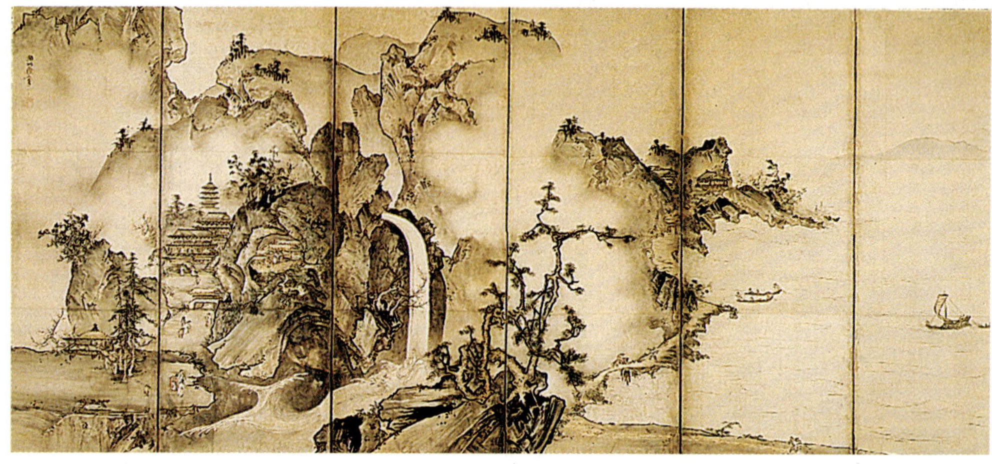

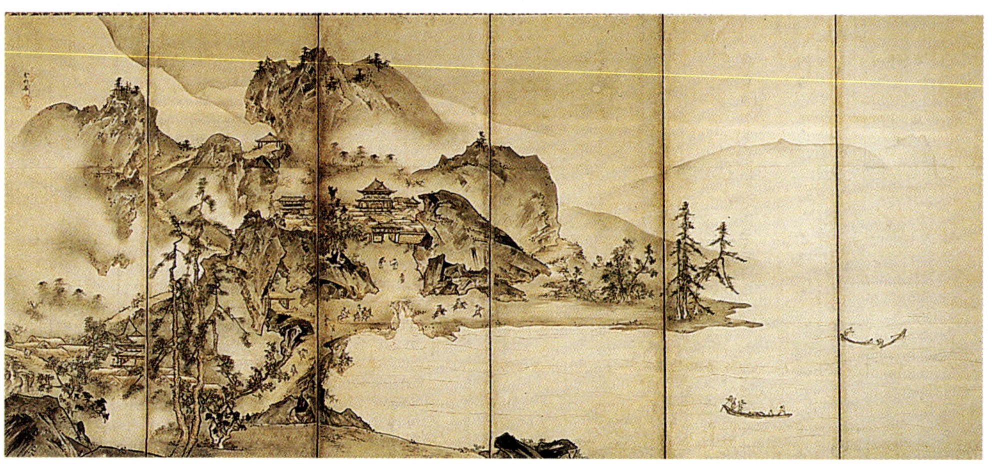

Fig. 4–19 **This pair of six-panel screens shows the four seasons. What elements of these screens reveal the artist's appreciation for the beauty of nature?**

Sesson Suikei, *Landscape of Four Seasons*, Muromachi period, 16th century. Ink and light colors on paper (one of pair of six-panel screens), 61 ⅜" x 133 ¼" (155.9 x 338.4 cm). Gift of the Joseph and Helen Regenstein Foundation, right side of pair/1958.167, left side of pair/1958.168. Photograph © The Art Institute of Chicago.

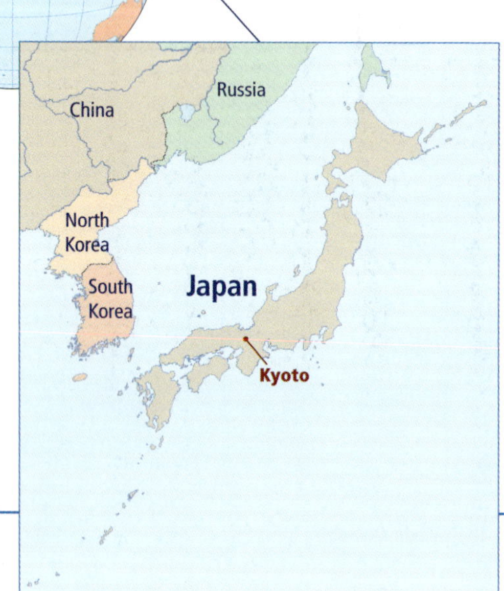


## Social Studies Connection

**Japan** is an island country in the Pacific Ocean. The four large islands and many smaller ones that make up Japan are spread out over 1300 miles of ocean. The islands lie along the northeastern coast of Asia and face Russia, Korea, and China. Because of the country's location along major trade routes, Japan's culture has been influenced by Korea, China, the South Pacific, Europe, and the Americas. The Japanese have adapted these influences into a unique artistic style that reflects Japanese culture.

Japan is called the "Land of the Rising Sun." Images of the sun, sea, sky, and mountains have always appeared in Japanese art. Japanese artists have a deep respect for nature. They are especially aware of the beauty of their surroundings. The Japanese are known for their painted scrolls, folding screens, and woodblock prints.

**Prints of Places** The Japanese made woodblock prints as early as the 700s. In the 1800s, Japanese landscape and nature prints influenced many artists in Europe and the United States. Western artists were interested in the lines, flat spaces, asymmetry, and close-up views shown in the images.

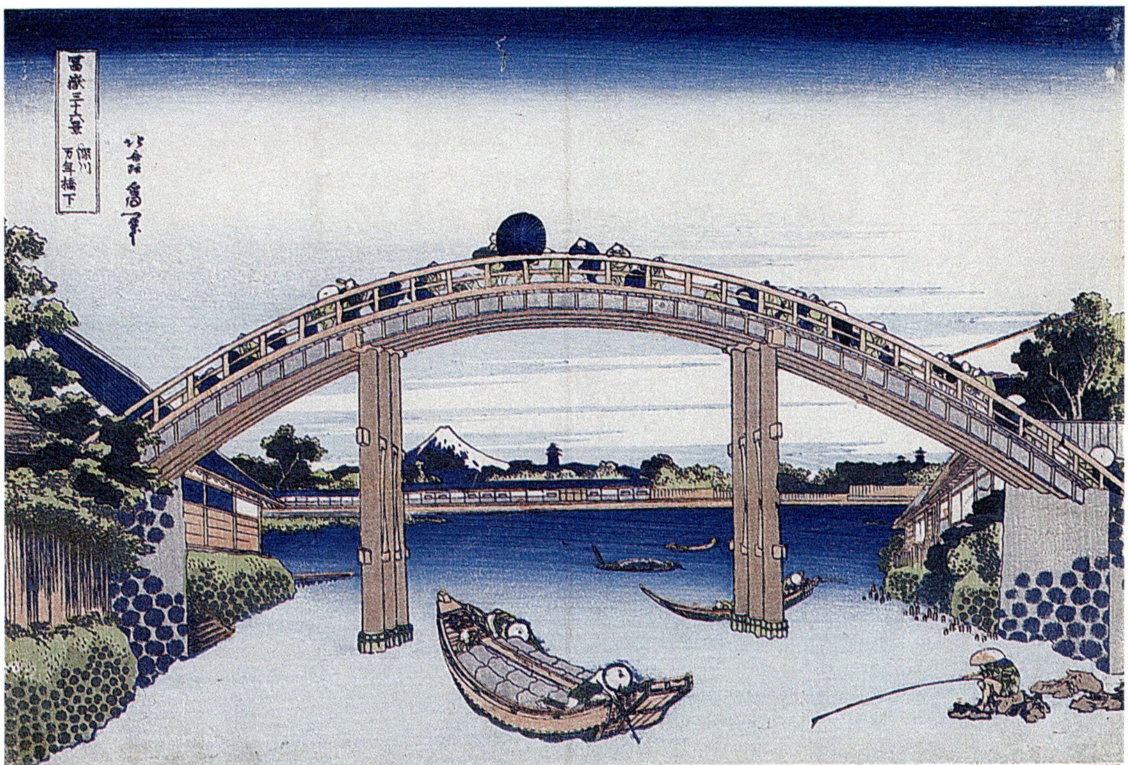

Fig. 4–20 **How does this print show Japanese life of the 1800s?**

Katsushika Hokusai, *Fukagawa Mannembashi*, from *36 Views of Mt. Fuji*, 1830. Multiple block woodblock print, 10 ¼" x 15" (26 x 38 cm). Courtesy of The Japan Ukiyo-e Museum.

## Visual Culture

In this lesson, you learned that Japanese artists are well known for their design of large folding screens. These folding screens function as visual barriers and to provide privacy.

Consider how, and why, people in your local community construct screens, walls, hedges, and fences in both interior and exterior spaces. Collect images and compare the visual qualities and materials used to create these visual boundaries.

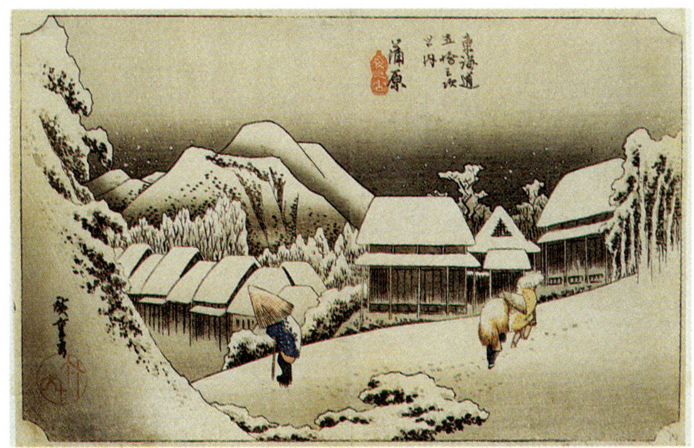

Fig. 4–21 **What details suggest that the village shown in this print is rural? What mood is expressed by the composition? Why do you think so?**

Utagawa Hiroshige, *Kanbara Evening Snow,* from the series *Fifty-Three Stations on the Tokaido*, ca. 1833. Woodblock print, 9 ½" x 14 ½" (24.1 x 36.8 cm). Clarence Buchingham Collection, 1925.3517. Photograph © of The Art Institute of Chicago.

**Ukiyo-e: The Floating World** *Ukiyo-e* (oo-key-OH-eh) is a style of Japanese art that shows colorful images of daily life. Translated, ukiyo-e means "pictures of the floating world." In the 1600s, when Japan was ruled by a strict military government, middle-class merchants and artists had no power in society. Instead, they built their own communities centered on the pleasures of money, theater, and worldly things. The word *ukiyo* was used to describe these communities. The ruling class frowned on this way of life.

Many ukiyo-e woodblock prints show life in middle-class communities. Japanese Kabuki theater was an important part of life there. By the mid-1800s, ukiyo-e was an accepted art style. Its subject matter began to include Japanese history, landscapes, and other natural images.

## Meet Okumura Masanobu

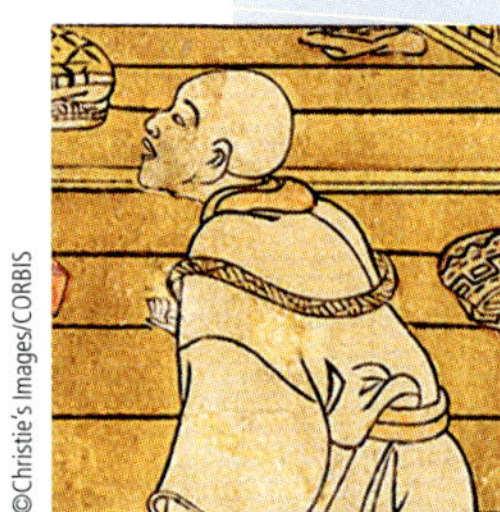



Little is known about Masanobu's life (1686–1764). He published his first book of prints when he was only fifteen. Later, he opened his own publishing shop, an unusual step for an artist of the time. It gave him the freedom to make whatever artworks he wished and to keep most of the profits. Masanobu is now admired for his technical skill and creativity.

**"With every new technical development, Masanobu was part of the creative vanguard."**

— Allen Memorial Art Museum

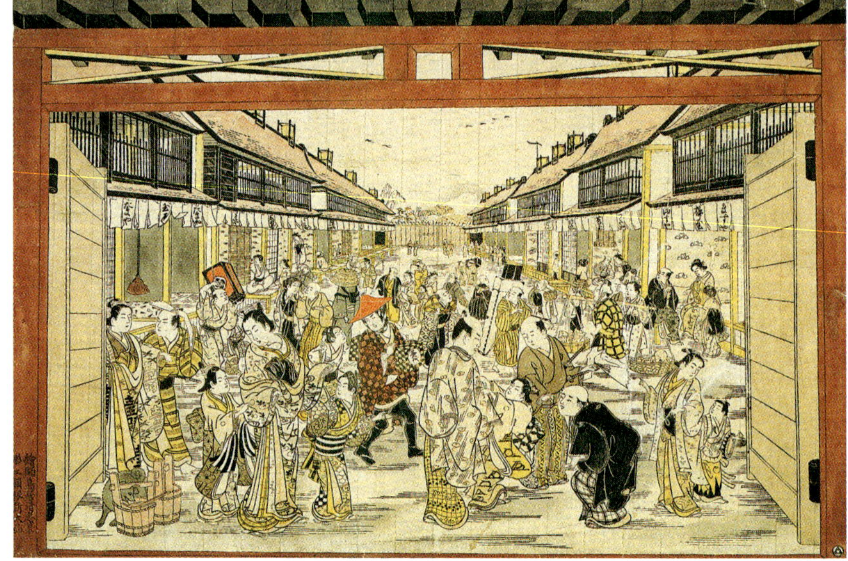

Fig. 4–22 **How would you describe the glimpse of Japanese daily life that you see in this print?**

Torii Kiyotada, *Main Gate of the Yoshiwara*, Edo period, ca. 1735. Handcolored woodblock print, 17" x 35 ¼" (43.2 x 89.5 cm). Clarence Buchingham Collection, 1939.2152. Photograph © of The Art Institute of Chicago.

## Check Your Understanding

1. What aspects of Japanese woodblock prints interested Western artists?
2. In what ways do Figs. 4–21 and 4–22 show different aspects of daily life in Japan?
3. What can we learn about Japan from its ukiyo-e woodcuts?

# Studio Time

## Linoleum Relief Print

### Safety Note

Handle cutting tools with extreme caution. Hold the block securely. Point the cutting edge of the tool away from hands, fingers, and body. Work slowly. Wear safety goggles.

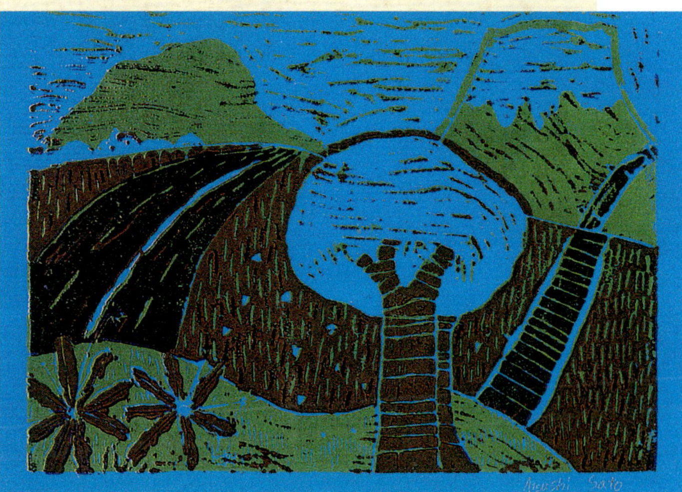

Fig. 4–24 Student artwork

Create a linoleum block print of a place that you remember. Show the mood of the place.

- Sketch your scene on paper first. How will you create the desired mood?
- Transfer the scene to a linoleum block using carbon paper. On the block, use a gouge to carve out areas that you do not want to print.
- Roll ink on the block's raised areas. Place paper over the inked block. Rub the back of the paper evenly.
- Carefully lift the print from the block.

Reflect on the mood of your scene.

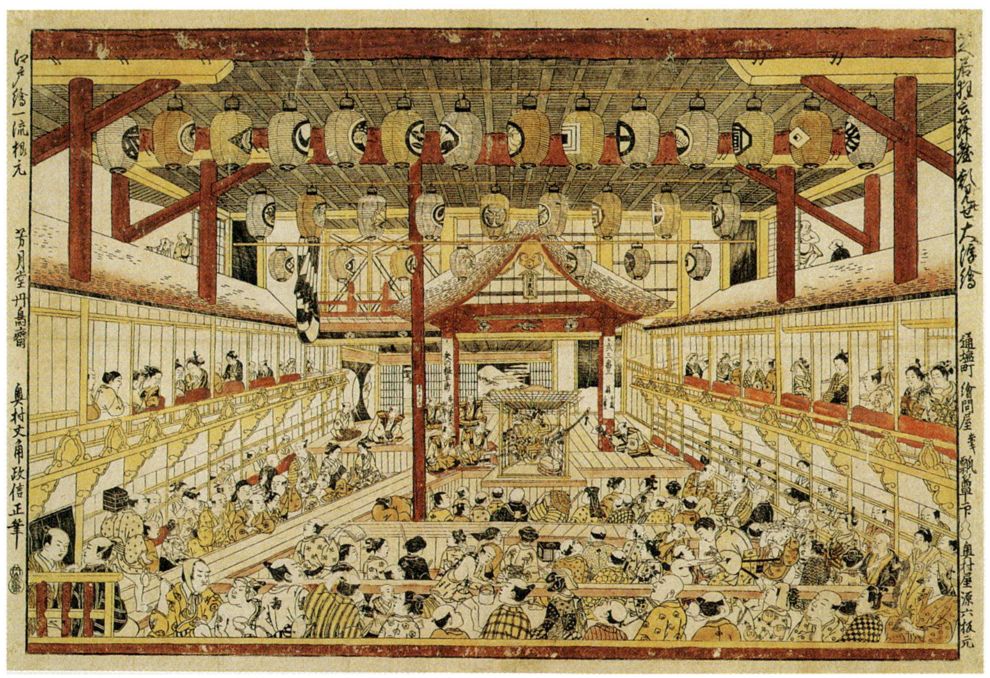

Fig. 4–23 **This print shows the inside of a theater. How has the artist used line and pattern to create the feeling of busyness in this scene?**

Okumura Masanobu, *A Performance of the Play "Ya no ne"*, 1740. Handcolored woodblock print, 18 ¼" x 26 ¾" (46.3 x 67.9 cm). Clarence Buchingham Collection, 1925.2285. Photograph © of The Art Institute of Chicago.

# A Postcard in Perspective

## Studio Background

If you were asked to design a postcard that shows a special place, what place would you choose? What details and mood would you want to capture?

**In this studio exploration, you will draw a postcard scene in two-point perspective.** Two-point perspective is a method of creating the illusion of deep space on a flat surface. Artists who use two-point perspective start with a horizon line. They place two vanishing points on the horizon line. If the lines that mark certain edges of objects are extended, those that seem to recede into the distance would meet at the vanishing points.

### You Will Need

- pencil
- ruler
- erasers
- large white drawing paper
- drawing media, such as pencils, markers, watercolors, or pastels

## Step 1 Plan and Practice

- Choose a special place to show on a postcard. The scene you choose should have objects in it that are up close and far away.
- Decide on the point of view you will show. Will you draw the scene at eye level, from above, or from below? Determine what other perspective techniques you will use.
- Decide what important details to include in your drawing. How will you show mood?

### Things to Remember:

- ✓ Start your drawing with a horizon line and use two vanishing points.
- ✓ Use detail to show that things are up close.
- ✓ Create a certain mood in your drawing.

## Inspiration from Our World

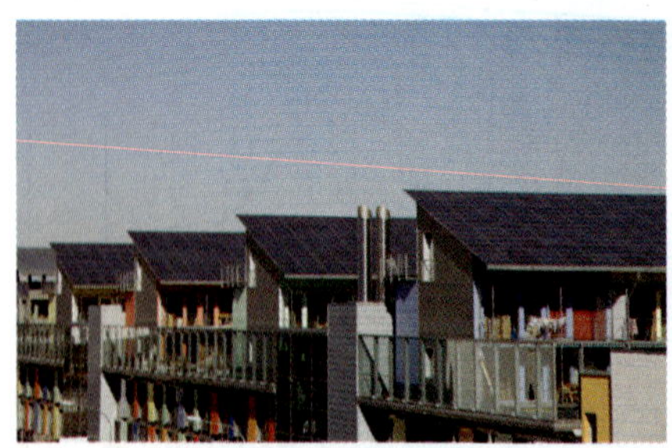

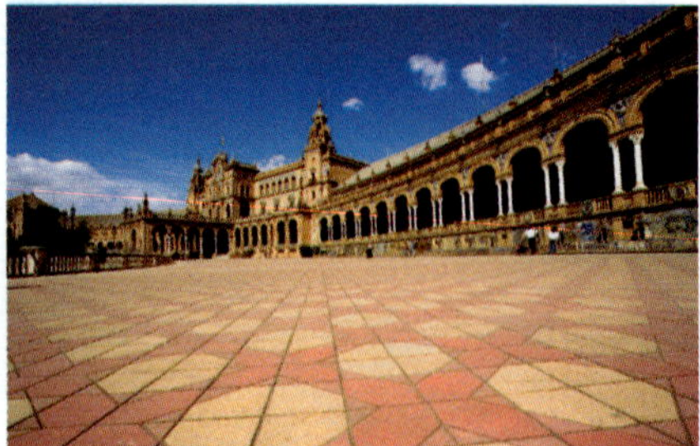

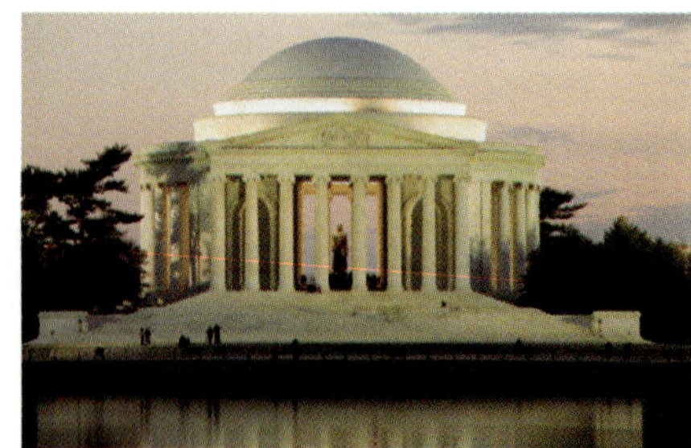

## Art Criticism

**Describe** What do you see in this drawing?

**Analyze** How did the artist plan the space in this drawing?

**Interpret** What words come to mind as you think about the building in this drawing?

**Evaluate** What makes this drawing special?

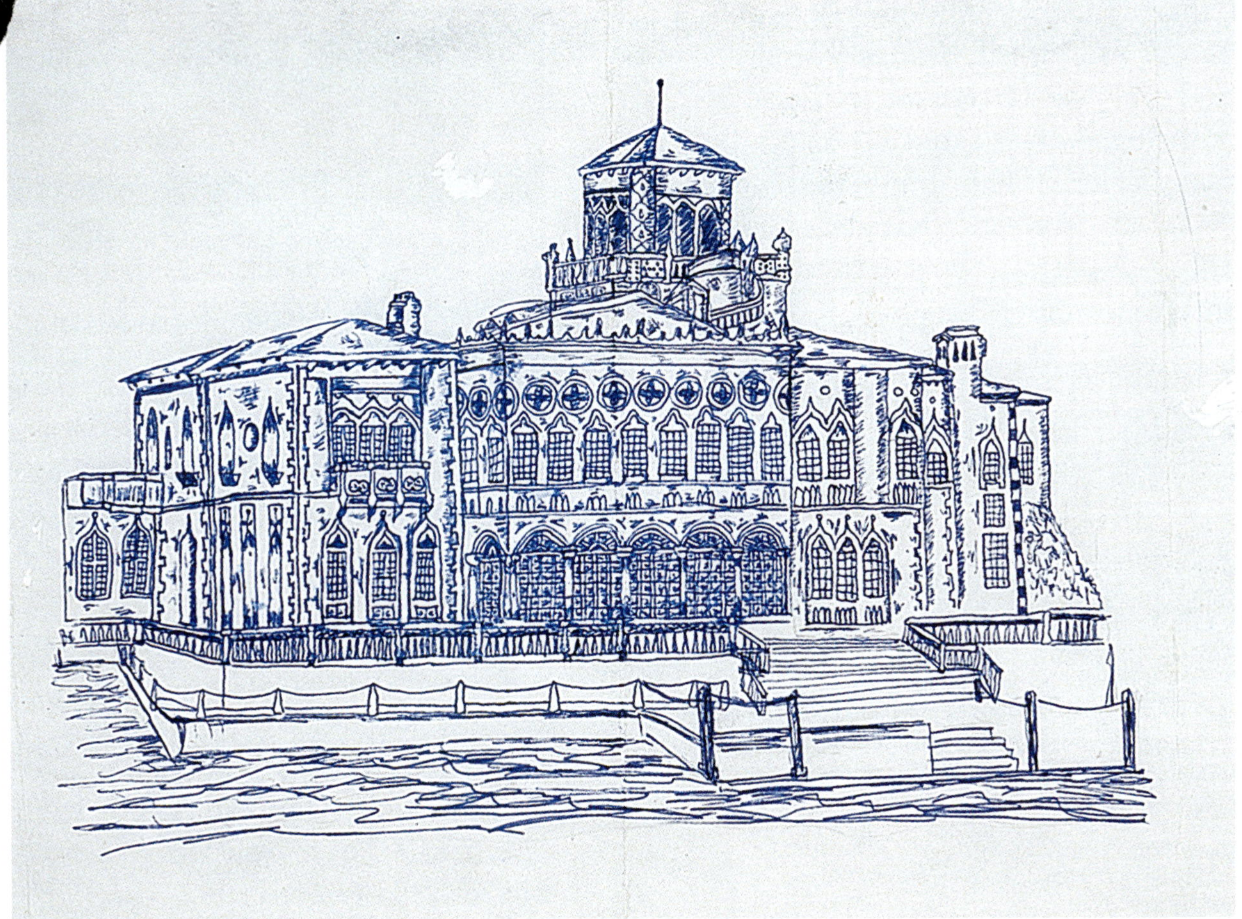

Fig. 4–26 Student artwork

## Social Studies

**Manifest Destiny was the belief that it was America's national mission to expand over the entire continent in the 1800s.** This expansion meant pushing Native Americans off their land. A number of artists played a role in westward expansion. They painted images of Native Americans, beautiful land, and other western subjects. These paintings were printed as posters and used back East to promote railroad travel to the West. What ideas about Native Americans do you think these images promoted?

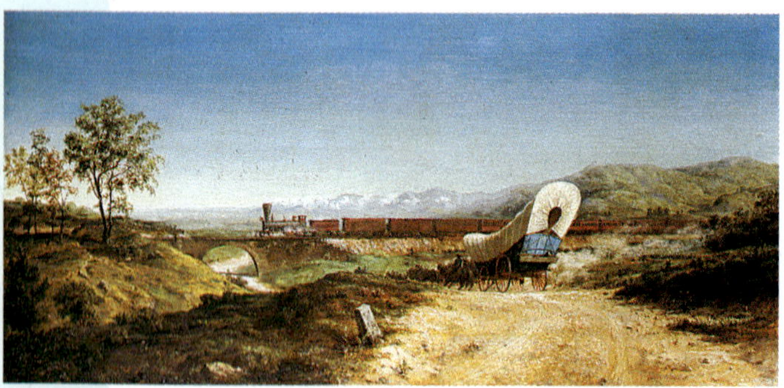

Fig. 4–27 **This artwork was painted in 1860. How has the artist contrasted the uncomfortable, dusty ride of the covered wagon with the smooth travel of the train?**

Thomas Otter, *On the Road*, 1860. Oil on canvas, 22" x 45 3/8" (55.8 x 115.3 cm). The Nelson-Atkins Museum of Art, Kansas City, Missouri (Purchase Nelson Trust).

## Music

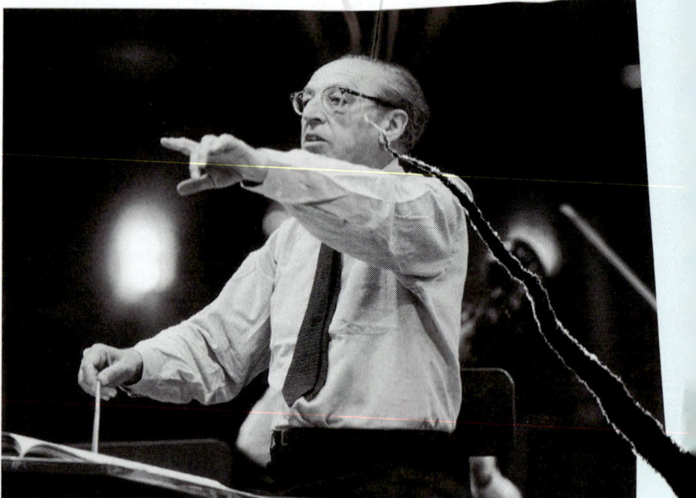

Fig. 4–28 **Aaron Copland was one of the great American composers. He also wrote several books on music and music appreciation.**

*Conductor Aaron Copland.* ©Bettmann/CORBIS.

**The identity of a culture can be expressed through its music.** Certain instruments identify regions: Caribbean steel drums, Scottish and Irish bagpipes, Japanese bamboo flutes. Beginning in the 1800s, many composers were inspired by a sense of national identity. They wrote music that reflected their particular culture. Aaron Copland (1900–1990) composed classic "American" music. Heitor Villa-Lobos (1887–1959) wrote music that mixed folk and popular music of his native Brazil. What type of music reminds you of the place you live?

## Careers **Landscape Architects**

**Large institutions like schools hire landscape architects to design the surrounding outdoor space.** Landscape architects prepare site plans and models. They select plants and flowers and work with others to complete the project. These architects must understand art and design, botany and ecology, climate and weather, and architecture and building codes. What buildings in your community have beautiful grounds or gardens?

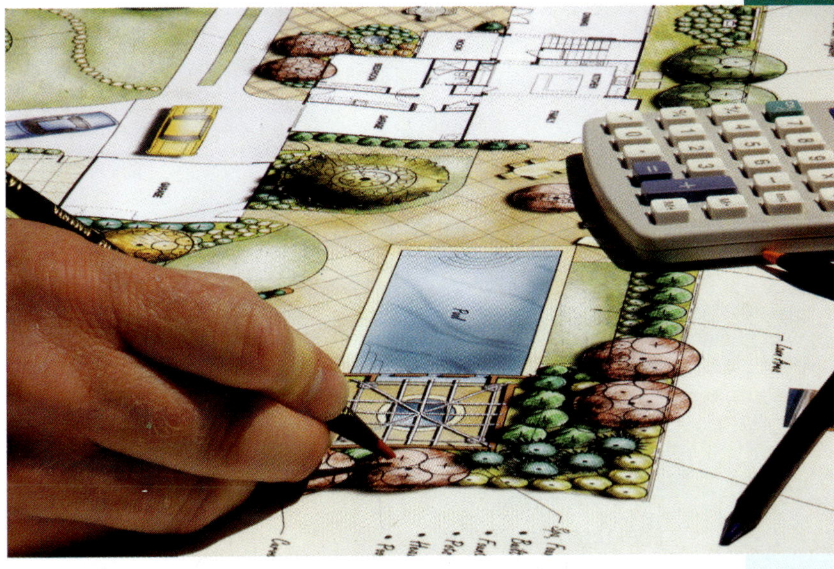

Fig. 4–29 **Drawing skills are essential to the work of any landscape architect.**

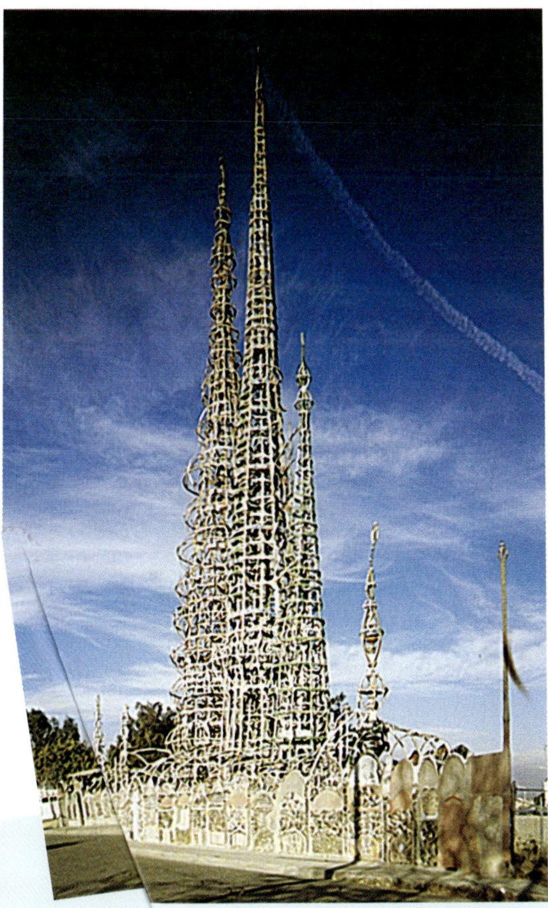

## Daily Life

**We attach special meanings to different places in our lives.** Think about a place that you feel connected to. It may be a specific building, like your home, a museum, or a community center. Or perhaps it's the street you live on, the town you live in, the state you live in, or even your country. Sometimes these special places bring people together and create a sense of community. What places are important to you? Why are they meaningful?

Fig. 4–30 **Artwork can inspire a sense of community. These sculptures symbolize the Los Angeles neighborhood of Watts. The community would not allow the structures be torn down.**

Simon Rodia, *Watts Towers*, 1921–54. Photograph ©Marvin Rand.

## Vocabulary Review

Match each art term below with its definition.

**memorial**

**Romantic style**

**document**

**linear perspective**

**Realistic style**

**ukiyo-e**

1. a style of art that shows foreign or exotic places, myths, legends, and imaginary events
2. to make or keep a record of
3. a technique used to create the illusion of space
4. a style of Japanese woodblock prints that often show scenes of nature or daily life
5. a style of art that shows people, scenes, and events of the artist's own time
6. an artwork or object that helps people remember where important events took place or where well-known individuals lived

## Aesthetic Thinking

Artists are often inspired by other artist's works. They sometimes use or change what another artist has done for their own artwork. Is this acceptable? If so, under what conditions? If not, why?

## Write About Art

Imagine that you have just walked down this cobblestone street in Paris and you want to send a postcard to a friend describing what you've seen. Compose a note to your friend that captures your experience.

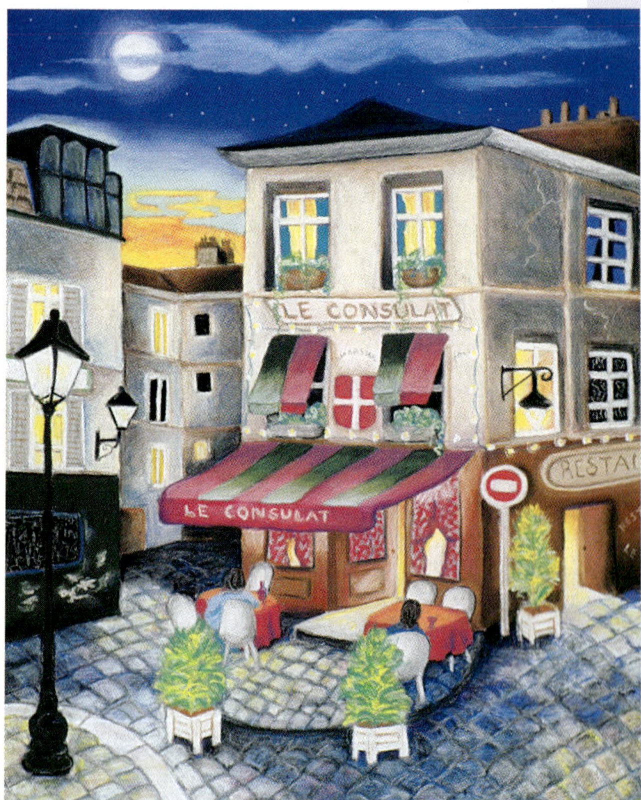


Fig. 4–31 **This artist created a drawing to help her remember a visit to Paris. Would this be a good image for a postcard? Why or why not?**

Linnea Pergola, *Le Consulat*, Fall 1998. Pastel, 16" x 20" (40.6 x 50.8 cm). Courtesy of the artist.

## Art Criticism

**Describe** What do you see in this mixed-media drawing?

**Analyze** How does the artist use pattern in this work?

**Interpret** Why do you think the artist selected a variety of poses for the ducks?

**Evaluate** What evidence points to the fact that Audubon made his artwork as documentation of the species?

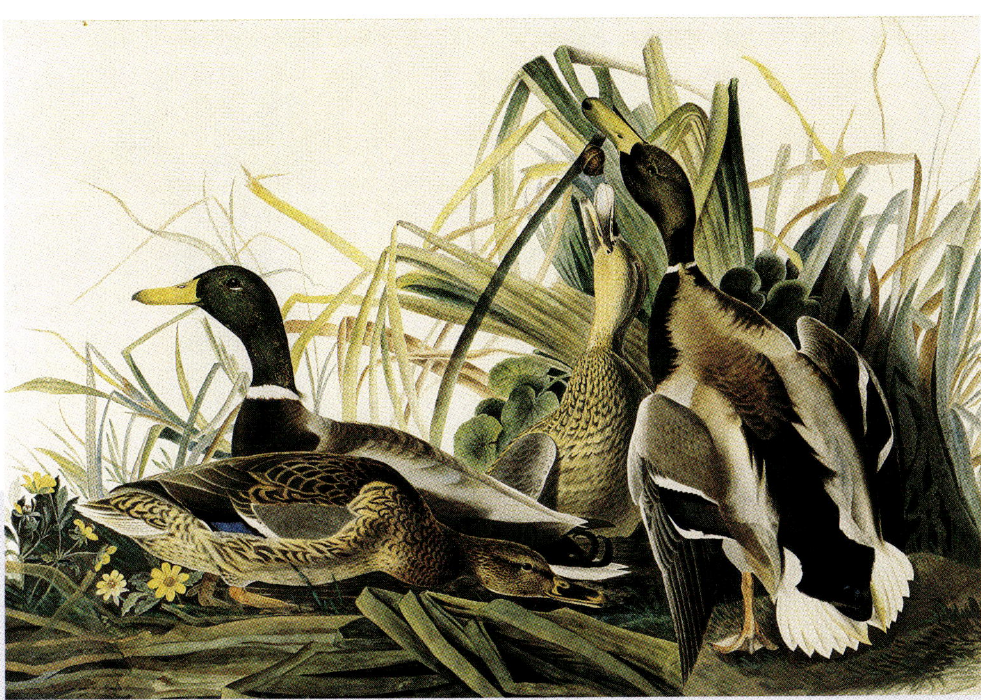

Fig. 4–32 John James Audubon, *Mallard* (Anas Playyrhynchos), ca. 1821–25. Watercolor, graphite, pastel, collage, selective glazing, metallic paint on paper, 25 5/8" x 38 1/4" (65.2 x 97.2 cm.) Collection of the New York Historical Society (1863.17.221).

## Meet the Artist

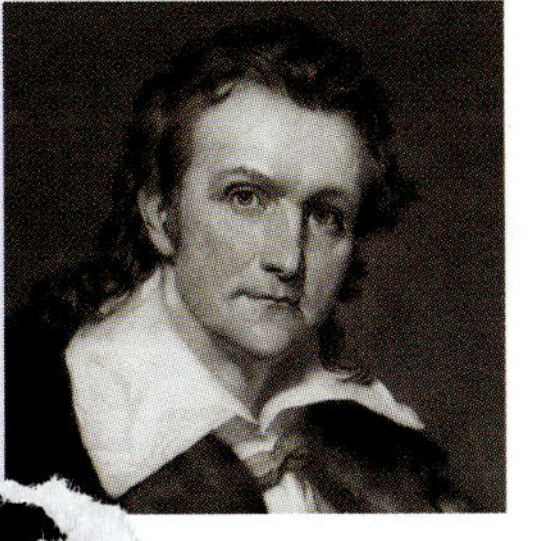

Michael Nicholson/Corbis

**John James Audubon** (1785–1851) was born in Haiti and later lived in France and the United States. He began hunting and studying birds and animals as a teenager; this work would become the focus of his career. Audubon traveled the United States making paintings of native birds for his book *The Birds of America*. He worked with a publisher to create etchings from these paintings so that the book could be widely distributed. *The Birds of America* documented nearly five hundred different species.

## For Your Portfolio

Select one of your artworks from this unit that sends a clear message about place. In a sentence, explain what the message is, and what you have done to make the message clear.

## For Your Sketchbook

Create sketches of gateways to special places and scenes that can be linked to human hopes, such as opportunity, success, and freedom.

Unit 5

# Art and Nature

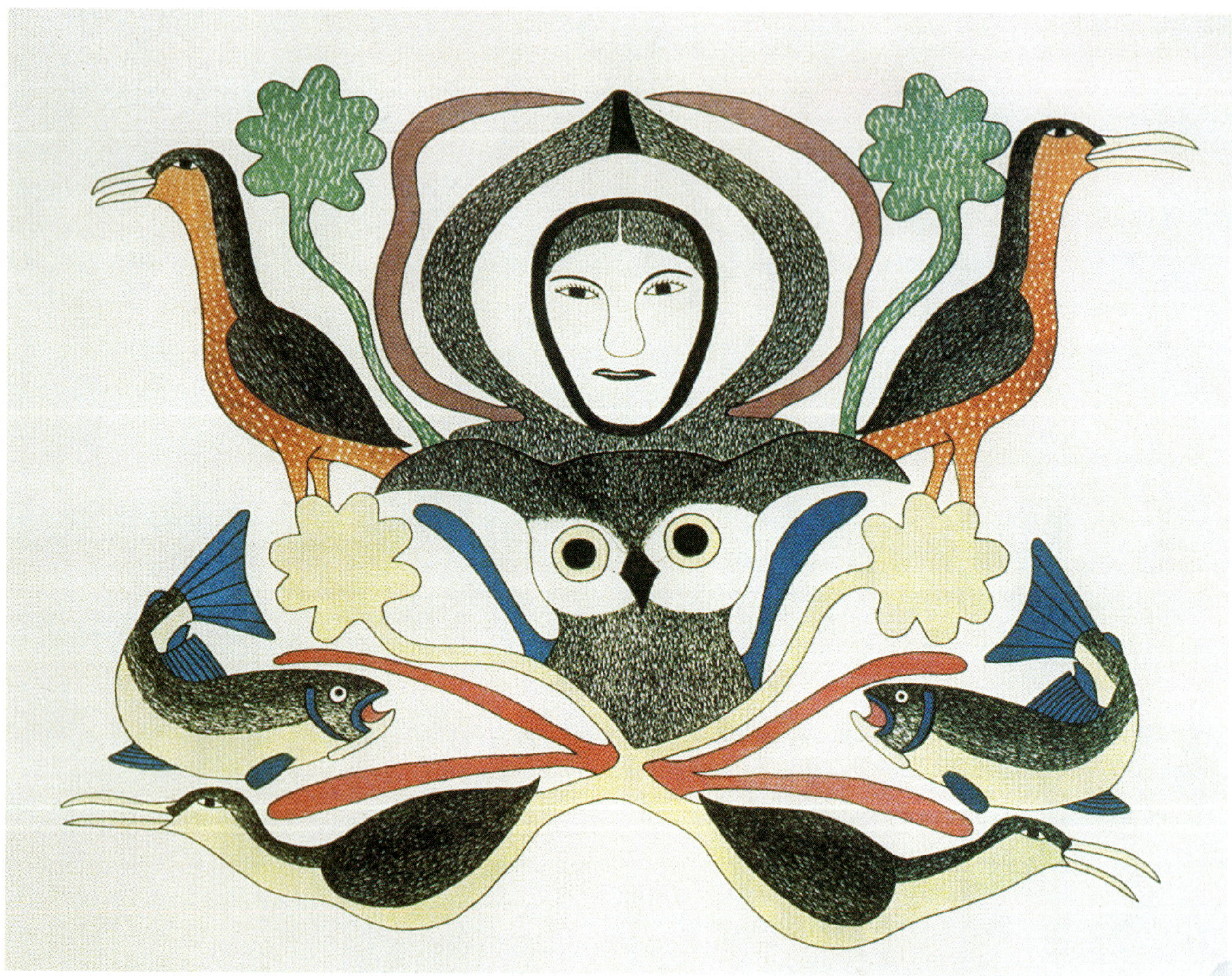

Fig. 5–1 **This artist has seen many changes in the northern arctic environment because of the expanding modern world. What message about nature does her artwork convey?**

Kenojuak Ashevak, *The World Around Me*, 1980. Lithograph, 22 ¼"x 31 ⅛" (56.5 x 79 cm). ©By permission of the West Baffin Eskimo Cooperative Ltd, Cape Dorset, Numavut, Dorset Fine Arts, Indian and Northern Affairs, Canada.

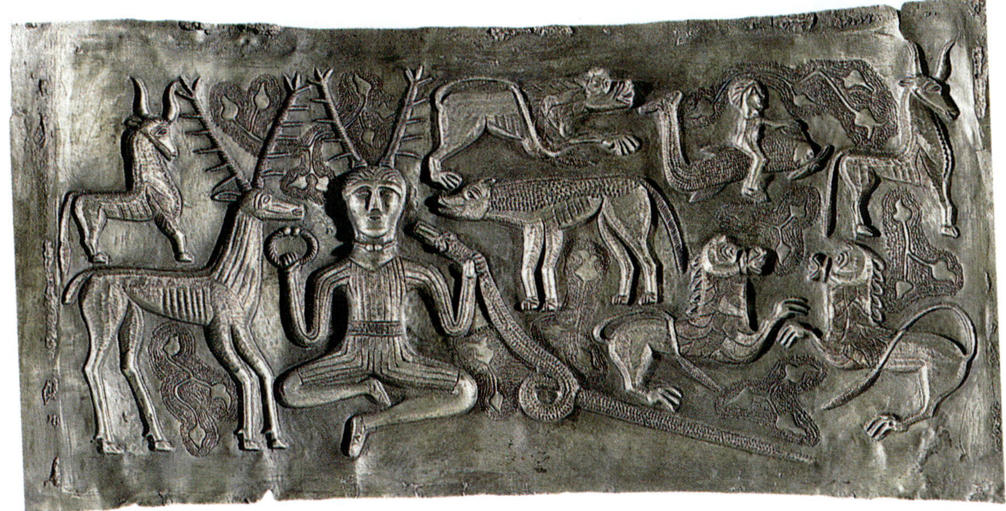

Fig. 5–2 **Cernunnos was an ancient god of the Celtic people. How does this artwork support the idea that he was lord of the beasts?**

Celtic, Gundestrup cauldron, inner plate: *Cerrunnos holding a snake and a torque, surrounded by animals*, 1st century BCE. Embossed silver, gilded. National Museum, Copenhagen, Denmark. Erich Lessing / Art Resource, NY.

**Think about nature's effect on your life. How does the weather influence your daily activities?** How do you relate to wild animals living in your area? With some thought, you'll realize how closely we are connected to nature.

Throughout history, artists have shown their connection to nature. Many use plants and animals as their subjects. Artworks have portrayed nature as powerful and ruthless as well as gentle and nurturing.

Today, people worldwide still witness nature's power and beauty in earthquakes, sunsets, blizzards, and other events. Artworks send messages about nature's power and beauty. They show us how nature affects our lives.

**In this unit, you will learn:**

- How artists reveal the many ways nature affects people.
- How to use elements of art and natural materials to create artworks that express feelings about nature.
- How to look at artworks as expressions of artists' attitudes toward nature.

# A Powerful Connection

Does nature sometimes frighten you? Even though we understand much about how nature works, nature's fury can still frighten people or spark their curiosity. Some people brave wind and rain to watch oceans launch huge waves over sea walls. Others tremble under the covers at night during thunderstorms.

Artworks from the past show the power of nature. Ancient communities tried to understand tornadoes and volcanoes through stories about gods and goddesses. Gods and goddesses often appear in artworks with the sun, moon, and other natural elements.

**Investigating Nature** Have you ever watched a line of ants and wondered where they were going? Can you name the kinds of plants in your yard or neighborhood? To learn about nature, you must carefully observe it. Out of curiosity, people have looked closely at natural things and tried to understand how nature works.

Artists help people investigate nature. Some artists make scientific records of plants and animals in a community. Scientific records are accurate, detailed works used to document exactly what something looks like. Other artists observe nature, and then express their own ideas and feelings about it in their artworks.

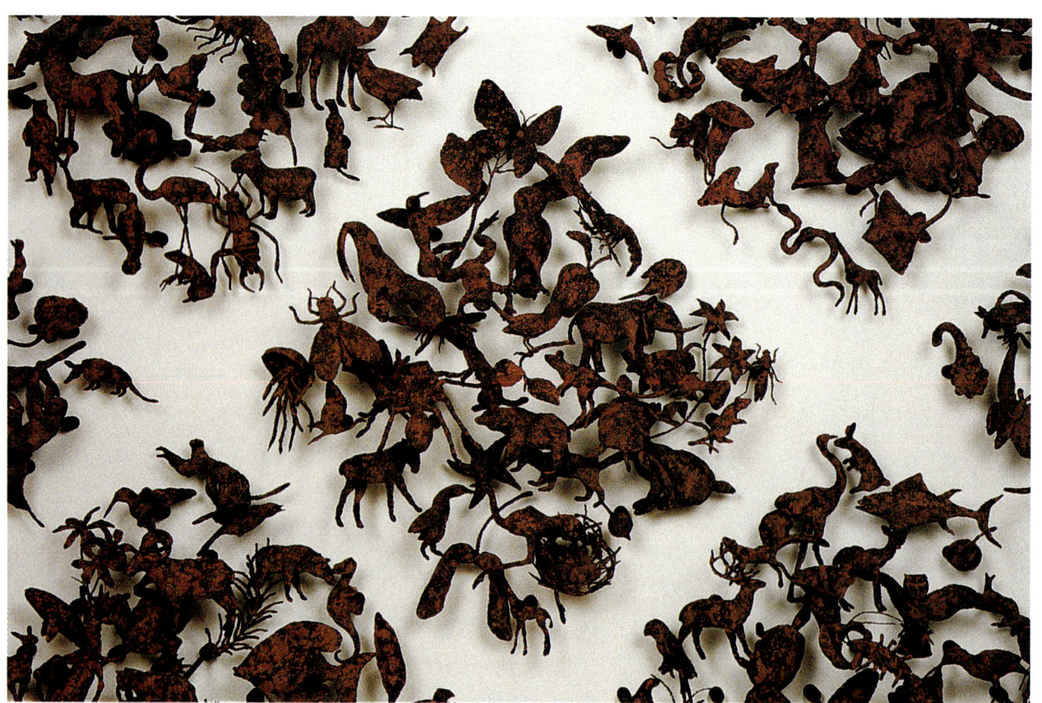

Fig. 5–3 **Why might this artwork be considered an example of an artistic expression of nature as opposed to a scientific record?**

Joe Walters, *Vignette #6 (butterfly, songbird)*, 1999. Aluminum, mesh, polymer clay, resin, glue, sand, paint, 32" x 32" x 10" (81.3 x 81.3 x 25.4 cm). Courtesy Bernice Steinbaum Gallery, Miami, FL.

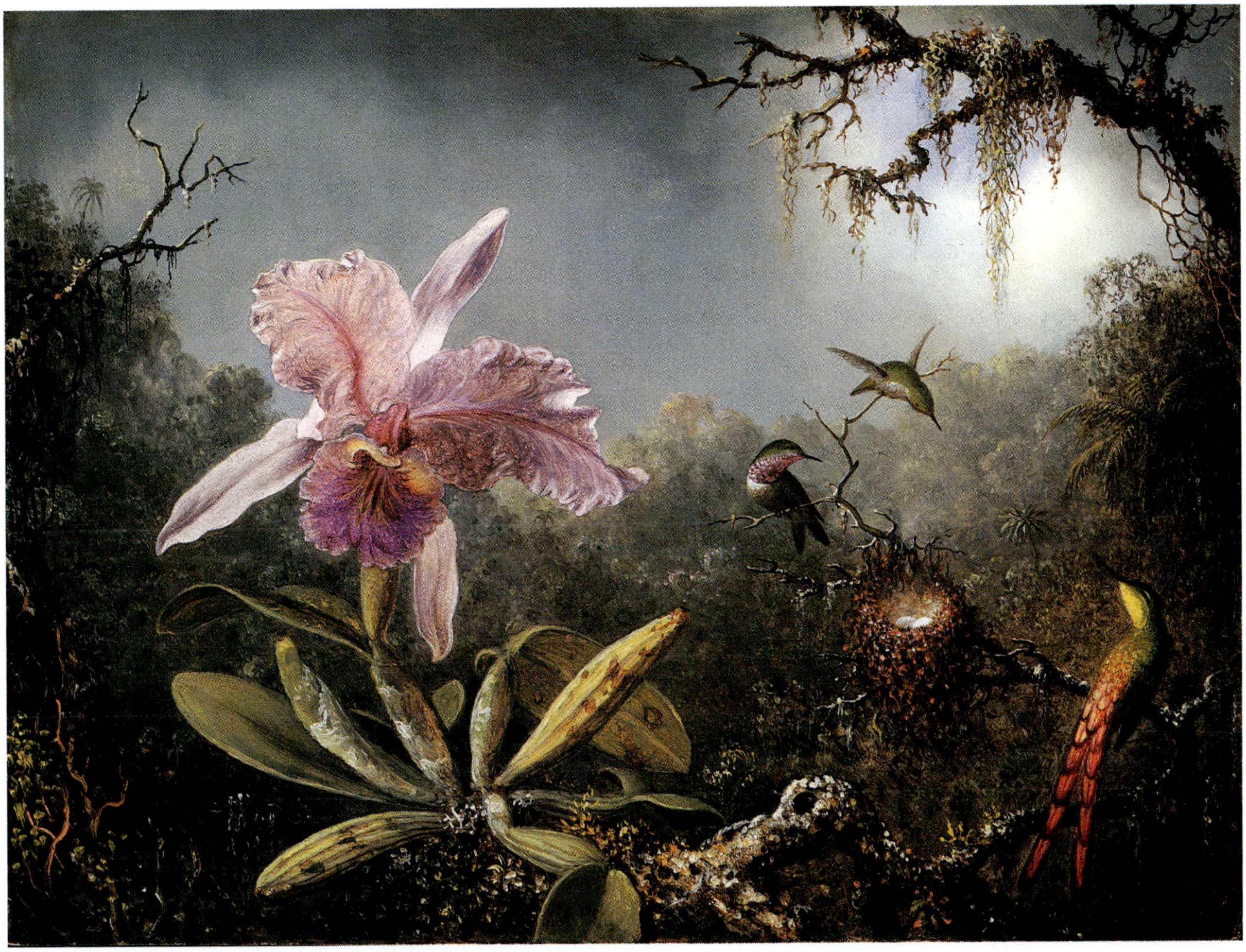

Fig. 5–4 **How is this painting like a photograph? How is it different from a photograph?**

Martin Johnson Heade, *Cattleya Orchid and Three Brazilian Hummingbirds*, 1871. Oil on wood, 13 ¾" x 18" (34.8 x 45.6 cm). Gift of The Morris and Gwendolyn Cafritz Foundation, ©1999 Board of Trustees, National Gallery of Art, Washington, DC.

## Meet Martin Johnson Heade

Martin Johnson Heade (1819–1904) was born in Lumberville, Pennsylvania. At 18, he studied art in Europe. He began his career painting portraits, but turned to landscapes and still lifes in his 30s. He traveled to South America, where he created a series of realistic hummingbird paintings. Other naturalist painters of the time often showed a variety of animals set against a solid background. Heade painted his hummingbirds within complete tropical landscapes.

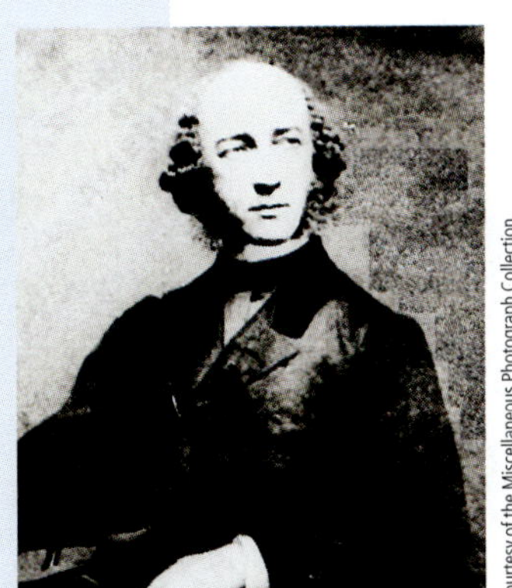

Courtesy of the Miscellaneous Photograph Collection, Archive of American Art, Smithsonian Institution.

Heade traveled for much of his life. He eventually settled in Saint Augustine, Florida, at age 64. There, he painted hummingbirds, orchids, and Florida swamps.

**“(Heade’s hummingbird paintings) are the very image of Eden.”**

— Theodore Stebbins, writing about Martin Johnson Heade in *A New World—Masterpieces of American Painting*

**Natural Beauty** Even though people have feared the power of nature, they have also enjoyed the natural world for its beauty. Delicate flowers, brightly colored birds, and magnificent scenery have given people great pleasure for thousands of years. People have been inspired by the beauty of nature to write poetry and to capture views in paintings and other artworks.

**A Message to Care** Today, environmental groups work hard to protect endangered species. They think about how the extinction of these plants and animals will upset the balance of nature.

Many artists reflect environmental concerns in their artworks. Much contemporary art calls our attention to this delicate balance in nature. Artists who create these artworks often use nontraditional art materials and sites.

The drawing of Agnes Denes' *Tree Mountain* **(Fig. 5–6)** shows the artist's plan for creating a living artwork. For *Tree Mountain*, 11,000 people from all around the world planted 11,000 trees in Finland between 1992 and 1996. The planters and their families to come will care for the trees.

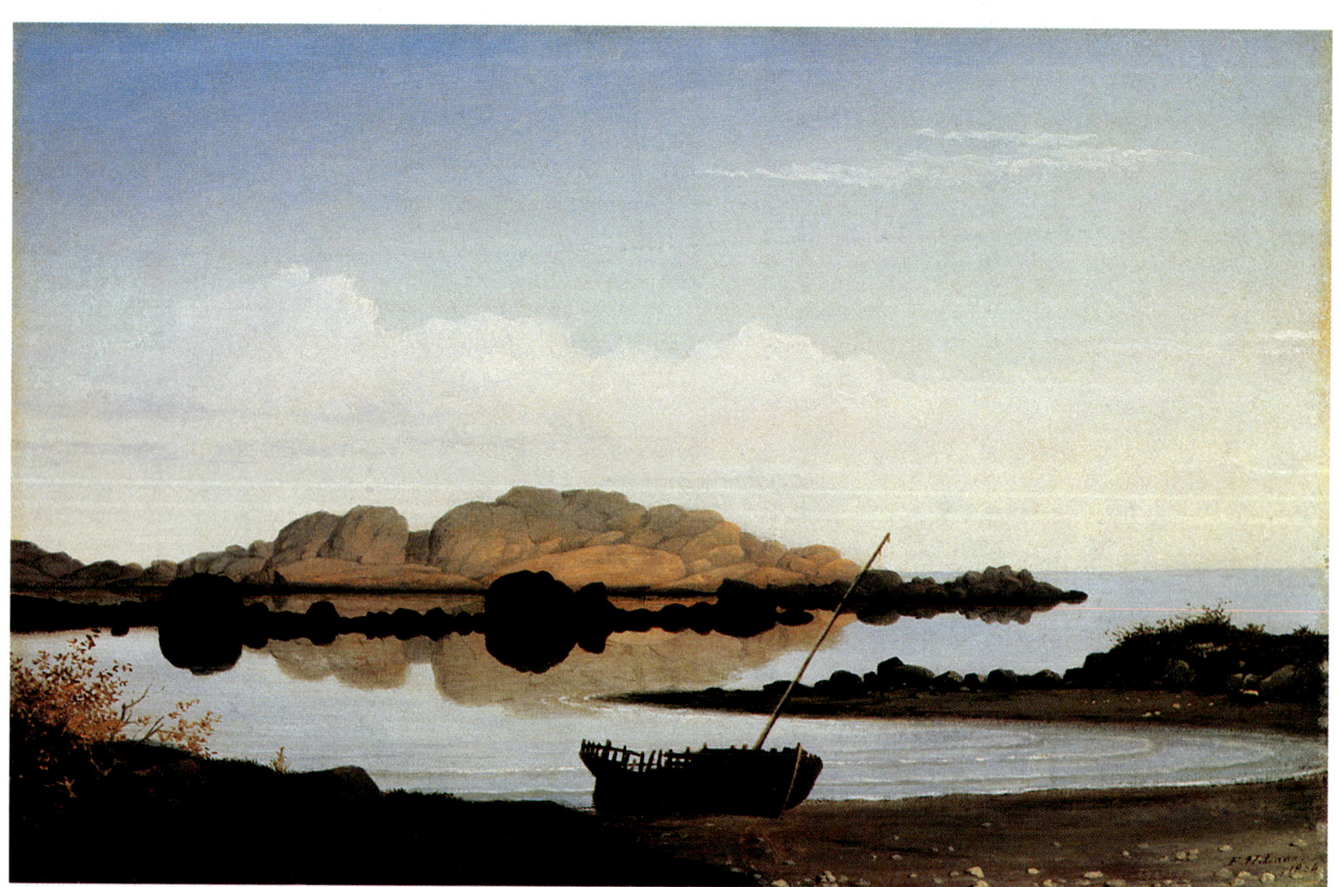

Fig. 5–5 **This artist painted a natural scene near his Massachusetts home. Where would you go to enjoy nature? How would you show that place in an artwork?**

Fitz Henry Lane, *Brace's Rock, Brace's Cove*, 1864. Oil on canvas, 10 ¼" x 15 ¼" (26 x 38.7 cm). Terra Foundation for the Arts, Daniel J. Terra Collection, 1999.83, Photograph courtesy of Terra Museum of American Art, Chicago.

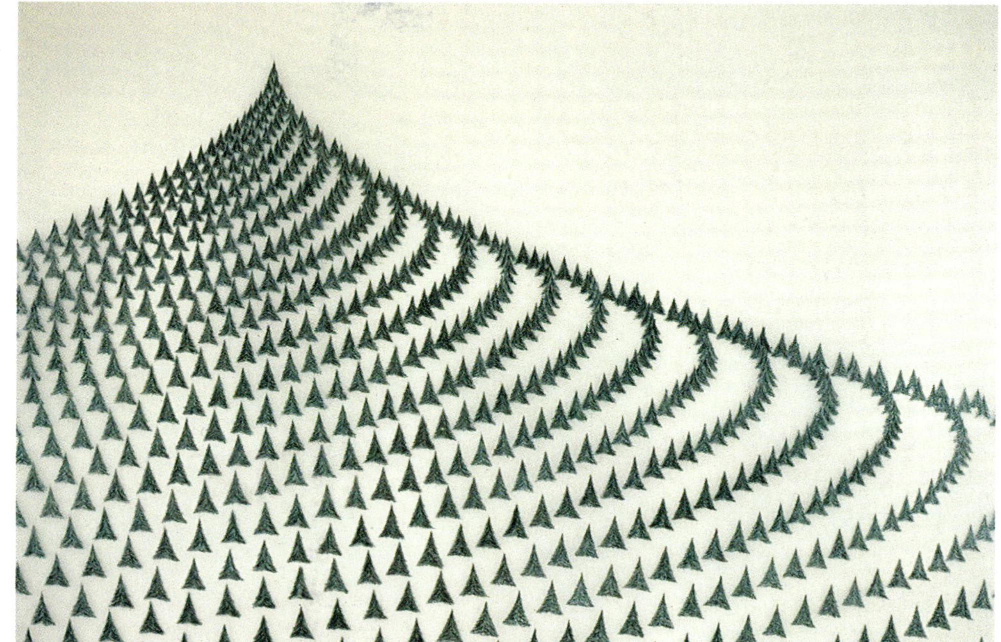

Fig. 5–6 **These trees will live for about 400 years. How is this artwork an expression of concern for the environment?**

Agnes Denes, *Tree Mountain—A Living Time Capsule, 11,000 Trees, 11,000 People, 400 Years*, 420 x 270 x 28 meters, Pinsio gravel pits, Ylojarvi, Finland, 1996. Metallic inks on mylar, 34 ¼" x 96 ½" (87 x 245 cm). ©Agnes Denes, 1996.

## Studio Time

### An Expressive Scene

Create a drawing that expresses your ideas or feelings about a scene you have observed in nature.

- Draw the scene from a close-up perspective using colored pencils. What elements will you show in a lifelike way? What might you change?
- Try to use color in a new or unexpected way to help express your ideas or feelings.
- Look at your drawing again and add any further details to finalize it.

Refect on how well you captured details in nature.

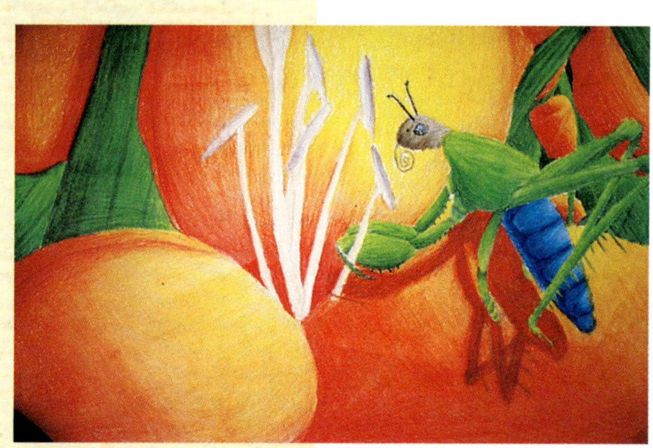

Fig. 5–7 Student artwork

### Check Your Understanding

1. What are two general kinds of messages that artworks send about nature?
2. Compare and contrast Martin Johnson Heade's painting (Fig. 5–4) with Agnes Denes's work (Fig. 5–6). How does each use color? Create a sense of space?
3. Suggest an idea for making an artwork that would include a message to care about the natural world.

# Crafts

Since the earliest times, people have needed shelters, various types of supports, and containers to help them survive. Early people used caves and cliff overhangs for shelters, tree branches or large rocks to sit on or eat from, and gourds or bird's nests for containers. Eventually, they learned to use natural materials, such as grass, wood, and clay, to make containers, furniture, and other useful objects.

**Craft Traditions** When people make useful objects out of natural materials, they are working in craft traditions. Crafts are decorative or useful works of art that are skillfully made by hand. Craft traditions vary from community to community depending on people's needs and the available materials. Older artists often teach a craft to younger artists and pass along ideas about how handmade objects should look and work.

Craft traditions may change from generation to generation. Other craft traditions, such as some methods for making Egyptian baskets, have remained the same for thousands of years.

The Cuna Indians of the San Blas Islands off the coast of Panama are known for their colorful blouses, or *molas* (Fig. 5–10). The front and back panels on each mola are made of many rectangular pieces of fabric of different colors and textures sewn together. Molas show scenes from nature, daily life, and traditional legends of the Cuna community. What craft traditions have been passed down to you?

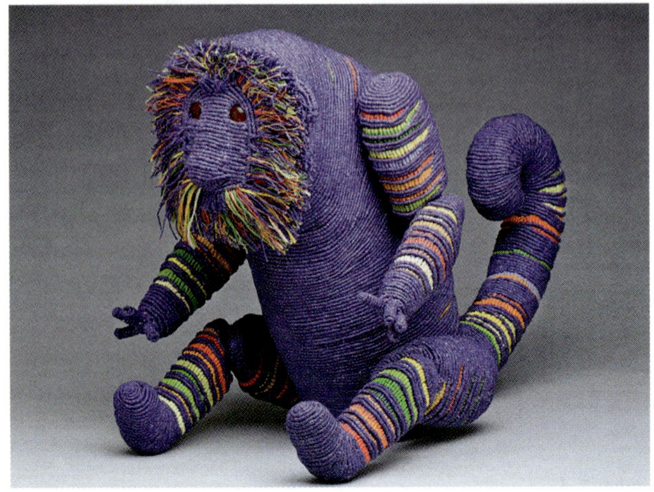

Fig. 5–8 **This artwork was created using the craft tradition of papier mâché. Why do you think the artist chose the title *Howler* for this artwork?**

Leah Danberg, *Howler*. Photo: Barnard Wolf.

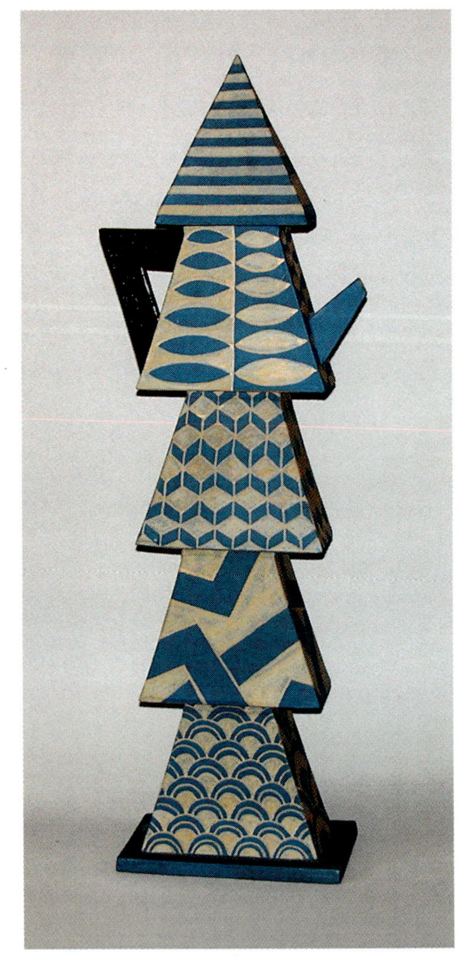

Fig. 5–9 **What elements of nature has the artist incorporated into this work?**

Kazuko Matthews, *Stacked Tea Pot*. Photo: P.T. Nunn. Courtesy of Craft in America, Los Angeles, CA.

**Observe** Look at Fig. 5–10. Notice the variety of colors and textures in the fabrics. Where do you see patterns? How have they been created?

**Tools:** Paper, pencil, and markers.

## Practice: Creating Patterns

- On a sheet of paper, draw three rectangles, each 2" deep x 6" wide.
- In the first rectangle, draw lines that form a repeated pattern. Fill the space. Use bright, contrasting colors.
- In the second rectangle, draw shapes that form a repeated pattern. As before, use bright colors to define the shapes.
- In the third rectangle, combine motifs from the first two rectangles to create a more complex pattern. Use colors from both previous sets of patterns.

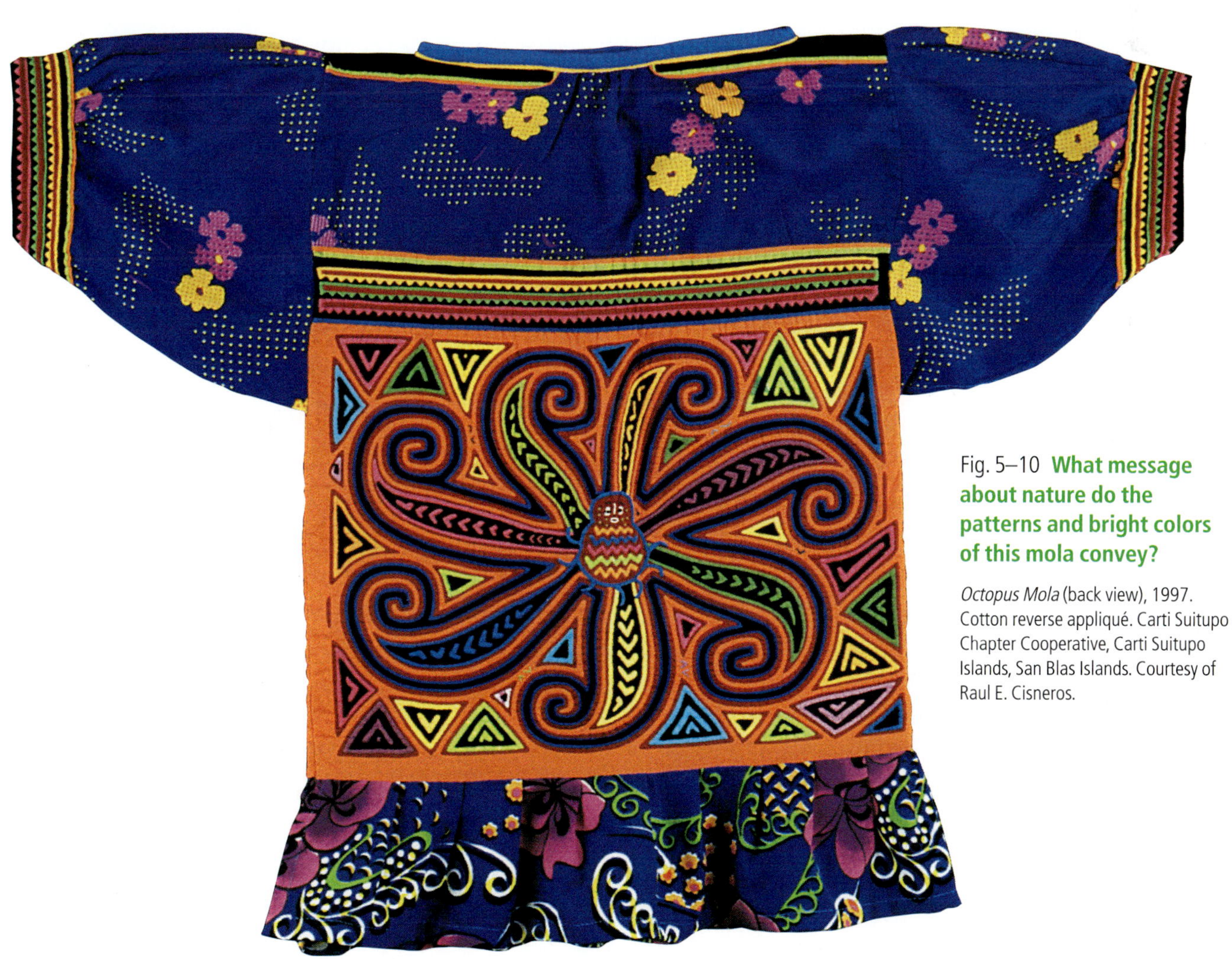

Fig. 5–10 **What message about nature do the patterns and bright colors of this mola convey?**

*Octopus Mola* (back view), 1997. Cotton reverse appliqué. Carti Suitupo Chapter Cooperative, Carti Suitupo Islands, San Blas Islands. Courtesy of Raul E. Cisneros.

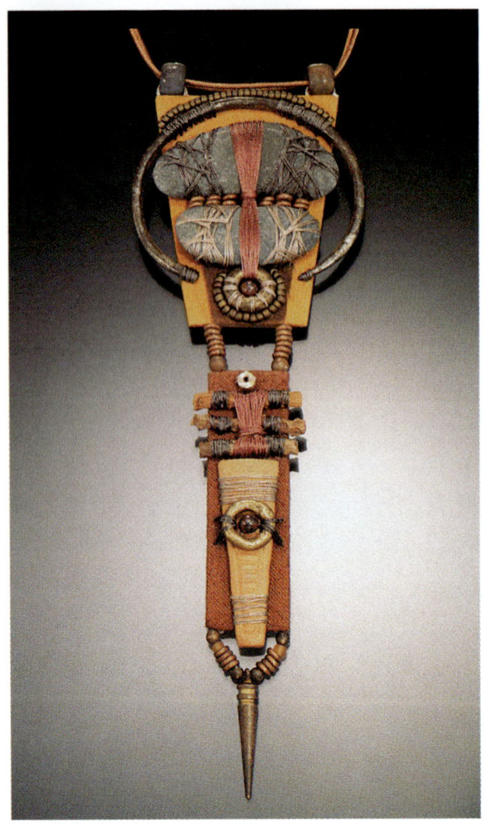

Fig. 5–11 **What materials do you see in this pendant? What ideas do the materials and the design of the pendant suggest?**

Kara Johns Tennis, *Untitled*, 1999. Hand-sewn mixed-media collage pendant, with fabric, linen, and nylon thread, coconut palm twigs, pebbles, polymer clay, African brass, and other found objects, 2" x 5 ½" (5.1 x 14 cm). Courtesy of the artist.

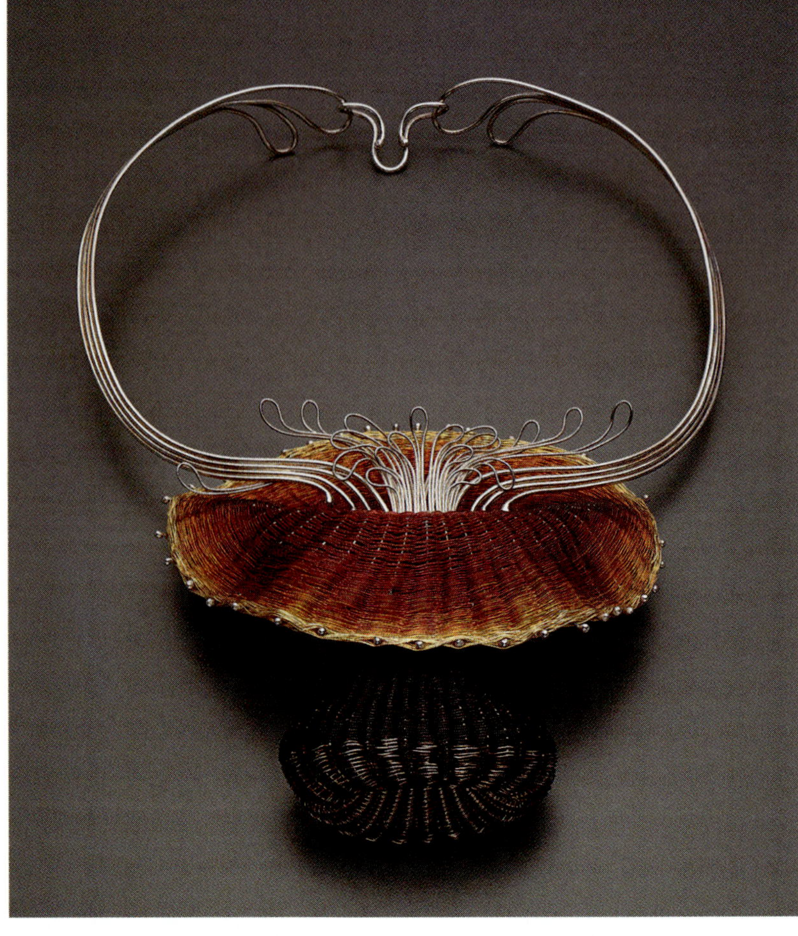

Fig. 5–12 **What natural forms can you find in this piece of jewelry?**

Mary Lee Hu, *Choker #48*, 1979. Fine and sterling silver, 24 kt gold, lacquered copper, twined, constructed, 9 ¼" x 7" x 1 ¾" (23.5 x 17.8 x 4.4 cm). Museum of Fine Arts, Boston, The Daphne Farago Collection, 2006.257.

**Experimenting for Beauty** People in almost every community embellish useful objects, such as clothing and pottery, so that they are pleasing to see and touch. These artists make careful decisions about form, color, texture, and pattern.

Sometimes they add designs and symbols to their objects that mean something to their community. Such designs might reflect religious beliefs or tell about other important community ideas. Artists also explore different ways to use craft materials to create new forms.

Jewelry making is another craft form that people use to express ideas. Artists often use natural materials, such as metals, gems, and shells, to craft objects that adorn the body or hold back hair. Sometimes these pieces of jewelry are not only made from natural materials, but also are inspired by leaves, flowers, or other natural objects.

**Observe** Look at the jewelry in Fig. 5–11. Notice the variety of materials, and the way the artist has attached one material to another. What holds the pieces in place?

**Tools:** Soft, flexible wire, pencils or dowel rods.

### Check Your Understanding

1. How do people learn craft traditions?
2. Compare and contrast crafts with another art form, such as painting or drawing. How are they similar? How are they different? Think about the reasons each type of artwork might be created.
3. Why do people create useful objects by hand?

### Practice: Working with Wire

- Make coils by wrapping the wire around pencils or dowel rods

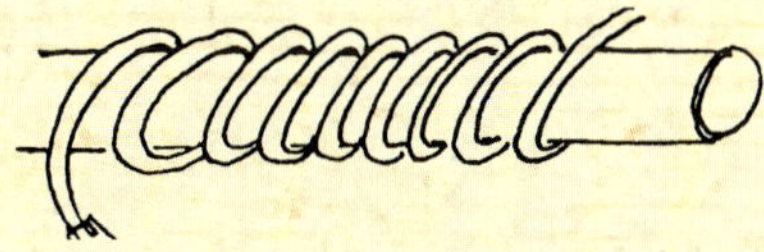

- Gently slip the coil off the pencil or dowel when complete.

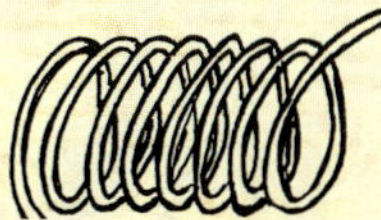

- Make loops by wrapping figure eights between two nails in a board.

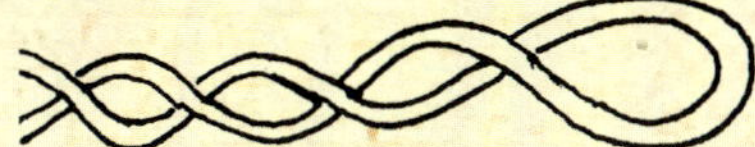

- Twist two strands of wire together. Braid three or more strands together.

## Studio Time

### Natural Forms in Jewelry

Create a piece of jewelry that suggests forms from nature. Use inexpensive materials, such as clay, paper, wood, wire, or leather scraps. You might also recycle parts of old jewelry, toys, or other objects.

- Think about what kind of jewelry you want to make. What can your piece of jewelry say about you? How will it echo natural forms?
- Decide what materials you will use. What materials will best express your ideas?
- Experiment with ways to connect your materials.

Show your jewelry to classmates and reflect on their responses.

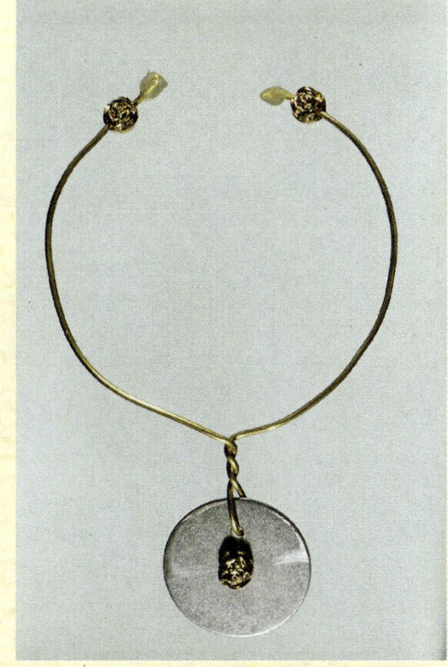

Fig. 5–13 Student artwork

# Coil Baskets: Natural Forms and Materials

## Studio Background

Long before people around the world made pots from clay or wove cloth from wool, they made baskets from tree bark and plant fibers. Whether they lived in wetlands, pine forests, or the high desert, they found everything needed to make baskets in the natural environment.

As people migrated to new lands, they adapted their techniques to the natural materials they found there.

Traditionally, basket makers use four basic techniques: weaving, plaiting, twining, and coiling. Plants and fibers used for making baskets include bamboo, banana leaves, bark, jute, raffia, rattan, cane, straw, grass, and sisal.

**In this studio exploration, you will create a coil basket using natural materials.** You might choose to make a basket with pine needles, straw, grass, raffia, rope, or cotton or wool yarns. You will have to make many decisions, research techniques, follow directions, and work patiently.

### You Will Need

- blunt end, #16 tapestry needle
- raffia, string, yarn
- 3⁄16" –cotton clothesline, jute, or pine needles
- masking tape
- found objects, seeds
- scissors

## Inspiration from Our World

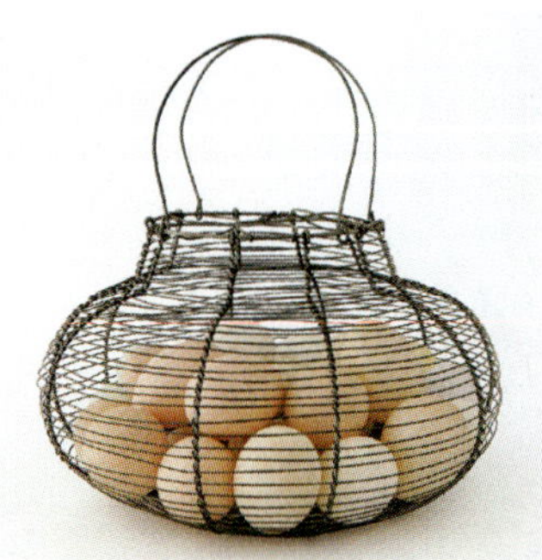

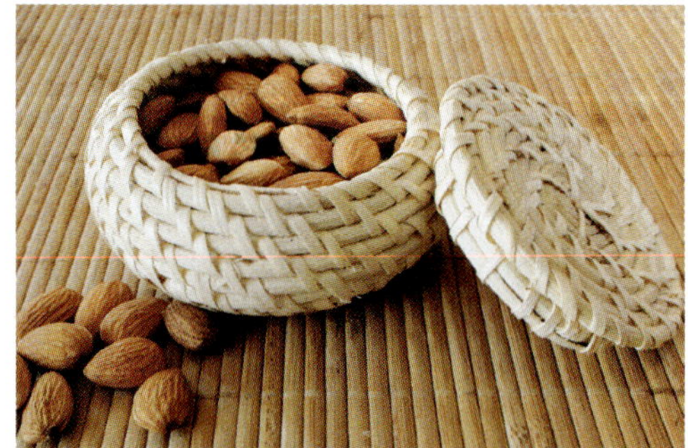

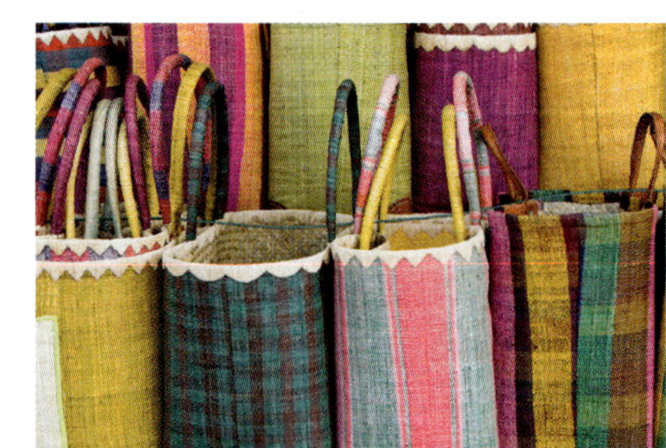

Step 1 **Plan and Practice**

- Decide what natural materials you will use for your basket. Will you use rope made from cotton or jute for your coils? Or will you try working with bunches of pine needles or raffia?
- Practice threading a needle with a long strand of raffia.
- Practice making and wrapping coils and sewing them together to form a flat coaster.

**Things to Remember:**

✓ Use at least two different natural materials with some contrast in color.

✓ Keep the form simple and natural.

✓ Maintain a tight and consistent weave.

## Inspiration from Art

For South Carolina artist Mary Jackson, weaving baskets is a family tradition. Her grandmother and mother taught her basic traditional designs and techniques when she was a child. Their ancestors brought the basket-making traditions with them from the West Coast of Africa more than 300 years ago.

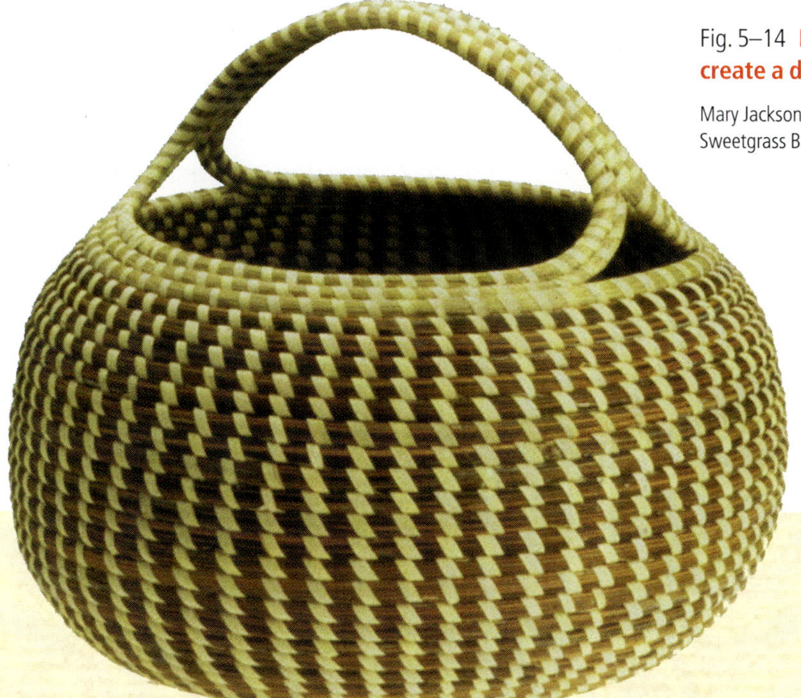

Fig. 5–14 **How did the artist create a design on this basket?**

Mary Jackson, *Cobra with Handle.* Sweetgrass Baskets, Charleston, SC.

### Step 2 Begin to Create

- **Shape the materials into a spiral** and, as each row is added, use needle and raffia or string to "sew" the coils together.

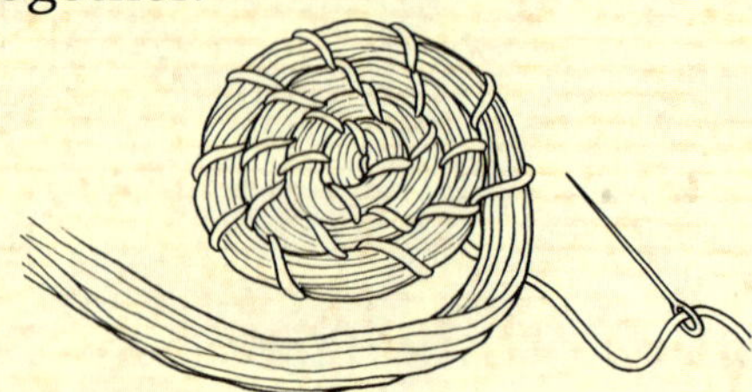

- Keep your work as flat as possible so your basket will sit flat. Continue wrapping and sewing until it is about four inches wide.
- **To continue, begin to stack and sew along the top of the last coil you completed.** Keep stacking so that your basket gets taller and taller.

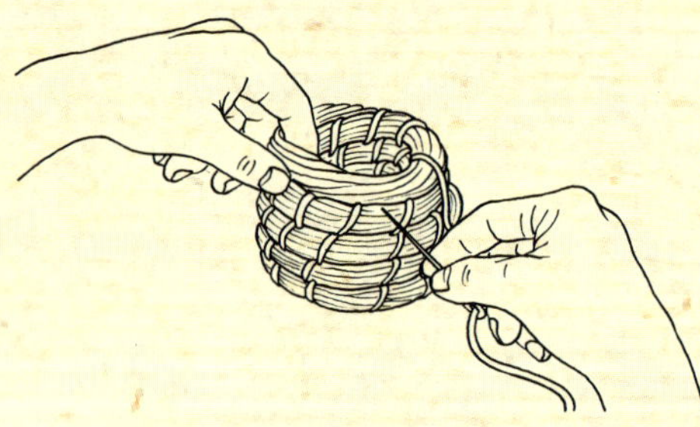

- How many coils will you stack?

### Step 3 Revise

**Did you remember to:**

- ✓ Use at least two different natural materials with some contrast in color?
- ✓ Keep the form simple and natural?
- ✓ Maintain a tight and consistent weave?

Adjust your work if necessary. In your sketchbook, make a note of your revisions and why you made them.

### Step 4 Add Finishing Touches

- Use a smaller needle and thread to sew seeds or dried leaves and twigs.
- Make a lid or handle for your basket.

### Step 5 Share and Reflect

- Arrange a display of the baskets. Create labels with titles based on the materials used or the natural form the basket resembles.
- Discuss similarities and differences with your classmates.
- Consider how the elements and principles of design are reflected in the construction of the baskets.

## Art Criticism

**Describe** What materials did the artist use to make this basket?

**Analyze** How do you think the form was created?

**Interpret** What might be the function of this kind of basket?

**Evaluate** What did the artist do especially well?

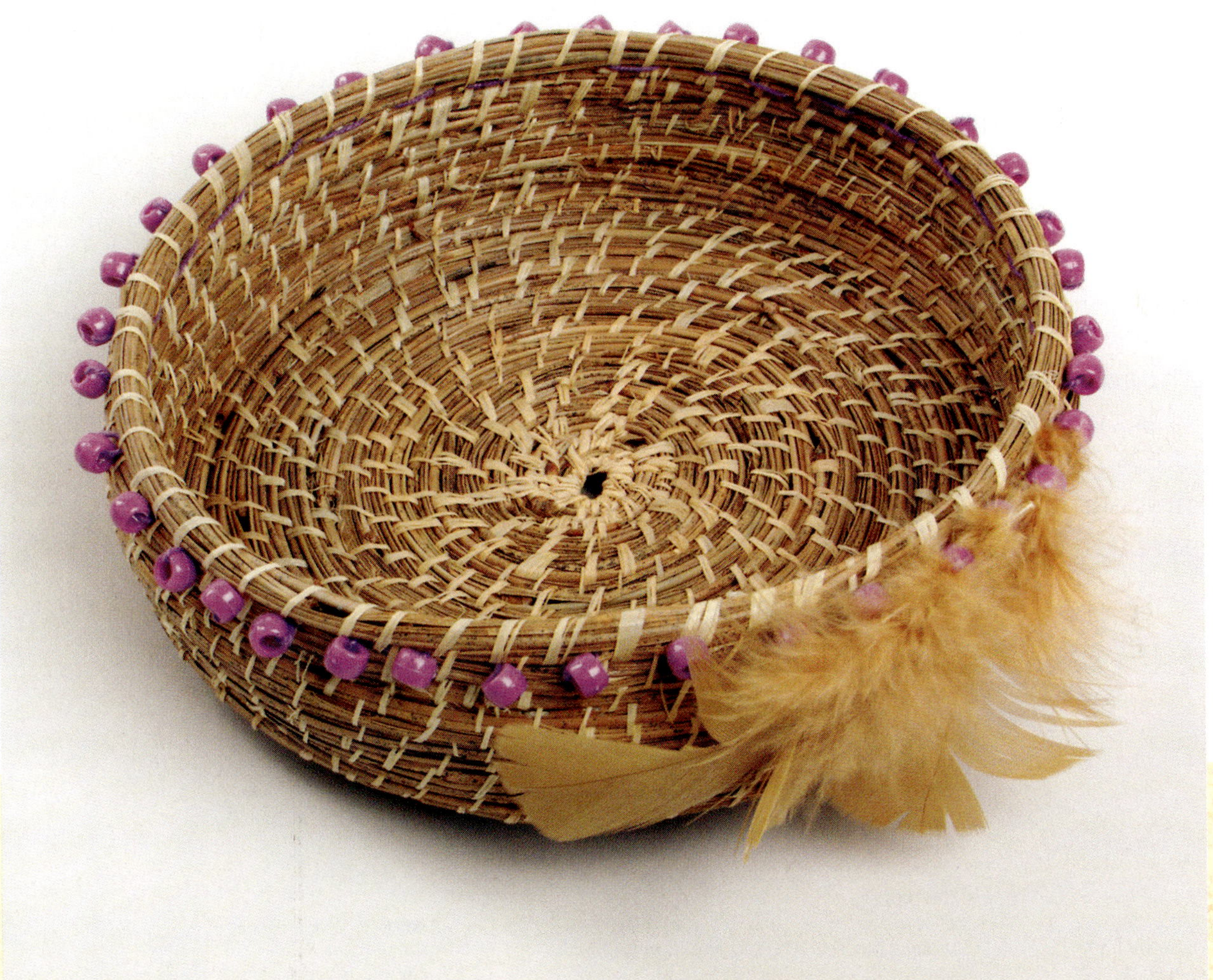

Fig. 5–15 Student artwork

# American Art: 1860–1900

Between 1860 and 1900, the nations of North America experienced times of peace and turmoil. In 1867, Canada became an independent nation. Mexico's politics were stable and its economy was growing. The United States, however, was fighting the Civil War from 1861 to 1865. Following the Civil War, cities grew rapidly as the age of industrialism began.

**The Appeal of Nature** A great demand for paintings of the natural environment arose during the late 1800s. People wanted to see the beauty of the North American wilderness they had heard about. In the years after the Civil War, the United States had a need to find new national symbols. People's interest in nature became something all communities could share. The first national parks in the United States were created at this time.

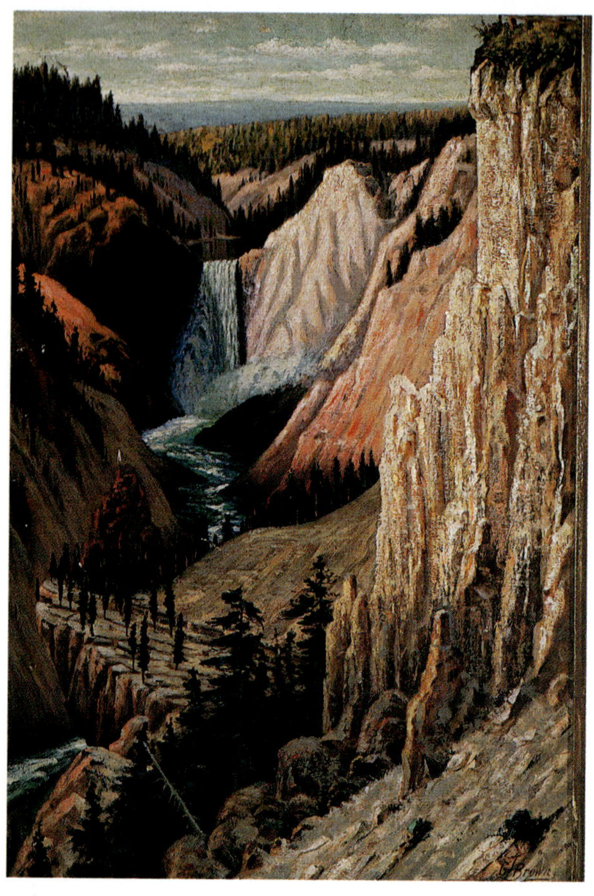

Fig. 5–16 **Brown was one of the first African-American artists to paint mountain scenes in California. Why would Americans during the late 1800s find this image exciting?**

Grafton Tyler Brown, *Grand Canyon of the Yellowstone from Hayden Point*, 1891. Oil on canvas, 24" x 16" (61 x 40.6 cm). Oakland Museum of California Founders Fund.

**1800s**

**1891** Brown, *Grand Canyon of the Yellowstone from Hayden Point*

**1892** John Muir founds the Sierra Club, an organization that protects the environment.

**1893** Katharine Lee Bates writes the words to "America the Beautiful."

**1895** Dewing, *Garden in May*

**1900s**

**ca. 1900** Tiffany, *Dragonfly Lamp*

**1906** Devils Tower in Wyoming becomes the first National Monument in the U.S.

**1908** Tiffany, *View of Oyster Bay*

**1914–15** Tiffany, *Necklace with grape and vine motifs*

**1915** Sullivan, *J.D. Van Allen Building*

**1916** The National Park Service is created to preserve historical and natural landmarks.

In response to the people's desire to see the wilderness, artists journeyed into unexplored regions of the United States. They took photographs and made sketches of the plants and features of the land. Back in their studios, they painted landscapes from these photographs and sketches. Landscape paintings, such as the one shown in **Fig. 5–16** by Grafton Brown, allowed communities to see the natural beauty of their nation.

**Natural Impressions** Impressionist artists painted the seasonal changes and weather of the areas where they lived. Impressionists worked outside and painted directly from nature. They used rapid brushstrokes to capture an impression of light and color. They painted what the eye sees at one particular moment. The American Impressionist artists considered this approach a way to explore color in art.

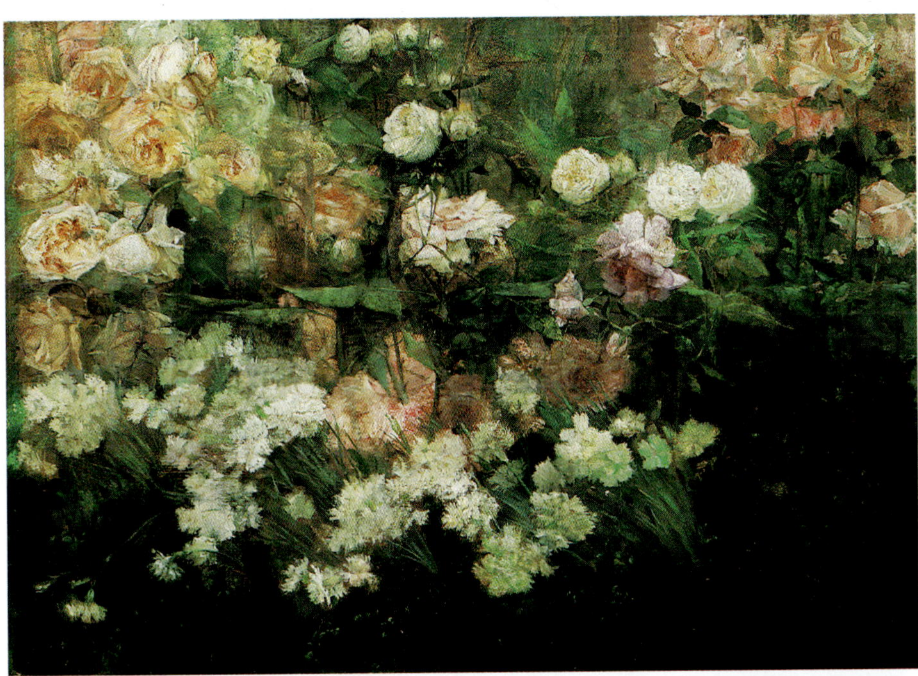

Fig. 5–17 **Dewing was an important flower specialist of this period. Where do you see brushstrokes that capture an impression of light and color?**

Maria Oakey Dewing, *Garden in May*, 1895. Oil on canvas. 23 ⅝" x 32 ½" (60.1 x 82.5 cm). National Museum of American Art, Smithsonian Institution, Washington, DC/Art Resource, NY.

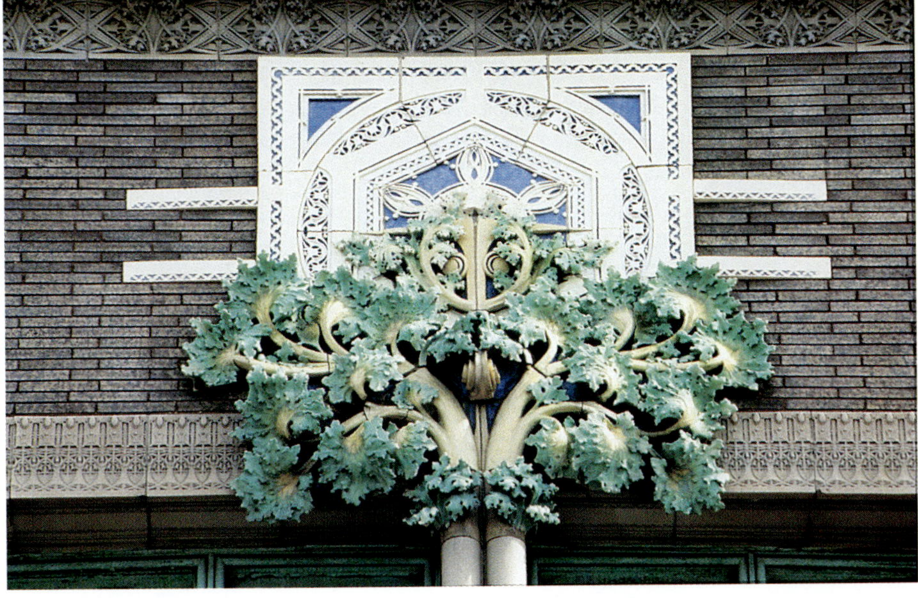

Fig. 5–18 **Some architecture from this period included a nature theme. Why do you think architects would choose to incorporate nature into their designs?**

Louis Sullivan, *J. D. Van Allen Building*, 1915. Detail of terra cotta leaf bursts on the 4th story attic. @ artonfile.com.

**Design Inspired by Nature** Painters, sculptors, and architects were not the only artists who were inspired by nature. Artists such as Louis Comfort Tiffany, who designed decorative items, also turned to nature for ideas. Patterns created from plant and animal forms, flames, smoke, waves, and other natural elements can be seen in jewelry, stained-glass windows, and home furnishings. Tiffany is known as the American pioneer of the Art Nouveau movement (ca. 1890–1918). Art Nouveau is a French term that means "new art." It is an art movement that explores the flowing lines, curves, and shapes of nature.

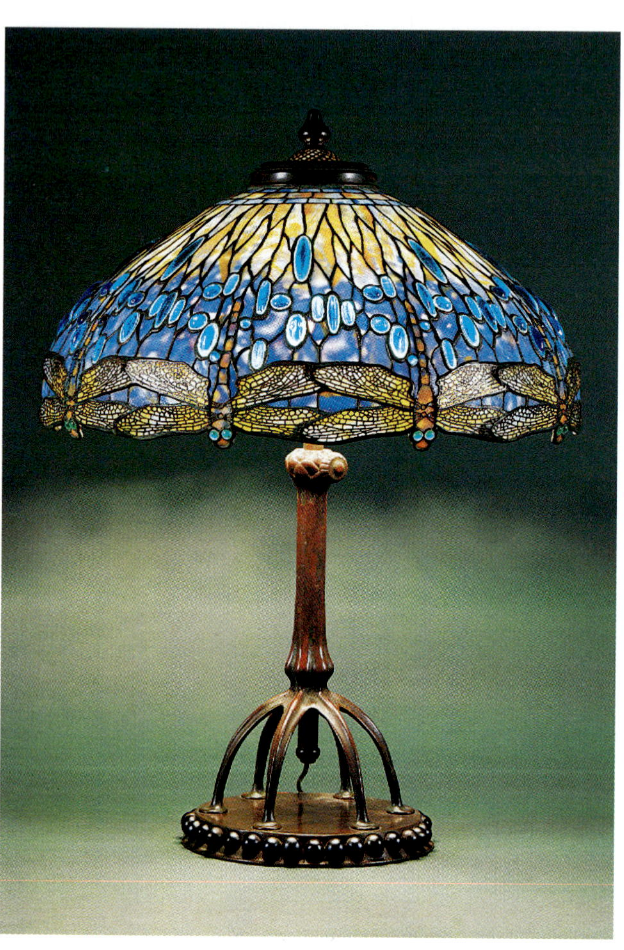

Fig. 5–19 **Notice how Tiffany created a pattern of dragonflies in this stained-glass lampshade. What other elements from nature do you see on the lamp?**

Louis Comfort Tiffany, *Dragonfly Lamp*, ca. 1900. Bronze base with color favrile glass, 28" x 22" (71.2 x 55.9 cm). Collection of the New York Historical Society (N84.113).

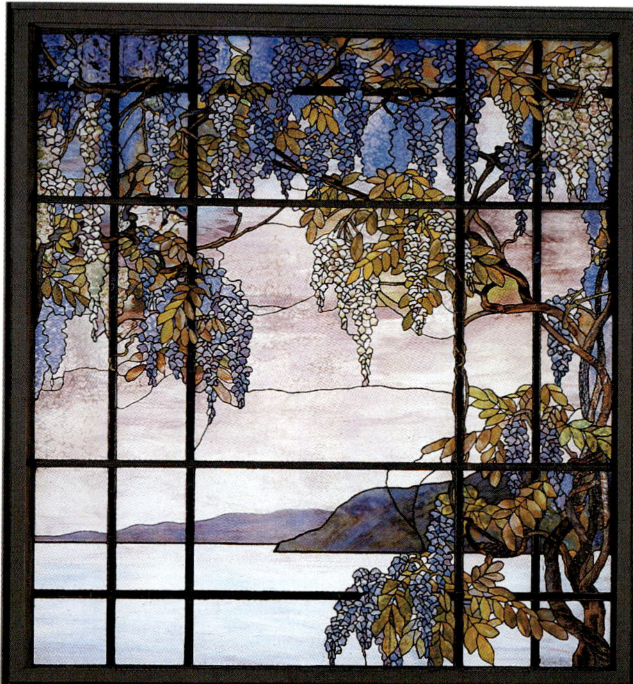

Fig. 5–20 **This stained-glass window is from Tiffany's home. Why might people recognize this window as an example of the Art Nouveau style?**

Louis Comfort Tiffany, *View of Oyster Bay*, Window from the William C. Skinner House, New York City, ca. 1908. Leaded favrile glass, 72 ¾" x 66 ½" (184.8 x 168.9 cm). The Metropolitan Museum of Art, Lent by the Charles Hosmer Morse Museum of American Art, Winter Park, Florida, in memory of Charles Hosmer Morse. (L.1978.19) Photograph ©1993 The Metropolitan Museum of Art.

Studio Time

## A Close-Up View

Create a close-up of a flower you found in nature using mixed media.

- Begin with a sketch. Let one or more main shapes fill your paper.
- Focus on the shapes, lines, and subtle changes in color, light, and shadow that you see.
- Choose media that will help you capture the beauty of the flower. Try creating a resist by combining crayon or oil pastel with watercolor.

Reflect on the effects of the techniques you used.

Fig. 5–21 Student artwork

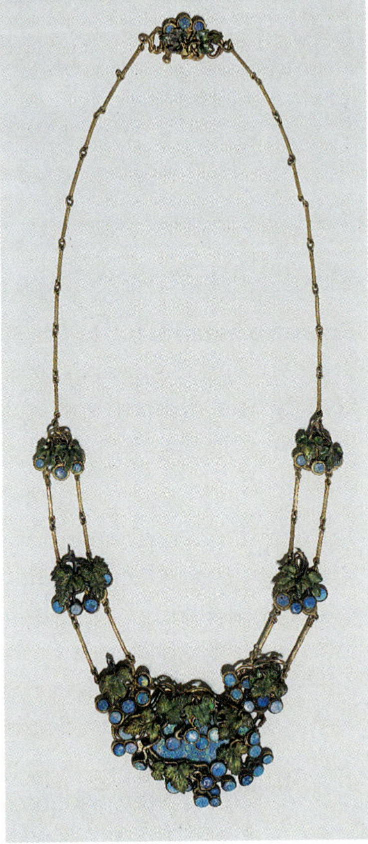

Fig. 5–22 **Tiffany created a pattern of grapes and vines in the design of this necklace. How has he simplified the forms of the grapes?**

Louis Comfort Tiffany, *Necklace with grape and vine motifs*, 1914–15. Opals, gold and enamel, length (open) 18" (45.7 cm). The Metropolitan Museum of Art, Gift of Sarah E. Hanley, 1946 (46.168.1) Photograph ©1988 The Metropolitan Museum of Art.

### Meet Louis Comfort Tiffany

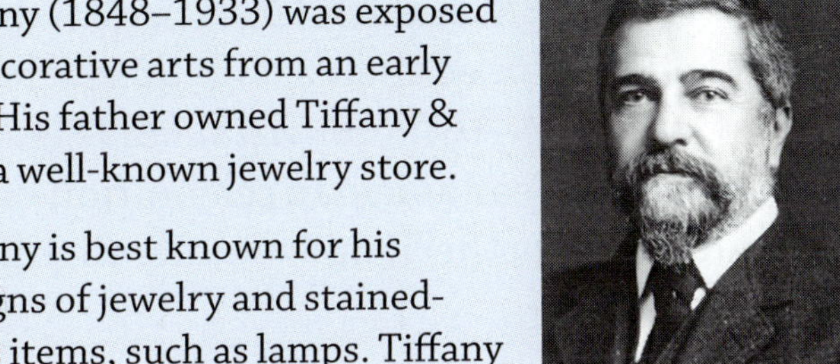

Photo by Pach, N.Y.

Born in New York City, Louis Tiffany (1848–1933) was exposed to decorative arts from an early age. His father owned Tiffany & Co., a well-known jewelry store.

Tiffany is best known for his designs of jewelry and stained-glass items, such as lamps. Tiffany founded Tiffany Studios in the 1880s. He wanted every piece produced to reflect his unique sense of design.

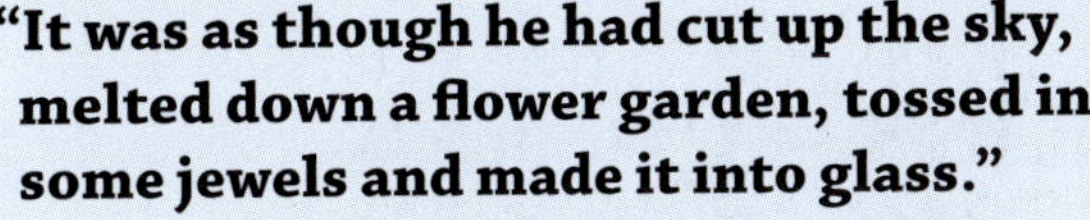

**"It was as though he had cut up the sky, melted down a flower garden, tossed in some jewels and made it into glass."**

— Hugh McKean, author of *The Lost Treasures of Louis Comfort Tiffany*.

### Check Your Understanding

1. Why was nature such an important theme in artworks of the late 1800s?
2. Compare and contrast the Impressionist and Art Nouveau styles.
3. Choose an artwork from this lesson and describe what it conveys about nature.

# Scandinavian Art

**Nature in Isolation** If you look at a map, you can see how the countries on the Scandinavian peninsula are somewhat isolated. The people who live there understand how nature can affect their communities. Scandinavian winters are long and dark, while in midsummer the sun does not set. As a result, annual festivals and traditions follow the cycles of nature. Scandinavian artists in the late 1800s focused their art on these cycles and traditions. *A Midsummerdance* **(Fig. 5–23)** shows a Scandinavian celebration of the unique northern midsummer night.

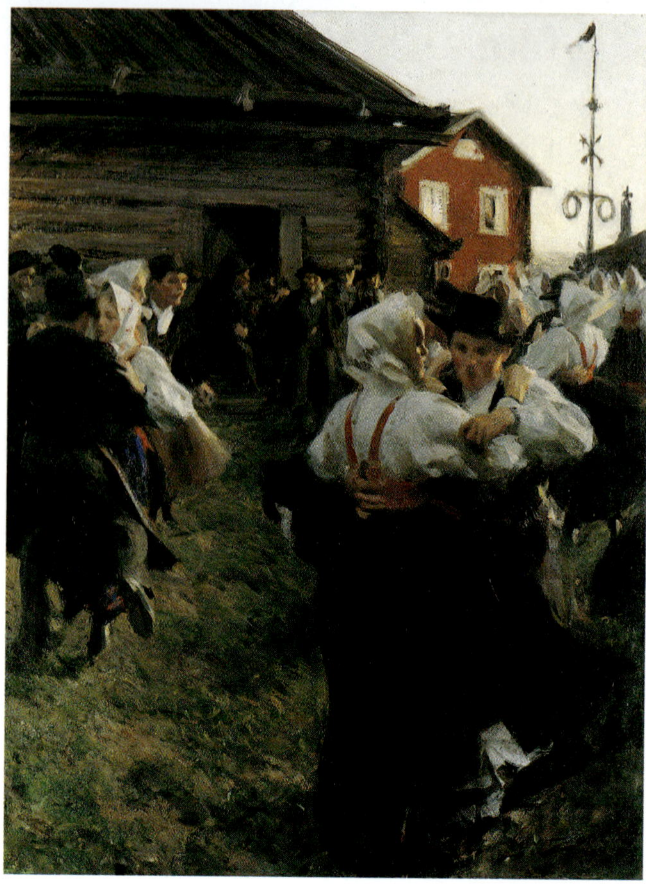

Fig. 5–23 **Notice the wispy, impressionistic quality of the brushstrokes. How would you describe the artist's use of light in this picture?**

Anders Zorn, *A Midsummerdance*, 1897. Oil on canvas, 55 ⅛" x 38 ⅝" (140 x 98 cm). Courtesy Nationalmuseum, Sweden.

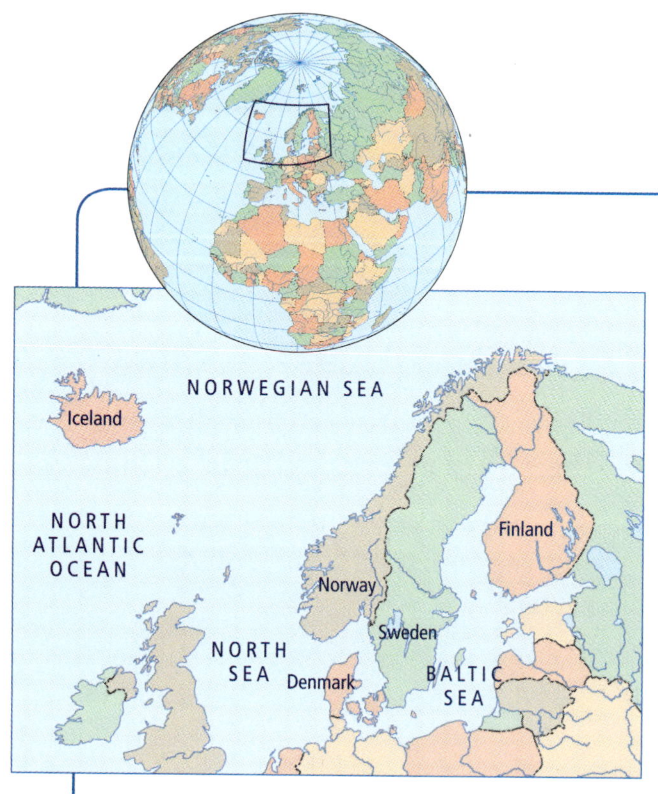


## Social Studies Connection

**Scandinavia** includes the countries of Norway, Sweden, and Denmark, although many experts also include Finland and Iceland in the list. Norway and Sweden make up the Scandinavian peninsula.

The Scandinavian countries share the seafaring Viking culture. Germany had some influence in the area during the Middle Ages. France influenced Scandinavia in the centuries that followed. However, there has always been a strong feeling of individualism in Scandinavia. "Every person's right" is an expression of freedom in Norway, Sweden, and Finland.

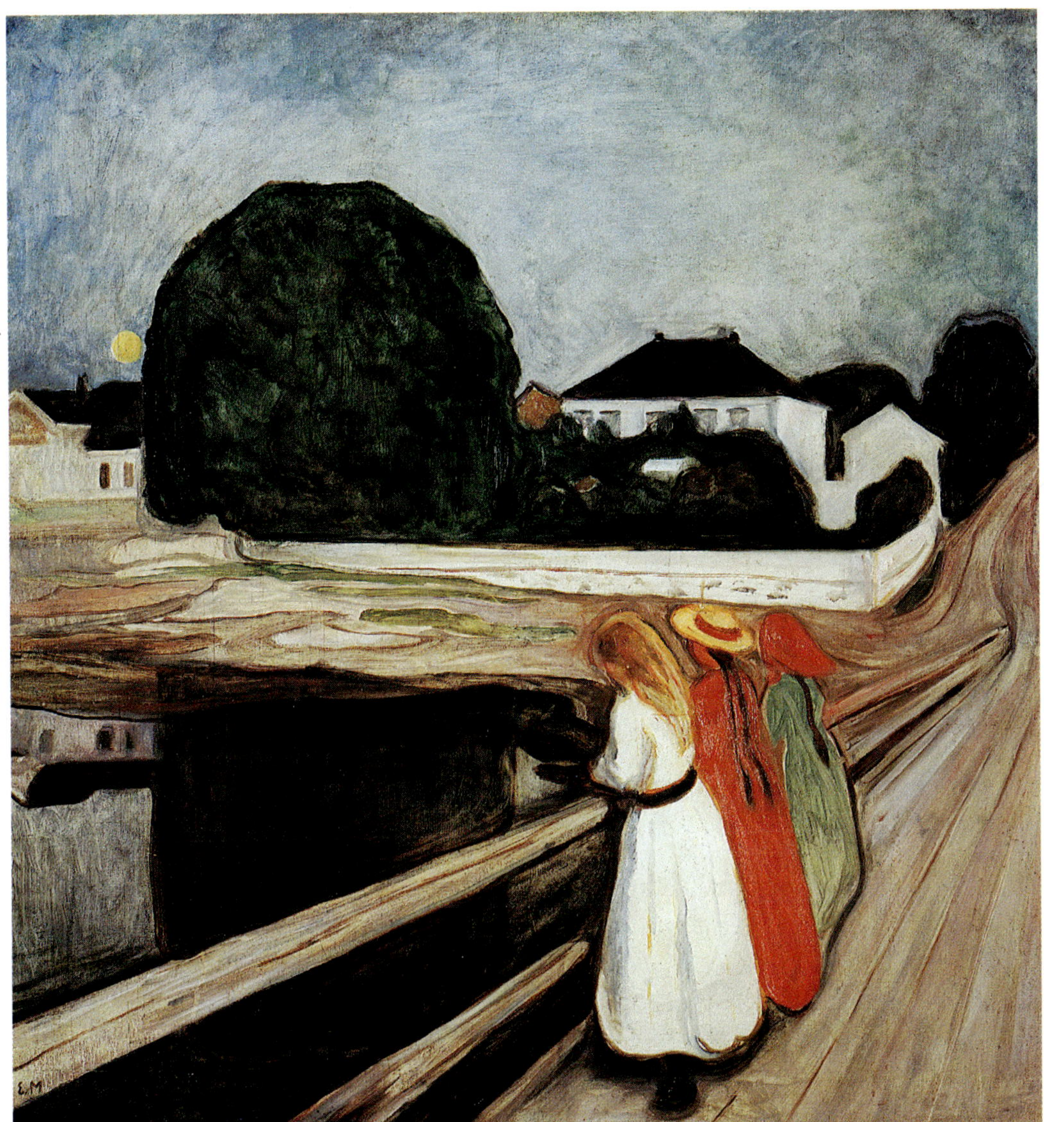

Fig. 5–24 **Munch's flowing brushstrokes add a dreamlike, fluid quality to this painting. How do his brushstrokes also suggest the closeness of the girls to their surroundings?**

Edvard Munch, *White Night*, 1904–07. Oil on canvas, 31 ½" x 27 ¼" (80 x 69 cm). Pushkin Museum of Fine Arts, Moscow, Russia. Scala/Art Resource, NY ©2000 The Munch Museum / The Munch-Ellingsen Group / Artist Rights Society (ARS), New York.

**French Influence** Many Scandinavian artists studied in Paris, where they discovered the expressive possibilities of their own country's light and landscape. French *plein-air* painting, which means painting outdoors, inspired Scandinavian artists to paint the beauty of their countryside. In their artwork, they captured the changing moods of nature. In *White Night* **(Fig. 5–24)**, Edvard Munch uses soft light to create a calm mood.

## Visual Culture

In this lesson you will learn about the importance of handcrafted items in Scandinavian cultures. You are also aware that most of the things we use and wear today are not handmade, but are mass-produced. Consider the pros and cons of handmade and mass-produced products. Think about the special qualities of design, personal meaning and significance, social status, and economical advantages associated with each way of producing useful objects.

**A Sense of Community** Scandinavian art and design reflect the Scandinavian sense of community. In the late 1800s, most people in Scandinavia lived in the countryside. Each villa, or house, within a community shared common design elements. Imagine a community in which all the houses are decorated in a similar way.

**A Scandinavian Style** In the late 1800s, the *Arts and Crafts Movement* influenced Scandinavian artists. This movement reacted against the industrialization of crafts design. The people involved were interested in the individuality of handmade items. Many were committed to preserving the Scandinavian design style known for its beauty and simplicity. There was a blending of old and new styles, and of painted and natural wood. Nature was the great source of ideas. Designs included *stylized*, or simplified, plant and flower motifs (Fig. 5–25), and clean, sharp lines. These ideals in Scandinavian design are still seen today.

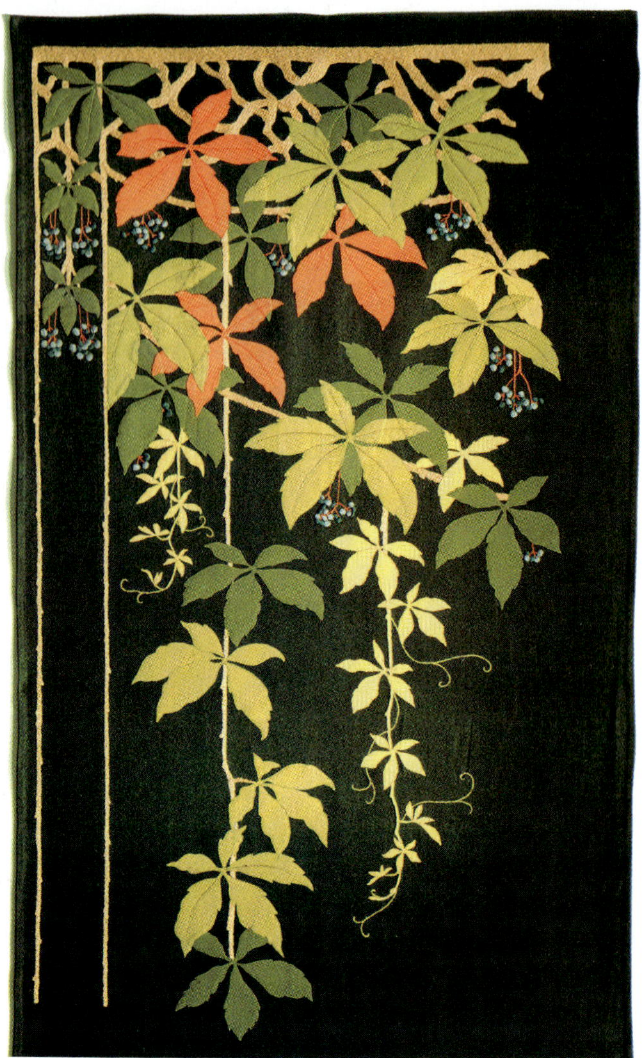

Fig. 5–25 **Why is this embroidered door curtain a good example of the Scandinavian design style?**

Gunnar Gunnarson Vennerberg, *Embroidered Door Curtain*, 1899. Made by The Association of Friends of Textile Art (Handarbetets Vanner). Photography Nordiska Museum. Nordiska Museum, Stockholm, Sweden.

## Check Your Understanding

1. Name three characteristics that are common to Scandinavian design style.
2. Compare and contrast Fig. 5–23 and Fig. 5–24. How is nature portrayed in each painting?
3. Why do you think it was important to Scandinavian communities that their villas share common design elements?

## Meet Carl Larsson

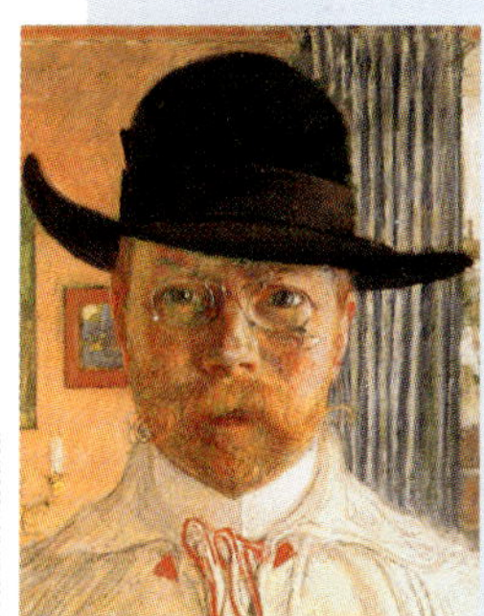



Carl Larsson was born in Stockholm, Sweden to poor parents. When he was 13, a teacher encouraged him to apply to the Royal Swedish Academy of Arts. He was accepted. After graduation, he worked as an illustrator. When he began to paint works that showed life in the house and garden he shared with his wife and eight children, he gained more and more notice. Some called the house itself a work of art, and said that it greatly influenced Swedish home furnishing.

**"I wanted the house my way, or else I would not feel at home in it, and then my work would suffer."**

— Carl Larsson (1853–1919)

## Studio Time

### Nature Monoprint

Make a monoprint using natural materials.

- Collect leaves, feathers, flower petals, and other flat natural objects.
- Evenly paint or ink a smooth plastic or glass surface. Lay your objects on the ink or paint. Place a sheet of paper on top.
- Rub evenly, but gently, over the entire paper. When you remove the paper, the shapes of your objects will be white.
- Paint or ink another surface with a different color. Reposition your objects on it, and place the same sheet of paper on top again. Rub.

Reflect on the quality of your impressions.

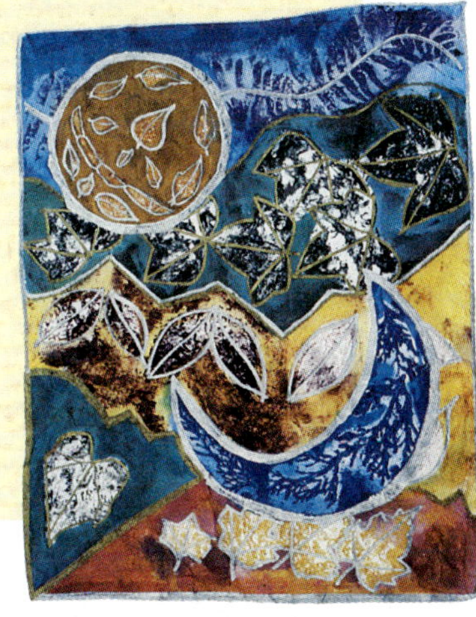

Fig. 5–27 Student artwork

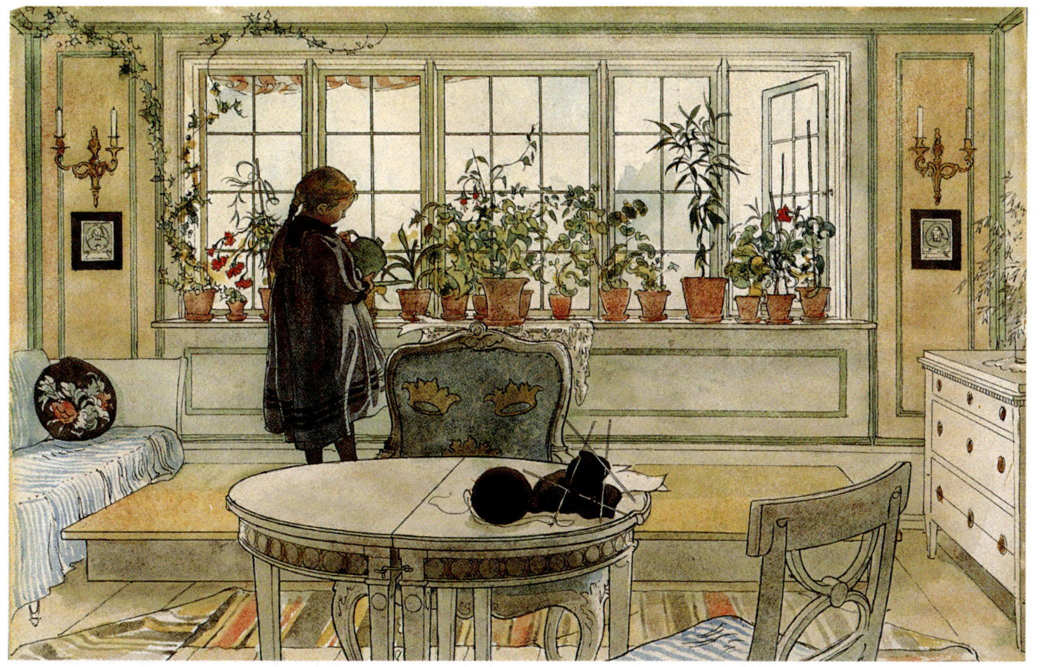

Fig. 5–26 **Notice the potted plants, open window, and plant motif. Why might a Scandinavian artist be attracted to nature and growing things as subjects for art?**

Carl Larsson, *Blomsterfonstret (Flowers on the Windowsill)*, 1894. Watercolor, ( x ) 32 x 43 cm. Nationalmuseum, Stockholm.

# Clay Relief Sculpture

## Studio Background

What do you think of when you see clay? Did you know that it is a fine-grained material that comes from the earth? When some people see clay, they think of mud. But some artists look at clay and imagine making a beautiful pot or vase with it. They know that moistened clay can keep its form when it's shaped by hand. And they know that firing clay can change it to a rocklike material. Firing means to bake at a high temperature.

Some artists use clay to create relief sculpture—sculpture with parts that are raised from a background. **In this studio exploration, you will create a relief sculpture that shows a natural environment.** What natural environment is in your area? A forest, an ocean, or a prairie? A mountain or a desert? A river, a flat plain, gentle hills? How can you show a natural environment in a relief sculpture?

### You Will Need

- sketch paper
- pencil and eraser
- clay
- two flat sticks
- rolling pin
- plastic knife
- dowel
- clay modeling tools
- sheet of plastic

## Step 1 Plan and Practice

- Decide which natural environment you want to show.
- Think about what kinds of plants and animals live there.
- Draw a sketch of what your relief sculpture will include.

**Things to Remember:**

✓ Choose one or two important elements to be the focus of your sculpture.

✓ Create a foreground, middle ground, and background.

✓ Use a variety of textures.

## Inspiration from Our World

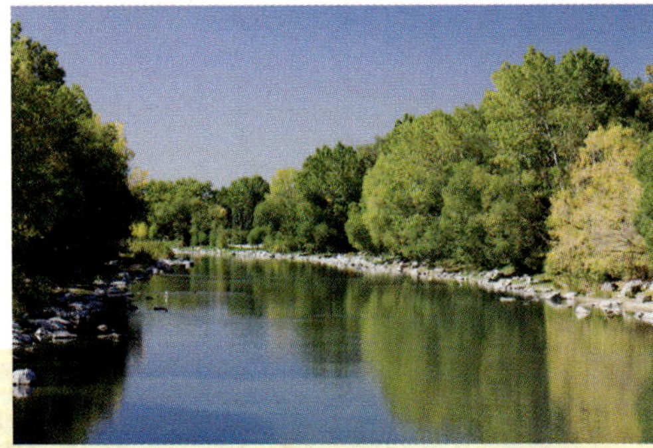

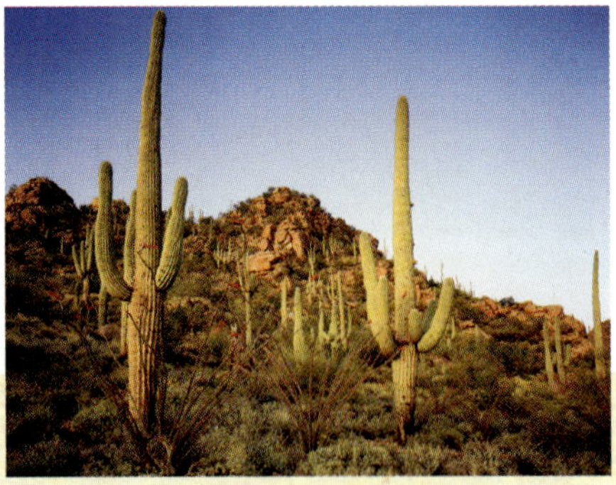

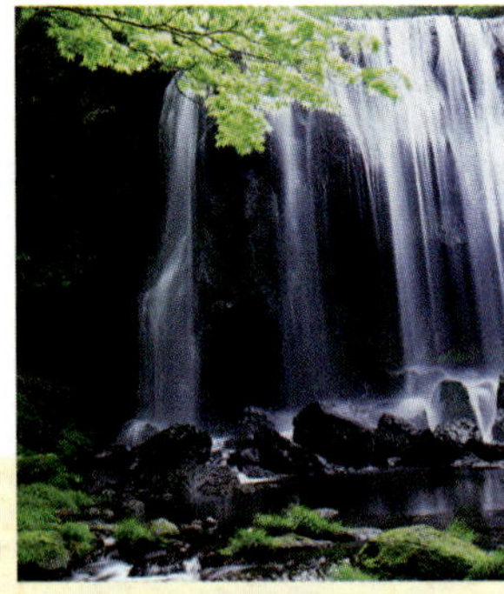

## Inspiration from Art

You may have seen fired clay tiles on floors or countertops. Ceramic tiles have been used as flooring for centuries. During the Arts and Crafts Movement of the late 1800s, decorative tiles became popular. These tiles have scenes, often from nature, impressed into their surfaces. They were used on floors and fireplaces, and served as decorative elements in kitchens and bathrooms.

Artists create art tiles by pressing layers of clay into a mold. The mold usually has a relief design in the bottom that forms an impression in the clay. After the layer of clay dries, it is removed from the mold. Colored slip is poured into the impression made by the mold. Slip is a runny mixture of clay and water. The slip fills the impression, creating a colored design. After the tile is dried slowly and fired, it can be used.

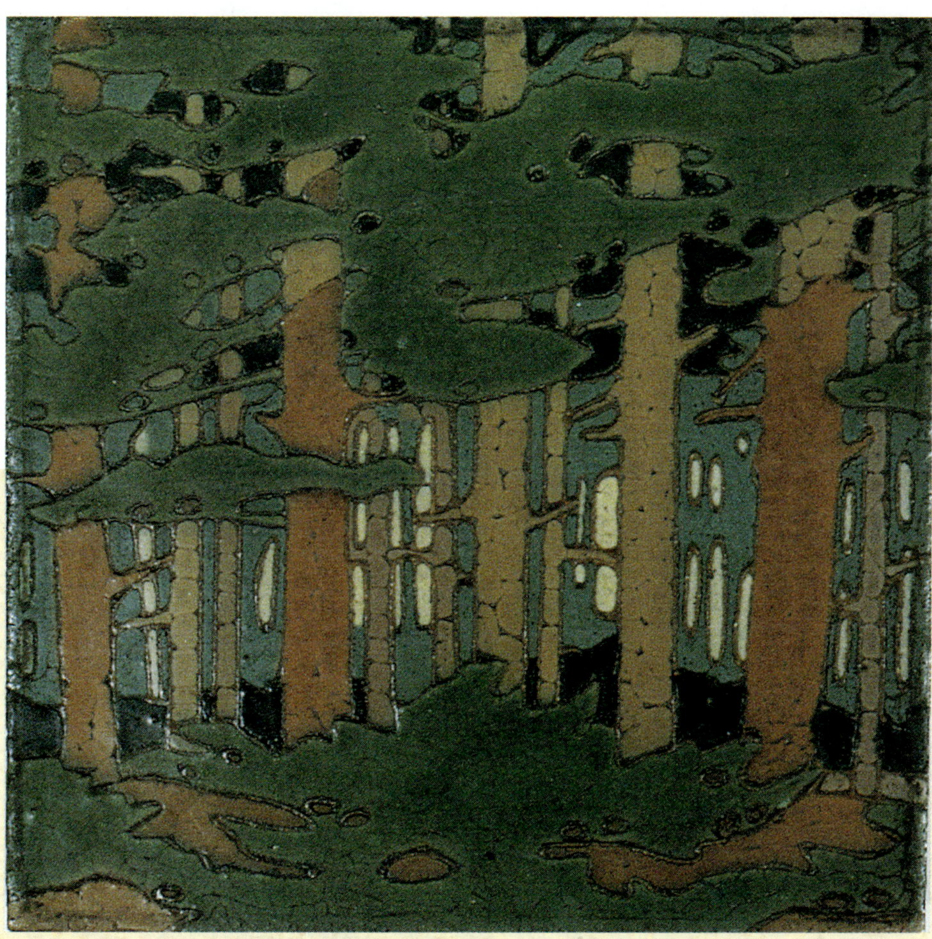

Fig. 5–28 **This tile comes from a series of tiles that show woodland scenes. How would you describe the lines and shapes in this scene?**

Grueby Faience Co., *Woodland Scene*, ca. 1895. Tile, 13" (33 cm). Courtesy of National Museum of American History, Smithsonian Institution, Washington, DC.

### Step 2 **Begin to Create**

- Place a ball of clay between two flat sticks. Roll out the clay with a rolling pin.
- Cut the slab of clay into the shape that will best represent your environment. Will you choose a rectangle, an oval, or another shape?
- **With a pencil, lightly draw the important features of your environment into the clay.**

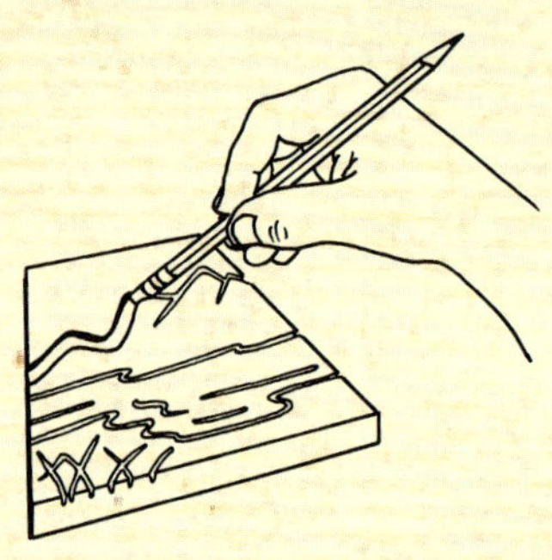

- Using the pencil eraser or dowel, carve along the guidelines to create a foreground, middle ground, and background. Foreground areas should be raised higher from the base than the middle ground and background areas.
- **Add textures to your sculpture.** Press objects into the clay to make patterns. Draw textures into the clay with a pencil or dowel.

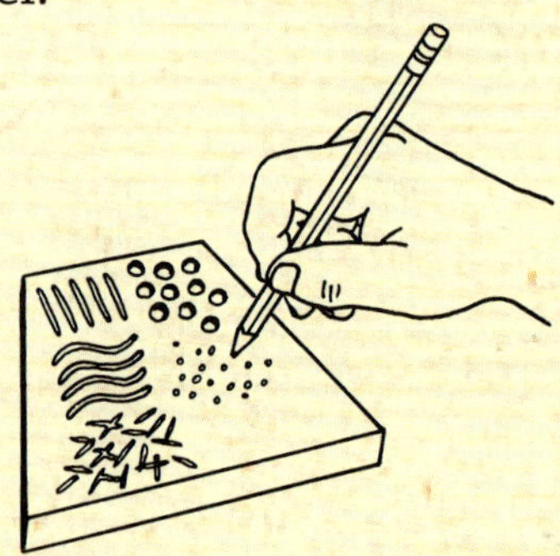

- **Shape the clay with your fingers. Add small shapes of clay onto the surface.** How will these techniques help you show the important features of your environment?

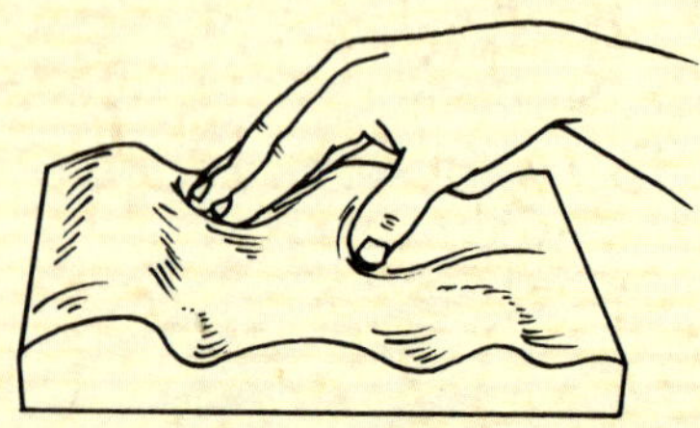

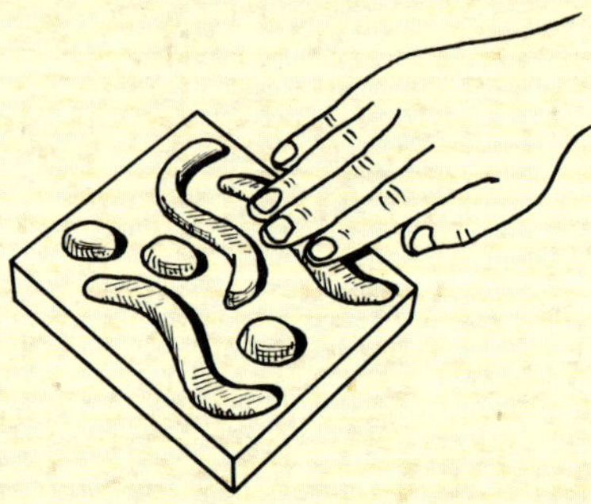

- When your sculpture is finished, cover it with plastic and allow it to dry slowly.

### Step 3 **Revise**

**Did you remember to:**

✓ Choose one or two important elements to be the focus of your sculpture?

✓ Create a foreground, middle ground, and background?

✓ Use a variety of textures?

Adjust your work if necessary. In your sketchbook, make a note of your revisions and why you made them.

### Step 4 **Add Finishing Touches**

- If available, use glaze to add color to your relief sculpture.
- Carve your name or initials into your sculpture.

### Step 5 **Share and Reflect**

- Share your relief sculpture with one or two classmates.
- Describe the environment and the features you chose to show.
- How did you come up with the idea for your relief sculpture?
- How did the clay techniques you used help to create the different features of the environment you chose?

## Art Criticism

**Describe** What natural environments did the artists show in these tiles?

**Analyze** How are the composition of these tiles similar and different?

**Interpret** What different ideas about nature do these tiles suggest to you?

**Evaluate** What makes each tile special and unique?

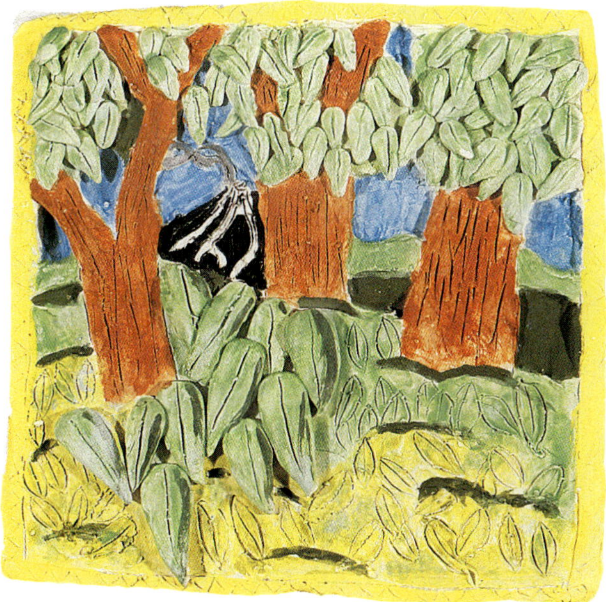

Fig. 5–29 Student artwork

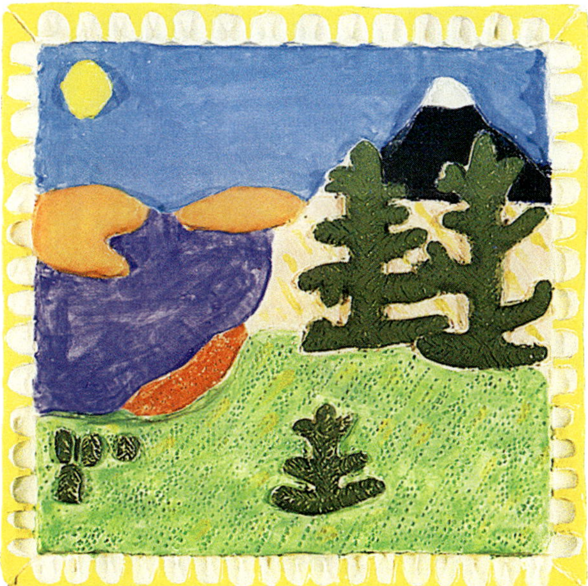

Fig. 5–30 Student artwork

## Social Studies

**Some ceremonies are connected to nature.** The tea ceremony was developed under the influence of Zen Buddhism. It symbolizes simplicity and the basic Zen principles of harmony, respect, purity, and tranquility.

The ceremony varies with the seasons. Suitable tea bowls, types of tea, flowers, and scrolls are chosen for each time of year. Participants follow rules that communicate the highest ideals of the tea ceremony. How could you find out about similar ceremonies in other cultures?

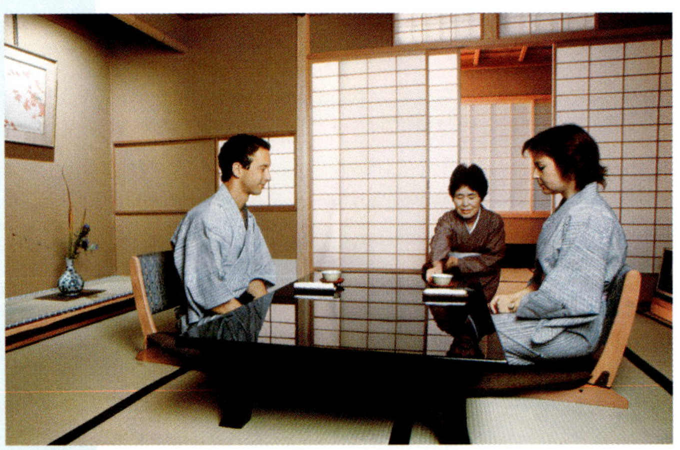

Fig. 5–31 **The Japanese word for tea is *cha* and the tea ceremony is called *Chaji*. Along with tea, guests are usually served a small meal.**

*Tea Room in a Japanese Inn*, 1989. ©Bob Krist/CORBIS.

## Music

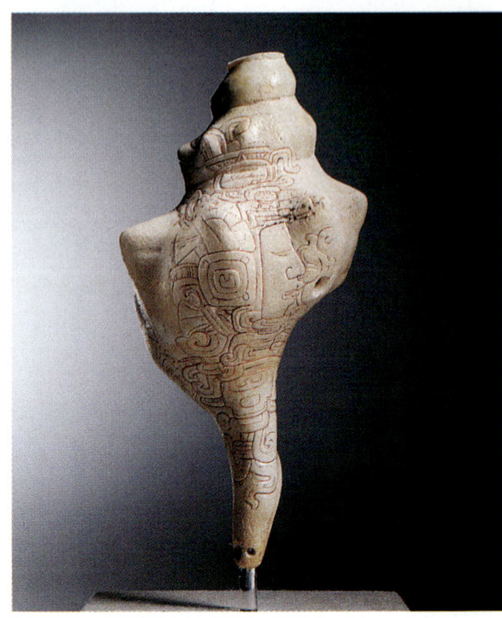

Fig. 5–32 **This Mesoamerican artist combined art, music, and nature by transforming a shell into a trumpet. Why do you think people have used natural objects as musical instruments?**

Pre-Columbian, Maya (Guatemala), *Incised Conch Shell*, 250–400 CE. Shell with cinnabar tracings, height: 11 9/16" (28.6 cm). Courtesy Kimbell Art Museum, Fort Worth, Texas.

**Musicians, like artists, have often been inspired by nature.** For example, Navajo musician R. Carlos Nakai plays a Native American flute made from natural materials. With this flute, he produces music that represents the connection that the Navajo feel with nature.

Nature plays an important role in the compositions of contemporary musician Paul Winter. He performed and recorded his album *Canyon* in the Grand Canyon. The natural sounds and the echoes of that huge outdoor space have made Winter's music appeal to many.

Careers **Ceramicist**

**What kind of artist would be most likely to use natural materials?** Since prehistoric times, ceramists (also called potters or clayworkers) have produced objects from clay. At first, pottery was made for practical purposes, such as to cook food or to use in ceremonies.

Today's ceramists still produce functional items, but they also create more artistic pieces. To work with clays and glazes, potters need some knowledge of chemistry. Ceramists enjoy the hands-on experience of working with the physical and natural qualities of clay.

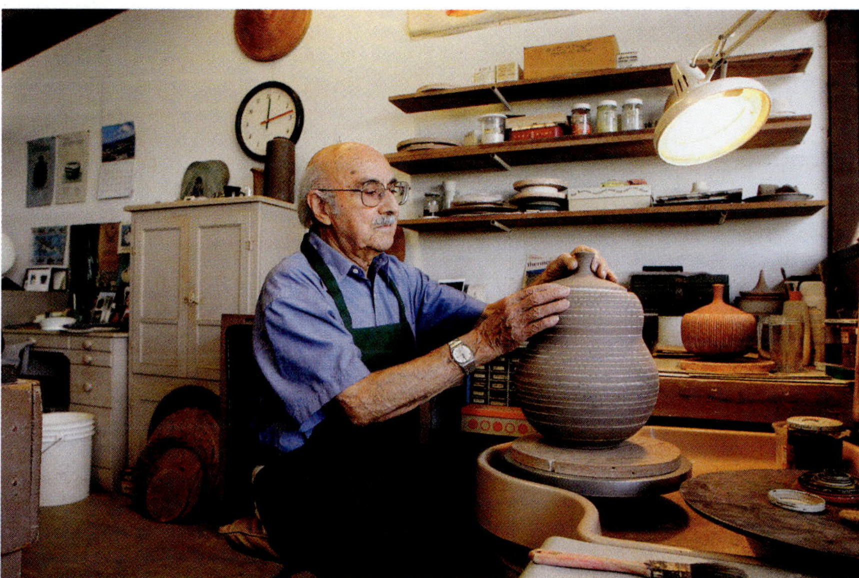

Fig. 5–33 Monica Almeida/The New York Times/Redux.

## Daily Life

**Are you always in a hurry, or do you take the time to notice what happens around you in the natural world?** It's easy to forget to slow down and really pay attention to the world around you. How can you develop a greater artistic awareness of the world's natural beauty? How can you learn to look more closely and appreciate the simplicity of a flower, the curve of a seashell, or a reflection in a puddle?

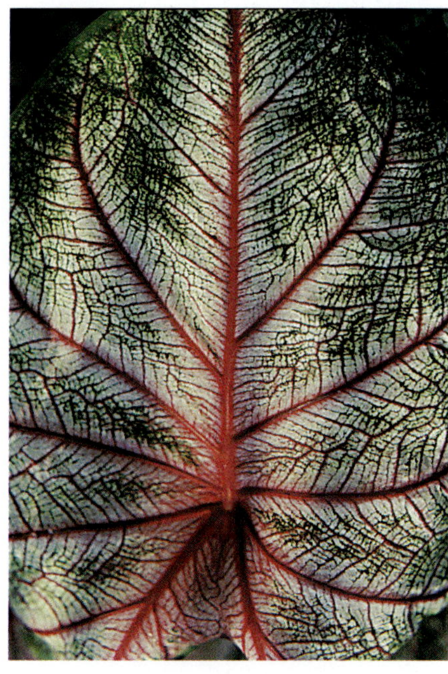

Fig. 5–34 **Nature is full of interesting shapes, colors, and designs. What color scheme does this leaf have? How is it like a work of art?**

Photo ©Karen Durlach.

## Vocabulary Review

Match each art term below with its definition.

**Art Nouveau**

**scientific record**

**crafts**

**Impressionists**

**relief sculpture**

1. a sculpture with parts that are raised from a background
2. an art movement that explores the flowing lines, curves, and shapes of nature
3. artists who worked outside and used rapid brushstrokes to capture a quick glimpse of light and color
4. accurate, detailed works used to document plants and animals in a community
5. decorative or useful works of art that are skillfully made by hand

## For Your Portfolio

Choose one of your artworks based on the theme of nature. Exchange your artwork with a peer and discuss each other's work. Make connections between what you see and the artwork's message about nature. Comment on strengths and offer suggestions for improvement.

## Write About Art

The Citizens' Stamp Advisory Committee receives all suggestions for stamp designs and reviews them on behalf of the United States Postal Service. Select an image from nature that you propose for a stamp design, and write a letter to the committee explaining your choice. Remember that United States' stamps must feature American subjects.

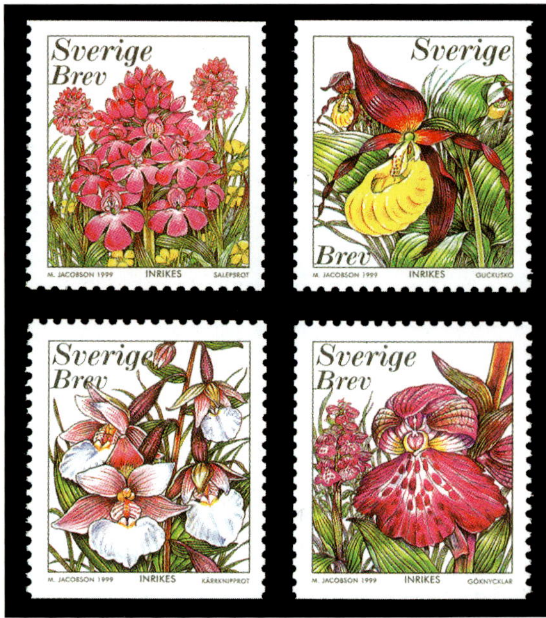


Fig. 5–35 **Artists and designers in Sweden often look to nature for subject matter. Here we see one designer's representation of flowers found in Sweden. In what other ways do these stamps look like they belong together in a set?**

Margareta Jacobson, *Swedish Orchids Stamps*, May 20, 1999. ©Sweden Post Stamps.

## Art Criticism

**Describe** What do you see in this painting?

**Analyze** How does the artist create movement in this painting?

**Interpret** Do you think the artist painted this picture outdoors or in her studio? What evidence supports your answer?

**Evaluate** Morisot aimed to capture the feeling of a forest rather than an exact likeness of one. Explain whether or not you think she was successful.

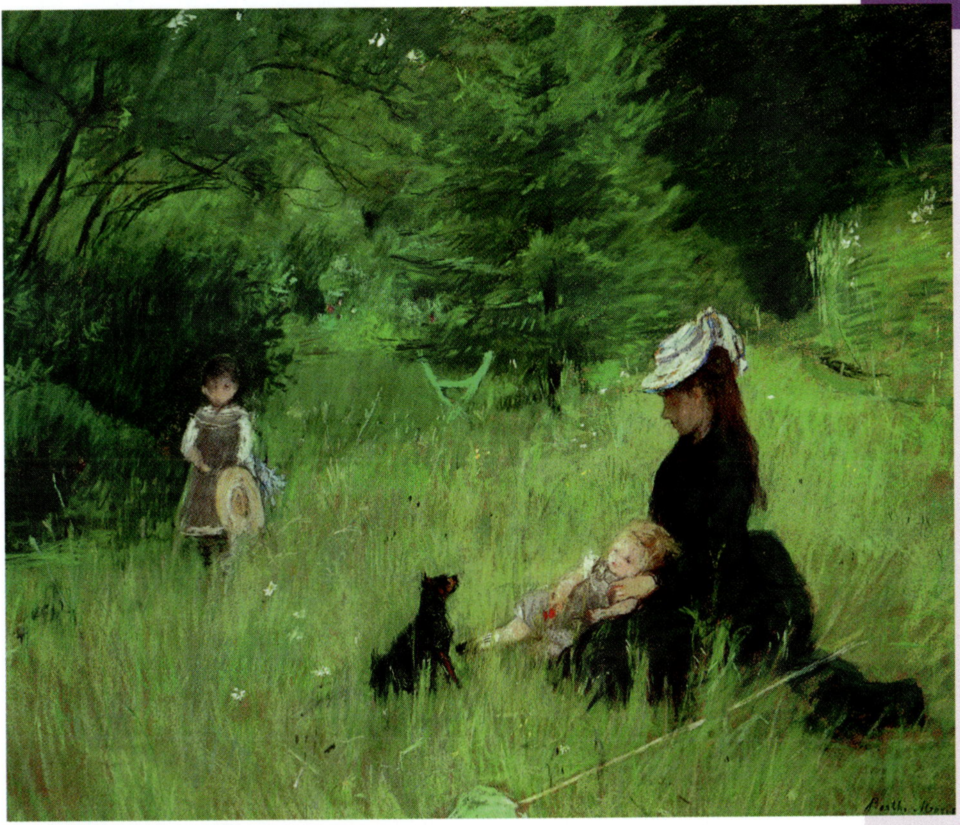

Fig. 5–36 Berthe Morisot, *In a Park,* 1876. Canvas. Musée du Petit Palais, Paris, France. Photo: Erich Lessing/Art Resource, NY.

## Meet the Artist

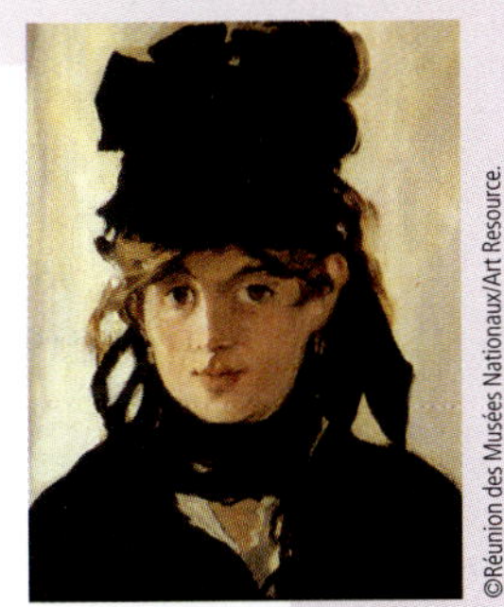



**Berthe Morisot** (1841–1895) was born in Bourges, France. Like most girls from well-to-do families at that time, Morisot and her sister studied painting from an early age. After moving to Paris, Morisot became a member of the Impressionists, a group of painters known for using loose brushstrokes to capture the essence of a scene. The Impressionists often painted outdoors and had a particular interest in the effects of light.

## Aesthetic Thinking

Judging by decoration found on everyday objects and modern architecture, would you say that imitating nature is important today? If so, give examples. If not, what is valued and how do you know?

## For Your Sketchbook

Select one thing from nature and draw it in many different ways, from different points of view. Use different color combinations and explore different media and technical effects.

Unit 6

# Art and Change

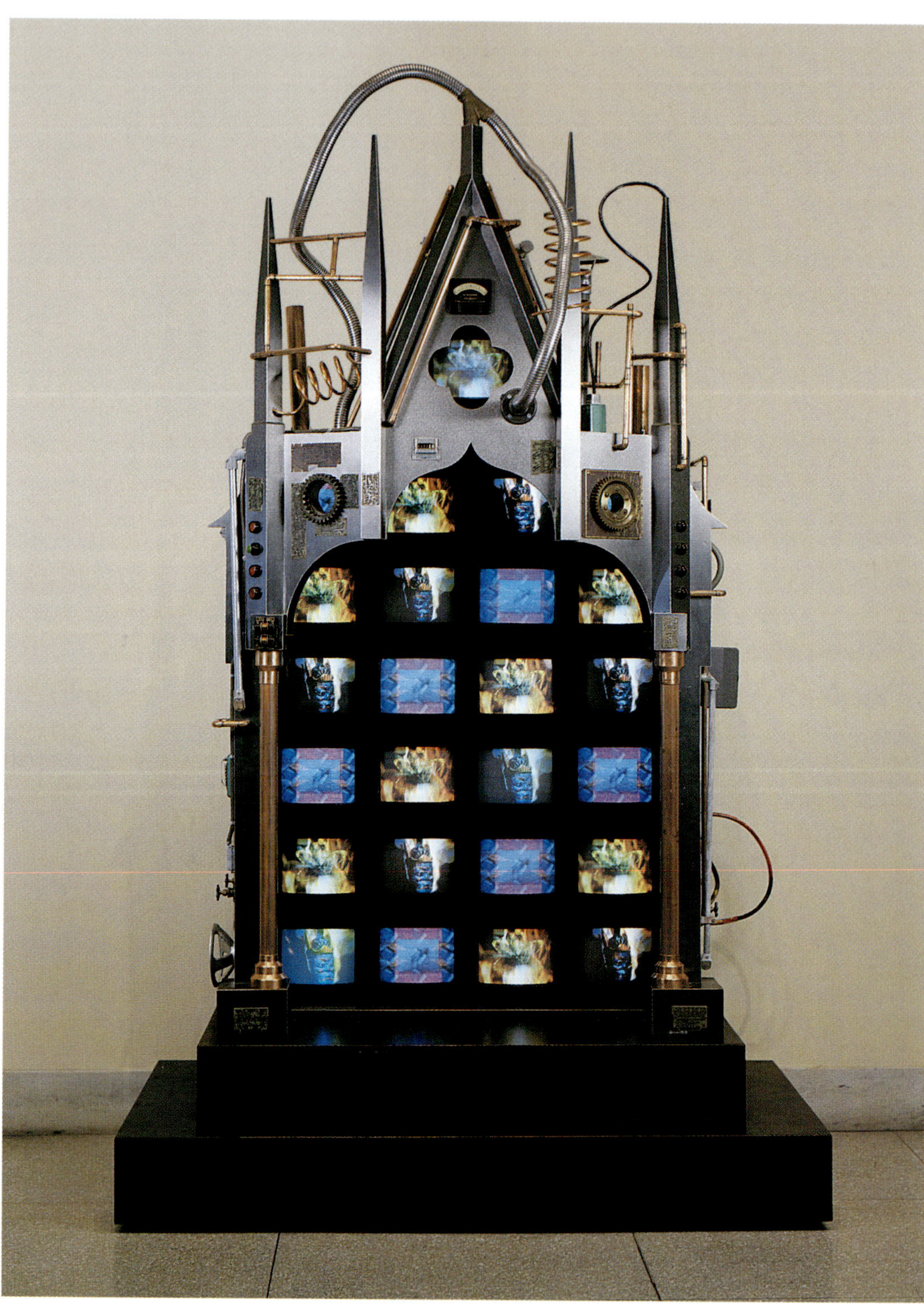

Fig. 6–1 **What message does this artwork send about television? What do you think it says about technology? Why do you think so?**

Nam June Paik, *Technology*, 1991. 25 video monitors, 3 laser disc players with unique 3 discs in cabinet. National Museum of American Art, Smithsonian Institution, Washington, DC./ Art Resource, NY.

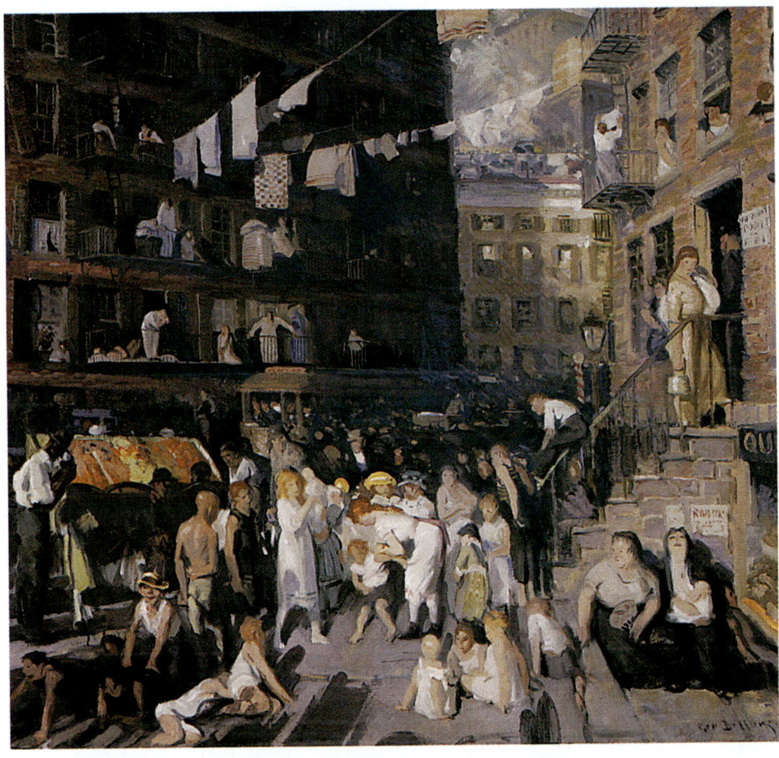

Fig. 6–2 **What does this painting say about city life during the early 1900s? How do you think city life has changed since that time?**

George Bellows, *Cliff Dwellers*, 1913. Oil on canvas, 40 3/16" x 42 1/16" (104.6 x 106.8 cm). Los Angeles County Museum of Art, Los Angeles County Fund. 

**As you've grown up, what kinds of changes have taken place that make your daily life easier or more enjoyable? Changes sometimes happen because of a new technology.** Technology can offer ways for people to meet their needs more quickly than they could before. New technology has also changed people's ability to communicate with each other. How did people communicate before cell phones and the Internet were invented?

As technology changes, so do the materials and tools used to create art. New technology and its influence on communities often inspires artists to create art that reflects these changes.

**In this unit, you will learn:**

- How artists observe changes in technology, ideas, and ways of life and reflect them in artworks.
- How to create artworks that express change using painting and sculpture media and techniques.
- How to look at artworks as records of and inspirations for change in communities.

# Art Reflects and Inspires

**Changes in Architecture** Throughout history, artists have used technology to create art and architecture. In ancient Rome, for instance, there were the inventions of the arch and dome. Centuries later, architects designed suspension bridges and factories. As cities grew, more people needed places to live and work. So, architects created high-rise buildings called *skyscrapers*. Skyscrapers provided space in a new and inventive way.

**Changes in Life** In the late 1800s and early 1900s, many factories were built in North American cities. People from around the world moved to the cities to find jobs. People crowded into apartments and had to adapt to many changes in life. Artists made artworks to show both the good and the bad sides of living in cities.

**Changes in Ideas** During the early 1900s, people everywhere were adapting to changes. A new form of government called *communism* began in Russia. The main idea of communism was to create communities in which people worked together and shared everything equally. Russian artists created artworks that reflected this change in people's lives.

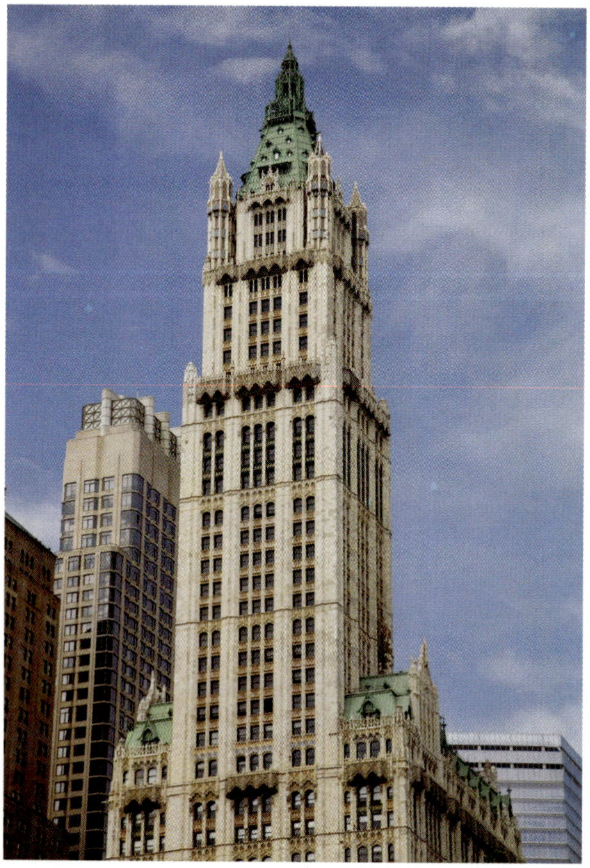

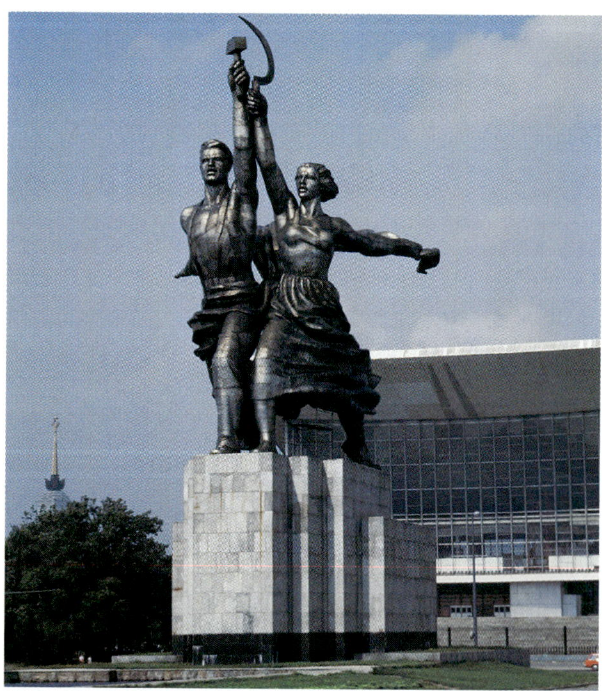

Fig. 6–4 **How do the poses of the figures in this sculpture help express the idea of equality?**

Vera Mukhina, *Industrial Worker and Collective Farm Girl*, 1937. Stainless steel, h. 79' (24 m), weight 75 tons, base h. 131' ½" (39.96 m). Courtesy of SovFoto/EastFoto. ©Estate of Vera Mukhina/Licensed by VAGA, New York, NY

Fig. 6–3 **The Woolworth Building is nestled in the center of this group of skyscrapers. Notice its decorative elements. How does it compare to the surrounding buildings?**

Cass Gilbert, *Woolworth Building, New York*, NY 1911–13. ©Peter Mauss/Esto. All Rights Reserved.

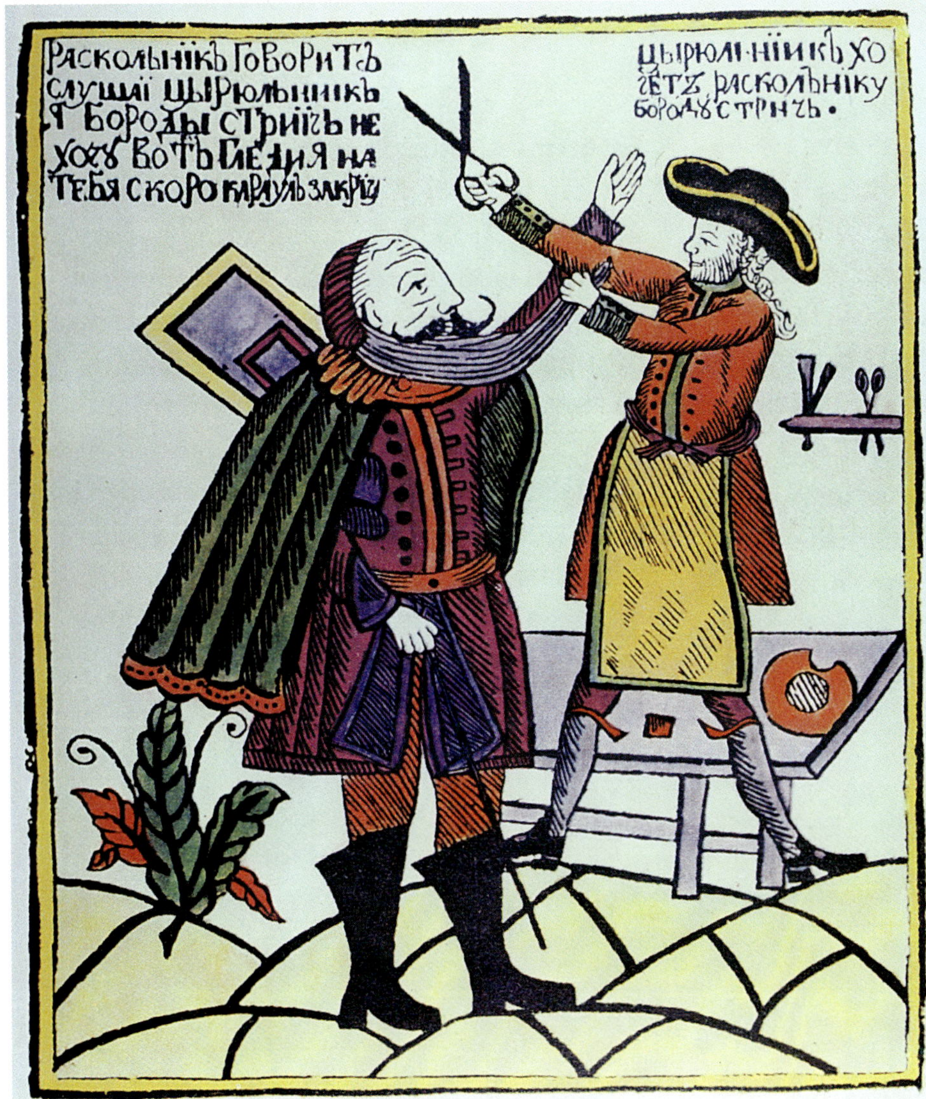


Fig. 6–5 **This Russian poster is about changing old ways. How does poster art influence people to think about artists' messages?**

Russia, *The Barber Wants to Cut the Old Believer's Whiskers*, ca. 1770. Woodcut, 38" x 30" (96.5 x 76.1 cm). Courtesy of Scott Archive.

## Meet Vera Mukhina

Vera Mukhina (1889–1953) was born into a wealthy Russian family. Although they disapproved of her decision to become an artist, her family supported her as she studied sculpture in France and Italy. As an artist, Mukhina created strong, dramatic artworks to express the ideals of communism. She especially loved enormous sculptures and, at age 48, she was able to create one. Mukhina led a team to make *Industrial Worker and Collective Farm Girl*, a 79-foot stainless steel sculpture weighing 75 tons. Today, it is shown in stamps, cards, and posters as a symbol of Russia.

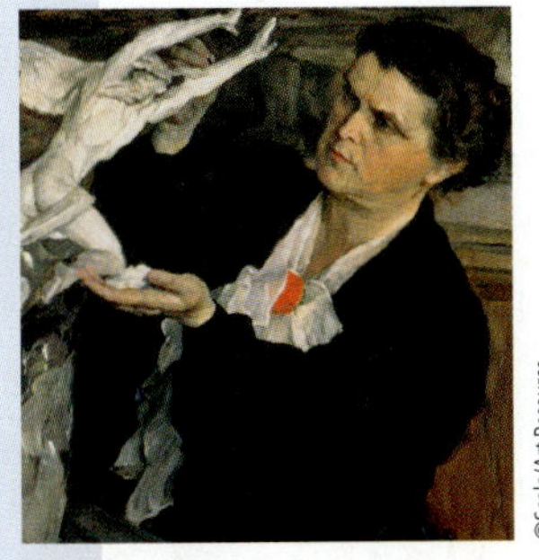



**"Mukhina's *Industrial Worker and Collective Farm Girl* is a monument to our time, to the Russian culture of the 20th century... It may be regarded as a symbol of this country."**

— Natalia Alexandrova

**Persuasion** One way people receive messages is through art. Art can influence people's views and opinions. For example, artworks can call attention to environmental concerns or political issues. Through their art, artists can inspire changes within their own communities.

When artists realized the possibilities of photography, they explored it as its own art form. Artists could document world events and viewers could see real people and real-life situations.

**Changing Minds Through Art** Artists can try to change people's minds in different ways. **Fig. 6–5** shows an example of art for political change. In 1705, a Russian law was passed that stated that all but certain groups of men had to be clean-shaven. In this poster, the bearded gentleman shows his resistance. **Fig. 6–6** shows how Lewis Hine used his photographs to draw attention to a need for change in child labor laws. Hine made people aware of the dangerous, brutal lives of child workers in factories.

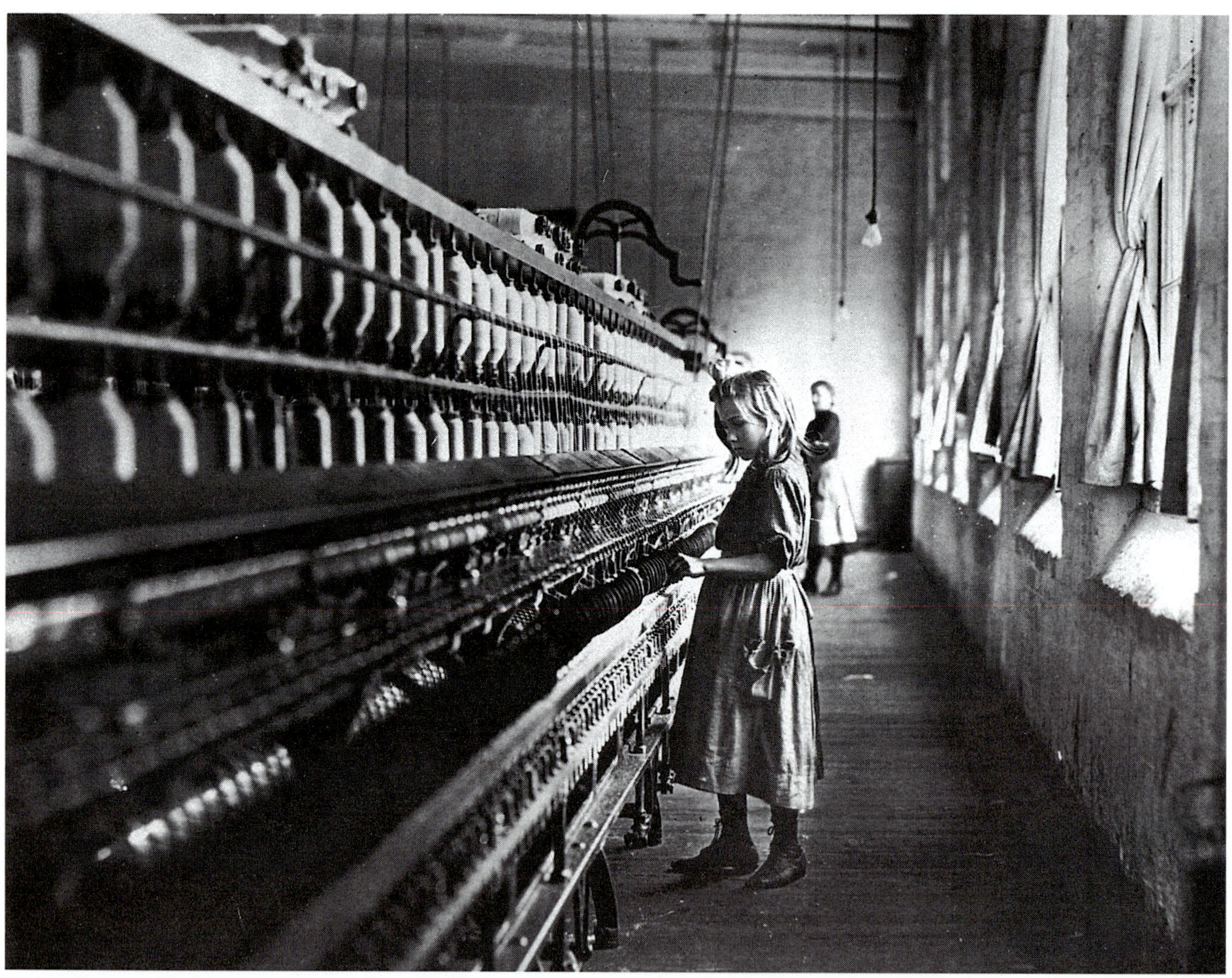

Fig. 6–6 **Why might the artist have thought that this image would be powerful enough to influence change in his community?**

Lewis Hine, *Little Girl in Carolina Cotton Mill*, 1908. Silver gelatin print. ©Corbis-Bettmann.

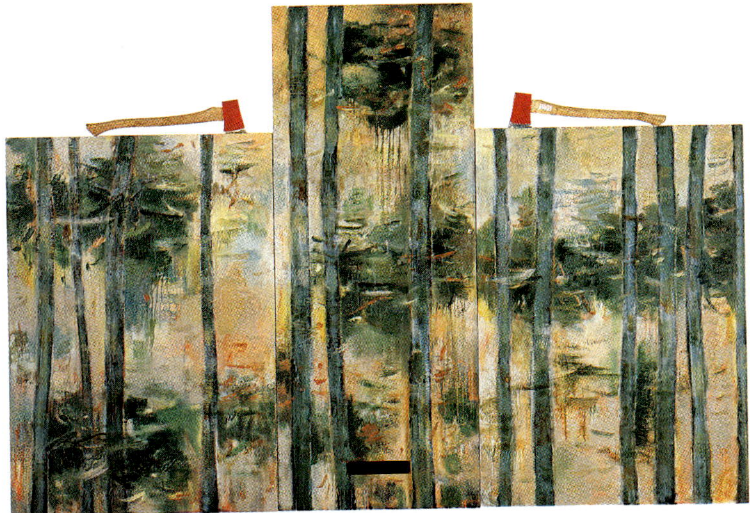

Fig. 6–7 **The timber industry is endangering the spotted owl by cutting old growth forest in the Northwest. What elements of the artwork symbolize the danger?**

Jaune Quick-to-See-Smith, *The Spotted Owl*, 1990. Oil and beeswax on canvas, 2 axes, wood panel, 80" x 116" (203.2 x 294.6 cm) triptych. Courtesy of the artist.

## Check Your Understanding

1. What are some ways that art reflects change in community life?
2. How do you think your life is different from the life of the girl shown in Fig. 6–6? How do you think your lives are similar?
3. What do changes in architecture say about communities?

## Studio Time

### A Model Skyscraper

Make a model of a skyscraper from cardboard or foam board.

- Sketch your ideas, showing the building's size and main shapes.
- Begin building your model. Cut the main shapes first. Glue or tape them together.
- Add details, colors, and textures. Consider adding windows and doors with drawing materials or cut paper.

Reflect on how your skyscraper model represents change or new directions in building design.

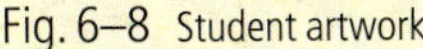

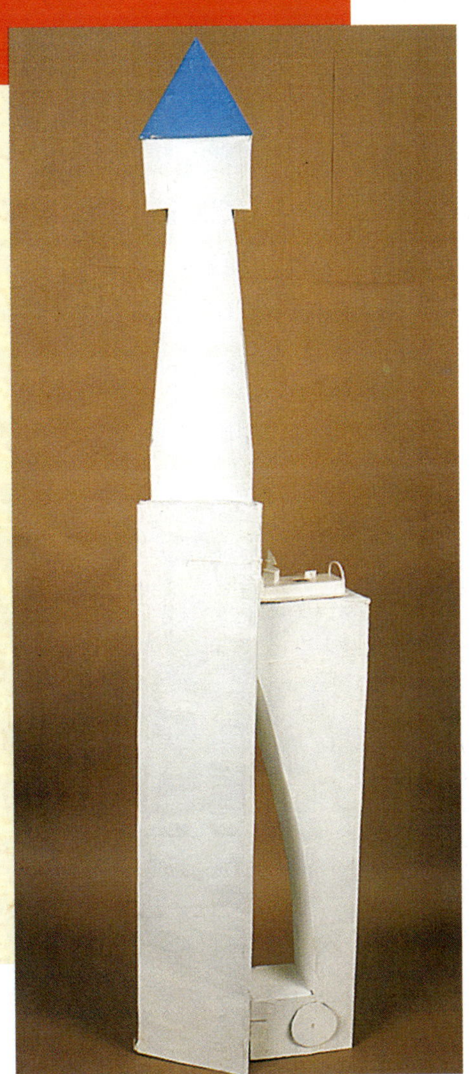

Fig. 6–8 Student artwork

# Painting

Painting is one of the oldest and most colorful forms of art. Subjects, themes, and styles of painting can reflect the culture, artistic traditions, and time period in which the artist lives.

**Changing Traditions** As communities change, so do painting traditions. Painters must make decisions about subject matter, materials, and techniques. Local traditions and changes in communities can influence these decisions. Painters' choices of subjects or themes may reflect the history and traditions found in the places where they live. An artist's decisions about tools and materials may depend on what is available at the time.

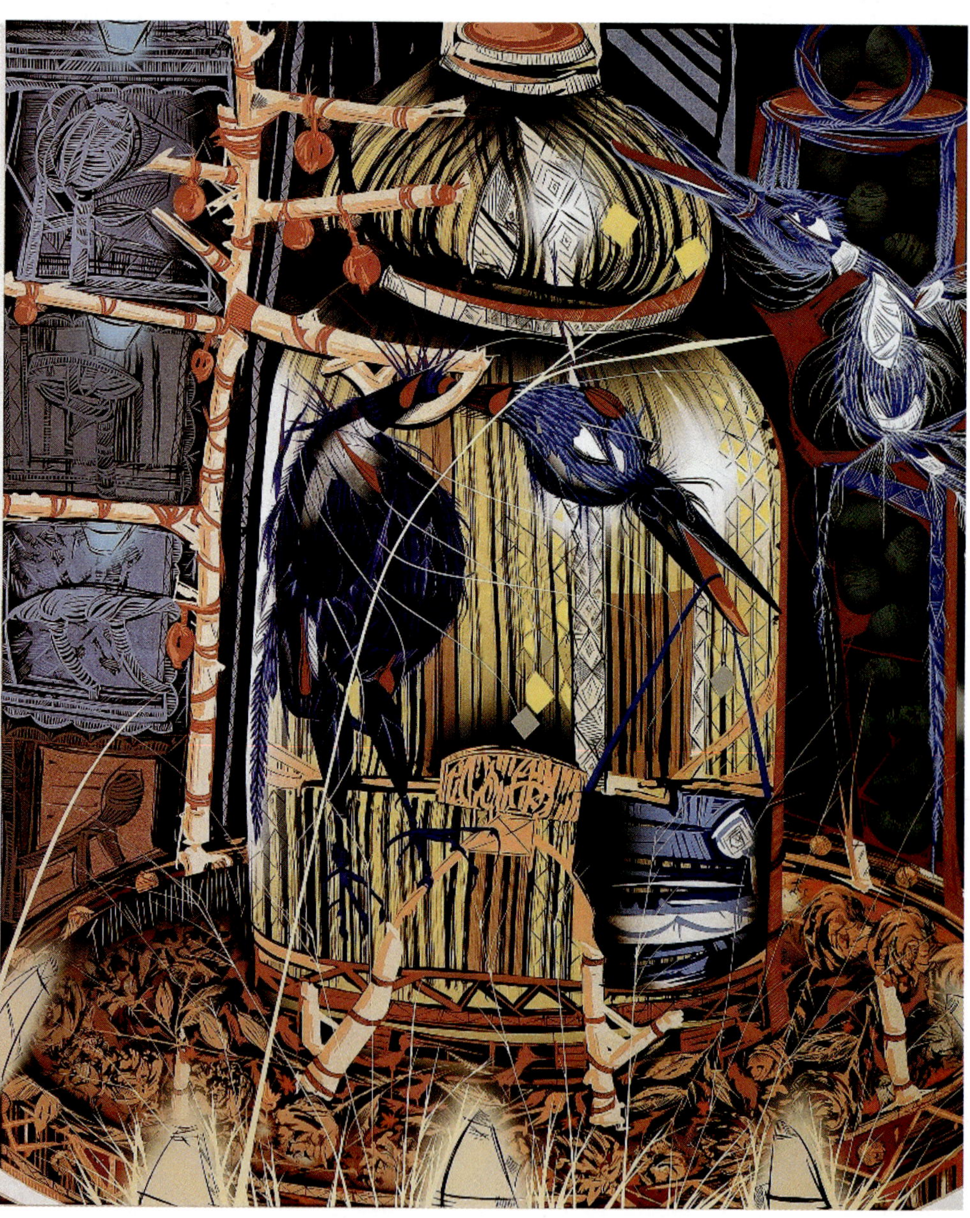

Fig. 6–9 **Why do you think this artist chose this painting medium and these colors to express his idea?**

Lari Pittman, *Palace*. Cel vinyl and aerosol on gessoed canvas over panel, 102" x 86" (259.1 x 218.4 cm). Courtesy of Regen Projects, Los Angeles.

**Different Kinds of Paint** Each painting medium has special qualities and limitations. Some paints are fluid and thin. Others are dense and thick. Most paints are made from powdered pigments. **Pigments** are coloring materials made from earth, crushed minerals, plants, or chemicals. Pigments are held together with glue, egg, wax, or oil. Examples of water-based paints are tempera, acrylic, and watercolor. Pastels are dry painting media. There are three kinds of pastel: chalk, oil, and wax.

**Observe** Notice how the artist's use of a specific painting medium produced the vibrant pigments shown in Fig. 6–9.

**Tools**: Acrylic and tempera paints, watercolors, water-based felt-tip markers, chalk or pastels, water, paper, and paintbrushes.

### Practice: Painting with Different Media

- Experiment with the listed painting media. Paint with each medium on both dry and wet paper. Use a dry brush first, and then try a wet one. Try blending colors and diluting the media with water. Make notes in your sketchbook about what you observe.

Fig. 6–10 **This artist has created a one-color scheme with shades of blue-green. What kind of mood does his use of color create? What makes this painting humorous?**

Mark Tansey, *Action Painting no. 2,* 1984. Diachrome, 76" x 100" (193 x 254 cm). Collection du Musée des beaux-arts de Montreal/The Montreal Museum of Fine Arts' Collection. Photograph: Brian Merrett, MMFA.

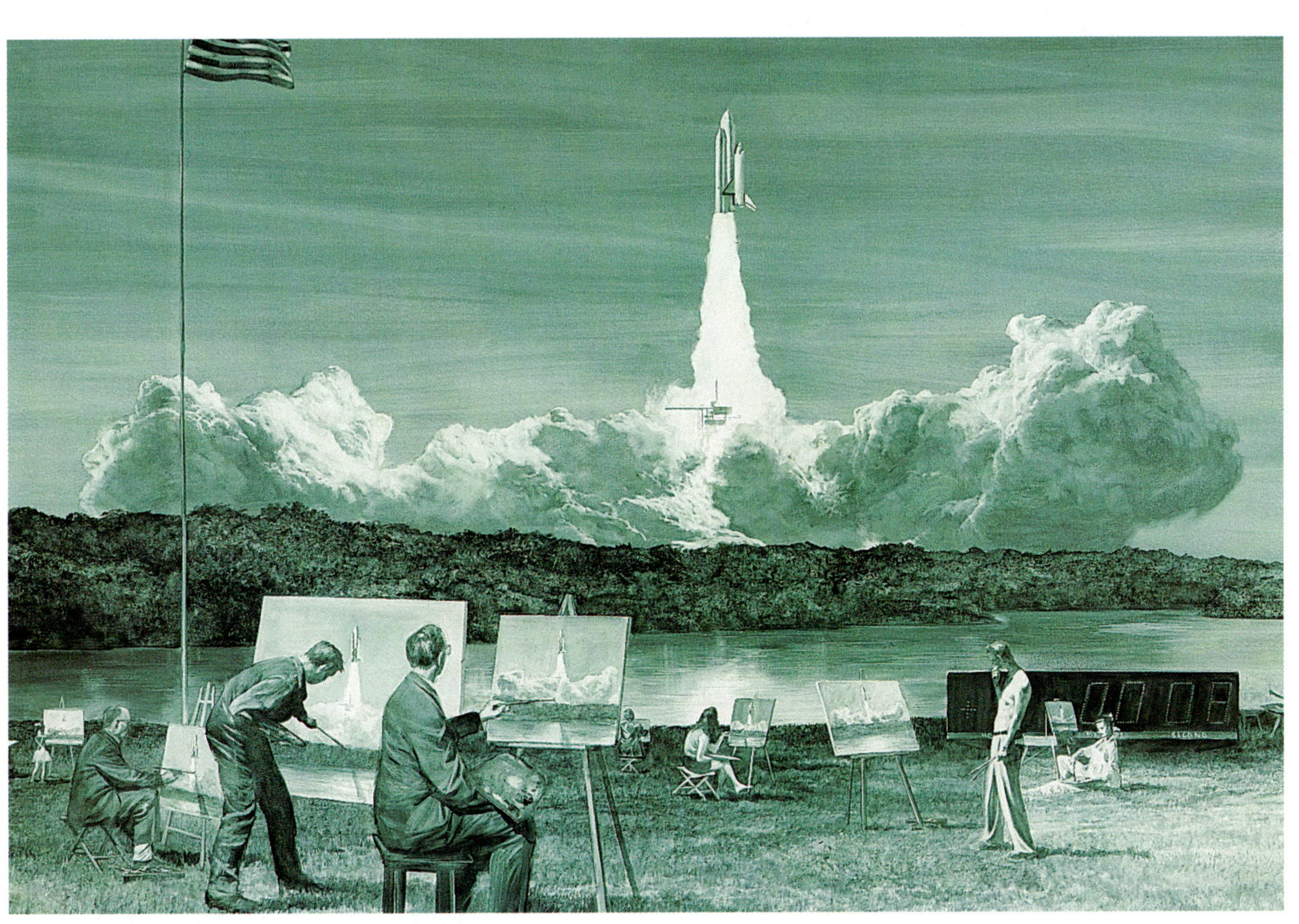

### Techniques, Tools, and Materials

Artists also experiment with painting techniques, tools, and materials. Artists apply paint to surfaces such as paper, canvas, wood, or plaster. They usually apply it with a paintbrush. Paintbrushes come in all sizes and shapes. Stiff bristle brushes are often used for oil, acrylic, and tempera. Soft hair brushes are usually best for watercolor. Some artists have recently used house paints and paints mixed with sand or other materials. They have applied paint with rollers, sponges, and their hands. Some pour, drip, or spray paint onto a surface, or squeeze it directly from the tube.

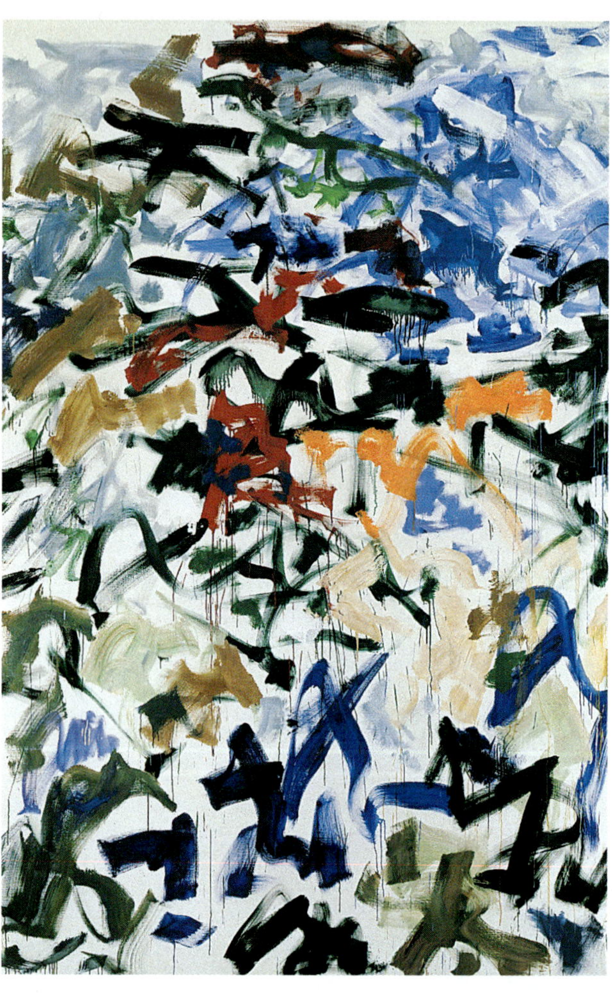

Fig. 6–11 **This style of painting is called Action Painting or Abstract Expressionism. Why might someone feel a sense of energy when looking at this painting?**

Joan Mitchell, *Mountain*, 1989. Oil on canvas, 110 ¼" x 157 ½" (280 x 400 cm). Photograph courtesy of Robert Miller Gallery, New York (RGM# MITC-0228) ©The Estate of Joan Mitchell.

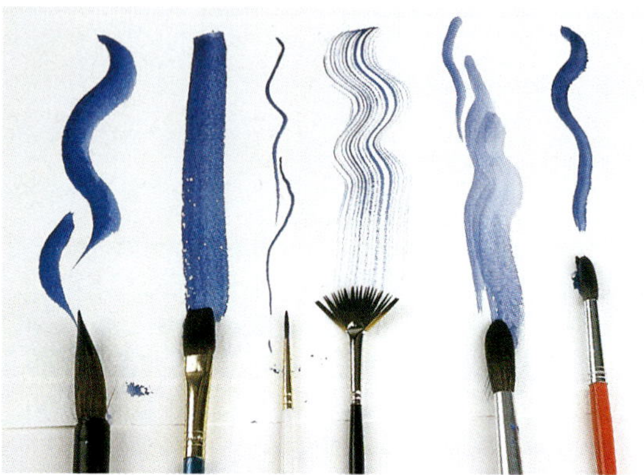

**Observe** Look at the painting shown in Fig. 6–11. Notice how the brushstrokes look as though they were placed anywhere and everywhere. What materials, tools, and techniques do you think the artist used to create this painting?

**Tools:** Stiff bristle brushes, soft hair brushes, sponges, oil paints, acrylic paints, tempera paints, watercolors, water, and paper.

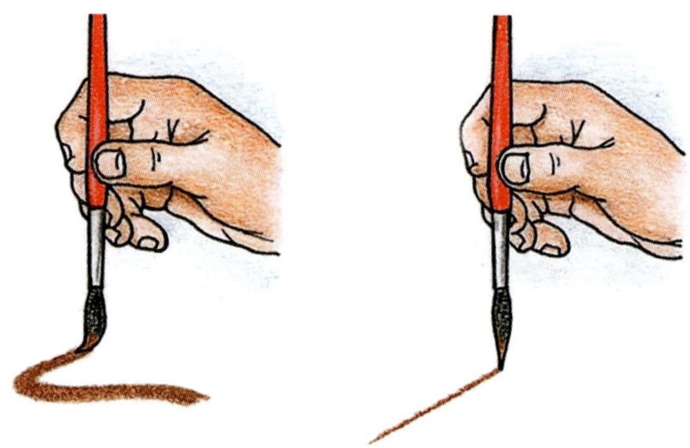

### Practice: Painting with Different Tools

- Practice on paper, using different tools with different types of paint. Which tools work better with which paints? Which work better for thin lines? Thick lines? What else did you learn by practicing with different painting tools?

### Check Your Understanding

1. How can changes in communities influence painters' decisions?
2. Choose two types of tools that you used in the practice exercises. How are their uses similar? How are they different?
3. Why is it important for painters to think about the tools, techniques, and materials they use in their artworks?

## Studio Time

### Experiments in Painting

Experiment with paints, techniques, tools, and materials to create a painting that conveys an idea about the theme of "change."

- What kinds of change do you see around you? Choose an idea to express in your painting.
- Decide how you will express your idea. How big will your completed work be? What painting media, tools, and techniques will best convey your idea?
- Look at many examples of painting in your book and elsewhere to help plan your work.

Reflect on how your painting suggests the idea of change.

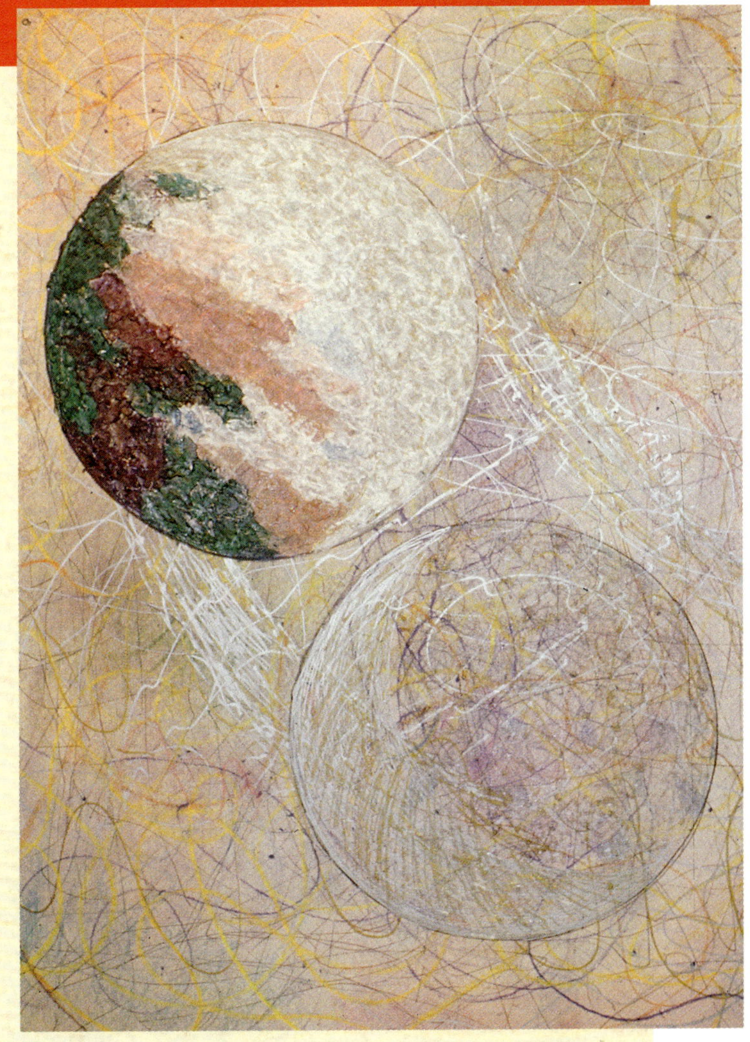

Fig. 6–12 Student artwork

# Experimenting with Materials

## Studio Background

Have you noticed that most of the paintings you learn about in this book or see in museums are rectangles? Some are vertical, some are horizontal, some are large, and some are small, but the basic shape of paintings has remained the same for thousands of years. However, artists in the last half of the 1900s changed that when they began experimenting with materials and techniques.

**In this studio exploration, you will experiment with Styrofoam or foam rubber and paint to create a three-dimensional painting.** You might choose to create an artwork with a humorous theme or one that focuses on the formal elements of shape, form, color, or pattern. Think about how you can use overlapping, balance, and emphasis to make your artwork three dimensional. Should you paint the parts with bright, bold colors? Should you emphasize pattern and texture?

### You Will Need

- sketch paper and pencil
- 1" Styrofoam™ or foam rubber
- coping saw, bread knife, or utility knife
- glue
- found objects
- tempera paints and brushes

**Safety Note** Use extreme caution when using sharp tools to prevent cuts and accidents.

## Step 1 Plan and Practice

- Decide what material you want to explore with your artwork. Will you experiment with the flexibility of foam rubber? Or will you practice using a coping saw to cut irregular shapes out of Styrofoam™? Will you use your work to send a message?
- Think about ways to stack and layer shapes to create dimensional forms. How can you combine parts to create a larger, irregular form?

## Inspiration from Our World

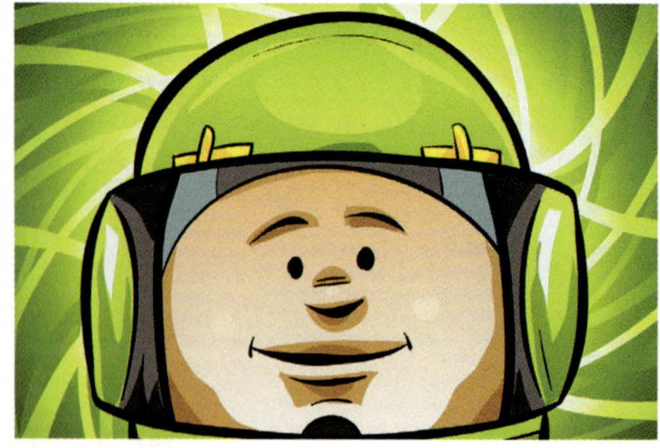

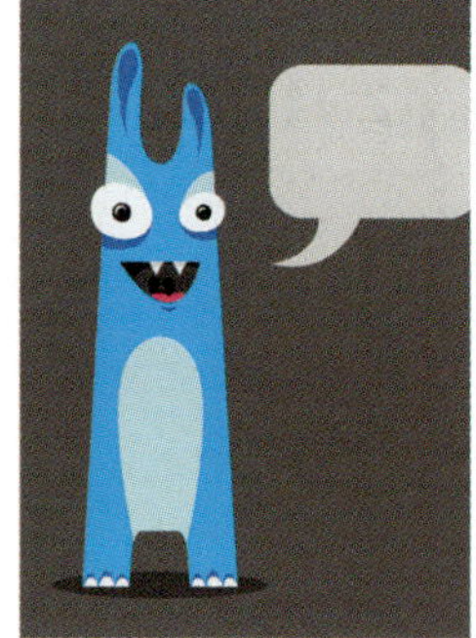

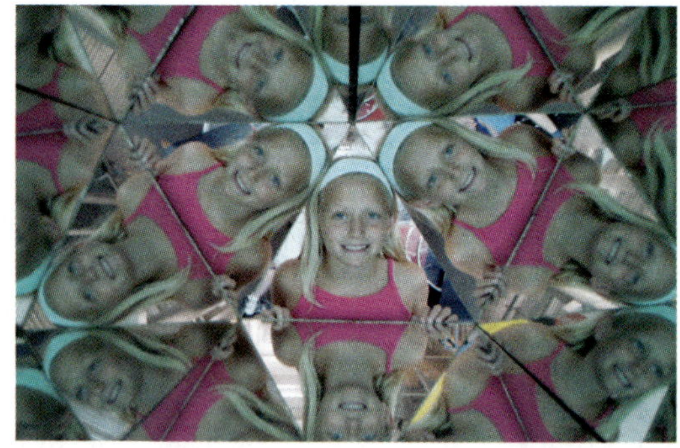

**Things to Remember:**

- ✓ Use overlapping and layering to create a relief or sculptural surface.
- ✓ Choose a color harmony or colors that go well together.
- ✓ Connect all pieces securely.

## Inspiration from Art

Contemporary artist Elizabeth Murray has really changed the way we think about traditional art forms such as painting and sculpture. Her stretched and irregularly shaped paintings are no longer rectangular. Her dimensional paintings pair goofy shapes and cartoonish images with familiar objects, jutting out from the wall like sculptures. Murray has blurred the line between paintings as objects hanging on a wall and paintings as a space for displaying objects.

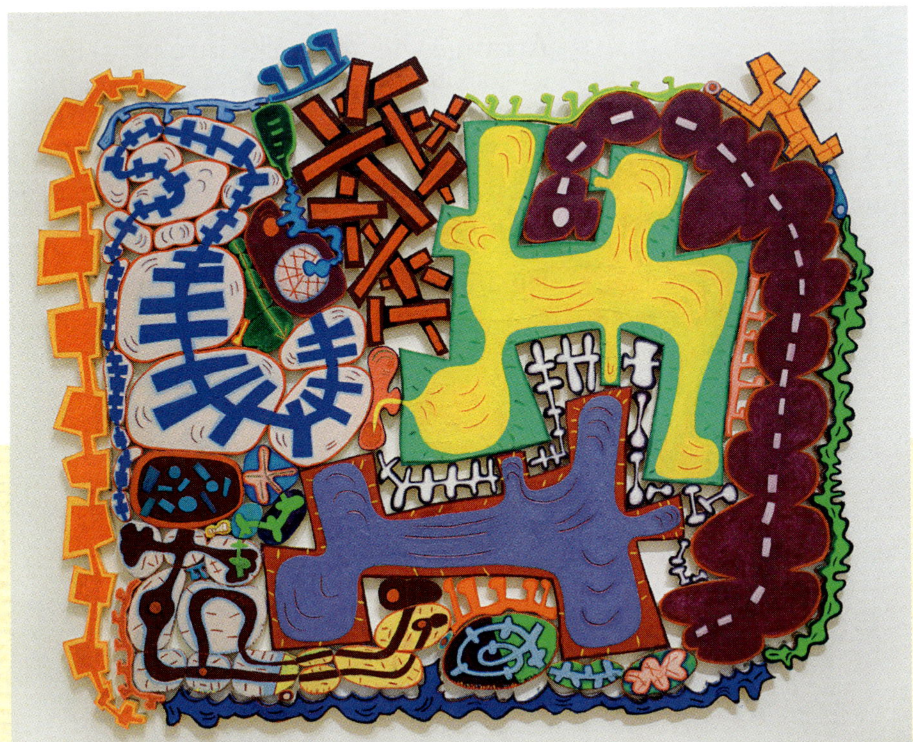

Fig. 6–13 **Why might someone consider this artwork to be a sculpture rather than a painting?**

Elizabeth Murray, *Do the Dance*, 2005. Oil on canvas on wood, 9' 5" x 11' 3" x 1 ½" (287 x 342.9 x 3.8 cm). Gift of Jo Carole and Ronald S. Lauder, Agnes Gund, and Arne Glimcher. Museum of Modern Art, New York, NY. ©The Museum of Modern Art. Licensed by SCALA/Art Resource, NY.

### Step 2 Begin to Create

- **Sketch your ideas. Decide what materials and tools you will need.** Will you use mostly geometric shapes? Or mostly organic?

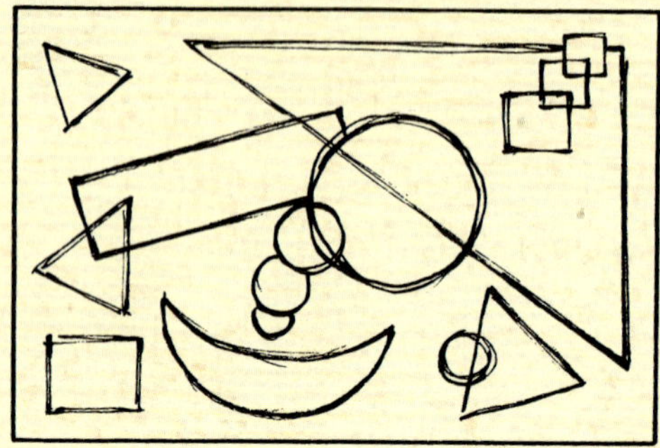

- **Cut and join your forms.**

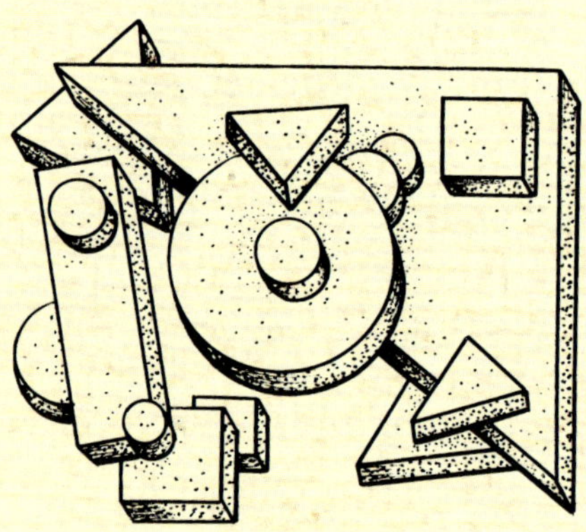

- How many layers of shapes will you overlap?

### Step 3 Revise

**Did you remember to:**

- ✓ Use overlapping and layering to create a relief or sculptural surface?
- ✓ Connect all pieces securely?
- ✓ Choose a color harmony or colors that go well together?

Adjust your work if necessary. In your sketchbook, make a note of your revisions and why you made them.

### Step 4 Add Finishing Touches

- Add found objects, glitter, or other materials if desired.
- On the back, mark the top of your artwork or the way it should hang.

### Step 5 Share and Reflect

- Arrange the artworks into mostly geometric or mostly organic and irregular shapes.
- Discuss similarities and differences with your classmates.
- Decide which ones are the most humorous, the most irregular, the most geometric, and the most colorful.

## Art Criticism

**Describe** What colors, textures, patterns, and forms do you see?

**Analyze** How did the artist blur the distinction between painting and sculpture?

**Interpret** What mood or feeling words can you connect with this sculpture?

**Evaluate** What did the artist do especially well?

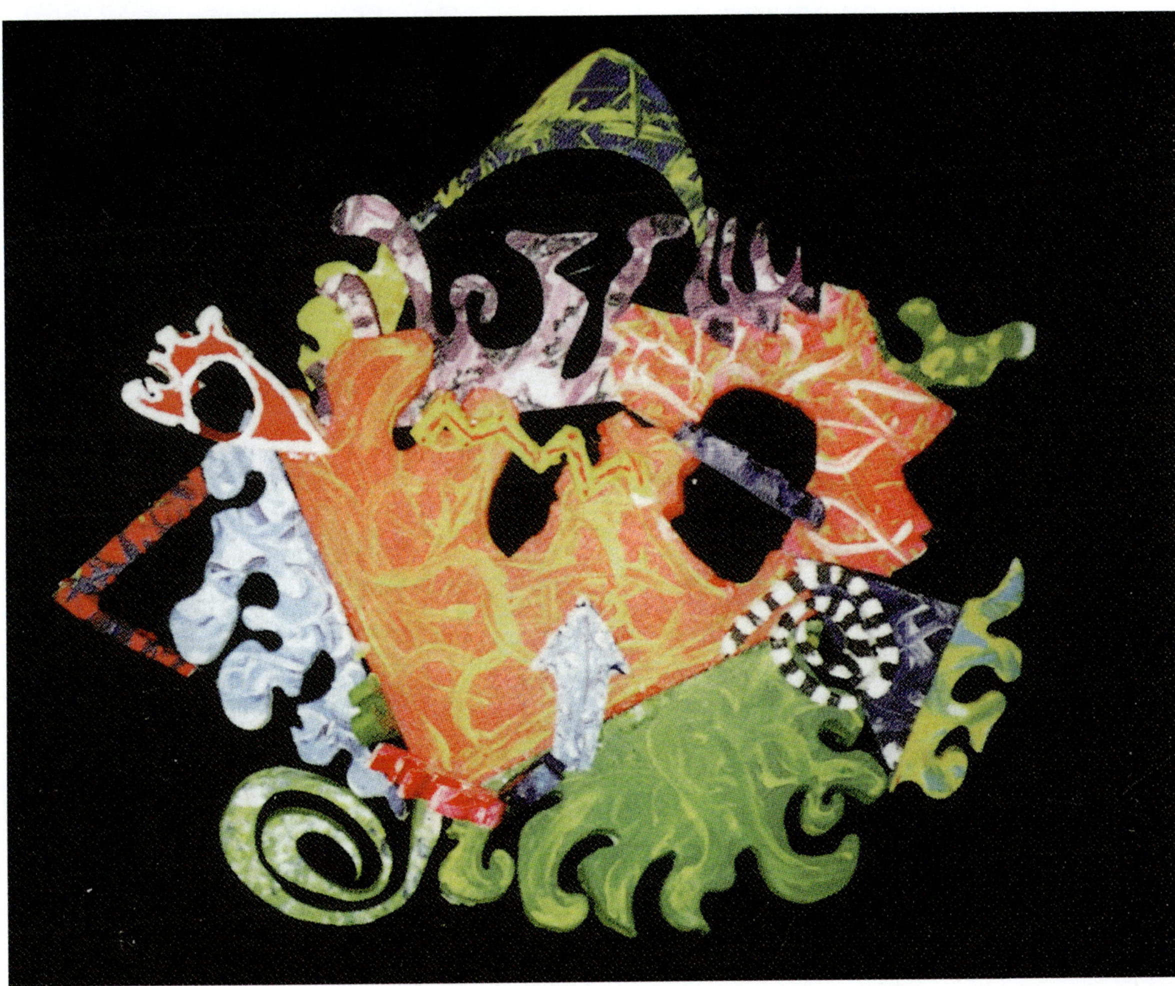

Fig. 6–14 Student artwork

# American Art: 1900–1920

During the first decade of the 1900s and the years before World War I, industry grew rapidly in the United States. The thousands of immigrants who arrived on American soil added to the growth of cities. For the nation's communities, this was a period of expansion and hope for the future.

**Cities as Subjects** During these years of industrial and economic strength in the United States, American artists turned their attention to cities. The subjects of their artwork were places where people gathered, such as streets, parks, and restaurants. Look at the cityscape shown in Fig. 6–15. A cityscape is an artwork that shows a view of a city. This view of buildings in New York City emphasizes the drama and excitement of nighttime, and reflects people's feelings that cities were good places to live.

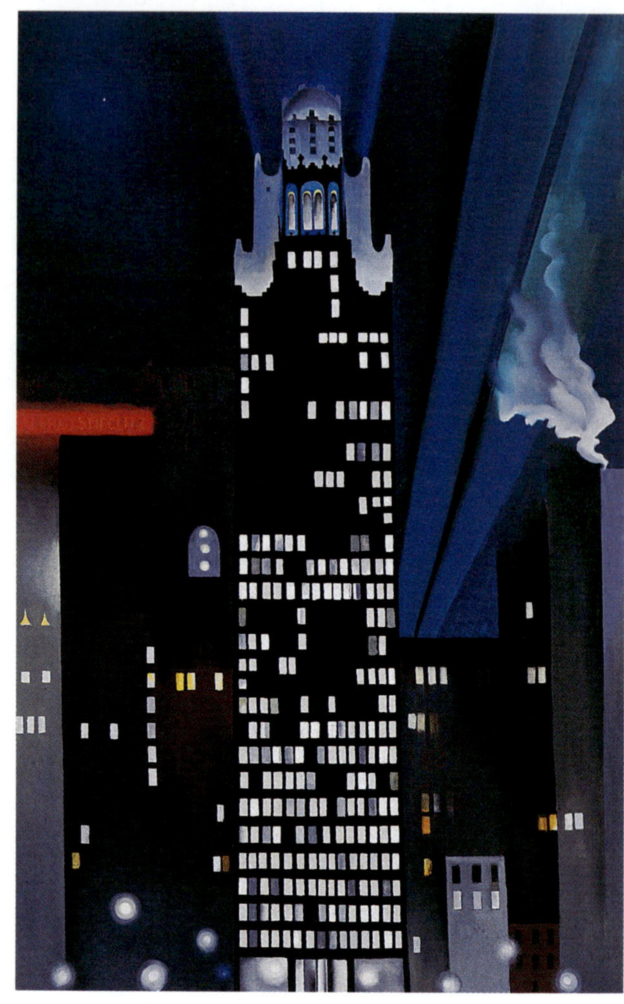

Fig. 6–15 **What moods or feelings does this artwork suggest? If you saw it in a travel brochure about New York, would it make you want to go there?**

Georgia O'Keeffe, *Radiator Building—Night, New York*, 1927. Oil on canvas, 48" x 30" (121.9 x 76.1 cm). The Carl Van Vechten Gallery of Fine Arts, Fisk University Galleries, Nashville, Tennessee. ©2000 The Georgia O'Keeffe Foundation/Artists Rights Society (ARS), New York.

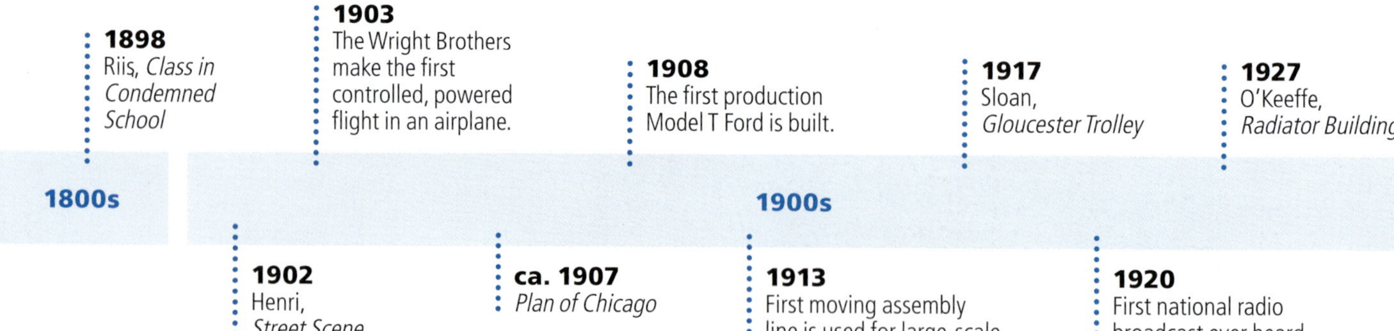

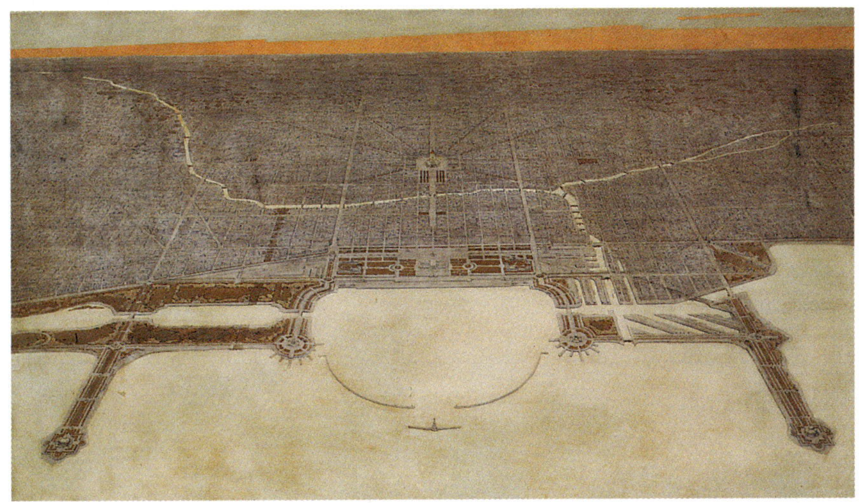

Fig. 6–16 **This plan of Chicago shows a proposed civic center, a park, and the waterfront. Why might newcomers at the time have found this plan exciting?**

Jules Gherin, (Daniel H. Burnham and Edward H. Bennett, Chicago, Illinois partnership 1903–12), *Chicago: View Looking West over the City Showing the Proposed Civic Center, the Grand Access, Grant Park and the Harbor; Plan of Chicago*, 1909. plate 87, 1907. Watercolor and graphite on paper, 57 1/8" x 91 3/4" (145.5 x 233 cm). Gift of Patrick Shaw, 1991-1381. Photograph courtesy of The Art Institute of Chicago.

**Art for Change** At first, artists of this time were mainly interested in how the change in cities gave them new subject matter for their art. After a while, however, artists and photographers wanted to use their art to influence new changes in communities. Their artworks called attention to social and economic problems, such as injustice, poverty, and overcrowding. In 1913, a New York art exhibition influenced change in American art. The show was called the "International Exhibition of Modern Art" (later called the "Armory Show"). After viewing this exhibition, Americans thought that American art was behind the times compared to the new European art. So, artists began shifting their attention away from the public community. Instead, they began to focus on using art as a way to express their personal feelings.

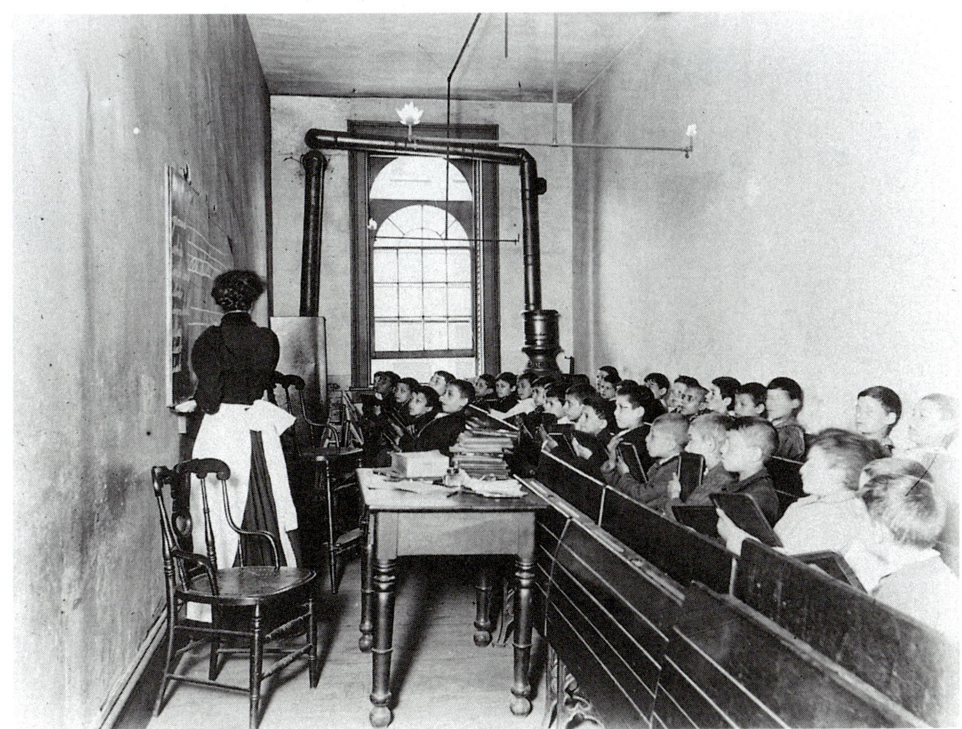

Fig. 6–17 **What do you think the artist was saying about the condition of schools in the late 1800s and the early 1900s? Notice the title.**

Jacob Riis, *A Class in the Condemned Essex Market School with Gas Burning by Day*, ca. 1898. Silver gelatin print. Museum of the City of New York. The Jacob A. Riis Collection.

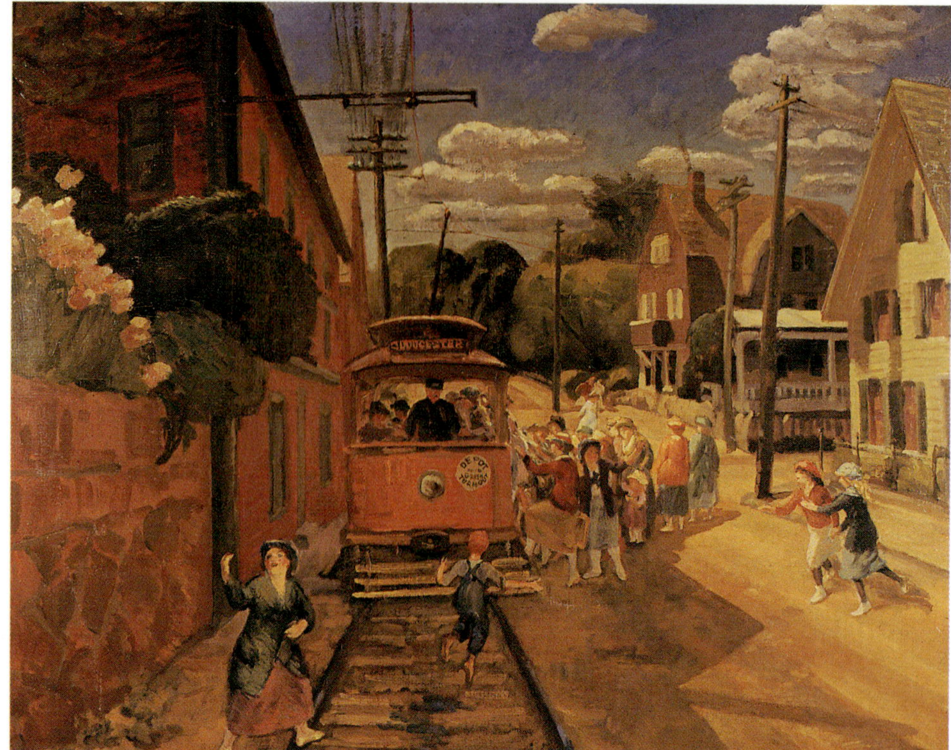

Fig. 6–18 **What colors help make this painting cheerful? How do they compare to the colors in *Street Scene with Snow* (Fig. 6–19)?**

John Sloan, *Gloucester Trolley*, 1917. Oil on canvas, 25" x 30 ½" (63.5 x 76.8 cm). Courtesy of Canajoharie Library and Art Gallery.

**Real City Life** One group of artists from the early 1900s, known as "The Eight," included Robert Henri, John Sloan, George Luks, William Glackens, Everett Shinn, Maurice Prendergast, Arthur B. Davies, and Ernest Lawson. They were also called the *Ash Can School* because they liked to show real scenes of city life in their artworks. They painted images from both the upper class and poorer neighborhoods of New York City. They did not create their artworks to express feelings about the differences between these neighborhoods. These artists thought this subject matter made their art interesting and lively. They showed the streets and people of city communities as they really looked. Some people didn't like this realistic look at city life.

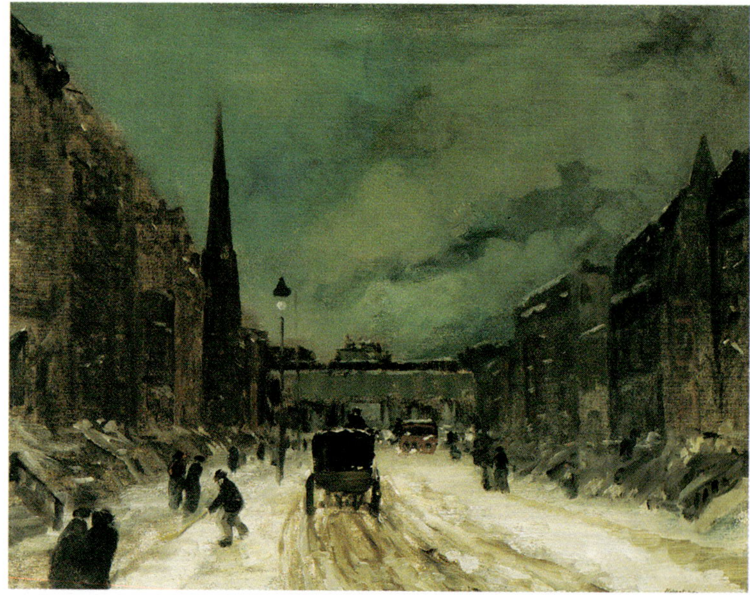

Fig. 6–19 **How has the artist created mood in this cityscape? How would you describe that mood?**

Robert Henri, *Street Scene with Snow, East 57th Street, New York*, 1902. Oil on canvas, 26" x 32" (66 x 81.3 cm). Yale University Art Gallery, Mable Brady Garvan Collection.

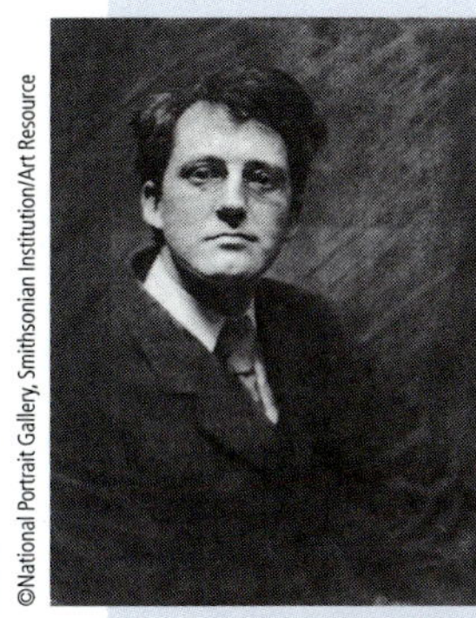



## Meet John Sloan

John Sloan was born in Pennsylvania. At 16, he quit school to help support his family. He worked as a magazine illustrator and took evening classes at the Pennsylvania Academy of Fine Arts.

Sloan met artist Robert Henri in 1904. Henri led Sloan and six other painters in a rebellion against the way art was taught at the Academy. Together, they formed a style that became known as the Ash Can School because it focused on dark street scenes, mostly of the poor. Sloan continued to paint until his death. His artworks reflect the enormous changes that occurred in and around American cities during the early 1900s.

**"When I painted the life of the poor, I was not thinking about them like a social worker—but with the eye of a poet who sees with affection."**

—John Sloan (1871–1951)

## Check Your Understanding

1. Why did artists turn their attention to cities as a source of subject matter?
2. How does your classroom differ from the one shown in Fig. 6–17? How are they similar?
3. How realistic is the scene shown in Fig. 6–19? Explain.

## Studio Time

### Paintings for Change

Create a painting that shows or promotes change in your community.

- Choose a style that will best express your ideas. (To learn more about art styles, see the Student Handbook.) Experiment with several styles before you begin your painting.
- When you have chosen a subject and the style in which you will create your painting, sketch your composition.
- Create your finished painting.

Reflect on how your style fits the change you show in your work.

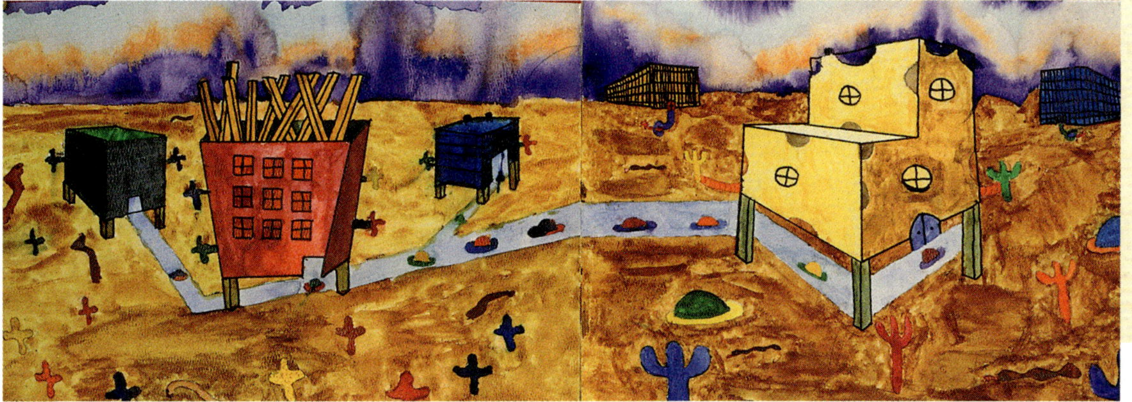

Fig. 6–20 Student artwork

# Russian Art

**A New Style** During the early 1900s, most Russian artists were affected by the Russian Revolution, and by changes in Western European art. Some began to do things differently than they had in the past. These artists became known as avant-garde. Avant-garde refers to a group or style that is at the front of artistic change. It generally describes very different or experimental art. Russian avant-garde artists wanted to modernize Russian art. They experimented with color and line, and created art that was not realistic in style.

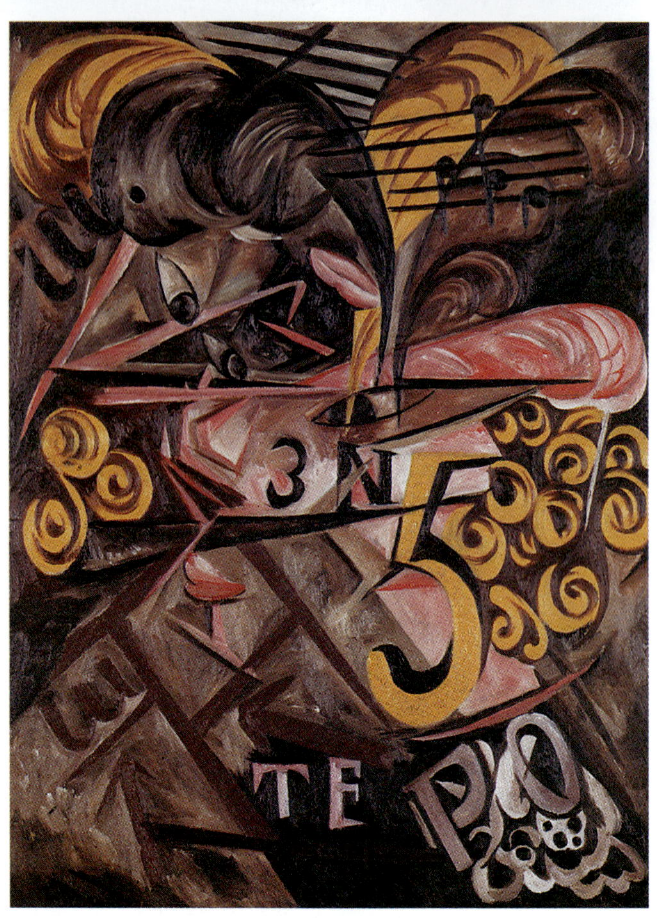

Fig. 6–21 **Look carefully at this painting. What qualities of abstract art do you see? Where is the lady that's referred to in the title?**

Natalia Goncharova, *Lady with Hat*, 1913. Oil on canvas, 35 ½" x 26" (90 x 66 cm). Musée National d'Art Moderne, Paris. Photo Philippe Migeat ©Centre Georges Pompidou. ©2000 Artists Rights Society (ARS), New York/ADAGP, Paris.

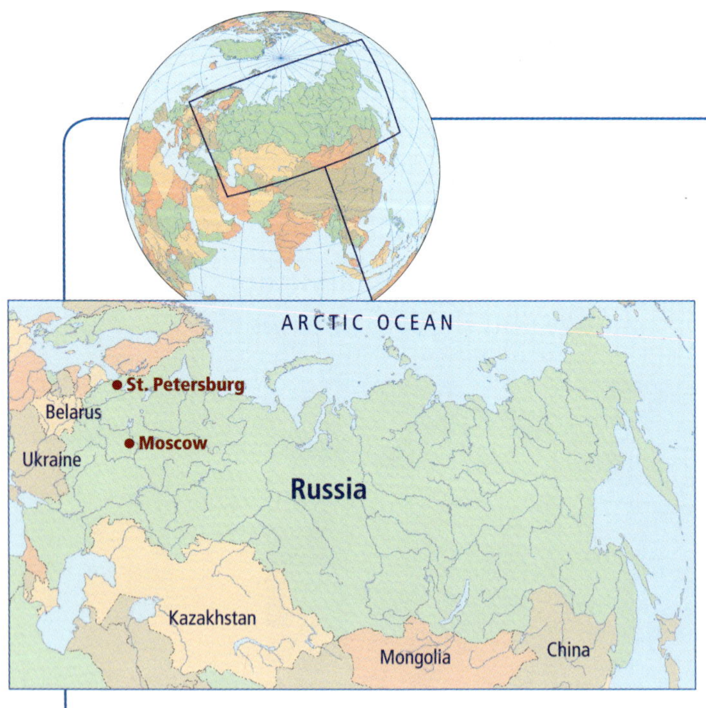


## Social Studies Connection

For many centuries, **Russia** looked west of its borders for cultural inspiration. One of Russia's best-known traditional art forms is religious icons. These are based on the Byzantine traditions. During the 1800s, Russian artists continued to rely on western European styles such as Realism, Impressionism, and Art Nouveau for ideas. In the early 1900s, however, Russian communities and their art changed. Revolutionary movements in Russia now interested western European artists. They began looking to Moscow for new and revolutionary ideas.

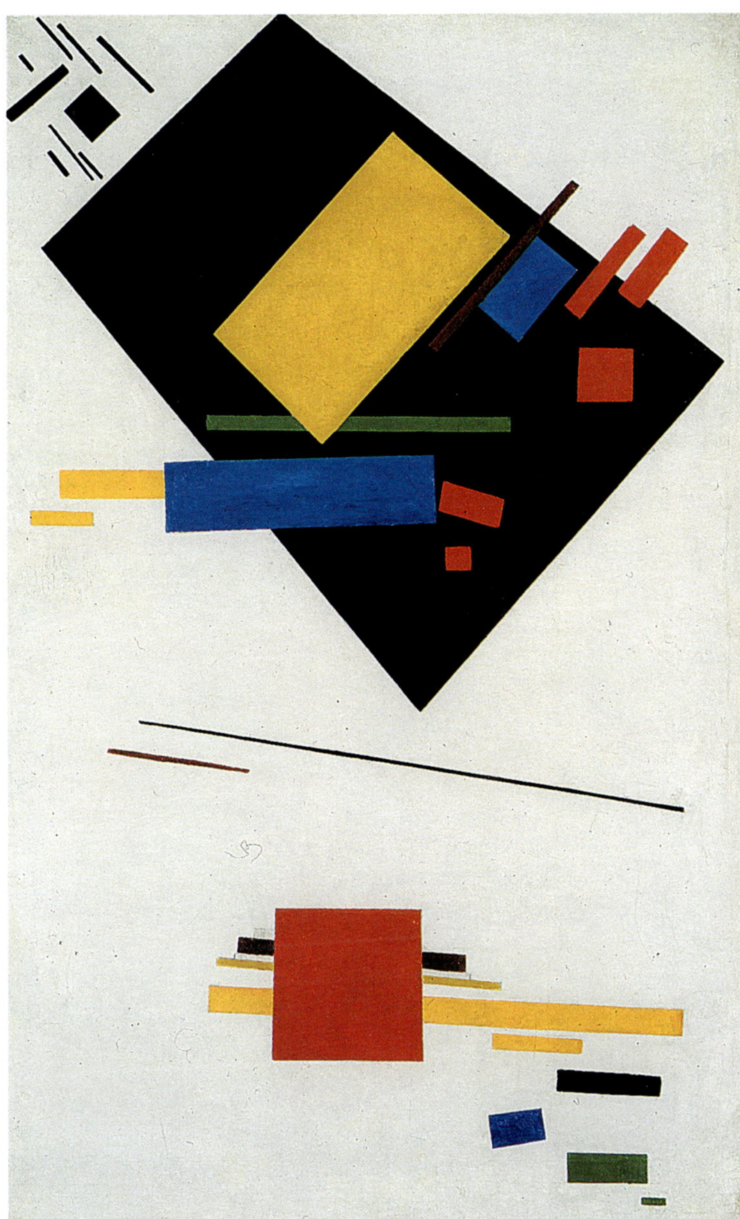

Fig. 6–22 **In 1913, Kasimir Malevich arranged simple geometric shapes to show pure colors and nonobjective forms. How is this an example of avant-garde art?**

Kasimir Malevich, *Suprematist Painting*, 1915. Oil on canvas, 40" x 24 ½" (101.5 x 62 cm). Stedelijk Museum, Amsterdam.

**Art for Beauty's Sake** Avant-garde artists continued to investigate new ideas, particularly abstract art. In abstract art, artists simplify, rearrange, or leave out colors, lines, and shapes in the objects they observe. Some artists based their ideas on things such as scientific theories of light and geometric shapes and forms. Avant-garde artists thought art should exist only to be looked at as beautiful forms, and not for a practical purpose. Some artists constructed abstract, freestanding, or suspended sculptural works. Others created kinetic sculptures. Kinetic sculptures are sculptures with moving parts.

### Visual Culture

During the early part of the 1900s in Russia, artists created posters and other visual images to promote ideas about political change. Consider how images and messages on television, billboards, posters, and brochures sent through the mail are used to influence people's attitudes and opinions about issues such as peace, war, employment, health care, and other social and political issues today. How do the artist's choices and arrangements of colors and symbols contribute to the persuasive power of these messages?

**Changing Society Through Art** Another avant-garde community of artists was called the *Productivists*. These artists wanted to be actively involved in reshaping society. They felt that the combined forces of art, craftsmanship, and industry could help build a better world. This group believed that art is useful to society. Artists played important roles in cultural activity and teaching. They were expected to concentrate on architecture, the design of household objects, and printing. Artists rejected any creativity that did not have a purpose. In these and other ways, the success of the Russian Revolution in 1917 brought many Russian artists together. This group shared an interest in promoting the Revolution's ideals of change. Later, some Russian artists who took part in these changes moved to Paris. They became part of Western European movements.

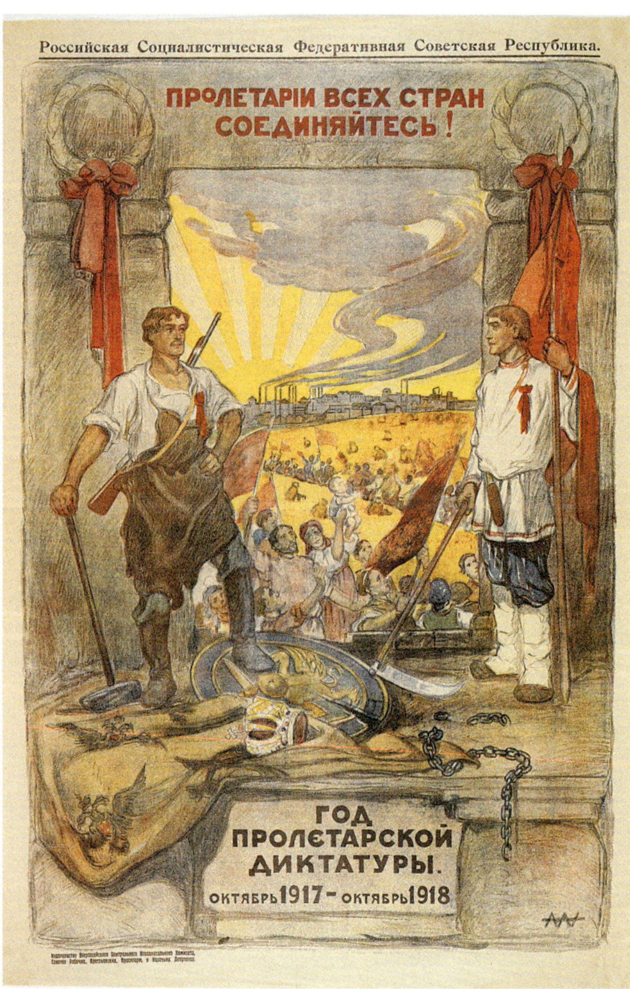


Fig. 6–23 **This poster illustrates Russia's political change to communism. It shows images of the past and the future. How is it an example of Productivist art?**

Alexander Apsit, *A Year of the Proletarian Dictatorship, October 1917–1918*, 1918. Poster. Courtesy of David King Collection.

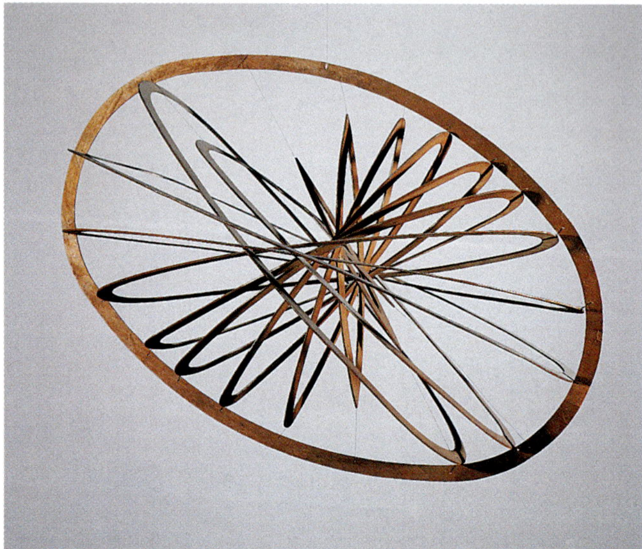

Fig. 6–24 **Take a close look at the shape and form of this kinetic sculpture. How do you imagine it might move?**

Aleksandr Rodchenko, *Oval Hanging Construction Number 12*, ca. 1920. Plywood, open construction partially painted with aluminum paint, and wire, 24" x 33" x 18 ½" (61 x 83.8 x 47 cm). The Museum of Modern Art, New York. Acquisition made possible through the extraordinary efforts of George and Zinaida Costakis, and through the Nate B. and Frances Spingold, Matthew H. and Erna Futter and Enid A. Haupt Funds. Photograph ©2000 The Museum of Modern Art, New York. ©Estate of Aleksandr Rodchenko/Licensed by VAGA, New York, NY.

## Studio Time

### A Changing Sculpture

Create a kinetic sculpture based on the theme of change. Remember that a kinetic sculpture has moving parts.

- Decide what the subject of your sculpture will be.
- Show change by planning the relationships between sizes, colors, and other visual elements in your sculpture. Will you use only flat shapes or three-dimensional forms? Will your shapes and forms be geometric or organic?
- Suspend or connect moving parts with string, wire, or wooden dowels.

Reflect on how your sculpture changes as it moves.

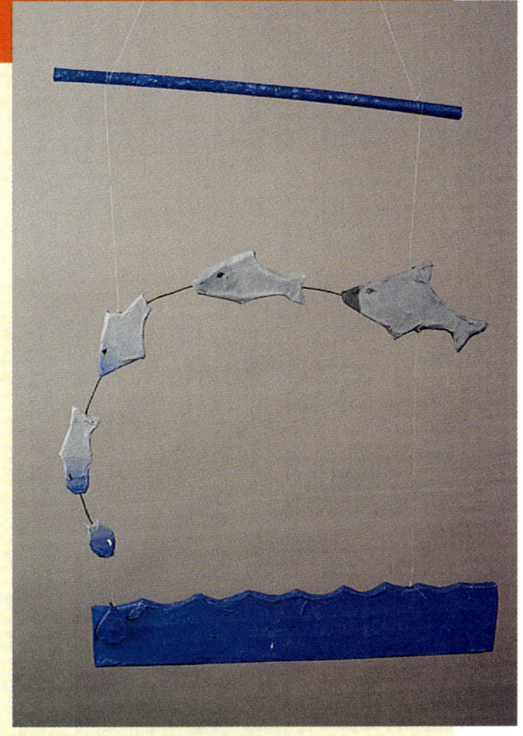

Fig. 6–25 Student artwork

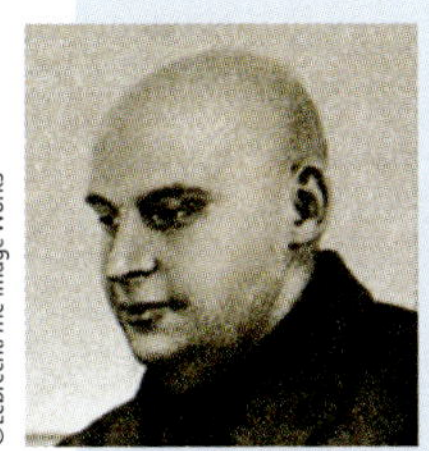



### Meet Aleksandr Rodchenko

Aleksandr Rodchenko was born in St. Petersburg, Russia. In the early 1900s, his family moved to Kazan, where Rodchenko attended art school. In 1914, he became a Futurist. Futurist artists were fascinated by speed and machines. They saw technology as the future of humanity, victorious over nature. Rodchenko made drawings using precise tools such as the compass. In 1921, Rodchenko's ideas about art changed and he became a Constructivist. He made only nonrepresentational artworks with minimal, geometric designs. He believed in replacing old ideas with new experiments.

**"In each of my works, I do a new experiment...Everything is experiment."**

— Aleksandr Rodchenko (1891–1956)

### Check Your Understanding

1. What is meant by avant-garde art?
2. How might the meaning of the Russian worker and peasant, standing on each side of the window in Fig. 6–23, be similar to the meaning of the figures in *Industrial Worker and Collective Farm Girl* (Fig. 6–4)?
3. Many Russian artists developed new styles simply because they wanted to do things differently. When do you want to change things? When might change not be appropriate or good?

# 6.6 Studio Exploration — Papermaking

## Painting with Paper

### Studio Background

What could you do with all the scraps of paper that people throw away every day? Today, many people take paper for granted. When paper was invented, it was a precious item because it was made by hand in small quantities.

**In this studio exploration, you will make your own paper from recycled paper scraps. You'll color your paper and use it as you would use paint. Make a paper painting that suggests change.**

**Slurry** is a watery mixture used to make paper. The mixture is made of **pulp**, which is mashed-up material usually made of wood or plant fibers. After the slurry is strained through a wire screen, the pulp that remains is carefully spread and shaped on blotters. When the pulp is completely dry, it is a sheet of paper.

### You Will Need

- scrap paper
- a blender
- water
- fine strainer and dishpan
- old nylon stocking
- cardboard
- felt or blanket scraps
- paint, ink, or dyes
- natural and printed materials
- paper towels
- an iron

### Step 1 Plan and Practice

- The paper you create will be a kind of collage of found materials. Decide how your paper painting will express thoughts about change.
- Select materials to put in your paper.

**Things to Remember:**

✓ Use materials that relate to your ideas about change.

✓ Make an interesting stencil shape.

✓ Think about your work as a collage.

## Inspiration from Our World

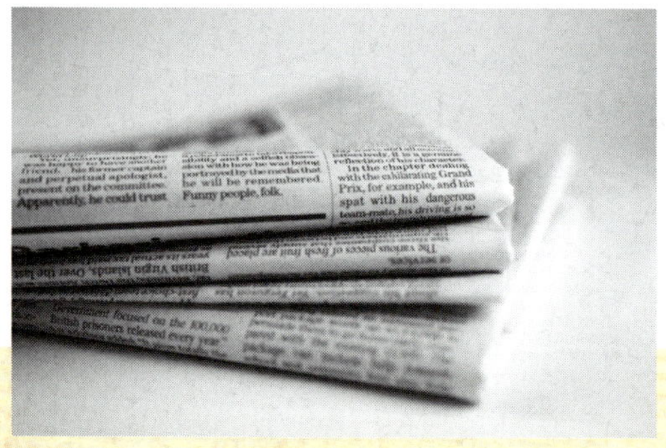

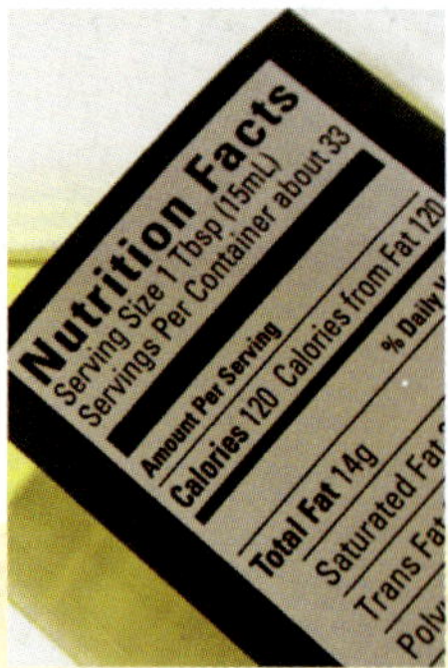


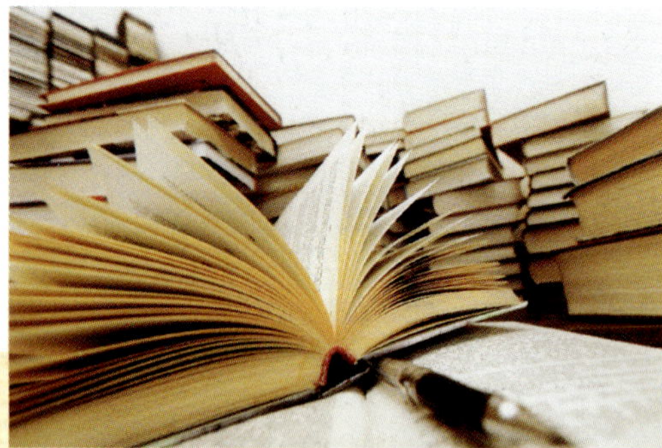

## Inspiration from Art

Artists and papermakers Doug and Helene Zucco founded White Crow Paper Mill in Fleetwood, Pennsylvania in the 1970s. They pioneered the craft of papermaking and the use of pigment introduced directly into paper pulp.

To create her "Sophia Series" of handcast paper pieces, Helene Zucco uses pigmented paper pulp to paint directly into a newly formed wet sheet of paper. For Zucco, pulp painting has the unique characteristics of both paint on wet paper and ink after the paper has dried. The medium allows her to achieve a fluid, painterly image at first. She then manipulates the pulp by applying textures, straight edges, and repetitive marks to her images. After the paper dries, she continues to rework the image, adding layers of depth and dimension. The images in Zucco's "Sophia Series" are based on architectural forms of the Hagia Sophia in Istanbul, Turkey.

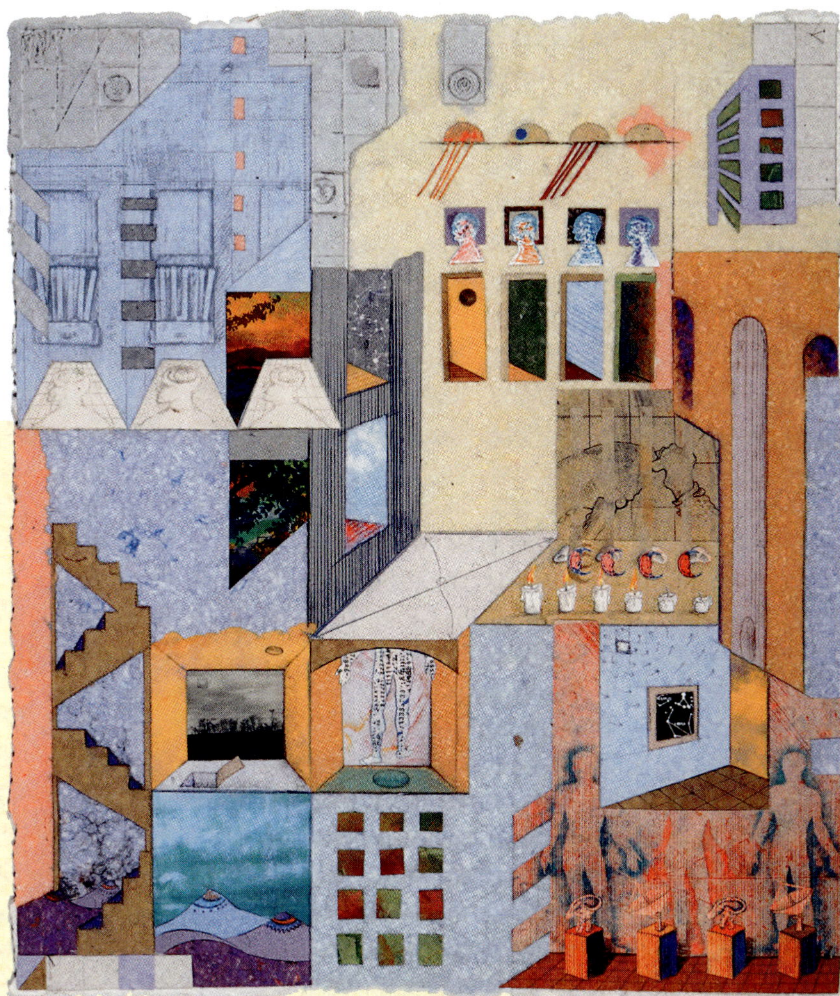

Fig. 6–26 **This is from Helene Zucco's "Sophia Series." Notice how she used paper to create different textures.**

Helene Zucco, *Sophia Series*. Photo by James R. Freeman.

## Step 2 Begin to Create

- **Mix two cups of pulp in a blender half-filled with water.** Run the blender for about thirty seconds. After blending the pulp, carefully mix in leaves, petals, and other natural materials by hand, if you wish.

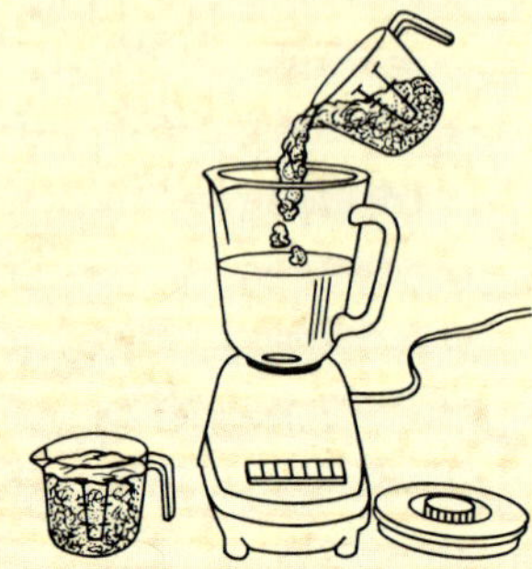

- **Line a fine strainer with a nylon stocking and hold it over a dishpan. Pour the pulp into the strainer.**

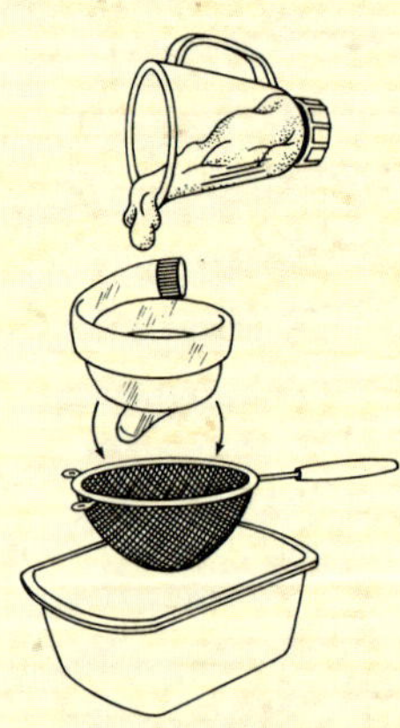

- **Choose a shape for your new sheet of paper. Cut a cardboard stencil in the shape you need.** Place the stencil on top of several layers of felt or blanket scraps.

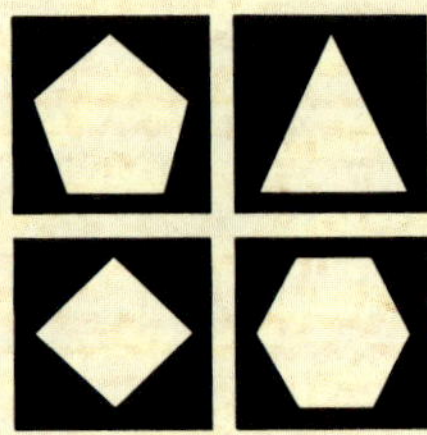

- **Press the pulp flat inside the stencil.** Add color with ink, paint, or dyes. Press additional materials into the paper form to create a collage-like effect.

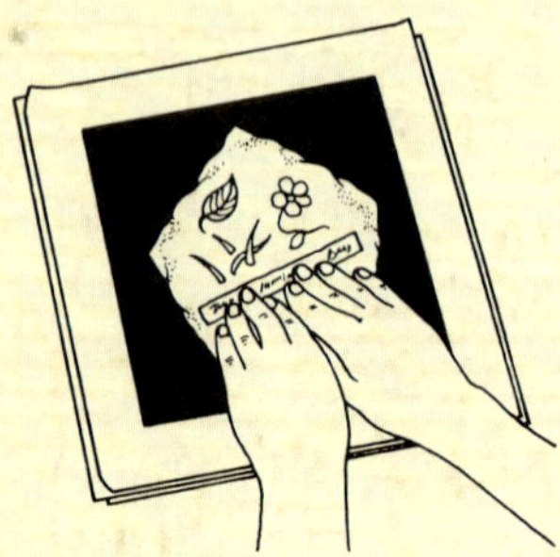

- Cover the form with paper towels and allow it to dry.

## Step 3 Revise

**Did you remember to:**

- ✓ Use materials that relate to your ideas about change?
- ✓ Make an interesting stencil shape?
- ✓ Think about your work as a collage?

Adjust your work if necessary. In your sketchbook, make a note of your revisions and why you made them.

## Step 4 Add Finishing Touches

- Remove towels, stencil, and blanket carefully.
- Place the newly formed sheet of paper between paper towels and press with a warm iron.

### Step 5 **Share and Reflect**

- Discuss your work with your classmates. What shapes and materials did you use to suggest change? What message does your paper communicate?
- How did you decide on a way to express ideas about change? What ideas did you have before you chose the one you used?
- Besides using it in a collage like this one, what are some other ways you can use handmade paper?

## Art Criticism

**Describe** What things do you recognize in this artwork?

**Analyze** How did the artist plan the picture space?

**Interpret** What do you think this picture is about?

**Evaluate** What makes this artwork special?

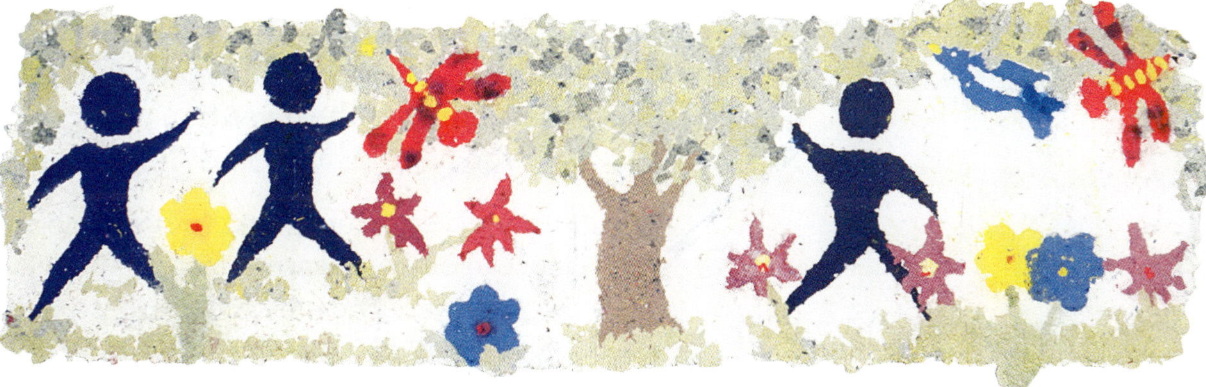

Fig. 6–27 Student artwork

## Language Arts

**When have you tried to change a friend's opinion?** Many writers use persuasive writing to change or influence the reader's opinion. Most articles written by art critics are persuasive pieces.

Try to find real-life examples of persuasive writing in the arts section of your local Sunday paper. Which articles use persuasive writing? How many of these articles are about art? Where else could you look for examples of persuasive writing about art?

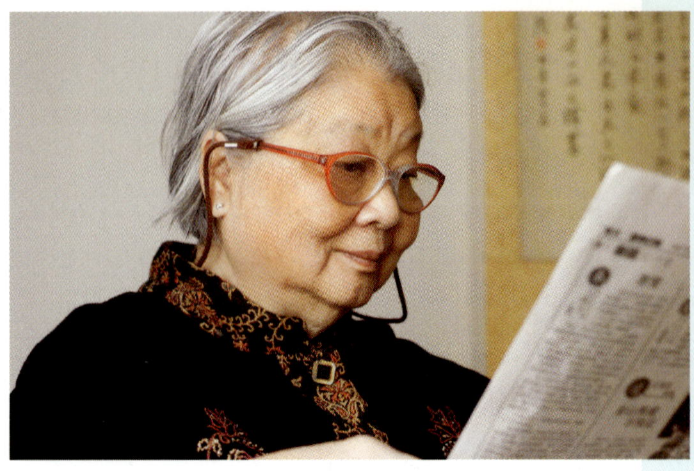

Fig. 6–28

## Theater

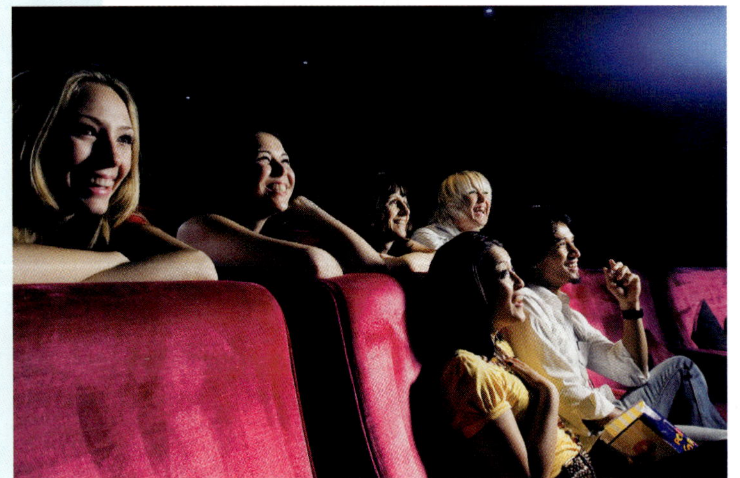

Fig. 6–29

**Advances in technology have changed visual arts and the art of theater.** The most important change in theater was the invention of the motion picture in the early 1900s.

Audiences started going to the movies instead of live theater performances. Movies were cheaper and more people could view them. To compete with all this, theater artists had to remind people why live theater was important. Compare and contrast live theater with recorded movies. How are they similar? How are they different?

## Careers **Toy Designer**

**How have toys changed since you were young?** Some toys have been popular for generations. The company that creates Lego blocks has been around since 1932! Toy designers research and design exciting new toys. They also consider things such as safety, packaging, and promotion. They may specialize in designing hard toys, soft toys, board games, or electronic games. Today, toy designers include advances in technology in their designs. If you could design a new toy, what would it be?

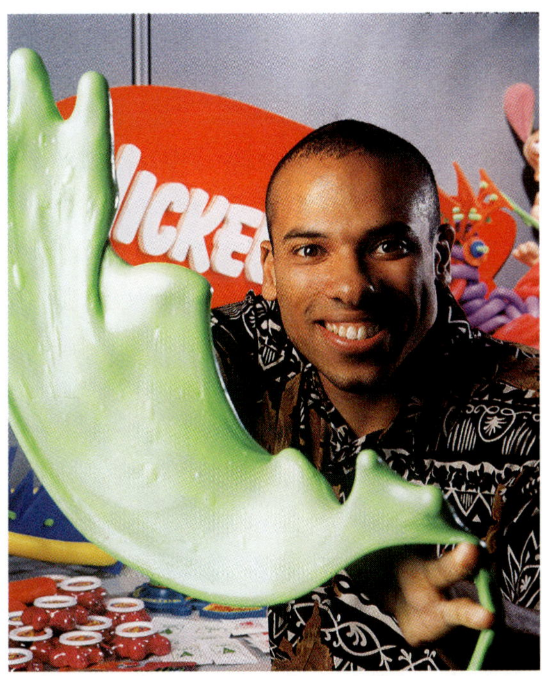

Fig. 6–30 **Toy designer Sean Lee enjoys every part of his job: from brainstorming new toy ideas to deciding how a toy will actually work.**



## Daily Life

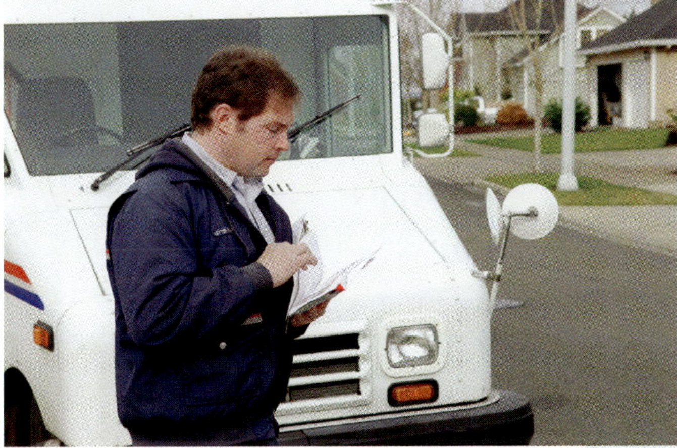

Fig. 6–31

**The way people communicate with others has changed a lot over the years.** How do you communicate with your friends? How has the way you communicate changed since you were a child? Technological advances have caused rapid changes in personal communications. E-mail and cell phones allow nearly instant contact with friends and family. This technology has replaced more traditional forms of communication for many people. When did you last write and mail a personal letter?

## Vocabulary Review

Match each art term below with its definition.

**pigments**
**cityscape**
**pulp**
**avant-garde**
**slurry**
**kinetic sculpture**

1. an art term that describes art that is original and different from traditional styles of art
2. a three-dimensional artwork that moves or has moving parts
3. artwork that shows a view of the city
4. a watery mixture used to make paper
5. colored materials made from earth, crushed minerals, plants, or chemicals
6. mashed-up material usually made of wood or plant fibers, used to make paper

## Aesthetic Thinking

Do artists have to take a lot of time to make good artworks? Why or why not? Consider artwork produced with a computer and artwork produced by hand in your argument.

## Write About Art

American artist Childe Hassam once said that the paintings of his friend John Henry Twachtman were "strong, and at the same time delicate." Study this painting and then write a short essay explaining what you think Hassam meant.

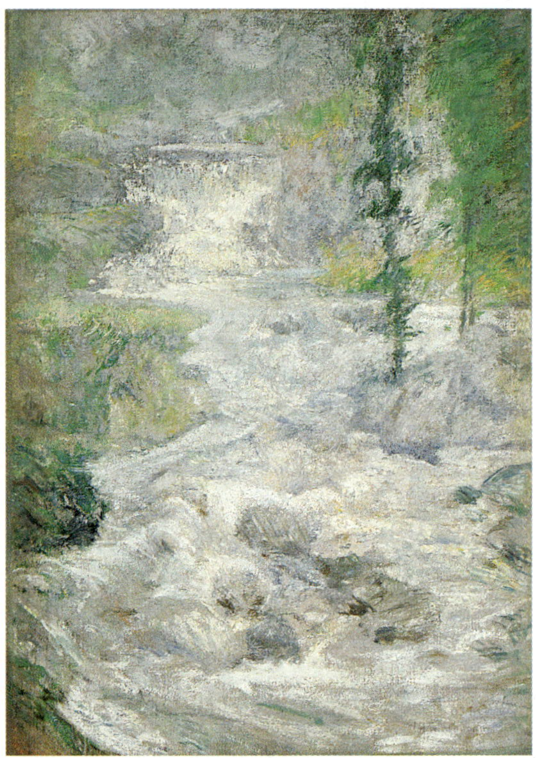

Fig. 6–32 **John Henry Twachtman was an American Impressionist painter. Look carefully at this painting. How would you describe the brushstrokes?**

John Henry Twachtman, *The Rainbow's Source*, ca. 1890–1900. Oil on canvas, 34 ⅛" x 24 ½" (86.7 x 62.2 cm). The St. Louis Art Museum (Modern Art), Purchase 124:1921. [ISN 3470]

## Art Criticism

**Describe** What do you see in this painting?

**Analyze** How does the artist create rhythm in this painting?

**Interpret** Thomas often gave her paintings titles that related to music. Why do you think this might be?

**Evaluate** Thomas's paintings have often been compared to mosaics. Explain whether or not you agree with that comparison.

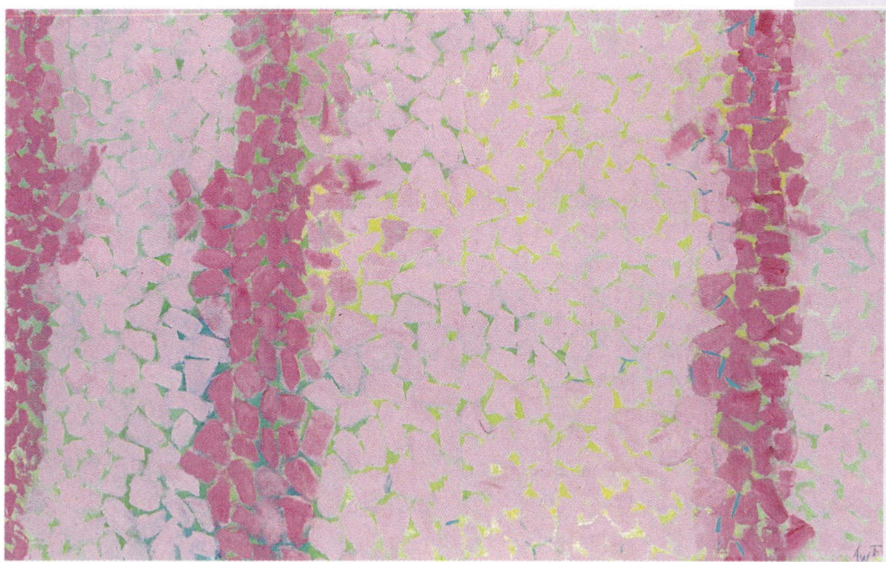

Fig. 6–33 Alma Woodsey Thomas, *Wind and Crepe Myrtle Concerto*, 1973. Acrylic on canvas, 35" x 52" (88.9 x 132.1 cm). National Museum of American Art, Smithsonian Institution, Washington, DC / Art Resource, NY

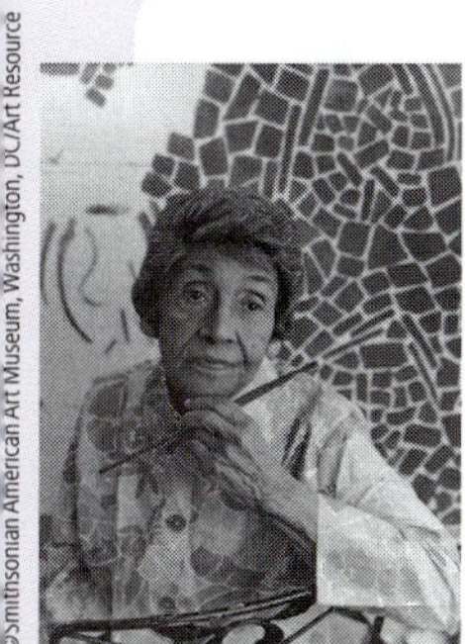



## Meet the Artist

**Alma Thomas** was born in Columbus, Georgia, and later moved with her family to Washington, DC. She was the first student to graduate from the art department at Howard University. Thomas spent more than thirty years teaching middle school. When she retired, she began to focus on the work she is known for today, brightly colored abstract paintings.

**"I got some watercolors and some crayons, and I began dabbling. Little dabs of color that spread out very free...that's how it all began. And every morning since then, the wind has given me new colors through the windowpanes."**

— Alma Thomas (1891–1978)

## For Your Portfolio

Select an artwork from your portfolio that best reflects the theme of change. Describe the work in detail. Why did you choose this particular artwork? Think about what you did well and on what you can improve.

## For Your Sketchbook

List characteristics or qualities that are consistent throughout your sketchbook. Also identify ways that your entries have changed. Summarize your findings on a blank page in your sketchbook.

# Art and Celebration

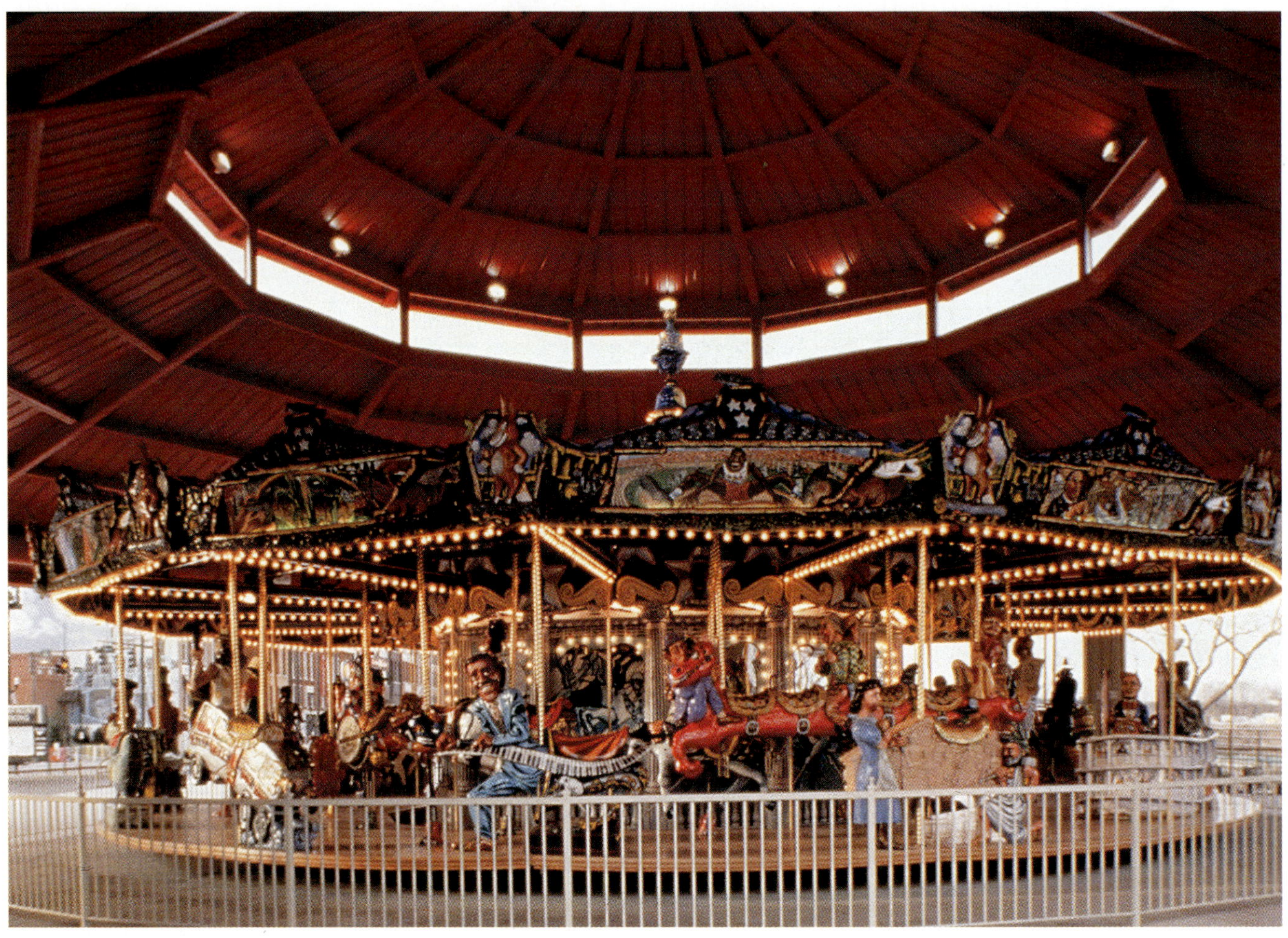

Fig. 7–1 **This carousel celebrates Tennessee history and culture. If you created a carousel to celebrate your own community, what people or events would you include?**

Red Grooms, *Tennessee Fox Trot Carousel,* Riverfront Park, Nashville, TN. Fiberglass over an aluminum frame, 35' x diam. 46' (88.9 x 116.8 cm). Illustration 1998 Red Grooms. Photo courtesy of Tennessee Fox Trot Carousel Operating Company. ©2000 Red Grooms/Artists Rights Society (ARS), New York.

**Does your town or city celebrate things that have special meaning to the community? Some places hold annual festivals.** Others celebrate the anniversary of the founding of their town or city. To celebrate something is to honor it.

There are many kinds of community celebrations and many ways to show these celebrations in artworks. Some artworks, such as the carousel in Nashville, Tennessee **(Fig. 7–1)**, are a celebration in themselves. This carousel focuses on the city's history and people.

Many artists create artworks that reflect community spirit. These artworks are often displayed in public. Where have you seen public art that honors your community or its heritage?

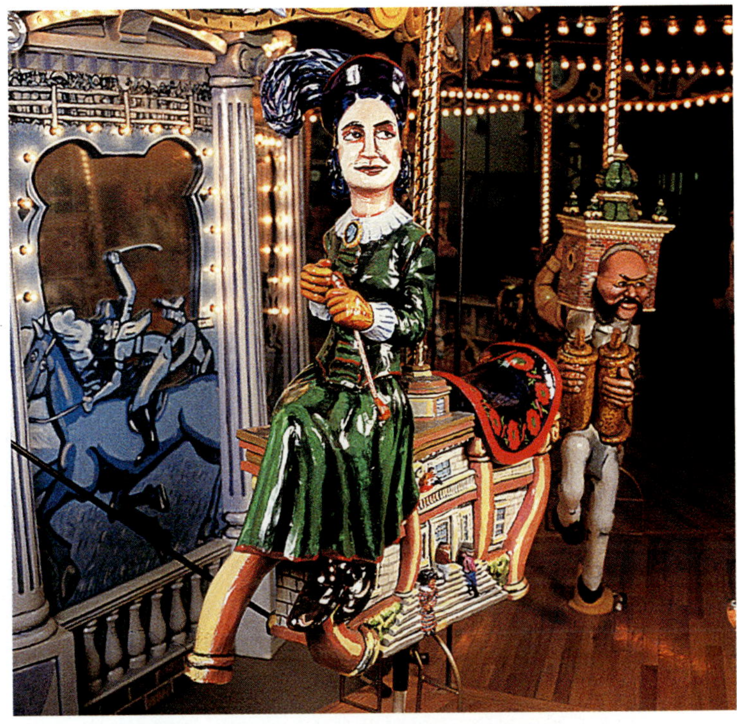

Fig. 7–2 **Adelicia Acklen is one of many Nashville figures featured on this carousel. Why might an artist create an artwork that celebrates a specific person?**

Red Grooms, *Tennessee Fox Trot Carousel* (detail).

### In this unit, you will learn:

- How artists express and promote community pride through their work.
- How to celebrate community through photography, paper sculpture, and other media.
- How to look at artworks as expressions of pride in communities.

# Community Honors

**Local Customs** A community's spirit comes in part from the pride its members have in their past. Language, clothing, and local customs can all add to the spirit of a community. To celebrate the spirit of a community is to celebrate its people and their way of life. Some artists show people going about their lives in local ways. These artworks help us learn about the different ways people live in other regions.

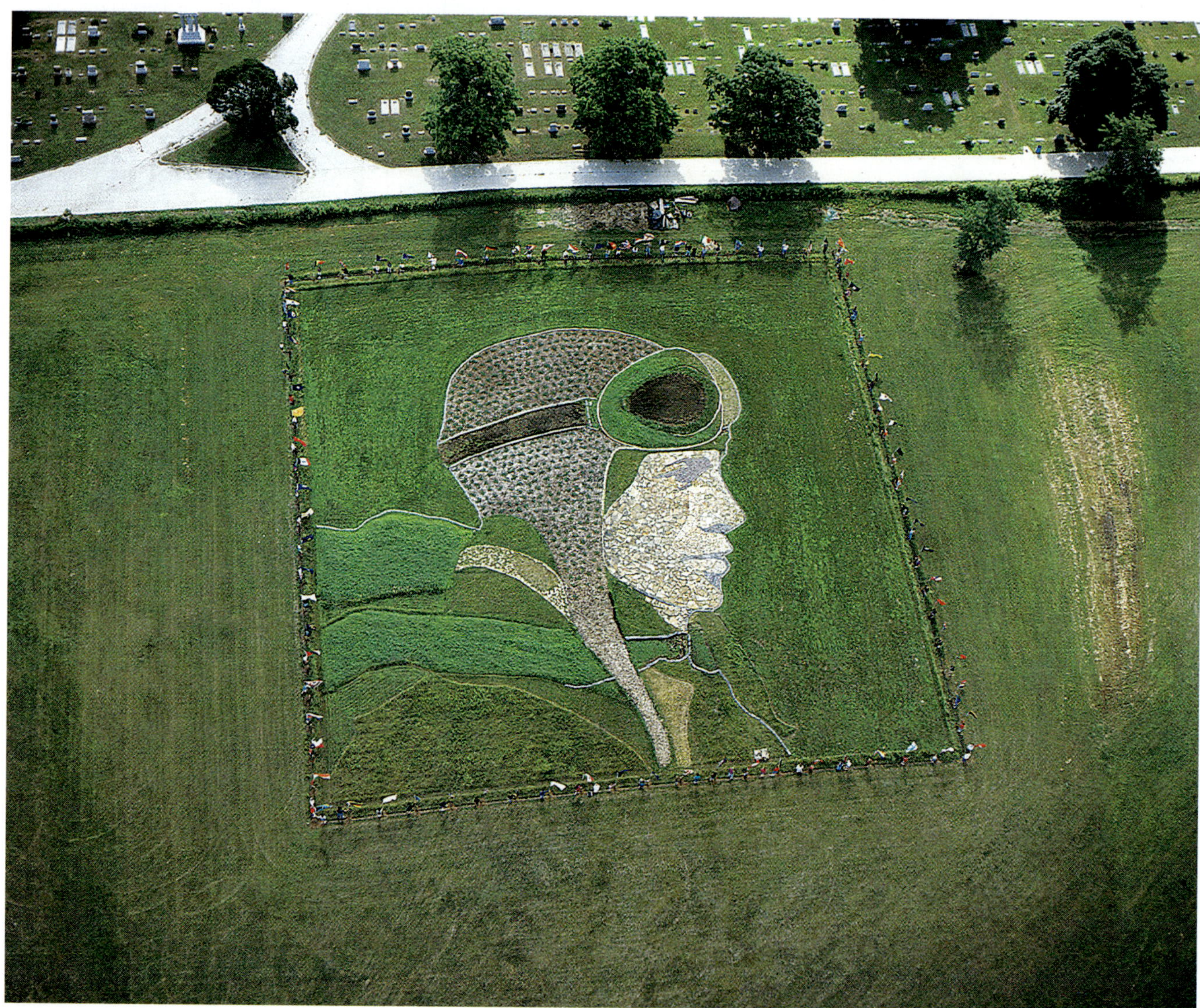

Fig. 7–3 **This portrait was made with native stones and grasses. Why might the artist have decided to honor this pilot with an artwork best seen from the air?**

Stan Herd, *Portrait of Amelia Earhart,* Atchison, Kansas, 1997. Native stone with perennial grasses and other ground covers. Photograph ©Jon Blumb, 1997.

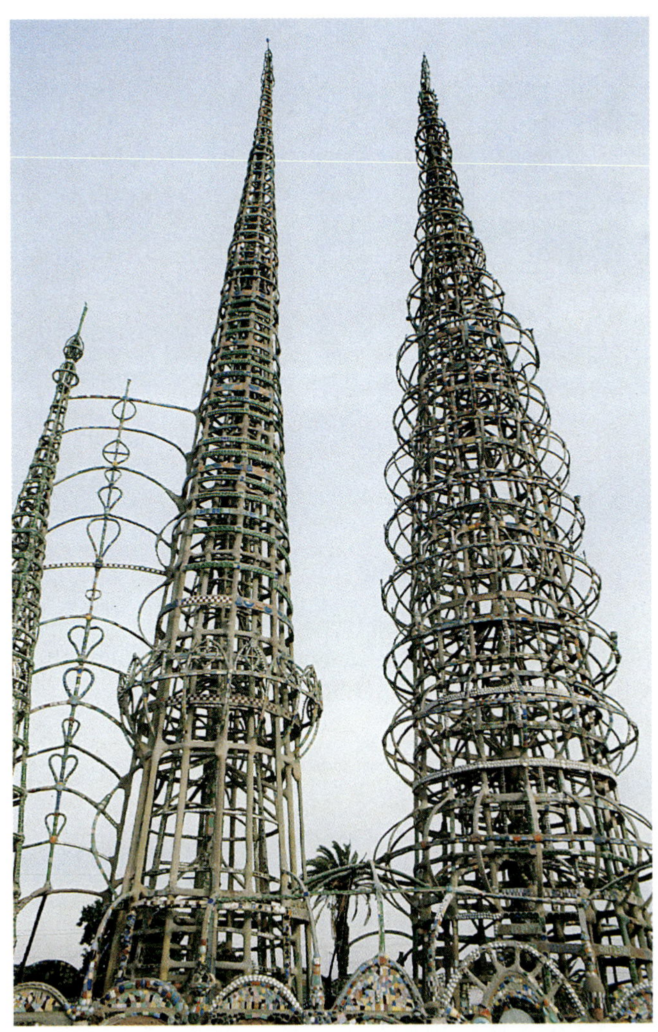

**Local Heroes** Another source of community spirit is the pride people have in their local heroes. As you travel into cities and towns, you may see welcome signs that tell about the well-known people who were born or lived there. Parks and restaurants are often named after favorite citizens.

Artists sometimes help communities create artworks that show the accomplishments of their citizens. In Atchison, Kansas, the hometown of aviator Amelia Earhart, volunteers helped Kansas artist Stan Herd commemorate Earhart's 100th birthday **(Fig. 7–3)**. As in most of Herd's artworks, the portrait of Amelia Earhart is best seen from the air.

Fig. 7–4 **One man used thousands of found materials to build these towers. Why might he still be considered a local hero after leaving the area?**

Simon Rodia, *Watts Towers*, Los Angeles, California, 1921–55. ©Rene Burri/Magnum Photos.

## Meet Simon Rodia

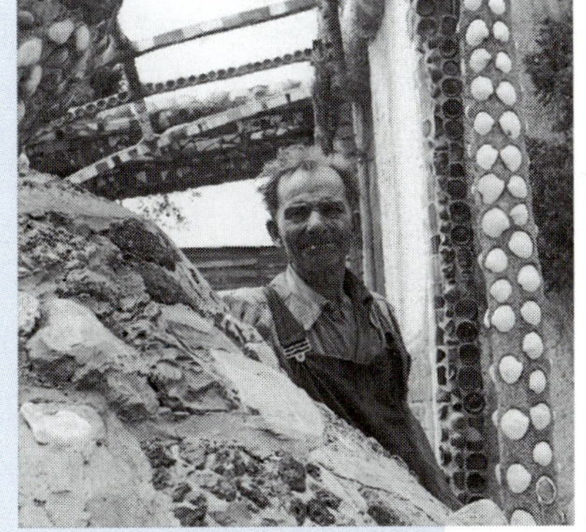

Getty Images

Simon Rodia was born on a farm in Italy. In his teens, he immigrated to America and worked as a coal mine laborer. At age 42, Rodia started constructing the *Watts Towers* beside his house in Los Angeles, California. He improvised everything and never let anyone else help him. He made towers, fountains, walkways, and a gazebo out of wire and concrete. Before the concrete dried, he pressed found objects into it, including jewelry, tiles, glass, and plastic. He worked for 33 years. Then he moved away from the area. Today, the towers are a tourist attraction and a source of local pride.

**"I had in mind to do something big and I did it."**

— Simon Rodia (1879–1965)

**Local Festivals** In a tour book for any North American region, you can usually find a list of local festivals. These celebrations provide opportunities for people to take part in cultural events and community traditions. Some festivals honor local heroes. Others celebrate local foods or crafts. Seasonal festivals highlight special activities associated with each time of the year.

**Common Customs** While community celebrations differ in many ways, festivals have some traditions in common. Traditions are customs or beliefs that are passed down from earlier generations. Parades and fireworks, for instance, are traditions in United States community celebrations. Flags, costumes, and artistic performances all add to the festivities. People with a common interest sometimes come from all around the world to attend festivals.

Imagine seeing a whole group of cars and vans that have been transformed into works of art! For several years, Houston, Texas, has been the destination for people interested in art cars or vehicles transformed into spectacular moving sculptures. Although people bring their art cars from many places, the community of Houston has adopted the festival as its own.

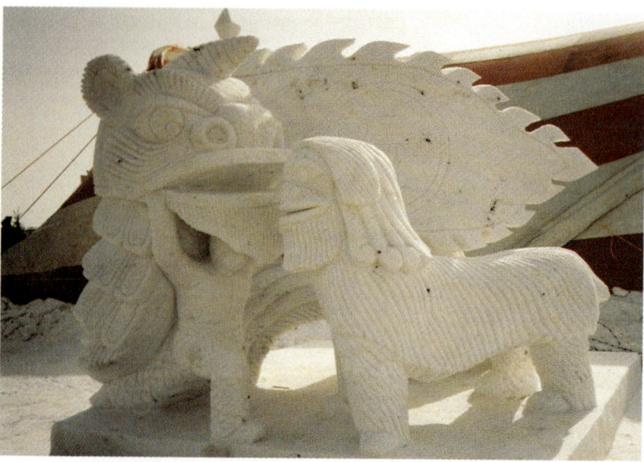

Fig. 7–5 **The largest winter festival in Canada is internationally known for its snow sculpture competition. What other types of competitions are often part of community celebrations?**

*Hong Kong's entry in the International Snow Sculpture Symposium,* 1993. Courtesy of Festival du Voyageur.

## Check Your Understanding

1. How might an artist show the spirit of a community?
2. Compare and contrast the *Watts Towers* (Fig. 7–4) and the *Camera Van* (Fig. 7–6). How are their connections to the community similar? How are they different?
3. Why do you think it is important to celebrate community spirit and pride through artwork?

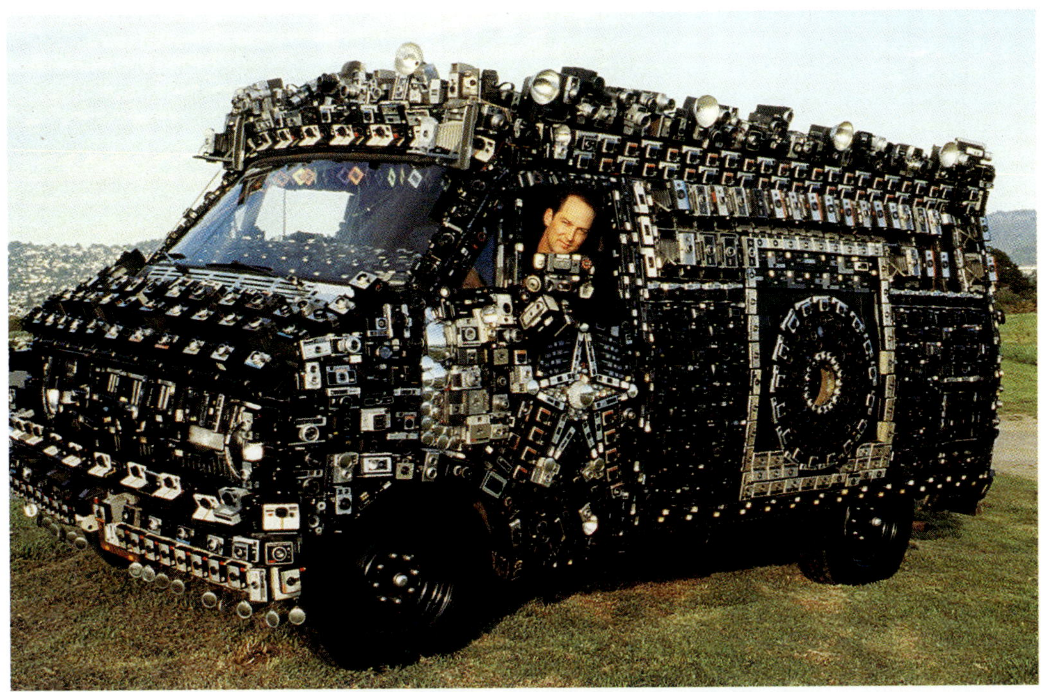

Fig. 7–6 **This artist used 2,000 cameras to make his van into a sculpture. What would you include on an art car you made to express yourself?**

Herrod Blank, *Camera Van,* 1995. 1972 Dodge van with 2000 cameras. Courtesy of the artist, cameravan.com.

## Studio Time

### A Community Celebration

Choose a community celebration to show in a drawing.

- Sketch your ideas for the scene. Will the point of view be from near or far?
- Decide which medium will best express your ideas for your drawing. Will you use markers, colored pencils, or pastels?
- Create your final drawing. Draw large shapes first, then add details.

Reflect on how details convey the theme of celebration.

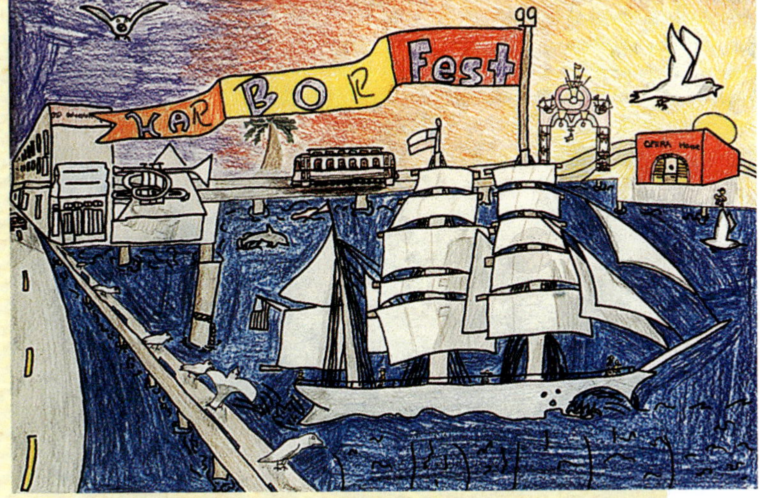


Fig. 7–7 Student artwork

# Photography

You have probably used a camera to capture a moment during a celebration with family and friends. People all around the world use cameras to record memorable times. After photography was invented in 1826, artists slowly began to realize the possibilities for creative expression. Using a camera, they could look around and frame pictures. Some artists have taken photographs as guides for later paintings. Others value photographs for their unique characteristics. For more than 175 years, artists have been using photography to explore their world and create unforgettable images.

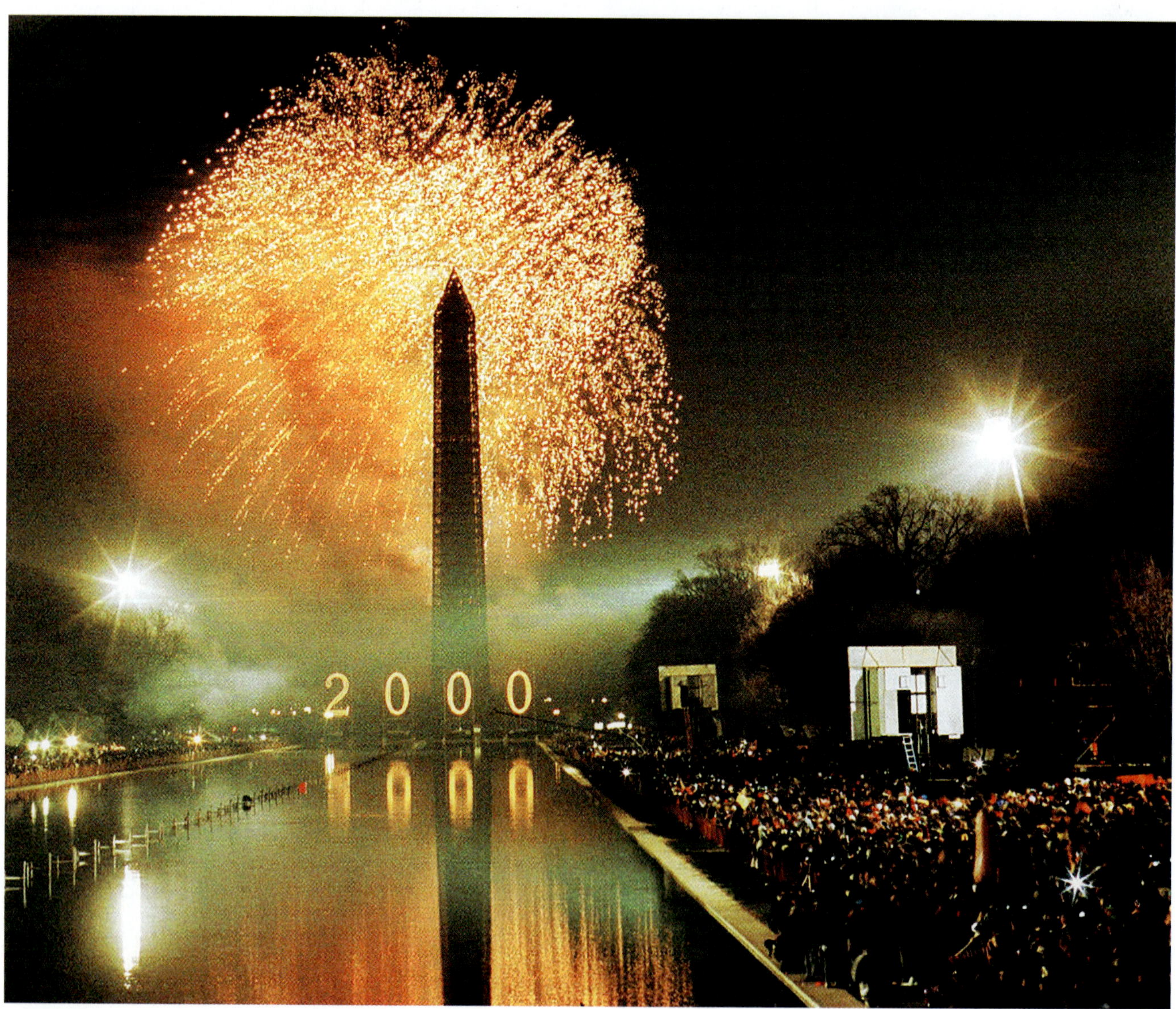


Fig. 7–8 **This photograph represents one city's perspective of a world celebration: the ringing in of the new millennium. Why might the photographer have included crowds of people in the frame?**

Fireworks in Washington, New Year's 2000 Celebration. ©Reuters Newmedia, Inc./Corbis.

Although almost everyone can take photographs with a camera, a photographer has several decisions to make that affect how each photograph finally looks. One factor that photographers consider is composition. Composition is the way the parts of the photograph or other artwork are arranged. Photographers consider which part of a scene they want to show and which part they may not want to capture. The way a photographer composes an image enables him or her to create a desired effect. Careful composition allows the photographer to create a clear center of interest.

Photographers also consider the point of view of an image. Point of view in photography means the position from which an artist takes a photograph. A close-up view often captures a small part of a scene in great detail, while a faraway view shows a larger scene and often provides less detail. Photographers can change the sense of distance in a photograph by moving closer to or farther away from a subject. Many cameras also have zoom lenses that enable the photographer to make it seem as though the photograph was taken from a closer or more distant view. Both the frame and point of view of an image affect the impact and emphasis of the photograph's subject.

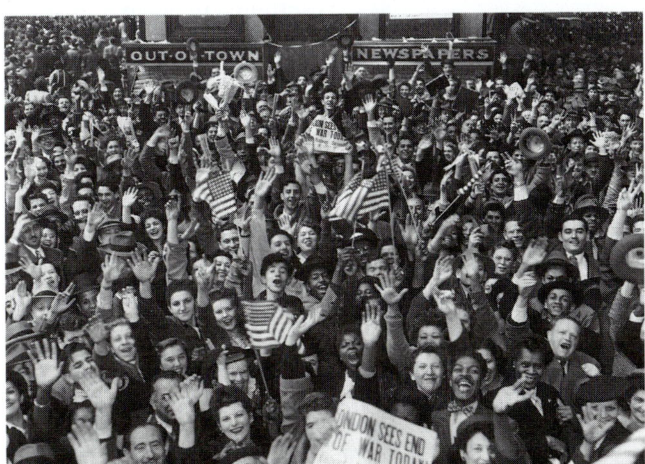

Fig. 7–9 **This community in New York City celebrated the surrender of German forces at the end of World War II. What makes this a powerful photograph?**

Large group of people celebrating V-E Day. Silver gelatin print ©Corbis/Bettmann-UPI.

**Observe** Look at Fig. 7–8. Why is the distant viewpoint the photographer chose best for capturing the moment?

**Tools:** Magazines and four half-inch strips of paper.

### Practice: Composing a Photograph

- Choose photographs from magazines that show different celebrations. Try to find photographs taken from far away and close up.
- Use the strips of paper to crop, or frame, the magazine photographs. Notice how cropping to the outside edge of the photograph can give you a distant view. Cropping to a smaller part of a photograph can give you a close-up view. Which view provides the most impact or emphasis?
- Cut the magazine photos into strips. Then shift the strips to create a distorted image. How does this change the impact or emphasis of the celebration?

Photographers make choices about point of view. Photographers also consider the balance and lighting of their shots. They decide how they want to present their subject within a photograph. Balance is a principle of design that describes the arrangement of the parts in a photograph. A balanced photograph has equal visual interest in all areas. An unbalanced photograph might show the subject to one side instead of in the center.

The lighting of a scene is another important choice for the photographer. The amount of light and the contrast that it creates influences the overall mood of the photograph. Lighting also affects the center of interest of a photograph because the brightest areas are usually seen first. The balance and lighting of a photograph contribute to the photograph's overall visual impact.

**Observe** Look at Fig. 7–10. How does the use of balance in this photograph help emphasize the celebration? How does the balance shown here differ from the balance shown in Fig. 7–8?

**Tools:** Camera

### Check Your Understanding

1. When is a photograph balanced?
2. Compare and contrast Figs. 7–9 and 7–10. How are the ways they capture a celebration similar? How are they different?
3. Why might the work of a professional photographer be considered artistic while a photograph taken by an average person might not be considered artistic?

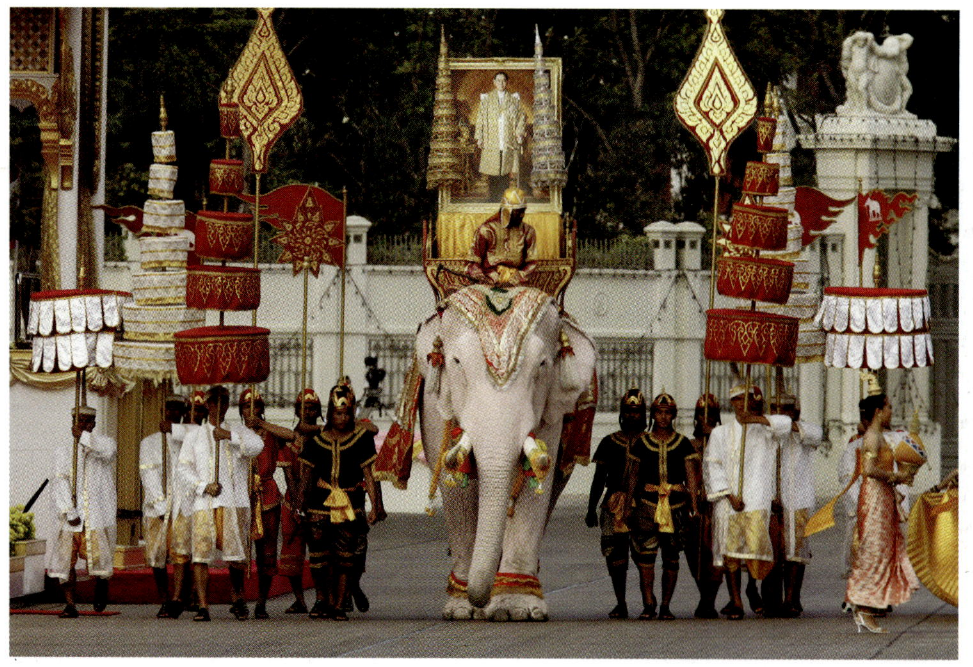

Fig. 7–10 **This photograph captures a moment during the week-long celebration of the king of Thailand's eightieth birthday. What can you learn about the celebration from this photograph?**

An elephant painted in pink carrying the portrait of the Thai King Bhumbol Adulyadej performs with performers prior to the trooping of the colors to honor the King's birthday in Bangkok, Thailand, Sunday, December 2, 2007. (AP Photo/ Apichart Weerawong) (07120205299)

### Practice: Taking a Photograph

- Hold the camera steady with your hands. Keep your elbows near to your body.

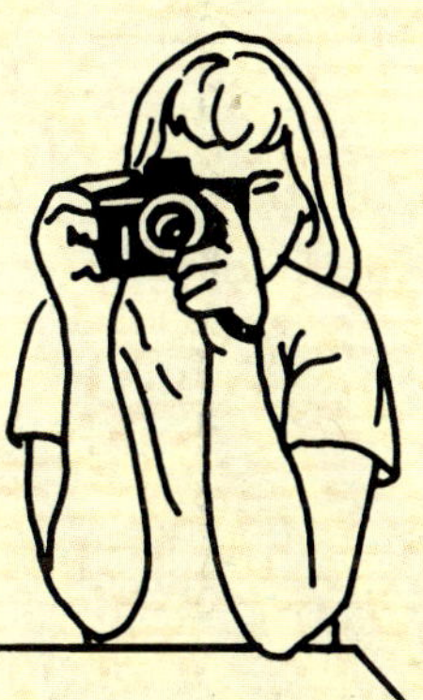

- Look through the viewfinder. Aim so your subject is in the center of the photograph. Then adjust your aim to achieve an unbalanced photograph.
- To include more of the space around the subject, move away from it. To include less space, move closer to the subject. Alternately, you may adjust your camera's zoom lens.
- Examine the photographs you have taken. How did the different points of view you used change the outcome of each image?

## Studio Time

### Documenting a Celebration

Take photographs of a birthday, festival, student assembly, or other community celebration.

- Take some close-up shots of important objects or moments. Take other photographs from far away.
- Have people pose for some of your photographs. Also take casual photographs while people are celebrating. Think about the lighting and balance of each shot.
- Organize the best photographs into a series that documents the event. Share your photographs with those who attended, and use them to tell others about the celebration.

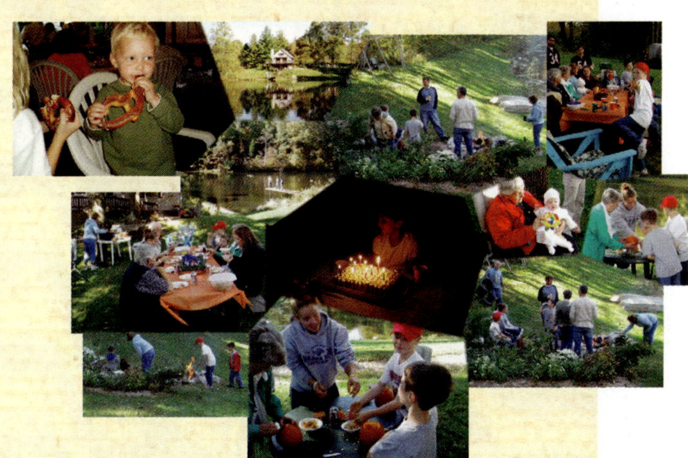

Fig. 7–11 Student artwork

Reflect on how the arrangement of your photographs contributes to the theme of celebration.

# An Essay in Photos

## Studio Background

Have you ever talked about a party or other event with a friend who attended it with you? Did you both remember the event in the same way? You both probably had a different experience, even though you attended the same event. Similarly, photography can serve as a way to capture an event or scene. The photographer chooses certain parts of a scene to capture. Some photographers take multiple photographs of the same scene, arranging them in a way that changes our perception and understanding of the scene.

**In this studio exploration, you will work in a group to create an essay in photographs.** You will take multiple photographs and assemble them to create an artwork that shows a particular way to understand an event, location, or experience.

### You Will Need

- camera
- mat board
- glue stick, double-sided tape, or other adhesive

### Step 1 Plan and Practice

- Divide into groups of four.
- Decide which group member will perform each of four specific tasks.
- One member should find out more information about the use and care of cameras.
- Another member should look at Fig. 7–12 and research other works of photography by artist David Hockney. Think about how and why Hockney includes several viewpoints in his work.
- A third member should find out more about composition and cropping photographs to create a center of interest.

## Inspiration from Our World

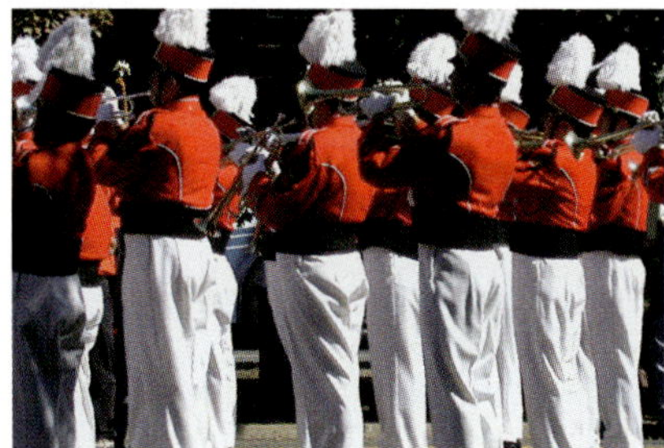

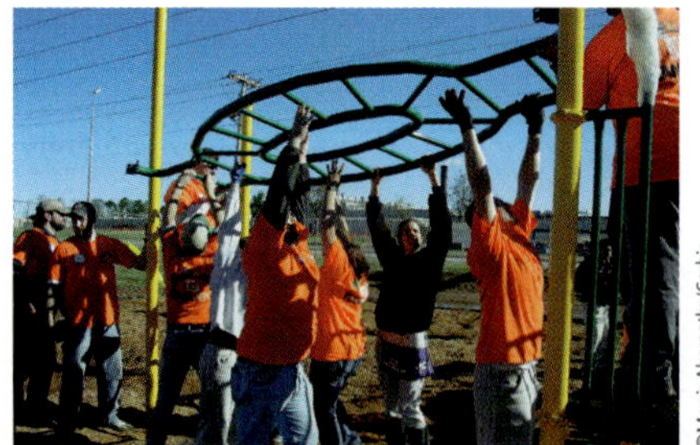



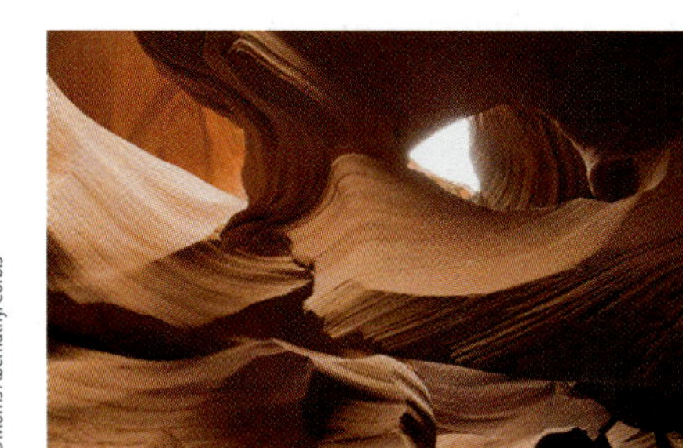

- The fourth group member should think about nearby locations or events in your school and community that could be the subject of your artwork. If you choose a location, consider how your artwork can celebrate certain aspects of it. If you choose an event, consider what is important about it, and what it suggests about your community.
- Each student should share his or her findings with the group.

**Things to Remember:**

✓ Work as a group.

✓ Take your photographs from different angles and viewpoints.

✓ Try different arrangements of your photographs.

## Inspiration from Art

By 1982, David Hockney was well known as a painter and portraitist. He had become interested in very wide views of landscapes, but disliked using wide-angle lenses to photograph these views. Wide-angle lenses can distort, or change, the look of the scene. One day he was grouping some snapshots that were to be the basis for a painting. He noticed that he could create the effect of seeing a scene from many different angles at once. For the next four years or so, Hockney experimented with this approach to photography, creating the pictures that he called "joiners." These pictures were made up of hundreds—sometimes thousands—of individual photographs.

At first Hockney used a Polaroid camera for his joiners. Polaroid cameras create an instant photograph that develops in seconds while you watch it. As his works became more complicated, however, Hockney switched to a 35mm camera. And after 1986 he began to experiment with color photocopies, faxes, and images made with computers.

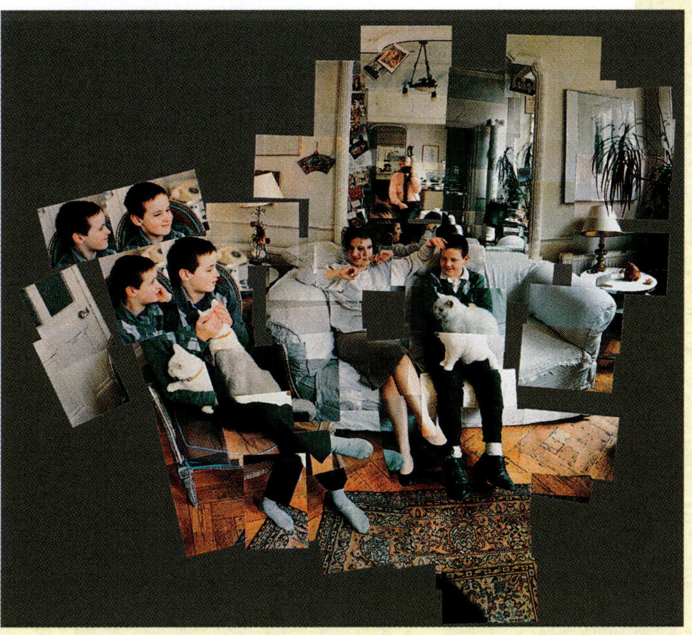

Fig. 7–12 **Notice how Hockney includes multiple views of the same subject. How does this affect your sense of time?**

David Hockney, *George, Celia, Albert and Percy,* London, 1983. Photographic collage, 44" x 47" (111.7 x 119.4 cm). ©David Hockney.

## Step 2 Begin to Create

- With your group, decide the subject of your photo essay.
- **Take photographs of your chosen location or event.** Some photographs may be taken from close up to capture details. Others may be taken from far away to capture a wider view. Try using the camera's zoom setting to change the distance.

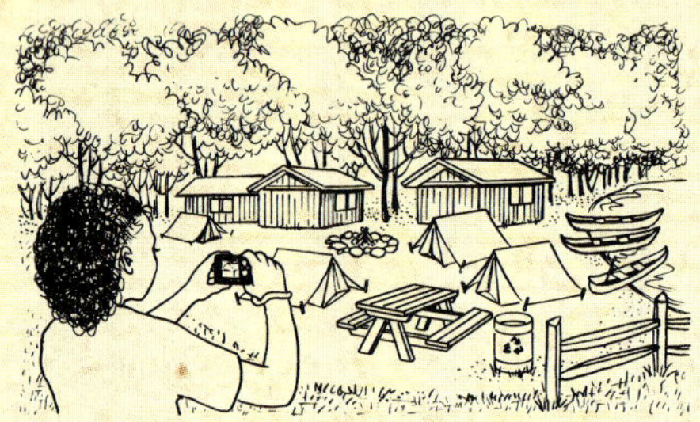

- Use the camera's flash to change the lighting in your photographs.
- Stand in different areas and take photographs from a variety of angles. Capture as many views as possible.
- Develop your photographs.
- **Work together to arrange your photographs on the mat board.** Experiment with different arrangements. Which photographs will you include? Which will be left out? Consider including only parts of some photographs.

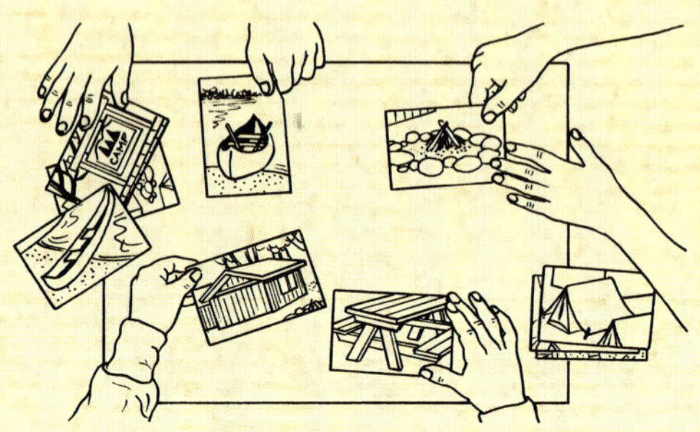

- Mount the final arrangement of photographs onto the mat board.

## Step 3 Revise

**Did you remember to:**

✓ Work as a group?

✓ Take your photographs from different angles and viewpoints?

✓ Try different arrangements of your photographs?

Adjust your work if necessary. In your sketchbook, make a note of your revisions and why you made them.

### Step 4 **Add Finishing Touches**

- Be sure all photographs are securely mounted.
- Create a title for your work and include it on the mat board.
- Each group member should sign the work.

### Step 5 **Share and Reflect**

- As a class, display all the photo essays. Discuss the experience of photographing your location or event and creating an artwork using multiple photographs of the same subject.
- Share how and why your group's artwork represents a celebration of community.
- What about your photo essay works well? How might the photographs be improved?
- Why is the photo essay a useful way to celebrate community?

## Art Criticism

**Describe** What do you recognize in these composite photographs?

**Analyze** How are these artworks composed?

**Interpret** What do these artworks suggest to you?

**Evaluate** What do you like best about these compositions?

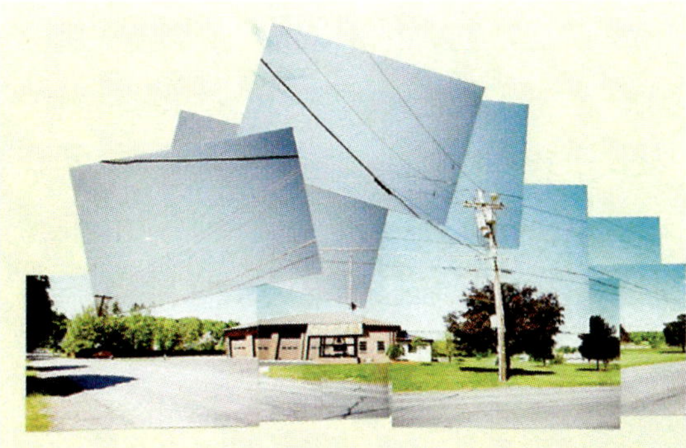

Fig. 7–13 Student artwork

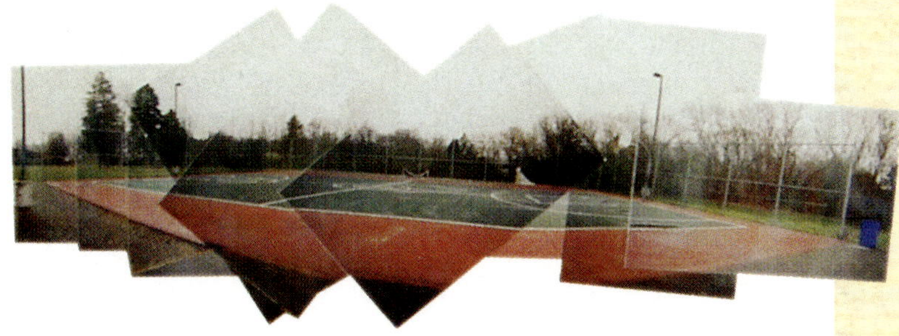

Fig. 7–14 Student artwork

# American Art: 1920–1950

Major international wars took place between the 1910s and the 1950s. In 1918, the United States was emerging from World War I, which was fought in Europe. Americans were tired of European political and economic affairs. They wanted to focus on the quality of life in the United States.

**Community and National Spirit** In the years following World War I, many Regionalist artists arose. Regionalist artists focused their attention on specific regions or sections of the country. Those artists who used the city as subject matter for their art are sometimes called Urban Regionalists. Their artworks celebrated the spirit of the community. They showed scenes crowded with people, new architecture, and changing styles of clothing. Away from the cities, artists searched for ways to celebrate a national spirit. Some, who became known as Rural Regionalists, captured American pride and traditions in their artworks. They often looked back to American folk art for inspiration. Fig. 7–15, for example, celebrates the spirit of the American West.

**Looking to Art in Difficult Times** In 1929, the American stock market crashed, triggering the Great Depression of the 1930s. Many people in the United States lost their jobs as well as everything they owned. During the Great Depression, the United States started one of the most extraordinary programs to support the arts. Inspired by the Mexican mural movement, the government paid artists minimum wages to create public works of art. These works included murals that focused on regional and community spirit. Many of these murals represent critical turning points in North American art history.

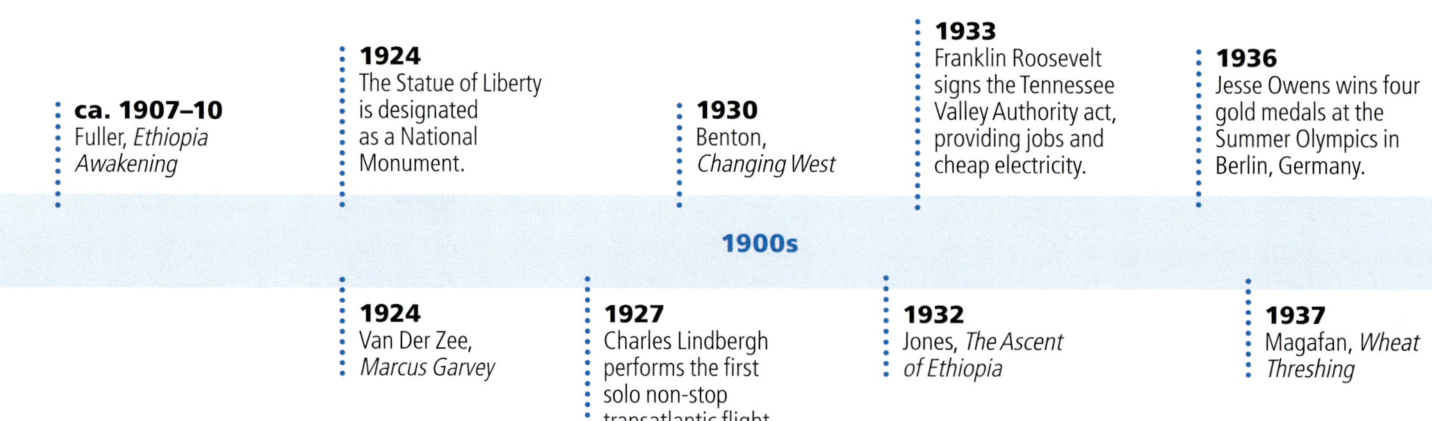

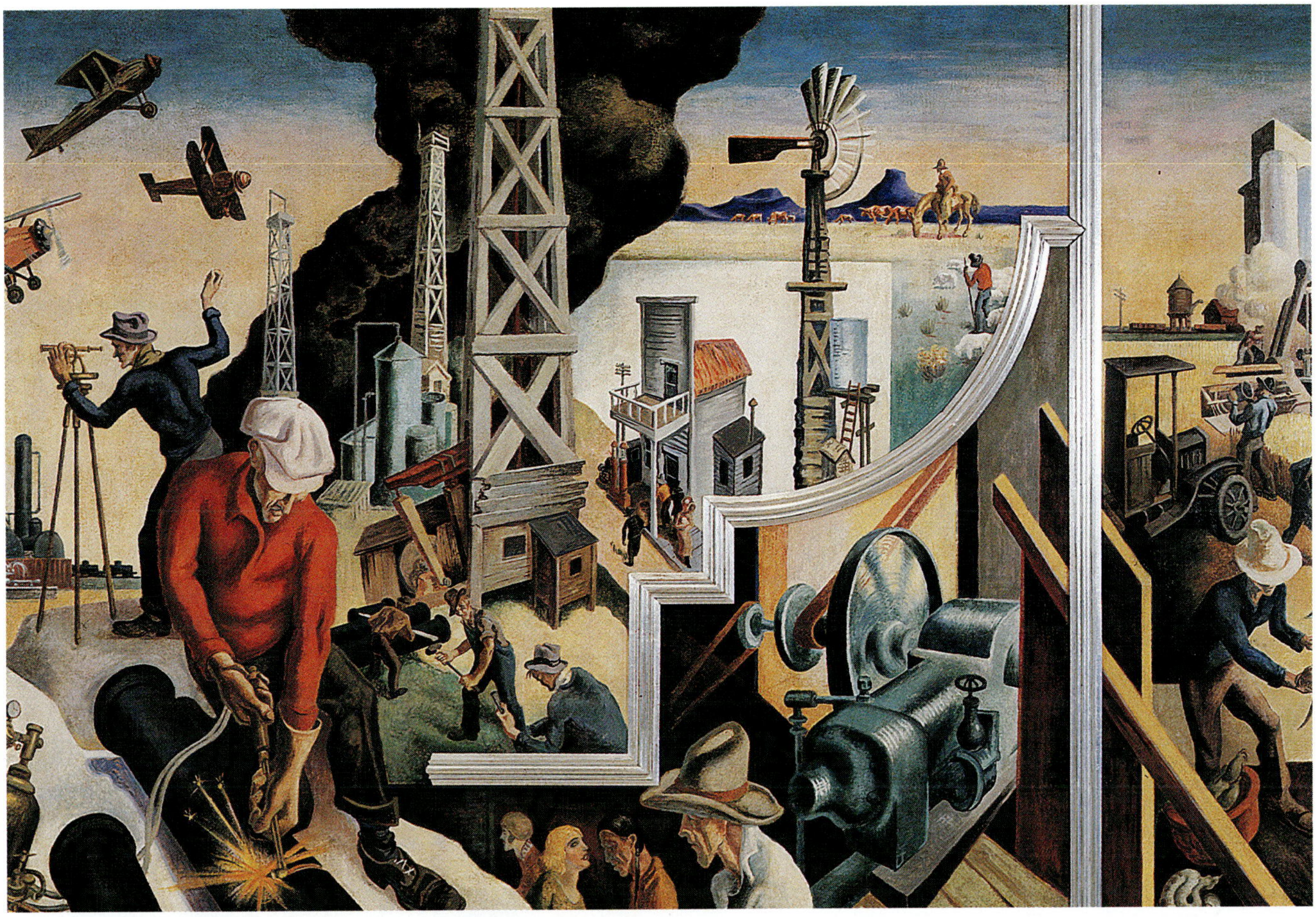

Fig. 7–15 **This artist painted a variety of "snapshots" of the American West. How does this painting convey the pride and traditions of the American West?**

Thomas Hart Benton, *The Changing West from America Today,* 1930. Distemper and egg tempera on gessoed linen with oil glaze, 92" x 117" (233.7 x 297.2 cm). Collection, AXA Financial. ©AXA Financial. ©T.H. Benton and R.P. Benton Testamentary Trusts/Licensed by VAGA, New York, NY.

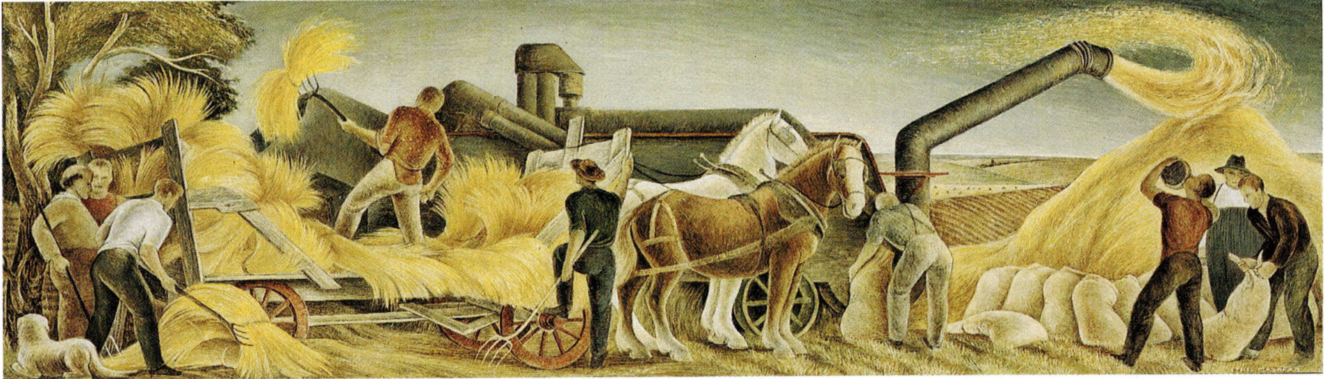

Fig. 7–16 **Government-funded murals often showed the things a community took pride in. What do you think the people in this community valued?**

Ethel Magafan, *Wheat Threshing,* 1937. Egg tempera on gessoed masonite panel, 17 ½" x 34 ⅛" (44.5 x 88.6 cm). Museum Purchase, Art Purchase fund, Friends of the Wichita Art Museum, Wichita Art Museum, Kansas. (1981.19).

**Harlem Renaissance** In the 1920s, a group of artists, writers, and entertainers gathered in Harlem, a section of New York City. The term Harlem Renaissance is used to describe the period when many artists who lived in Harlem used various forms to express their lives as African Americans. *Renaissance* means "a rebirth of culture." These artists helped the African-American community explore its history and express pride in its culture.

The Harlem Renaissance ended with the stock market crash in 1929. In the decades that followed, artists including Lois Mailou Jones **(Fig. 7–19)** continued to create important works. These artists spread cultural pride to African-American communities throughout the country. Although less publicized, creative activities were taking place in the African-American communities of other cities, such as Philadelphia, Chicago, Boston, and San Francisco.

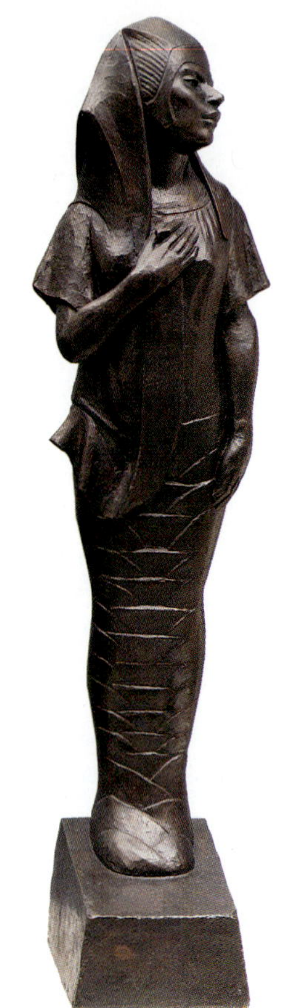

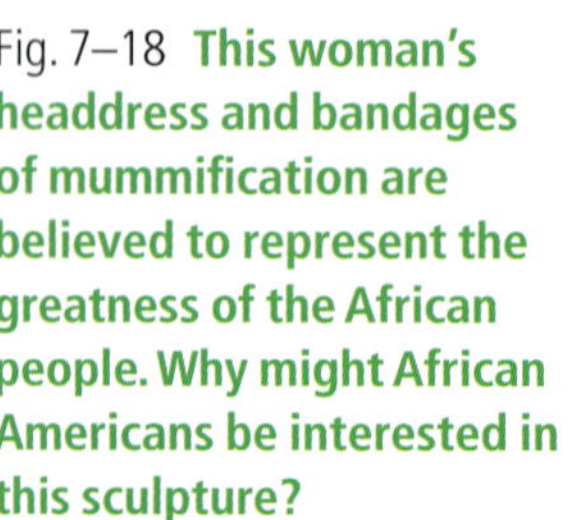

Fig. 7–18 **This woman's headdress and bandages of mummification are believed to represent the greatness of the African people. Why might African Americans be interested in this sculpture?**

Meta Warrick Fuller, *Ethiopia Awakening*, ca. 1907–10. Plaster (bronze cast), 67" x 16" x 20" (170 x 40.6 x 50.8 cm). Art and Artifacts Division, Schomburg Center for Research in Black Culture, The New York Public Library, Astor, Lenox and Tilden Foundations. Photo by Manu Sassoonian.

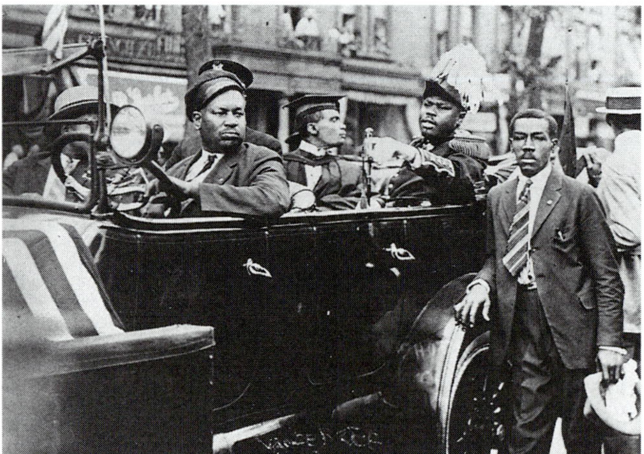

Fig. 7–17 **This photograph shows Marcus Garvey, an important community leader of the time. Why do you think the artist captured important African-American figures in his photographs?**

James VanDerZee, *Marcus Garvey in Regalia*, 1924. Silver gelatin print, 5 5⁄16" x 10" (15.2 x 25.6 cm). ©Donna Mussenden VanDerZee.

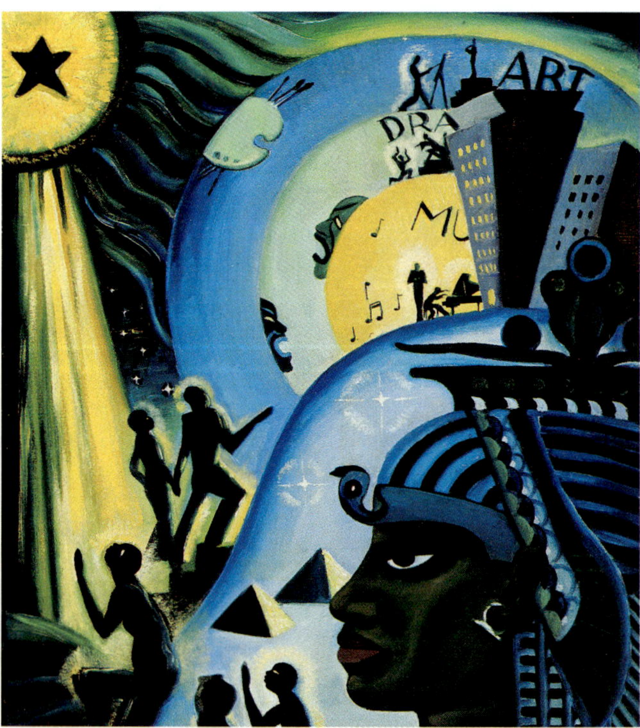


Fig. 7–19 **How does this painting celebrate the heritage of African-American people?**

Lois Mailou Jones, *The Ascent of Ethiopia*, 1932. Oil on canvas, 23 ½" x 17 ½" (59.7 x 43.8 cm). Milwaukee Art Museum, Purchase, African American Acquisition Fund, matching funds from Suzanne and Richard Pieper, with additional support from Arthur and Dorothy Nelle Sanders. Photo credit: Larry Sanders.

## Meet Lois Mailou Jones

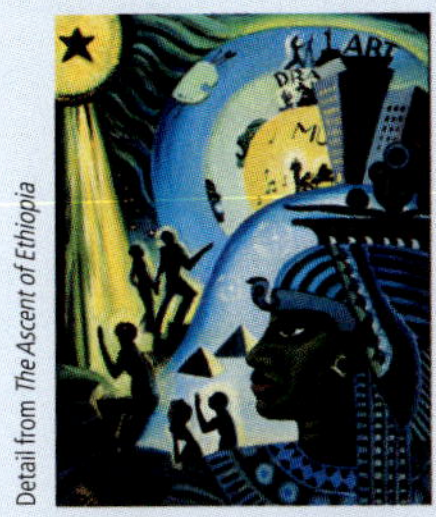

Detail from *The Ascent of Ethiopia*

Lois Mailou Jones was an African American born in Boston, Massachusetts. A passionate, talented artist, she went to the High School of Practical Arts and the School of the Museum of Fine Arts. She earned a master's degree in textile design, then successfully sold her textiles to department stores. However, she wanted to be well known and textile designers were usually anonymous, so she switched to painting.

At 23, Jones started and ran the art department at the Palmer Memorial Institute in North Carolina. Then she taught at Howard University in Washington, DC for 47 years.

Influenced by the Harlem Renaissance, Jones explored her African heritage in her art. She led students on trips to Africa. At 48, she married a Haitian artist and began exploring his heritage in her art as well. She created hundreds of paintings celebrating the roots of African-American culture.

**"By combining the motifs from various regions of Africa, I try to explore on canvas a sense of the underlying unity of all of Africa."**

— Lois Mailou Jones (1905–1998)

## Studio Time

### A School Spirit Mural

Design a mural that celebrates the spirit of your school.

- Sketch your ideas on a large sheet of paper. What will be the focus of your mural?
- Color your mural with paints or markers. Think about how the colors will attract attention.

After displaying your mural, reflect on how other students respond.

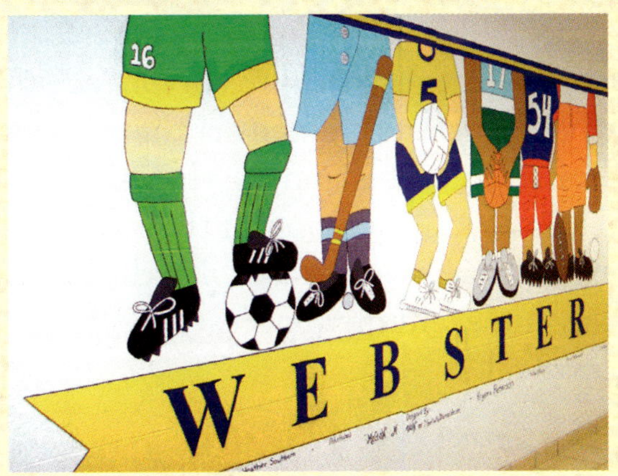


Fig. 7–20 Student artwork

## Check Your Understanding

1. What role did artists have in the Harlem Renaissance?
2. Compare and contrast Urban Regionalism and Rural Regionalism. How were their ideas similar? How were they different?
3. Why do you think art helped to bring the nation and its communities together during the difficult time of the 1920s to 1950s?

# Caribbean Art

**Artistic Beginnings** The Caribbean was not known for its artwork until after about 1750. By that time, the Caribbean population was a mixture of European cultures, African slave groups, and a Creole society. The European influence on Caribbean artworks of the late 1700s is easy to see. During this time, religious artworks were in great demand by the upper classes and remained popular through the 1800s.

**Cultural Celebration** In the early 1900s, Caribbean artists created art that showed the daily work of islanders, the gaiety of life and leisure, and symbols of their culture. Their artworks were filled with the bright colors and excitement of festivals, such as carnival.

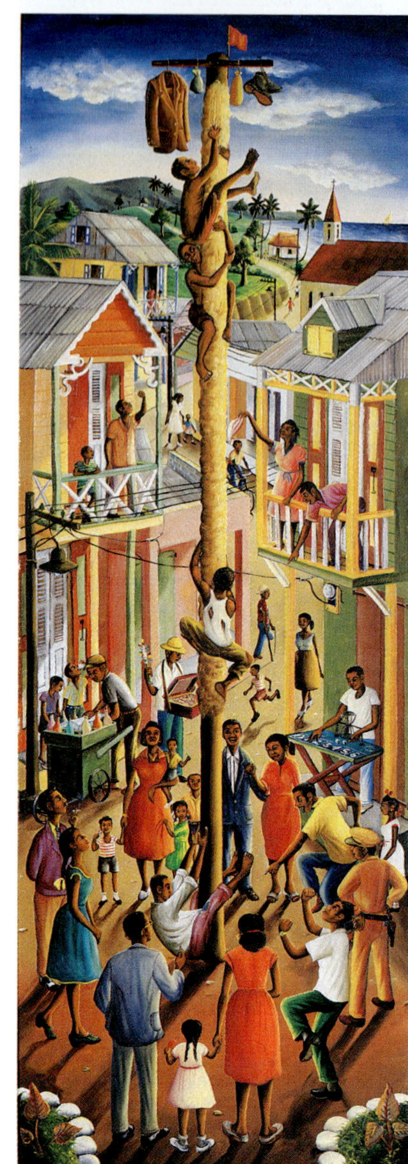

Fig. 7–21 **Why might the artist have chosen a tall and narrow format for this festive scene?**

Andre Normil, *The Greased Pole,* 1966. Oil on masonite, 49 ½" x 17 ½" (125.7 x 44.5 cm). Milwaukee Art Museum, Gift of Richard and Edna Flagg. Photo by Larry Sanders (M1991:136)

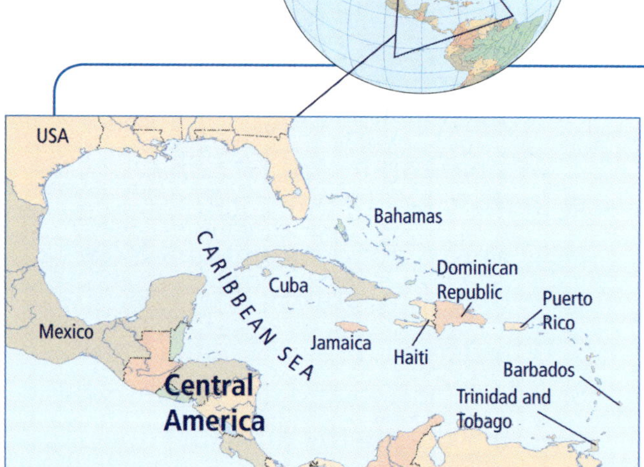


## Social Studies Connection

**The Caribbean** is a chain of many large and small islands. The communities of these islands do not all share the same culture and language. The four main language groups of the Caribbean are Spanish, French, English, and Dutch. West African and Asian languages are also spoken on the islands. All the island communities of the Caribbean, however, have two things in common: religious icons and carnival or festival traditions. These traditions are important to the art of the Caribbean.

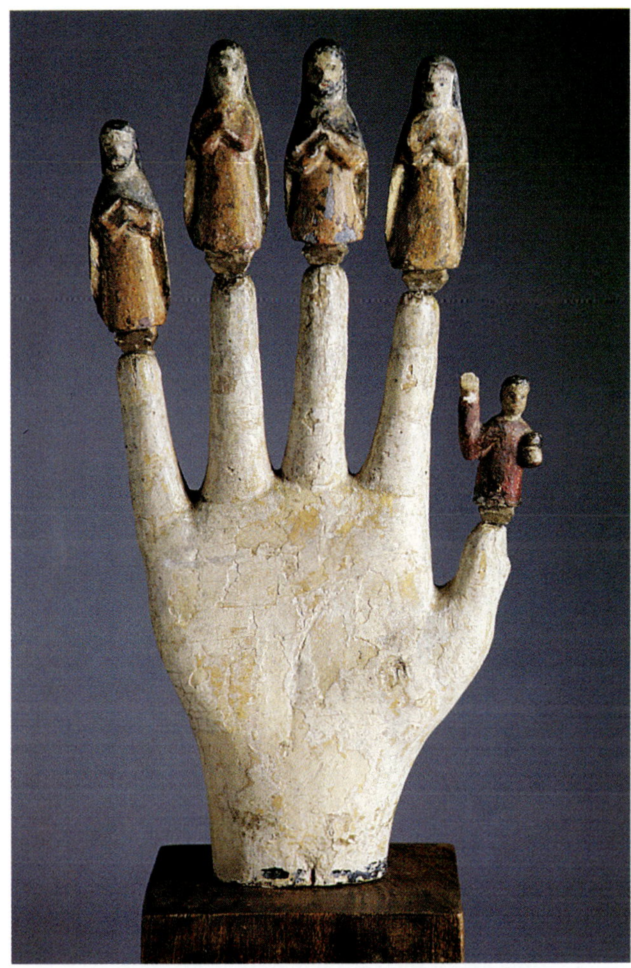

Fig. 7–22 **In the Caribbean, small woodcarvings such as this are used in the home for religious rituals. The figures on the ends of the fingers are probably saints.**

Anonymous, Caban family member, *La Mano Poderosa*, Camuy area, Puerto Rico, 19th century. Wood, 10" (25.5 cm) Private Collection, San Juan, Puerto Rico. Courtesy of Galeria Botello, Hato Rey, P.R.

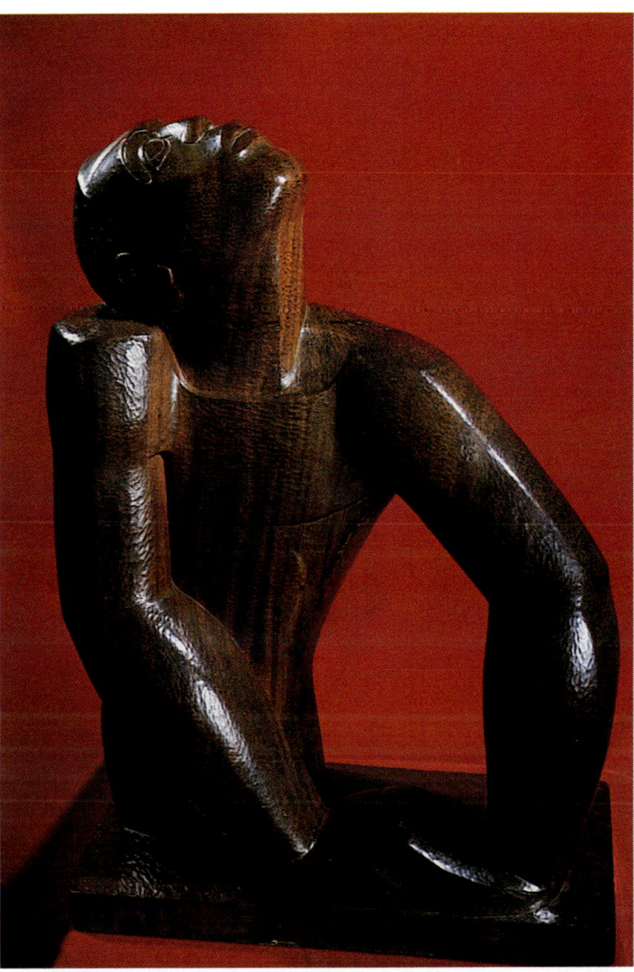

Fig. 7–23 **Edna Manley created some of her works during the Harlem Renaissance. Notice the upturned face and strong arms of this sculpture. How might these features suggest rebirth or reawakening?**

Edna Manley, *Negro Aroused,* 1935. Mahogany, height: 51" (129.5 cm). National Gallery of Jamaica, Kingston. Photograph ©2000, Denis Valentine.

Caribbean artists also were inspired by communities around the world. Artists of Spanish descent began to create images showing local conditions, such as poverty, similar to the Mexican muralists of the time. The connection between African-American communities and the Caribbean became strong. Several Caribbean artists were key figures in the Harlem Renaissance.

### Visual Culture

Most people celebrate special occasions—holidays, birthdays, and the like. Consider the origins and traditions of celebrations that occur in your town, community, or region. What colors, symbols, images, performances, and other activities do you associate with these celebrations?

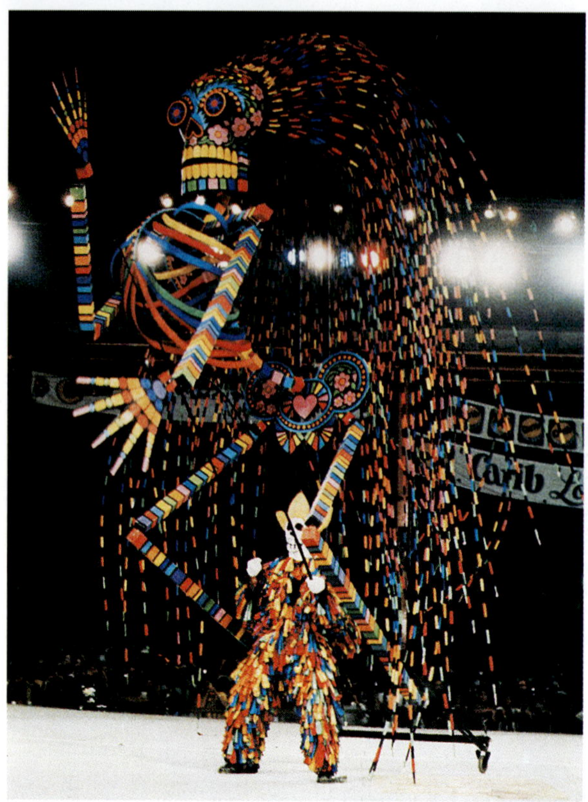

Fig. 7–24 **The theme of this elaborate costume, made from strips of cloth, is life and death. Which features represent life? Which features represent death?**

Peter Minshall, *The Merry Monarch*, Caribbean Festival of Arts, 1987. Courtesy of John W. Nunley.

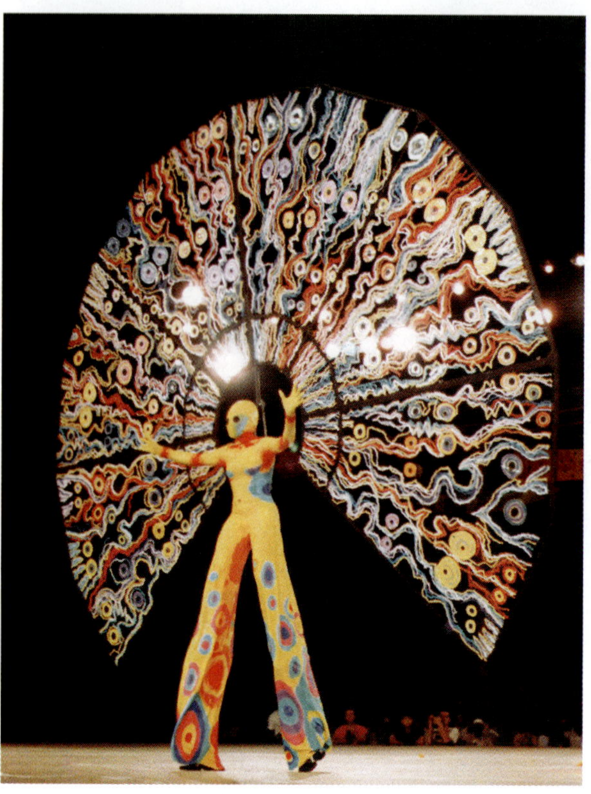

Fig. 7–25 **How might this costume have been influenced by East Indian Islamic cultures?**

The individual mas character "Maco Jumbie," from the mas presentation "Jumbie" by Peter Minshall, Trinidad Carnival 1988. Performed by Sherry Ann Coelho. Photo by Noel Norton.

**Carnival as Art** At carnival, there is only one rule: to have fun. People wear bright costumes, eat traditional foods, and parade through the streets. Latin communities around the world hold this festival each spring. It's a celebration of life and what it means to belong to a community.

Traditionally, carnival comes from ancient celebrations of many civilizations: European, African, Asian, and Middle Eastern. African traditions combine music, dance, costume, sculpture, and drama in a single performance. The influence of East Indian Islamic cultures contributes abstract, geometric, colorful patterns to costumes, parade floats, and other artworks.

Some consider Caribbean carnival to be performance art at its best. As an art of celebration, carnival is an opportunity to be part of the energy and spirit of a community. Individuals become a part of something larger than themselves. For many, it provides a means of expressing community pride.

## Meet Peter Minshall

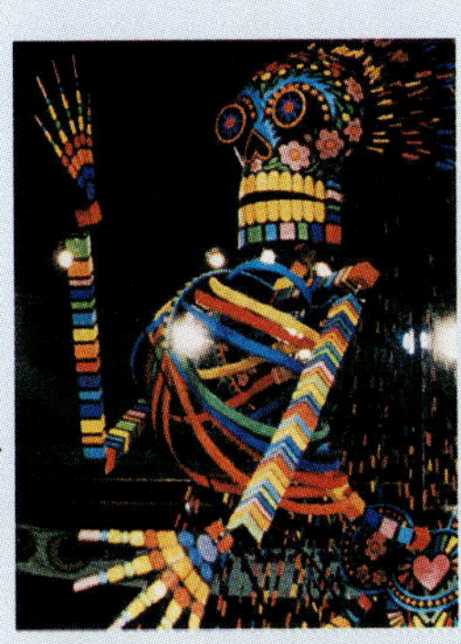

Detail from The Merry Monarch

Peter Minshall grew up in Trinidad and Tobago, where the yearly Carnival Masquerade, or mas, is the nation's biggest event. A masquerade is an event at which people wear costumes or disguises. Minshall studied theater design at the Central School of Art and Design in London. Today, he is the master of dancing mobiles, which are large-scale sculptures worn as costumes by human performers. Sometimes hundreds of dancing mobiles are involved in one choreographed performance. Minshall's Callaloo Company in Trinidad produces mas performances at Carnival and worldwide, including opening shows for the Olympics.

**"A mas band is the closest thing to...symphonic music....There are characters that lead sections, section leaders, and floor members. There's balance, color, shade, tone and form among all these arrangements. It's a cinematic experience, and its great beauty is that it is live."**

— Peter Minshall (born 1941)

## Check Your Understanding

1. What traditions are associated with carnival?
2. How is carnival similar to celebrations in your community? How is it different?
3. Why do you think Caribbean art might boost community spirit?

## Studio Time

### Festive Figures

Create a festive figure using a variety of paper sculpture techniques.

- Design a figure that combines human and animal features. What theme will your figure have?
- Curl or fold brightly colored paper to create abstract, geometric shapes. You might draw patterns on some pieces of paper before you add them to your figure.
- Use glue or tape to attach the pieces of paper together. Add details to help show your theme.

Reflect on the festive features of your sculpture.

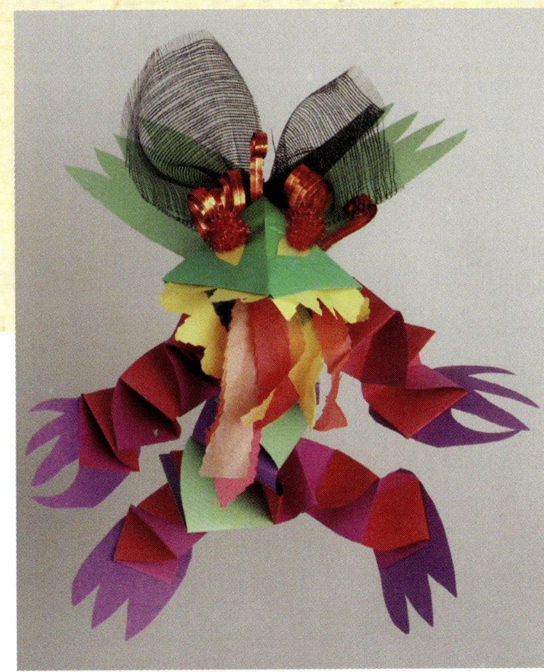

Fig. 7–26 Student artwork

# Masks for Celebration

## Studio Background

Have you ever worn a mask, hat, or costume? During many festivals, people wear masks to add to the fun of the celebration. In some cultures, masks are an important part of rituals and ceremonies. Masks often depict characters in myths or plays.

**In this studio exploration, you will make a festive mask.** You will create textures in metal tooling foil and use ink and paint to add contrast and color. What will your mask celebrate? Will it look like a human face with an exaggerated expression? Will it be based on the traits of an animal?

### You Will Need

- newsprint paper
- pencils
- metal tooling foil
- felt
- wooden craft stick
- India ink
- small paintbrushes
- steel wool
- metallic acrylic paints

## Step 1 Plan and Practice

- Consider what your mask will celebrate. Will it celebrate community? When might it be worn?
- Decide what kind of unusual face your mask will have. Sketch some ideas.
- Think about where your mask might have areas of relief. Where might you add texture?
- Use a wooden craft stick to experiment with creating different patterns and textures on scrap pieces of metal foil.

**Things to Remember:**

- ✓ Break up the space into a variety of shapes.
- ✓ Create areas of high relief.
- ✓ Use a variety of textures to add interest to your mask.

## Inspiration from Our World

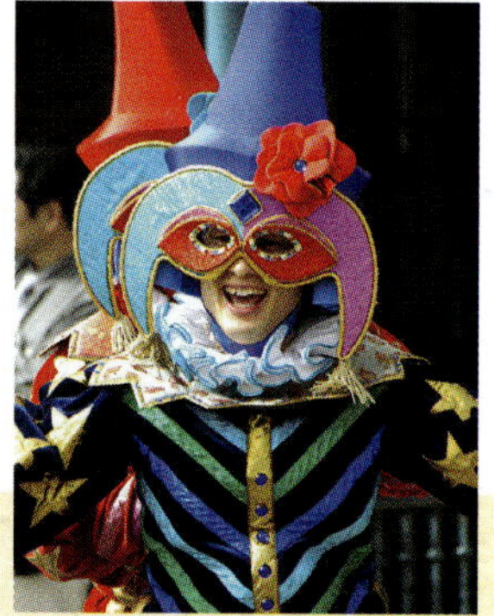

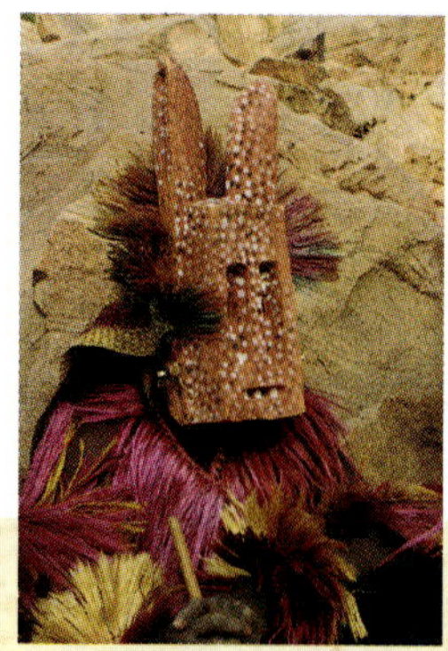

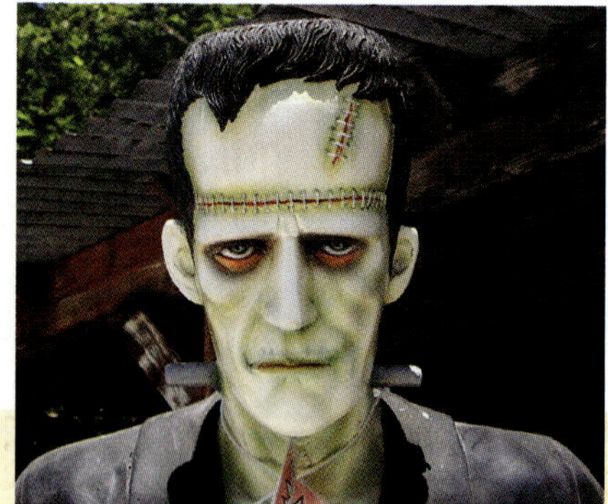

## Inspiration from Art

Maskmaking is an art that has been part of human culture for many thousands of years. One of the earliest known clues to mask use by humans is a cave painting in France that shows a hunter wearing the head and antlers of a deer. Masks have been made of wood, grasses, clay, leather, feathers, bone, gold, silver, and many other materials.

Most masks throughout history have had serious purposes. Masks have been used in religious ceremonies and rituals, and as symbols in temples and mosques. Death masks were made by the ancient Mycenaeans to honor rulers. The Kwakiutl people of the Northwest Coast of North America carve large, heavy wooden masks that open and close to reveal multiple animal figures. Metal masks from India often feature Hindu gods.

In Western culture, decorative masks today are more often used for light-hearted purposes, and appear in parades, at Halloween, at Mardi Gras celebrations, and in theatre performances.

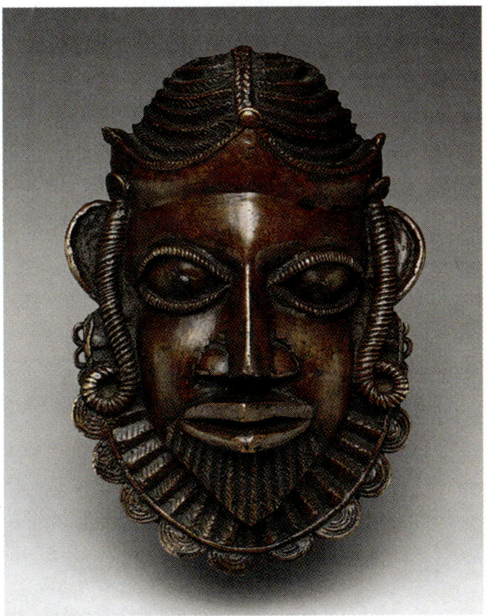

Fig. 7–27 **Not all masks are created for the face. Why might someone have worn this mask as a hip ornament?**

*Hip Ornament: Portuguese Face.* 16th–19th century. Brass, iron, 7 5/8" (19.4 cm). Gift of Mr. And Mrs. Klaus G. Perls, 1991 (1991.162.9). The Metropolitan Museum of Art, New York, NY. ©The Metropolitan Museum of Art/Art Resource, NY.

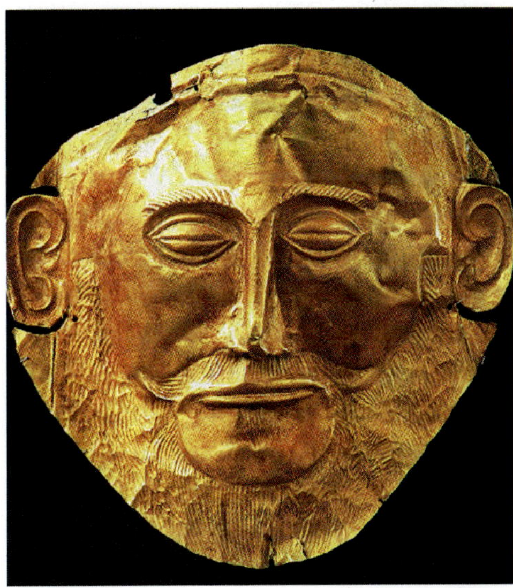

Fig. 7–28 Mycenae Death Mask (also known as Mask of Agamemnon), about 1500 B.C.E. Beaten gold, about 12" (30 cm) high. Royal tombs, Mycenae. Photo ©2001 Thomas Sakoulas.

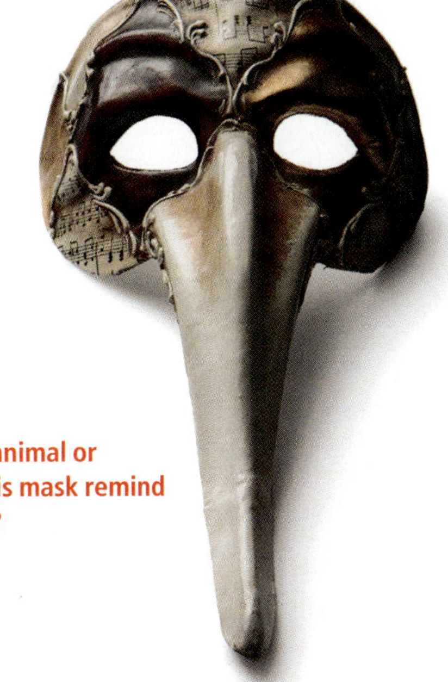

Fig. 7–29 **What animal or animals does this mask remind you of and why?**

### Step 2 **Begin to Create**

- Fold a piece of newsprint paper in half.
- **Draw an outline of one half of a face along the fold.** All lines within the outline should touch the edge of the paper or another line to create different shapes.

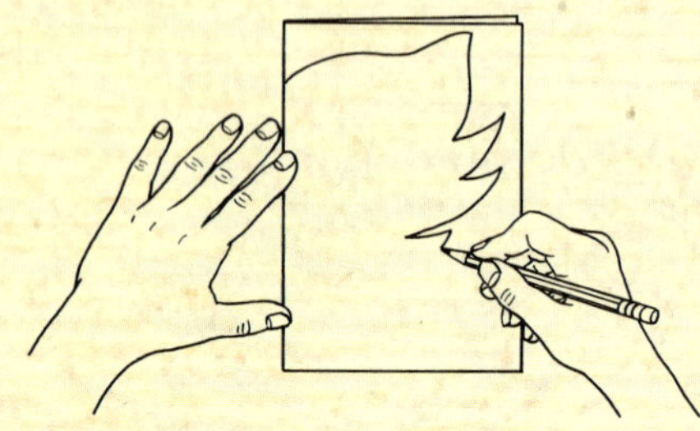

- Once the outline is complete, turn the paper over and trace the lines onto the other half. This creates a symmetrical face.
- Tape your design to a piece of metal foil and place felt underneath it.
- **Use a dull pencil or wooden craft stick to trace over your drawing.**

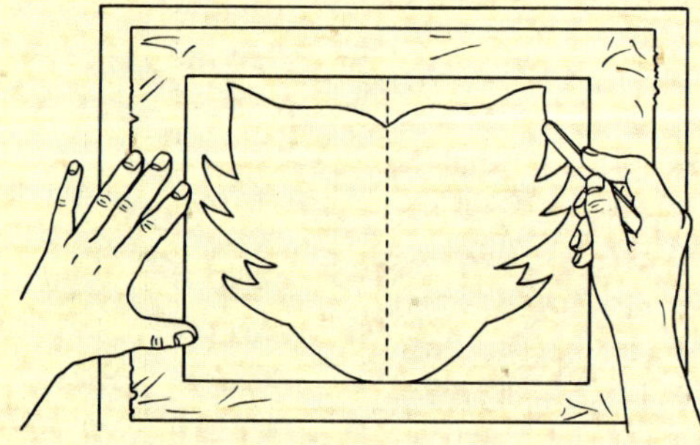

- After removing the paper, trace the lines in the metal again to make them deeper.
- Turn over the foil. Using a craft stick, rub gently back and forth inside one of the shapes to create a relief. The foil stretches slightly as you rub it. Repeat this process with several other shapes.
- **Add textures to your mask.** Try spirals, dots, dashes, or scribble marks. Apply textures to areas of relief from the back. Other areas can have texture applied from the front.

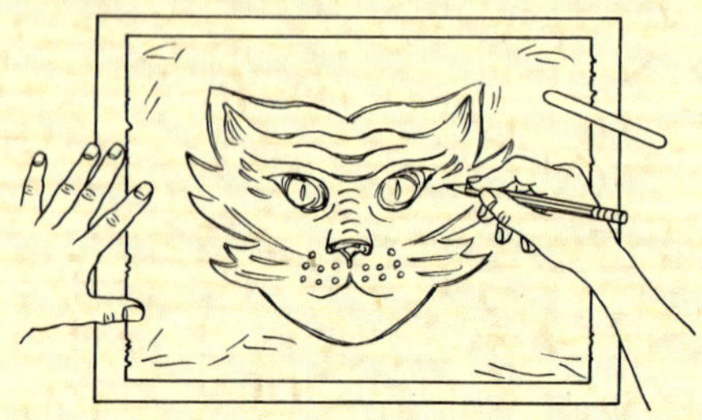

- To create greater contrast, paint your mask with India ink and allow it to dry.
- Using fine steel wool, rub off most of the ink, and add shine to your mask.
- If you like, add color to some areas with diluted acrylic paints.

### Step 3 **Revise**

**Did you remember to:**

✓ Break up the space into a variety of shapes?

✓ Create areas of high relief?

✓ Use a variety of textures to add interest?

Adjust your work if necessary. In your sketchbook, make a note of your revisions and why you made them.

### Step 4 **Add Finishing Touches**

- Add any extras to your mask, such as jewelry, headdresses, or antlers, using scrap foil or wire.
- Trim your mask, leaving ¼" of foil around the design.

### Step 5 **Share and Reflect**

- Share your mask with a partner. Take turns talking about your design and what your mask celebrates.
- As a class, display all the masks. Discuss where you chose to create a relief and how you added different textures.
- What did you like about working with metal foil? What was the most challenging?
- What might you do differently the next time you create a mask?

## Art Criticism

**Describe** How would you describe the features of this mask?

**Analyze** How did the artist create variety and unity in forming this mask?

**Interpret** What words would you use to describe your reaction to this mask?

**Evaluate** What do you think are some of the outstanding qualities of this mask?

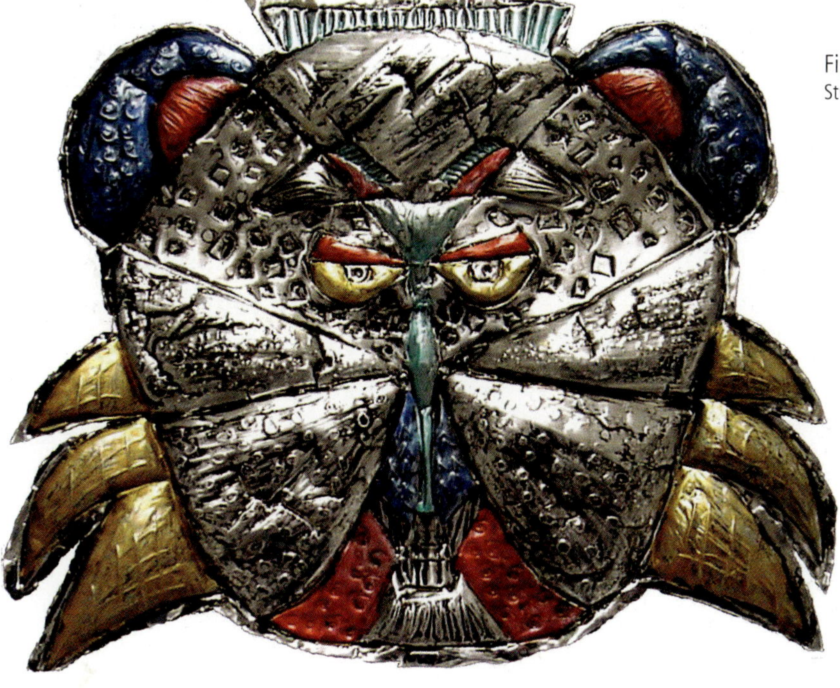

Fig. 7–30
Student artwork

## Social Studies

**Artists often use traditional foods of individual cultures as their subject.** In his artwork, Mexican artist Diego Rivera celebrates maize (corn), an important food plant in the Americas. The Maya and other Mesoamerican civilizations were founded on the farming of corn, the basis of their diet. Corn-based foods are still prepared for special celebrations. For example, cornbread dressing is an important part of many Thanksgiving dinners. What particular food do you enjoy on special occasions?

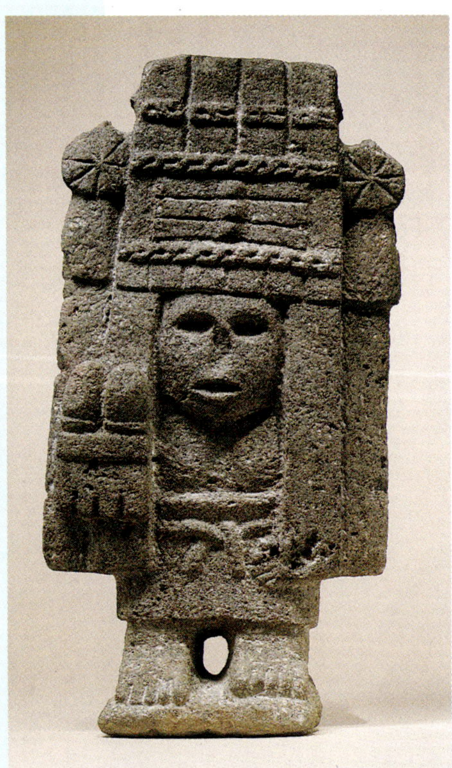

Fig. 7–31 **This sculpture shows the Aztec corn goddess, Chicomecoatl (che-co-ME-co-ah-tul). Which features of this sculpture are lifelike? Which are less realistic?**

Mexico Aztec (1325–1519/21), *Chicomecoatl (Corn Goddess)*. Stone, height: 13 ½" (34.3 cm). The Metropolitan Museum of Art, Purchase, 1900 (00.5.51). Photograph ©1981 the Metropolitan Museum of Art.

## Music

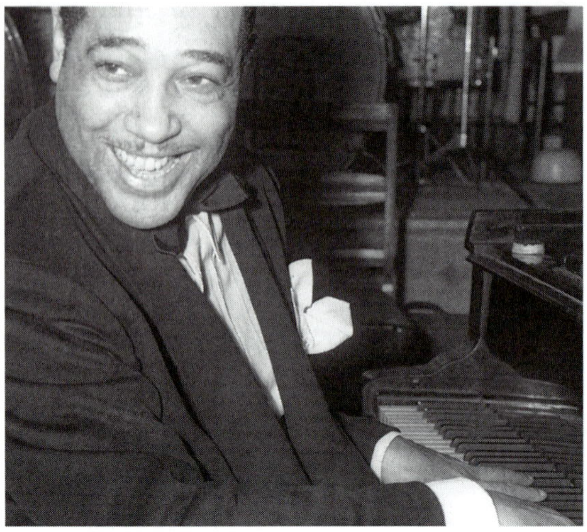

Fig. 7–32 **Duke Ellington**

**Musicians, like artists, celebrate their community.** Duke Ellington, a well-known jazz composer and performer, wrote the symphony *Harlem* to celebrate the greatness of his community. In *Opelousas Hop*, Clifton Chenier celebrates his Louisiana home, where Cajun music developed from a blending of European and African-American traditions. Here, the sounds of Chenier's "squeeze box" (accordion) celebrate one French contribution to Cajun music. Listen to the two pieces of music. How did each composer celebrate his community? What would a song that celebrates your community sound like?

## Careers **Children's-Book Illustrators**

**What were your favorite picture books when you were a child?** The artists who create images for picture books, nonfiction and fiction, and textbooks for young people are children's-book illustrators. A children's-book illustrator may have a special style that he or she is known for. For example, Carmen Lomas Garza illustrates and writes bilingual storybooks that celebrate her childhood memories. Her books honor images that are recognized and appreciated by Mexican Americans. They also serve to inform those who are unfamiliar with the culture.

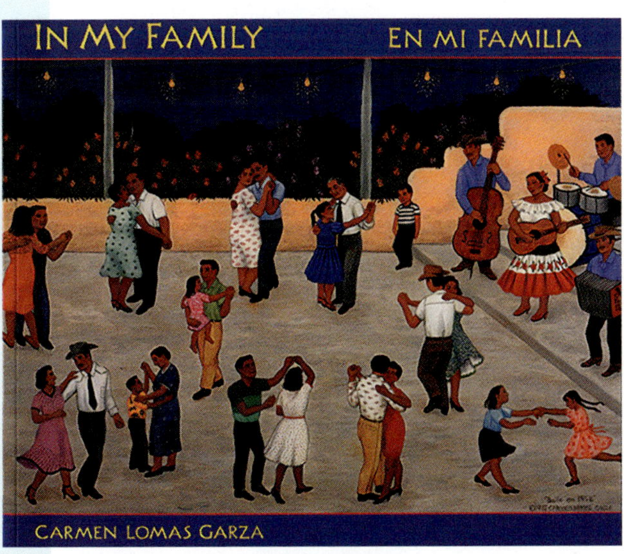


Fig. 7–33 ©Michael Ochs Archives/Corbis

## Daily Life

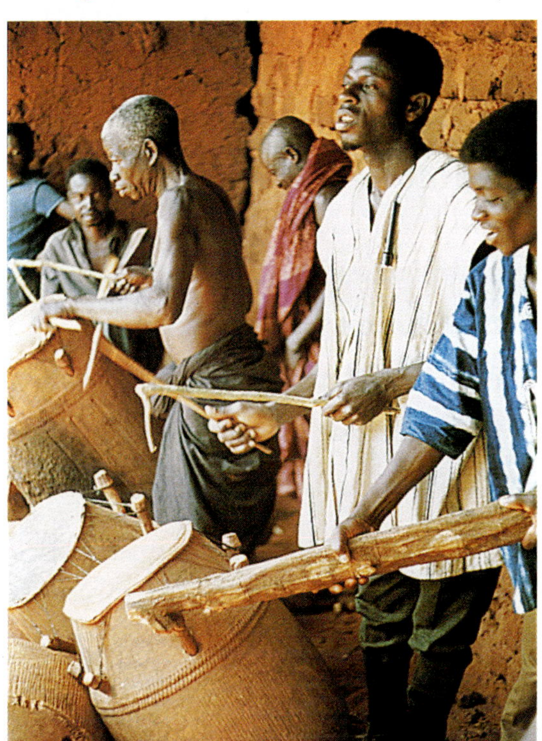

Fig. 7–34 **This festival in Africa celebrates community. Why do you think people enjoy getting together for events like this?**

Ghana, Africa, Bono peoples, *Festival*. Courtesy of Davis Art Images.

**Festivals and other celebrations are common in communities throughout the world.** Some neighborhoods celebrate by holding a street fair, a block party, or a barbecue. How does your community celebrate? Communities may have a parade for a sports victory, a returning hero or celebrity, or a holiday. These celebrations allow neighbors to meet and get to know one another. What other benefits might these celebrations have?

## Vocabulary Review

Match each art term below with its definition.

**celebrate**

**traditions**

**composition**

**Regionalist**

**Harlem Renaissance**

1. artists who focused their attention on specific regions or sections of the country
2. to honor
3. the period when many artists who lived in Harlem used various forms to express their lives as African Americans
4. customs or beliefs that are passed down from earlier generations
5. the way the parts of an artwork are arranged

## Aesthetic Thinking

What is the difference, if any, between artwork that depicts a celebration and artwork that helps celebrate?

## Write About Art

Shadow puppet shows are featured in festivals throughout Indonesia. Traditionally, they tell stories from Hindu mythology. Themes include the battle between good and evil as well as morality tales. Choose a myth or story you think would work well for a shadow puppet show, and write a page of dialogue between two or more characters.

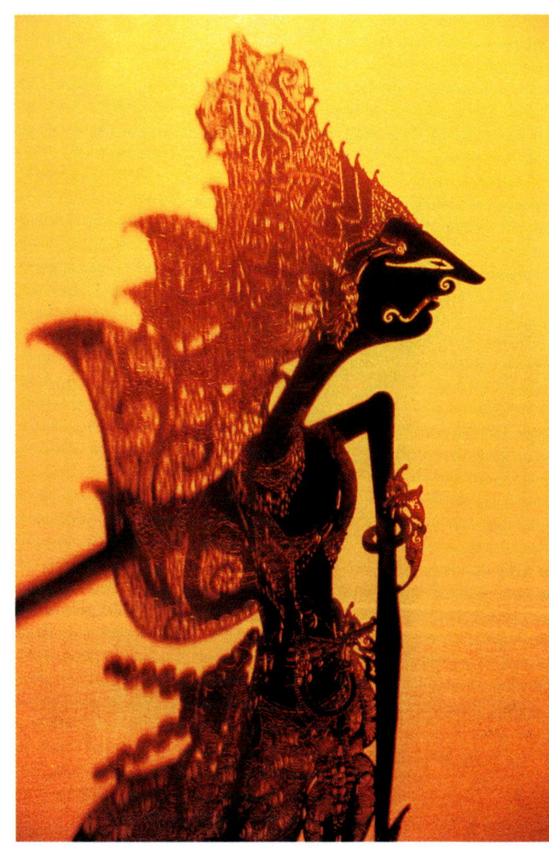

Fig. 7–35 **Shadow puppet shows are featured in festivals throughout Indonesia. Traditionally, they tell stories from Hindu mythology. The shows start late and last all night.**

Indonesia, Central Java, *Shadow Puppets.* ©Luca Tettoni/Viesti Associates, Inc.

## Art Criticism

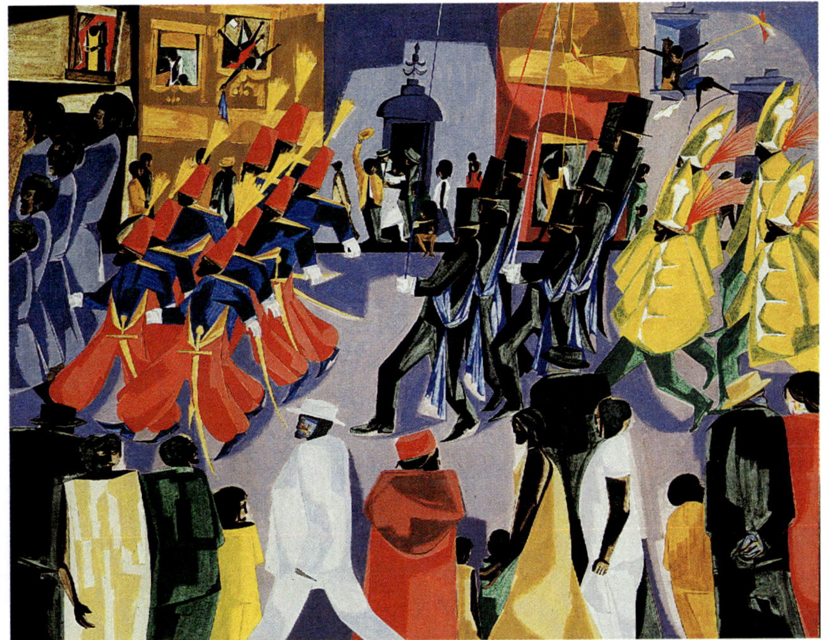

Fig. 7–36 Jacob Lawrence, *Parade*, 1960. Tempera with pencil underdrawing on fiberboard, 23 7/8" x 30 1/8" (60.6 x 76.5 cm). Hirshhorn Museum and Sculpture Garden, Smithsonian Institution, Gift of Joseph H. Hirshhorn, 1966. Photographed by Lee Stalsworth. Artists Rights Society (ARS), NY.

**Describe** What do you see in this painting?

**Analyze** How does the artist create unity in this painting?

**Interpret** What makes this painting feel like a celebration?

**Evaluate** One of Lawrence's goals as an artist, especially early in his career, was to capture and celebrate life in Harlem. Explain whether you think he succeeded in this painting.

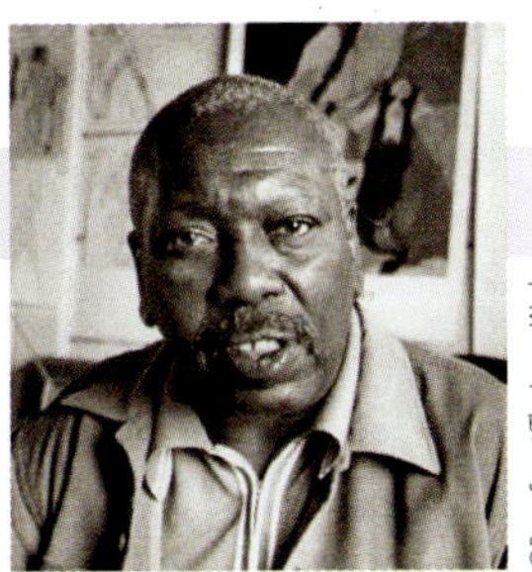

©Barry Sweet/The Image Works

## Meet the Artist

**Jacob Lawrence** (1917–2000) was born in Atlantic City, New Jersey. He studied art in New York. Lawrence was known for his social realist painting, in which he showed the struggles and triumphs of everyday people. The streets and people of Harlem was one major theme in his work. He also created series that told the stories of African-American heroes including Harriet Tubman and Toussaint L'Ouverture, a leader of the Haitian revolution. Lawrence taught art at the University of Washington in Seattle for many years.

## For Your Portfolio

Choose one of your artworks based on the theme of celebration. With a peer, discuss each other's work. Interpret the meaning of the work, making connections between what you see and what the work is about. What is its message about celebration?

## For Your Sketchbook

Create a rough design for a series of four postage stamps to commemorate your community. Focus on the theme of celebration and feature your community in connection with four different celebrations.

# Unit 8

# Art and Making a Difference

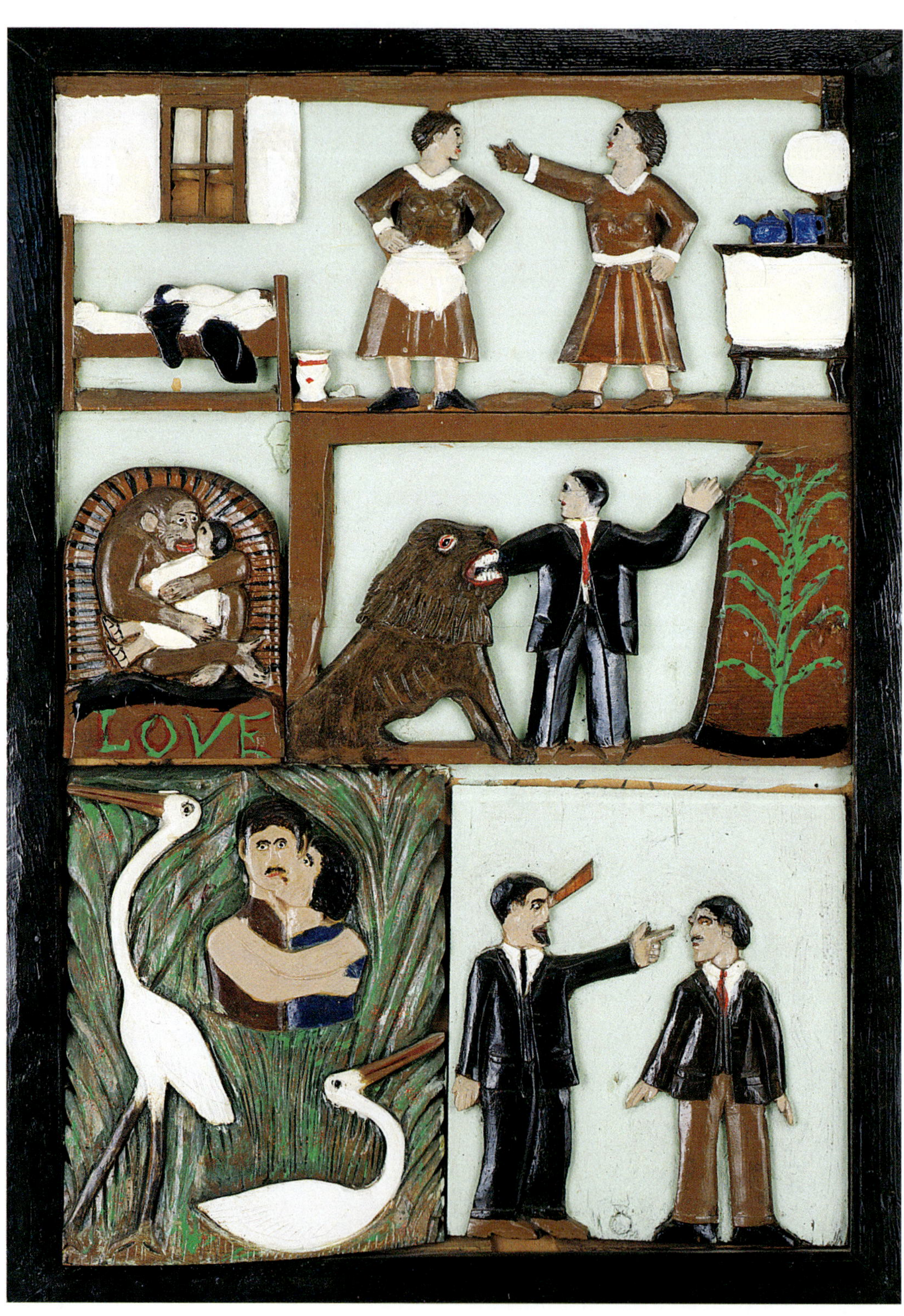


Fig. 8–1 **People could view Elijah Pierce's art in his barbershop and learn lessons about how to live a good life. What story could you tell in an artwork?**

Elijah Pierce, *Monday Morning Gossip*, 1934. Carved and painted wood relief with glitter, mounted on painted panel, 33 ½" x 24" (85.1 x 61.0 cm). Collection of Michael D. Hall. Courtesy of the Columbus Museum of Art.

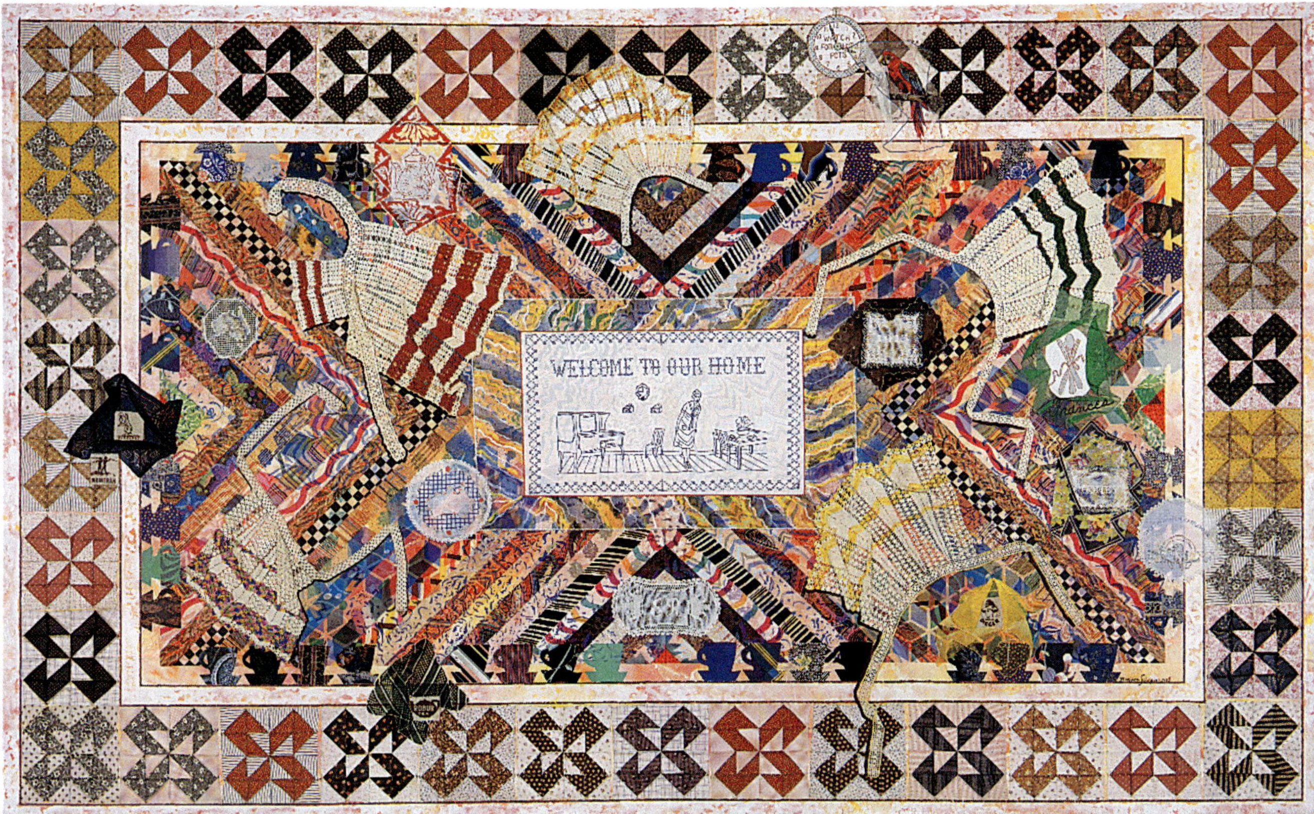


Fig. 8–4 **In many of her artworks, Schapiro focuses on the beautiful items that women have created. What details in this artwork celebrate the creative work of women?**

Miriam Schapiro, *Wonderland*, 1983. Collage: acrylic, fabric and plastic beads on canvas, 35 ½" x 56 ¾" (90 x 144 cm). National Museum of American Art, Washington, DC/Art Resource, NY.

## Meet Miriam Schapiro

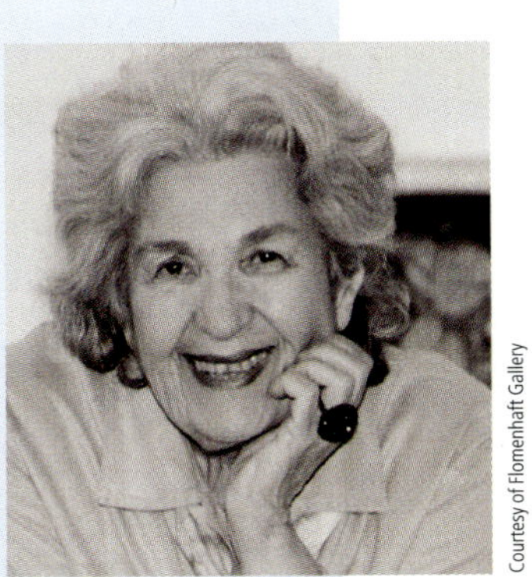

Courtesy of Flomenhaft Gallery

Miriam Schapiro was born in Toronto, Canada, and studied painting at the University of Iowa. Her career started with Action Paintings and geometric art.

At 49, Schapiro and Judy Chicago, another renowned artist, founded the Feminist Art Program at the California Institute of the Arts. Their class converted an empty mansion into *Womanhouse*, an art installation exploring women's roles. Schapiro realized that traditional women's arts are usually considered decorations, while fine art is traditionally made by men and valued more. Schapiro started making fine artworks that include embroidery, appliqué, hearts, and flowers. These works blur the line between decoration and fine art, showing the value of traditional women's arts.

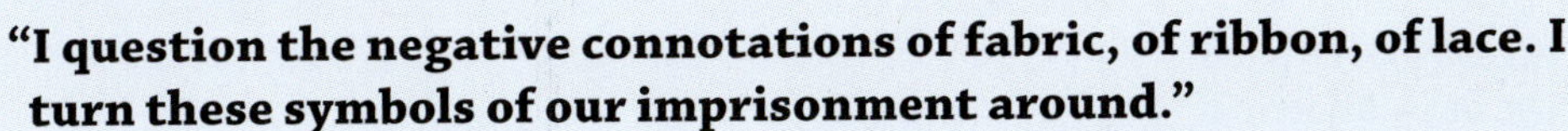

**"I question the negative connotations of fabric, of ribbon, of lace. I turn these symbols of our imprisonment around."**

—Miriam Schapiro (born 1923)

### Collaborating to Make a Difference

Sometimes artists collaborate, or work together, with communities to create artworks. Collaborations can involve any number of people—from two people to thousands. Group work can express powerful feelings that we share as human beings.

There are many examples of people working together to make a difference through art. One example is the *AIDS Memorial Quilt* (Figs. 8–5 and 8–6). As thousands of Americans faced the loss of loved ones to the AIDS disease, they were invited to create a quilt square in memory of those people. The AIDS quilt was displayed at a public space in Washington, DC, and in other places around the country. This enormous quilt was a collaborative artistic effort. It provided a solemn comfort for those who contributed to it. It also brought public attention to the need for medical research to find a cure for AIDS.

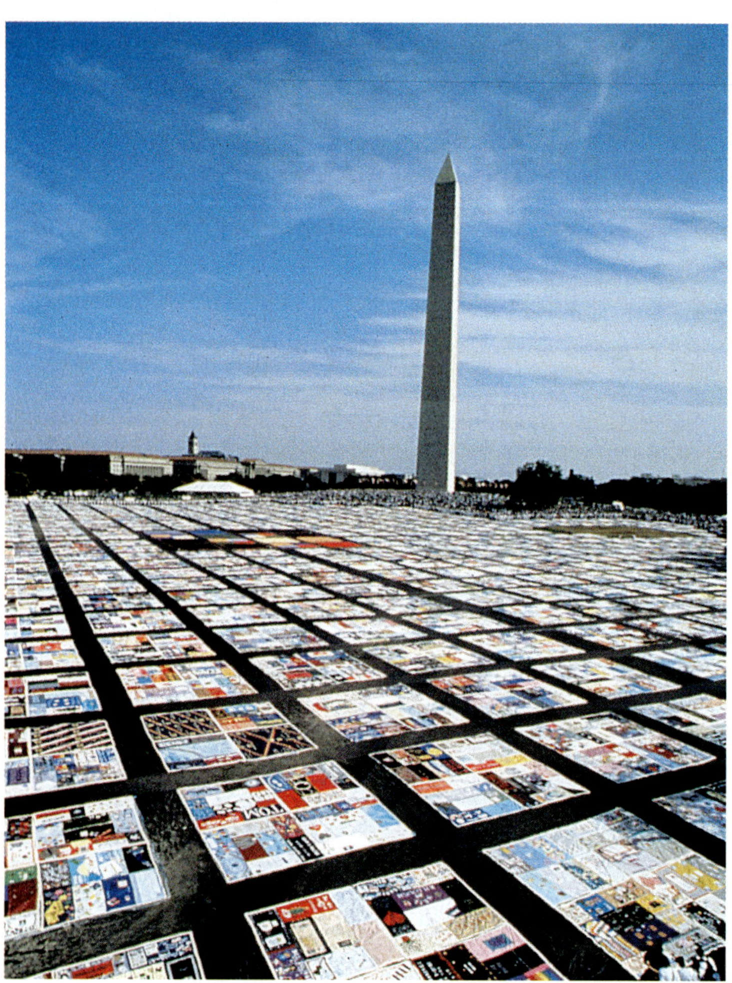

Fig. 8–5 **Sometimes people help each other accept a loved one's death. How might this healing experience have been different if people created their memorial artworks independently?**

Cleve Jones, Founder, *AIDS Memorial Quilt*, 1985–present. Fabric and mixed media, each panel measures 36" x 72" (91.4 x 182.9 cm) (over 43,000 panels as of 1999). Photo by Mark Theissen. Courtesy of the NAMES Project Foundation.

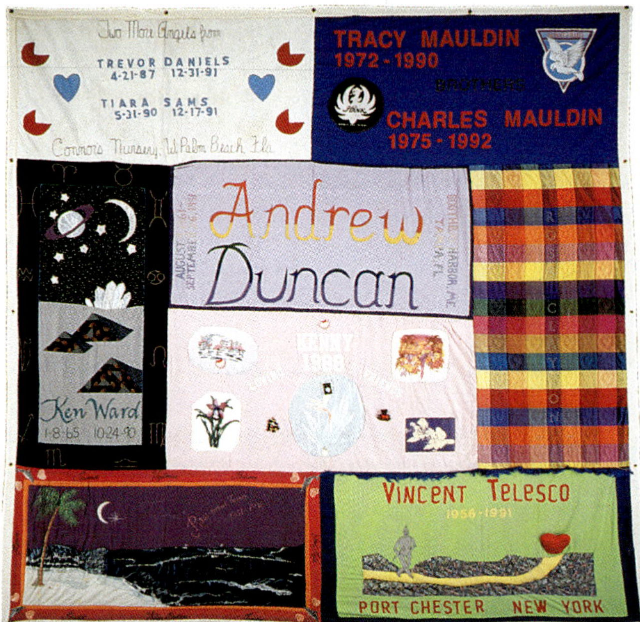


Fig. 8–6 **Each panel on this quilt square is a personal expression of loss. How do you think the quilt makes a difference?**

*AIDS Memorial Quilt* (detail) 1985–present. Fabric and mixed media, each panel measures 36" x 72" (91.4 x 182.9 cm). Photo by Paul Margolies. Courtesy of the NAMES Project Foundation.

## Studio Time

### Art With Power

Make a montage that expresses a powerful opinion. What subject do you feel strongly about? What would you like to express about that subject?

- Look for photographs that illustrate the main idea of your montage.
- Create background shapes and details with assorted colored and printed papers. Try cutting some shapes with scissors, and tearing the edges of others for a different effect.
- Arrange your pieces on tag board. Try several arrangements until you are satisfied with your composition. Glue the pieces in place.

Reflect on how you think your visual image can make a difference.

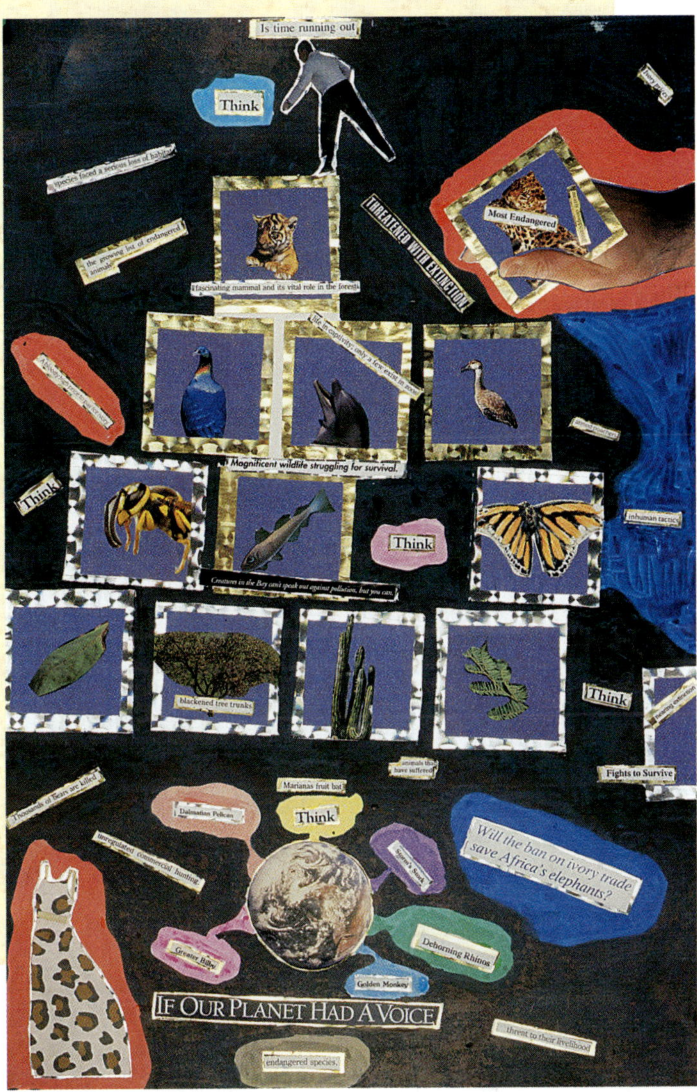


Fig. 8–7 Student artwork

### Check Your Understanding

**1.** How have artists used their art to address problems people face in communities?

**2.** Compare and contrast the way *Guernica* and the *AIDS Memorial Quilt* send messages that make a difference.

**3.** Make a list of good reasons for artists to collaborate with others to make art. When is collaboration not such a good idea?

# Printmaking

In the simplest terms, printmaking is a process of transferring an image or words from one surface to another. Artists use printmaking techniques to tell stories, express ideas, and create beautiful designs.

**Types of Prints** There are three basic steps for making any print. Create an image on a printing plate. Ink the plate. Transfer the image by pressing the inked plate against paper or cloth. By varying the three basic steps, artists make different kinds of prints.

- A relief print is created using a printing process in which ink is placed on the raised portions of a block or plate. When the block is pressed on to paper, the raised part of the block prints.

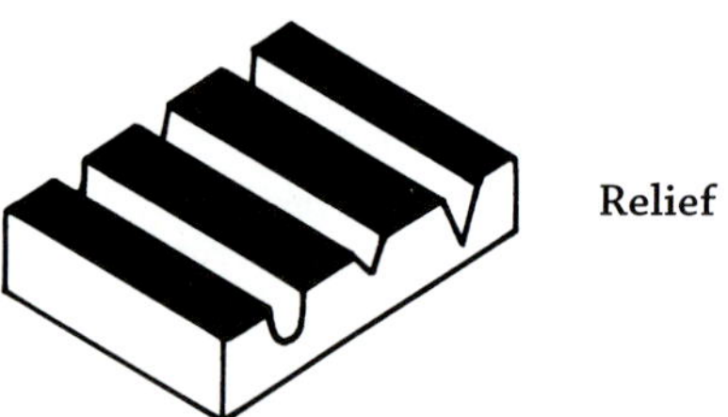


- For an intaglio print, the artist scratches lines into a smooth metal plate. After the ink is rubbed into the grooves and the surface of the plate is wiped clean, artists use a printing press to transfer the ink from the grooves onto the paper.

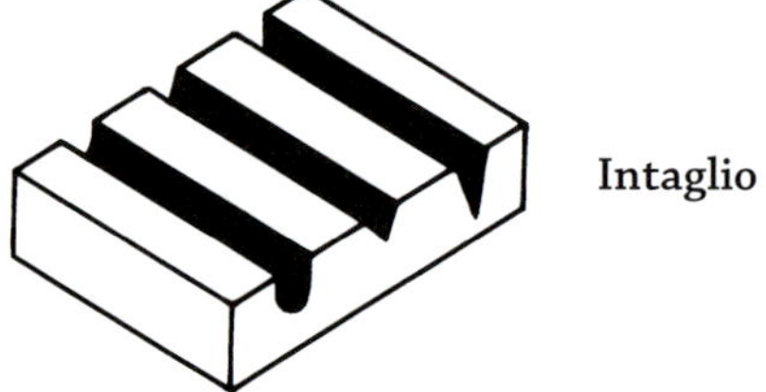


- To make a lithographic print, the artist draws an image on a flat slab of stone (or a special metal plate) with a greasy crayon. Then the artist coats the blank areas of the stone with a special chemical. The ink sticks to the drawn areas, but will not stick to the chemical. The print is made using a printing press.

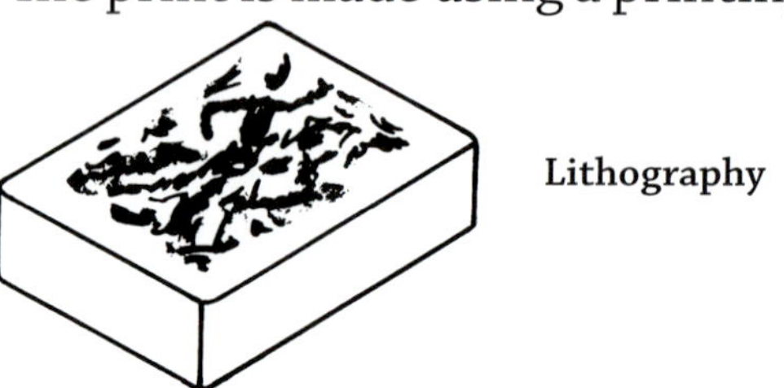


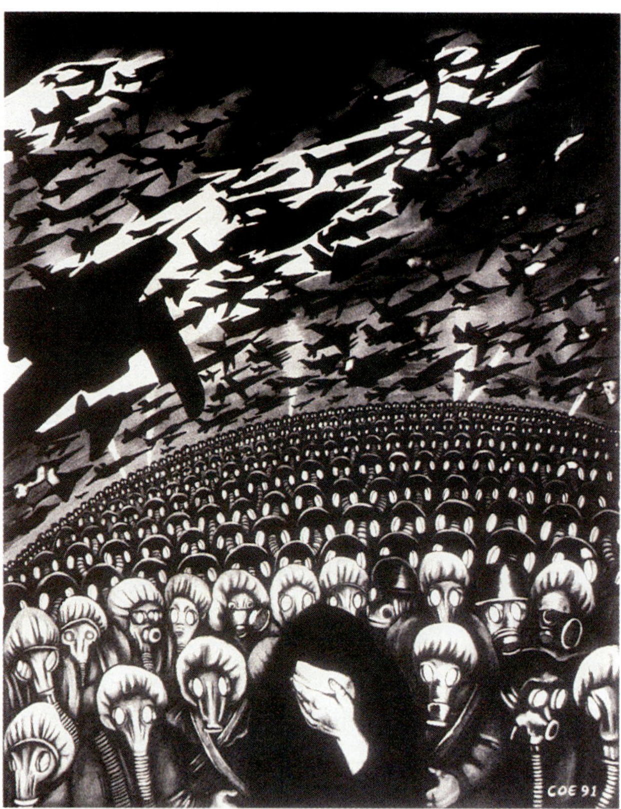


Fig. 8–8 **The lines and shapes in this intaglio print are bold. How might the artist's message be different if she had used fine lines and soft shadows?**

Sue Coe, *The New World Order*, 1991. Photo-etching, 13 3/8" x 10 5/8" (34 x 27 cm).

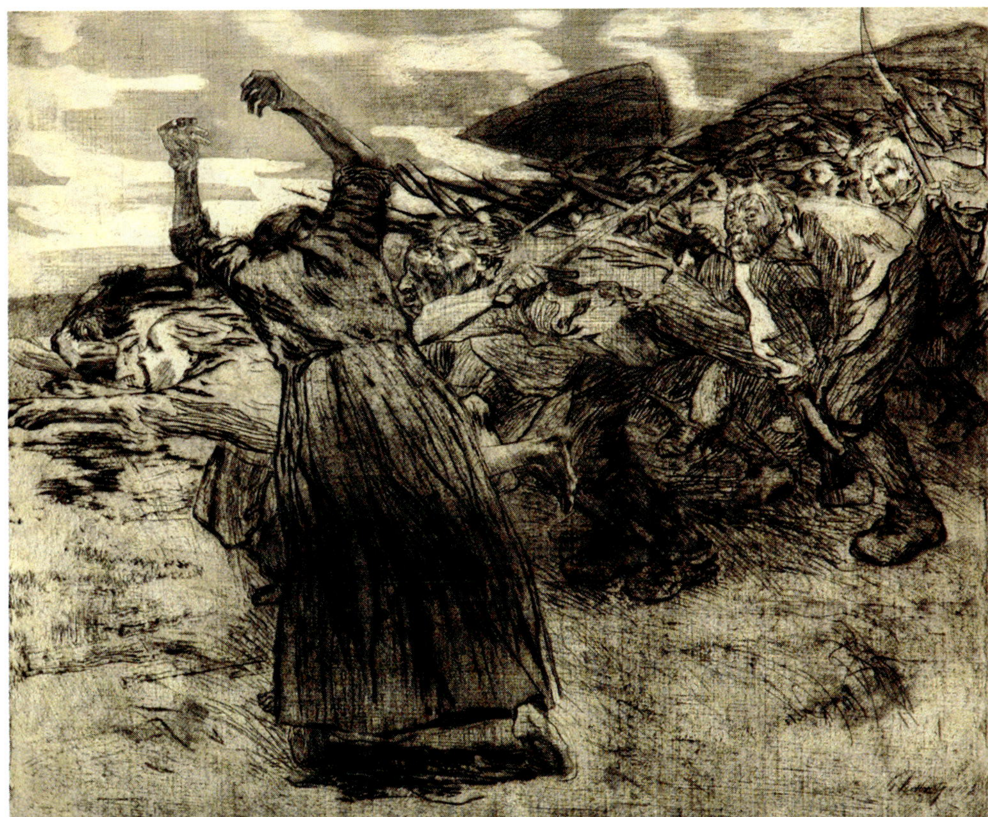

Fig. 8–9 **This print is one of a series about a revolution among peasants in Germany in the 1500s. How does the artist's use of line give the work a sense of forward motion?**

Käthe Kollwitz, *Peasant Revolt.* Courtesy of Spaightwood Galleries, Inc. Upton, MA. Artists Rights Society (ARS), NY.

- In the serigraph, or silkscreen, printing process, artists use stencils to overlap colors. A stenciled image is placed on a fine screen mounted to a frame. The print is made by pulling ink across the screen, transferring the image to the paper below.

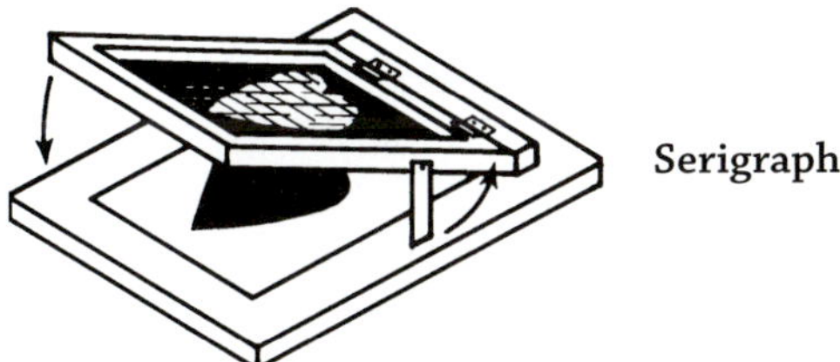

**Serigraph**

**Observe** Look at the examples of prints (Figs. 8–8 and 8–9) on these pages. Images on any printing plate are the reverse (a mirror image) of images when they are printed. Imagine what the original printing plate for each print looked like.

**Tools:** Soft lead pencils, newsprint or other thin paper.

## Practice: Reverse Images

- On thin paper, draw a simple arrangement of shapes, a still life, or a basic landscape.
- Turn the paper over and trace your drawing from the other side.
- How does your drawing change? Which arrangement do you like better?

**Stencil Prints** A stencil print is made by placing a stencil on a sheet of paper and applying ink or paint through the opening. Stencils can be created using a special stencil paper that is lightly waxed, a stiff paper such as a manila folder, or a piece of thin cardboard. A stencil brush, with short bristles, is the traditional way to apply the ink or paint in a stencil print. The serigraph, or silkscreen print, is a type of stencil print.

**Observe** Notice the simple shapes in the stencil print **(Fig. 8–10)**. Note how a few lines can be used to create detail.

**Tools:** Stiff paper, scissors or craft knife, printmaking paper, ink or paint, stencil brush, cloth (optional), and tape (optional).

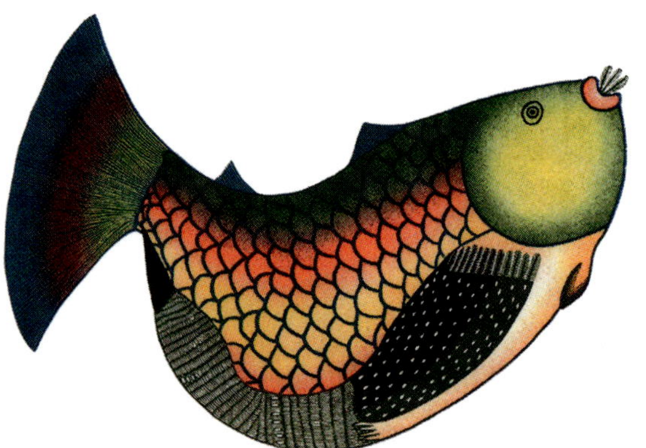

Fig. 8–10 **The artist created this print using a stencil. How many different shapes do you notice? Which stand out to you?**

Ningeo Kuluk Teevee, *Rainbow Reflection,* 2006. Stonecut and stencil. Courtesy of Dorset Fine Arts.

## Practice: Cutting and Inking a Stencil

- Draw a simple design on a sheet of stiff paper.
- Cut out your design. Make sure all cuts are neat and clear.
- Lay your stencil on final paper. Use tape on outer edges to hold the stencil in place.
- Dip your brush into the ink or paint, and wipe it on a piece of newspaper to eliminate any excess.
- Apply ink to the open area of the stencil, using a light stippling motion (up and down) or a light "feathery" stroke to apply the ink.
- Be careful when applying ink or paint near the edges of the stencil. Ink or paint flowing under the stencil will ruin the crispness of the image.

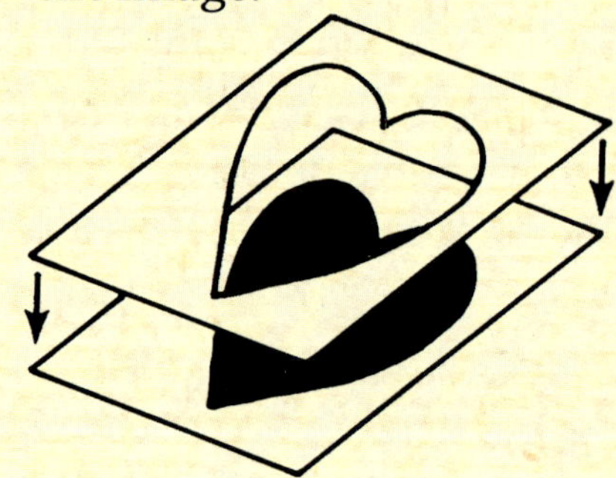

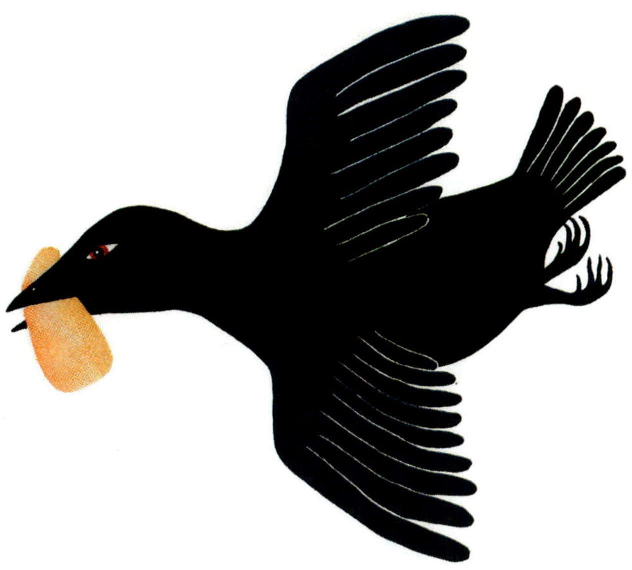

Fig. 8–11 **How did the artist use line and color to create unity and variety in this print?**

Mialia Jaw, *Stolen Bannock,* 2006. Stonecut and stencil. Courtesy of Dorset Fine Arts.

### Check Your Understanding

1. What are the three basic steps of printmaking?
2. Compare and contrast the printmaking techniques used for intaglio prints and silkscreen prints.
3. Why might some artists prefer printmaking to other forms of art? When might it be helpful to create many prints of the same image?

## Studio Time

### Make a Difference with a Print

Create a stencil print that will make a difference in the way people think and feel about an environmental issue that is important to you. Plan your design.

- Cut your stencil design into stiff paper. For "fuzzier" edges, consider tearing some of the edges.
- Place your stencil over a piece of paper or cloth. Tape the stencil in place.
- Apply ink or paint to the stencil. Remember to wipe off excess ink or paint before beginning. Move your brush with an up-and-down motion.

Reflect on how planning ahead made your print more successful.

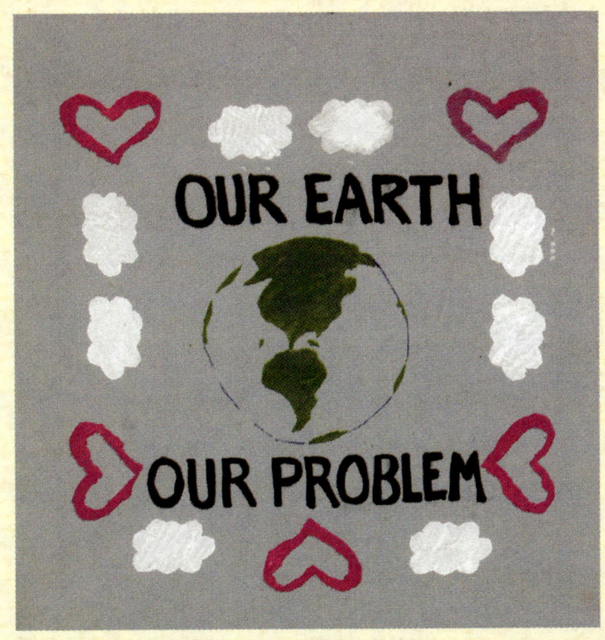


Fig. 8–12 Student artwork

## 8.3 Studio Exploration — Printmaking

# A Collagraph with an Opinion

### Studio Background

You have seen artworks that are created to make a positive difference or address problems within a community. You have also been introduced to artists who have used their artworks to express strong opinions or ideals. What do you feel strongly about?

A collagraph is a print made from a collage with raised areas. **In this studio exploration, you will create a collagraph print related to an issue that you feel strongly about.** Use materials and objects with interesting shapes and textures that will make your message clear.

**You Will Need**

- corrugated cardboard (the block)
- collage materials
- glue
- acrylic gel medium
- paintbrushes
- printing ink
- drawing paper, 3 or 4 sheets

### Step 1 Plan and Practice

- Choose an issue to use as a focus for your print. Are you concerned about war, climate change, injustice? What images will help you express your concern?
- Sketch some of your ideas.
- Collect materials with unusual textures. Choose textures that will help express your ideas.

**Things to Remember:**

✓ Use collage materials with rich textures and interesting shapes.

✓ Arrange your collage materials in a way that best projects your message.

✓ Experiment with the amount of ink you use on the plate.

## Inspiration from Our World

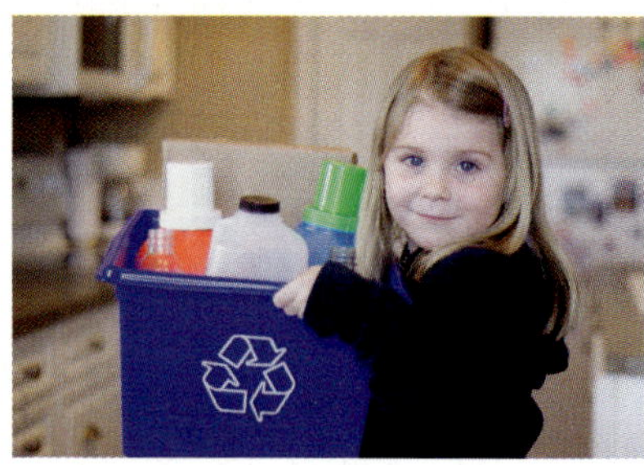

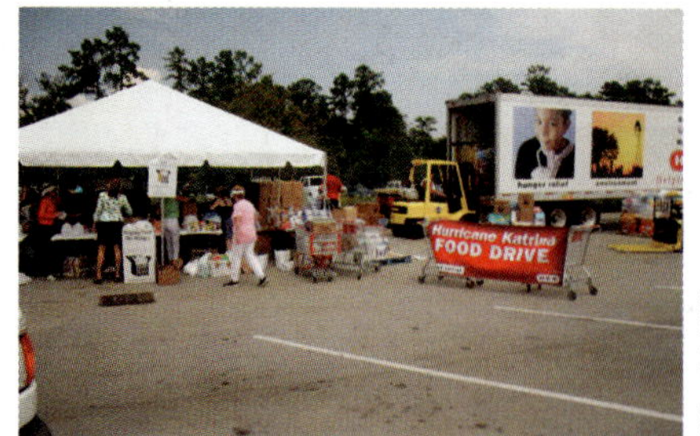


PR News Foto/H/E/B.

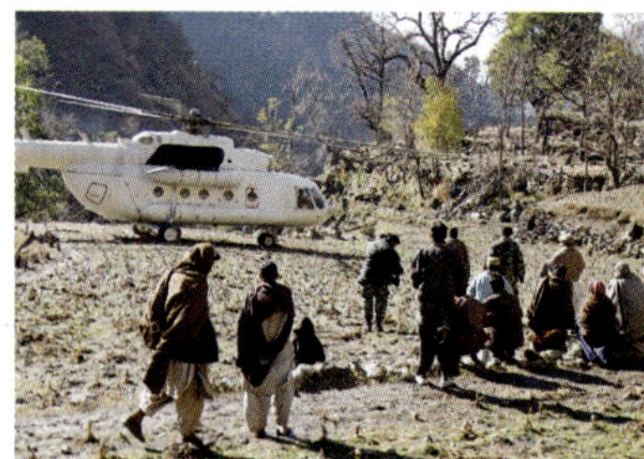

## Inspiration from Art

In the early 1900s, European artists began experimenting to create new and different kinds of art. They pasted flat objects on their paintings and invented the *collage* (from a French word meaning "to glue"). They also produced the *montage* (a collage made from photographs or other pictures) and the collagraph. Artists who create *collagraphs* add textures to a collage before printing. After pulling the first print, the artist may add objects before printing again.

Australian artist Dorothy Winnert used a variety of texture materials to create a collage. She then produced a collagraph print about the dangers of pesticides and herbicides. Her print illustrates some Australian wildlife that could be affected by the overuse of chemicals. What does the title, *Worth Their Weight*, suggest to you?

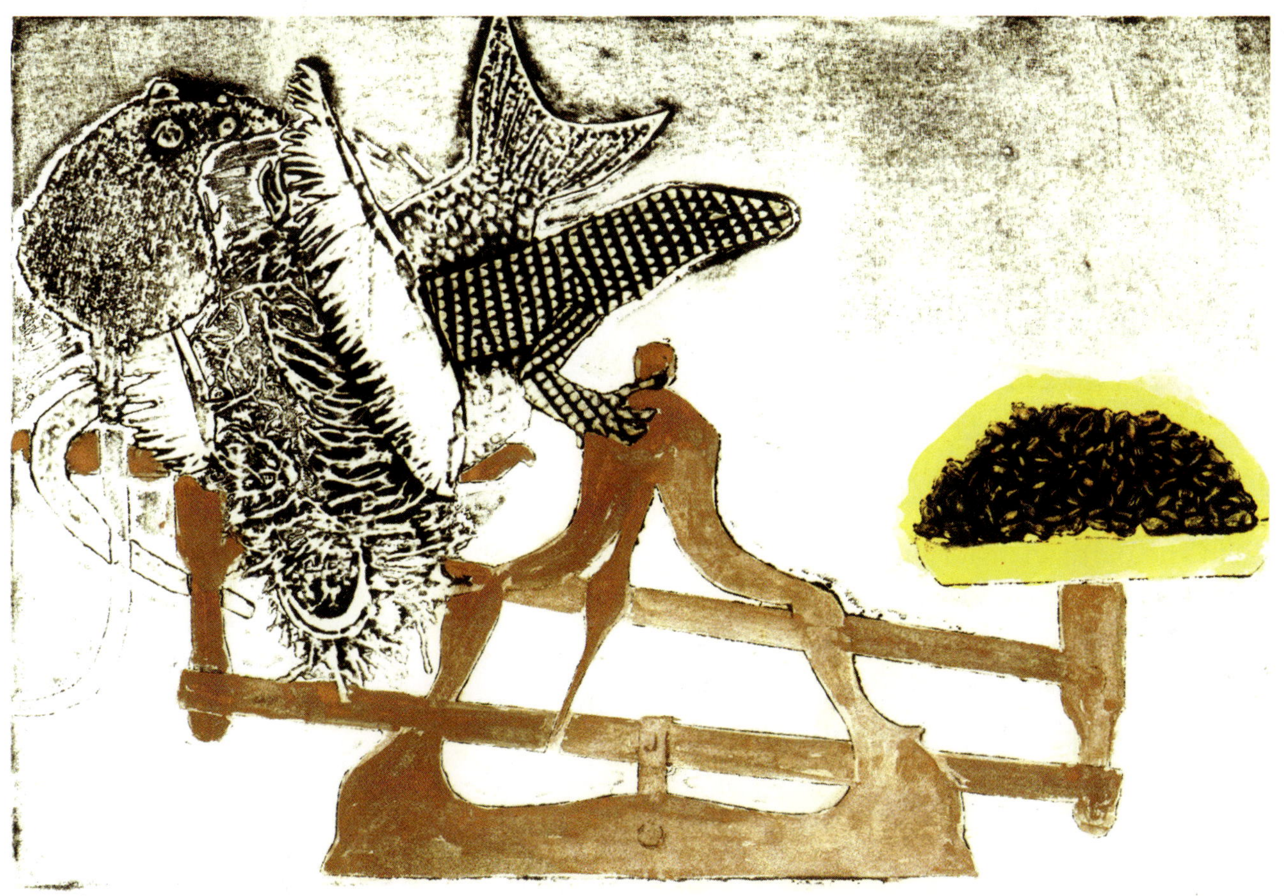

Fig. 8–13 **What different textures do you notice in this collagraph? How do they create a mood or feeling?**

Dorothy Winnett, *Worth Their Weight*. Collagraph on 310 gm Dutch aquatint, hand colored with Ecoline and Reeves drawing inks. Courtesy of the artist.

### Step 2 Begin to Create

- **Arrange your collage materials on the cardboard block.** Think about texture, placement, and the message your artwork will send.

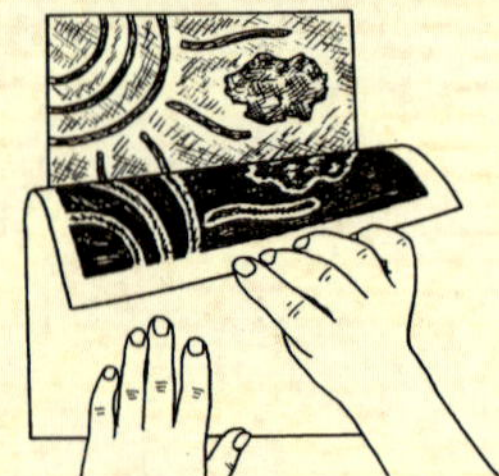

- Experiment with the arrangement of materials.
- **When you are pleased with the arrangement, glue the materials in place.**

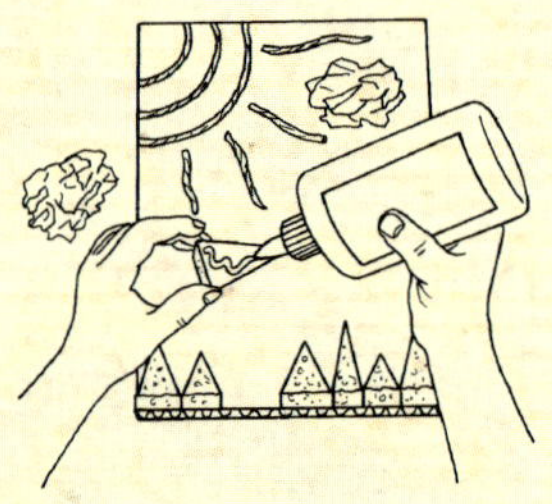

- Coat the plate with acrylic gel medium.
- Brush ink onto the plate surface. Place paper on the inked plate, and gently rub the paper with your hand. **Remove the paper by lifting the corners and carefully peeling the print away from the plate.**

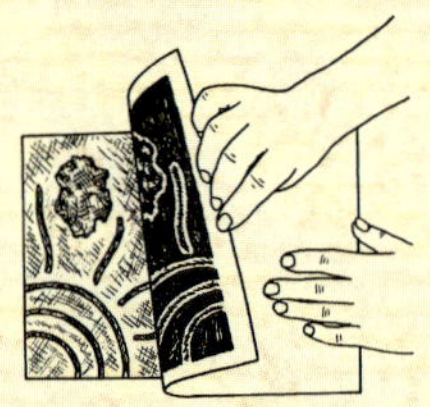

- Ink the plate again, and experiment. Wipe the ink off the plate surface, but leave ink in the crevices. Place another sheet of paper on the plate, and gently rub the paper with your hand. **Peel away the print as before.**

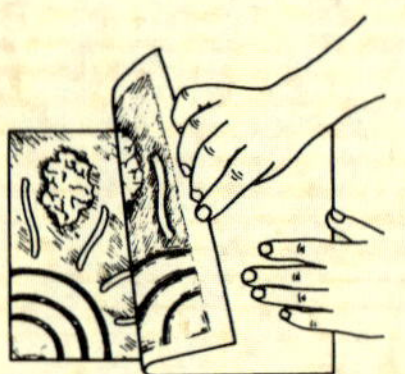

### Step 3 Revise

**Did you remember to:**

✓ Use collage materials with rich textures and interesting shapes?

✓ Arrange your collage materials in a way that best projects your message?

✓ Experiment with the amount of ink you use on the plate?

Adjust your work if necessary. In your sketchbook, make a note of your revisions and why you made them.

### Step 4 Add Finishing Touches

- Check the results from each printing method. Which is more interesting? Which method shows a better variety of textures?
- Experiment with different printing colors.

### Step 5 **Share and Reflect**

- Display your collagraph printing plate and one of your completed prints with those of your classmates.
- Make judgments about the prints and the plates. In what ways are they pleasing or interesting? What messages are presented in the prints? Discuss your experiments.

## Art Criticism

**Describe** What does the artist show in this collagraph?

**Analyze** How do you think the artist created the various textures in this print?

**Interpret** What message is presented in this print?

**Evaluate** What did the artist do especially well?

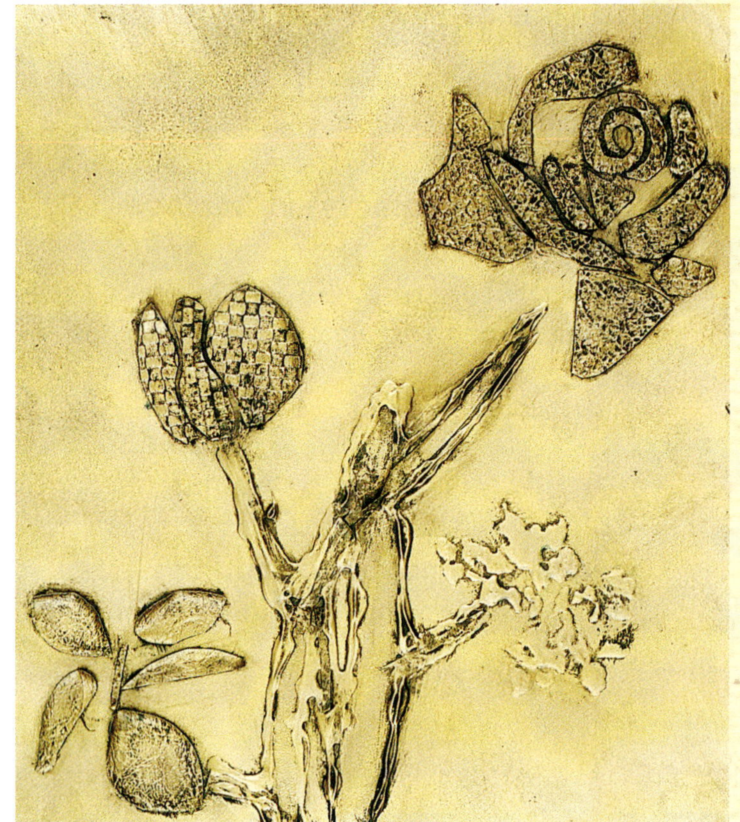

Fig. 8–14 Student artwork

# Making a Difference: 1950–1980

**Art and Social Causes** You've probably heard the expression "that's a good cause" or "that cause is worth supporting." A cause is a movement that focuses on an issue. Causes spring up when a group of people share a belief that something needs changing.

Following World War II, groups began to focus on social causes such as civil rights, women's issues, and the environment. This was also a time of antiwar protests. Many artists of the time, such as Robert Rauschenberg **(Fig. 8–15)**, addressed these issues through artworks, believing that art could make a difference in social and political causes.

Marisol Escobar **(Fig. 8–17)** and other sculptors of the time focused on social issues in all kinds of communities, from family groups to national and international concerns.

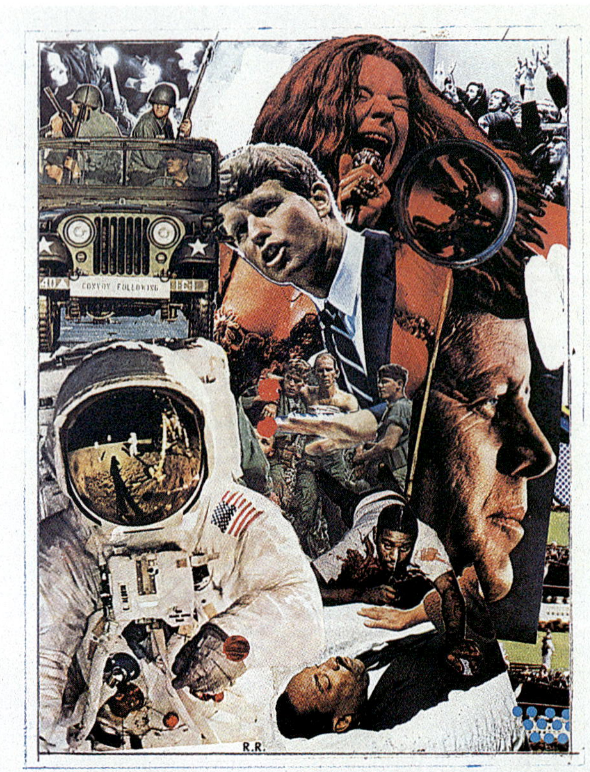

Fig. 8–15 **Each image in this print is a powerful expression of the turmoil America faced in the 1960s and 1970s. What images do you recognize?**

Robert Rauschenberg, *Signs*, 1970. Silkscreen print, 43" x 43" (109 x 109 cm). Edition: 250. Published by Castelli Graphics. © Untitled Press, Inc. / Licensed by VAGA, New York, NY.

**1955**
Rosa Parks refuses to give up her bus seat and is arrested.

**1962**
Escobar, *The Family*

**1962**
Rosenquist, *A Lot to Like*

**1963**
Martin Luther King, Jr. delivers his well-known "I Have a Dream" speech.

**1969**
250,000 people gather in Washington, DC, to protest the Vietnam War.

**1970**
Rauschenberg, *Signs*

**1974–75**
Chicago Mural Group, *History of Mexican American Worker*

**1977**
President Carter pardons civilians who resisted the Vietnam War draft.

**1900s**

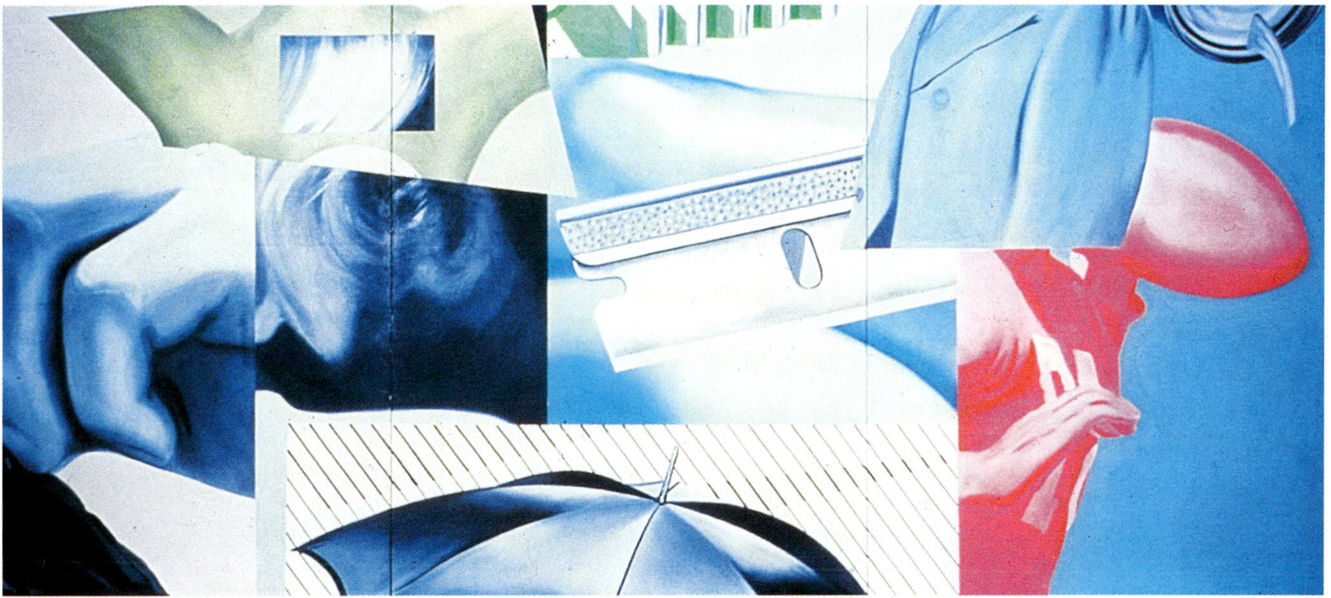

Fig. 8–16 **Does this painting remind you of a collage? How does it compare to *Signs* (Fig. 8–16)? What do you think this painting means?**

James Rosenquist, *A Lot to Like*, 1962. Oil on canvas, 93" x 204" (236 x 518.2 cm) (triptych). The Museum of Contemporary Art, Los Angeles. The Panza Collection. © James Rosenquist / Licensed by VAGA, New York, NY.

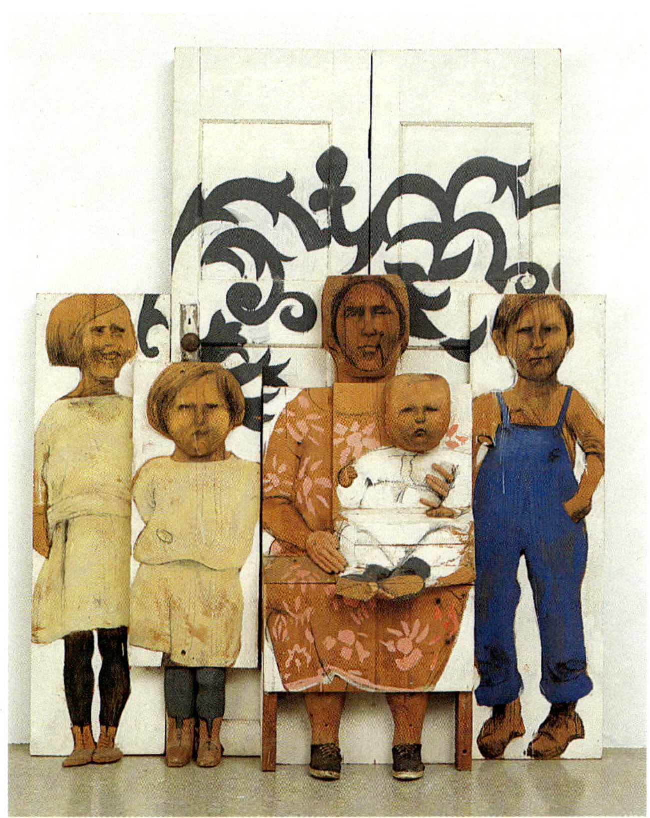

Fig. 8–17 **What might this artist be saying about the American family in this artwork? How might she be trying to make a difference?**

Marisol Escobar, *The Family*, 1962. Painted wood and other materials in three sections, overall, 6' 10 5/8" x 65 ½" x 15 ½" (209.8 x 166.3 x 39.3 cm). The Museum of Modern Art, New York. Advisory Committee Fund. Photograph © 2000 The Museum of Modern Art, New York. © Marisol / Licensed by VAGA, New York, NY.

**Art and Art Issues** Not all of the art during this period, however, was about social causes. Some artists chose not to use their art for making a difference in society. For these artists, making a difference in the way art is made and viewed seemed most important. These artists explored the qualities and effects of lines, shapes, colors, and surfaces. *Pop Art* featured products and images from popular culture. Pop artists such as James Rosenquist **(Fig. 8–16)** responded to the world of advertising, billboards, commercial products, television, comics and other images from the human-made environment. The Pop artists invited other artists to create art in new ways.

### Art and Community Involvement

Does your community have a mural? What message does it send? In the early 1970s, artists began a mural movement. The mural movement was an effort by artists to create murals in many cities all over the country. The murals helped add beauty to city neighborhoods and gave people an opportunity to express pride in where they live.

The Chicago Mural Group included about a dozen artists, both men and women, of different races and backgrounds. The group has created more than fifty outdoor murals (Fig. 8–18) and twenty-four indoor murals.

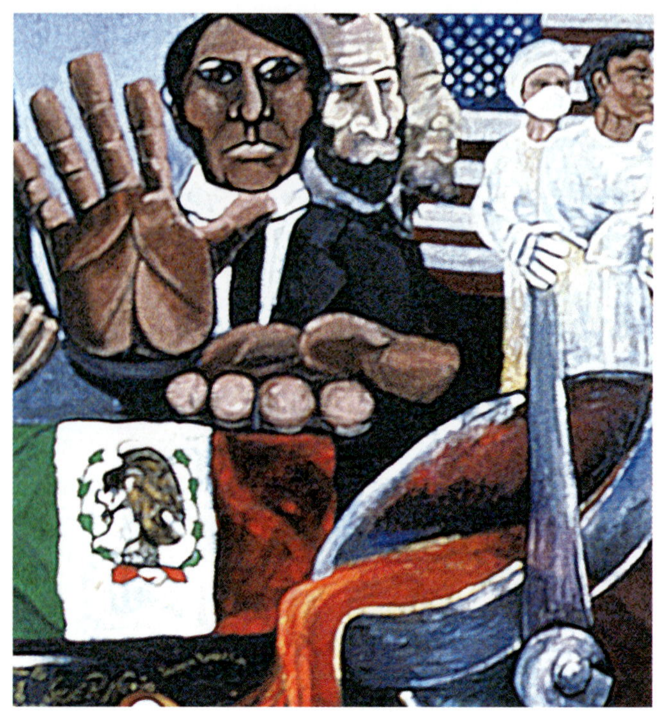

Fig. 8–19 Chicago Mural Group, Chicago, *History of Mexican American Worker* (close detail), 1974–75. (13337 South Western). Courtesy of Chicago Public Art Group.

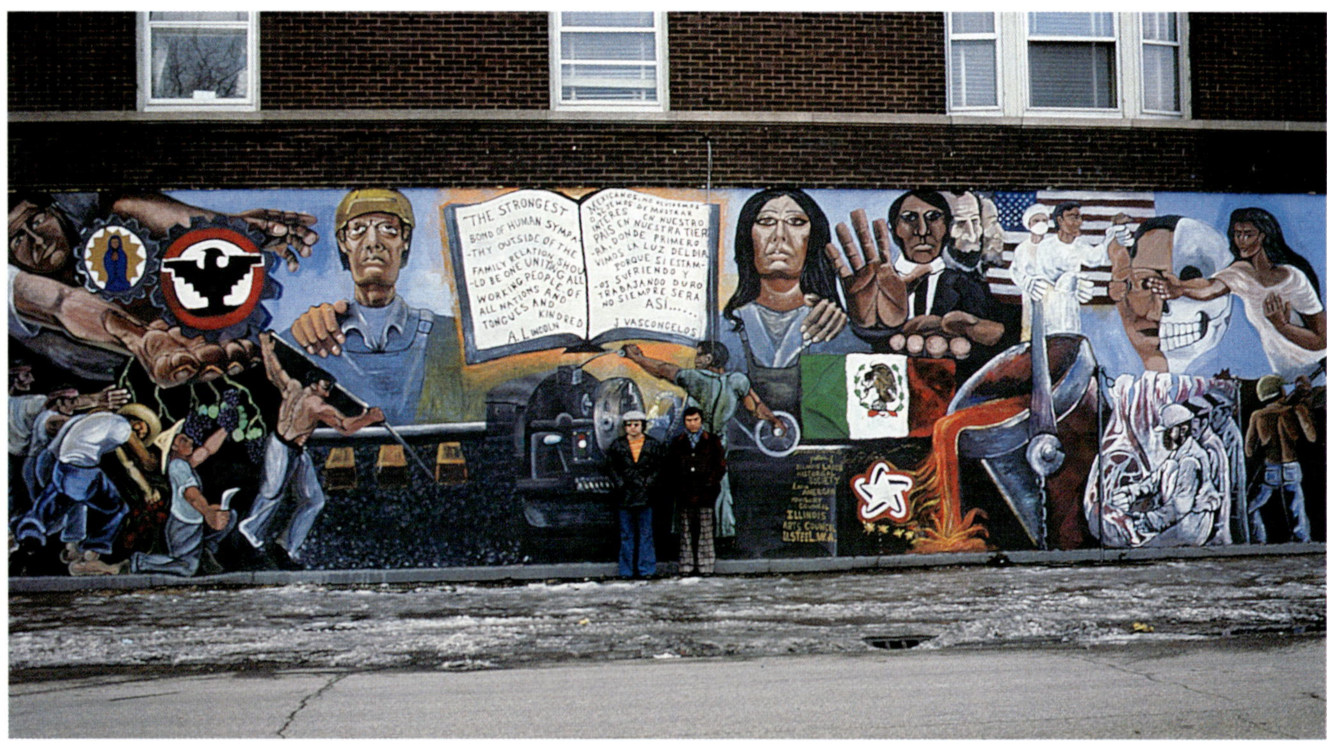


Fig. 8–18 **City neighborhoods can differ from one another in terms of the people who live there and the issues they're concerned about. What ideas are expressed in this mural?**

Chicago Mural Group, Chicago, *History of Mexican American Worker*, 1974–75. (13337 South Western). Courtesy of Chicago Public Art Group.

The success of the Chicago Mural Group inspired artists to create murals on walls in neighborhoods from Boston to Los Angeles. Often, the residents of the neighborhoods participated. Through these murals, artists have helped people in communities make a difference in their lives.

## Meet the Chicago Mural Group

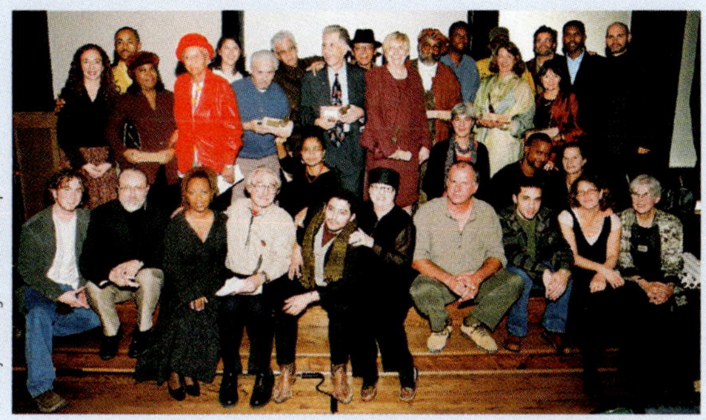

Courtesy of Chicago Public Art Group.

The Chicago Mural Group was founded in 1971 by a group of artists. They wanted to help communities create public art in their neighborhoods. Later, the group renamed itself Chicago Public Art Group (CPAG), because it had expanded its activities. Besides murals, it also began to create mosaics, sculptures, and landscapes.

CPAG teaches artists how to work with communities. Sometimes artists think of a good idea, and approach community leaders to ask for support. Sometimes communities come to CPAG with their ideas, and ask for help. Usually a team of one or two CPAG artists works with a group of volunteers, often residents or students. The group decides together what the artwork will look like. They explore issues of race, class, gender, place, identity, and justice. Sometimes, making the artwork helps bring its values to life. For example, high school students of mixed races worked together to build a mosaic about racial harmony.

**"Through art, communities develop a sense of their history and future."**

— Chicago Public Art Group

## Check Your Understanding

1. For what purposes did artists use artworks in the period following World War II?
2. How is the mural pictured in Fig. 8–18 similar to and different from the silkscreen print in Fig. 8–15?
3. How did artists make a difference in the second half of the 1900s?

## Studio Time

### A Message About Caring

Create a drawing that sends a message about the benefits of caring about others and listening to and investigating their concerns.

- Use colored pencils, markers, or mixed media.
- Choose and arrange elements to send a clear message.
- Use color, shape, and texture to present your message.

Reflect on how your classmates respond to your message.

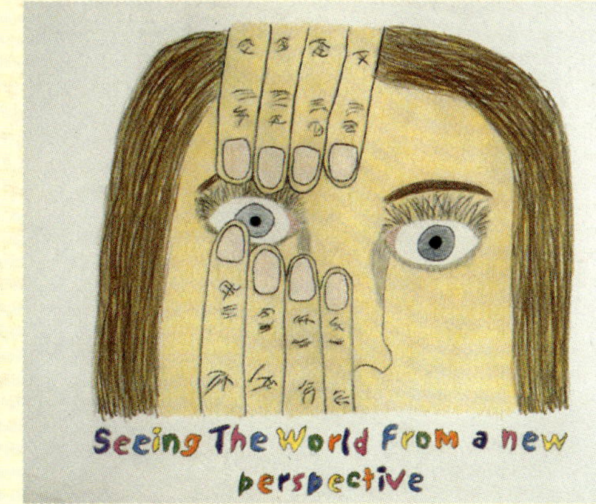


Fig. 8–20 Student artwork

# African Art Today

Fig. 8–21 **In traditional African house painting, the designs usually have some symbolic meaning. What geometric or organic designs do you see?**

Africa, Nigeria, Giwa, Hausa People, *Painted house*, 20th Century. Façade, left side. ©Maude Wahlman

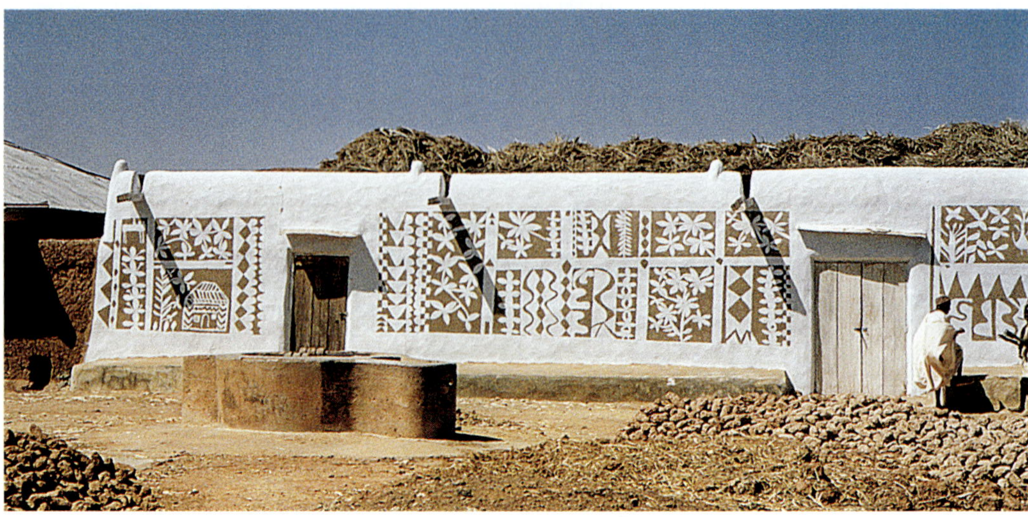

Africa is a vast continent with two major regions of culture and geography. In the north, there are many records of the artwork of ancient Egypt. This art influenced the Greek and Roman civilizations and the development of Western art. In the region south of the Sahara, African kingdoms have a long artistic heritage. Four types of art have made a difference in the way we think about African art today: traditional art, Christian art, tourist art, and new African art.

**Traditional Art** Traditional art in Africa includes textiles, masks, power figures used in rituals, sculptured heads, wall embellishments, and ceremonial and everyday objects. Although they vary greatly from one region of Africa to another, most of these traditional art forms have been created to serve religious or social needs in the community. Traditional art forms, styles, and processes of working with wood, fibers, metal, and clay have survived throughout Africa's history.

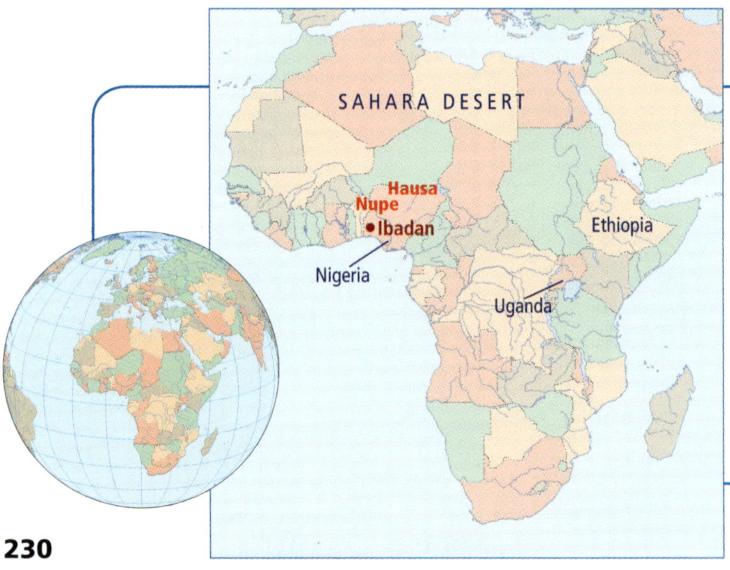


## Social Studies Connection

After Asia, **Africa** is the largest of the continents, stretching nearly 5,000 miles from north to south. During the last half of the 1900s, African communities have experienced great changes in their political, economic, social, and religious ideas. These community changes have caused changes in art as well.

**Other Traditions in Art** Among the most widely recognized forms of African art is tourist art. Tourist art is another word for souvenirs. Travelers buy tourist art to help them remember places they visited in Africa. Most tourist art realistically depicts the animals of Africa or shows scenes of village life. It is often made of recycled materials such as tin, plastic, and telephone wire. Tourist art is sold in art stalls at African markets **(Fig. 8–22)**, and provides income to the African economy.

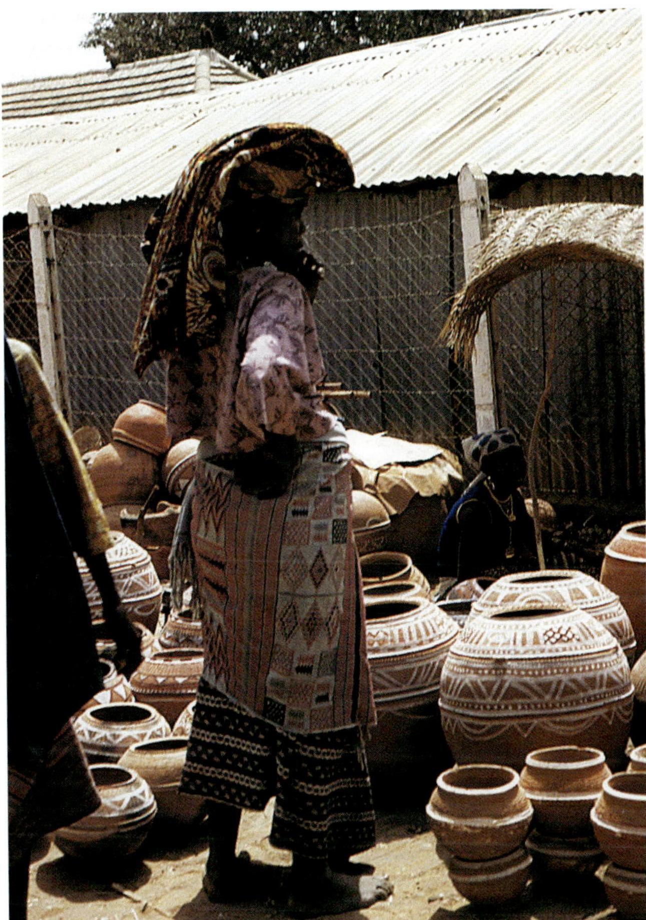

Fig. 8–22 **In a traditional market, like the one you see here, all kinds of objects are bought and sold. What examples of traditional art do you see?**

Africa, Nigeria, Nupe People, *Market Scene: Selling Bide-Pottery*, 1974.

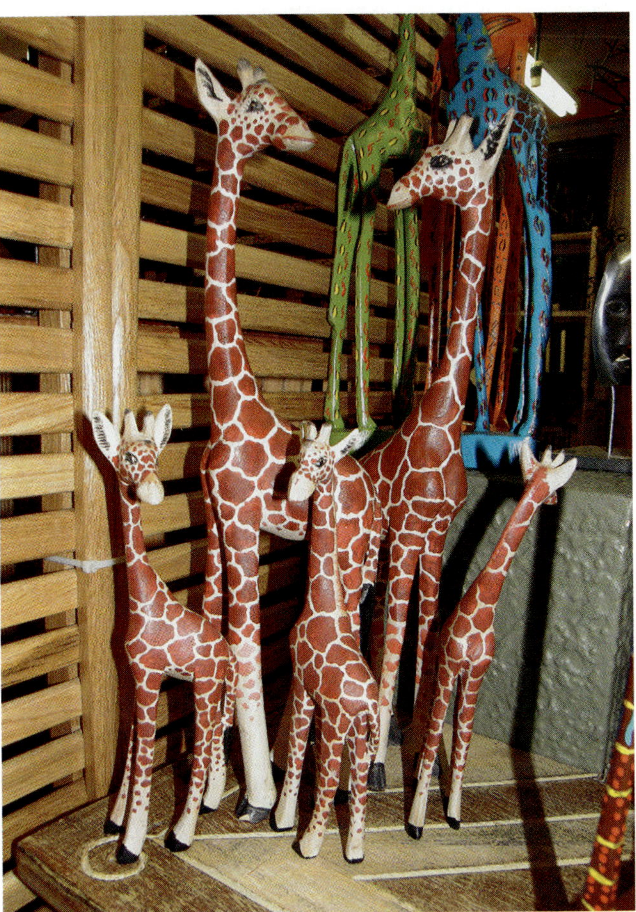

Fig. 8–23 **This artist combined painting and sculpture to create tourist art. How does the combination of two forms of art create an accurate depiction of a giraffe?**

*Kenyan wood carvings*, 2008. Photo courtesy of Eldon Katter and Bamboula, Ltd., Kutztown, PA.

### Visual Culture

Many people, when they travel, buy souvenirs to remind them of the places they have been. Consider the type and variety of objects that are sold as souvenirs in your state or region. What do they represent? How, and by whom, are they made? If you were going to design a souvenir to help people remember a visit to your town or community, what would it look like?

**New African Art** Since the mid 1900s, a new African art has caught the attention of art museums and collectors around the world. The majority of these artists have been trained in art schools such as Makerere School of Fine Arts in Uganda. These artists are aware of both historic and modern art traditions in Africa and other parts of the world.

The style of new African art is similar to modern art movements around the world, but the subject matter and themes are distinctly African. These artworks show African subjects in African settings, and deal with African political and social issues. The new African art shows the artists' views of scenes from their world. In the last half of the 1900s, African artists have continued to make a difference as they use their talent, training, and ideas to describe the exciting and unique experience of life in African communities.

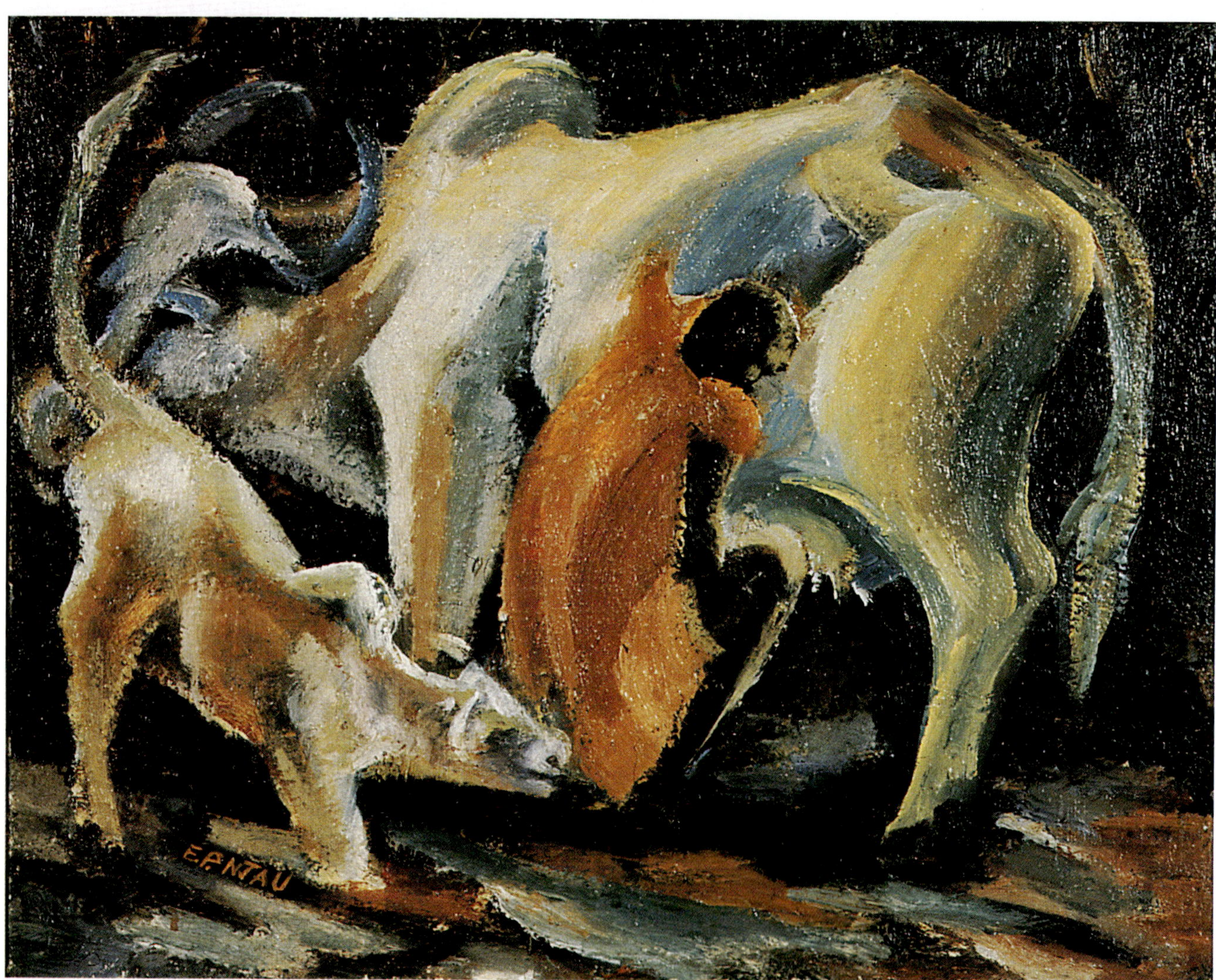


Fig. 8–24 **How is this artwork an example of new African art?**

Elimo Njau, *Milking*, undated. Oil on canvas, 20 ⅛" x 15 ¾" (51 x 40 cm). Photo: Maria Obermaier.

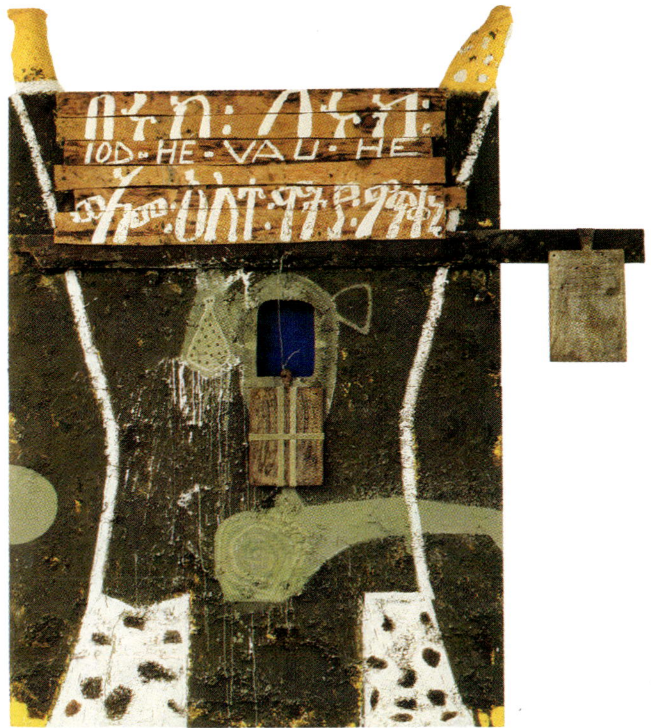


Fig. 8–25 **How is this artwork different from traditional African art? What modern art style does it make you think of?**

Ouattara, *Masada*, 1993. Acrylic, electric cord, and mixed media on 2 wood panels, 116 ½" x 101 ½" x 7 ½" (296 x 257.8 x 19 cm). Signed and dated on the reverse. Courtesy Cavaliero Fine Arts, New York.

## Meet Ouattara

Detail of *Masada*.

Drawing was the first love of Ouattara, an artist born and raised in the West African country of Ivory Coast. He was self-taught as a child, but went to Paris at age nineteen to study at the École des Beaux-Arts.

Ouattara's artworks combine materials and beliefs from his West African upbringing with the influences of European artists such as Pablo Picasso, Joan Miro, and Marcel Duchamp. His works are often political, raising such issues as slavery, consumerism, and the conflict between traditional and modern beliefs and values.

**"My vision...refers to the cosmos."**

— Ouattara (born 1957)

## Check Your Understanding

1. Describe some of the traditional forms of African art.
2. How does the art of the new African artists differ from other African styles of art?
3. African tourist art represents the community from which it comes. What kind of tourist art could be created to represent your community?

## Studio Time

### Recycled Expressions

Create a sculpture of a person or animal using recycled wire, tin, or plastic.

- Plan your work before you begin. Think about how you can use your sculpture to make a difference in the way people think about something. What subject matter might catch people's attention? How can you inspire viewers to think about your subject matter differently?
- Remember to consider all angles of your sculpture during the creation process.

Reflect on how your classmates respond to your work.

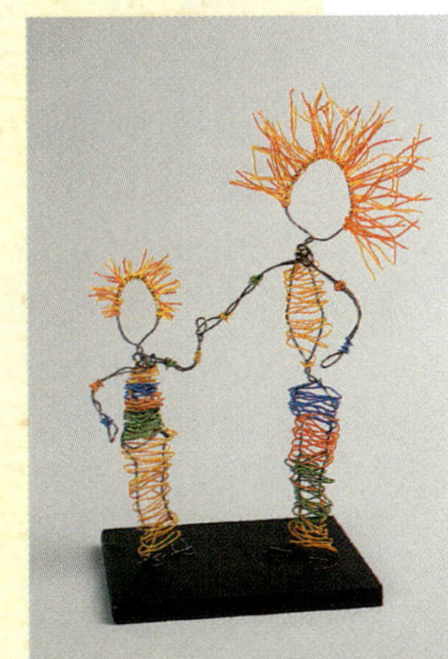

Fig. 8–26 Student artwork

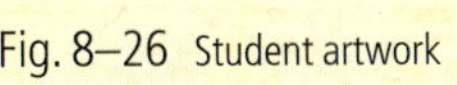

# Two-Color Relief Print

## Studio Background

Look around you. There are natural environments everywhere. A seaside beach is an environment of crabs, seaweed, and barnacles. A garden is an environment of flowers, vegetables, animals, and insects. A marsh is an environment of grasses, cattails, and waterfowl. Some natural environments are in danger of being destroyed. How can you show an endangered environment in a positive way?

For many years, printmaking has been used to create multiple copies, to get a message out to many people quickly. **In this studio exploration, you will make a two-color relief print of a natural environment that is in danger of being destroyed.** You might think of a slogan that sums up what you want to say about this environment. Then try to illustrate your thought.

### You Will Need

- thin paper
- soft pencil
- carbon paper
- linoleum block
- cutting tools
- ink, inking slab, and brayer
- printing paper

## Step 1 Plan and Practice

- Choose an endangered environment to show in a relief print. Will you choose an environment that you know or one that you have heard about?
- Sketch your image on thin paper that is the same size as your printing block. Make the main shapes of your subject simple and strong.
- When you are finished, turn your sketch over and hold it up to a strong light. This will show you how your final print will look.

**Things to Remember:**

✓ Simplify main shapes.

✓ Use colors and textures that help emphasize your message.

✓ Apply ink evenly.

## Inspiration from Our World

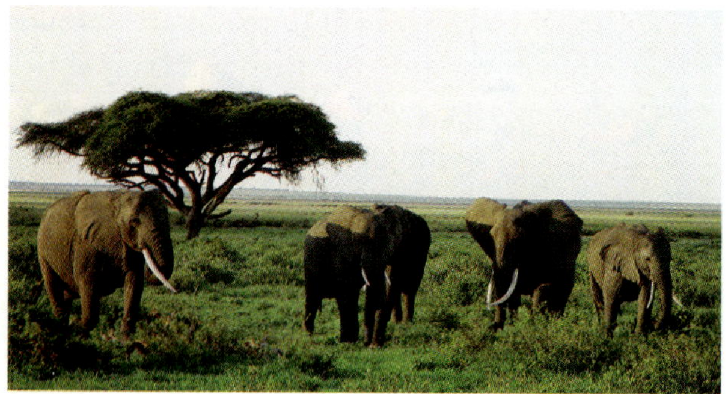

## Inspiration from Art

Do you remember the first time you accidentally left a fingerprint of ink or paint on a sheet of paper? You may not have realized it, but you made a relief print. The fine lines of the print were made by the ridges or raised areas of the fingertip itself. The shallow areas between the ridges remained free of ink or paint.

A linoleum cut is a relief print made from a linoleum block. When an artist makes a linoleum cut, he or she uses cutting tools, such as gouges, veiners, and knives, to cut an image on the block.

Depending on the size of the cutting tool, an artist can make thick or thin lines, or remove entire areas of the block's surface. The areas that are left uncut will be covered with a thin coat of ink. When the print is made, the areas of the block that are cut away will be the color of the paper.

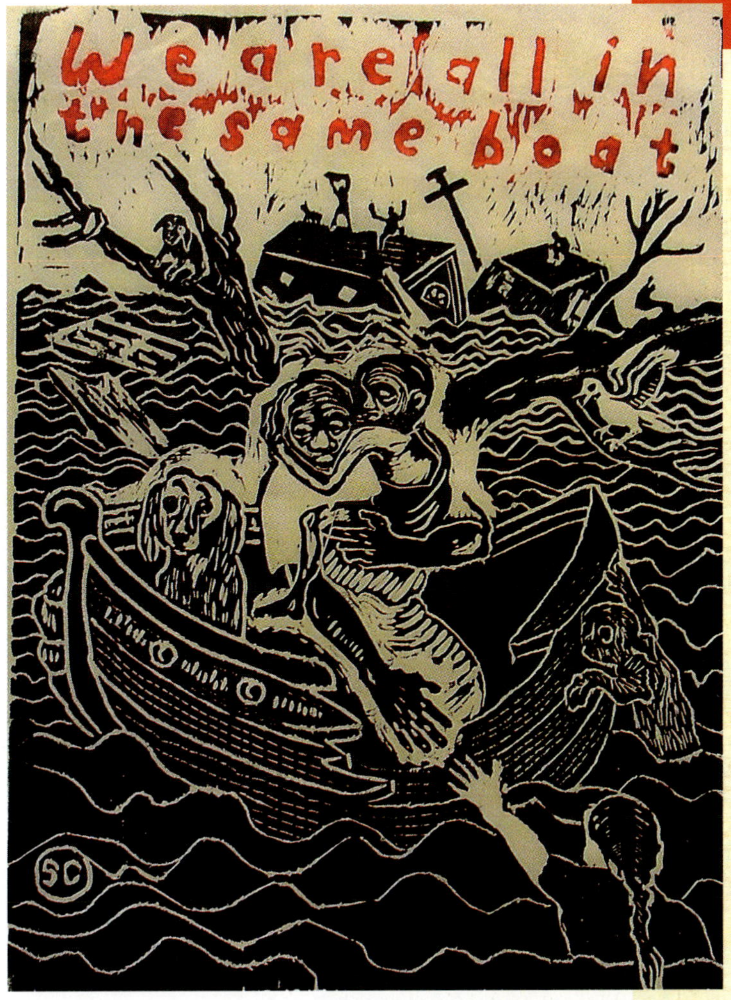


Fig. 8–27 **Based on these words and images, what message about caring for the world or its people is the artist trying to express?**

Sue Coe. *We Are All in the Same Boat.* Woodcut. ©2005 Sue Coe. Courtesy of Galerie St. Etienne, New York.

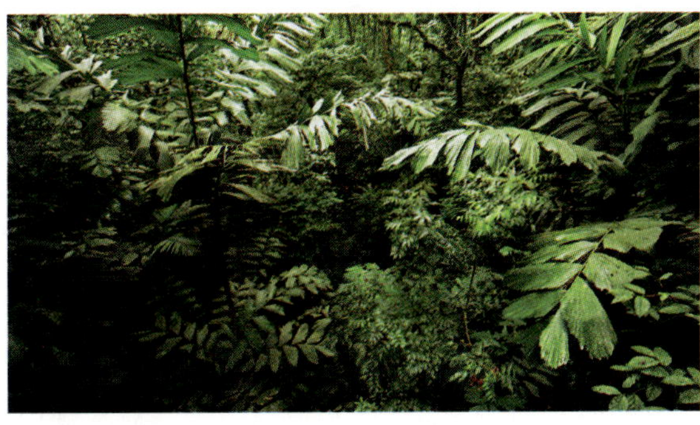

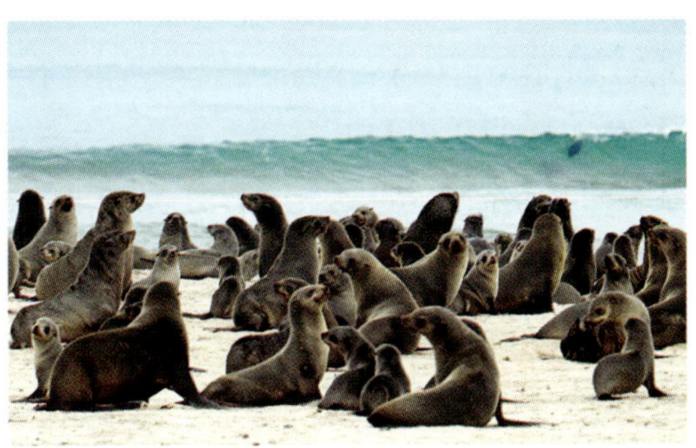

## Step 2 Begin to Create

- Use carbon paper to transfer your design onto the block. **Place the carbon paper face down on your block. Lay your design face up over the carbon paper.** Carefully trace over the design.

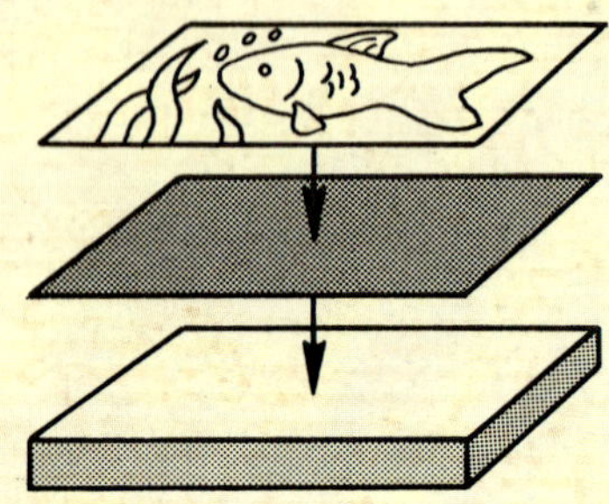

- With your pencil, lightly fill in the areas on your block that you want to print in the first color. Check your design when you are finished. Make changes as needed.
- **Carefully cut away the areas you do not want to print.**

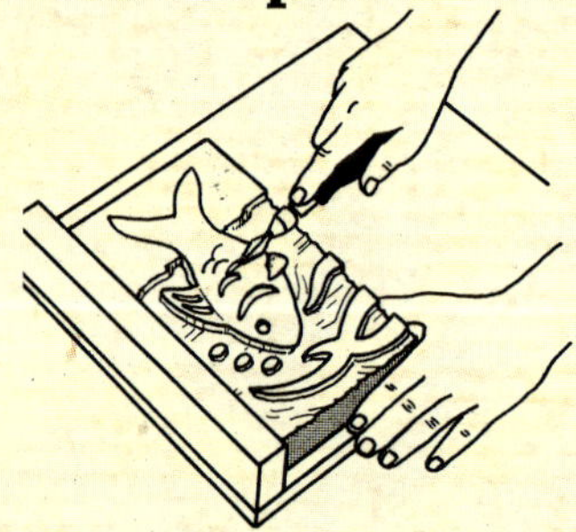

### Safety Note

Cutting tools must be handled with extreme caution. Always hold the block securely and point the cutting edge of the tool away from your hands, fingers, and body. Work slowly. Wear safety goggles.

- **With a brayer, apply a thin, even coat of ink to the raised areas of your design.**

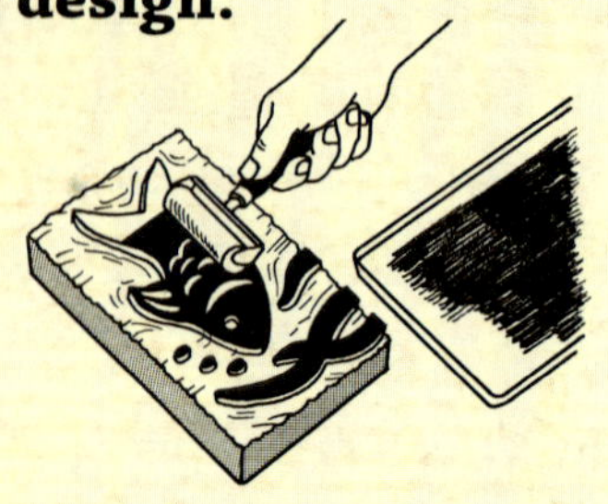

- Carefully place the printing paper over the block. Gently rub the paper with your hand. When you can see your design faintly through the back of the sheet, **slowly pull the print away from the block.**

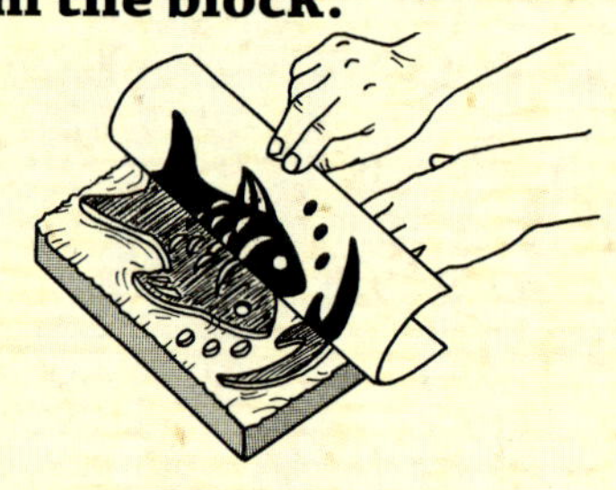

## Step 3 Revise

**Did you remember to:**

✓ Simplify main shapes?

✓ Use colors and textures that help emphasize your message?

✓ Apply ink evenly?

Adjust your work if necessary. In your sketchbook, make a note of your revisions and why you made them.

### Step 4 **Add Finishing Touches**

- To add a second color to your print, create a stencil that exposes the part of your design that you wish to cover with the second color. Place the stencil over your print.
- By inking the block with another color and printing over the first color, the stencil area remains unchanged.

### Step 5 **Share and Reflect**

- Display your artwork for your classmates to see.
- Discuss what your print says about the natural environment you've shown. How might it make a difference in the way viewers think about the environment?

## Art Criticism

**Describe** What objects do you recognize in this artwork?

**Analyze** How has the student combined shapes to call attention to an environmental issue?

**Interpret** What do you think is the message of this block print design?

**Evaluate** What did the artist do especially well?

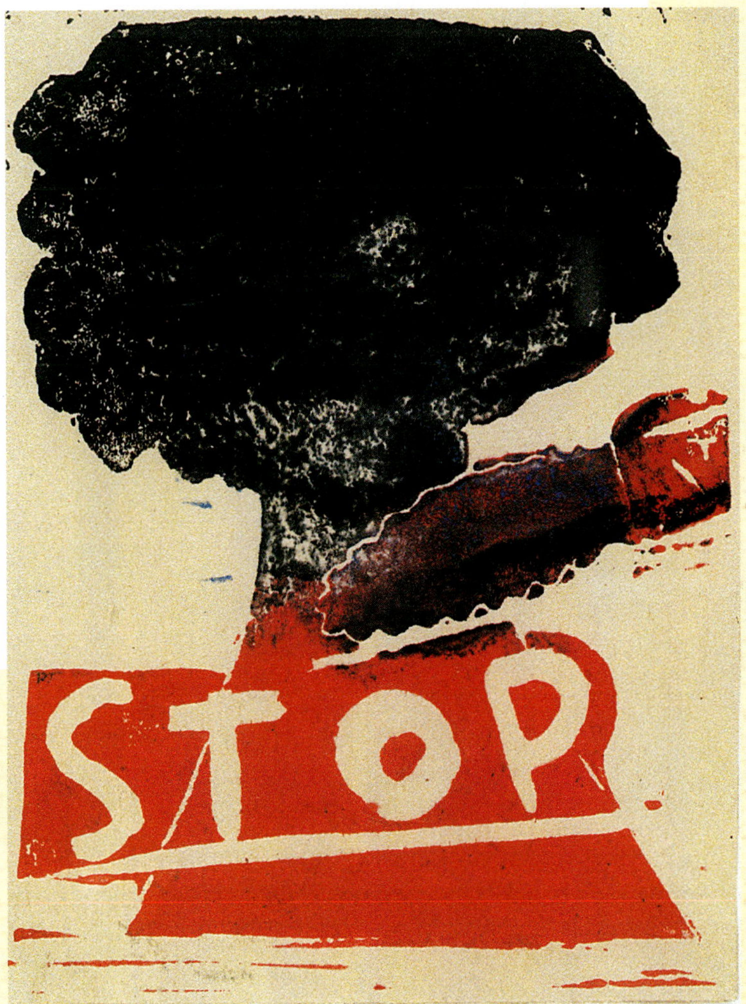


Fig. 8–28 Student artwork

## Language Arts

**Computers make a huge difference in our lives.** How well do you understand computers? Some people believe that computers are necessary for learning and education. Software for creating text and graphics has had a huge impact on language arts. We now have access to many websites that provide meaningful content and excellent graphic design. To benefit from this, students must be knowledgeable about what they see and read. Why do you think it's important to know how to use a computer?

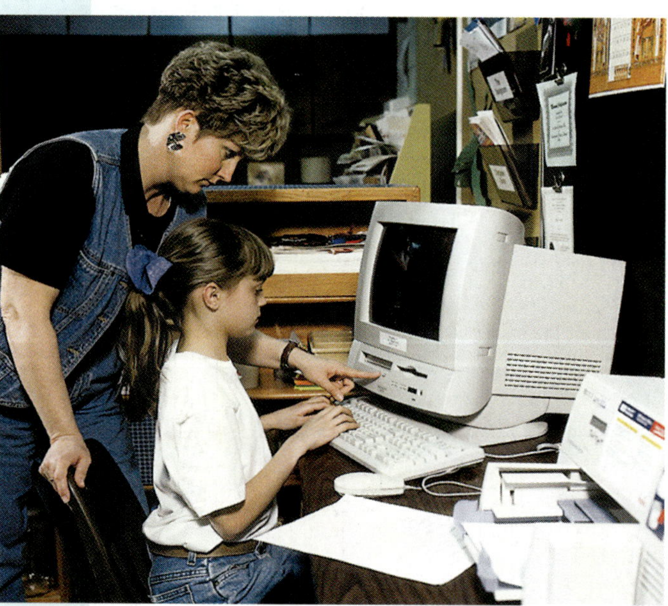

Fig. 8–29 **Many schools and local libraries have computers available for student use. Why do you think it's important for students to have access to computers?**

Photo courtesy of *SchoolArts*.

## Theater

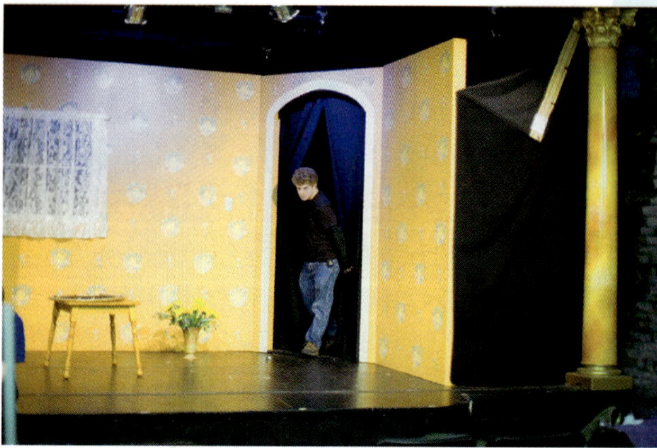

Fig. 8–30

**Theater artists, like visual artists, work to make a difference in their communities.** During the early 1900s, cities and towns across the United States began to create community theaters to serve local interests and needs. Early on, many community theaters held large pageants in which many people could take part and learn about theater. However, these productions became too large, and community theaters began staging smaller productions that were meant to entertain as well as educate. How might a community benefit from a local theater?

## Careers Photojournalist

**How might you use a camera to make a difference?** You could choose a career in photojournalism. Photojournalists work for newspapers, TV stations, magazines, and news services. They provide photographs that tell a news story. Photojournalists may work with a reporter to cover a particular story. Or they might cover an event alone, working to create a photo-essay, a story in pictures. By capturing an image artfully, a photographer can make a powerful statement.

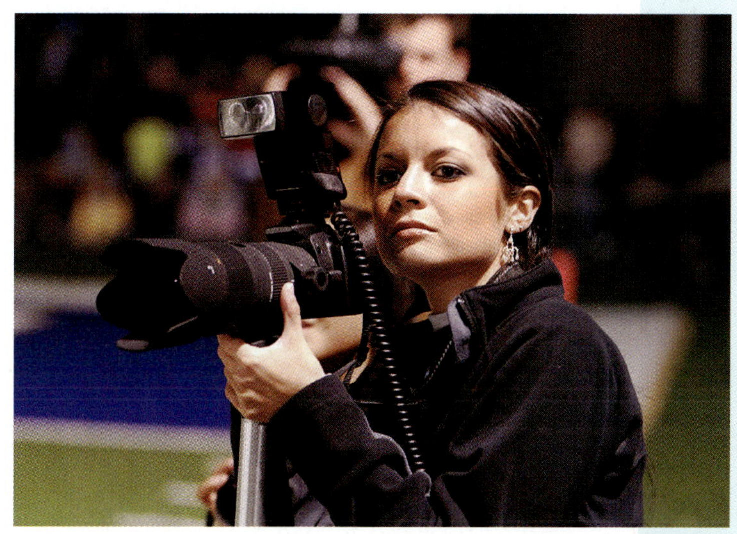

Fig. 8–31

## Daily Life

**What can each of us do to make a difference?** By combining our efforts with those of others, we can make the world a better place. For example, you can volunteer in a hospital or a food bank or donate clothing to organizations such as the Salvation Army and Goodwill. You may even help prepare or deliver meals to the sick or a family in need. What other charitable efforts could you make?

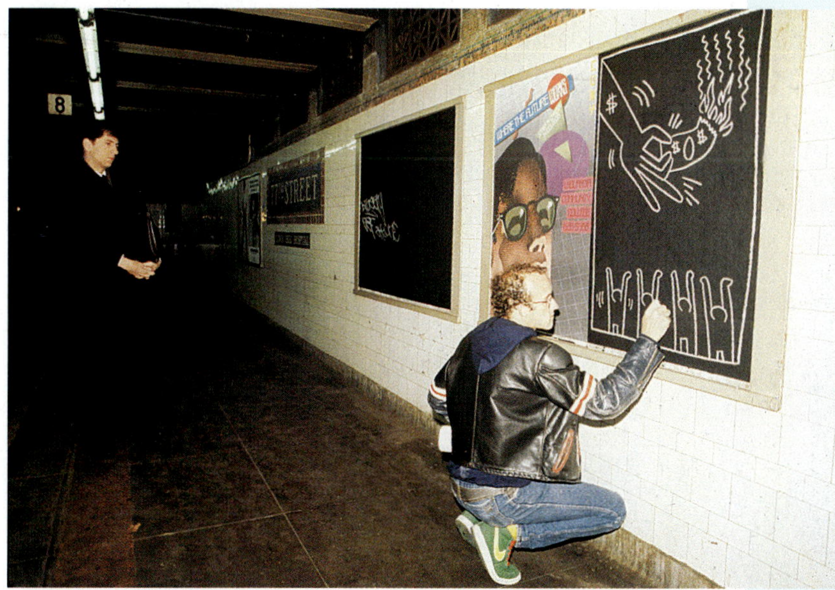

Fig. 8–32 **Art can be used to make a difference. Keith Haring used this subway station for his art. What message does this artwork seem to send?**

*Keith Haring photographed by Chantal Regnault in NYC subway*, 1981. ©The Estate of Keith Haring.

## Vocabulary Review

Match each art term below with its definition.

**serigraph**
**cause**
**collagraph**
**relief print**
**mural movement**
**traditional art**

1. helped add beauty to city neighborhoods and gave people an opportunity to express pride in where they live
2. a print, also known as a silkscreen print, made by squeezing ink through a stencil and silk-covered frame to paper below
3. artwork created using a process in which ink is placed on the raised portions of a block or plate
4. a print made from a collage with raised areas
5. artwork created in almost the same way year after year because it is part of a culture, custom, or belief
6. a movement that focuses on an issue

## Aesthetic Thinking

Can someone without formal training in art, like Elijah Pierce, be considered an artist? What makes someone an artist? Must you consider yourself an artist to be one?

## Write About Art

Lynne Hull creates sculpture that solves an ecological problem—in this case, providing a safe place for birds to roost. She has said: "I believe that the creativity of artists can be applied to real-world problems and can have an effect on urgent social and environmental issues." Write a short essay that explains whether or not you agree with her. Then select a social or environmental problem you care about and describe what type of an artwork might help draw people's attention to that issue.

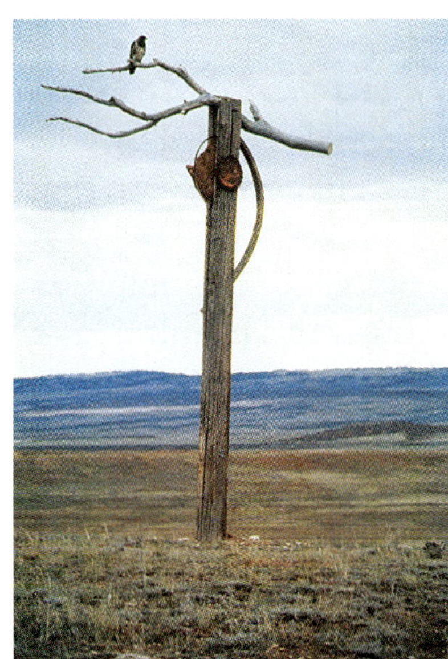

Fig. 8–33 **Artist Lynne Hull was concerned that hawks and eagles were being electrocuted when they roosted on telephone poles. So, she created structures for them.**

Lynne Hull, *Raptor Roost L-1 with Swainson's Hawk: a safe roosting sculpture for hawks and eagles*, 1988. Wood, found metals, stone from site, height: 16' (4.9 m). Photo by Bertrand de Peyer. Courtesy of the artist.

## Art Criticism

**Describe** What do you see in this print?

**Analyze** What techniques does Warhol use to create drama in this image?

**Interpret** In what way to you think Warhol hoped to make a difference with this print?

**Evaluate** Do you think Warhol succeeded at making a difference? Does the dramatic style he chose work well for this type of message?

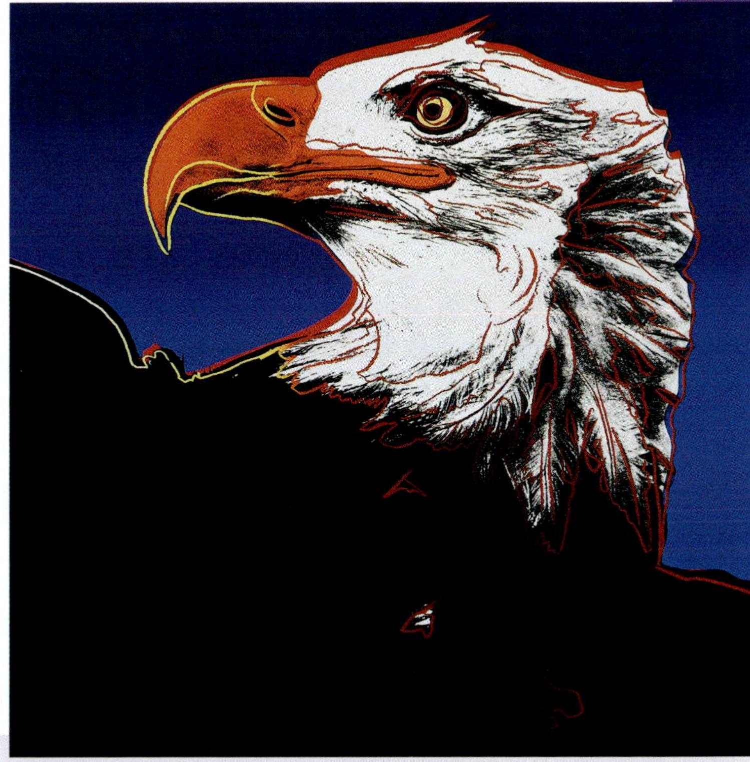

Fig. 8–34 Andy Warhol, *Bald Eagle, Endangered Species Series,* 1983. One of a portfolio of ten screen prints and colophon printed on Lenox Museum Board, 38" x 38" (96.5 x 96.5 cm). ©The Andy Warhol Foundation for the Visual Arts/ARS, NY. Photo: The Andy Warhol Foundation, Inc./Art Resource, NY.

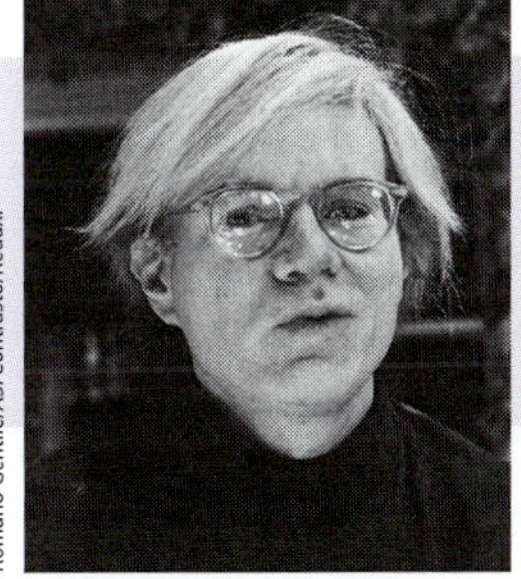

Romano Gentile/X3/Contrasto/Redux.

## Meet the Artist

**Andy Warhol** was born in Pittsburgh, Pennsylvania. He graduated from Carnegie Mellon University before moving to New York City to become a commercial artist. Warhol founded the movement known as "Pop Art," short for "popular." He used familiar images like Campbell's Soup cans and photographs of celebrities like Marilyn Monroe in his work. Warhol was one of the first artists to successfully blend aspects of commercial art with more traditional fine art techniques.

**"Art is what you can get away with."**

— Andy Warhol (1928–1987)

## For Your Portfolio

Keep your portfolio well organized. Choose what to keep in your portfolio and what to remove. Check that each entry is well presented and identified with your name, date, and title of work. Protect each entry with newsprint or tissue paper.

## For Your Sketchbook

Think about your portfolio artworks in terms of how they might make a difference. Which pieces express an opinion? What ideas do you explore most often? Describe your findings in your sketchbook.

# Art and New Directions

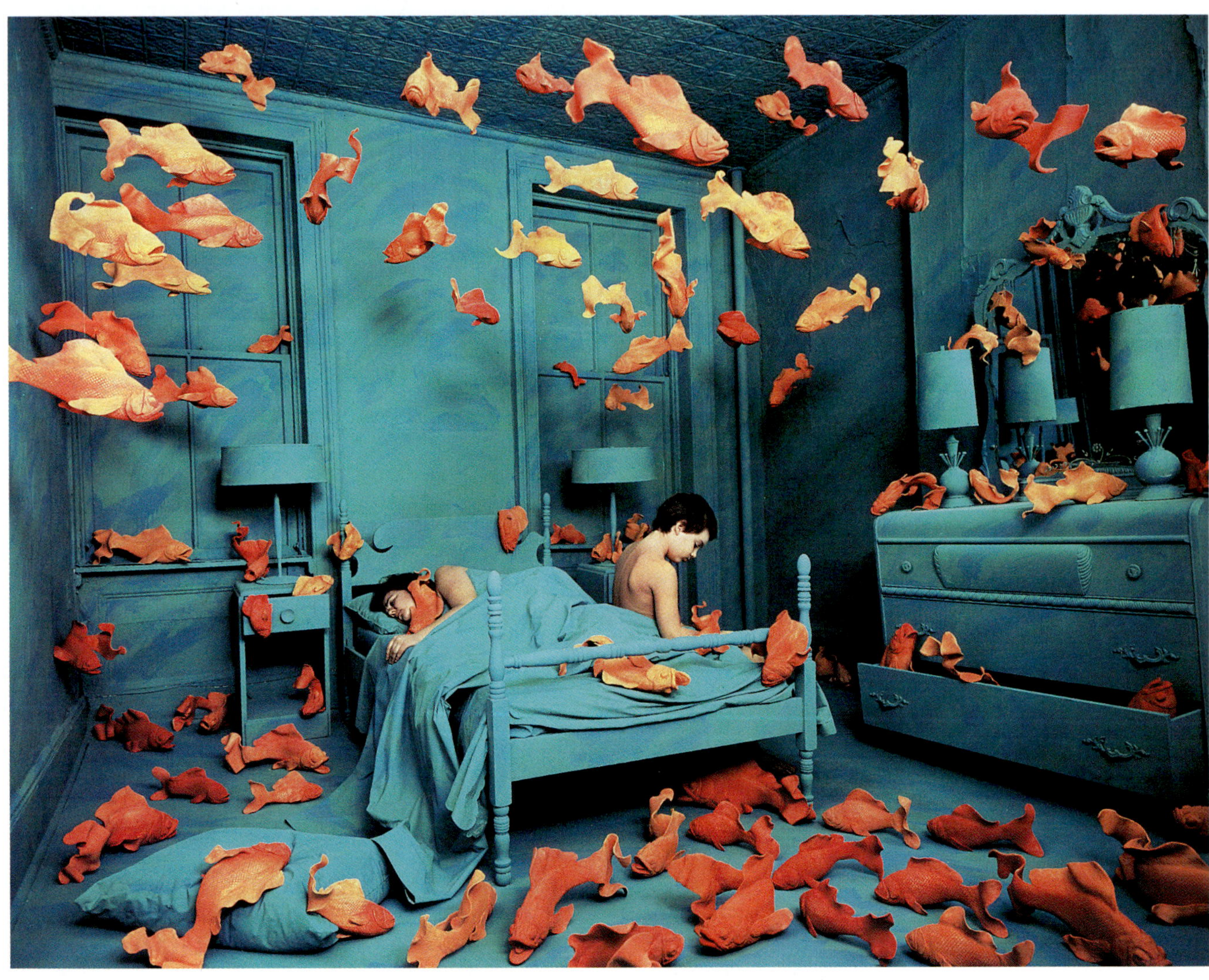

Fig. 9–1 **When we look at this image, it's easy to think that we're viewing someone's dream. Whose dream might it be? What might it mean?**

Sandy Skoglund, *Revenge of the Goldfish*, 1981. Cibachrome color photograph, 30" x 40" (76.1 x 101.6 cm), ©1981, Sandy Skoglund.

**Let's face it. The image shown in Fig. 9–1 is strange. Parts of it are familiar: a bedroom, a person sleeping. But everything is blue-green except the people and those fish.** What are they doing there? Is this scene underwater? Are the fish flying in the air? This is the sort of image that could take place only in a dream.

Since early times, artists have helped people imagine other worlds. Sometimes, these worlds remain fantasy. Other times, the dreams of artists and community members become reality in the future. Every invention begins as an idea of what someone imagines for the future.

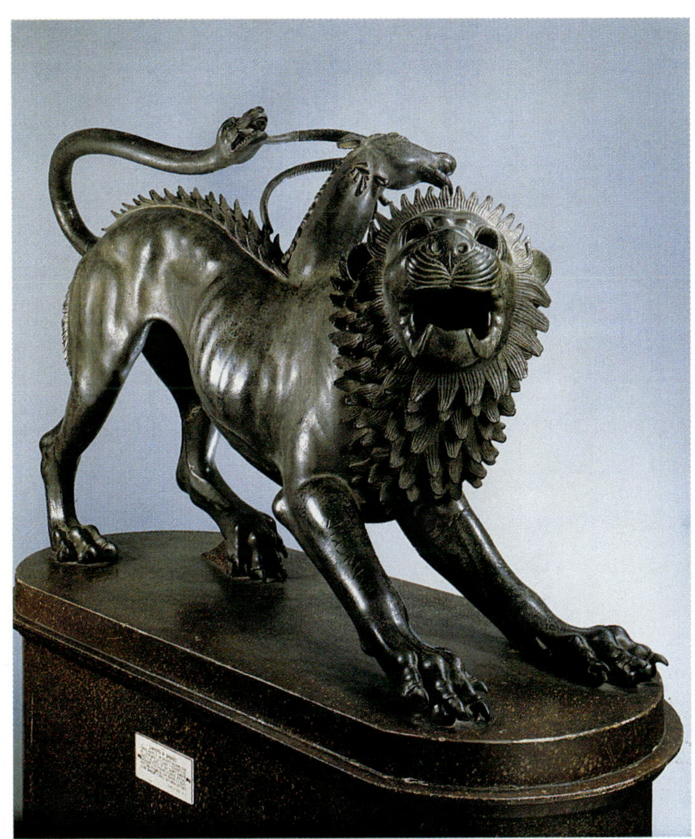

Fig. 9–2 **Chimera was a Greek mythical creature. What creatures from mythology are you familiar with? How might they be shown in an artwork?**

Etruscan, *Chimera of Arezzo*, 6th century BCE. Bronze. Museo Archeologico, Florence, Italy. Scala/Art Resource, New York.

**In this unit, you will learn:**

- How artists help people explore new ways to imagine the future.
- How to use new and traditional media to create imaginative worlds.
- How to look at art as expressions of the future.

# Imagining the Unfamiliar

**New Ideas** Have you ever wished for a machine that could help you with your chores? Artists design futuristic objects to help communities imagine possibilities. Leonardo da Vinci, for example, drew flying machines. For everyone who lived in the late 1400s and early 1500s, such machines only existed on paper or in dreams.

Community members dream about improving their surroundings. They ask architects and other artists to help in their planning. In some cases, teams of people help imagine these new places. Students, parents, and other community members worked together to create the plan of the school shown in **Fig. 9–3**.

**New Kinds of Art** Contemporary artists around the world experiment with new materials and technology to create new kinds of art. Many artists create installations. Installations are temporary arrangements of objects in galleries, museums, and outdoors. Some artists include sound and video or computer technology in an installation, such as the work by Jenny Holzer **(Fig. 9–4)**. Occasionally, an artist will become part of the artwork, engaging in a kind of performance.

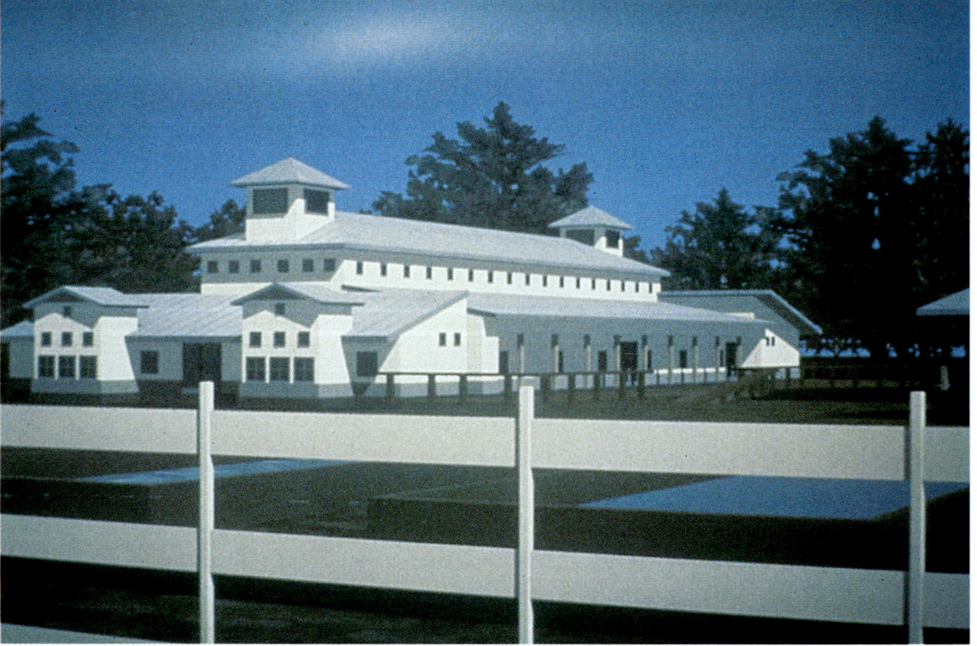

Fig. 9–3 **Which parts of this school resemble a farm?**

Stephen Bingler, *Lincoln High School Environmental Resource Center*, 1996. Digital graphic illustration. Courtesy of Concordia Architects.

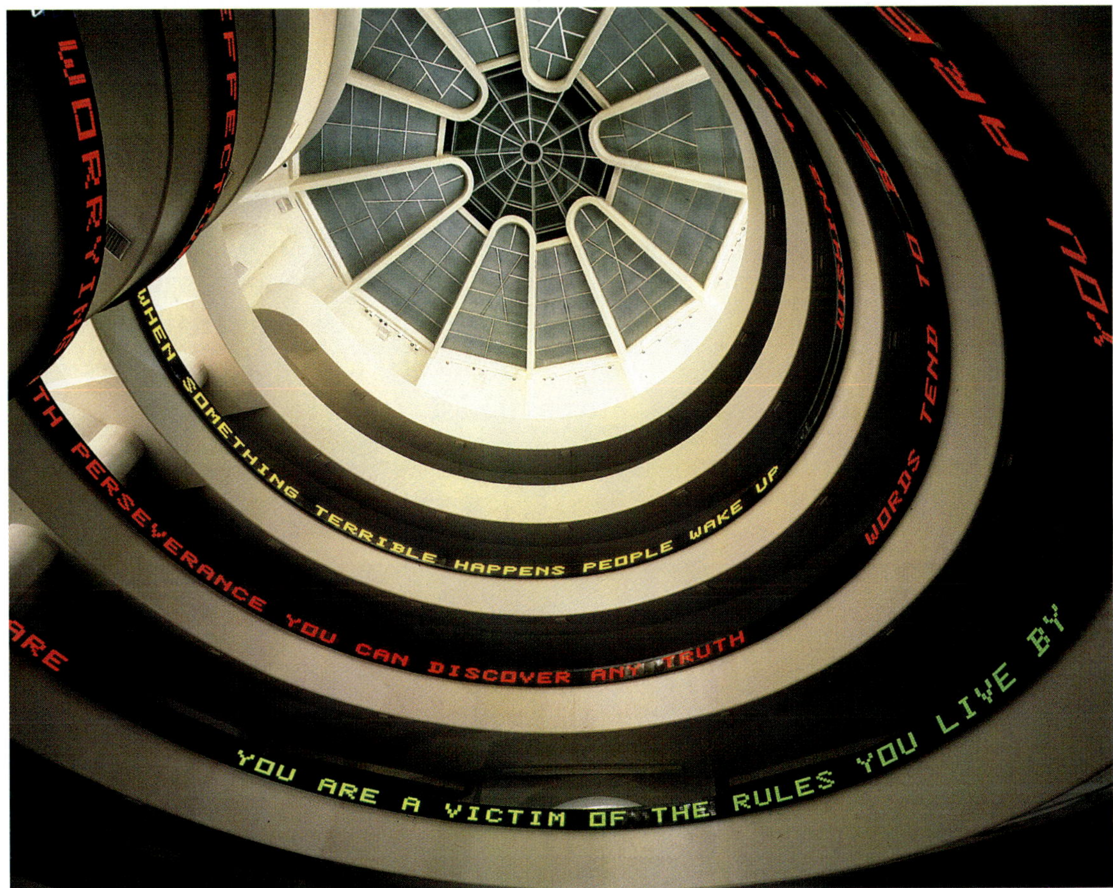


Fig. 9–4 **Compare the experience of seeing this installation to the experience of seeing a painting. How does this work change your ideas about what art is?**

Jenny Holzer, *Untitled* (Selections from *Truisms, Inflammatory Essays, The Living Series, The Survival Series, Under a Rock, Laments*, and *Child Text*), 1989. Extended helical tricolor L.E.D. electronic-display signboard, dimensions subject to change with installation. Solomon R. Guggenheim Museum, NY. Partial gift of the artist, 1989. Photo by David Heald © The Solomon R. Guggenheim Foundation, NY. (FN89.3626)

## Meet Jenny Holzer

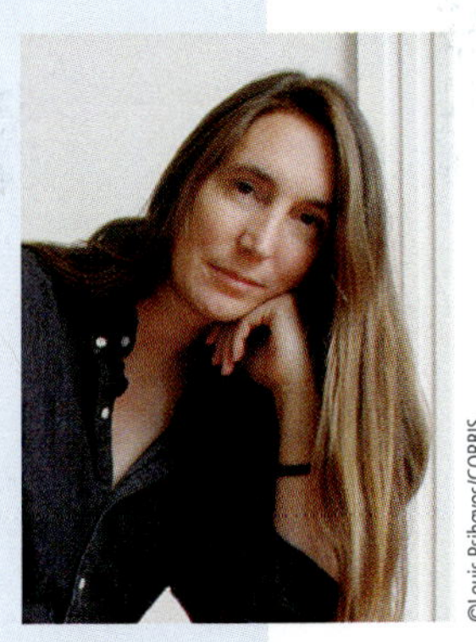

©Louis Psihoyos/CORBIS.

Jenny Holzer was born in Ohio and earned her bachelor's degree in printmaking and painting. While studying for her master's degree, Holzer began to display powerful words in public places. For her *Truisms* series, she made posters of wise sayings and posted them anonymously on the streets of New York.

Holzer's artworks often look like advertisements. Their words are surprising because of their contrast with actual advertisements. She uses electronic signs, posters, T-shirts, stone sarcophagi, bronze plaques, billboards, and light projections. She tries to get people in public places to stop and think about humanitarian issues and about their own lives.

**"I don't sign my work because I think that would diminish its effectiveness...I want people to concentrate on the content of the work and not 'whodunit.'"**

— Jenny Holzer (born 1950)

**Beyond the Familiar** Think about the legends and stories you know. Remember *Paul Bunyan, Peter Pan*, and *Alice in Wonderland*? In cultures around the world, stories passed down through generations have inspired artists to create imaginary monsters and other creatures. They appear as decorations for buildings, on everyday objects, and in paintings and sculptures.

Artists also create their own fantasy worlds for others to consider. Artist Paul Klee created dreamlike worlds in which creatures, plants, and people floated. Many of Klee's images resulted from his free use of line. He also scratched lines into painted surfaces, revealing colors underneath **(Fig. 9–5)**.

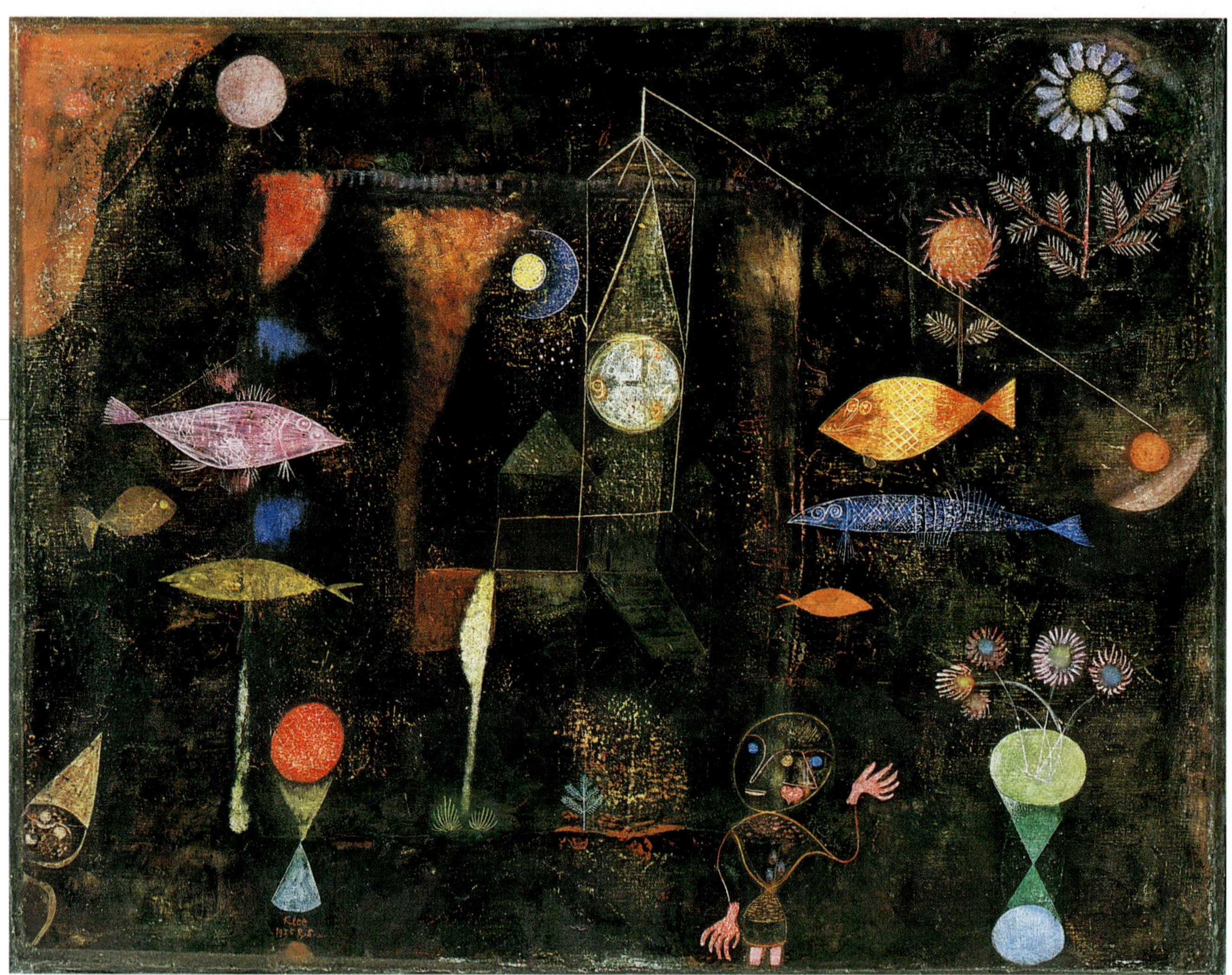

Fig. 9–5 **Paul Klee was very interested in the drawings he made as a child. How is this image like those made by children you know?**

Paul Klee, *Fish Magic*, 1925. Oil on canvas, mounted on board, 30 ⅜" x 38 ¾" (77.4 x 98.4 cm). Philadelphia Museum of Art, The Louise and Walter Arensberg Collection. Photo by Graydon Wood, 1994. Acc. # 1950-134-112 ©2000 Artists Rights Society (ARS), New York / VG Bild-Kunst, Bonn.

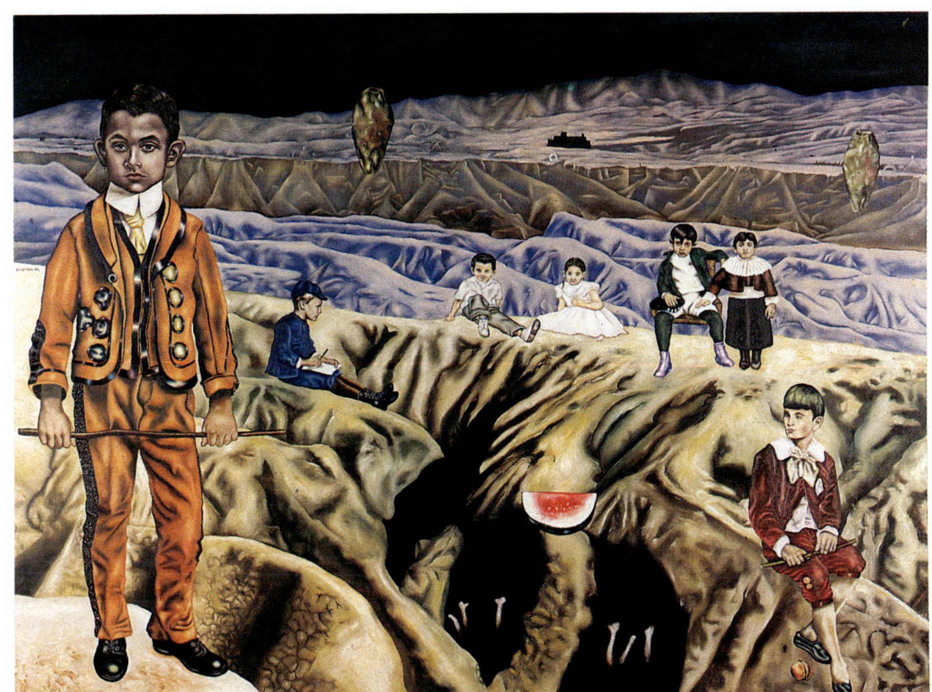

Fig. 9–6 **How would you describe this landscape? How does the title help you understand the meaning of this artwork?**

Arturo Elizondo, *Nostalgia*, 1995. Oil on canvas, 78" x 103 ¼" (198 x 262 cm). Courtesy of Galeria OMR, Mexico City.

Some artists create artworks by placing things together as if by chance, as often happens in dreams. In *Nostalgia* **(Fig. 9–6)**, the artist placed a chunk of watermelon in a bare landscape. Even though the watermelon seems out of place, it is in the foreground of the picture.

### Check Your Understanding

**1.** Identify two ways that artists help communities imagine what might be possible.

**2.** Compare and contrast the dreamlike images in **Figs. 9–5** and **9–6**.

**3.** What type of media do you think has the most possibilities for showing new and innovative artworks? Why?

## Studio Time

### Art That Looks Beyond

Create a collage of a futuristic world that you have imagined.

- Plan your collage. Collect magazine, newspaper, or photocopied images that will help show your ideas. Cut or tear shapes from other colored or patterned papers.
- Carefully arrange your materials. Create unity by repeating shapes and colors.
- Carefully glue the images.

Reflect on how well your collage shows a fantasy world.

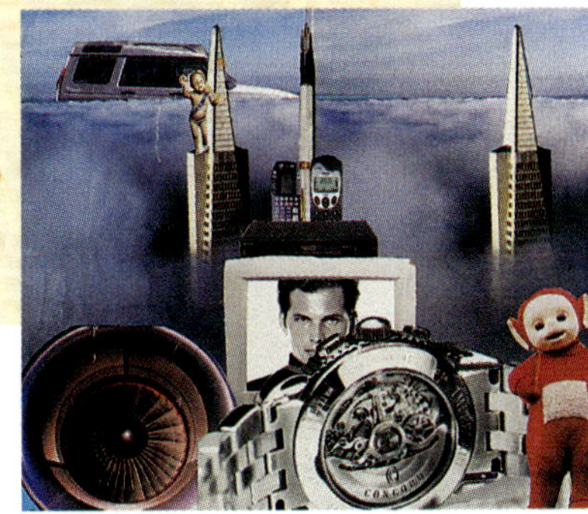

Fig. 9–7 Student artwork

# New Media

As you have learned, some artists use traditional media to create artworks in new ways. Other artists explore nontraditional media for making new kinds of artworks.

**Computers** What do most people use a computer for? Your answers might include school, work, games, e-mail, or access to the Internet. Some artists use computers to create art. "Paint" and "draw" software allows artists to create original digital images. Artists can also scan objects and drawn or painted images into the computer. Or they can take photographs with a digital camera, then import the photos into the computer. Once the images are on the computer, artists can edit them, change the colors, "draw" or "paint" on them, create a collage effect...the possibilities seem endless!

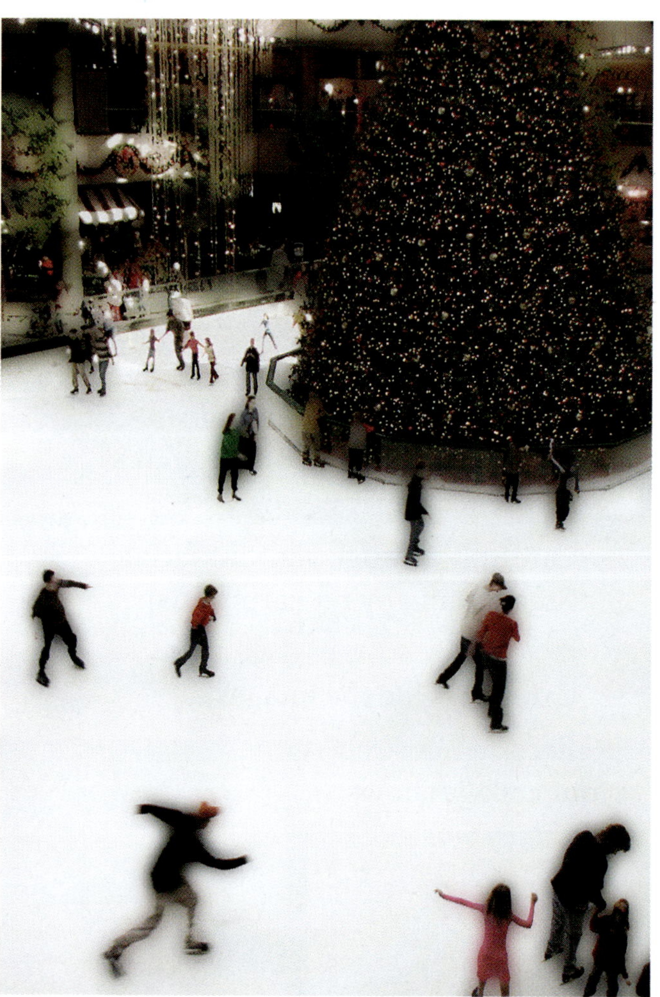

Fig. 9–8 **What suggests that this artwork was made on a computer?**

Dan Burkholder, *Iceskaters at Christmas.* Pigment over platinum palladium.

Some artists want their work to be viewed on a monitor. Other works are printed as two-dimensional images.

**Scanners** Flatbed scanners combine the features of a copier and a digital camera. Scanners create digital copies of flat objects, like photographs, drawings, paintings, maps, pages of text, and film. In addition to copying two-dimensional objects, these scanners can also handle any three-dimensional object that will fit on the scanner's glass surface.

How might you use a scanner to create art? Would you scan actual objects? Your own artwork or photography? Photographs from magazines?

**Observe** Look at the artworks on these pages. Are they more like photographs or more like paintings? How do you think they were made?

**Tools:** Flatbed scanner, two-dimensional images, and three-dimensional objects that fit on the scanner's glass surface.

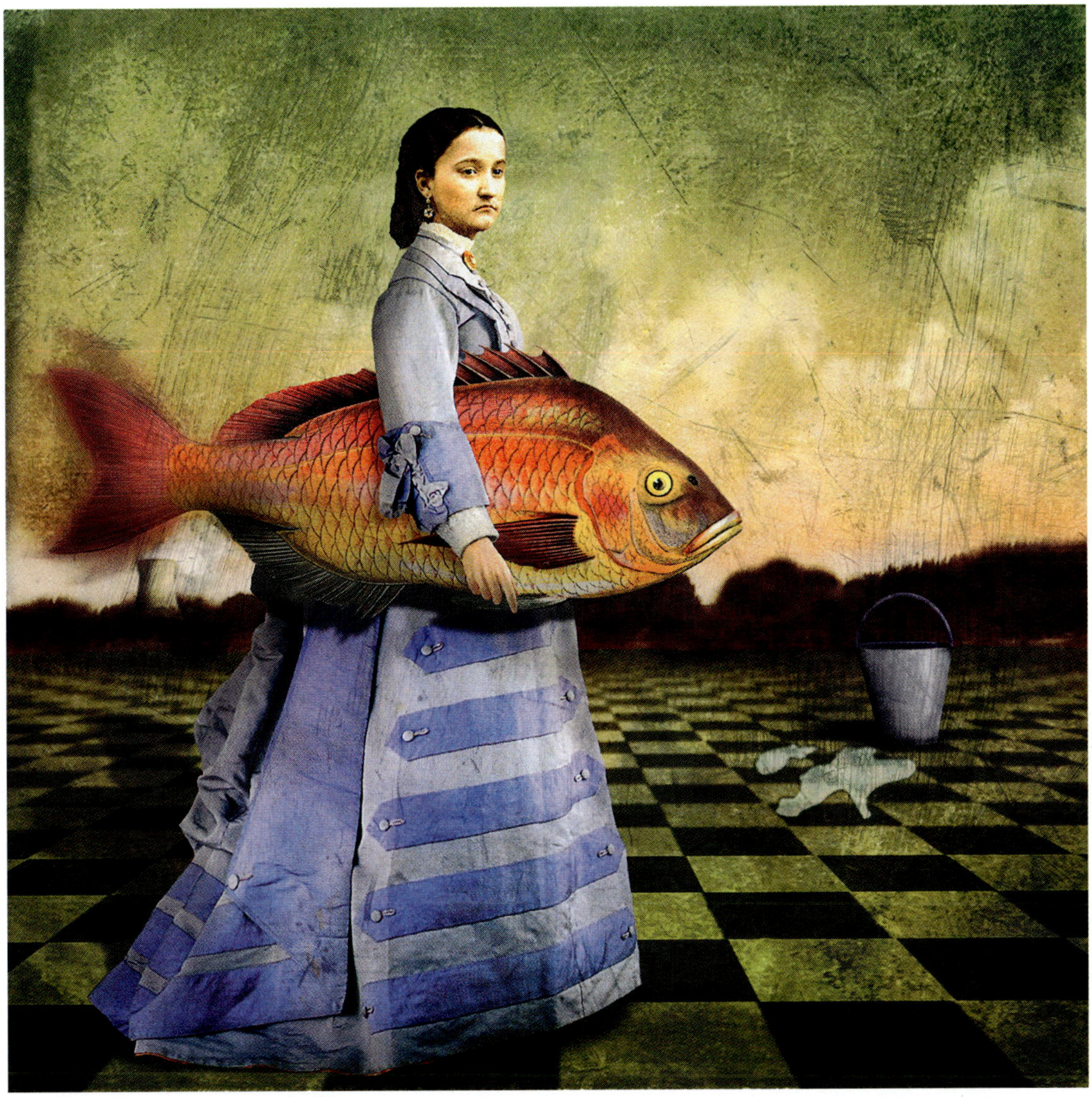

Fig. 9–9 **What mood or feeling does this artwork suggest? Why?**

Maggie Taylor, *Woman Who Loves Fish*. Courtesy of the artist.

## Practice: Scanning and Saving

- Select an image and an object.
- Lay the image face down on the glass, and close the lid.
- To scan the object, leave the scanner's cover up and out of the way. Either cover the object and scanner with a piece of dark cloth or turn off the room lights for a dark background. Then start the scan.
- Save each image as a TIFF (Tagged Image File Format), because this provides the highest-quality images.

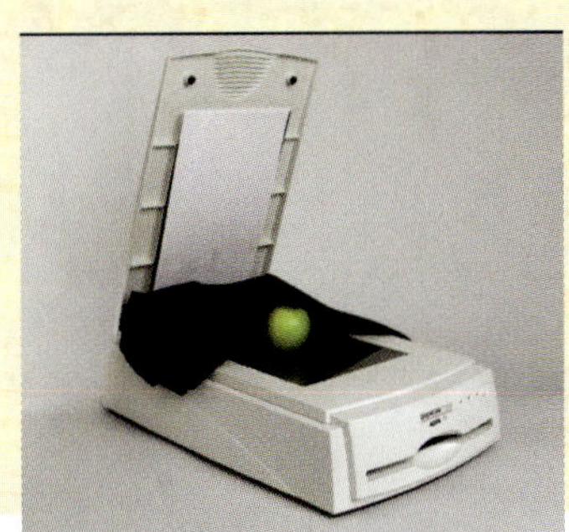

**Video Art** Video allows you to record and view moving images immediately. Many artists use video technology to create movies, documentaries, individual images, and other kinds of art. Once they have collected video images, artists can take out or rearrange parts, blur, and distort the images. Video artists have projected their artworks on the sides of buildings, on fabric, and into gallery wall corners.

**Multimedia** Many artists can express their ideas best when they use multimedia. Multimedia means the tools and techniques of more than one medium. For instance, in multimedia installations such as *Mantle* **(Fig. 9–11)**, the artist includes many different objects. Some installations combine sculpture and architecture. Digital technology allows artists to create a single file that contains still and moving images, text, and sound.

**Observe** Look at your original saved images from page 249 of this lesson. Think about how you might rotate, crop, and resize them to change them further.

**Tools:** TIFF images, a computer installed with an image manipulation program such as Photoshop® or Paint Shop Pro®.

### Practice: Rotating and Cropping

- Go to **Image > Rotate Canvas**, and select the correct option.
- Use the **Crop Tool** from the Tool Bar. Place the crop box in the image and move some, or all, of the sides. When you have the placement you want, double-click the mouse inside the box to select that framing.

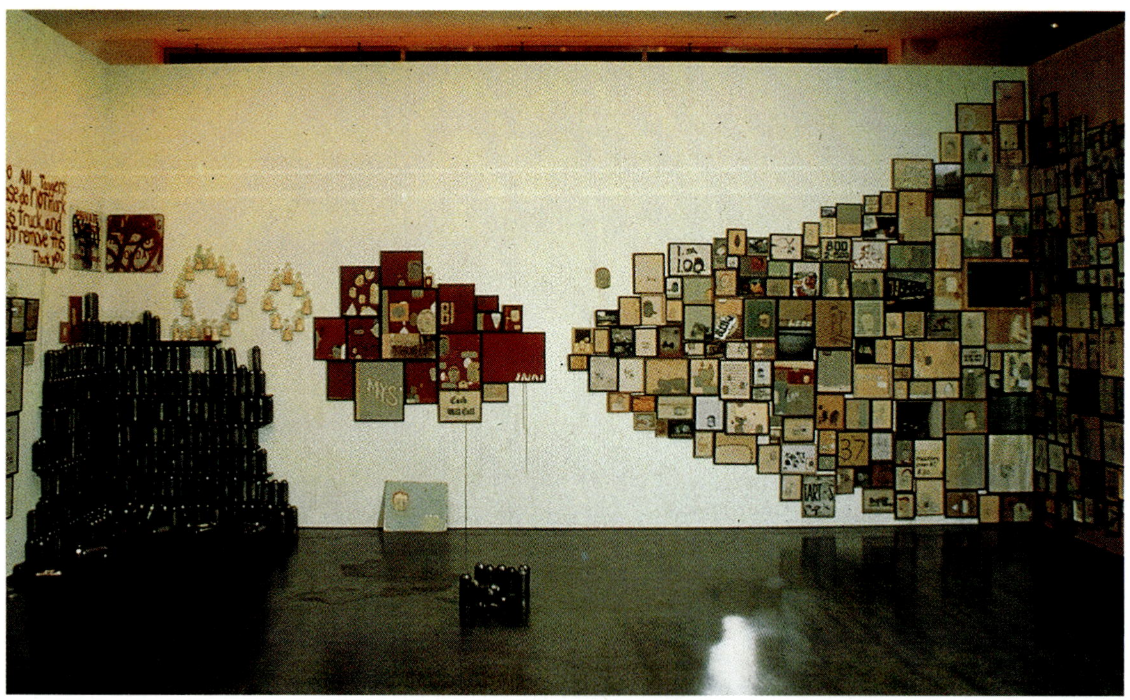

Fig. 9–10
**Which tools and techniques from different media did this artist use?**

Barry McGee, *Installation view at UCLA/Armand Hammer Museum, Los Angeles.* Photo: Robert Wedemeyer. Courtesy of Deitch Projects, NY.

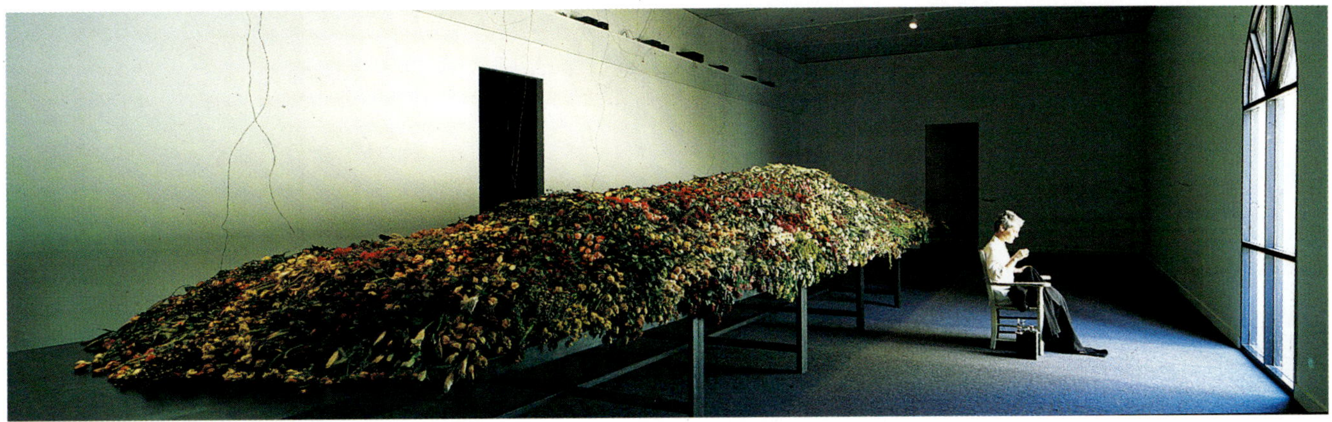

Fig. 9–11 **This installation includes flowers, radios, a window, coats, and the artist. Do these seem like things you would normally see together? Why or why not?**

Ann Hamilton, *Mantle*, 1998. Installation view, Miami Art Museum, April 2–June 7, 1998. Courtesy of Miami Art Museum. Photo by Thibault Jeanson.

### Check Your Understanding

1. What does TIFF stand for? Why should you save images in this format?
2. Compare and contrast the process of using a computer to manipulate an image to the process of manipulating an image without using a computer.
3. Why might artists choose to use computers to create art?

## Studio Time

### From Photo to Fantasy

Manipulate a photograph of an object to create a fantastic interpretation.

- Choose an image to scan, and scan it. Save the image as a TIFF.
- Using image manipulation software such as Photoshop, change your image. If you like, scan and add other images.
- Change colors and textures, rotate or crop the image, add lines, shapes, shadows, and other enhancements. Remember to save your work as you go along.

Reflect on how you changed the original image. What have you done with the computer that you could not have done as easily with traditional media?

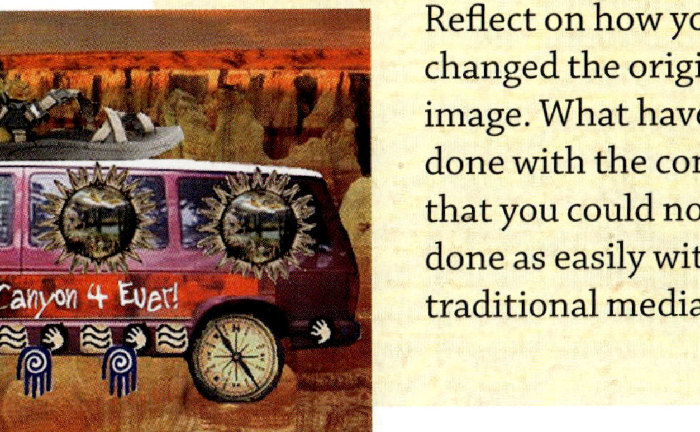


Fig. 9–12 Student artwork

# A Digital Collage

## Studio Background

Have you ever looked at pictures of a beautiful place and wished you could be there? Or perhaps you have seen photos of a car sitting on top of a steep mountain peak and wondered, "How did they get that car up there?" With digital photography and computer program tools, it's possible to manipulate images to make strange things look real. It's also possible to put yourself into a picture of a place you have never been.

**In this studio exploration, you can explore the possibilities for creating a digital collage using more than one photo.** Digital photo collages are similar to what you did in lesson 1, but you aren't physically going to be gluing images onto paper. Instead, you will be digitally "gluing" them on your computer to create a printable collage of your favorite photos or images like those you scanned in lesson 2.

### You Will Need

- computer
- digital photo software
- flatbed scanner
- photographs
- magazine or postcard images
- color printer

### Step 1 Plan and Practice

- Photo collage possibilities are extensive, ranging from an arrangement of horizontal and vertical images to an overlapping mosaic of photographic tiles. What format and arrangement will you use for your collage?
- Decide on a theme or dominant subject matter. What will you show? How many images will you have? Which images will you feature?

## Inspiration from Our World

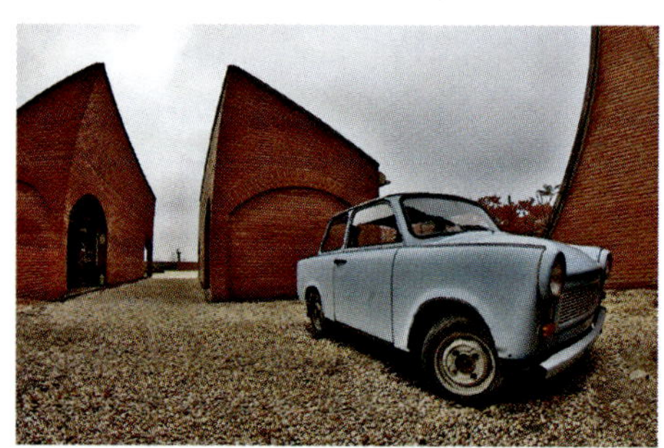

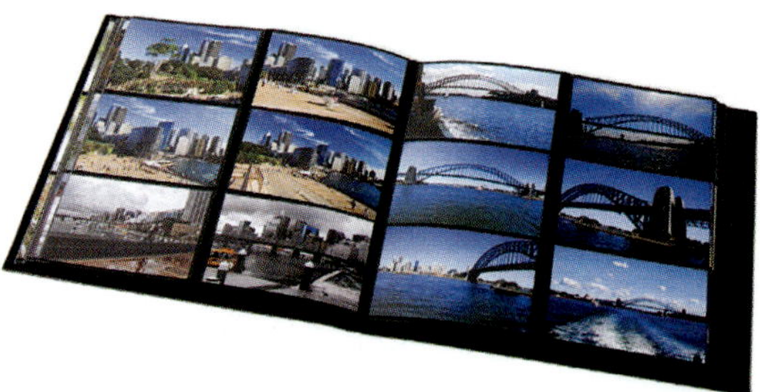

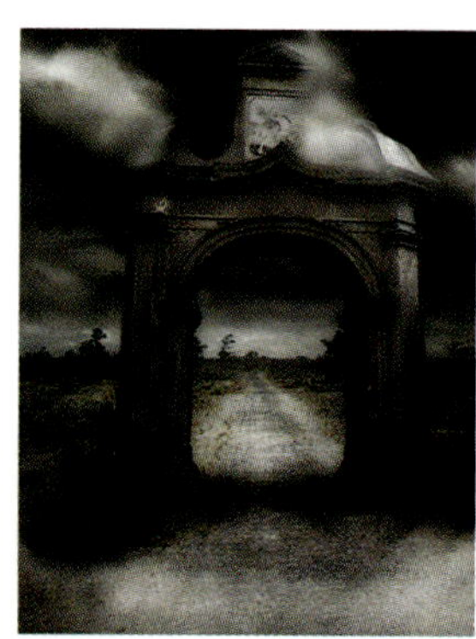

- Scan photos and images in different sizes and arrange them in an image file on your computer. Will you arrange them by subject matter? By dominant color? By size?
- Practice using the editing tools in your digital-imaging program.

**Things to Remember:**

✓ Create a collage based on a theme.

✓ Use layers and several photos to create a composite.

✓ Use a variety of functions on your tool bar.

## Inspiration from Art

Artists sometimes put objects or images together that we don't expect to see together side by side. Sometimes the objects or images are in different sizes than we expect. These artworks might show parts of a world that seem real and other parts that don't seem normal to us. This style of art is called Surrealism.

Surrealist artists create artworks that look beyond what is real. They show fantasy or imaginary worlds where realistic objects are combined in unusual ways or with unfamiliar scenes.

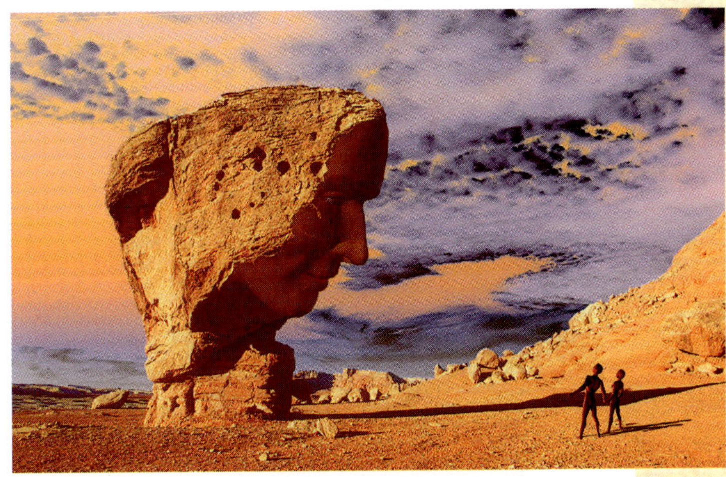

Fig. 9–13 **How does this digital photo fit the definition of Surrealism?**

Dale O'Dell, *Martian Face*. ©Dale O'Dell 2002.

For contemporary artist Dale O'Dell, digital photography is a surreal art form. With his camera, he collects bits and pieces of landscapes and other images for later rearrangement on the computer. The numerous collage techniques available on the computer allow him to copy and paste, work with layers and layer masks, and manipulate colors and intensities. By rearranging existing natural elements, he creates places that he'd like to visit, yet do not exist.

## Step 2 Begin to Create

- **Open your photo-editing program and create a new canvas.**

- Open all the photos you would like to use in your collage.
- **Decide what you want your background to be. Move the picture to your working canvas.**

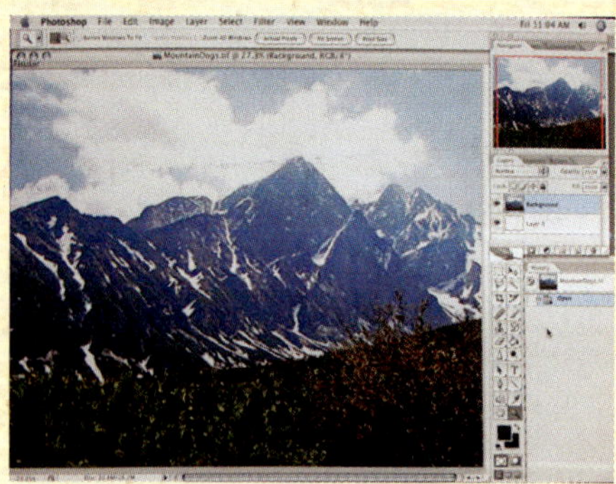

- **Manually drag and drop additional images onto the collage.**

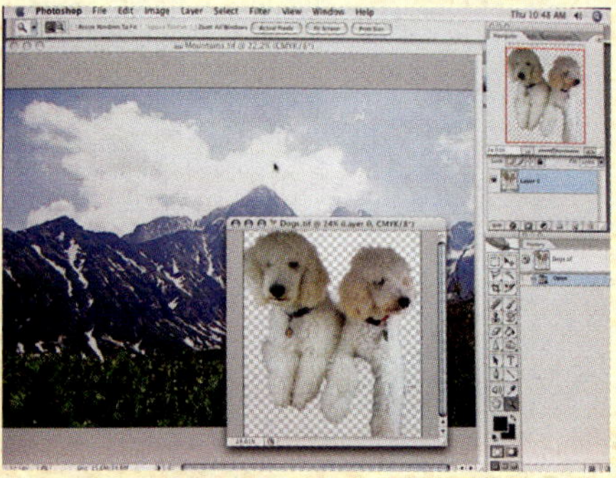

## Step 3 Revise

**Did you remember to:**

✓ Create a collage based on a theme?

✓ Use layers and several photos to create a composite?

✓ Use a variety of functions on your tool bar?

Adjust your work if necessary. In your sketchbook, make a note of your revisions and why you made them.

## Step 4 Add Finishing Touches

- You can also use the computer to add words and text to your collage.
- When you are finished with your composite, print it out. Will you mount it on mat board?
- Remember to save your composite on a disk.

## Step 5 Share and Reflect

- View the completed collages created by you and your classmates.
- Discuss the theme and dominant subject matter of each collage.
- What tools did you use for your collage? Which tools were most useful? Most successful?
- What would you change for the next time?

## Art Criticism

**Describe** What do you recognize in this artwork?

**Analyze** How did the artist manipulate and rearrange the parts in this image?

**Interpret** What do you think is the theme of this artwork?

**Evaluate** What's special about this artwork?

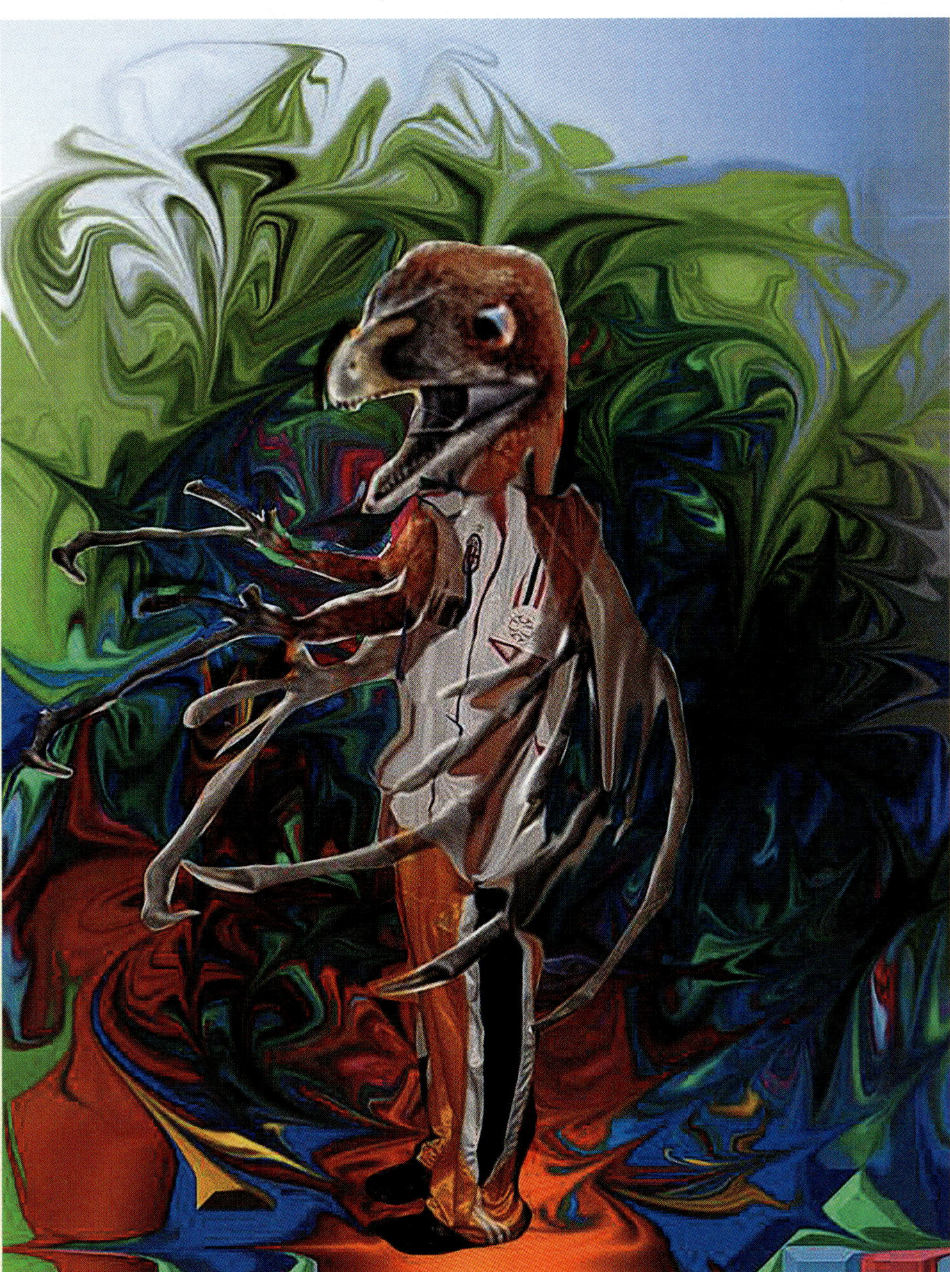

Fig. 9–14 Student artwork

# New Directions in Art: 1980–present

**New Approaches** You've probably said to yourself after an exciting adventure, "Where do we go from here?" Many artists were thinking the same thing in the 1990s.

Artists tried new technologies as tools and materials for making art. They displayed and exhibited their work in new settings. They recycled the art of the past. Artists also reused traditional styles, humorously copied classical works, and created new looks at familiar images. Pat Steir, for example, created her own interpretation of the artwork of Jan Brueghel (Fig. 9–15).

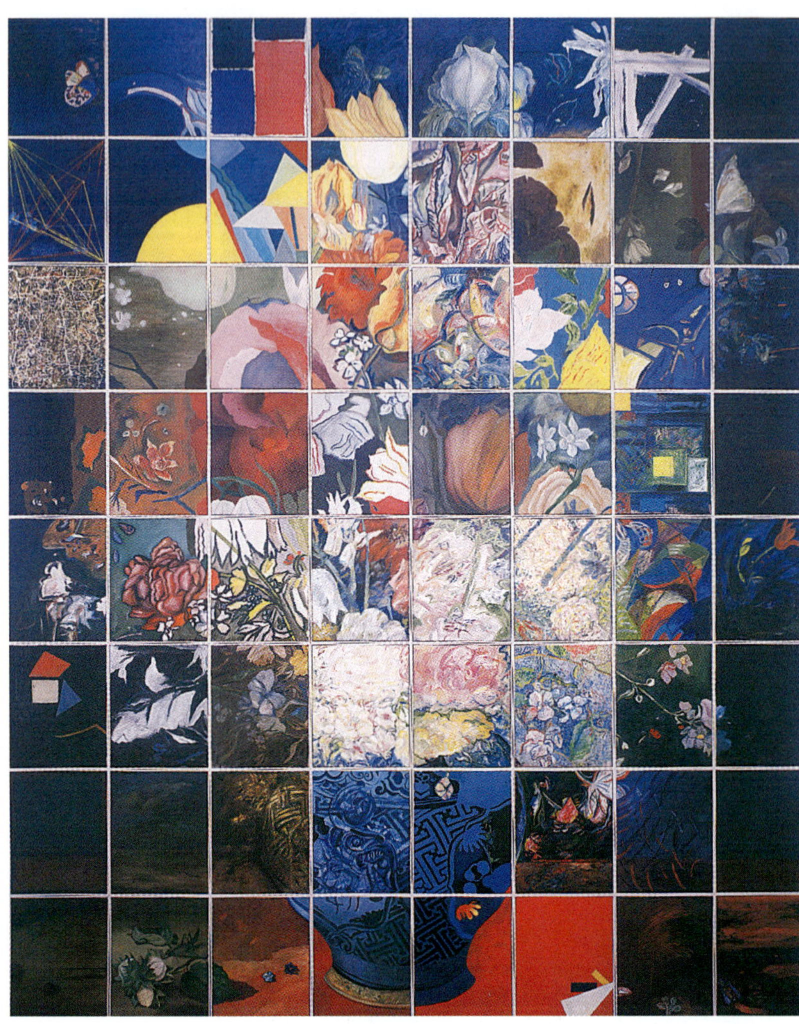

Fig. 9–15 **Look carefully at each panel that makes up this artwork. What styles and techniques in each remind you of other artists you have studied?**

Pat Steir, *The Brueghel Series (A Vanitas of Styles)*, 1997. Oil on Canvas, 64 panels, each panel 28 ½" x 22 ½" (72.4 x 57.2 cm). Courtesy of the artist.

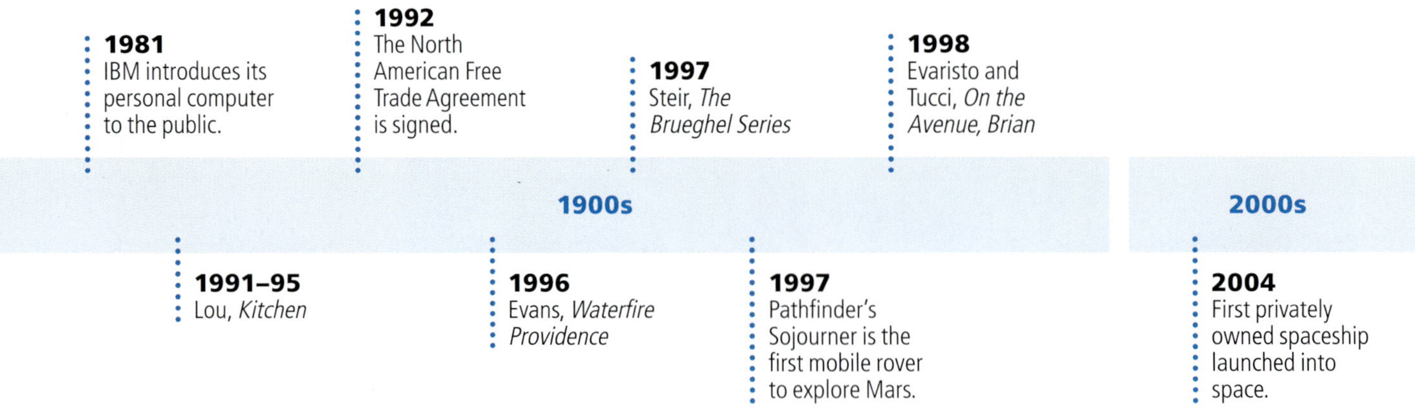

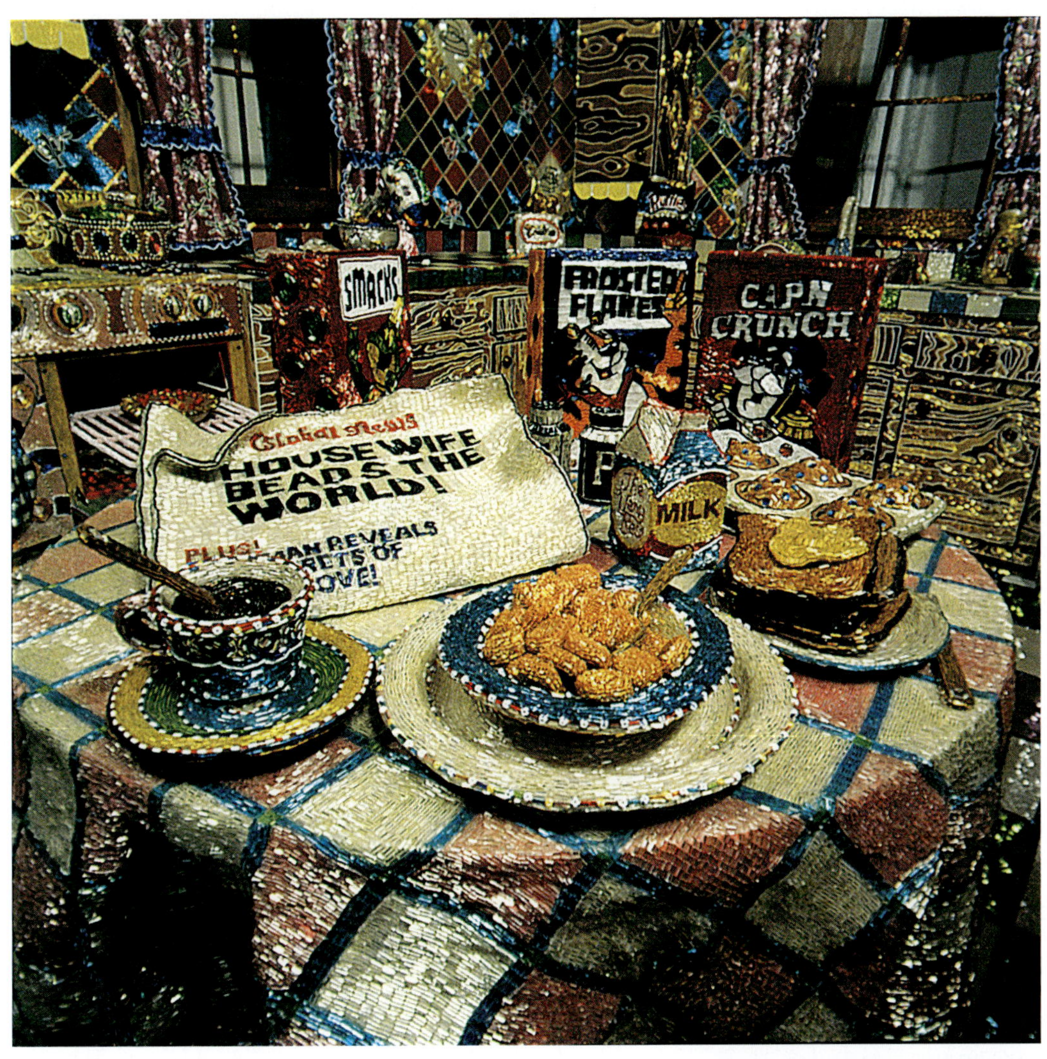


Fig. 9–16 **Each of the objects in this life-size room is made of tiny beads. What words can you think of to describe this work?**

Liza Lou, *Kitchen*, 1991–95 (detail). Mixed media with glass beads, 168 square feet (51.3 m). Courtesy of the artist.

**Working without Boundaries** Since 1980, artists have created work that spans a range of styles, materials, and techniques. They made artworks that were realistic, abstract, serious, and humorous. Some artworks were large-scale outdoor art created with industrial equipment. Others were handcrafted work with tiny details. Liza Lou made her artworks entirely of beads **(Fig. 9–16)**.

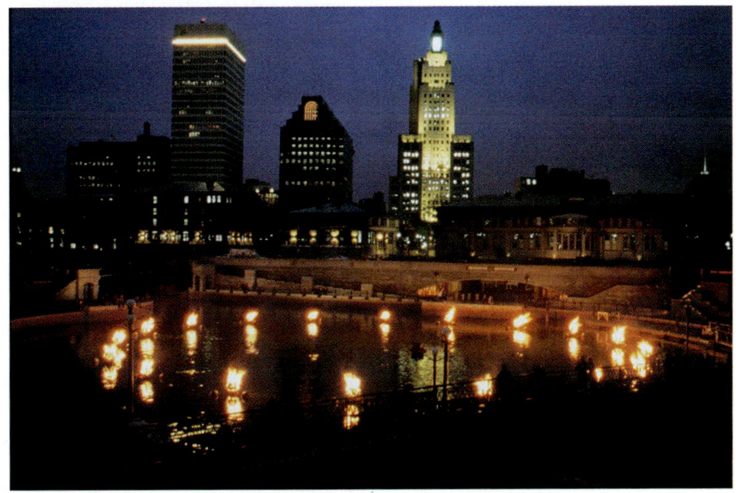

Fig. 9–17 **How does this artwork exceed the boundaries of traditional art?**

Barnaby Evans, *Waterfire Providence,* Water Place Park, Providence, Rhode Island, various dates, June 1996–present.

**Community Involvement** By 2000, artists were continuing to use collaboration, activism, and performance art to involve communities in art creation. Activism means working to change opinions or beliefs related to politics or other issues within a community. Performance art combines expressive forms such as poetry, theater, music, painting, or film. Banners are one example of a community's involvement in creating art. Communities often help design and create banners about their neighborhoods to decorate public spaces.

**The Future of Art** What's ahead for the world of art? Imagine using new technologies to develop artworks in which viewers experience new realities of time, space, and form.

New technology is exciting, but it also challenges artists to preserve pride in craftsmanship and traditional skills. As new technologies make art easier to produce, handmade objects may increase in value. And we hope that the value of individual skill and accomplishment will never be lost.

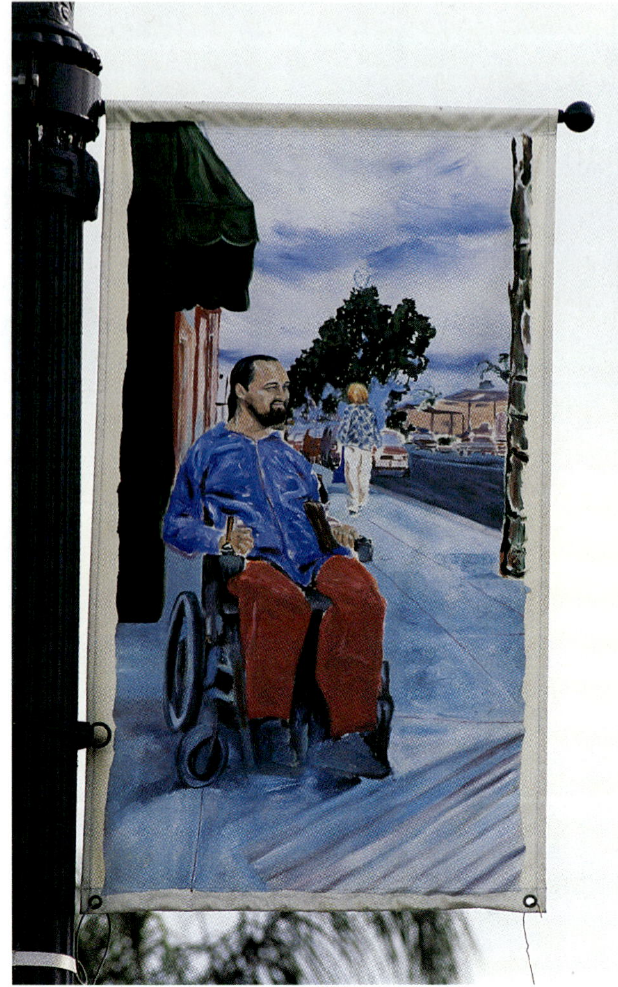

Fig. 9–18 **The banners that were created for this project show people who have made a difference in the community.**

Pete Evaristo and Jodi Tucci, *On the Avenue, Brian*, from Adams Avenue, one of 110 unique street banners, 1998. Mixed media on canvas, 27" x 48" (68.6 x 121.9 cm). Courtesy of the artists.

### Check Your Understanding

1. What are some of the ways that artists challenged traditional ideas and explored new possibilities in the 1990s?
2. Compare and contrast performance art and banner projects.
3. What are some examples of activism from your own community?

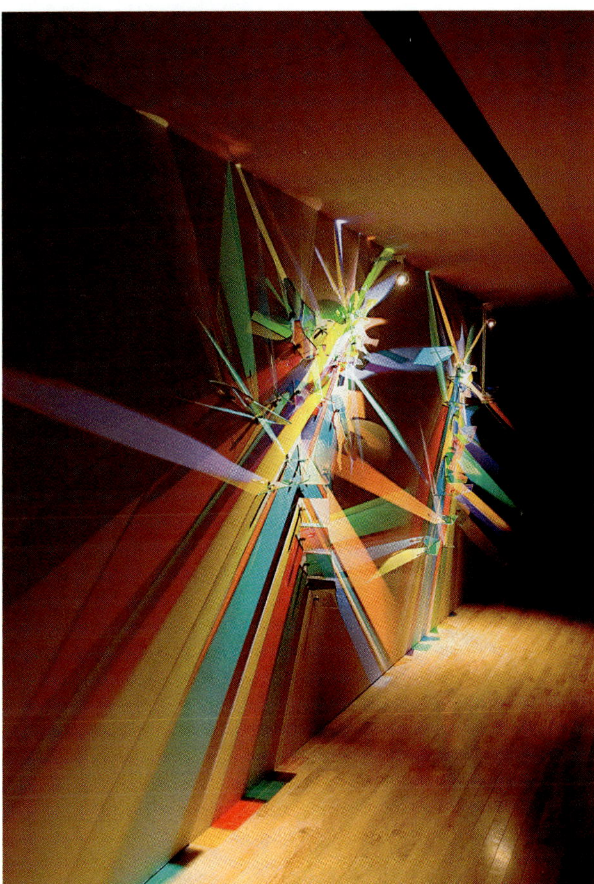

Fig. 9–19 **Why might this be considered a work of art?**

Stephen Knapp, *Temporal Meditations Lightpainting.*

## Meet Stephen Knapp

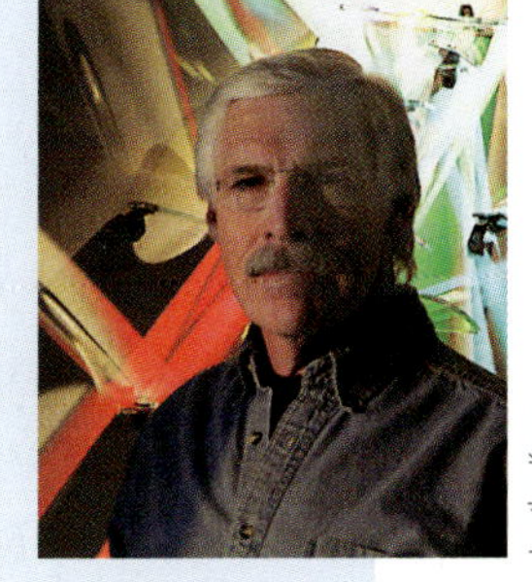

Jonathan Knapp.

Stephen Knapp was born in Worcester, Massachusetts. He began his career as a photographer, photographing the architecture and interiors of buildings. Understanding the value of research and experimentation, Knapp changed his focus to working and creating with materials such as ceramic, metal, stone, and glass.

Knapp is an artist who has always been intrigued by art made with light. In his recent artworks, he secures small pieces of glass to a wall with highly polished stainless steel brackets. He then projects light onto the glass and steel to form "lightpaintings."

**"There is no right answer hidden within each piece, only a shared journey."**

—Stephen Knapp (born 1947)

## Studio Time

### Imaginative Drawing

Explore new directions in art by creating an imaginative drawing.

- Combine unrelated ideas in your drawing. For example, you might combine parts of different animals in one creature.
- Select a drawing medium that will help you express an imaginative idea.
- Your work might be bold and startling or show distortion or exaggeration.

Reflect on what you did to make your work imaginative.

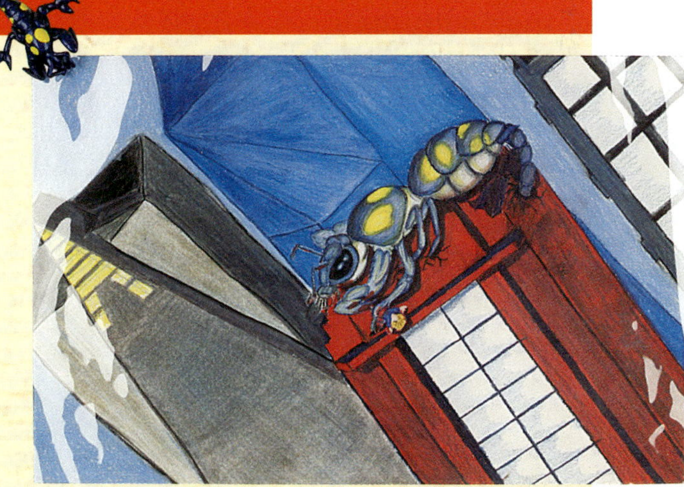

Fig. 9–20 Student artwork

# Global Changes

**Preserving Traditions** Remembering the past is an important part of the human experience. The preservation of cultural, ethnic, and religious heritage is as important to artists as exploring new possibilities.

Within the history of art, many artistic treasures and the techniques and processes used to create them have been lost. As cultures change, traditional art forms are often forgotten. If people and artists do not continue to use traditional techniques and media, these art forms can disappear from our cultures.

In exhibitions of today's Native American art, you can find artists who use traditional styles. Sometimes, artists continue to create art that is directly related to the artistic traditions and traditional beliefs of their cultures.

In other instances, artwork might only reflect some of their artistic traditions. The Native American artworks shown in Figs. 9–21 and 9–23 were made recently, but they preserve the techniques and images of ceremonial costumes and rituals within the artists' communities.

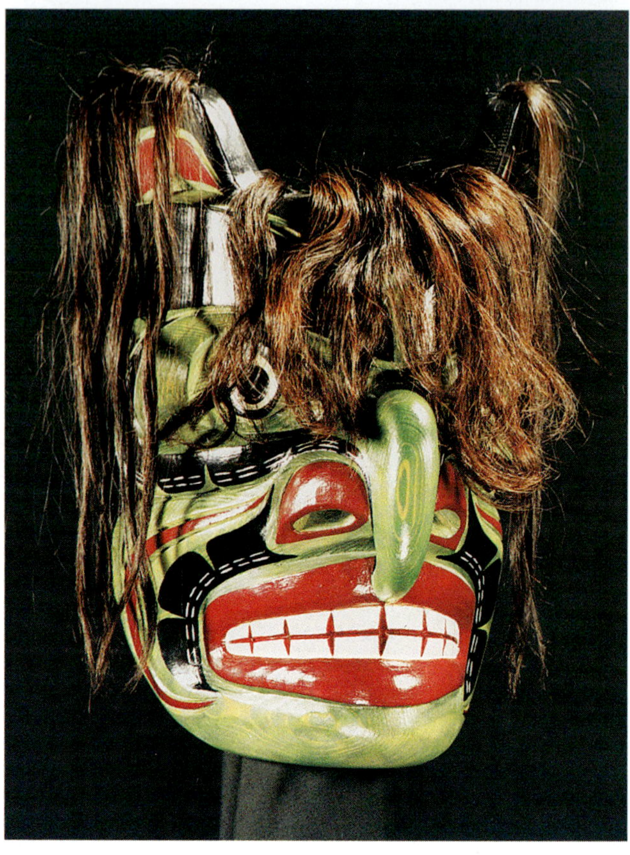

Fig. 9–21 **The Bookwus is an exciting figure of Pacific Northwest Coast legend. What features of this mask might be traditional? What features might be contemporary?**

Bill Henderson, *Bookwus Mask: Wildman of the Woods*, 1999. Painted red cedar with real hair, 12" x 9" (33 x 22.9 cm). Courtesy of the artist.

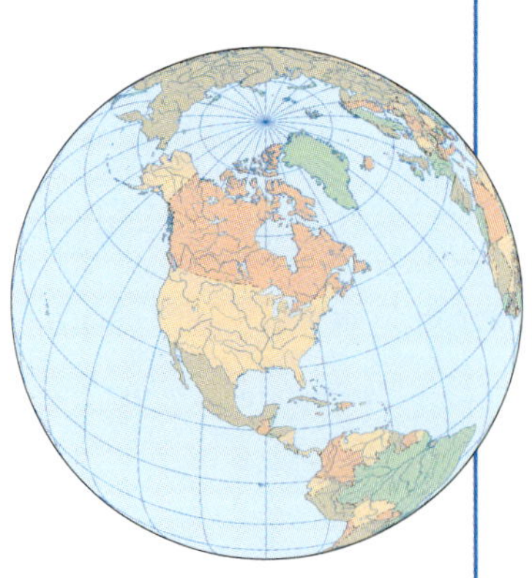

## Social Studies Connection

Today, advances in transportation, communication, motion pictures, and television cause ideas to cross cultural and geographic boundaries quickly in the global community. The global community is the interaction of ideas and knowledge of people and populations all over the world.

Increasingly, artists are working in what might be called a global style. A global style cannot be linked to just one culture or tradition of art. It comes from the exchange of ideas among artists of many nations and cultures around the world.

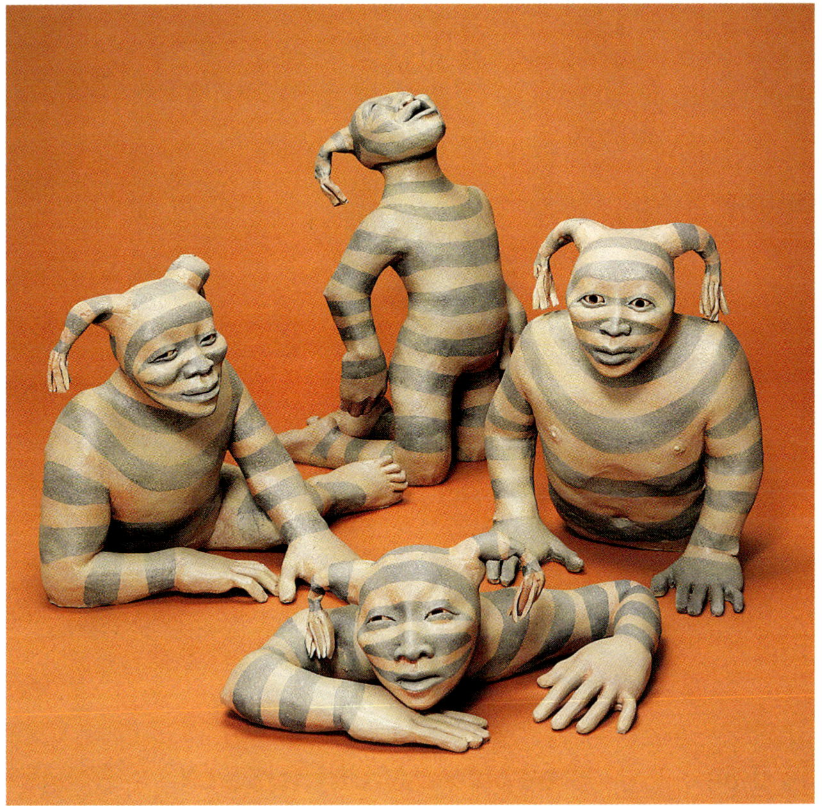

Fig. 9–22 **These clown images recall an example of traditional Native American ceremonial costumes. What emotions do you think the artist tried to capture in these sculptures?**

Roxanne Swentzell, *The Emergence of the Clowns*, 1988. Mixed media clay, 7" x 19" x 11" (17.8 x 48.3 x 27.9 cm). Shared Visions Collection, Heard Museum, Phoenix, Arizona.

## Visual Culture

We are all unique, yet we share many things in common. People may go to the same school, yet they have many different influences upon their lives. Think about who you are and the things you do and then try this: Create a diagram with a series of concentric circles. Label the circles from the center outward: personal, national, ethnic, religion, gender, clubs, teams, other. Create a pattern of visual symbols and colors for each concentric band. Talk with your classmates about commonalities and differences.

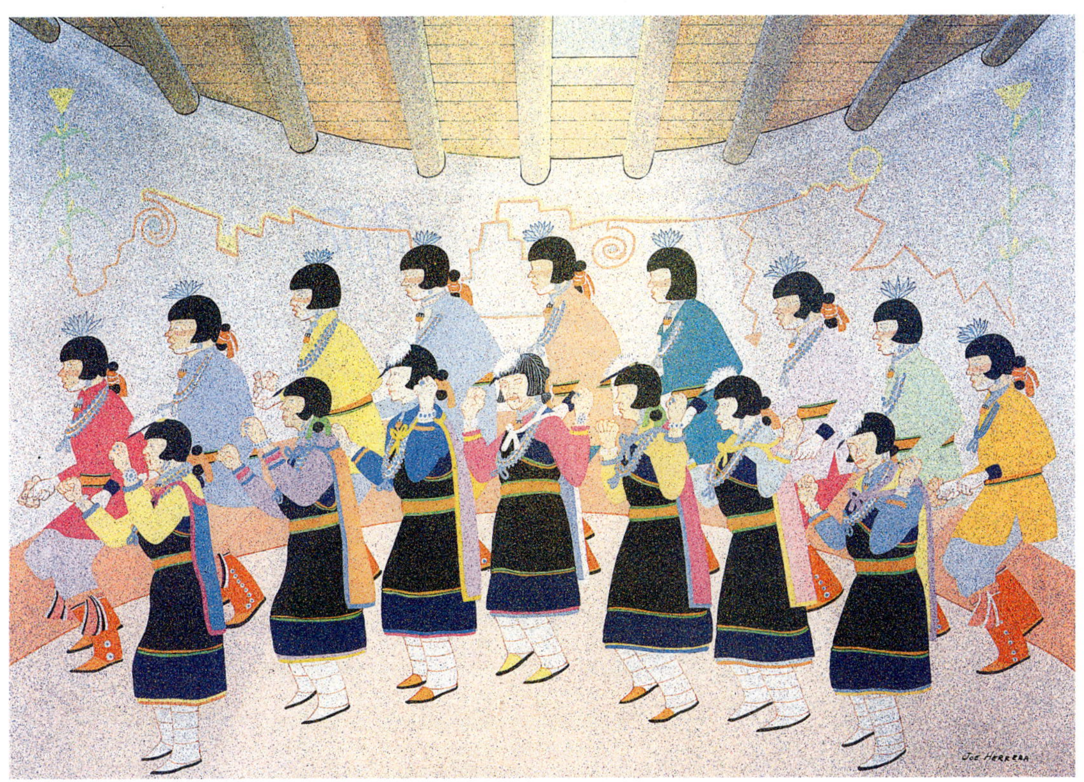

Fig. 9–23 **How did the artist combine traditional and nontraditional elements in this artwork?**

Joe Herrera, *Spring Ceremony for Owah*, 1983. Watercolor on paper, 29" x 37" (73.7 x 94 cm). Courtesy of Shared Visions Collection, Heard Museum, Phoenix, Arizona.

## Breaking New Ground

Today, Native American artists, like many other artists, are expressing their ideas about issues such as identity, how they fit into the world, and how people relate to one another. These artists are working with new materials and meeting the challenge of new trends. Their artworks invite us to examine the past and to question the present.

The Native American artworks shown here combine traditional and nontraditional media and techniques. The artists make statements about their cultural traditions and the changes they see in their communities. Mary Adams **(Fig. 9–25)** blends the traditions of several cultures. Robert Haozous **(Fig. 9–26)** adorned an image of a traditional pueblo with symbols of modern transportation. Kay WalkingStick **(Fig. 9–24)** uses abstract imagery and suggests boundaries between people, cultures, or countries.

The direction of art will depend on social, moral, and political changes within communities. Artists will share new ideas by using technology. They will continue the tradition of observing and interpreting the world.

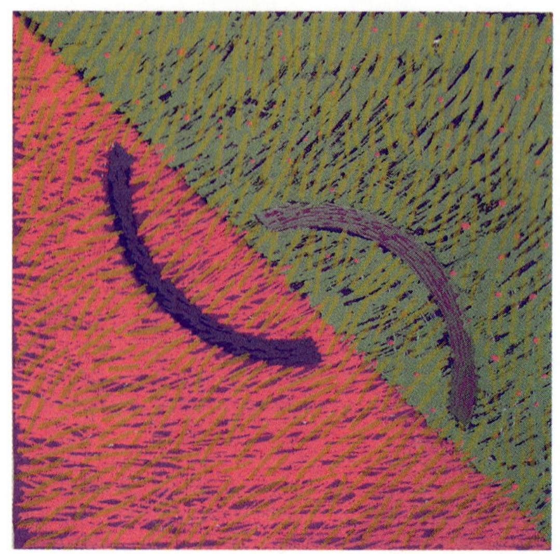

Fig. 9–24 **What message do you think Kay WalkingStick was trying to send in this artwork?**

Kay WalkingStick *Columbus Boogie,* 1985. Screen print, Edition of 25, 22" x 22" (55.9 x 55.9 cm). ©Kay WalkingStick.

### Meet Kay WalkingStick

Kay WalkingStick was born in Syracuse, New York. She started painting landscapes in the 1980s. Many of her landscapes include mountains as symbols of her body. She believes in the importance of touch, so WalkingStick frequently paints with her hands instead of brushes. Because she is half Cherokee, her paintings often deal with mixed heritage.

Courtesy of Manu Sassonian.

**"I want all people to hold onto their cultures...but I also want to encourage a mutual recognition of shared being."**

—Kay WalkingStick (born 1935)

### Check Your Understanding

1. What is the global community?
2. Compare the mask shown in Fig. 9–21 to a type of mask that you are familiar with. How does tradition play a role in each one?
3. Using what you know about global style, describe the aspects of some artworks in this unit that reflect that style.

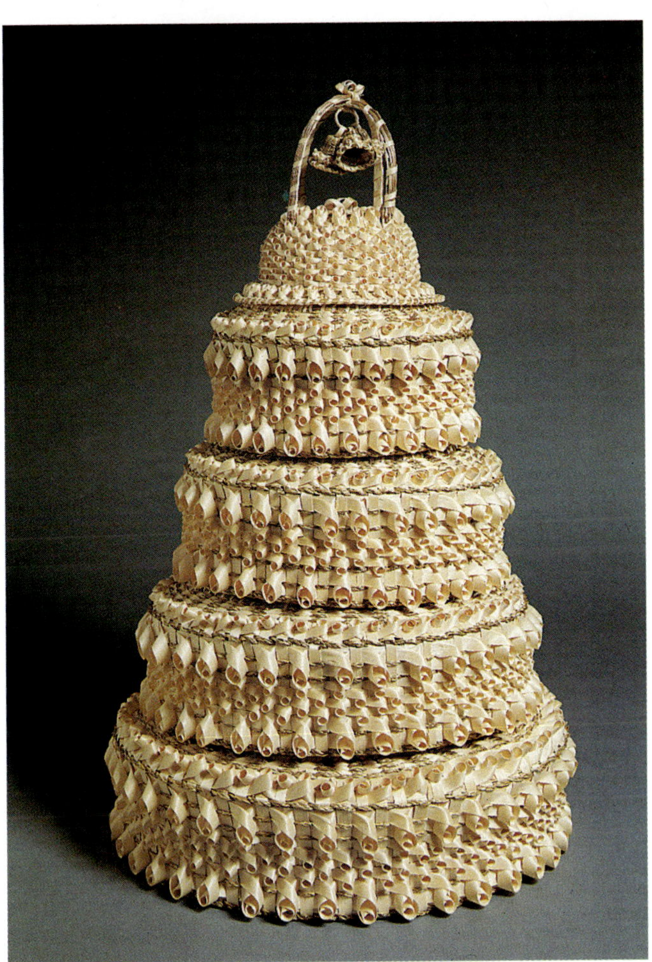

Fig. 9–25 **This artist used traditional Native American basketweaving techniques to create a traditional wedding cake form. What might this suggest about the relationship between Native American and European cultures?**

Mary Adams (b. 1920s), *Wedding Cake Basket*, 1986. Woven sweet grass and ash splints, 25 ½" x 15 ¾" (64.8 x 40 cm). Gift of Herbert Waide Hemphill, Jr., National Museum of American Art, Smithsonian Institution, Washington, DC/Art Resource, NY.

## Studio Time

### Expanding Traditions

Create a weaving with nontraditional materials or forms.

- Consider materials such as licorice, wire, or twisted plastic bags.
- Explore ways to twist and tie as you weave over and under.
- Try weaving between natural objects such as branches or use found objects as a framework.

Reflect on how you have expanded the weaving tradition.

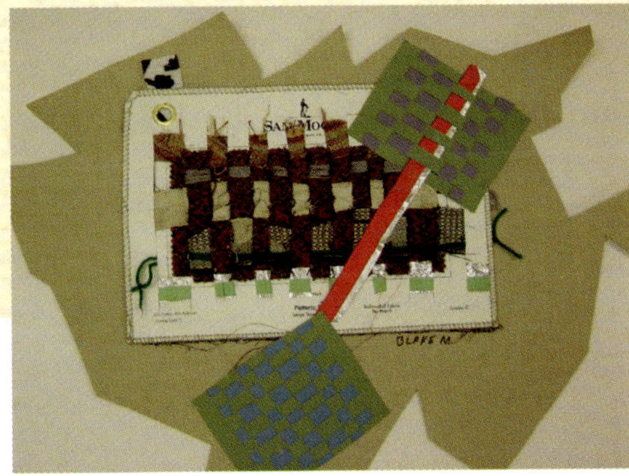

Fig. 9–27 Student artwork

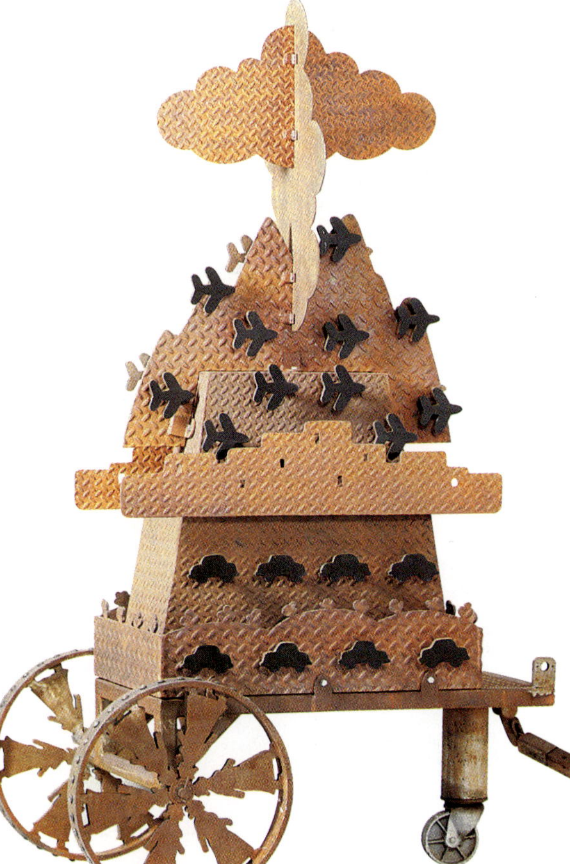

Fig. 9–26 **This sculpture is about how tourists visit pueblo communities, staying only long enough to shop for artworks. What details of this sculpture suggest tourists?**

Robert Haozous, *Portable Pueblo*, 1988. Steel, 94" high (with cloud), 78" long (101" with handle extended), 33" deep (239 x 198 x 83.8 cm). Joselyn Art Museum, Omaha, NE.

# A Digital Story

## Studio Background

What do you like best about your favorite movie or television show? The characters? The plot? There is probably some element of storytelling that you enjoy, too.

**In this studio exploration, you will make a short film that uses new media to bring to life the traditional form of storytelling.** Think about several movies or television shows you know well. How do they tell a story? Do they follow one character or a group of characters? What is the story based on? What events happen? How is the movie or show shot? Notice how the camera moves in for close-ups, moves out for long (distant) shots, and pans, or follows, the action or view of a scene.

### You Will Need

- pencil and paper
- costumes and props
- source of music or other sounds
- camcorder
- a computer with video-editing software
- tripod (optional)

## Step 1 Plan and Practice

- As a group, choose or create a simple story or presentation that you would like to film.
- Plan your presentation. How many characters will your story have? What events will you show?
- Decide on a sequence of events.
- List the images that come to mind as you discuss your ideas. Create a visual outline of scenes from your list.

**Things to Remember:**

- ✓ Use traditional storytelling techniques.
- ✓ Use a storyboard to plan out each shot.
- ✓ Use the camera to take different types of shots.

## Inspiration from Our World

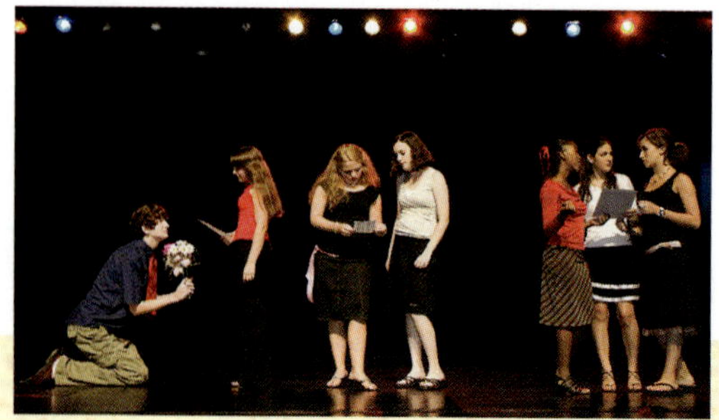

©Thinkstock/CORBIS.

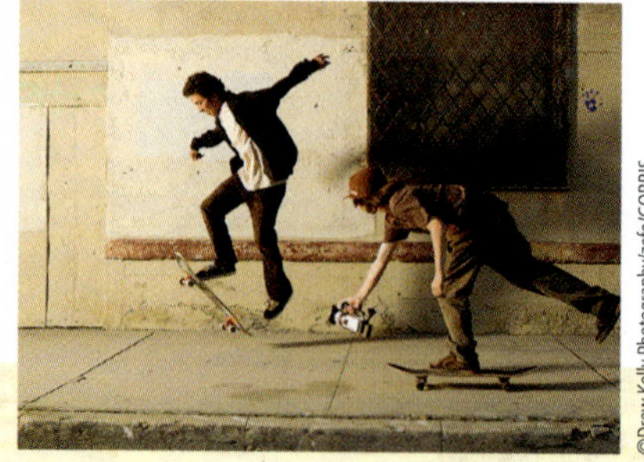

©Drew Kelly Photography/zefa/CORBIS.

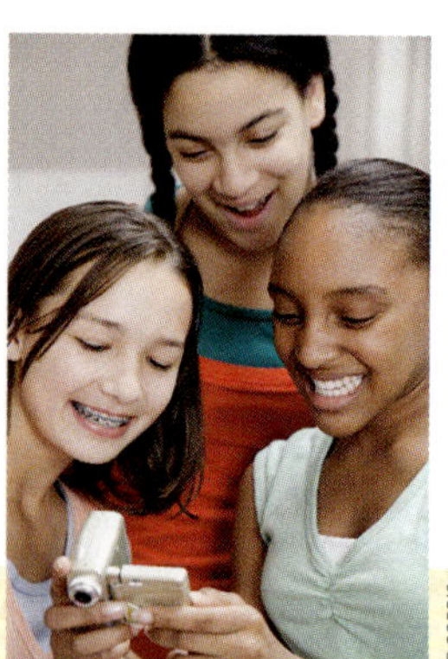

©CORBIS.

## Inspiration from Art

Many people collaborate to make a movie. First, the screenwriter writes the script. Then, the director hires the actors. A producer raises money to pay for everything, including the cameras, lights, and other equipment. The producer also hires a film crew, which operates the cameras and lighting and helps the actors with their costumes, makeup, and props.

Before filming starts, film artists sketch storyboards that show each scene in the order it will appear. When the storyboard is finished, filming begins. Each day, everyone views the film shot the day before; then they shoot the footage and prepare for the following day's filming. Shooting a film can last for months. Finally, film editors use all of the footage and the storyboard to put the shots together so they look as if the entire movie has been filmed without stopping.

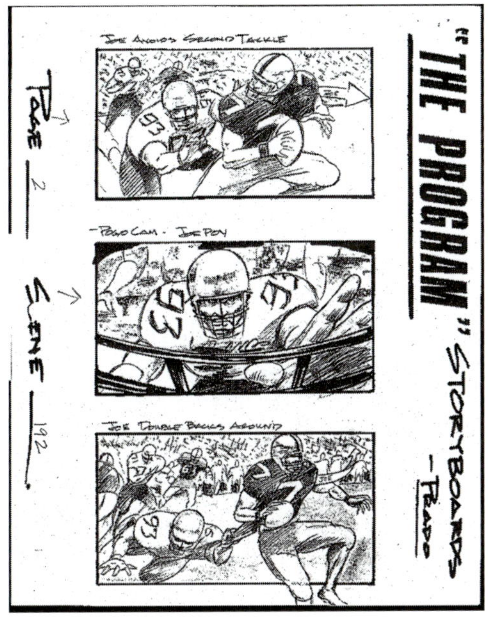


Fig. 9–28 **A storyboard is made up of hundreds of small, quick sketches like these. Based on this storyboard, what might this movie be about?**

Raymond C. Prado, *The Program.* Illustration storyboard. Courtesy of the artist.

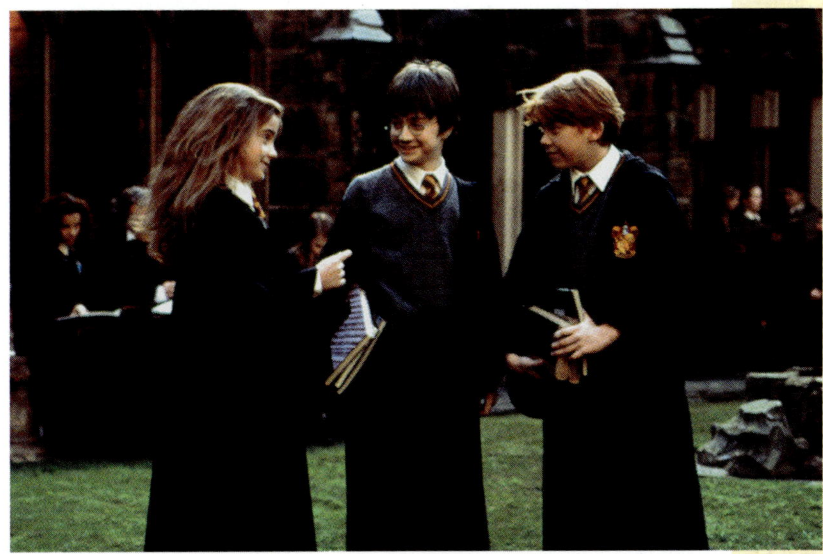

Fig. 9–29 **The Harry Potter films combine amazing special effects with traditional storytelling techniques, such as character development and plot, to tell a fascinating tale.**

©Warner Brothers/courtesy of the Everett Collection.

### Step 2 **Begin to Create**

- **Using your outline as a guide, create a storyboard.** Indicate whether the camera should zoom in for a close-up, zoom out for a long shot, or pan the scene.

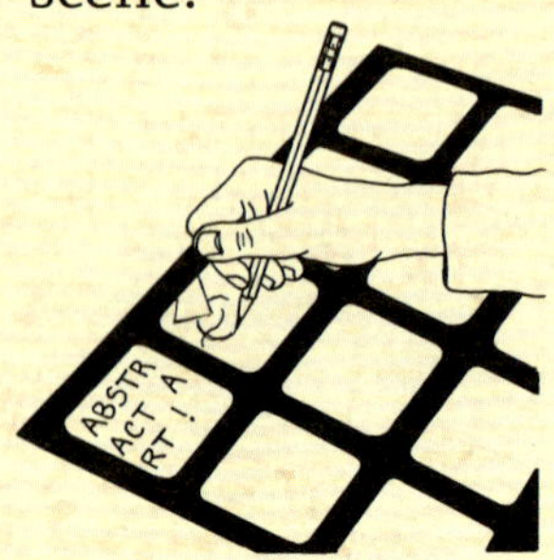


- Write a script for your film. Will there be dialogue or a single narrator?
- **Select whatever actors, costumes, props, and music or other sounds that you need.**

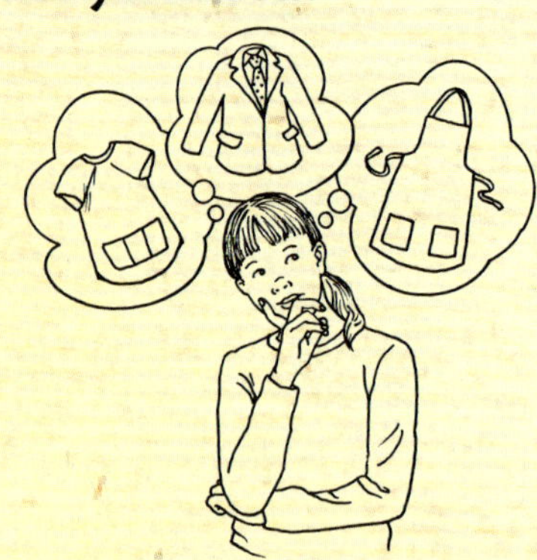

- **Shoot the film scene by scene.**

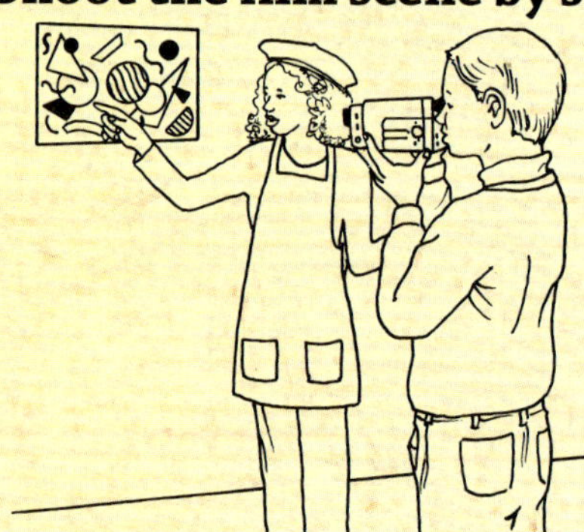

### Step 3 **Revise**

**Did you remember to:**

✓ Use traditional storytelling techniques?

✓ Use a storyboard to plan out each shot?

✓ Use the camera to take different types of shots?

Adjust your work if necessary. In your sketchbook, make a note of your revisions and why you made them.

### Step 4 **Add Finishing Touches**

- When you are finished with your film, view it with your group. Edit the film as needed. Then make the final copy.
- You can also use a computer to add titles, credits, or different effects to your film.

### Step 5 **Share and Reflect**

- With your class, view the completed films created by you and your classmates.
- Discuss how the films tell a simple story or make a presentation that teaches viewers something.
- What type of format did you choose for your film? Why did you select this format?
- What did you like best about making the film? What would you change for the next time?

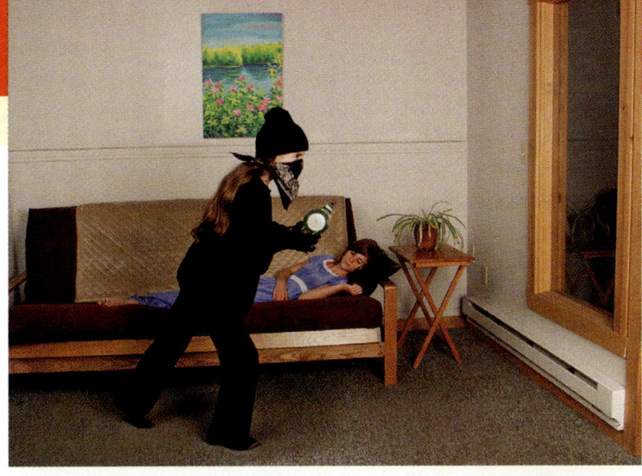

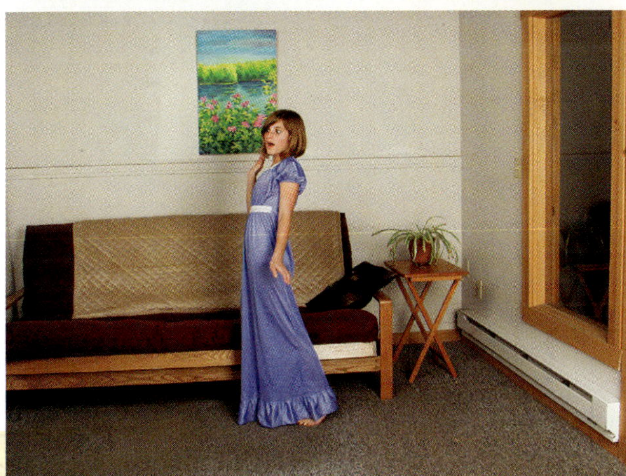

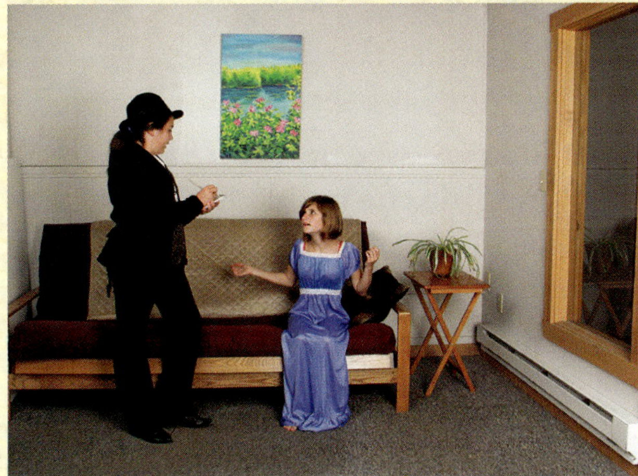

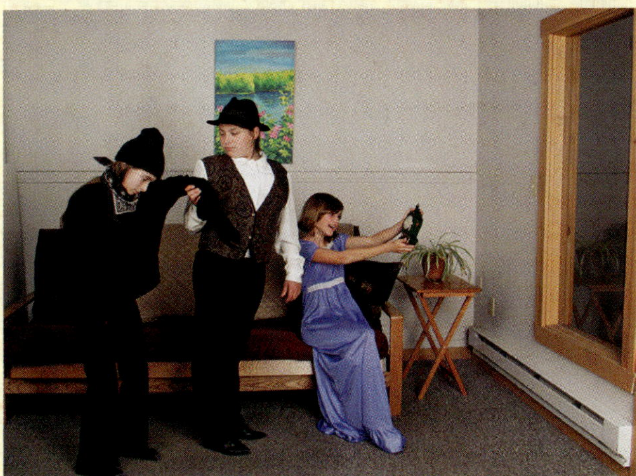

## Art Criticism

**Describe** Describe the characters, props, and settings you see.

**Analyze** How is each scene photographed?

**Interpret** What could the story be about?

**Evaluate** What makes this a good example of effective storytelling?

Fig. 9–30 Student work

## Language Arts

**Have you ever read a book online?** This is now a possibility through Project Gutenberg. Named for Johannes Gutenberg, the developer of movable type and the printing press, the project is an online effort to make thousands of books available in electronic form. Project Gutenberg is a free service that allows anyone who has access to the Internet to read online books and other documents in the public domain. What impact might Project Gutenberg have on the world of language arts?

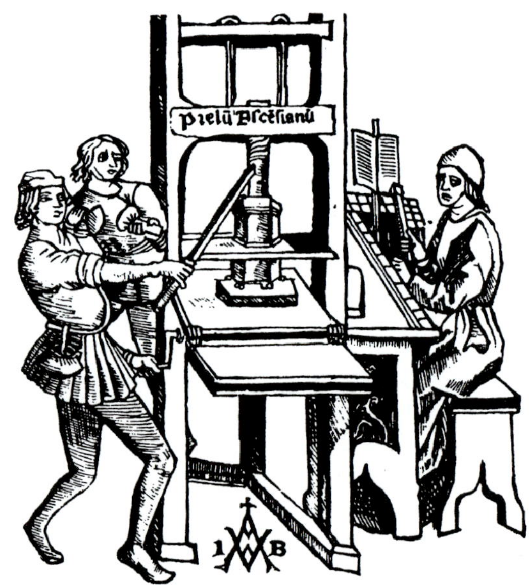

Fig. 9–31 **Johannes Gutenberg began using movable type, individual letters made from metal, in Europe around 1438. This new process revolutionized the printing of books.**

## Theater

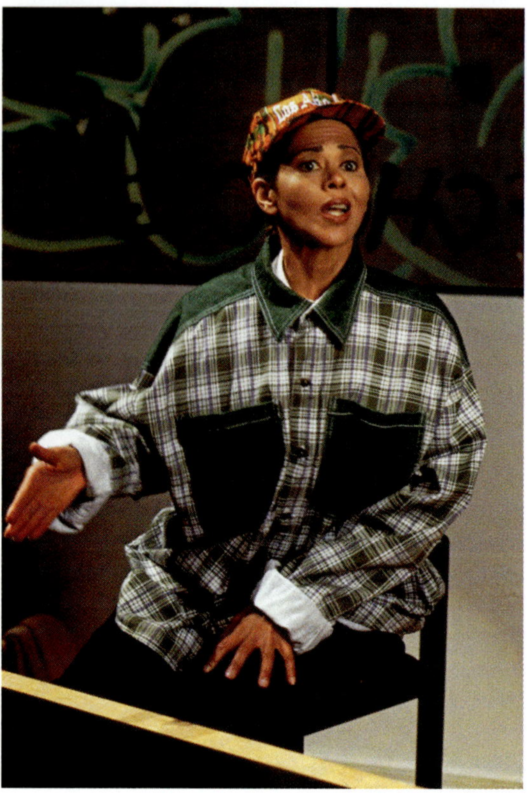

Fig. 9–32 ©Jim McHugh/CORBIS.

**Theater, like art, can help people imagine the unfamiliar.** In theater, the telling of a story can help people imagine what characters feel, what another time was like, or what the future may hold. Performance artist Anna Deavere Smith does this through the medium of video performance. In *Fires in the Mirror: Crown Heights, Brooklyn and Other Identities* (1992), Smith helps viewers understand one community's conflicts. She explores issues of race, ethnicity, and identity through role-playing the people who experienced the events.

## Careers **Space Artist**

**Space artists use astronomy and space exploration as inspiration and subjects for their art.** Space artists may be science, science-fiction, or fantasy illustrators, or even fine-art painters. They all share an interest in the possibilities of space exploration. NASA artist Robert T. McCall and astronaut Alan Bean paint "spacescapes" in response to ideas and images that have arisen from over forty years of space exploration. What do you think might be a future discovery in space that space artists can record?

Fig. 9–33 **Astronaut Alan Bean has experienced firsthand the "spacescapes" he paints. Your imagination can help you create artworks based on the theme of space exploration.**

*Alan Bean in His Studio.* Photograph by David Nance. ©The Greenwich Workshop, Inc. Courtesy of Alan Bean.

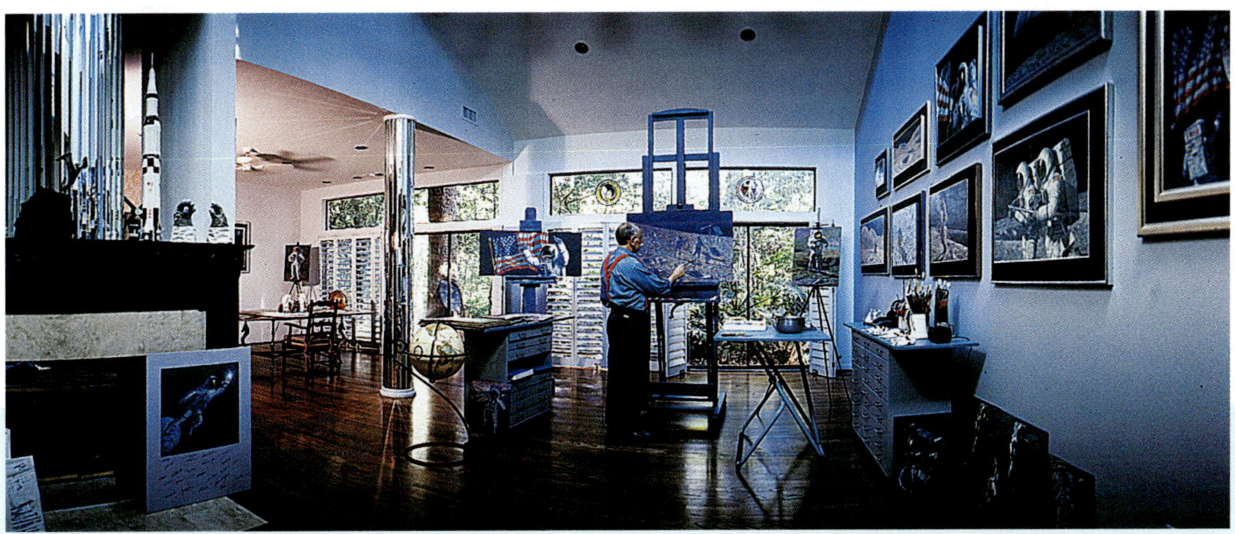

## Daily Life

**How do you think daily life will be different in 100 years?** One exciting prediction is that cars will practically drive themselves. They will run on automatic pilot, guided by magnetic sensors to keep them in their lane, control their speed, and avoid obstacles. Cars of the future may also be more environmentally friendly and safer to drive. How do you think the cars of the future will look in your lifetime?

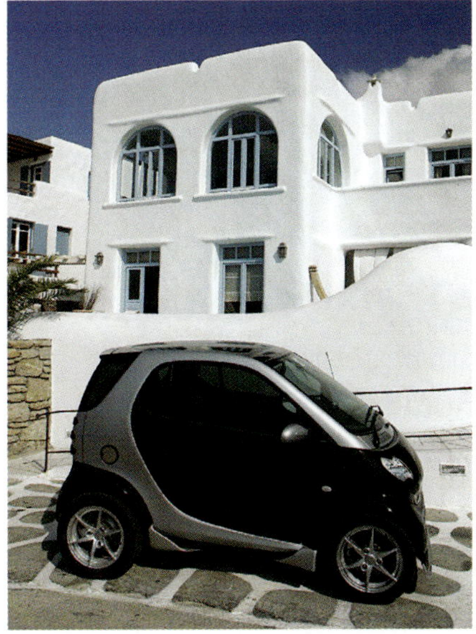

Fig. 9–34

## Vocabulary Review

Match each art term below with its definition.

**installations**

**activism**

**global style**

**Performance Art**

**global community**

1. the practice of working to change opinions or beliefs related to politics or other issues within a community
2. a visual art related to theater that combines creative forms of expression
3. the interaction of ideas and knowledge of people and populations all over the world
4. a style that cannot be linked to just one culture or tradition of art
5. temporary arrangements of objects in galleries, museums, and outdoors

## Aesthetic Thinking

Should limits be set for art? For example, should we censor works of art? If so, why and under what conditions? If not, explain why it is important that artists should not follow rules.

## Write About Art

Compare this painting to Jacob Lawrence's *Parade* from unit 7, p. 211 **(Fig. 7–36)**. Make a list of the major differences between these two paintings. For example, how did the artists use color differently? What part of the parade did they decide to show? Then determine if there are any similarities. Which parade would you like to attend?

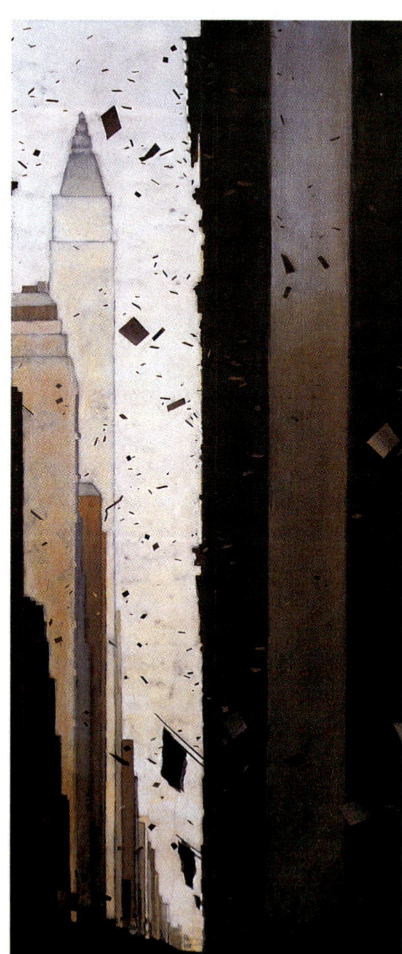

Fig. 9–35 **Celebration is a common theme in art. This artist shows it in a new way.**

Mark Innerst, *Parade*, 1999. Acrylic on board, 45 3/8" x 23 3/8" (115 x 59.4 cm). Courtesy of Paul Kasmin Gallery.

## Art Criticism

**Describe** What do you see in this painting?

**Analyze** How does the artist use proportion in this painting?

**Interpret** What is the effect of the way the artist has used proportion? Do you think this painting is funny? Scary? Strange? Why?

**Evaluate** Why do you think Magritte chose to portray the room and the apple very realistically, apart from the apple's size?

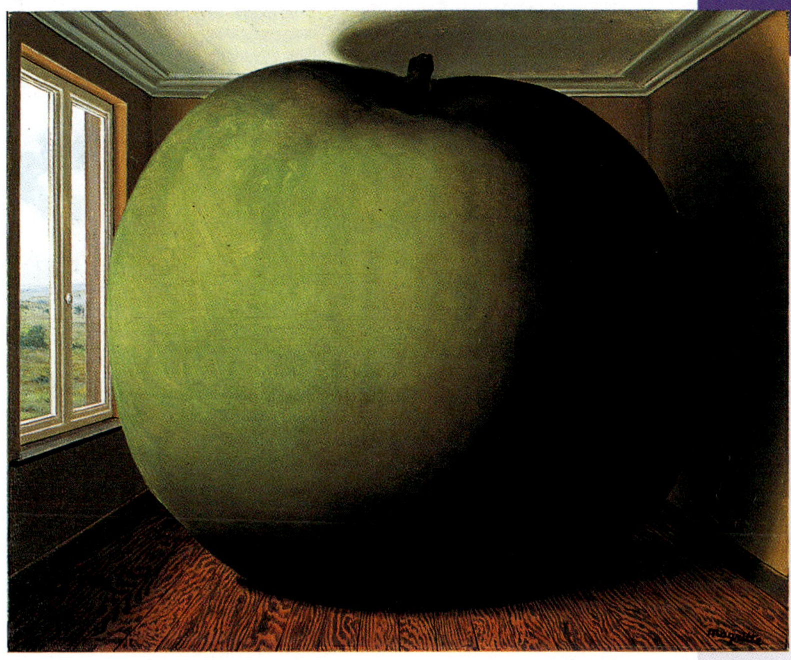

Fig. 9–36 Magritte, *La Chambre d'ecoute (The Listening Chamber),* 1952. Oil on canvas, 17 5/8" x 21 5/8" (45 x 55 cm). The Menil Collection, Houston. Gift of Philippa Friedrich, Photographed by Paul Hester, Houston. ©Charly Herscovici, Brussels/Artists Rights Society (ARS), New York.

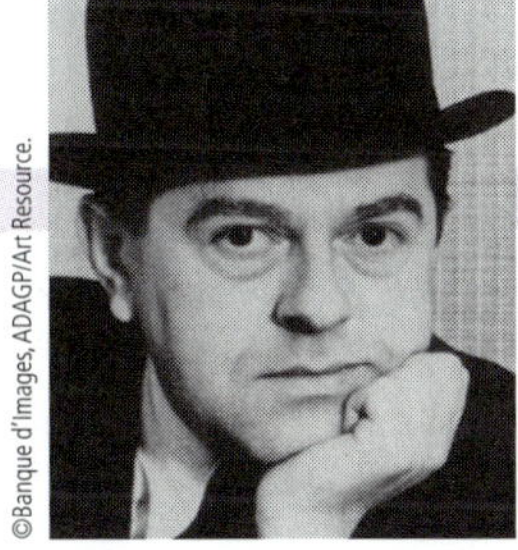



## Meet the Artist

**René Magritte** was born in Lessines, Belgium. He began to paint as a child and later studied art in Brussels. With several friends, Magritte founded the Belgian Surrealist group. Unlike some types of Surrealism that relied on dreams, Magritte took his images from real life, but he combined them in strange ways in an otherwise realistic style.

**"[W]hen one sees one of my pictures, one asks oneself this simple question 'What does that mean?' It does not mean anything, because mystery means nothing either, it is unknowable."**

— René Magritte (1898–1967)

## For Your Sketchbook

Design a series of masks in the style of a particular culture or with some distinguishing characteristic associated with a cultural area. Refer to the Global View lessons in this text.

## For Your Portfolio

Select four examples from your portfolio to demonstrate your ability to create artworks with meaningful themes. For each artwork, explain how the piece is a good example of your skill and ability to focus on a theme.

# Student Handbook Contents

# Studio Safety

Stay safe when you create! No matter what art materials you use, developing safe habits is important. Read labels, follow common safety procedures, and always wash your hands thoroughly after working with art materials.

## Avoid breathing dust.

**Why?** Chalk, pastel, charcoal, and plaster dust can harm your lungs and might trigger an allergic reaction.

**What to do?** Wear a mask over your nose and mouth if necessary. When carving plaster, keep your work damp and place it in a shallow tray lined with damp newspapers.

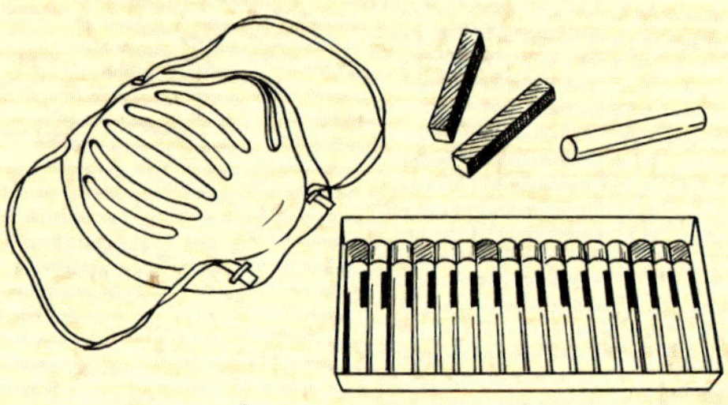

## Keep art materials away from your eyes.

**Why?** Chemicals in paints, solvents, and photo developing solutions can irritate your eyes and skin. Chemicals can also be absorbed through your skin.

**What to do?** Keep your hands away from your face when you work with art materials. Wear disposable latex or rubber gloves.

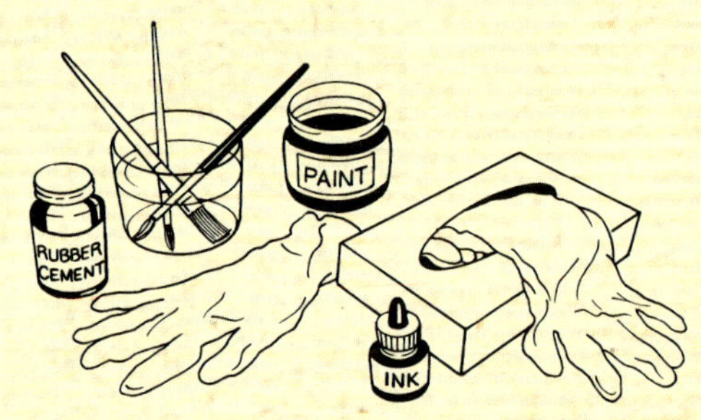


## Do not breathe sprays or vapors.

**Why?** Permanent markers, some paints, some solvents, photo developing solutions, and spray fixatives all give off fumes that can be harmful.

**What to do?** Do not use permanent markers for any art activity. Use sprays and other chemicals only in areas with active ventilation.

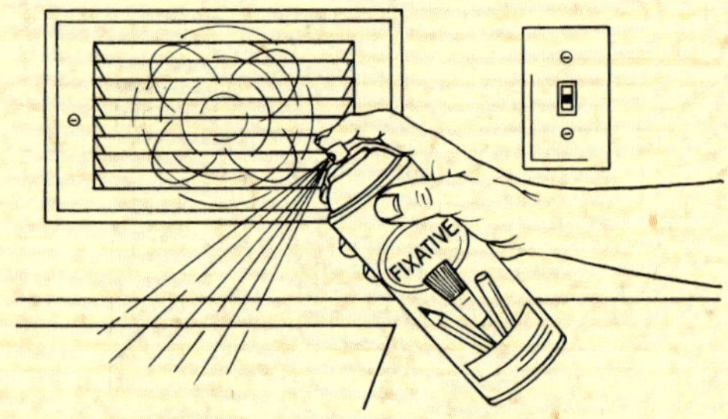

## Read labels carefully.

**Why?** Be sure labels say the materials are *nontoxic*, which means they are *not* poisonous. The word *toxic* or a picture of a small skull and crossbones means the material is poisonous.

**What to do?** Ask your teacher how to handle the material. Be sure to wash your hands thoroughly after use.

## Point scissors and sharp tools away from you.

**Why?** Scissors, knives, wood or linoleum block cutting tools, clay tools, needles, pins, and tacks are sharp and if mishandled can cause injury.

**What to do?** Always direct a sharp edge or point away from you and others. When you use the tools, hold your work securely or use a vise. Wear safety goggles. Work slowly.

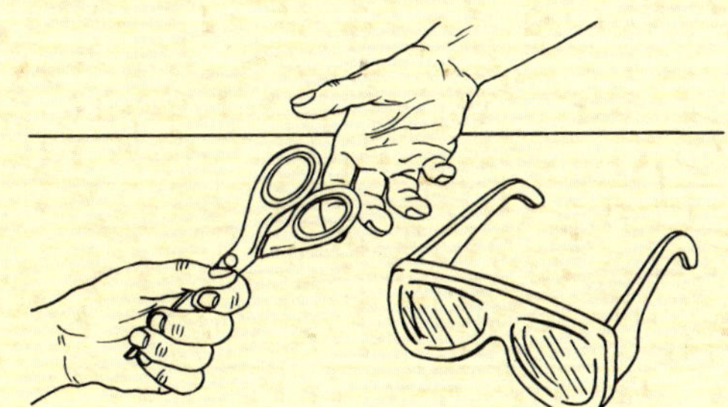

## Do not eat or drink in the artroom.

**Why?** Chemicals from art materials may get into your food or drink. Foods that are part of an edible creation can also become contaminated.

**What to do?** Always leave the artroom when you want to eat or drink. Create edible artwork in the kitchen using only food preparation tools and materials.

## Clean up spills immediately and keep the floor clear of objects.

**Why?** Liquids are slippery. Liquids and clutter on the floor can cause falls.

**What to do?** Clean up spills immediately, following your teacher's directions. Keep backpacks, books, and materials in or under your worktable.

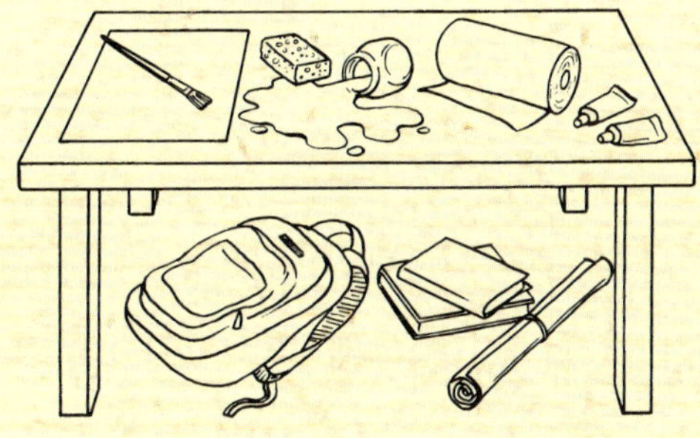

# Elements of Art

The *Elements of Art* are the basic building blocks that an artist uses when creating a work of art. Understanding the elements of art can also help you appreciate the artworks of others.

## Line

- A mark that has length and direction.
- Outlines shapes and forms or suggests movement.
- *Implied* line is not actually drawn, but suggested by part of an image, such as a path of footprints.
- Line affects the mood of artworks. Thick zigzag lines will give a different "feel" from light, curved lines.

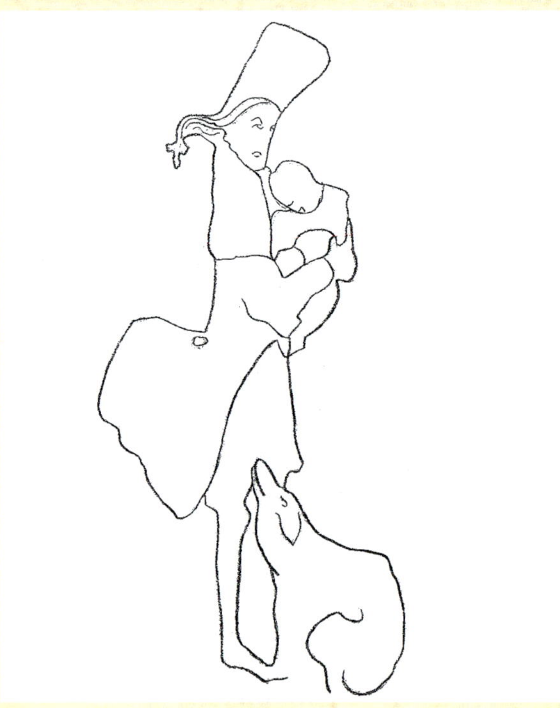

**Even a simple outline can convey much information.**

Romaine Brooks, *The Soldier at Home*, 1930.

## Shape and Form

### Shape

- Created when a line encloses a space or color.
- Flat and two-dimensional (2-D).
- Examples: circle, square.
- *Positive* shapes are the main shapes in an artwork.
- *Negative* shapes are the shapes that surround the positive shapes.
- Artists often plan their work so that the viewer's eyes move back and forth between positive and negative shapes.

### Form

- Has height, width, and depth.
- Is three-dimensional (3-D).
- Examples: sphere, cube.

### Shapes and Forms

- Can be *organic*, meaning irregular, such as leaves or shells.
- Can be *geometric*, meaning precise and regular, such as circles, spheres, triangles, and pyramids.

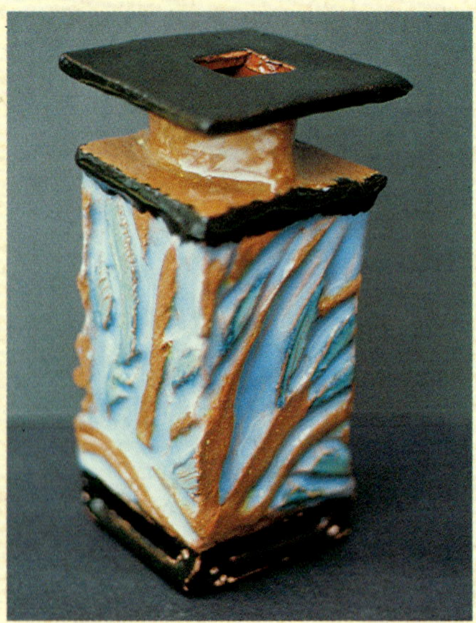

**This ceramic work contains geometric shapes and forms.**

Student artwork.

## Space

- In three-dimensional work, artists use actual space.
- In two-dimensional work, artists create the illusion of space.
- *Positive* space is the space filled by a work.
- *Negative* space is the space that surrounds the work.
- Ways to create the illusion of space or depth include:
  - making closer objects larger, farther objects smaller
  - overlapping objects
  - placing distant objects higher in the picture
  - *linear perspective*, a special technique in which lines meet at a specific point in the picture.

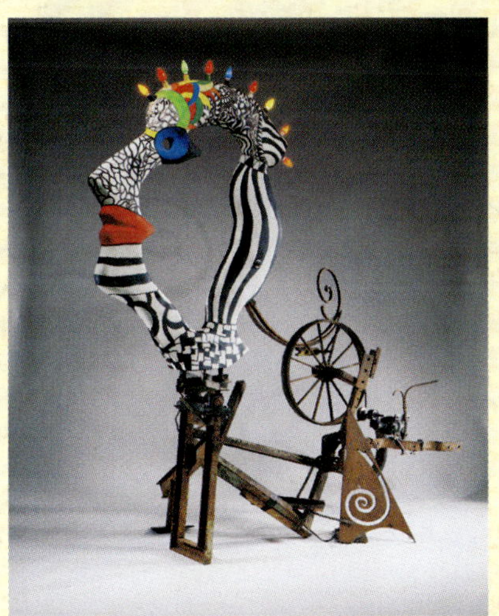

**You can see negative space through the open parts of this sculpture.**

Nikki de Saint Phalle and Jean Tinguely, *Illumination*, 1988.

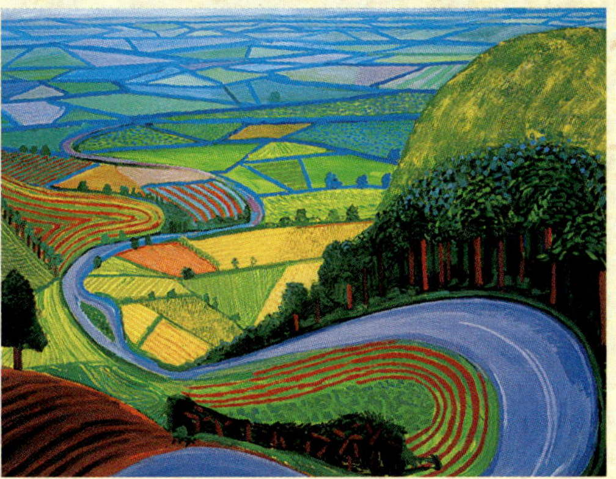

**Smaller and smaller fields help create the illusion of space in this painting.**

David Hockney, *Garrowby Hill*, 1998.

## Texture

- The way a surface feels or seems to feel, such as rough, sticky, prickly.
- *Real* textures are those you can actually feel.
- *Implied* textures are textures that do not feel the way they look, such as soft fur created by painting many fine lines.

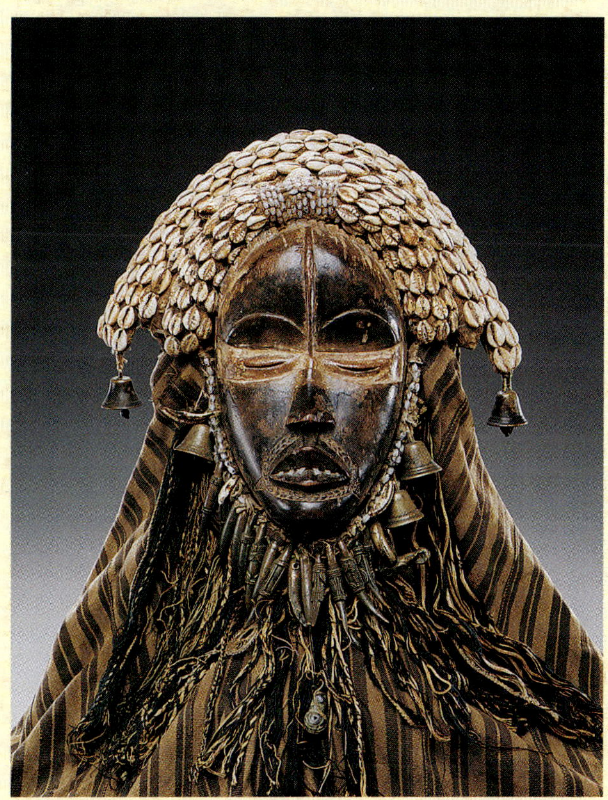

**The textures in this mask are real—you could feel them if you touched it.**

Africa, Dan Culture (Liberia, Ivory Coast), *Ga-Wree-Wre-Mask*, 20th century.

## Color

- The *color spectrum* is created when light passes through a prism.

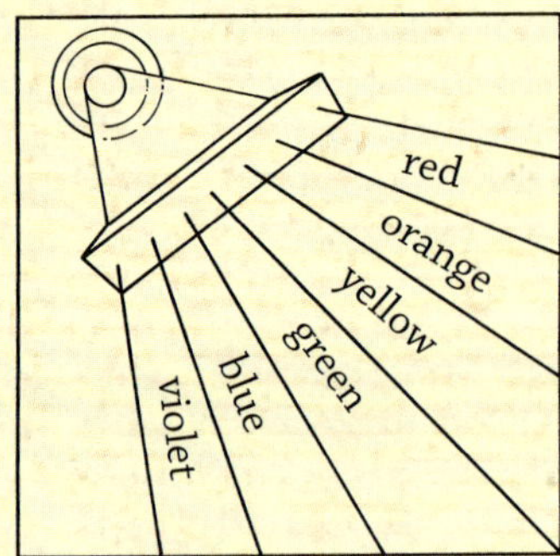


The Spectrum

- Colors of the spectrum are red, orange, yellow, green, blue, indigo, and violet.
- The *primary hues* or colors are red, yellow, and blue. Primary colors cannot be created by mixing other colors.
- The *secondary* colors are orange, green, and violet. Mix two primary colors to create a secondary color.
- To create an *intermediate* color, mix a primary color with the secondary color next to it on the color wheel.
- Use the primary colors, plus black and white, to mix almost every other imaginable color.
- *Intensity* is the brightness or dullness of a color.
- To create dull colors, mix complementary colors, those that are opposite each other on the color wheel.
- A *color scheme* is a specific group of colors an artist works with to create an artwork.

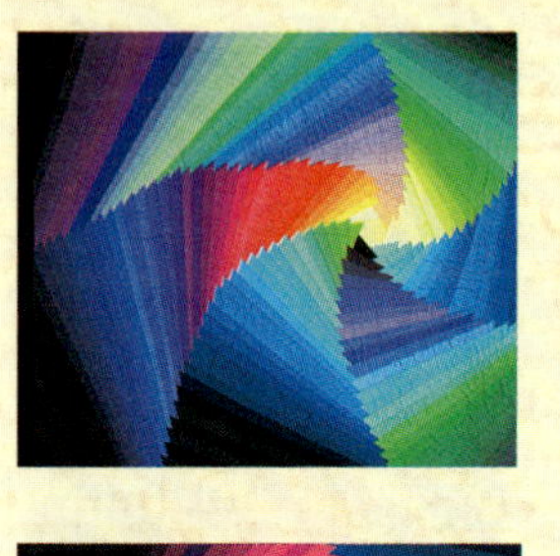
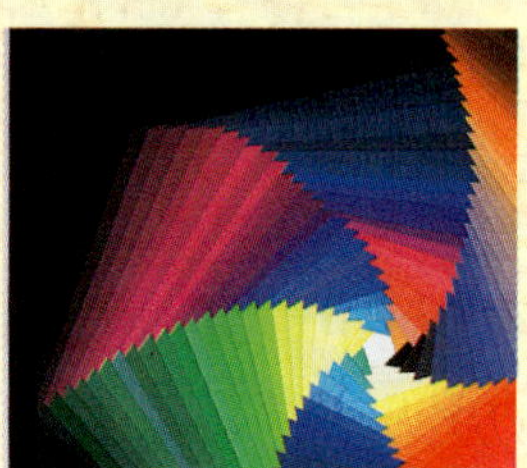
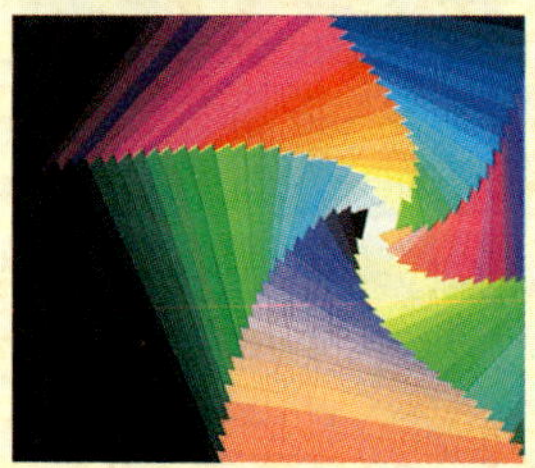
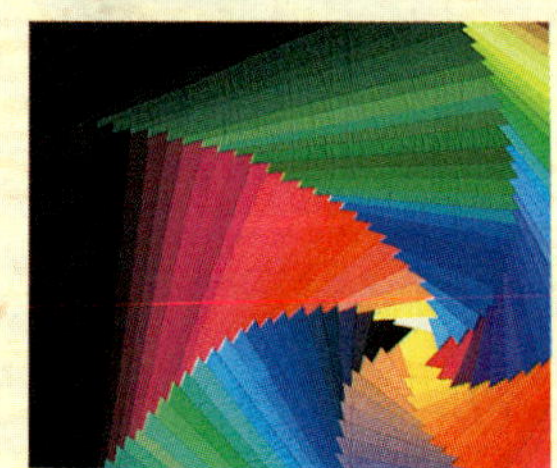

Caryl Bryer Fallert, *Refraction #4–#7*

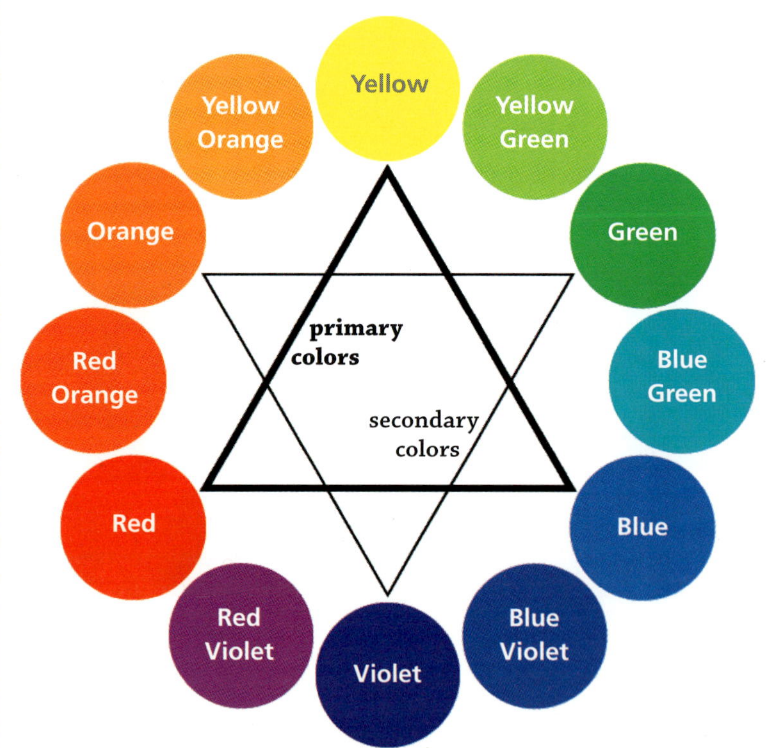


The Color Wheel

### Common Color Schemes

- *Warm:* colors that remind people of warm places, things, and feelings.

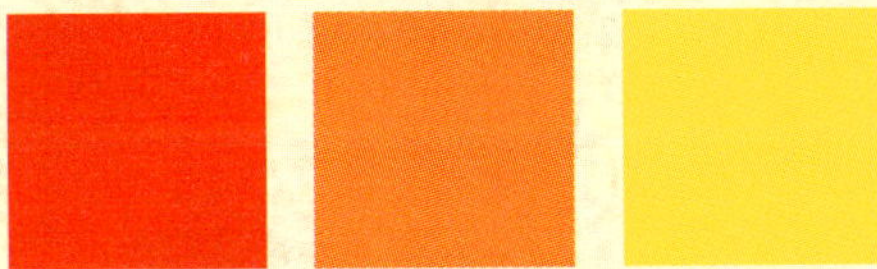

- *Cool:* colors that remind people of cool places, things, and feelings.

- *Neutral:* colors that are not associated with the spectrum.

- *Monochromatic:* the range of values of one color (*monochromatic* means "one color").

- *Analogous:* colors that are next to each other on the color wheel and share a common hue.

- *Split complement:* a color and the two colors on each side of its complement.

- *Triad:* any three colors spaced at an equal distance on the color wheel, such as the primary colors or the secondary colors.

## Value

- The lightness or darkness of a color.

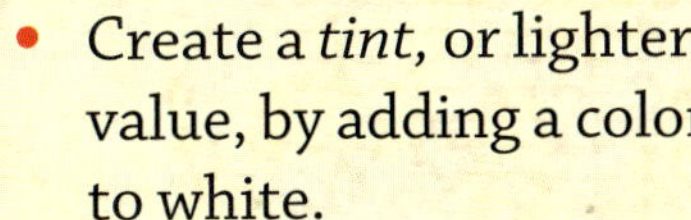

- Create a *tint,* or lighter value, by adding a color to white.

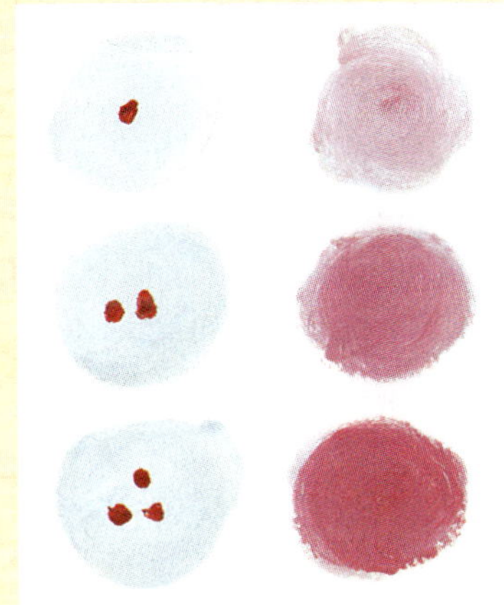

- Create a *shade,* or darker value, by adding black to a color.

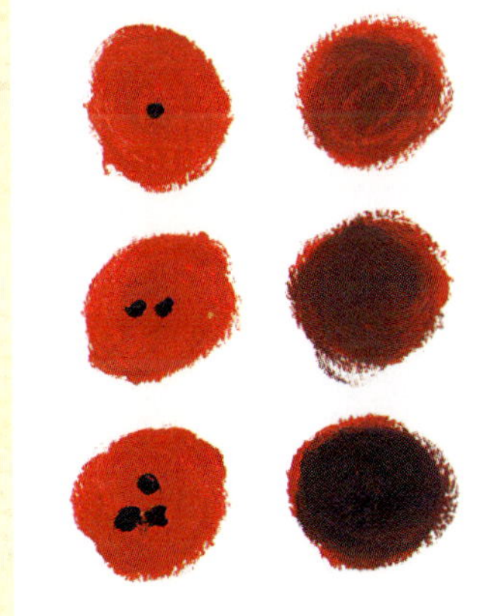

# Principles of Design

The principles of design are guidelines that help artists plan relationships among visual elements. These guidelines include balance, emphasis, unity, variety, pattern, proportion, movement and rhythm, and contrast.

## Balance

Artists use balance to give the parts of an artwork equal "visual weight" or interest. The three basic types of visual balance are symmetrical, asymmetrical, and radial.

- In **symmetrical balance**, the halves of a design are mirror images of each other, which creates a look of stability and quiet.

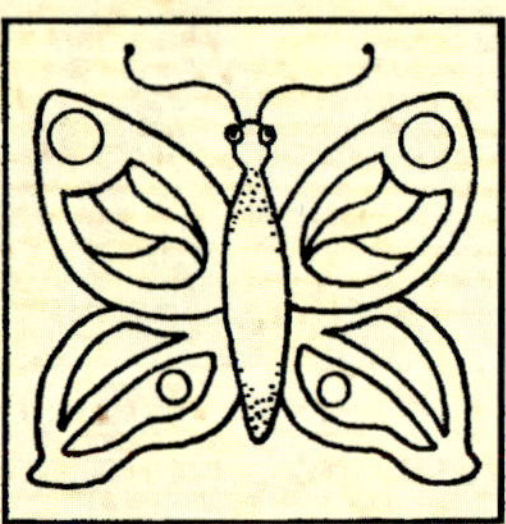

- In **asymmetrical balance**, the halves of a design are visually equal, yet not exactly the same.

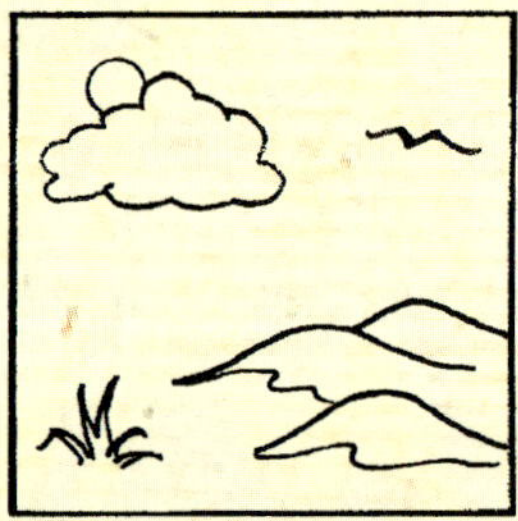

- In **radial balance**, the parts of a design seem to "radiate" from a central point, like the petals of a flower. Designs that show radial balance are often symmetrical.

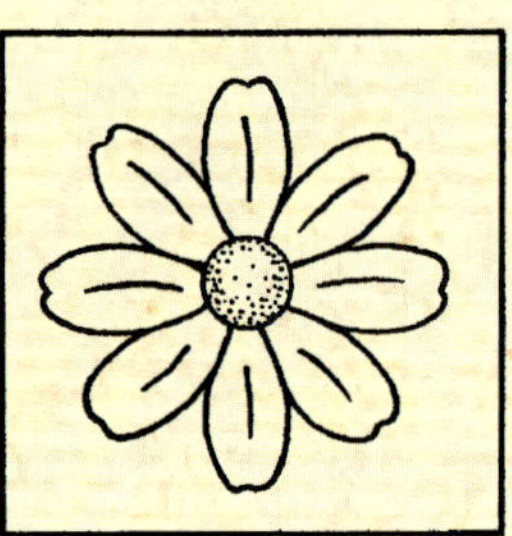

## Emphasis

When artists design an artwork, they use emphasis to call attention to the main subject. Emphasis makes objects, shapes, or even white space more noticeable than other elements.

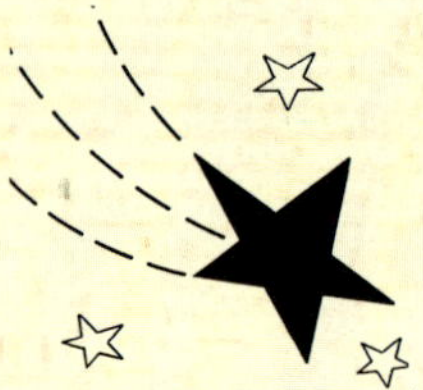

- The **size** of the subject and **where it is placed** are two key factors of emphasis.
- Create emphasis by arranging other elements in the artwork to **lead the viewer's eyes** to the important subject.
- **Group certain objects together** in a design and **use contrasting elements** to create emphasis.

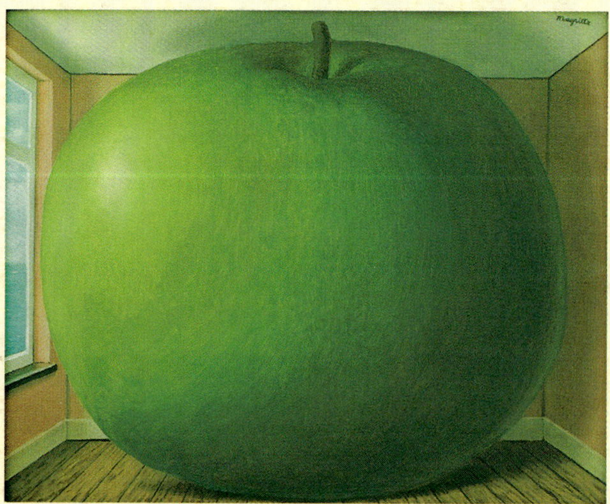

**Making the apple unusually large calls your attention to it.**

René Magritte, *The Listening Room,* 1958.

## Unity

Unity is the feeling that all parts of a design belong together or work as a team. Here are several ways that artists can create unity:

- **repetition:** the use of a shape, color, or other visual element over and over
- **dominance:** the use of a single shape, color, or other visual element as a major part of the design
- **harmony:** the combination of colors, textures, or materials that are similar or related

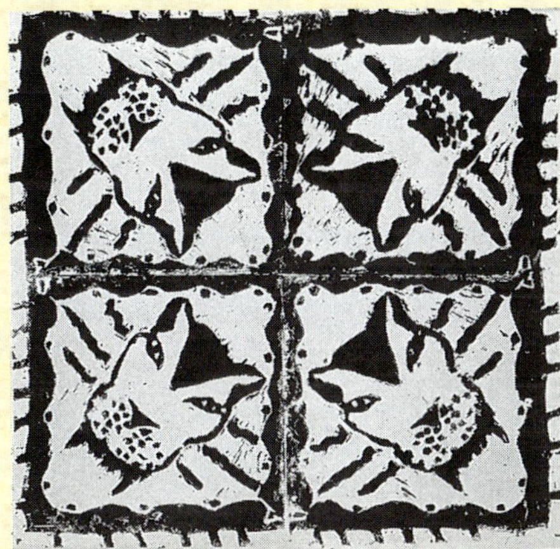

**Repeated shapes give this work unity.**
Student artwork.

## Variety

Variety adds visual interest to a work of art. Artists create variety by combining elements that contrast or are different from one another.

- A painter might draw **varying sizes** of shapes and paint them in contrasting colors.

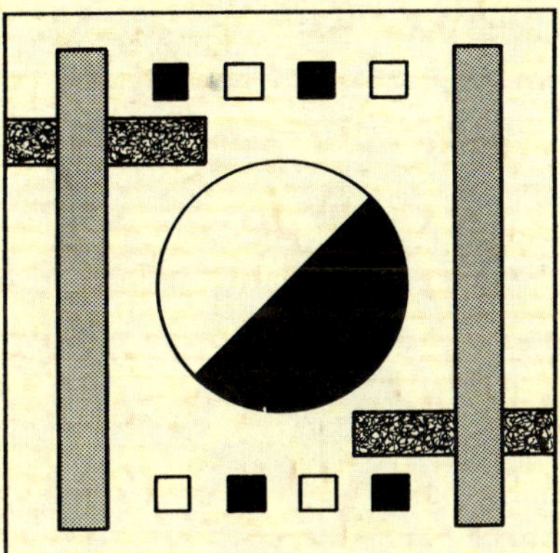

- A sculptor might **combine media** or **vary the texture** of one material.
- Architects create variety when they **use different materials**, such as stone, glass, and concrete, together in one building.

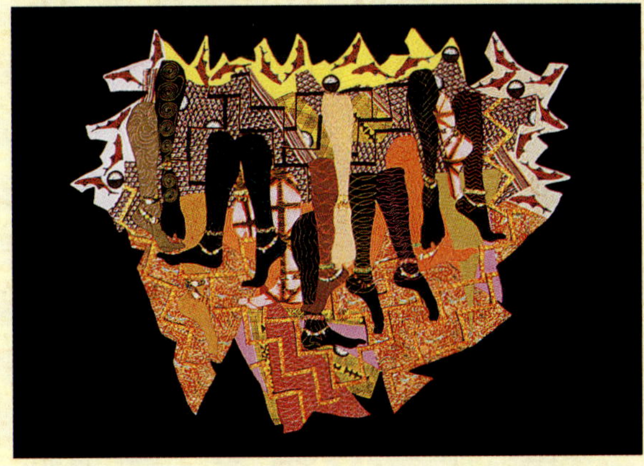

**This artist used many different materials to create variety.**
Frances Hare, *Sixteen Feet of Dance: A Celebration, A Self-Portrait*, 1996.

## Pattern

Artists create pattern by repeating lines, shapes, or colors in a design. Patterns help organize designs and create visual interest. Patterns are either *planned* or *random*.

- In a **planned** pattern, the element repeats in a regular or expected way.
- In a **random** pattern, elements appear scattered throughout the design. Random patterns are usually more exciting than planned ones.

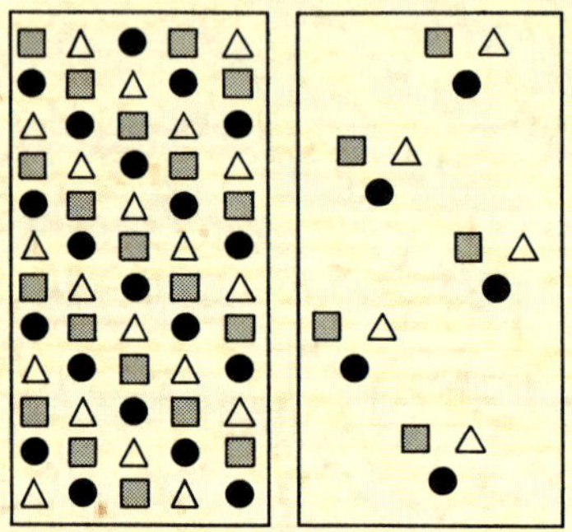


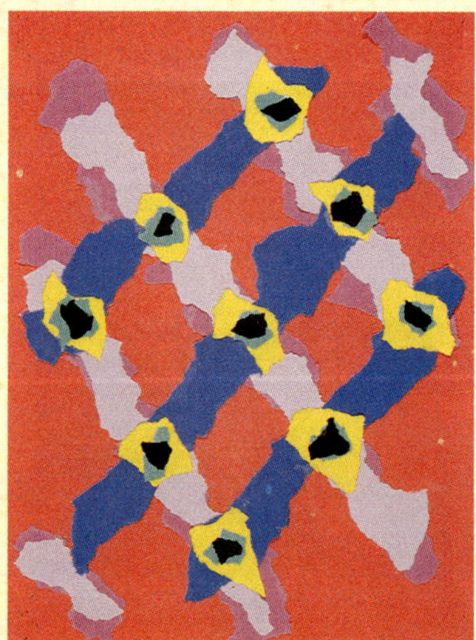

**This planned pattern is formed by the color, shape, and position of paper shapes.**

Student artwork.

## Proportion and Scale

Proportion is the relationship of size, location, or amount of one thing to another.

- In art, **proportion** is mainly associated with the human body. Cartoonists exaggerate human proportions for humorous purposes.

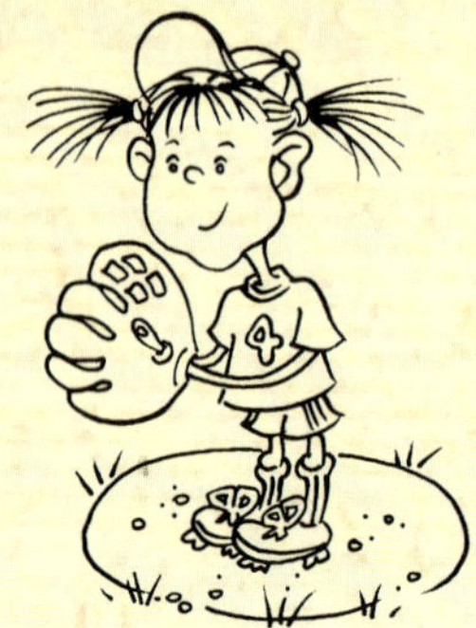

- **Scale** is the size of one object compared to the size of something else.
- Artists sometimes exaggerate the scale of objects in an artwork.

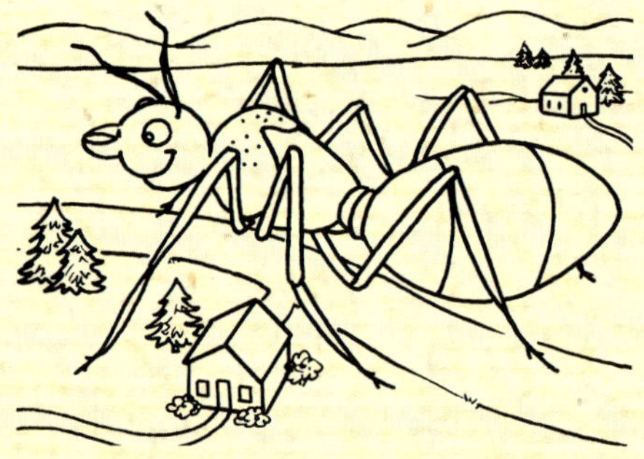

- Drawing an object on a larger scale can make it seem more important or allow the artist to use it in an unexpected way.

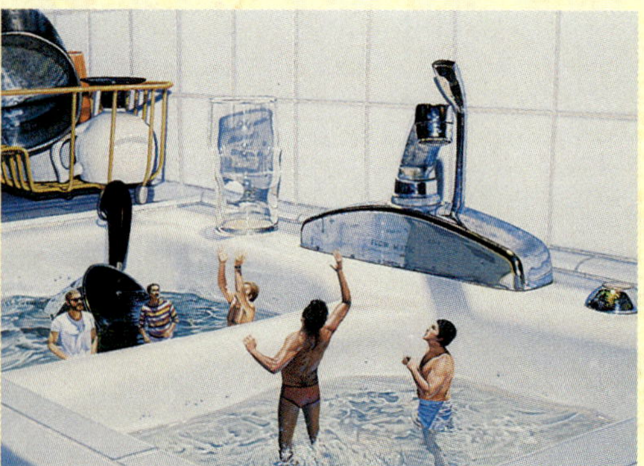

**Here, the scale of the sink is greatly enlarged.**

Doug Webb, *Kitchenetic Energy*, 1979.

## Movement and Rhythm

Artists often use movement to create excitement and energy in their artwork. Rhythm, which is related to both movement and pattern, is created by repeating elements in a particular order.

- Kinetic art, such as mobiles, actually moves, while other forms of art only record the movement of their subjects.

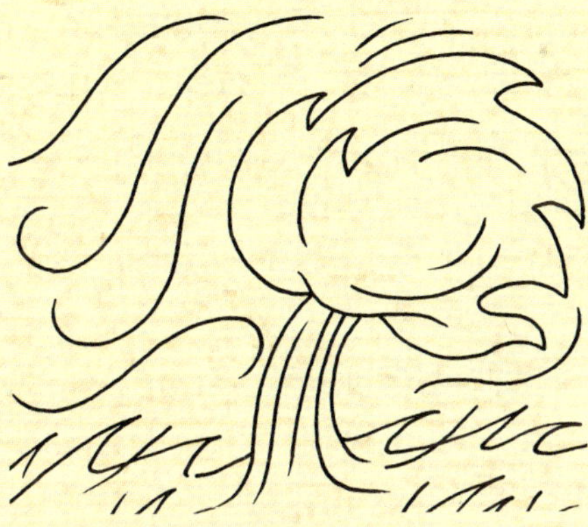

Even simple lines can show rhythmic movement.

- Sometimes movement is added to an artwork to lead the eye to a center of interest or add to a mood.
- Rhythm may be simple and predictable, such as the lines in a sidewalk, or it may be complex and unexpected.
- Artists use rhythm, like pattern, to help organize a design or add visual interest.

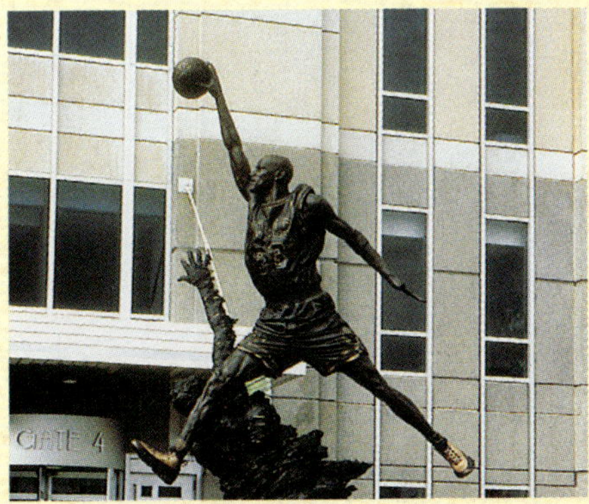

Showing a figure with both feet off the ground helps suggest movement.

Omri Amrany and Julie Rotblatt-Amrany, *The Spirit, Michael Jordan*, 1994.

## Contrast

Contrast is a difference between two things. The greater the difference, the greater the contrast.

- The area of greatest contrast captures your attention first.
- Value is one element artists contrast in their work. Contrast in values creates a noticeable difference between light and dark. It adds excitement or drama.
- Artists also create contrast through the use of strong differences in colors, shapes, textures, and lines.
- Some artists use contrast to create a particular mood or feeling.

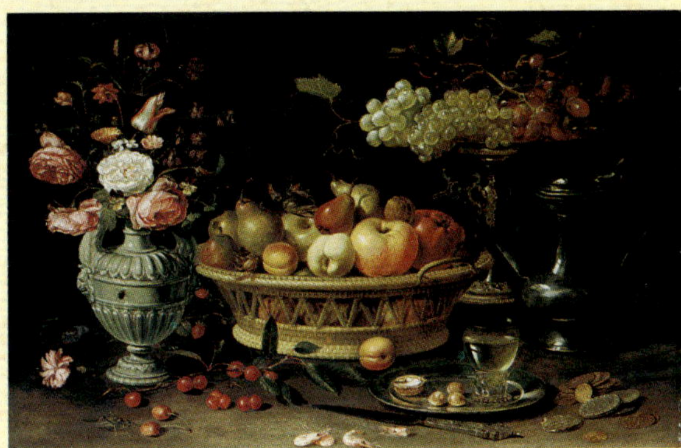

Contrast between bright and dark areas adds drama to this painting.

Clara Peeters, *Still Life with Fruit and Flowers*, after 1620.

# New Directions in Design

**Design** is the act of making a plan for a specific outcome such as a website, an appliance, a building, or a video game. Unlike fine artists, who create for self-expression, designers plan products, structures, and systems for people to use. Designers consider questions such as *How can this object best serve its user? How can its appearance match the way it functions? How can this object use specific materials or the environment for maximum efficiency?*

## Information Design

- Information designers and graphic designers consider the different ways to communicate information.
- *Graphic design* is the use of visual art to communicate information.
- Graphic designers use typography (fonts), images, and page layout as part of their overall design.
- They are responsible for creating advertisements, animation, logos, road signs, diagrams in textbooks, book layouts, and websites.

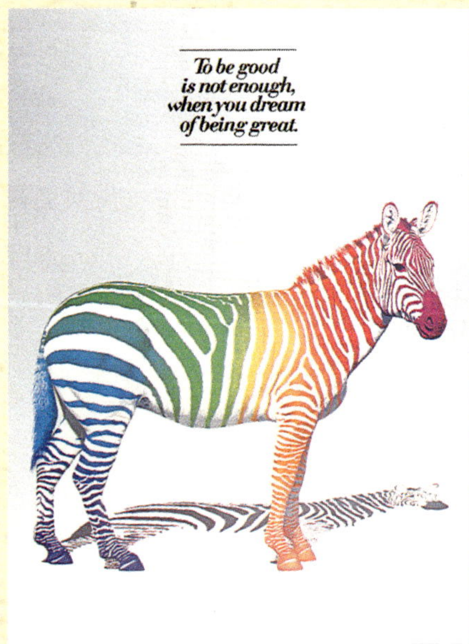


**Graphic designers use words and images together to send their messages.**

Marvin Mattelson (illustrator), *Subway Poster for School of Visual Arts.*

## Object Design

- Object designers create new designs for everyday objects such as automobiles, clothing, furniture, and appliances.
- Many of these objects are intended for mass production. The design of mass-produced consumer products is called *industrial design.*
- Industrial designers are often trained as architects or as visual arts professionals. Many work with a larger creative team to create products that work well, look attractive, and will sell well in a competitive market.

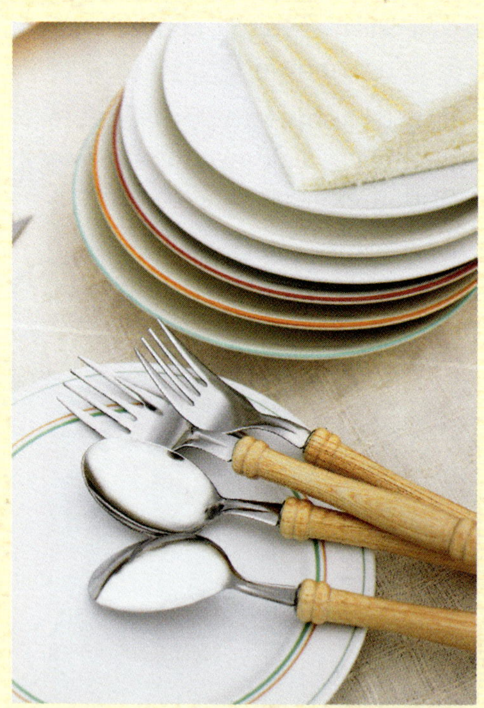

**These utensils and plates were designed and then mass-produced.**

"Tableware," Bloomimage/Corbis.

## Space and Place Design

- Space and place designers plan and determine how a structure—including its interior—interacts with space, objects, and the environment.
- *Architects* design buildings and other structures. They consider the function their structure will serve, how stable and durable it will be, and how its form will communicate ideas.
- *Interior designers* focus on the smaller, more intimate spaces within a building and use a mix of space and objects to create certain moods.
- *Urban planners* work with much larger spaces, so they have much to consider as they design. They focus on how society uses structures and space and the impact society has on both. They also plan the development of open land and the renewal of existing parts of cities.

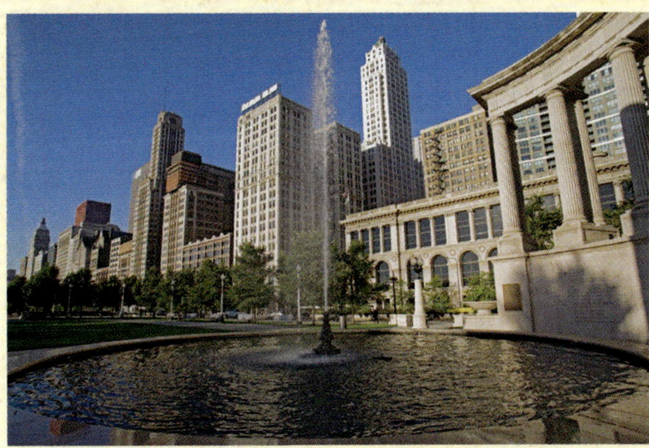

**A city's buildings are usually designed by many different architects at various times in history.**

Art on File/Corbis.

## Experience Design

- Experience designers plan products, processes, services, events, and environments with which people can interact. The results of these designs provide experiences for people.
- Computer-human interface (CHI) designers create products that allow people to physically interact with computers. The computer mouse, the touch screen, and pull-down menus are examples of CHI technology.
- The video games, theme parks, toys, and games you enjoy were all created by experience designers.

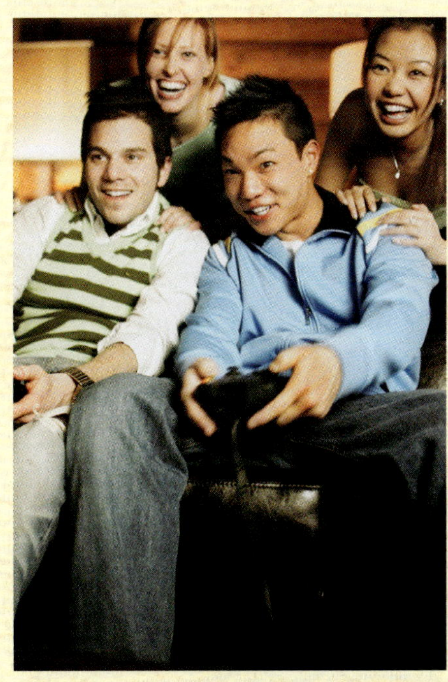

**Products that interface with computers should be designed for ease of use.**

Brand X/Corbis.

# Major Western Art Styles and Movements

For thousands of years, people all over the world have created art. In the following pages, you can observe how artists in western Europe and North America have expressed themselves and how art styles have developed and changed over time.

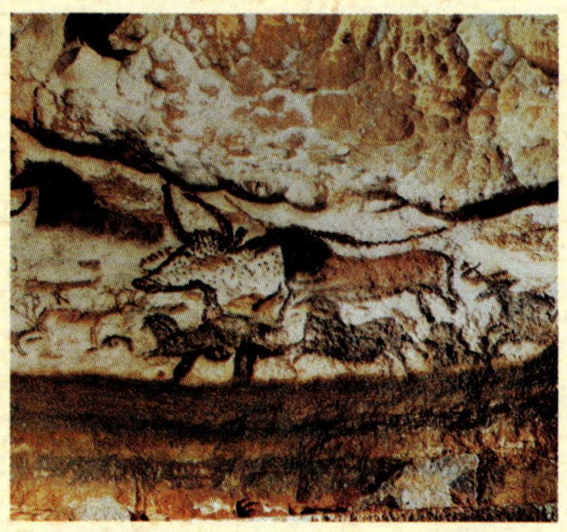

*Hall of Bulls*, detail, Lascaux, c.15,000–13,000 BC.

## Stone Age Art 30,000–2000 BCE

- The earliest known artworks are paintings discovered in caves in Spain, France, and Africa.
- Animals in cave paintings are usually shown in profile with lifelike proportions, details, and actions. People are shown as stick figures with spears.
- Cave paintings may have been used to communicate hope for a successful hunt, to record events, or to educate children.

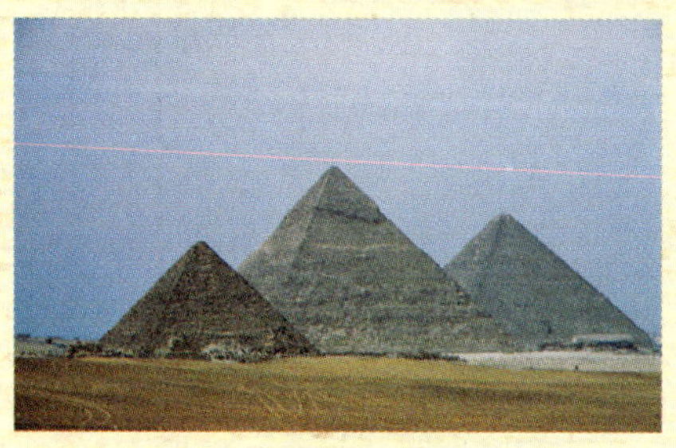

Giza, Egypt, *The Pyramids of Mycerinus, Chefren, and Cheops,* built between 2589 and 2350 BC.

## Ancient Egyptian Art 3000–500 BCE

- Pharaohs built pyramid-shaped tombs filled with furniture and jewelry to take with them in the afterlife.
- Wall paintings, relief sculptures, and small models were common art forms.
- Artists worked according to strict rules: head, arms, and lower body in profile, eye and upper torso in front view.

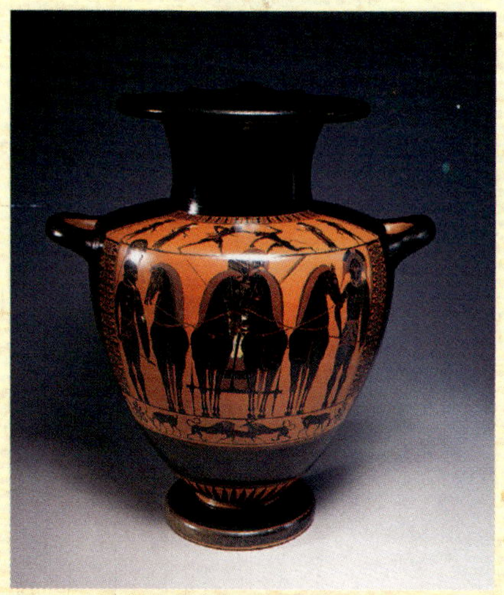

Ancient Greece, Athens, (attributed to the Antimenes painter), *Hydria*, c. 530–510 BC.

## Ancient Greek Art 600–150 BCE

- Known for its elegant proportions and perfection of form.
- Mosaic murals were created in many buildings.
- Sculptures were often decorated with paint, gold, and colorful stones.
- Athletes, heroes, myths, and important events were common art subjects.
- Architecture, especially temples and outdoor theaters, featured carved columns and new building techniques.

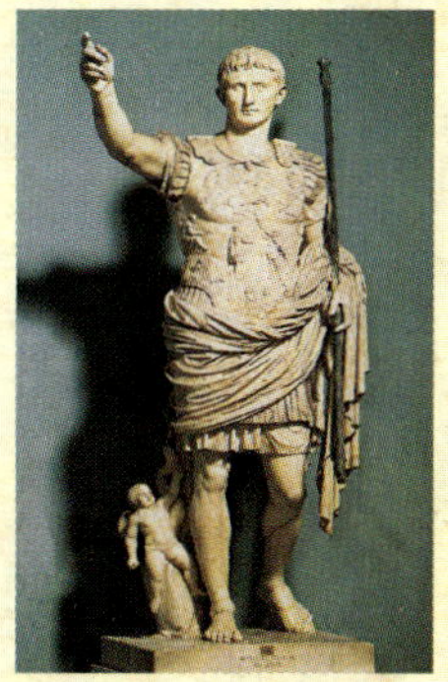

*Augustus of Prima Porta*, Roman Sculpture, Early first century AD.

## Ancient Roman Art 753 BCE–476 CE

- Reflects ideas from Greece, but with a greater interest in naturalistic details
- Emphasized realistic features, showing rulers, ancestors, and peers as they looked in real life.
- Used for practical and political purposes. Exact facial features let people in any part of the vast Roman Empire know what their ruler looked like.

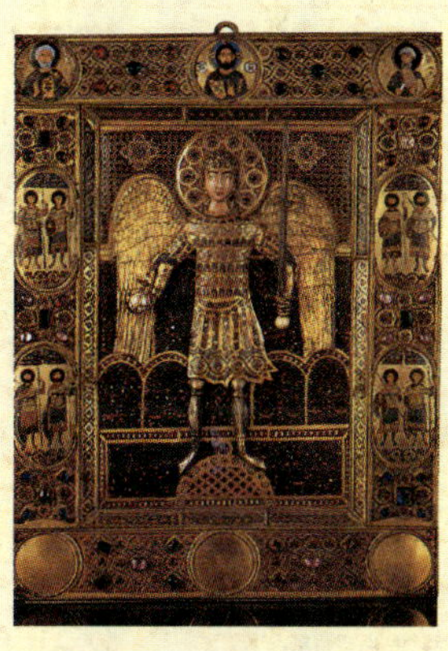

*The Archangel Michael with Sword*, Byzantine, 11th century.

## Byzantine Art 300–1500

- Developed in eastern Roman Empire as a response to the rise of Christianity.
- Rejected Greek and Roman ideals of the perfect human being, physical beauty, and strength.
- Focused on religious themes, using symbols and icons to tell stories about how to live a Christian life.
- Artworks feature a rich use of color and flat, stiff figures.

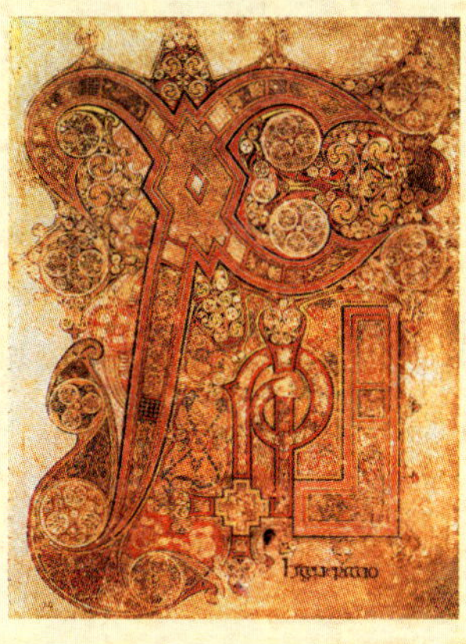

*Chi-rho Gospel of St. Matthew, chapter 1 verse 18*, Irish (vellum). *Book of Kells*, c. 800.

## Medieval Art 400–1400

- Heavily influenced by Christianity, Judaism, and Islam.
- Because many people could not read, art was used to communicate important religious lessons.
- Illustrated scriptures show scenes painted with complex geometric patterns, figures, and fantastic animals. Often, a layer of gold is used to emphasize parts of an image.
- Artworks, in the forms of books and objects of adornment, were small and could be carried easily.

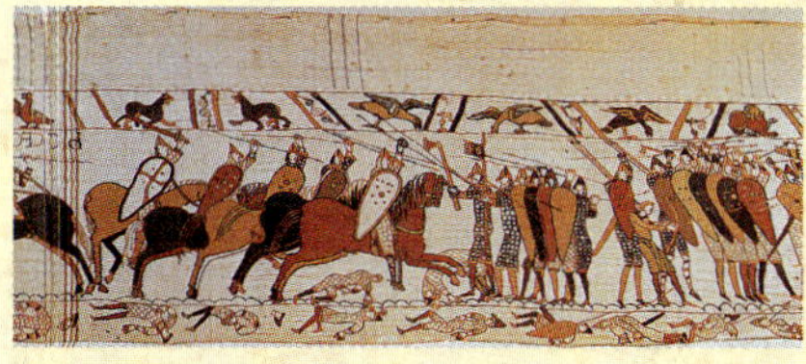

*Bayeux Tapestry*, 1100 CE.

## Romanesque Art 1000–1200

- Developed in western Europe during the Middle Ages.
- Brought back the Greek and Roman tradition of carving large-scale sculptures.
- Cathedrals have thick walls, rounded arches, and sculpted religious scenes.
- Items created for use in worship were often decorated with gold, silver, pearls, and gemstones.

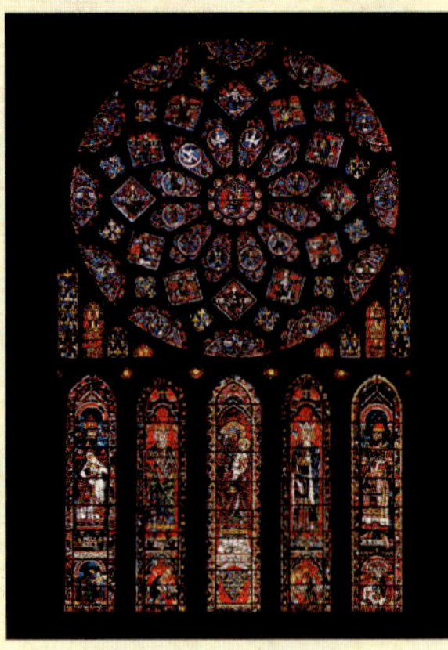

Chartres Cathedral, *North Transept Rose and Lancet Windows,* 13th century.

## Gothic Art 1000–1200

- French style that was adopted in parts of Europe and England.
- Art and architecture characterized as vertical, open, delicate, and light.
- Churches used stained-glass windows to let in light.
- Biblical scenes in windows taught churchgoers lessons.

**Artists:** Giotto di Bondone, Cenni di Pepi Cimabue, Ambrogio Lorenzetti, Simone Martini, Gentile da Fabriano, The Limbourg Brothers (Paul, Jean, and Herman) (painters); Nicola Pisano, Sabina von Steinbach, Claus Sluter (sculptors)

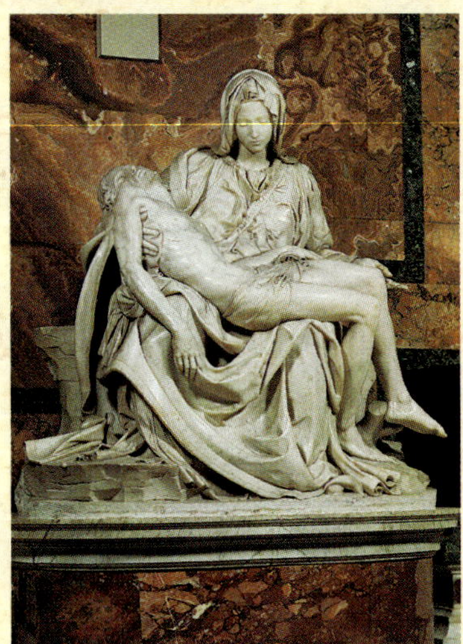

Michelangelo Buonarroti, *Pietà*, 1499.

## Renaissance Art 1400–1600

- Began in Italy and gradually spread to the rest of Europe.
- Paintings show realistic textures such as metal, wood, and skin.
- The invention of oil paint allowed artworks to have smooth, glowing surfaces and clear colors.
- Artists focused on light and perspective, and used new techniques to show order, depth, and graceful movements.

**Artists:** Fra Angelico (painter), Giovanni Bellini (painter), Filippo Brunelleschi (architect), Michelangelo Buonarroti (sculptor), Donatello (sculptor), Jan Van Eyck (painter), Leonardo da Vinci (painter)

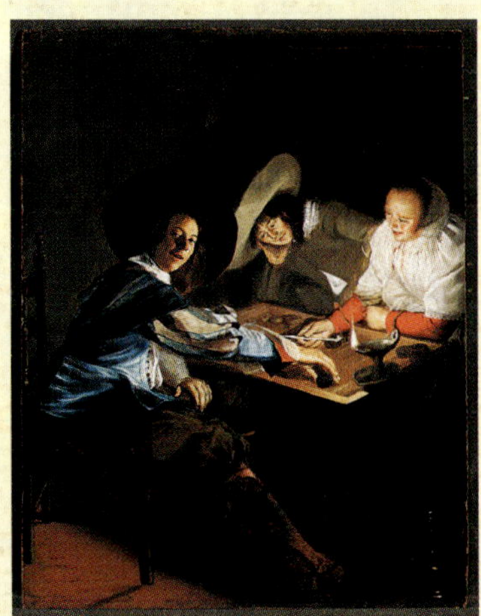

Judith Leyster, *Game of Tric-Trac*, ca. 1630.

## Baroque Art 1600–1700

- Lively motion, dramatic contrasts in light and shade, and asymmetrical design are typical.
- Artists used rich colors and textures and swirling curves.
- Still lifes, everyday objects and events, portraits, and landscapes were popular subjects.
- Artists shaped metal and stone into fluid forms.

**Artists:** Michelangelo da Carravaggio, Artemisia Gentileschi, Francisco de Zurbarãn, Bartolomé Murillo, Diego Velásquez, Peter Paul Rubens, Anthony van Dyck, Nicholas Poussin, Claude Lorraine, Frans Hals, Judith Leyster, Jan Vermeer, Jacob van Ruisdael, Clara Peeters, Racel Ruysch, Sibylla Maria Merian (painters); Francesco Borromini, Guarino Guarini, Jakob Prandtauer, Christopher Wren (architects)

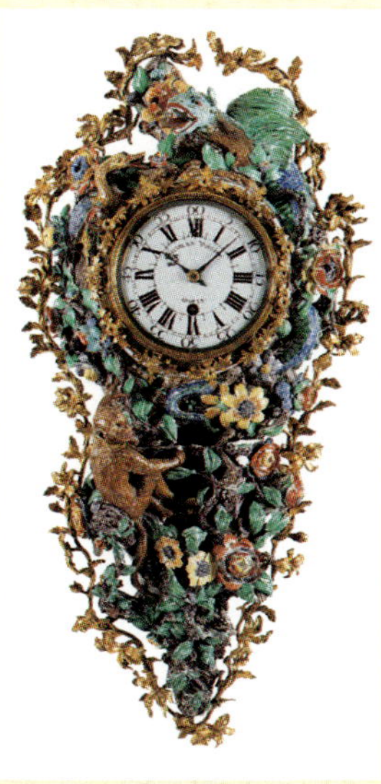

Movement made by Charles Voisin and Chantilly manufactory, *Wall Clock*, c. 1740.

## Rococo Art 1700–1800

- Whimsical, decorative variation of Baroque art created for aristocrats in France, Spain, England, and Italy.
- Delicate colors, playful use of lines, and graceful movement show aristocrats at carefree leisure.
- Ordinary household items showed the elegance and charm favored by the upper class.

**Artists:** Rosalba Carriera, Jean-Baptiste Chardin, William Hogarth, Benjamin West, (painters)

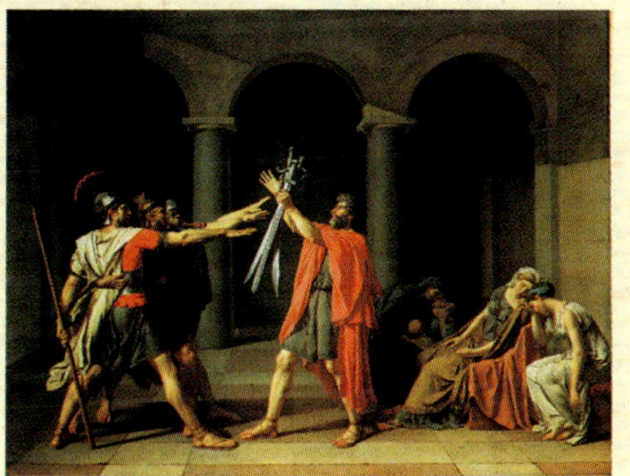

Jacques-Louis David, *Oath of the Horatii*, 1784–1785.

## Neoclassicism 1750–1875

- Unearthed classical art at ancient Roman cities Pompeii and Herculaneum inspired the movement.
- Greek and Roman ideals of beauty, courage, sacrifice, and patriotism applied to artworks.
- Formal lines, shapes, proportions, and simple orientation are features of this style.
- In architecture, renewed emphasis on classical arches and columns.

**Artists:** Antonio Canova (sculptor), Jacques-Louis David (painter), Thomas Jefferson (architect), John Trumbull (painter), Elizabeth Vigée-Librun (painter), Thomas Walter (architect)

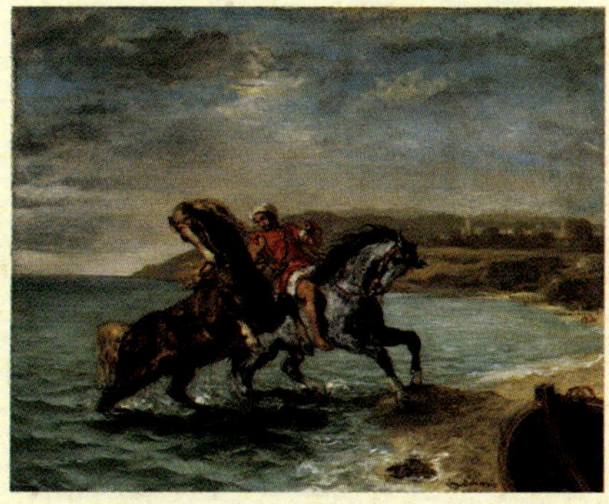

Eugène Delacroix, *Horses Coming Out of the Sea*, 1860.

## Romanticism 1815–1875

- Rejected the ordered style of Neoclassical art.
- To show emotion, artists applied color with wild, active brushstrokes.
- Themes included dramatic action, exotic settings, imaginary events, faraway places, or strong feelings.

**Artists:** Thomas Cole (painter), John Constable (painter), Eugène Delacroix (painter), Sophia Hayden (architect), H.H. Richardson (architect), François Rude (sculptor)

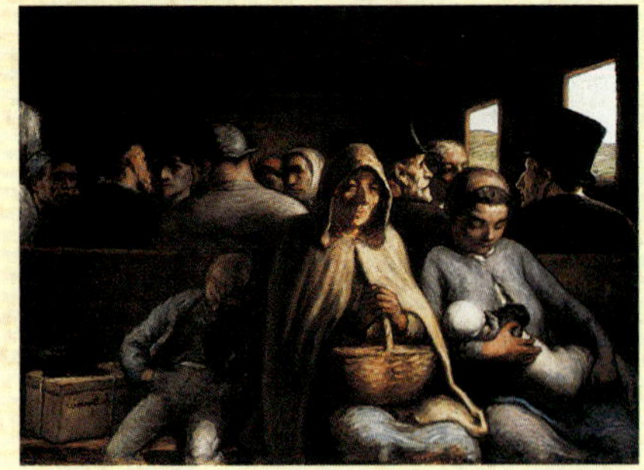

Honoré Daumier, *The Third Class Carriage,* ca. 1863–65.

## Realism 1850–

- Rejected Neoclassicism and Romantic styles.
- As subjects, artists chose scenes from real life—rural and city life, people at work, the poor, and political strife
- Realists believed their art recorded simple ways of life that were being destroyed by new technologies.
- Buildings' designs matched their functions.

**Artists:** Rosa Bonheur (painter/sculptor), Honoré Daumier (painter), Gustave Eiffel (architect), Jean-François Millet (painter), Edouard Manet (painter), Joseph Paxton (architect), John Singer Sargent (painter)

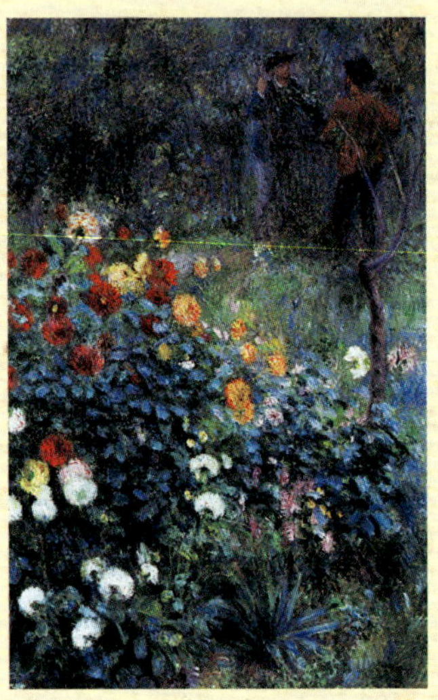

Pierre-Auguste Renoir, *The Garden in the Rue Cortot, Montmarte,* 1876.

## Impressionism 1875–

- Began in France; artists created an "impression," capturing a brief moment in time.
- Space and form are suggested by varying the intensity of light and color.
- Paintings are created using short, quick brushstrokes, which cause shapes to merge together.
- Small strokes of color make artworks shimmer and sparkle.

**Artists:** Daniel Burnham (architect), Mary Cassatt (painter), Edgar Degas (painter/sculptor), Claude Monet (painter), Berthe Morisot (painter), Auguste Rodin (sculptor), Georges Seurat (painter)

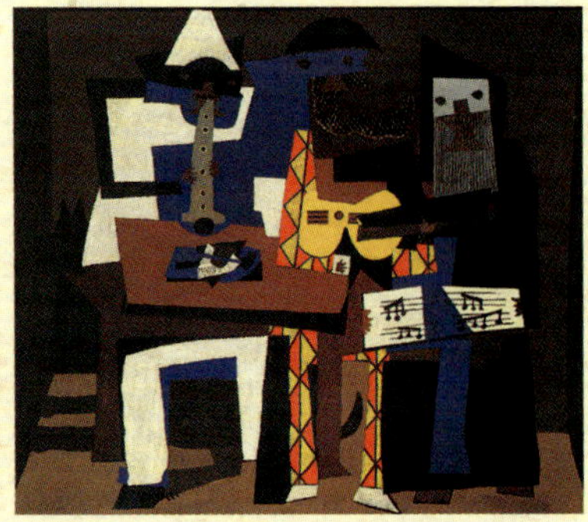

Pablo Picasso, *Three Musicians,* 1921.

## Cubism 1907–

- Based on an interest in showing multiple and partial views of objects on the flat surface of a page or canvas.
- Artworks have an abstract, often puzzle-like design with features broken into pieces.
- Another characteristic of this style is the use of hard-edged, geometric forms.

**Artists:** Georges Braque (painter), Sonia Terk Delaunay (painter), Jacques Lipchitz (sculptor), Georgia O'Keeffe (painter), Pablo Picasso (painter/sculptor)

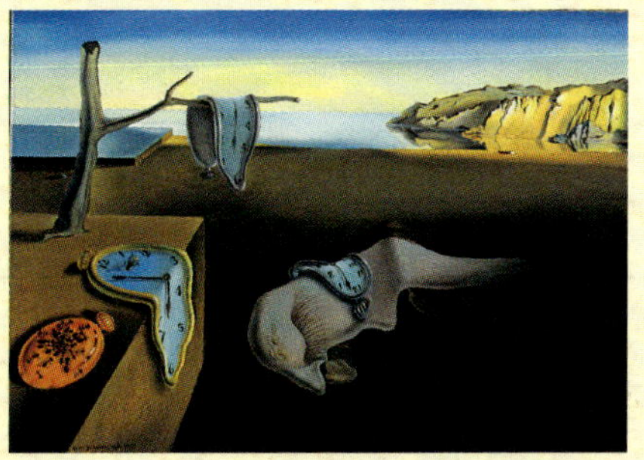

Salvador Dali, *The Persistence of Memory,* 1931.

## Surrealism 1924–

- Artists emphasized dream worlds and the subconscious.
- Unrelated objects are often shown realistically in an illogical or unnatural setting.
- Artworks often include visual surprises.

**Artists**: Marc Chagall, Salvador Dali, René Magritte, Joan Miró, Meret Oppenheim, Henri Rousseau, Kay Sage Tanguy, (painters)

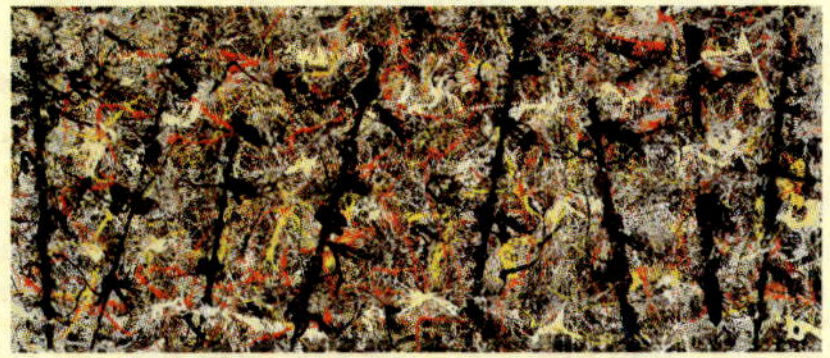

Jackson Pollack, *Blue Poles,* 1952.

## Abstract Expressionism 1945–

- Refers to large paintings that are meant to suggest feelings or ideas.
- Artworks are based on emotion and feeling, with little or no recognizable subject matter.
- Artists explore ways of painting. They drip, pour, or splash paint on the canvas.

**Artists:** Hans Hofmann, Jackson Pollack, Arshile Gorky, Hale Woodruff, Mark Tobey (painters); Louise Nevelson, Nancy Graves, David Smith (sculptors)

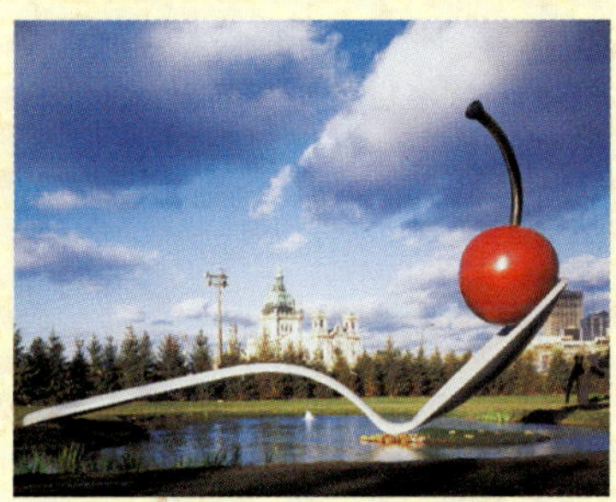

Claes Oldenburg and Coosje van Bruggen, *Spoonbridge and Cherry,* 1988.

## Pop Art 1950–

- Everyday objects are used as subject matter.
- Artists draw their ideas from popular and consumer culture: comic strips, hot dogs, movie stars, and so on.
- Artworks often show wit, satire, or humor.

**Artists:** Roy Lichtenstein, Jasper Johns, Andy Warhol, David Hockney (painters); Claes Oldenburg, George Segal, Duane Hanson (sculptors)

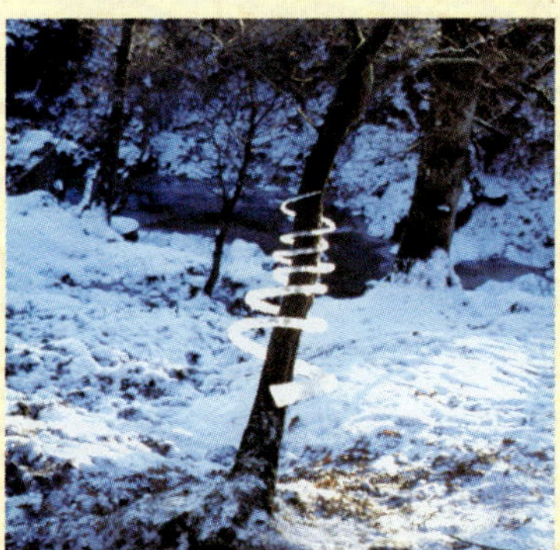

Andy Goldsworthy, *The coldest I have ever known in Britain,* 1995.

## Environmental Art/Earthworks 1960–

- Artworks draw attention to environmental issues.
- Movement celebrates the environment.
- Artists often use earth, wind, and water as sculptural media.
- Artworks are often impermanent.

**Artists:** Robert Smithson, Mary Miss, Christo/Jeanne-Claude, Andy Goldsworthy

# Techniques

The following basic art techniques can be used as a guide while drawing and painting.

## Contour Drawing

### Studio Background

A contour drawing is a drawing that describes the overall shape of an object or figure. It may include some interior details. Contour drawings are usually done slowly.

There are different kinds of contour drawings. In **blind contour drawing** you do not look at the paper while you are drawing.

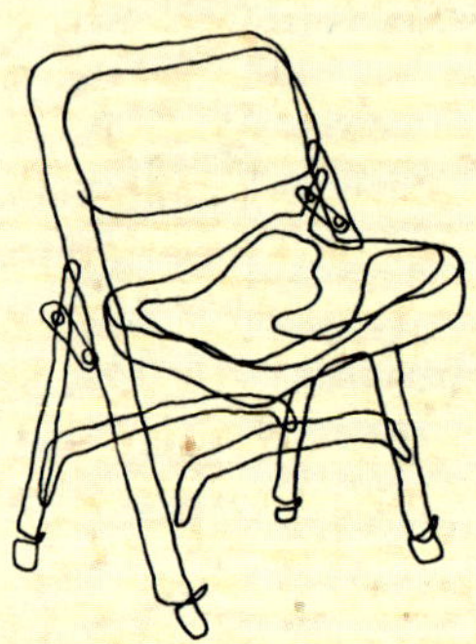

Blind contour drawing

In **modified contour drawing** you use the same technique as blind contour drawing, but you may pause at times to check the position of your drawing tool.

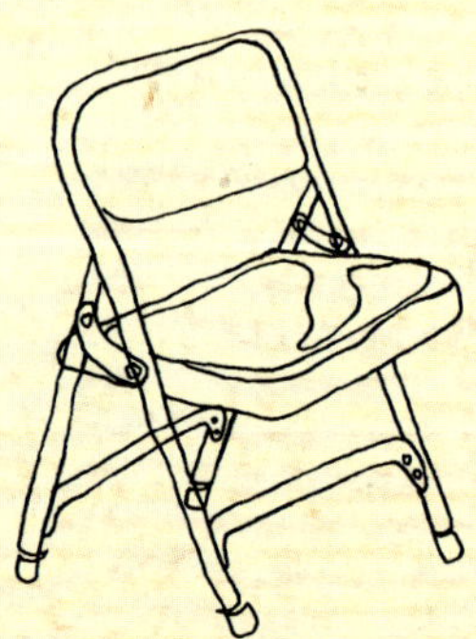

Modified contour drawing

### Making a Contour Drawing

- Look only at the object you are drawing, not at your paper.
- First practice drawing the object's outline without letting your drawing tool touch the paper.

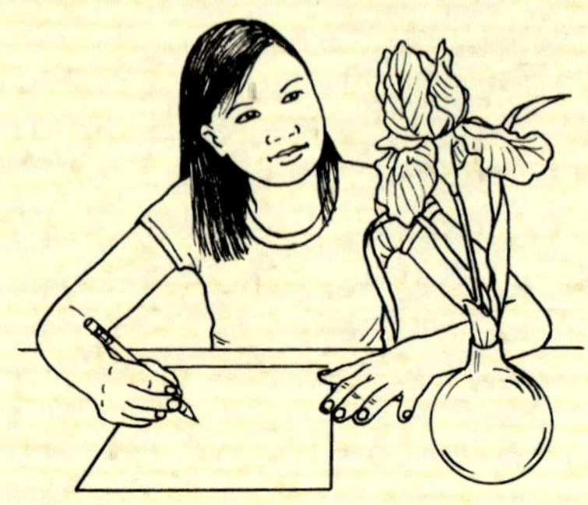

Look only at the object.

- Begin to draw, using a continuous line. Draw slowly.
- Follow the contours of the object, including its wrinkles and folds.
- Do not lift your pencil from the paper until you have finished.

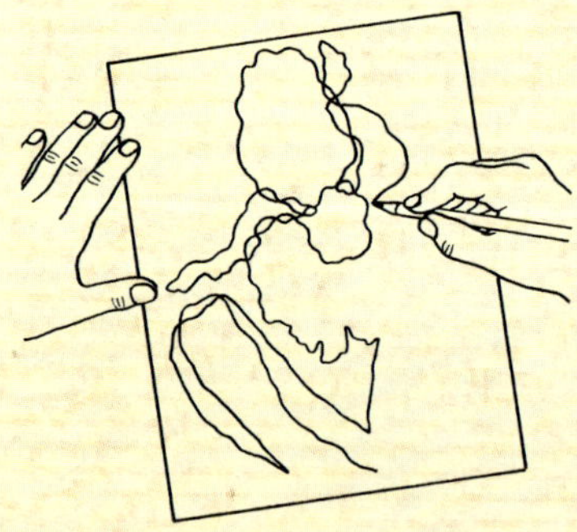

Don't lift your pencil from the paper until you are finished.

# Perspective

## Studio Background

Artists use an assortment of techniques to create **perspective**. These techniques include overlapping, shading and shadow, placement, size, and focus. Some artists invent ways to combine these techniques.

## Basic Perspective Techniques

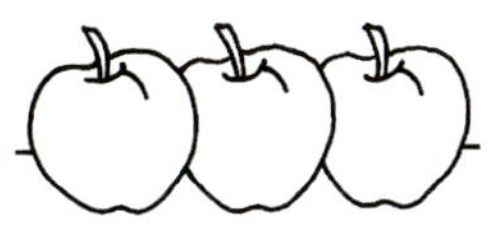

Overlapping

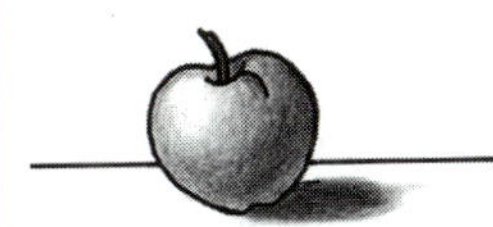

Shading and shadow

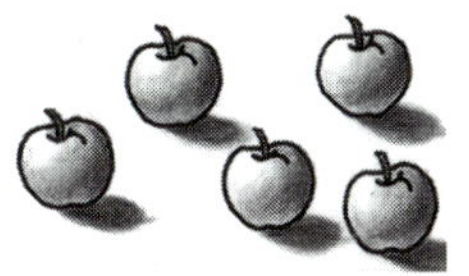

Placement: Objects near top seem more distant

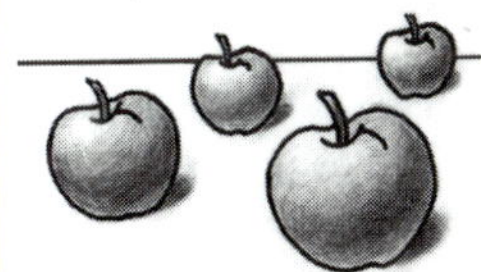

Size: Smaller objects seem more distant

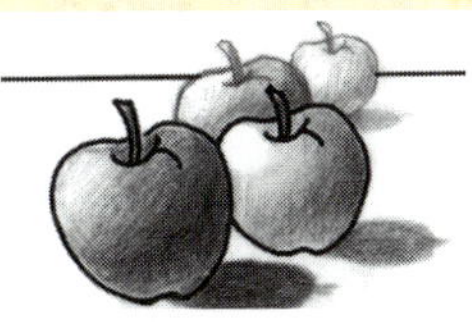

Focus: Sharp detail suggests nearness

## Using Linear Perspective

Linear perspective is a system of lines used to create the illusion of three-dimensional space.

### One-Point Perspective

- Use a yardstick or ruler to lightly draw a horizon line (HL) across the paper.
- Mark a vanishing point (VP) at the center of your horizon line. Add diagonal guides that recede to the vanishing point.

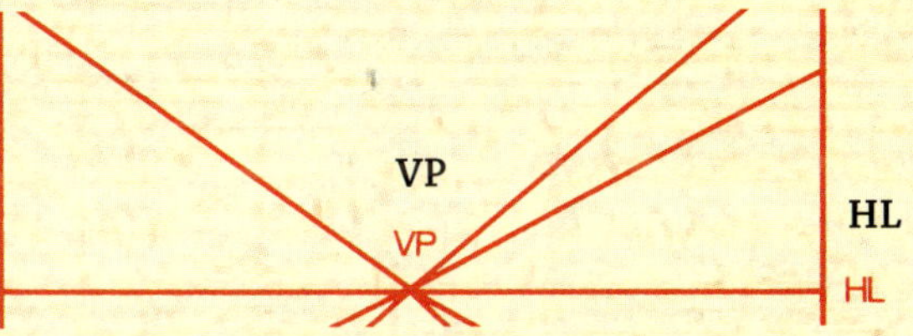


- Draw buildings, houses, or other box-like objects that recede as they approach the vanishing point.
- Vertical lines should be parallel to the side of the paper; horizontal lines should be parallel to the top and bottom of the paper.

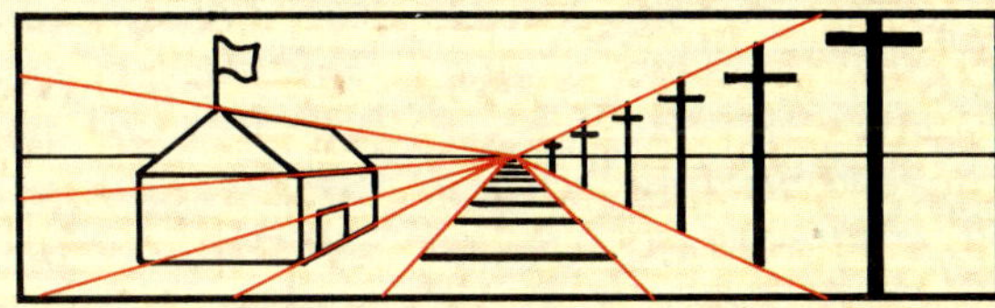

### Two-Point Perspective

- Begin your drawing with two vanishing points (VP) on the horizon about the same distance from the edges of the paper.

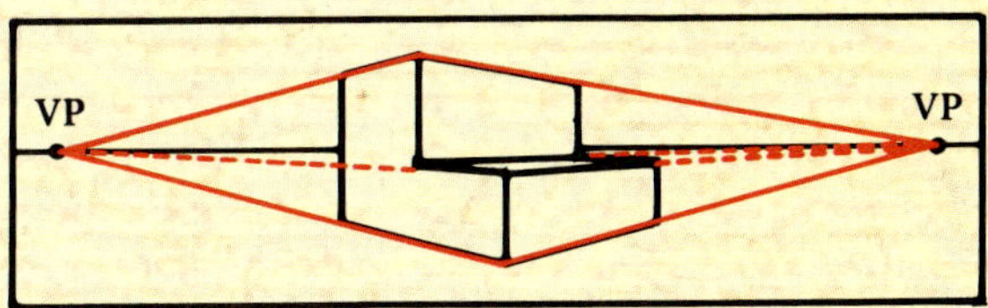

# Drawing with Chalk, Crayon, and Pen and Ink

## Studio Background

Before they draw, artists think about the medium they will use. Pencils, charcoal, pastels, and crayons are **dry media**. Inks, applied with a pen or brush, are **wet media**. The effects of drawing media can change depending on whether they are used on wet or dry paper. Once artists choose their medium, they experiment with it to find the techniques they like best.

## Drawing with Chalk and Crayons

- Colored chalk, or pastels, can be used on wet or dry paper.
- Practice using the tip of the chalk to make solid and dashed lines.

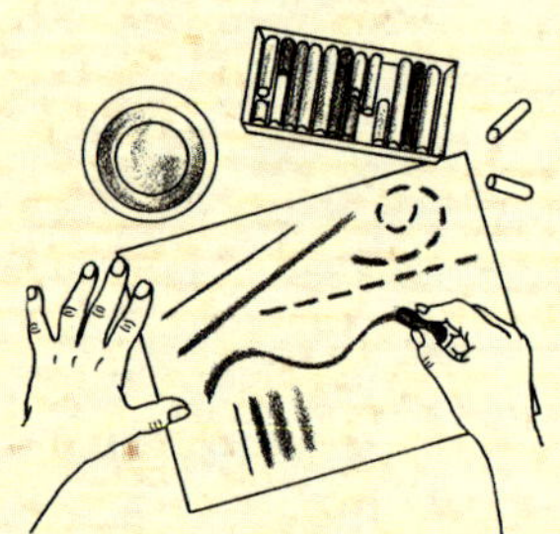

Practice making many kinds of lines.

- To make clean, sharp lines, dip the chalk into water or liquid starch.
- Use the side of the chalk to make wide lines.
- Press harder to make the line darker and more solid. Use less pressure for a lighter, less solid line.

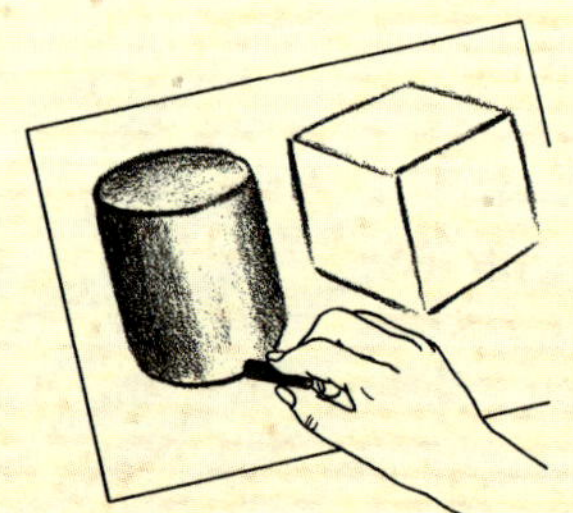

Press hard to make dark lines.

- To mix colors, apply one on top of the other. Use a tissue to blend the colors together.
- Use a kneaded eraser, or putty rubber, to add highlights or small corrections.

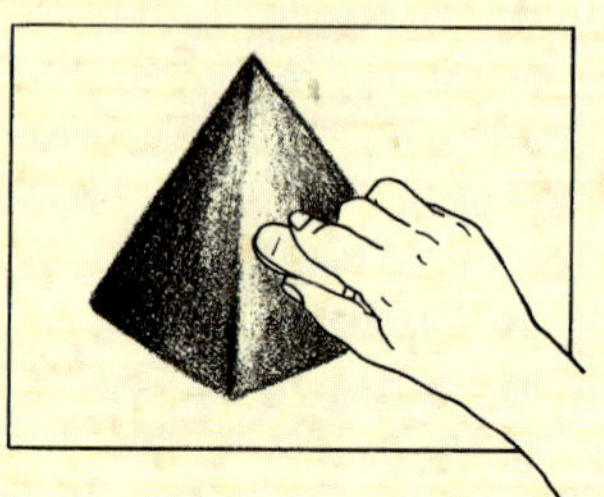

Add highlights with an eraser.

- Practice with crayons in the same way as chalk, but on dry paper only.

## Drawing with Pen and Ink

- Ink can be applied with a variety of tools—natural pens like quills, ballpoint pens, nibs, twigs, cotton swabs, or small sponges.

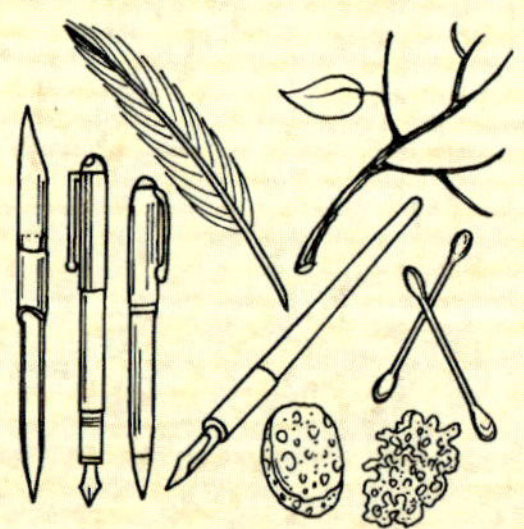

Try a variety of tools.

- Pen and ink can be used on wet or dry paper, but smooth paper gives a more pleasing result.
- Draw your design in pencil first.
- Go over the lines with a pen. Work from one side of the paper to the other so you do not smear the ink.

# Brushstrokes

## Studio Background

The type of brush and paint you choose, and the brushstrokes you use in your artwork, affect the way your paintings look. The brushstroke techniques below work well with tempera paints, watercolors and thinned acrylic paint.

## Making Brushstrokes

- Try different kinds of brushes. Feel how their bristles differ from one another. Certain brushes work best with specific types of paint.

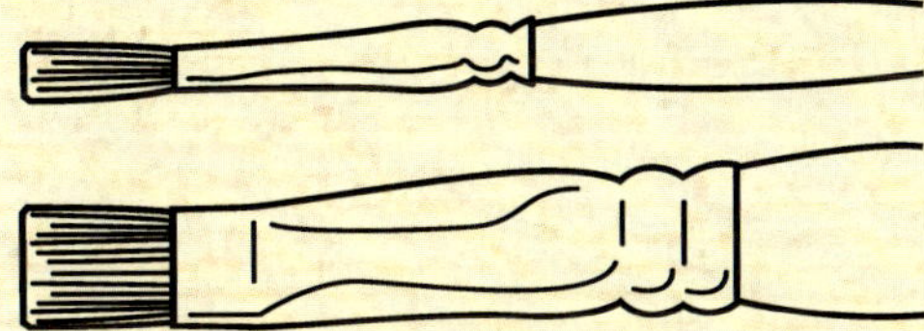

Stiff bristle brush for thick paint

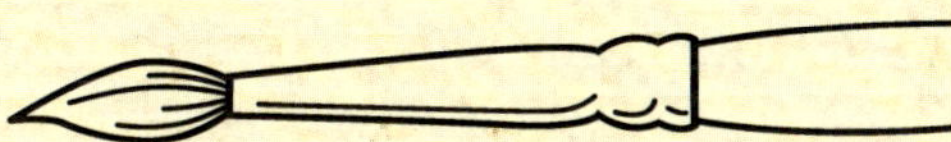

Soft hair-type brush for washes and details

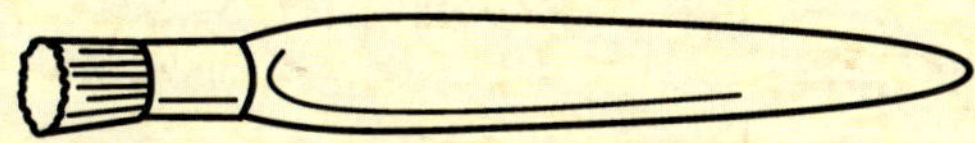

Stiff bristle brush for stencil work

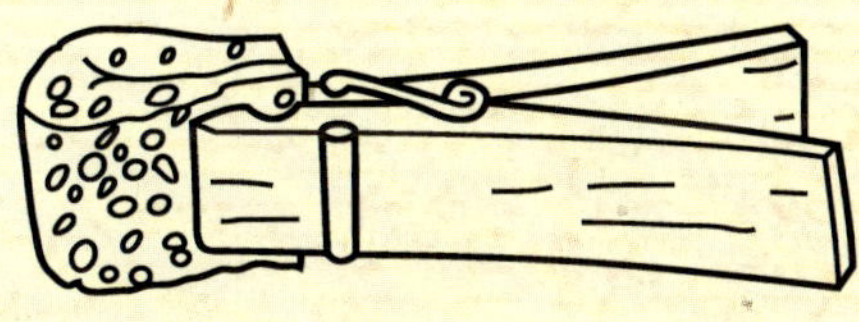

Simple sponge brush

- Choose a soft-hair brush for watercolors or thinner paints. Hold the brush with the bristles pointing down.

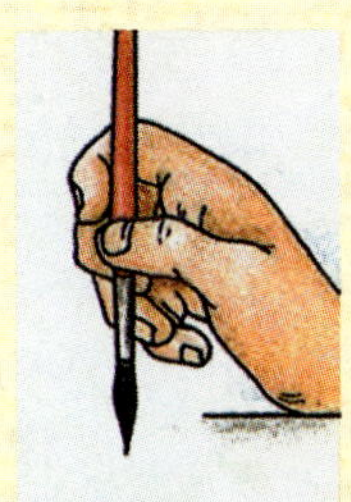

- Press hard for a wide brushstroke. Lift the brush up for a thin stroke. Use one stroke for a shape.

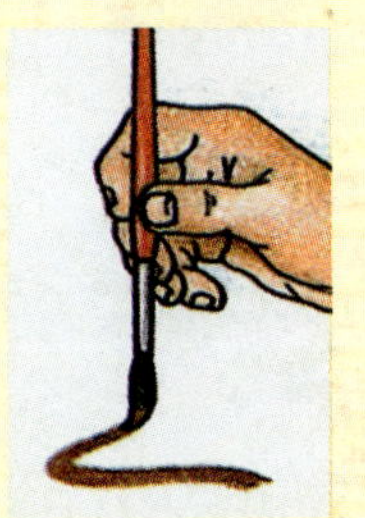
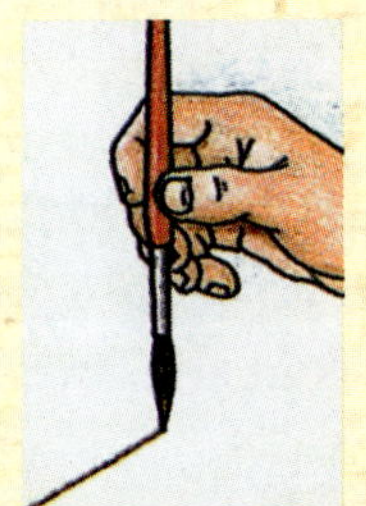
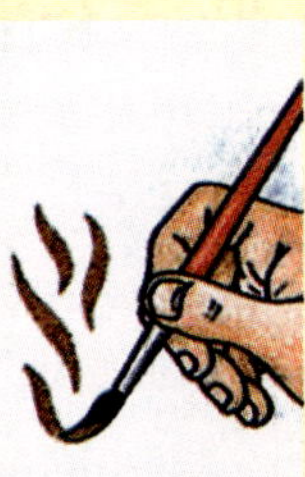

- Practice strokes using different amounts of water in your brush and different amounts of pressure. Observe how the lines change.
- Wash, wipe, and blot your brush before putting it away.

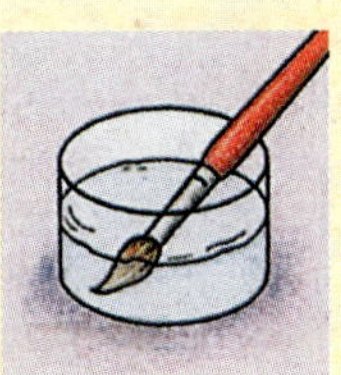
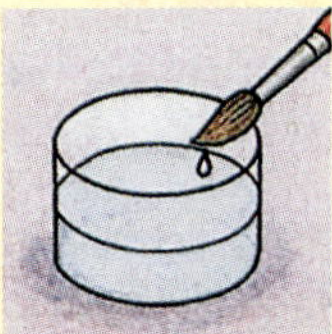

# Art Forms and Media

The materials an artist uses to create an artwork are called **media**. Watercolors, pen and ink, pencil, clay, and digital cameras are different kinds of media.

## Digital Photography

### Studio Background

Instead of using film, digital cameras capture images and movies by changing them into thousands of **pixels**, tiny squares or dots of color, and storing them in the camera's memory. A screen allows you to preview, plan, or review images, hundreds of which can be stored in the camera's memory. You can then either delete these images or download them to a computer to be saved or printed.

### Using a Digital Camera

Digital cameras are easy to use. Follow these steps to take pictures and store them in your computer.

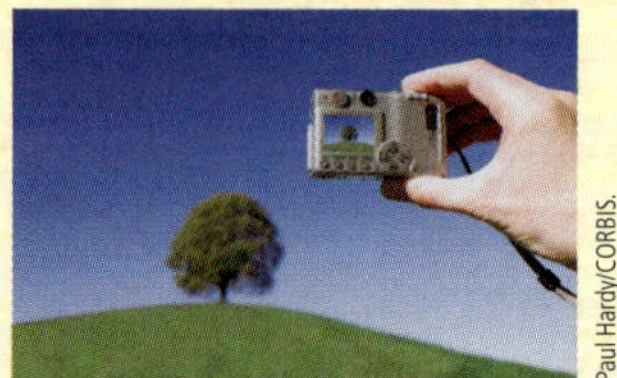
Paul Hardy/CORBIS.

**Taking a Picture**

- Turn the camera on.
- Your digital camera should be in automatic mode. In this mode, the camera selects all settings.
- To view your subject, look through the viewfinder. If your digital camera does not have one, look at the screen.
- Focus on your subject. Then press the shutter button to take the picture.
- Review the image when it appears on the screen. You may delete it or save it to your camera's memory.

**Saving Pictures to Your Computer**

- Make sure your camera's software is installed on your computer.
- Connect your camera to the computer using a USB cable.
- Turn the camera on.
- The camera's software should open on your computer.
- Select the images from the camera that you want downloaded to your computer.
- Save or print the images.

**Keep In Mind**

- Make sure your digital camera has enough power by inserting or replacing the batteries. Keep extra batteries on hand. Digital cameras require a lot of power, so you may need to change the batteries again during use.
- Check that your digital camera has enough memory to record your images and movies. You can either delete images stored in the memory to free up space, or you can use memory cards with higher capacities for image storage.
- Images can be stored in different file formats. The most common file format is JPEG, which does not take up much room in the camera's memory and is processed faster than other file formats. TIFF files use more space in the memory, but they are higher-quality images. RAW files are the least common format and are used mostly by professional photographers because they have editing options.

# Multimedia Presentations

## Studio Background

A **multimedia presentation** uses a variety of media—text, video, slides, photographs, art, music, and charts—to communicate information about a subject. Presentation software allows you to combine these media to deliver a successful and effective multimedia presentation.

## Making a Multimedia Presentation

### Gather Your Media

- First, decide what you want to present. If you plan to present your portfolio, gather your artworks. If you plan to present a topic, such as an artist or an art movement, research and record information on that topic.
- Once you know what you will present, think about the kinds of media that you will include. Choose specific artworks from your portfolio. Search your local library or the Internet for audio and video clips, music, or art.

### Prepare Your Media

- Scan your artworks so that you can view them on your computer. Save all other media files you might have to your computer.
- Presentation software uses *slides*—individual screens that can contain images, text, sound or animation files—to show information. Use slides to organize your media and information.

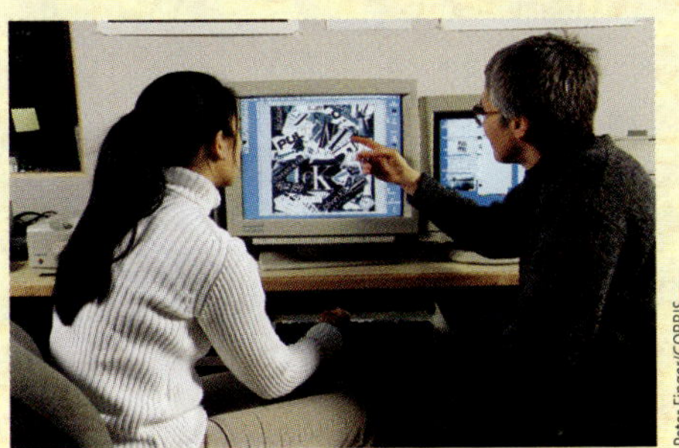

Peter Finger/CORBIS.

### Prepare Your Presentation

- Consider *slide transitions*, the movement of one slide to the next. You can choose transitions in which your slides dissolve into each other, push each other off the screen, or open up like blinds. Using many different transitions can be distracting for your audience, so use only one or two kinds of transition throughout your presentation.
- Consider the layout of your slide. Make sure it is readable and visually pleasing. Put the title at the top and important information below it. To keep all your slide layouts consistent, use a *design template*, a model into which you insert your text and files.

### Keep In Mind

- The amount of time a slide appears on the screen is very important. Do not change the slides quickly, because your viewers will not get a chance to read or look closely at your artwork or information. Do not keep your slides up for too long, or your viewers may lose interest.
- Electronic media require additional equipment such as projectors that you or your school must provide. If you plan to use your school's equipment, alert your teacher in advance so the equipment will be available on the day of your presentation.

# Watercolors

## Studio Background

Watercolor paints are transparent, and come in tubes or pans. Start with just a few basic colors, and then mix them to create a wider range.

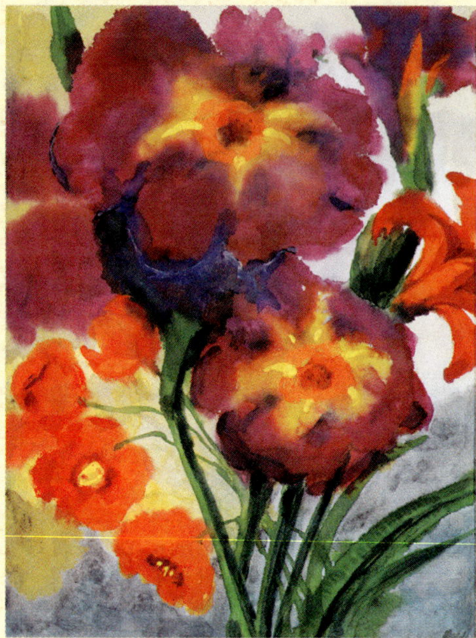

Notice how you can see one color through another in this watercolor painting.

Emile Nolde, *Summer Flowers*, 1930.

## Using Watercolors

- To create **sharp edges**, apply wet paint to dry paper.
- To create **soft edges**, apply wet paint to damp paper.
- Paint light colors first, darkest colors last.
- To create a **light value** of a hue, dilute the paint with plenty of water.
- To create a **darker value**, use more pigment and less water.

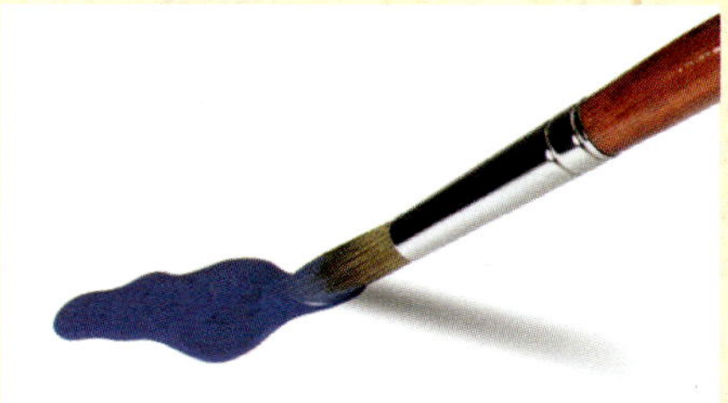

A dark value of blue

- A wash is a thin layer of paint spread over a large area.

A green wash

- You can let a wash dry and then paint over it.
- You can paint over a wash before it has dried.
- To make a white area, do not apply paint. Let the white paper show through.

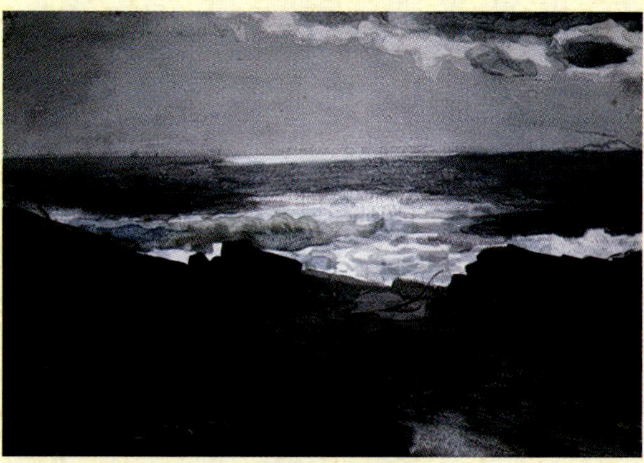

This artist let the white paper show in some areas to create highlights.

Winslow Homer, *Sunshine and Shadow, Prout's Neck*, 1984.

# Tempera Paints

## Studio Background

Tempera paints come in both liquid and powder form and in brilliant hues. They dry quickly, developing a dull, chalky appearance when dry. They can be layered to produce intense color.

## Using Tempera Paints

- Use a stiff bristle brush and short, swift brushstrokes to paint large areas of color first.

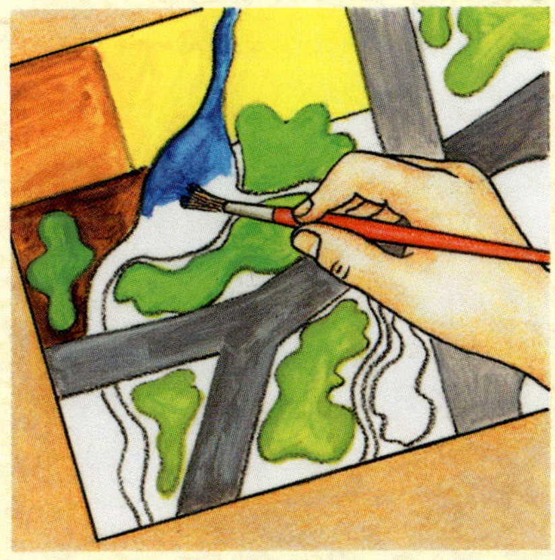

Paint large areas first.

- Allow area to dry before adding small details. Brushing large areas of wet paint over dry paint will cause the paint to run.

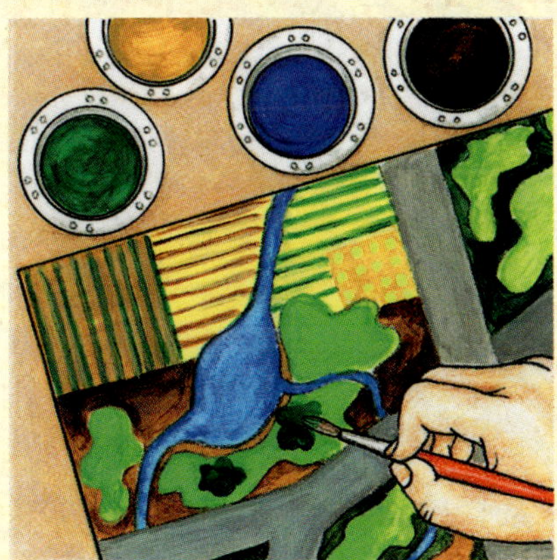

Add small details after the paint dries.

- To mix a **tint**, add small dots of colored paint to white paint.

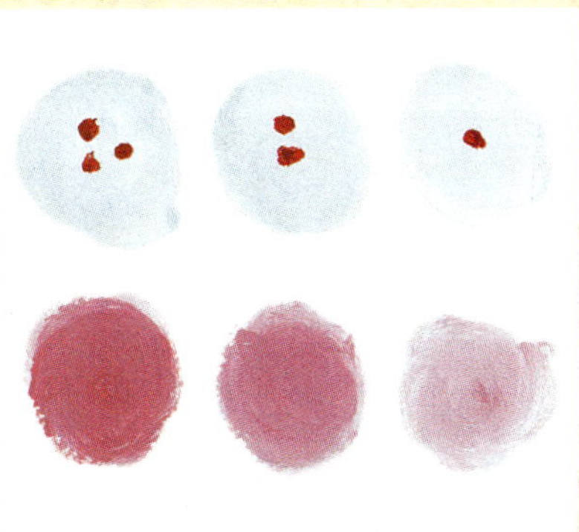

- To mix a **shade**, add small amounts of black to a color.

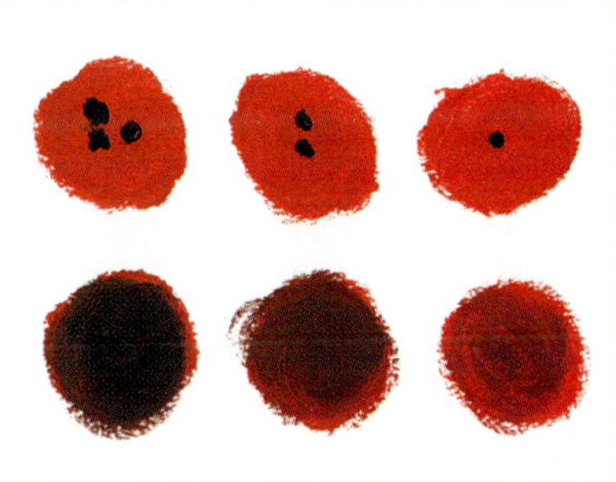

- To mix a new color, add small amounts of a different color to the original color.
- When you change colors, wash, wipe, and blot the brush. Do not dip the brush directly into the bottle.

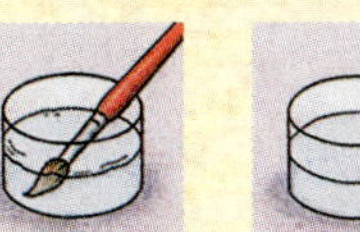
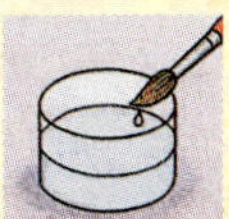
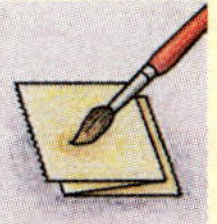

- Once a bottle is opened, use it as quickly as possible. Keep bottles tightly closed. Do not return unused paint to the bottles.

# Oil Pastels

## Studio Background

Oil pastels are pigments mixed with oil and wax. Unlike chalk pastels, they do not make dust when you use them, but they never dry completely. This means your works will not crack, but they will smudge unless you frame them and cover them with glass or plastic.

## Using Oil Pastels

- Use oil pastels to sketch the main shapes and colors.
- Press heavily for a brilliant-colored line. Press lightly to create a fuzzy line.

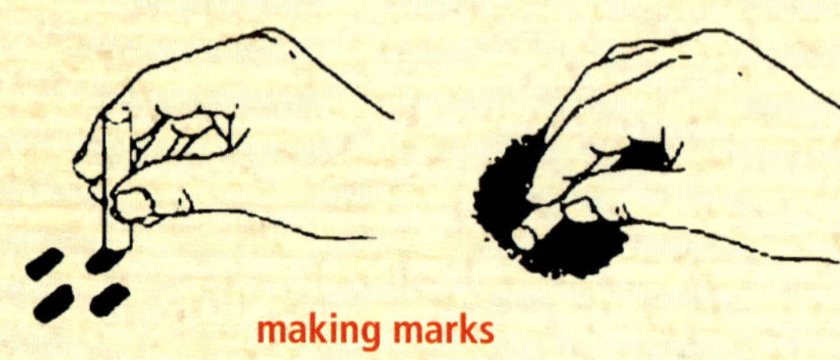

making marks

- Blend colors together using your fingers, a tissue, or cotton swab.

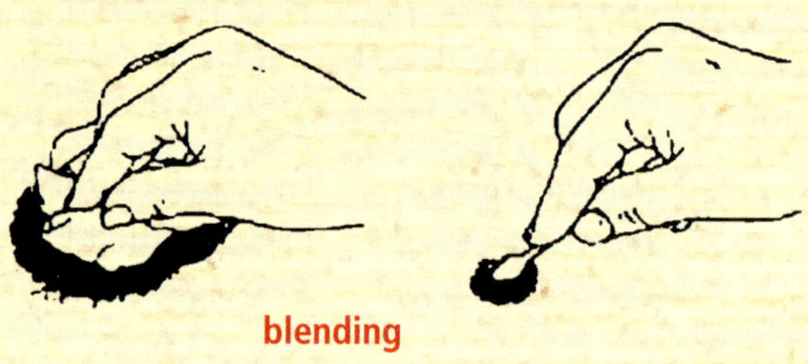

blending

- With your fingers or blending tool, add small swirls or strokes that mimic the details of your subject.
- Change colors of details by blending a new color with the base pastel. Use white or black to make a tint or shade of a color.

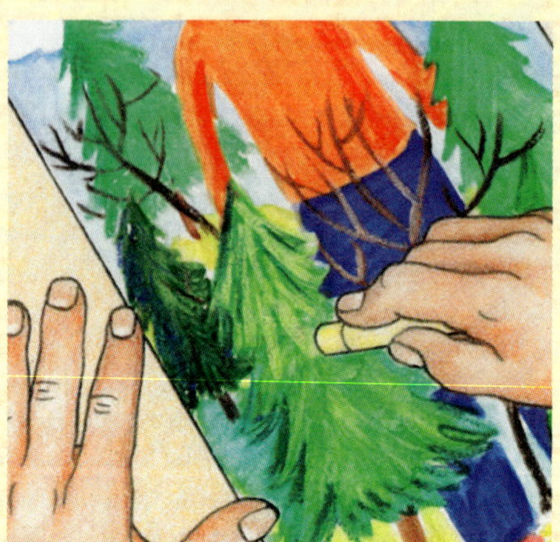

Add one color over another.

- If you are using colored paper or trying a new technique, apply a layer of white first. Scrape away the result if you do not like it, and begin again.

# Monoprinting

## Studio Background

A monoprint is an edition of only one print. In other forms of printmaking, you can make many prints from the same plate. When you create a monoprint, you can prepare the plate in several ways, but usually the preparations do not survive after the first print.

## Making a Monoprint

### Method 1

- Roll out a thin, even layer of ink on a smooth, nonabsorbent surface.

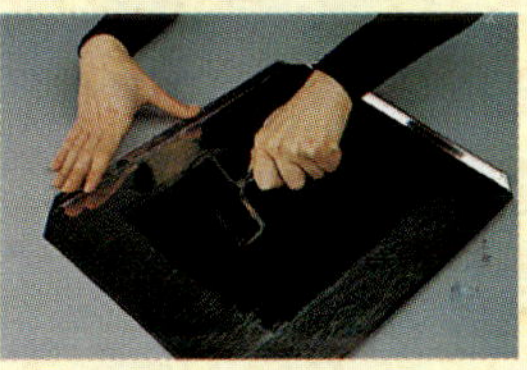

- Draw directly into the ink with a tool such as a toothpick, pencil eraser, cotton swab, facial tissue, or old comb.

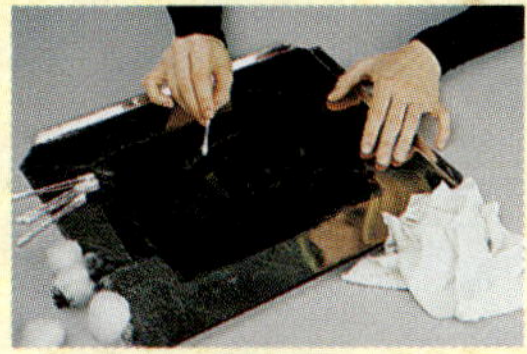

- Place a sheet of paper over the design, and rub it evenly but lightly with your hand.
- Pull the print by lifting the paper away from the surface.

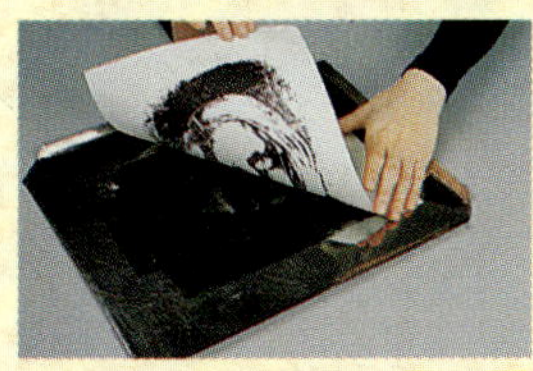

### Method 2

- Working quickly, paint an image with tempera paint on a smooth, nonabsorbent surface.

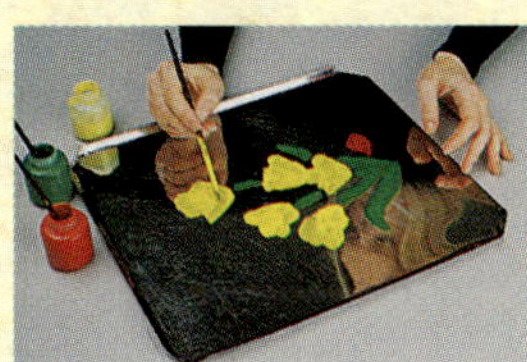

- Place a sheet of paper over the painted image, and rub it evenly but lightly with your hand.

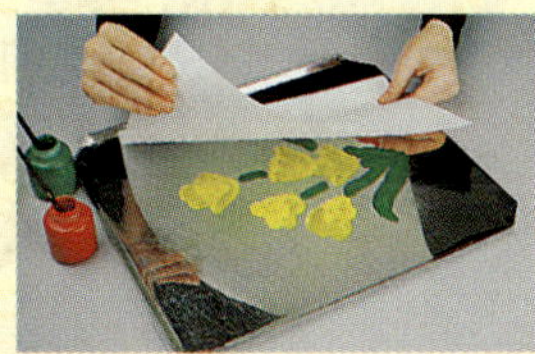

- Pull the print by lifting the paper away from the surface.

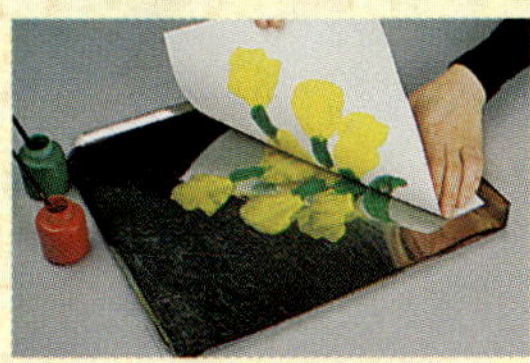

### Method 3

- Roll out a thin, even layer of ink on a smooth, nonabsorbent surface. Place a sheet of paper over the inked surface, but do not rub it.

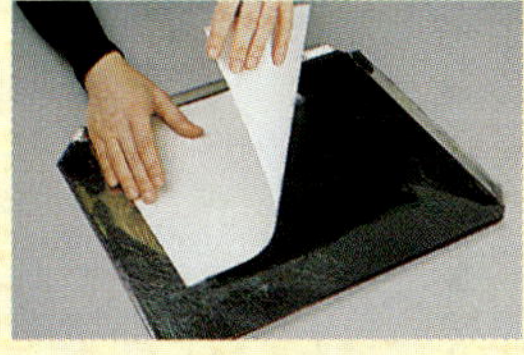

- Using a pencil, draw an image on the paper.

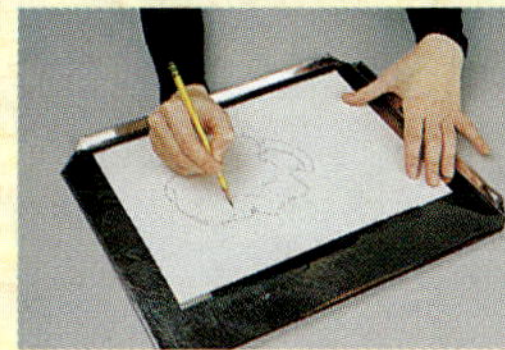

- Pull the print by lifting the paper away from the surface.

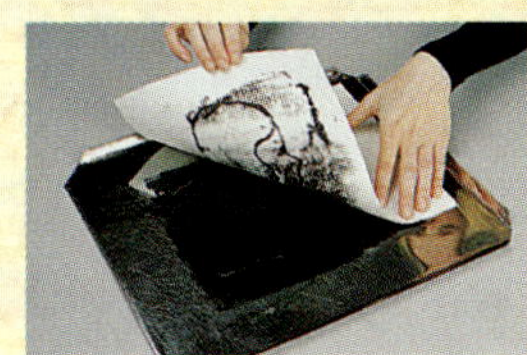

# Relief Printmaking

## Studio Background

Relief printmaking is one of several basic printmaking processes. A **relief print** is made from a design that is raised from a flat background, usually a wood or linoleum block. Ink is applied to the raised surfaces and then paper or another material is pressed down on the print to leave an image. Printmakers can make many identical prints using this method.

## Making a Relief Print

- Create a design on paper.
- Place your design and carbon paper on top of a wood or linoleum block. Alternatively, you can use a dark pencil to black the back of your design.
- Trace over your design to transfer the image to the printing block.

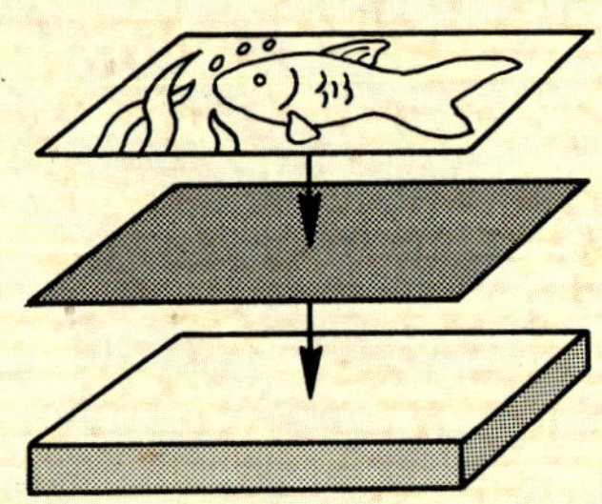

- Use wood-carving or linoleum gouges to carve out areas of your design. These areas will not print.
- Be sure to cut away from your fingers.

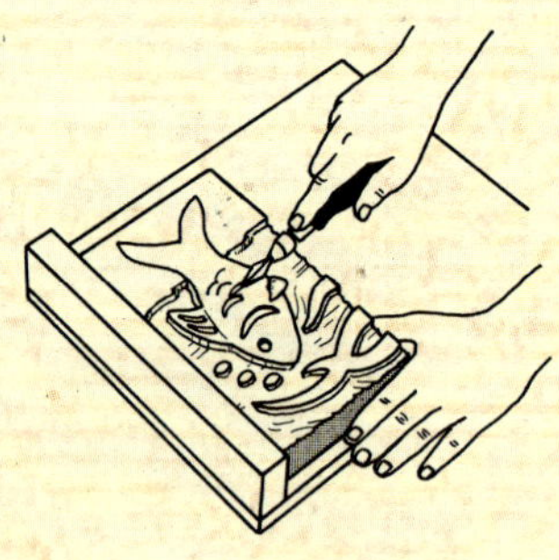

- To keep your block firmly in place, secure it with a bench hook.
- Roll printing ink on a flat surface until it is tacky.
- Roll ink on the printing block surface.
- Place a sheet of paper over your inked block.

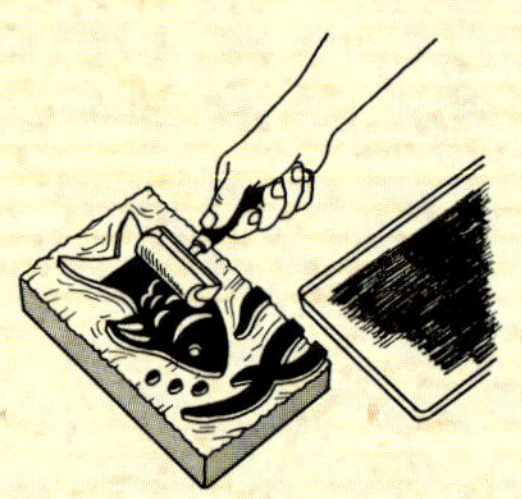

- Rub the back of the paper gently and evenly to transfer ink to the paper.
- Carefully pull the printed paper away.

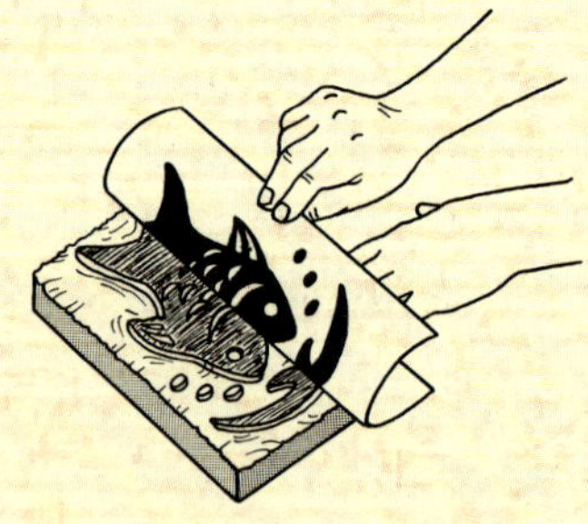

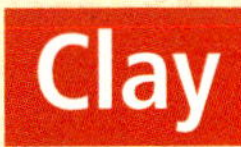

# Clay

## Studio Background

Clay is earth mixed with oil or water. Oil-based clay is reusable, so it is good to use for planning your artwork or to make molds. Water-based clays harden and your artwork will become permanent when you fire it in a kiln.

## Getting Ready to Use Clay

- Protect your desk or work area with a plastic mat or canvas.
- Prepare a *slip*, or liquid clay, to join pieces of clay together. Slip is a creamy mixture of water, clay, and a few drops of vinegar.
- Keep your fingers moist when working with clay. Dip your fingers into water and then spread the water over your palms with your fingers.
- Press or knead the air bubbles out of your clay.

## Making a Clay Figure

- Create a five-point star with a ball of clay by pulling out a point for the head, each arm, and each leg.

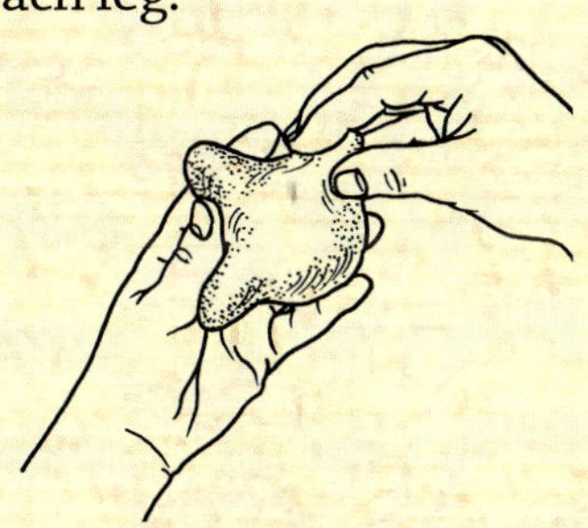

- To shape, pinch and pull the points. Think about the pose of your figure. Twist or bend the shape as needed.

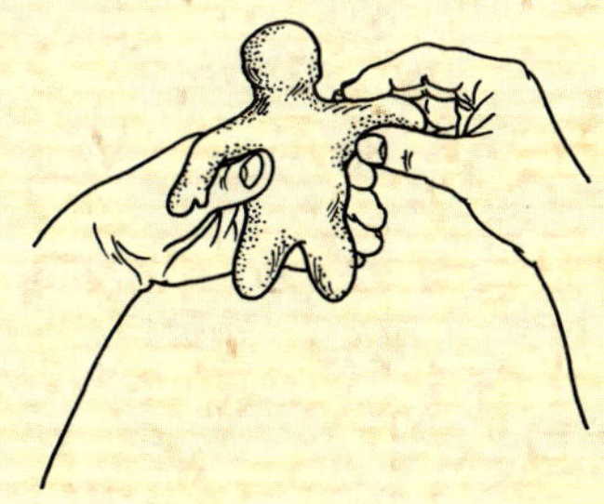

- Add details, such as facial features, hair, and clothing patterns. Press tiny coils or bits of clay into the figure, or press textures onto the surfaces.

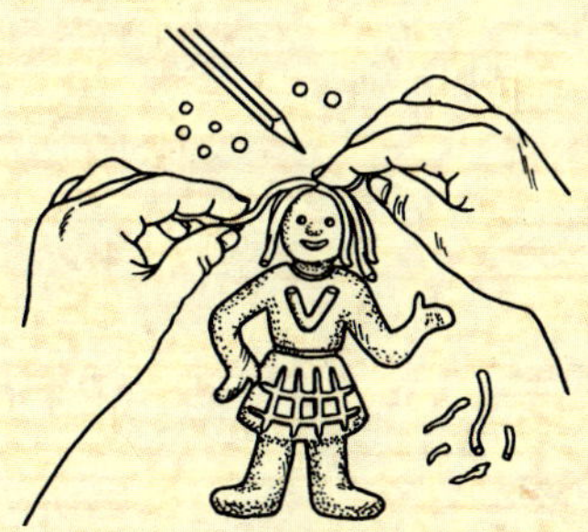

## Making a Pinch Pot

- Press your thumb into a ball of clay.
- Slowly turn the pot as you pinch the clay between your thumb and fingers.

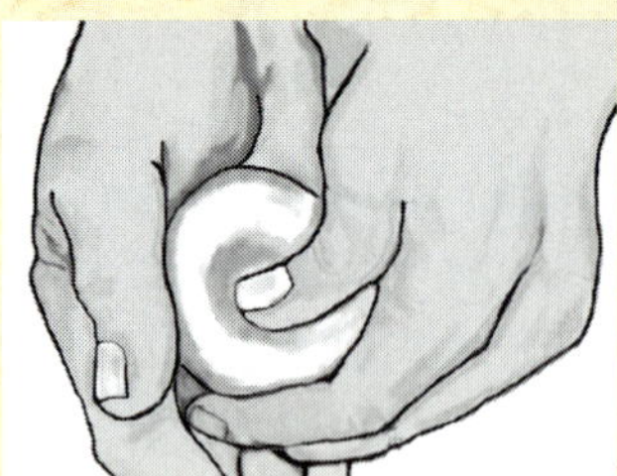

- Continue turning and pinching the pot until the walls are an even thickness all around. Smooth the inside and outside of the pot with a scraper.

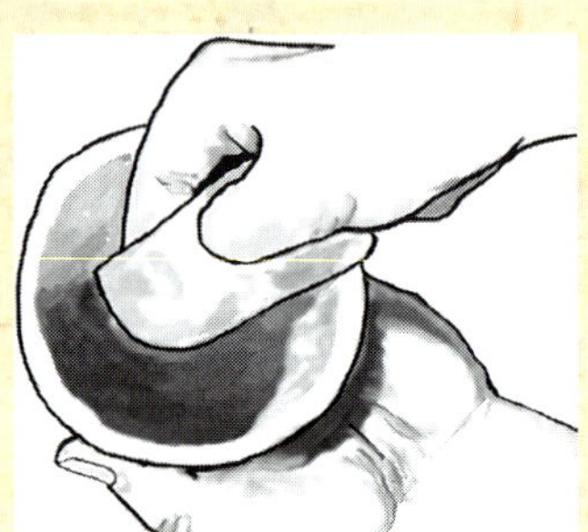

## Making Clay Coils

- Roll clay coils to about the thickness of your thumb.

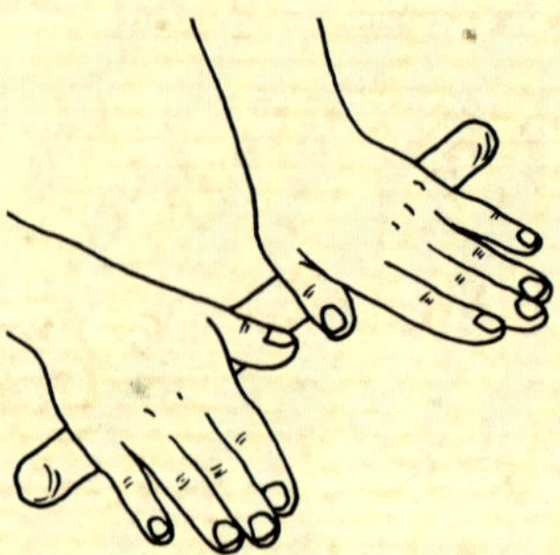

- Form a flat base. Score the edge with a plastic fork. Add slip.

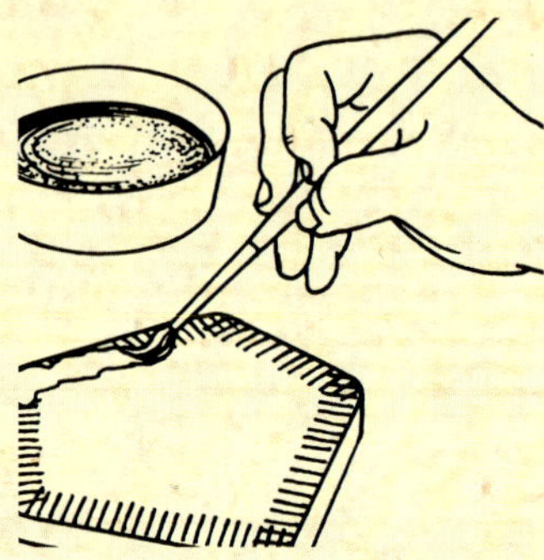

- Bend and press coil to base. Add more coils. Score each new layer and add slip.

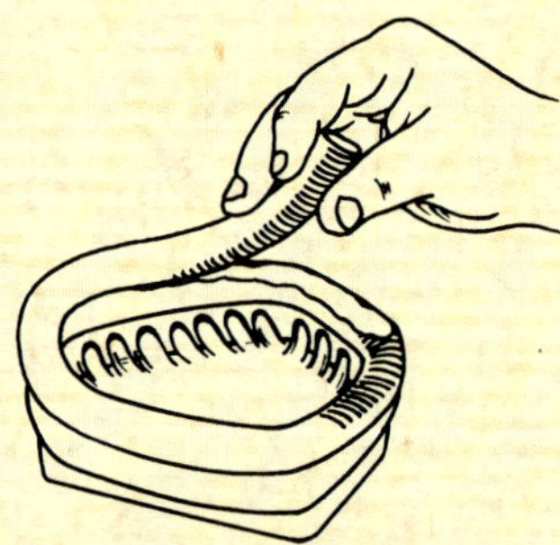

- Smooth coils together with your fingers or a clay tool.

## Making a Slab Form

- With a rolling pin, roll clay flat between two sticks of the same thickness.

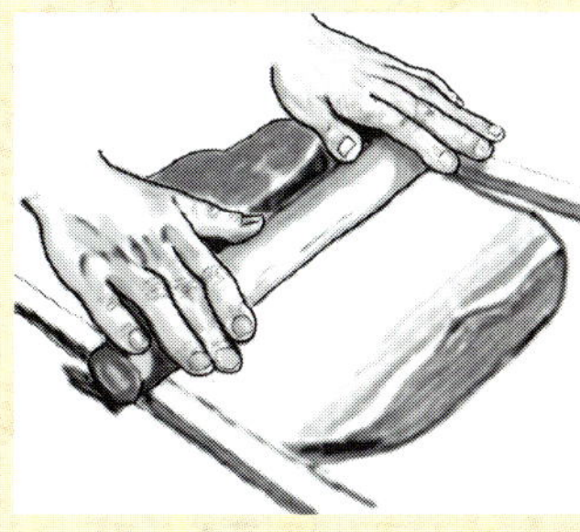

- Cut the slab into shapes that can be joined into a container. Use a plastic fork to score the edges.

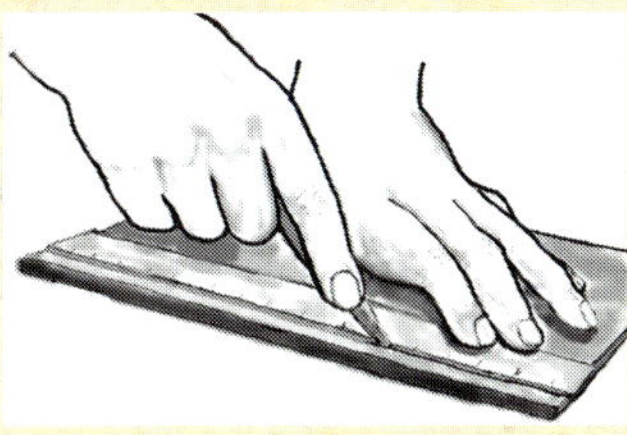

- Use your fingers to apply slip to the edges and join the shapes. Reinforce the inside of the joints with coils.

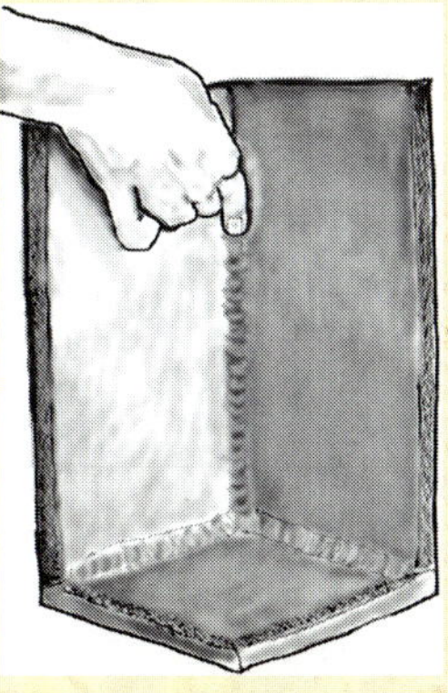

- Pinch the outside edges together and smooth.

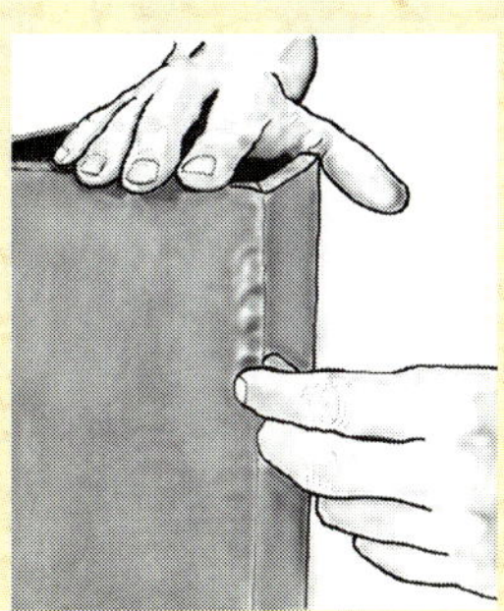

## Making a Clay Object With a Press Mold

- Find an appealing form: seashell, plastic bowl, cooking utensil, and so on.
- Roll out a thin, clay slab on a piece of canvas.
- Grasping the edges of the canvas, pick up the slab and invert the clay over the mold.

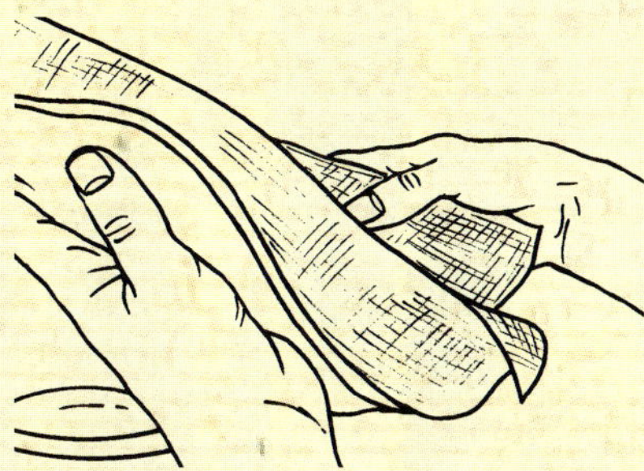

- Using your fingers, gently press the clay into the mold.

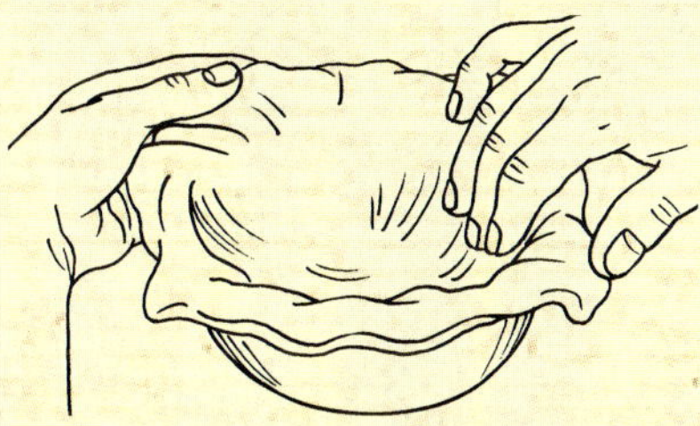

- Smooth surface with a rib tool, and let stiffen till leather-hard.

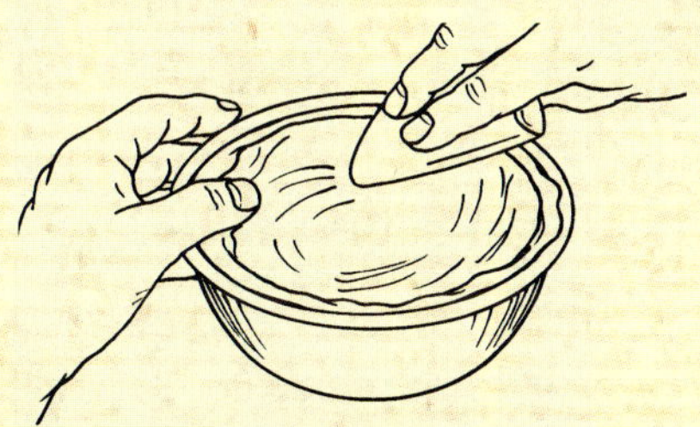

- Turn mold upside down and ease clay out. If clay sticks, let it dry some more.
- Decorate your clay piece.

# Papier-Mâché

## Studio Background

Papier-mâché comes from French words meaning "chewed paper." This lightweight sculpture material is made from a soupy mixture of wheat paste and paper. The paste-soaked paper is generally applied over an armature, or support. Then the sculpture becomes hard when it dries. When dry, hardened papier-mâché can be painted to be realistic or fantastic.

## Using Papier-Mâché

- Begin with an armature , or support, made of wire, folded paper or foil, or recycled objects.

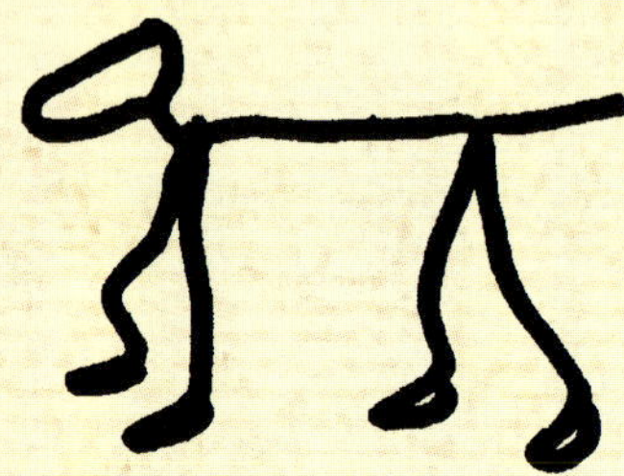

- Add paper with tape to fill out your sculpture's form.

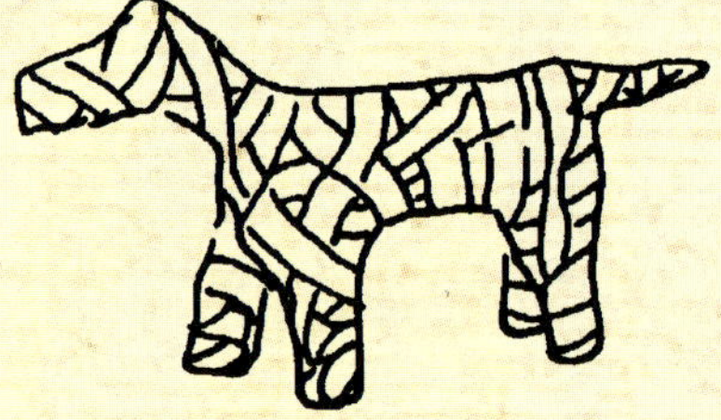

- Tear newspaper or paper towels into strips at least 1" wide.
- Dip the strips into papier-mâché paste. Remove extra paste from the strips with your fingers.

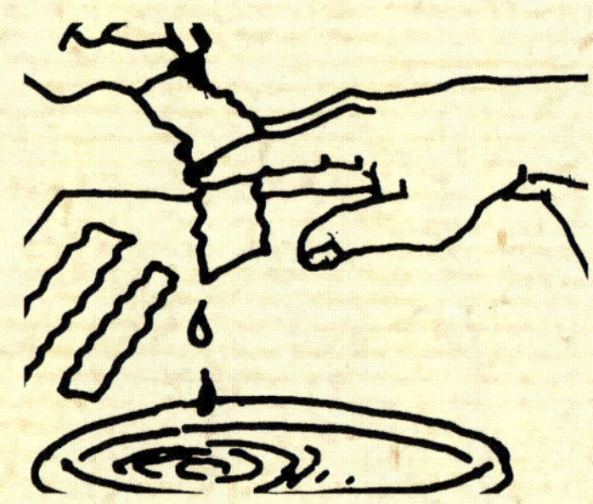

- Place the strips in layers over the support. Use wide strips for large shapes, and thinner strips for smaller shapes. Apply at least two layers.

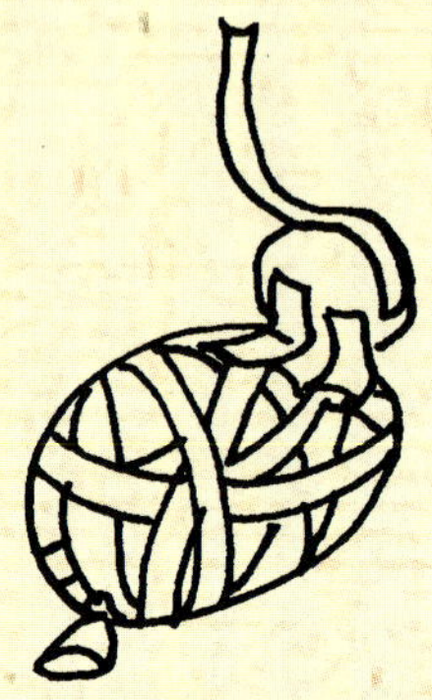

- Use paint and other materials to decorate your dried sculpture.

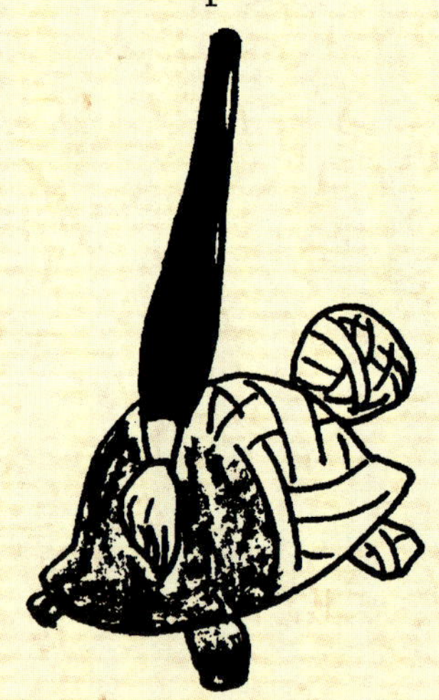

# Relief Sculpture

## Studio Background

A relief sculpture projects from a background surface. It is not freestanding. Depending on how far the sculpture projects from its background, it can be either *low relief* or *high relief*.

## Making Relief Sculptures

Use oil-based or water-based clay to form a slab. Use any of the following techniques to create relief and texture in your sculpture.

- Use clay tools to carve away areas of the clay slab.

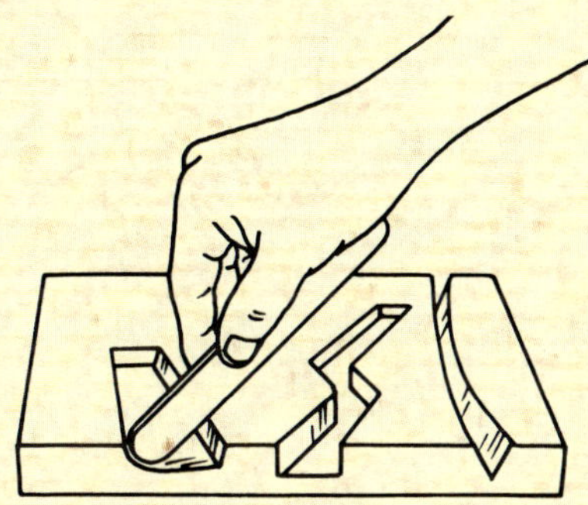

- Press and pull clay to mold lower and higher areas.

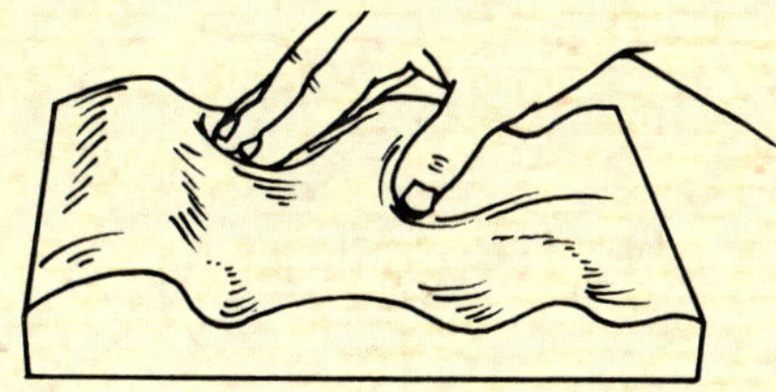

- Press textured objects (seashells, spools, rope, leaves, etc.) into the clay slab.

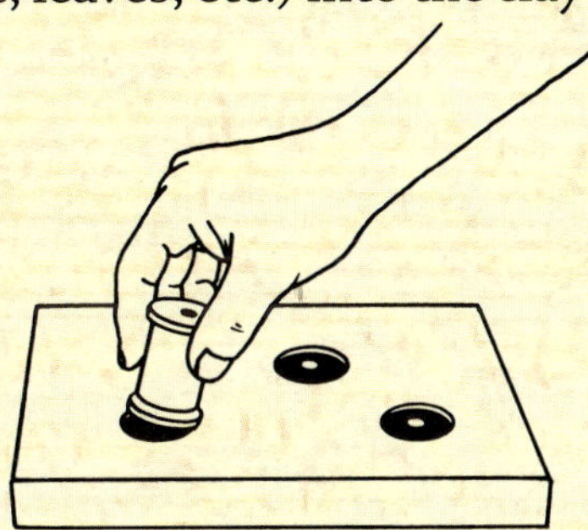

- Attach small coils and clay balls, or scratch lines into the surface to create a variety of textures.

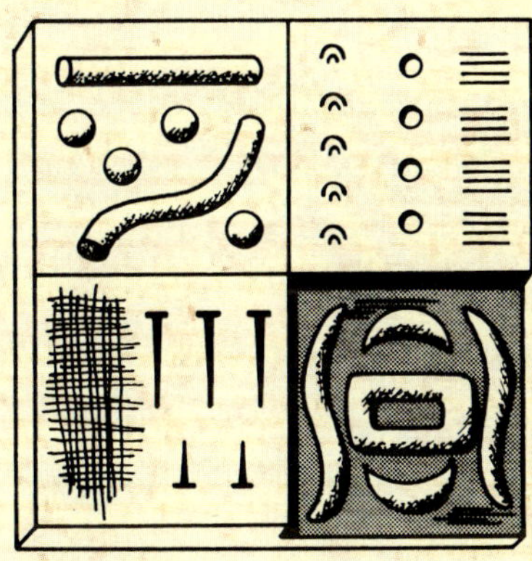

# Paper Sculpture

## Studio Background

Paper has many purposes in art. Artists draw on paper, of course, but they also use it to create sculptures. The many colors and varieties of paper, as well as paper's ability to be bent, torn, and shaped into forms, make it an exciting medium.

## Paper Sculpture Techniques

Gather a variety of paper samples—heavy or light, smooth or rough—and experiment with the techniques shown here. The forms you make can be used to create paper sculptures, or can be added to papier-mâché or other sculptural forms.

**1.** Make a cut partway across circle; overlap and glue to form a cone.

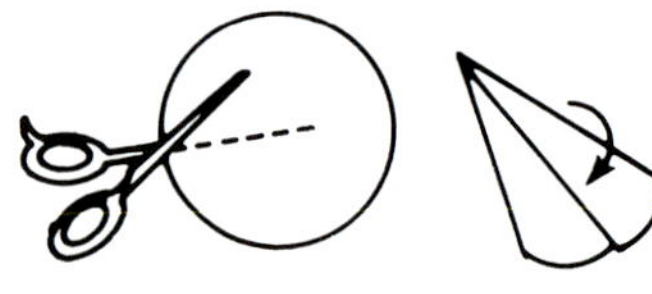

**2.** Cut tabs at bottom of cone and glue to surface to make it stand or project.

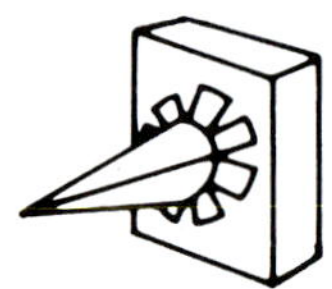

**3.** Accordion fold, or make folds progressively smaller.

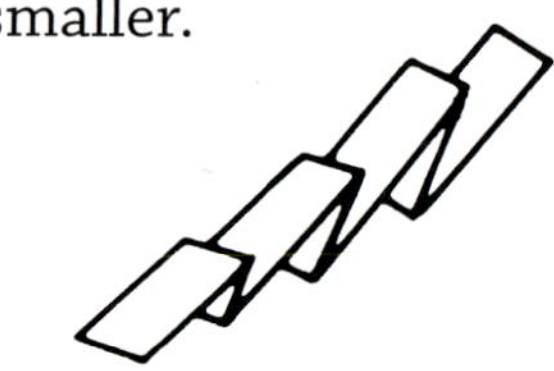

**4.** Cut triangular or half-circular notches in paper; bend cut pieces upward.

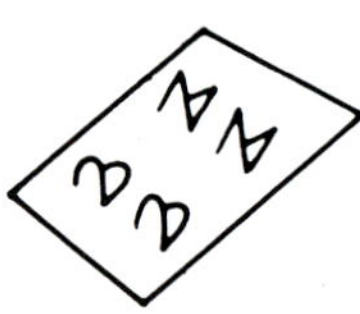

**5.** Make slots in paper or light cardboard; join pieces by slotting together.

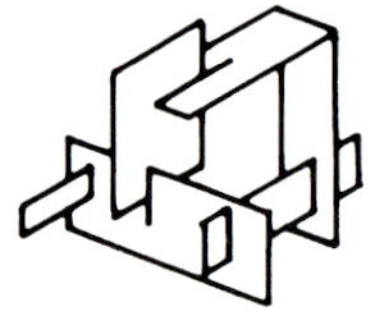

**6.** Join paper loops by gluing.

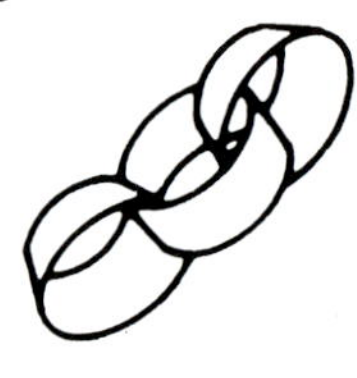

**7.** Slide scissors blade along strips to form curls.

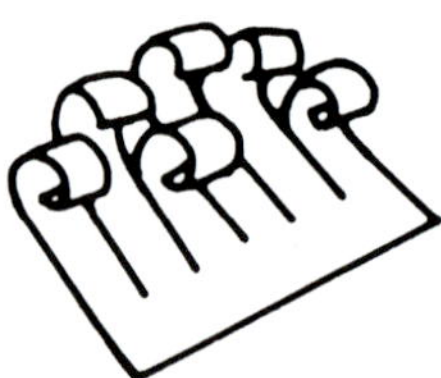

**8.** Roll paper around pencil to form large curls.

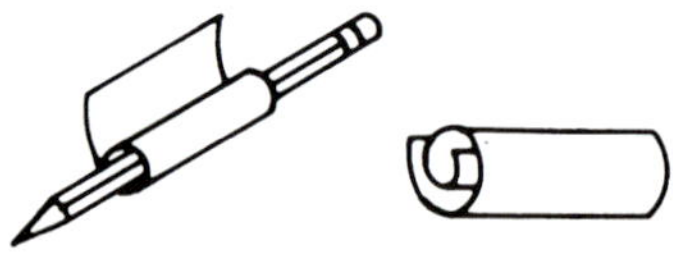

**9.** Cut crescent shapes; score between points; bend to make forms.

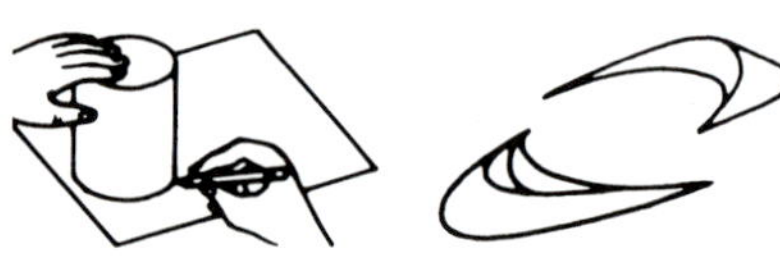

# Basic Skills

Whether drawing, painting, making a collage, or sculpting, there are some basic skills that every artist should learn.

## Brush Cleaning

Regular and proper brush cleaning is key to ensuring that your brushes last a long time.

- Immediately clean your brush when you change a color or finish a painting. If the brush dries before cleaning, the paint will be difficult to remove and may stain the bristles.
- Most brushes can be cleaned with warm water.
- Try to use most of the paint on the brush before cleaning. Then, wash the brush, wipe excess water on the side of the container, and dry the brush.

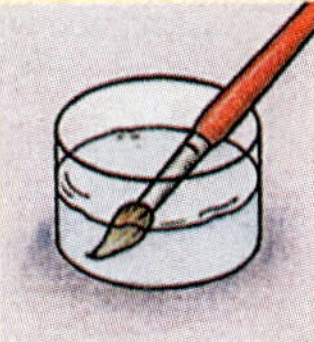

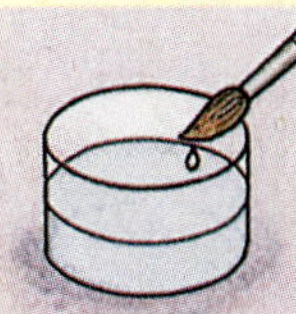

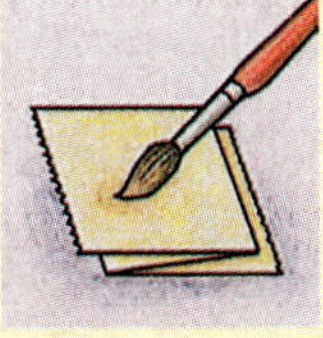

## Making a Viewfinder

When drawing or painting, a viewfinder can help focus your vision by isolating parts of an artwork or scene.

- You can make a viewfinder by cutting a square or rectangle in a sheet of paper. Use the viewfinder to plan your artwork.

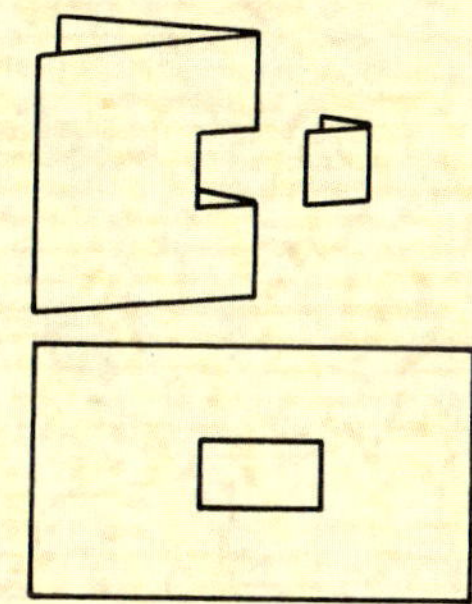

- Look at a scene or subject through a viewfinder to notice shapes formed by the edge of the viewfinder and subject, and to determine which parts of a subject are most interesting.

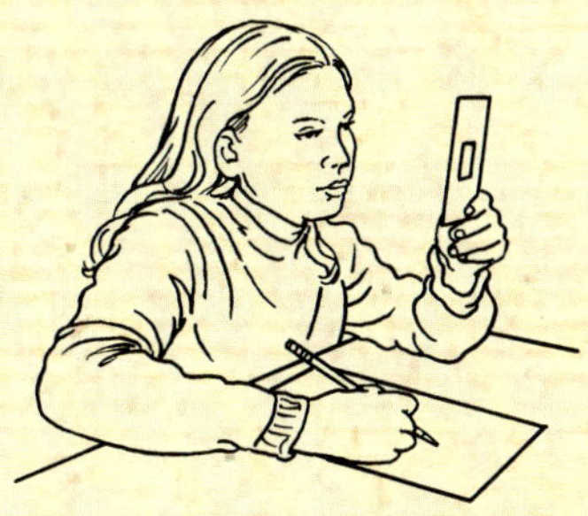

- You can also construct a viewfinder with two L-shaped pieces of paper or cardboard. By sliding these L shapes together or moving them apart, you can see the shape and proportion of the area around your subject.

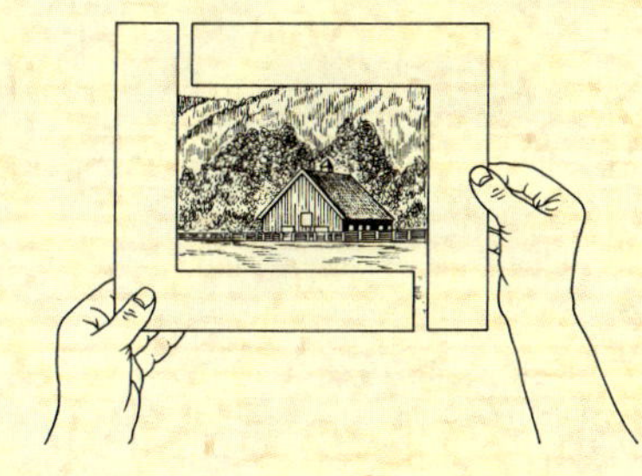

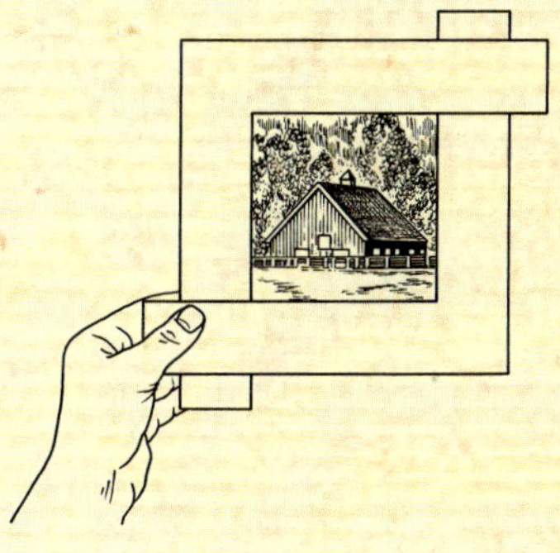

# Mixing Paint

- Use tempera paint to mix colors.
- Select a disposable palette.
- Mix colors on a large sheet of paper.
- Clean your brush after each use.

## Mixing Primary Colors

### Mix Red and Blue

- Paint three circles of red.
- Add one drop of blue paint to the first circle. Use your brush to mix. Add two drops of blue paint to the second circle, and mix. Then add three drops of blue paint to the third circle, and mix.

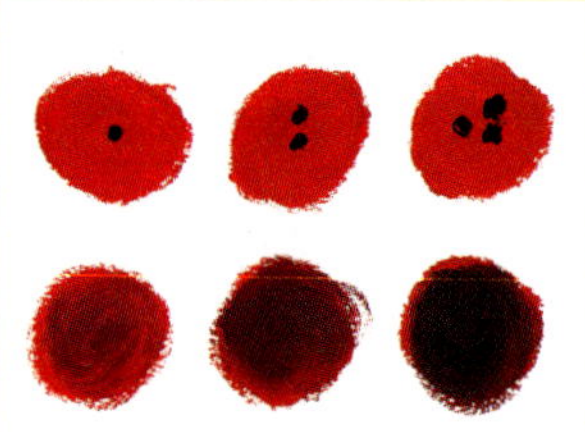

### Mix Yellow and Red

- Paint three circles of yellow. Add drops of red, and mix.

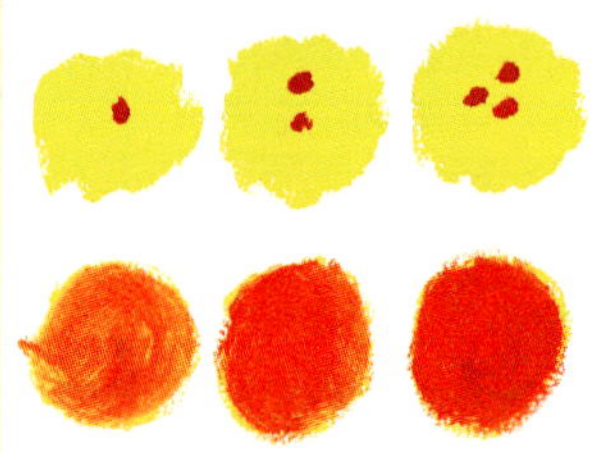

### Mix Yellow and Blue

- Paint three more circles of yellow. Add drops of blue, and mix.

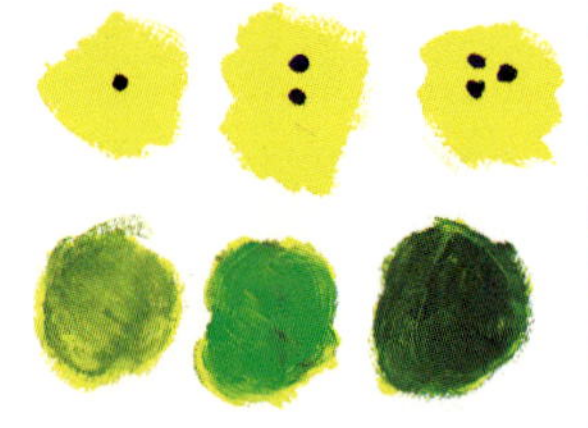

## Mixing Tints

- Paint three circles of white. Add drops of a color, and mix.

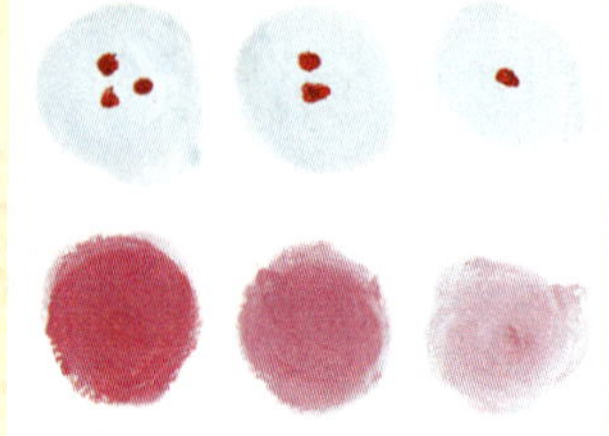

## Mixing Shades

- Paint three circles of one color. Add drops of black, and mix.

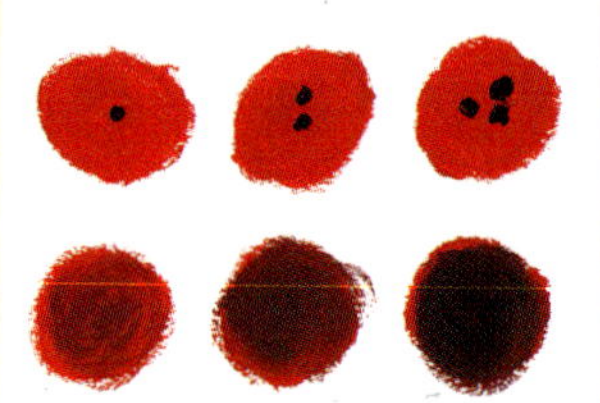

## Changing Intensity

- Paint three circles of one color. Leave the first circle alone. Add one drop of the color's complement to the second circle, and mix. Add two drops of the color's complement to the third circle, and mix. Compare intensities.

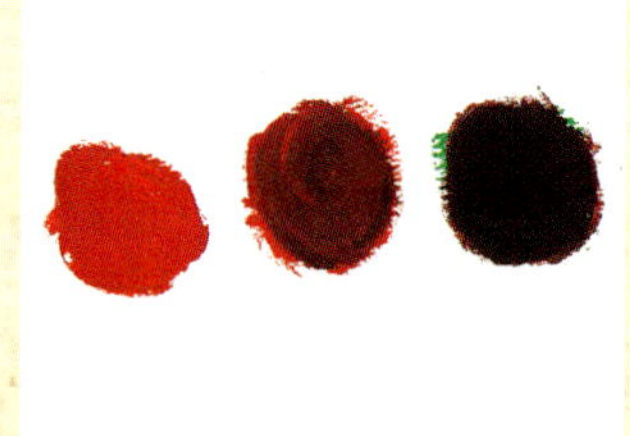

## Making a Grid

Grids are networks of squares formed by horizontal and vertical lines. They can be used to recreate or enlarge an existing artwork. The grid lines help transfer the proportions of the original artwork to the copy or enlargement.

- Use a yardstick or ruler to draw horizontal and vertical lines over your artwork.

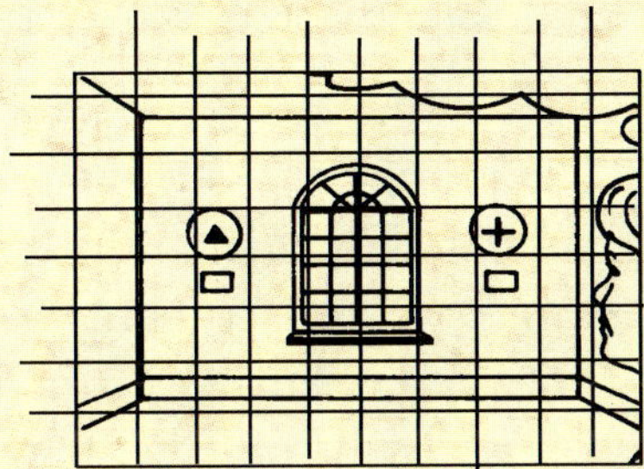

- Draw a second grid on another sheet of paper.
- If you are enlarging the artwork, use a larger sheet of paper for the second grid, and make the squares on this grid proportionally larger than the first grid.
- Carefully copy the contents of each square on the first grid into the corresponding squares on the second grid.

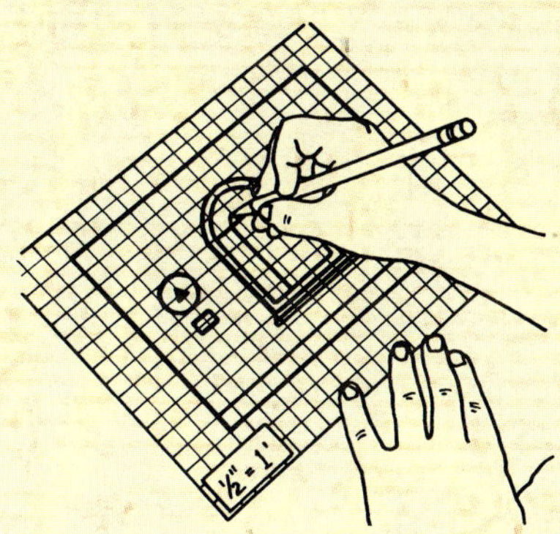

## Mounting

Any drawings, prints, photos, or paintings you plan to exhibit should be mounted and accompanied with a label that identifies your work. Follow these steps to mount your work:

- Choose a piece of heavy paper or board that is larger than the artwork you will exhibit. Select a color for your mount that will enhance or match the colors in your artwork.
- Center your artwork on the mount.
- Measure the borders to check that they are even.
- Use a pencil to lightly trace the corners of your artwork.
- Apply glue or double-sided tape to the back of your artwork.
- Position your artwork inside the corner marks.
- Press your artwork onto the mount.
- Print a label that includes your name and other information about the artwork, such as title, date, medium, your grade, and the name of your teacher and school.

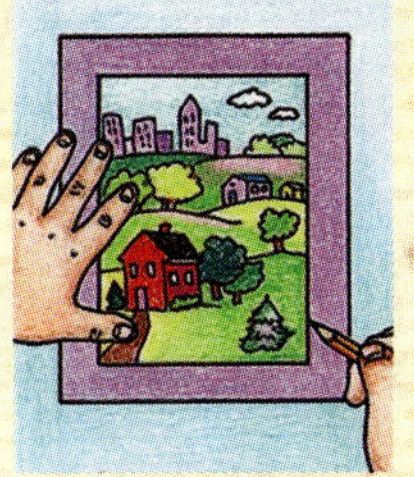

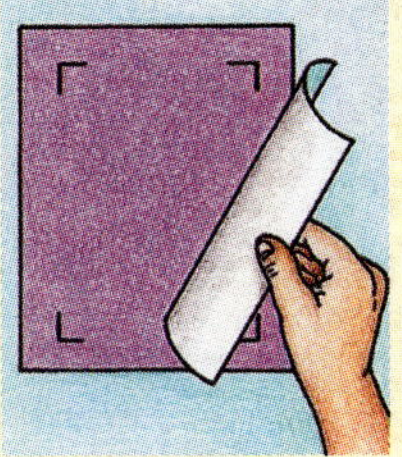

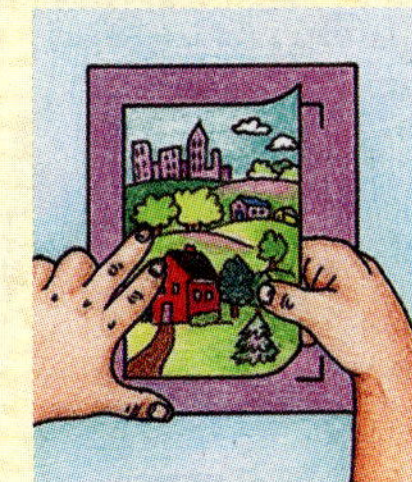

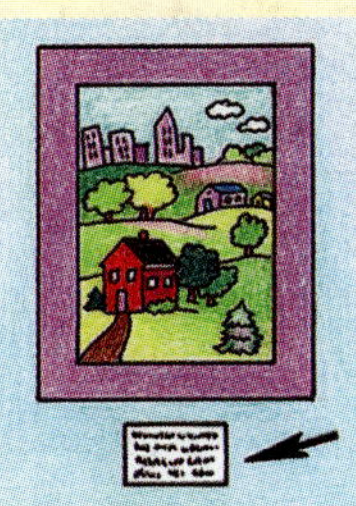

# Making a Mat

A **mat** is a colored piece of board or paper that frames an artwork. The purpose of a mat is to enhance and protect an artwork. You can make a mat for an artwork that you want to display in your home or in your school.

- Choose a colored piece of poster or mat board. Be sure to select a color for your mat that will match the colors in your artwork or make the existing colors stand out.
- On the back of your artwork, draw in light pencil a line ¼" from the edges.
- Find the center point of your art. Lightly draw lines dividing your paper into four equal parts.

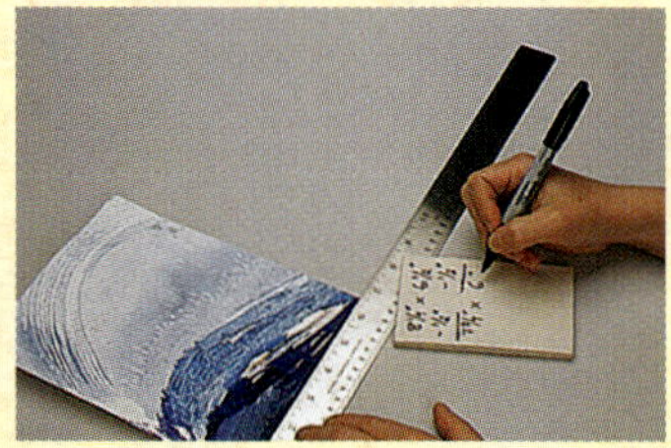

- Cut poster or mat board 6" longer and 6" wider than your artwork.
- To find the center of your mat, on the back, draw a vertical line down the middle of the mat. Then draw a horizontal line across the middle. Where the lines intersect is the center.

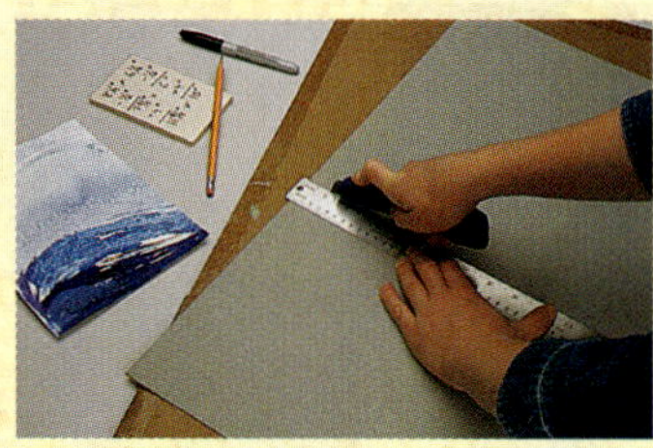

- Place your artwork face down on the back of the mat board. Line up the pencil lines.
- Attach your art to the mat using several small pieces of tape.
- Trace the corners of your artwork.

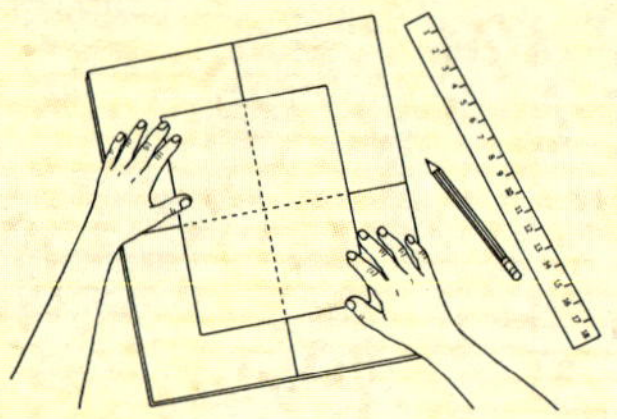

- Locate the four points on your artwork where the ¼" guidelines cross. At each point, press a pin through your artwork, into the mat board, and through to the front of the mat to make pinholes in the mat board. Remove the pins and your artwork.

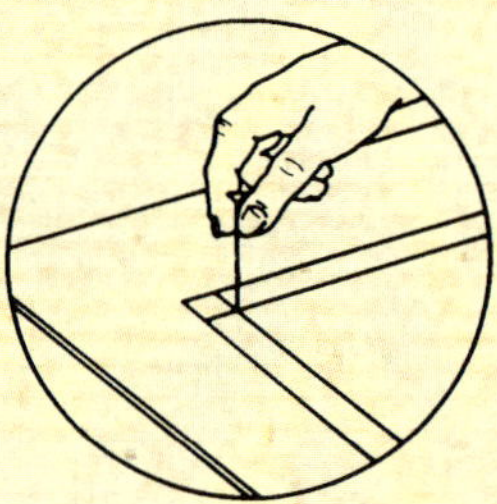

- Place the mat face up on a sheet of cardboard.
- Lay a metal ruler or yardstick between two pinholes and parallel to the mat edge.
- Cut along the edge of the ruler with a sharp mat knife. Repeat, cutting between the other pinholes to create the mat “window.”
- Remove the window.
- Place your artwork on the back of the mat over the opening.

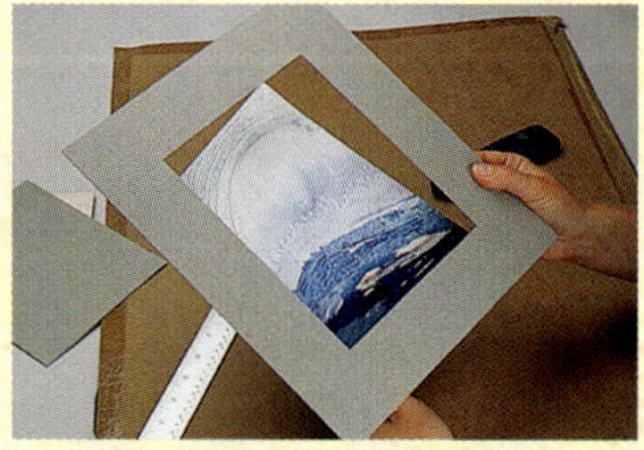

- Secure the artwork to the mat with tape. Check that the artwork is straight. Add more tape if necessary.

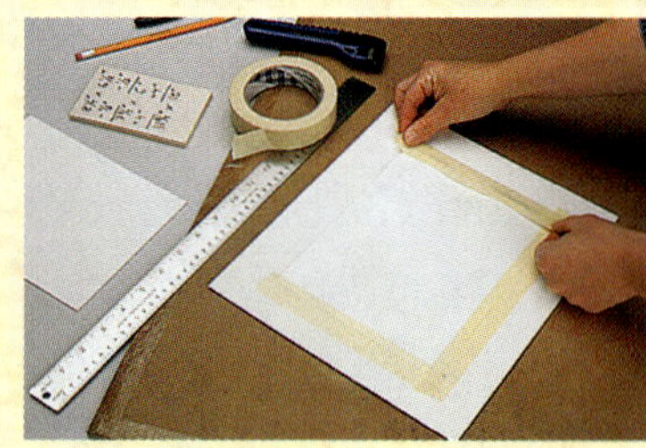

# Photographic Credits

## An Introduction to Art

### Page xviii

*Dome of the Rock*, late 7th century. Jerusalem, Israel.

Massachusetts Bay Colony, *Bradford Chair*, 1630. Black ash, seat: wood, 46" x 24" x 19" (116.8 x 61 x 48.3 cm). Pilgrim Society, Pilgrim Hall Museum, Plymouth, MA.

China, Qing dynasty, *Wedding Ensemble*, ca. 1860. Silk with embroidery and couched gold threads; robe: 43" x 38" (109 x 97 cm); skirt: 39" x 46" (99 x 117 cm). Pacific Asia Museum Collection, Gift of Dr. and Mrs. Milton Rubini 80.86.1AB. ©Pacific Asia Museum.

Dorothea Lange, *Migrant Mother, Nipomo, California*, 1936. Gelatin silver print. Reproduced from the Collections of the Library of Congress.

### Page xix

Paul Klee, *Fish Magic*, 1925. Oil on canvas, mounted on board, 30 ⅜" x 38 ½" ( 77.3 x 97.8 cm). Philadelphia Museum of Art, The Louise and Walter Arensberg Collection. Photo by Graydon Wood, 1994 Acc # '50-134-112 © 2000 Artists Right Society (ARS), New York / VG Bild- Kunst, Bonn.

### Page xx

David Hockney, *Garrowby Hill*, 1998. Oil on canvas, 60" x 72" (152.4 x 182.9 xm). David Hockney No. 1 Trust.

Diego Rivera, *Learning the ABC's (Alfabetizacion)*, 1923–28. Mural, 6 ¾' x 4 ⁹⁄₃₅' (2.06 x 1.33 m). Court of Fiestas, Level 3, West Wall. Secretaria de Educacion Publica, Mexico City, D.F., Mexico Photo Credit: Schalkwijk / Art Resource, NY.

Peter Paul Rubens, *Portrait Study of His Son Nicolas*, 1621. Black, red, and white chalk, 25.2 x 20.3 cm. Inv. 17.650. Graphishe Sammlung Albertina, Vienna, Austria. Erich Lessing / Art Resource, NY.

### Page xxi

Mongolian (Casas Grandes style), *Macaw Bowl*, Tardio Period, 1300–1350. Earthenware with polychrome slip painting, 5 ¼" x 8" x 6 ¼" (13.3 x 20.3 x 15.9 cm). Museum of Fine Arts, Houston (Gift of Miss Ima Hogg).

Winold Reiss, *Langston Hughes (1902–1967), Poet*, ca. 1925. Pastel on artist board, 76.3 x 54.9 cm. Gift of W. Tjark Reiss in memory of his father, Winold Reiss. National Portrait Gallery, Smithsonian Institution, Washington, DC / Art Resource, NY.

Anna Mary Robertson Moses, called Grandma Moses, *Summer Party*, 20th century. Oil on masonite, 23 ⁹⁄₁₆" x 15 ¾" (59.9 x 40 cm). The Museum of Fine Arts, Houston; Wintermann Collection of American Art, gift of Mr. and Mrs. David R. Wintermann.

### Page xxii

Charles Willson Peale, *The Peale Family*, ca. 1770–73 and 1808. Oil on canvas, 56 ½" x 89 ½" (143.5 x 227.3 cm) Collection of the New York Historical Society (1867.298).

Etruscan, *Chimera of Arezzo*, 6th century BCE. Bronze. Museo Archeologico, Florence, Italy. Scala / Art Resource, New York.

### Page xxiii

William H. Johnson, *Soap Box Racing*, ca. 1939–40. Tempera, pen and ink on paper mounted on paperboard, 14 ⅛" x 17 ⅞" (35.9 x 45.5 cm). National Museum of American Art, Smithsonian Institution, Washington, DC / Art Resource, NY.

### Page xxiv

China, Tang dynasty, *Tomb Figure of a Saddle Horse*, early 8th century. Earthenware, three- color lead glazes, length: 31 ½" (80.5 cm). Victoria & Albert Museum, London / Art Resource, New York.

Frida Kahlo, *Portrait of Mrs. Christian Hastings*, 1931. Drawing. Fundacion Dolores Olmedo, Mexico City, D. F., Mexico. Photo credit: Schalkwijk/ Art Resource, New York. © Banco de Mexico Trust.

### Page xxv

Warren Smith, *Cloak of Heritage*, 1991. Acrylic and collage on canvas, 24" x 36" (61 x 91.4 cm). © 1991 Kevin Warren Smith.

Marsha Burns, *Jacob Lawrence*. Photograph.

### Page xxvi

Marc Chagall, *I and the Village*, 1911. Oil on canvas, 75 ⅝" x 5 ⅝". (192 x 151 cm). The Museum of Modern Art, New York/Art Resource, NY. © The Museum of Modern Art/Licensed by SCALA/Art Resource, NY/ARS NY/ADAGP, Paris.

### Page xxvii

North American Indian, *Acoma Polychrome Jar.* Museum of Indian Arts and Culture/ Laboratory of Anthropology, Museum of New Mexico. Photograph by Douglas Kahn. (18947/ 12).

Louis Comfort Tiffany, *Dragonfly Lamp*, ca. 1900. Bronze base with color favrile glass, 28" x 22" (71.2 x 55.9 cm). Collection of the New York Historical Society (N84.113).

### Page xxviii

Vincent van Gogh, *The Starry Night*, 1889. Oil on canvas, 29" x 36 ¼" (73.7 x 92.1 cm). Acquired through the Lillie P. Bliss Bequest. Museum of Modern Art, New York. © The Museum of Modern Art/Licensed by SCALA /Art Resource, NY.

### Page xxix

Claude Monet, *Japanese Footbridge and the Water Lily Pond, Giverny*, 1899. Oil on canvas, 35 ⅛" x 36 ¾" ( 89.2 x 93.3 cm). Philadelphia Museum of Art: The Mr. and Mrs. Carroll S. Tyson, Jr. Collection.

*Cathedral of St. Basil*, 1554–1566. Moscow.

Japan, Momoyama period (1568–1615), *Ewer for Use in Tea Ceremony*, early 17th century. Shino-Oribe ware. Stoneware with overglaze enamels, 7 ¾". (19.7 cm) high. The Metropolitan Museum of Art, Purchase, Friends of Asian Art Gifts, 1988 (1988.156ab). Photograph © 2001 The Metropolitan Museum of Art.

Rosa Bonheur, *Ploughing in the Nivernais*, 1849. Oil on canvas, 52 ½" x 102" (133.4 x 259.1 cm). Musee d'Orsay, Paris, France. Photo Credit: Réunion des Musées Nationaux / Art Resource, NY

Thomas Cole, *View on the Catskill, Early Autumn*, 1837. Oil on canvas, 39" x 63" (99 x 160 cm). The Metropolitan Museum of Art, New York, gift in memory of Jonathan Sturges by his children, 1895.

### Page xxx

Sakino Hokusai IITSU, *Fukagawa Mannembashi*, from *36 Views of Mt. Fuji*, 1830. Multiple block wood blockprint, 10 ¼" x 15" (26 x 38 cm). Courtesy The Japan Ukiyo-e Museum.

Faith Ringgold, *The Wedding Lover's Quilt No. 1*, 1986. Acrylic on canvas, quilted with pieced border, 77 ½" x 58" (196.9 x 147.3 cm). Private collection. © Faith Ringgold, 1986.

Miriam Schapiro, *Master of Ceremonies*, 1985. Acrylic on fabric on canvas, 90" x 144" (228.6 x 365.8 cm). Collection of Elaine and Stephen Wynn. Courtesy of the Steinbaum Krauss Gallery, New York, New York.

Alberto Giacometti, *Three Men Walking*, 1948–49. Bronze, height: 29 ½" (74.9 cm). Edward E. Ayer Endowment in memory of Charles L. Hutchinson, 1951.256. Photograph courtesy The Art Institute of Chicago. © 2000 Artist Rights Society (ARS), New York/ ADAGP, Paris.

### Page xxxi

I. M. Pei, *Addition to the Louvre*, 1988. Glass, steel rods, and cable, I. M. Pei, Paris, France.

Makonde, Tanzania, *Family Group*, 20th century. Wood, 31" (78.7 cm). Gift of Nancy Gray, Collection Bayly Art Museum of the University of Virginia, Charlottesville. (1981.94.75)

Anne Coe, *Migrating Mutants*, 1986. Acrylic on canvas, 61" x 61" (154.9 x 154.9 cm). Horwitch Newman Gallery, Scottsdale, Arizona. Courtesy of the artist.

### Page xxxii

Paul Cézanne, S*till Life with Apples and Peaches*, ca. 1905. Oil on canvas, 31 ⅞" x 39 ½" (81 x 100.5 cm). © National Gallery of Art, Washington, Gift of Eugene and Agnes Meyer.

### Page xxxiii

Student artwork.

## Student Handbook

### Page 276

Romaine Brooks, *The Soldier at Home*, 1930. Pencil on paper, 9 ⁹⁄₁₆" x 7 ⅛" (24 x 18 cm). Gift of Romaine Brooks. Smithsonian American Art Museum, Washington, DC/Art Resource, NY.

### Page 277

Niki de Saint Phalle and Jean Tinguely, *Illumination*, 1988. Mobile sculpture, mixed media, height: 9' (2.75 m). Courtesy Galerie Bonnier, Genevia. © 2001 Artists Rights Society (ARS), New York/ADAGP, Paris.

David Hockney, *Garrowby Hill*, 1998. Oil on canvas, 60" x 72" (152.4 x 182.9 cm). David Hockney No. 1 Trust.

**Page 277**

Africa, Dan Culture (Liberia, Ivory Coast), *Ga-Wree-Wre-Mask*, 20th century. Wood, metal, fiber, cowrie shells, glass beads, brass, bone, hand-woven cloth, 47" x 16" x 22" (119.4 x 40.6 x 55.9 cm). Virginia Museum of Fine Arts, Richmond. The Adolph D. and Wilkins C. Williams Fund. Photo: Katherine Wetzel. © Virginia Museum of Fine Arts.

**Page 278**

Caryl Bryer Fallert, *Refraction #4–#7*. Hand-dyed cotton fabric, machine pieced and quilted, 88" x 88" (224 x 224 cm). Courtesy of the artist.

**Page 280**

René Magritte, *The Listening Room*, ca. 1958. Oil on canvas 15" x 18" (38 x 46 cm). Kunsthaus, Zürich, donated by Walter Haefner. Photo AKG London. ©2001 C. Herscovici, Brussels/Artists Rights Society (ARS), New York.

**Page 281**

Frances Hare, *Sixteen Feet of Dance: A Celebration, A Self-Portrait*, 1996. Cotton fabrics, beads, braided cloth, 69" x 56" (175.2 x 152.2 cm). Courtesy the artist.

**Page 282**

Doug Webb, *Kitchenetic Energy*, 1979. Acrylic on linen, 30" x 40" (76.2 x 101.6 cm). Courtesy of the artist.

**Page 283**

Omri Amrany & Julie Rotblatt-Amrany, *The Spirit, Michael Jordan*, 1994. Bronze, height (including base): 16' (5 m) United Center, Chicago, Illinois.

Clara Peeters, *Still Life of Fruit and Flowers*, after 1620. ©Ashmolean Museum, University of Oxford.

**Page 284**

Marvin Mattelson (illustrator), *Subway Poster for School of Visual Arts*. Art Director: Silas H. Rhodes; Designer: William J. Kobasz; Copywriter: Dee Ito.

"Tableware", Bloomimage/CORBIS

**Page 285**

Art on File/CORBIS

Brand X/CORBIS

**Page 286**

Lascaux, *Hall of Bulls*, detail, c. 15,000–13,000 BC, Dordogne, France. Color photo Hans Hinz.

Giza, Egypt, *The Pyramids of Mycerinus, Chefren, and Cheops*, built between 2589 and 2350 BC. Limestone. Erich Lessing/Art Resource, NY.

Ancient Greece, Athens (attributed to the Antimenes painter), *Hydria*, c. 530–510 BC. Black-figure earthenware, height: 16 5/8" (42.2 cm). Cleveland Museum of Art. Purchase from the J. H. Wade Fund. 1975.1.

**Page 287**

*Augustus of Prima Porta*, Roman Sculpture, Early first century AD. Vatican Museums, Vatican State. Scala/Art Resource, New York.

*The Archangel Michael with Sword*, Byzantine, 11th century. Gold, enamel, and precious stone. Framed icon. Tesoro San Marco, Venice. Cameraphoto/Art Resource, New York.

*Chi-rho Gospel of St. Matthews, chapter 1, verse 18*, Irish (vellum). *Book of Kells*, c. 800. The Board of Trinity College, Dublin, Ireland/Bridgeman Art Library.

*Bayeux Tapestry, William preparing his troops for combat with English Army.* Musée de la Tapisserie, Bayeux, France. Giraudon/Art Resource, New York.

**Page 288**

*North Transept Rose and Lancet Windows (Melchizedek & Nebuchadnezzar, David & Saul, St. Anne, Solomon & Herod, Aaron & Pharaoh)*, 13th century. Stained glass, 42' (12.8 m) Diameter. Chartres Cathedral, France. Scala/Art Resource, New York.

Michelangelo Buonarroti, *Pietà*, 1499. Marble, height: 5' 6" (1.7 cm). St. Peter's Basilica, Vatican State. Scala/Art Resource, New York.

Judith Leyster, *Game of Tric-Trac*, c. 1630. Oil on panel, 16" x 12 ¼" (40.7 x 31.1 cm). Worcester Art Museum, Worcester, Massachusetts. Gift of Robert and Mary S. Cushman.

**Page 289**

Movement made by Charles Voisin and Chantilly manufactory, *Wall Clock*, c. 1740. Soft-paste porcelain, enameled metal, gilt-bronze, and glass, 29 ½" x 14" x 4 3/8" (74.9 x 35.6 x 11.1 cm). The J. Paul Getty Museum, Los Angeles.

Jacques-Louis David, *Oath of the Horatii*, 1784–85. Oil on canvas, 129 11/12" x 167 5/16" (330 x 425 cm). Louvre, Paris, France. Erich Lessing/Art Resource, New York.

Eugène Delacroix, *Horses Coming Out of the Sea*, 1860. Oil on canvas, 20 ¼" x 24 ¼" (5.4 x 61.5 cm). The Phillips Collection, Washington, DC. (0486).

**Page 290**

Honoré Daumier, *The Third Class Carriage*, ca. 1863–65. Oil on canvas, 25 ¾" x 35 ½" (65.4 x 90.2 cm). National Gallery of Canada, Ottawa. Purchased 1946.

Pierre-Auguste Renoir, *The Garden in the Rue Cortot, Montmarte*, 1876. Oil on canvas, 59 ¾" x 38 3/8" (151.8 x 97.5 cm). Carnegie Museum of Art, Pittsburgh. Acquired through the generosity of Mrs. Alan M. Scaif, 65.35. Photography by Peter Harholdt.

Pablo Picasso, *Three Muscians*, Fontainebleu, summer 1921. Oil on canvas, 6' 7" x 7' 3 ¾" (22.07 x 222.9 cm). The Museum of Modern Art, New York. Mrs. Simon Guggenheim Fund. Photograph ©2000 The Museum of Modern Art, New York. ©2000 Estate of Pablo Picasso/Artists Rights Society (ARS), New York.

**Page 291**

Salvador Dalì, *The Persistence of Memory*, 1931. Oil on canvas, 9 ½" x 13" (24.1 x 33 cm). The Museum of Modern Art, New York. Given anonymously. Photograph ©2000 The Museum of Modern Art, New York. ©2000 Artists Rights Society (ARS), New York.

Jackson Pollock, *Blue Poles*, 1952. Enamel and aluminum paint with glass on canvas. 6' 10 7/8" x 15' 11 5/8" (212.09 x 488.95 cm). Collection: National Gallery of Australia, Canberra (NGA Acc. No. 74.264). © The Pollock-Krasner Foundation/Artists Rights Society (ARS), New York.

Claes Oldenburg and Coosje van Bruggen, *Spoonbridge and Cherry*, 1988. Aluminum painted with polyurethane enamel and stainless steel, 29'6" x 51'6" x 13'6" (9 x 15.7 x 4.1 m). Minneapolis Sculpture Garden, Walker Art Center, Minneapolis, Photography by Attilio Maranzano. Courtesy of the artists.

Andy Goldsworthy, *The coldest I have ever known in Britain/as early/worked all day/reconstructed icicles around a tree/finished late afternoon/catching sunlight, Glenn Marlin Falls, Dumfriesshire, 28 december 1995*, 1995. Cibachrome print, 23" x 19" (58 x 48.3 cm) square. Galerie Lelong, New York, New York. Courtesy of Private Collector, New York.

**Page 300**

Emile Nolde, *Summer Flowers*, 1930. Watercolor painting.

Winslow Homer, *Sunshine and Shadow, Prout's Neck*, 1984. Watercolor painting.

# Artist Guide

**Abbott, Berenice** (AB-bet, BER-a-nees) US, 1898–1991, p. 95

**Adams, Mary** US, b. 1920s, p. 263

**Ahearn, John** (AY-hern) US, b. 1951, p. 32

**Al-Fuzula, Miftah** (ahl-foo-ZOO-lah, miff-tah) India, 1600s, p. 50

**Ali, M.** (ah-LEE) Persia, 1500s, p. 51

**Amish artists** (AH-mish) US, p. 4

**Ancestral Puebloan (Anasazi) artists** (ah-nah-SAH-zee) Southwestern US, pp. 18, 30

**Apsit, Alexander** Latvia, 1880–1844, p. 172

**Ashevak, Kenojuak** (ASH-eh-vack, ken-OH-joo-ack) Canada, b. 1927, p. 122

**Audubon, John James** (AW-doo-bahn) US, 1785–1851, p. 121

**Aztec artists** (AZ-tek) Mexico, 1200s–1500s, pp. 22–23, 208

**Barthé, Richmond** (BAR-tay) US, 1901–1989, p. 67

**Bean, Alan** US, b. 1932, p. 269

**Bearden, Romare** (BEER-den, ro-MAIR) US, 1911–1988, p. 13

**Beg, Farrukh** (begg, fah-ROOHK) Persia, 1547–1615, p. 52

**Bellows, George** (BELL-ohs) US, 1882–1925, p. 153

**Benton, Thomas Hart** US, 1889–1975, p. 197

**Bierstadt, Albert** (beer-shtaht) Germany, 1830–1902, p. 107

**Bingler, Steven** US, b. 1948, p. 244

**Blank, Harrod** US, b. 1963, p. 187

**Brown, Grafton Tyler** US, 1841–1918, p. 136

**Burgis, William** (burr-jiss) US, born England, active early 1700s, p. 47

**Burkholder, Dan** (BERK-hold-ur) US, b. ca. 1950, p. 248

**Callot, Jacques** (kah-low, zhak) France, 1592–1635, p. 33

**Carter, Dennis Malone** US, 1827–1881, p. 66

**Celtic artists** (KELL-tik) Western and Central Europe, p. 123

**Chicago Mural Group (Chicago Public Art Group)** US, founded 1971, pp. 228–229

**Chin, Mel** US, b. 1951, p. 213

**Christopher, Roy** US, b. ca. 1936, p. 29

**Coe, Sue** England/US, b. 1951, p. 218

**Copley, John Singleton** (KOPP-lee) US, 1738–1815, p. 48

**Cortor, Eldzier** (CORE-tore, ELLD-zeer) US, b. 1916, p. 31

**Cover, Sally** (KUH-ver) US, 1853–1936, p. 108–109

**Danberg, Leah** Canada, b. 1934, p. 128

**Das, Manohar** (dahs, mahn-oh-hahr) India, 1500s–1600s, p. 60

**Degas, Edgar** (deh-gah, ed-gahr) France, 1834–1917, pp. 61, 98

**Delano, Pablo** (de-LAN-o) Puerto Rico, b. 1954, p. 62

**Denes, Agnes** (DEN-niss, AG-ness) US, b. 1931, p. 127

**Dewing, Maria Oakey** US, 1845–1927, p. 137

**Disney, Walt** (DIZ-nee) US, 1901–1966, p. 94

**Duncanson, Robert Scott** US, 1821–1872, p. 108

**Durand, Asher Brown** US, 1796–1886, p. 106

**Elizondo, Arturo** (ay-lee-ZAHN-doe, arr-TOO-roh) Mexico, active 2000s, p. 247

**Escobar, Marisol** (ESS-koh-bahr, MAHR-ee-sohl) Venezuela, b. 1930, p. 227

**Escobedo, Helen** (ess-koh-BAY-doh) Mexico, b. 1934, p. 69

**Etruscan artists** (eh-TRUSS-ken) ancient Etruria, p. 243

**Evans, Barnaby** US, b. 1953, p. 257

**Evaristo, Pete, and Tucci, Jodi** (eh-VAR-ist-o) (TOOCH-ee) US, b. 1955, b. 1956, p. 258

**Fuller, Meta Warrick** US, 1877–1968, p. 198

**Martínez, María Montoya** (mar-TEE-nes) US, 1887–1980, pp. 55, 58

**Masanobu, Okumura** (mah-sahn-o-boo, oh-koo-moor-a) Japan, 1686–1764, pp. 112–113

**Matthews, Kazuko** (kah-zoo-koh) US, active late 1900s and early 2000s, p. 128

**Mayan artists** (MYE-en) pre-Columbian Mexico, pp. 20, 148

**McGee, Barry** US, b. 1966, p. 250

**Mimbres artists** (MIM-brayz) artists Southwestern US, p. 17

**Minshall, Peter** Trinidad, b. 1941, pp. 202–203

**Mitchell, Joan** US, 1926–1992, p. 160

**Mixtec artists** (MISH-tek) pre-Columbian Mexico, pp. 3, 7

**Morisot, Berthe** (mo-ree-zoh, bairt) France, 1841–1895, p. 151

**Mughal School artists** (MOH-gull) India, ca. 1690–1710, p. 43

**Mukhina, Vera** (moo-KEE-nah, vair-ah) Russia 1889–1953, pp. 154–155

**Munch, Edvard** (moongk, ED-vart) Norway, 1863–1944, p. 141

**Murray, Elizabeth** US, 1940–2007, p. 163

**Nagano, Paul T.** (NAH-gah-noh) US, b. 1938, p. 25

**Njau, Elimo** (nn-jaow, eh-LEE-mo) Tanzania, b. 1932, p. 232

**Normil, Andre** (nor-mill) Haiti, b. 1934, p. 200

**Nupe artists** (NOO-pay) Nigeria, p. 231

**O'Dell, Dale** US, b. 1959, p. 253

**O'Keeffe, Georgia** US, 1887–1986, p. 166

**Otter, Thomas P.** US, 1832–1890, p. 118

**Ouattara (Watts)** (wah-tah-rah) Ivory Coast, b. 1957, p. 233

**Paik, Nam June** (NAWM joon PIKE) Korea, b. 1932, p. 152

**Peale, Charles Willson** US, 1741–1827, p. 34

**Pennsylvania German artists** US, settled 1600s–1700s, pp. 78–79

**Pergola, Linnea** (per-GOLE-ah, linn-AY-ah) US, b. 1953, p. 120

**Picasso, Pablo** (pee-KAHS-soh, PAH-bloh) Spain, 1881–1973, p. 214

**Pierce, Elijah** US, 1892–1984, p. 212

**Pittman, Lari** US, b. 1952, p. 158

**Pueblo artists** (PWEB-lo) Native American, Southwestern US, p. 87

**Qin Dynasty** (chin) China, 221–206 BCE, p. 85, 91

**Quick-to-See Smith, Jaune** (kwik-too-see smith, zjhohn) US, b. 1940, p. 157

**Rauschenberg, Robert** (RAO-shen-berg) US, 1925–2008, p. 226

**Revelle, Barbara Jo** (reh-VELL) US, b. 1946, p. 25

**Revere, Paul** US, 1734–1818, p. 49

**Riis, Jacob** (rees) Denmark, active US, 1849–1914, p. 167

**Rodchenko, Aleksandr** (ROTE-chen-ko) Russia, 1891–1956, pp. 172–173

**Rodia, Simon** (roh-dee-ah) Italy, 1875–1965, pp. 119, 185

**Rodin, Auguste** (roh-dan, oh-goost) France, 1840–1917, pp. 64–65

**Romero, Frank** (ro-MAY-ro) US, b. 1941, p. 96

**Rosenquist, James** (RO-zen-kwist) US, b. 1933, p. 227

**Saint-Gaudens, Augustus** (saynt-GOD-enz) US, 1848–1907, pp. 63, 73)

**Schapiro, Miriam** (shuh-PEER-o, MEER-ee-um) US/Canada, b. 1923, p. 215

**Schofield, David** (skoh-feeld) US, b. 1958, p. 103

**Scott, Douglass** US, b. 1947, p. 8

**Segal, George** (SEE-gel) US, 1924–2000, p. 35

**Skoglund, Sandy** (SKOH-glend) US, b. 1946, p. 242

**Sloan, John** US, 1871–1951, pp. 168–169

**Smith, Kevin Warren** US, Cherokee, b. 1958, p. 13

**Steir, Pat** (steer) US, b. 1938, p. 256

**Stoltzfus, Rebecca Fisher** (STOLTS-fuhss) US, active early 1900s, p. 28

# Glossary

**abstract art** Art that is based on a subject you can recognize, but the artist simplifies, leaves out, or rearranges some elements so that you may not recognize them. *(arte abstracto)*

**activism** The practice of working to change attitudes or beliefs related to politics or other issues within a community. *(activismo)*

**Art Nouveau** *(art noo-voh)* 1900–1915. A French phrase that means "New Art." A design style that explored the flowing lines, curves, and shapes of nature. *(art nouveau)*

**Ash Can School** 1908–1914. A group of American artists who painted pictures of real scenes of city life. The group's original name was "The Eight." *(escuela "Ash Can")*

**avant-garde** *(ah-vant-gard)* An art term that describes art that is original and different from traditional styles of art. Avant-garde artists often experiment with new materials and ways of expressing ideas. *(vanguardismo)*

**balance** A principle of design that describes how parts of an artwork are arranged to create a sense of equal weight or interest. An artwork that is balanced seems to have equal visual weight or interest in all areas. Types of balance are symmetrical, asymmetrical, and radial. *(equilibrio)*

**bisqueware** *(BISK-wair)* Ceramic that has been fired once but not glazed. *(bizcocho de porcelana)*

**cause** A belief or issue that moves people to action. *(causa)*

**celebrate** To observe an event or local tradition with other members of a community. *(celebrar)*

**cityscape** An artwork that shows a view of a city (buildings, streets, shops) as subject matter. *(paisaje urbano)*

**codex** A type of book whose pages are hinged together at both sides, similar to an accordion. *(códice)*

**collaborate** To work together with others. *(colaborar)*

**collage** *(coh-LAHZ)* A work of art created by gluing bits of paper, fabric, scraps, photographs, or other materials to a flat surface. *(collage)*

**collagraph** A print made from a collage with raised areas on its surface. *(colografía)*

**commemorate** To honor the events and people that have shaped the histories of towns, cities, and countries.

**communication** The exchange of information, thoughts, feelings, ideas, opinions, and so on, either in spoken, written, or visual form. *(comunicación)*

**composition** The way the parts of an artwork are arranged. *(composición)*

**contour drawing** A drawing that shows only the edges (contours) of objects. *(dibujo de contorno)*

**crafts** Works of art, either decorative or useful, that are skillfully made by hand. *(artesanías)*

**Dada** 1915–1923. An art movement that was known for rejecting traditional art styles and materials. These artists created artworks based on chance, and often used found objects to create new art forms. Many artists involved in the Dada movement became leaders of Surrealism and other new styles of art. *(dadaísmo)*

**designer** An artist who plans the organization and composition of an artwork, object, place, building, and so on. Designers plan clothing (fashion design), outdoor spaces (landscape design), indoor spaces (furniture and interior design), signs and ads (graphic design), and so on. *(diseñador)*

**document** *(DOK-you-ment)* To make or keep a record of. *(documentar)*

**dry media** Art materials such as pencils, chalk (pastels), and crayons that are not wet and do not require the use of a liquid. *(medios secos)*

**earthwork** Any work of art in which land and earth are important media. Often, large formations of moved earth, excavated by artists in the surface of the earth, and best viewed from a high vantage point. *(obras de tierra)*

**fire** To bake at a high temperature. *(cocer)*

**form** An element of design; any three-dimensional object such as a cube, sphere, pyramid, or cylinder. A form can be measured from top to bottom (height), side to side (width) and front to back (depth). Form is also a general term that means the structure or design of a work. *(forma)*

**found objects** Materials that artists find and use for artwork, such as scraps of wood, metal, or ready-made objects. *(objetos encontrados)*

**genre scene** A scene or subject from everyday life. *(escena costumbrista)*

**geometric** Includes mechanical-looking shapes or forms such as squares or triangles. *(geométrico)*

**geometric shapes** Shapes with smooth, even edges such as circles, squares, and triangles. *(figuras geométricas)*

**gesture drawing** A quick drawing that captures the gestures or movements of the body. *(dibujo gestual)*

**global community** The interaction and sharing of ideas and knowledge of people and populations worldwide. *(comunidad global)*

**global style** A style of art that cannot be linked to just one culture or tradition of art. Global style comes about from exchanges of ideas among artists of many nations and cultures around the world. *(estilo global)*

**graphic design** A general term for artwork in which letter forms (writing, typography) are often an important part of the artwork. *(diseño gráfico)*

**Harlem Renaissance** *(HAR-lem ren-eh-SAHNSS)* 1920–1940. A name of a period and a group of artists who lived and worked in Harlem, New York City. They used a variety of art forms to express their lives as African Americans. *(Renacimiento de Harlem)*

**horizon line** A level line where water or land seem to end and the sky begins. It is usually on the eye level of the observer. If the horizon cannot be seen, its location must be imagined. *(línea de horizonte)*

**Impressionists** 1875–1900. A group of artists who worked outside and painted directly from nature. Impressionist artists used rapid brushstrokes to capture an impression of light and color. *(impresionistas)*

**installations** Temporary arrangements of art objects in galleries, museums, or outdoors. *(instalaciones)*

**intaglio print** *(in-TAH-lee-oh)* A print in which the artist scratches lines into a smooth metal plate, inks the plate, and then pulls the print using a printing press to apply even pressure between the plate and the paper. *(impresión en huecograbado)*

**kinetic sculpture** A sculpture that moves or has moving parts. The motion may be caused by many different forces, including air, gravity, and electricity. *(escultura cinética)*

**limner** *(LIM-ner)* An early American self-taught artist who painted signs, houses, portraits. *(limner)*

**linear perspective** *(LIN-ee-er per-SPEK-tiv)* A technique used to show three-dimensional space on a two-dimensional surface. *(perspectiva lineal)*

**linoleum cut** A relief print that is made from a linoleum block. The linoleum is cut away. The uncut relief areas are covered with ink, paper is placed on top, and the print is made by rubbing the back of the paper. *(impresión en linóleo)*

**lithographic print** *(lith-oh-GRAF-ik)* A print made when an artist draws an image on a flat slab of stone (or a special metal plate) with a greasy crayon or paint. A special acid removes the part of the stone not covered with crayon. The crayoned part is then inked, and the print is made using a printing press. *(litografía)*

**maquette** *(mah-KET)* A small-scale model of a larger sculpture. *(maqueta)*

**medium** A material or technique used by an artist to create a work of art. Singular of media. *(medio)*

**memorial** An artwork or other objects that help people remember things, such as important events or people. *(obra conmemorativa)*

**miniature** A very small, detailed painting. *(miniatura)*

**mixed media** Any artwork that is made with more than one medium, such as ink and watercolor, painting and collage, and so on. *(medios mixtos)*

**montage** *(mahn-TAHZH)* A special kind of collage, made from pieces of photographs or other pictures. *(montaje)*

**monument** An artwork created for a public place that preserves the memory of a person, event, or action. *(monumento)*

**motif** *(moh-TEEF)* A single or repeated design or part of a design or decoration. *(motivo)*

**multimedia** Artworks that use the tools and techniques of more than one medium. *(multimedia)*

**mural movement** A movement begun by American artists in the 1970s that focused on adding beauty to city neighborhoods through the creation of large, public paintings, often on the walls of public buildings. *(movimiento muralista)*

**Neoclassicism** 1750–1875. A style of art based on interest in the ideals of ancient Greek and Roman art. These ideals were used to express ideas about beauty, courage, sacrifice, and love of country. *(neoclasicismo)*

**organic** Includes irregular shapes from nature. *(orgánico)*

**organic shapes** Shapes that are irregular in outline, such as things in nature. *(formas orgánicas)*

**Performance Art** A form of visual art closely related to theater that combines any of the creative forms of expression, such as poetry, theater, music, architecture, painting, film, slides, and so on. *(arte de la representación)*

**perspective** *(per-SPEK-tiv)* Techniques for creating a look of depth on a two-dimensional surface. *(perspectiva)*

**pigments** Coloring materials made from earth, crushed minerals, plants, or chemicals. Pigments are mixed with a liquid or binder (such as glue, egg, wax, or oil) to make paint, ink, dyes, or crayons. *(pigmentos)*

**point of view** The position from which an artist creates an artwork. *(punto de vista)*

**portrait** An artwork that shows a specific person or group of people. *(retrato)*

**portraiture** The art of creating portraits. *(retratismo)*

**Pre-Columbian art** 7000 BCE to about 1500 CE. An art history term used to describe the art and civilizations in North and South America before the time of the Spanish conquests. *(precolombino)*

**Productivists** A group of Russian avant-garde artists who believed that art is useful to society. They felt that combining art, craftsmanship, and industry could help build a better world. *(productivistas)*

**proportion** The relation of one object to another in size, amount, or number. Proportion is often used to describe the relationship between one part of the human figure and another. *(proporción)*

**pueblo** A Native American village of the southwestern United States. *(pueblo)*

**pulp** Mashed up material, usually wood or plant fibers, used to make paper. *(pulpa)*

**Realistic Style** 1850–1900. A style of art that shows places, events, people, or objects as the eye sees them. Realist artists did not use the formulas of Neoclassicism and the drama of Romanticism. See Neoclassicism, Romanticism. *(estilo realista)*

**Regionalist** An artist whose artworks focus on a specific region or section of the country. *(regionalista)*

**relief print** A print made by inking the raised surface of a block or plate. *(grabado en relieve)*

**relief sculpture** A three-dimensional work designed to be viewed from one side, in which surfaces are raised from a background. *(escultura a relieve)*

**Romantic Style** *(ro-MAN-tick)* 1815–1875. A style of art that developed as a reaction against Neoclassicism. Themes focused on dramatic action, exotic settings, adventures, imaginary events, faraway places and strong feelings. *(estilo romántico)*

**scientific record** Accurate and highly detailed artworks or written works, used to help document or classify species. *(récord científico)*

**sculpture** Artworks that have three dimensions. *(escultura)*

**serigraph** *(SEHR-i-graf)* A print, also known as a silkscreen print, made by squeezing ink through a stencil and silk-covered frame to paper below. *(serigrafía)*

**sgrafitto** *(sgra-FEET-toh)* A pottery technique in which designs are scratched onto a clay object through a thin layer of colored slip before the pottery is glazed and fired. *(esgrafiado)*

**shading** A gradual change from light to dark. Shading is a way of making a picture appear more realistic and three-dimensional. *(sombreado)*

**slip** A runny mix of clay and water. *(barbotina)*

**slurry** A watery mixture used to make paper. *(lechada)*

**subtractive process** Sculptural process in which material (clay, for example) is carved or cut away to create form. In an additive process, material is added to create form. *(proceso de substracción)*

**Surrealism** A style of art in which dreams, fantasy, and the human mind are the source of ideas for artists. Unrelated objects and situations are often set in unnatural surroundings. Artists who work in this style are known as Surrealists. *(surrealismo)*

**Surrealist** An artist for whom dreams, fantasy, and the human mind are sources for ideas. *(surrealista)*

**tohunga** *(toh-HUN-gah)* A Maori term that means "craftsman-priest." A great master carver of the Maori of New Zealand. *(tohunga)*

**tourist art** Souvenirs created to help travelers remember the places they visit. In African cultures, these souvenirs are often made from recycled materials and realistically depict native animals and village life. *(arte turístico)*

**traditional art** Artwork created in almost the same way year after year because it is part of a culture, custom, or belief. *(arte tradicional)*

**traditions** Customs, actions, thoughts, or beliefs that are passed on or handed down from generation to generation, either by word of mouth or by example. *(tradiciones)*

**two-point perspective** A method of creating the illusion of deep space on a flat surface. In two-point perspective there are two vanishing points on the horizon line. *(perspectiva de dos puntos)*

**ukiyo-e** *(oo-key-OH-eh)* Japanese pictures of the "floating world" district of Edo. These were first made in paint, but were more commonly created in editions of woodcuts of many colors. They are the unique creation of the Edo period (1603–1868). The term *ukiyo*, meaning temporary or floating, was used to describe these communities. *(ukiyo-e)*

**value** An element of art that means the darkness or lightness of a surface. Value depends on how much light a surface reflects. Tints are light values of pure colors. Shades are dark values of pure colors. Value can also be an important element in works of art in which there is little or no color (drawings, prints, photographs, most sculpture and architecture). *(valor)*

**vanishing point** In a perspective drawing, one or more points on the horizon where parallel lines that go back in space seem to meet. *(punto de fuga)*

**wet media** Drawing and painting materials that have a fluid or liquid ingredient. *(medios húmedos)*

# Index



*Italicized page numbers refer to artworks.*

*Italicized page numbers refer to artworks.*

*Italicized page numbers refer to artworks.*

## M



## N



## O

*Italicized page numbers refer to artworks.*

*Italicized page numbers refer to artworks.*